# Afro-Latin American Studies

Alejandro de la Fuente and George Reid Andrews offer the first systematic, book-length survey of the humanities and social sciences scholarship on the exciting field of Afro-Latin American Studies. Organized by topic, these essays synthesize and present the current state of knowledge on a broad variety of topics, including Afro-Latin American music, religions, literature, art history, political thought, social movements, legal history, environmental history, and ideologies of racial inclusion. This volume connects the region's long history of slavery to the major political, social, cultural, and economic developments of the last two centuries. Written by leading scholars in each of those topics, the volume provides an introduction to the field of Afro-Latin American Studies that is not available from any other source and reflects the disciplinary and thematic richness of this emerging field.

ALEJANDRO DE LA FUENTE is the Robert Woods Bliss Professor of Latin American History and Economics and Professor of African and African American Studies at Harvard University. He is the Director of the Afro-Latin American Research Institute and the co-chair of the Cuban Studies Program at Harvard. He is the author of *Diago: The Pasts of This Afro-Cuban Present* (2017), *Havana and the Atlantic in the Sixteenth Century* (2008), and of *A Nation for All: Race, Inequality, and Politics in Twentieth-Century Cuba* (2001). He is the editor of the journal *Cuban Studies* and of *Transition: Magazine of Africa and the Diaspora*.

GEORGE REID ANDREWS is Distinguished Professor of History at the University of Pittsburgh. He received his PhD from the University of Wisconsin in 1978 and has taught Latin American history at the University of Pittsburgh since 1981. His books include *The Afro-Argentines of Buenos Aires, 1800–1900* (1980), *Blacks and Whites in São Paulo, Brazil, 1888–1988* (1991), *Afro-Latin America, 1800–2000* (2004), *Blackness in the White Nation: A History of Afro-Uruguay* (2010), and *Afro-Latin America: Black Lives, 1600–2000* (2016).

# Afro-Latin America

*Series Editors*

George Reid Andrews, *University of Pittsburgh*
Alejandro de la Fuente, *Harvard University*

This series reflects the coming of age of the new, multidisciplinary field of Afro-Latin American Studies, which centers on the histories, cultures, and experiences of people of African descent in Latin America. The series aims to showcase scholarship produced by different disciplines, including history, political science, sociology, ethnomusicology, anthropology, religious studies, art, law, and cultural studies. It covers the full temporal span of the African Diaspora in Latin America, from the early colonial period to the present and includes continental Latin America, the Caribbean, and other key areas in the region where Africans and their descendants have made a significant impact.

*A full list of titles published in the series can be found at:*
www.cambridge.org/afro-latin-america

# Afro-Latin American Studies

## An Introduction

Edited by

**ALEJANDRO DE LA FUENTE**
*Harvard University*

**GEORGE REID ANDREWS**
*University of Pittsburgh*

CAMBRIDGE
UNIVERSITY PRESS

# CAMBRIDGE
## UNIVERSITY PRESS

University Printing House, Cambridge CB2 8BS, United Kingdom

One Liberty Plaza, 20th Floor, New York, NY 10006, USA

477 Williamstown Road, Port Melbourne, VIC 3207, Australia

314–321, 3rd Floor, Plot 3, Splendor Forum, Jasola District Centre,
New Delhi – 110025, India

79 Anson Road, #06–04/06, Singapore 079906

Cambridge University Press is part of the University of Cambridge.

It furthers the University's mission by disseminating knowledge in the pursuit of
education, learning, and research at the highest international levels of excellence.

www.cambridge.org
Information on this title: www.cambridge.org/9781107177628
DOI: 10.1017/9781316822883

© Alejandro de la Fuente and George Reid Andrews 2018

First published 2018

Printed in the United States of America by Sheridan Books, Inc.

*A catalogue record for this publication is available from the British Library.*
*Library of Congress Cataloging-in-Publication Data*
NAMES: Fuente, Alejandro de la, 1963- author. |
Andrews, George Reid, 1951-
TITLE: Afro-Latin American studies : an introduction /
edited by Alejandro de la Fuente, George Reid Andrews.
DESCRIPTION: Cambridge ; New York, NY : Cambridge University Press, 2018. |
Series: Afro-latin america | Includes bibliographical references and index.
IDENTIFIERS: LCCN 2018000002 | ISBN 9781107177628 (Hardback) |
ISBN 9781316630662 (pb)
SUBJECTS: LCSH: Blacks–Latin America. | Latin America–Race relations.
CLASSIFICATION: LCC F1419.N4 A394 2018 | DDC 980/.00496–dc23
LC record available at https://lccn.loc.gov/2018000002

ISBN 978-1-107-17762-8 Hardback
ISBN 978-1-316-63066-2 Paperback

# Contents

# Figures

vii

# Tables

# Contributors

**Paulina L. Alberto** is Associate Professor in the Department of History and the Department of Romance Languages and Literatures at the University of Michigan. She is the author of *Terms of Inclusion: Black Intellectuals in Twentieth-Century Brazil* (2011) and multiple articles on racial activism and racial ideologies in modern Brazil and Argentina. She is coeditor with Eduardo Elena of *Rethinking Race in Modern Argentina* (2016). Her current book manuscript on the (in)famous *porteño* street character Raúl Grigera ("el negro Raúl") explores the power of racial stories to construct whiteness and blackness in nineteenth- and twentieth-century Argentina and to shape individual fates.

**George Reid Andrews** is Distinguished Professor of History at the University of Pittsburgh, where he has taught since 1981. His publications include *The Afro-Argentines of Buenos Aires, 1800–1900* (1980), *Blacks and Whites in São Paulo, Brazil, 1888–1988* (1991), *Afro-Latin America, 1800–2000* (2004), *Blackness in the White Nation: A History of Afro-Uruguay* (2010), and *Afro-Latin America: Black Lives, 1600–2000* (2016).

**Alejandro de la Fuente** is the Robert Woods Bliss Professor of Latin American History and Economics, Professor of African and African American Studies, and founding Director of the Afro-Latin American Research Institute, Harvard University. He is the author of *A Nation for All: Race, Inequality and Politics in Twentieth-Century Cuba* (2001), *Havana and the Atlantic in the Sixteenth Century* (2008) and *Diago: The Pasts of This Afro-Cuban Present* (2017). He is the curator of three art exhibits dealing with race, history, and justice in Cuba: Queloides: Race and Racism in Cuban Contemporary Art (2010–2012),

Grupo Antillano: The Art of Afro-Cuba (2013–2016), and Diago: The Pasts of This Afro-Cuban Present (2017). He is also the editor of the journals *Cuban Studies* and *Transition: Magazine of Africa and the Diaspora*.

**Roquinaldo Ferreira** is Vasco da Gama Associate Professor of History at Brown University and the author of *Cross-Cultural Exchange in the Atlantic World: Angola and Brazil during the Era of the Slave Trade* (2012).

**Brodwyn Fischer** is Professor of History at the University of Chicago, where she also directs the Center for Latin American Studies. Her research focuses on the histories of cities, law, race, inequality, slavery, and social movements in Brazil and Latin America. Her publications include *A Poverty of Rights: Citizenship and Inequality in Twentieth-Century Rio de Janeiro* (2008) and *Cities from Scratch: Poverty and Urban Informality in Urban Latin America*, coedited with Bryan McCann and Javier Auyero (2014). She is currently completing two new books: one is a history of relational power and inequality in urban Brazil, and the other is a coedited volume with Keila Grinberg on Brazilian slavery and abolition.

**Keila Grinberg** is Associate Professor of History at the Federal University of Rio de Janeiro State and a researcher at the National Council for Scientific and Technological Development (CNPq, Brazil). She has been a visiting professor at Northwestern University and the University of Michigan and a Tinker Visiting Professor at the University of Chicago. Her books include *Liberata* (1994), *Código civil e cidadania* (2001), and *O fiador dos brasileiros: cidadania, escravidão e direito civil no tempo de Antonio Pereira Rebouças* (2002, currently being translated into English). Her current research examines nineteenth-century cases of kidnapping and illegal enslavement on the southern Brazilian border and their larger effects on the making of South American international relations. With Hebe Mattos and Martha Abreu, she is currently directing the public digital history project "Pasts Present: Memories of Slavery in Brazil."

**Frank A. Guridy** is Associate Professor of History and African American Studies at Columbia University. He is the author of *Forging Diaspora: Afro-Cubans and African Americans in a World of Empire and Jim Crow* (2010), and coeditor, with Gina Pérez and Adrian Burgos, Jr., of *Beyond el Barrio: Everyday Life in Latino/a America* (2010). His current research has shifted to US sport and urban history, focusing on the relationship of sport to urban political economies and recreational life in the United States. He is currently at work on two book projects: *Assembly in the Fragmented City: A History of the Los Angeles Memorial Coliseum* and *When Texas Sports Became Big Time: A History of Sports in Texas after World War II* (forthcoming).

**Jesse Hoffnung-Garskof** is Associate Professor of History and American Culture at the University of Michigan. He is author of *A Tale of Two Cities: Santo Domingo and New York after 1950* (2008) and of *Racial Migrations: New York City and the Revolutionary Politics of the Caribbean, 1850–1902* (2019).

**Juliet Hooker** is Professor of Political Science at Brown University. She is a political theorist specializing in multiculturalism, racial justice, Latin American political thought, Black political thought, and Afrodescendant and indigenous politics in Latin America. Her publications include *Race and the Politics of Solidarity* (2009) and *Theorizing Race in the Americas: Douglass, Sarmiento, Du Bois, and Vasconcelos* (2017). Her most recent publications are a coedited (with Barnor Hesse) special issue of the journal *South Atlantic Quarterly* on "After #Ferguson, After #Baltimore: The Challenge of Black Death and Black Life for Black Political Thought" and an article on "Black Protest/White Grievance: On the Problem of White Political Imaginations Not Shaped by Loss," *South Atlantic Quarterly* (2017). Hooker has been the recipient of fellowships and awards from the National Endowment for the Humanities, the Woodrow Wilson International Center for Scholars, the DuBois Institute for African American Research at Harvard, and the Advanced Research Collaborative at the Graduate Center of the City University of New York.

**Paul Christopher Johnson** is Professor of History, the Doctoral Program in Anthropology and History, and Afroamerican and African Studies at the University of Michigan. He is the author of *Secrets, Gossip and Gods: The Transformation of Brazilian Candomblé* (2002), *Diaspora Conversions: Black Carib Religion and the Recovery of Africa* (2007), and co-author (with Pamela E. Klassen and Winnifred Fallers Sullivan) of *Ekklesia: Three Inquiries in Church and State* (2018). Johnson is editor of the volume, *Spirited Things: The Work of "Possession" in Afro-Atlantic Religions* (2014) and is currently coeditor (with Geneviève Zubrzycki) of the interdisciplinary journal *Comparative Studies in Society and History* (CSSH). He is finishing a new book entitled *Automatic Religion: On Nearhuman Agents in Brazil and France.*

**Jennifer A. Jones** is Assistant Professor of Sociology and a Faculty Fellow in the Institute for Latino Studies at the University of Notre Dame. Her research has been published in *Latino Studies, Ethnic and Racial Studies, Sociology of Race and Ethnicity, Sociological Perspectives*, and *Law and Contemporary Problems*. With Petra Rivera-Rideau and Tianna Paschel, she is the coeditor of *Afro-Latinos in Movement: Critical Approaches to Blackness and Transnationalism in the Americas* (2016) and the author of the forthcoming *The Browning of the New South: Race, Immigration, and Minority Linked Fate*.

**Hebe Mattos** is Titular Professor of History at the Federal Fluminense University and a researcher at the National Council for Scientific and Technological Development (CNPq, Brazil). She has been a visiting professor at the University of Michigan, the School for Advanced Studies in the Social Sciences (Paris), and the Federal University of Pernambuco as well as Ruth Cardoso Chair Visiting Professor at Columbia University (2013/2014). Her publications include *Escravidão e Subjetividades no Atlântico Luso-brasileiro e Françês,* coedited with Myriam Cottias (2016), *Diáspora Negra e Lugares de Memória* (2013), *Memórias do Cativeiro. Família, Trabalho e Cidadania no Pós-Abolição*, with Ana Lugão Rios (2005), *Das Cores do Silêncio. Significados da Liberdade no Sudeste Escravista* (1995, 1998, 2013), and *The Abolition of Slavery and the Aftermath of Emancipation in Brazil*, with Rebecca Scott et al. (1988). She is currently working on a book based on self-narratives of free men descended from enslaved Africans in Brazil. She is the coordinator of The Oral History and Image Lab of the Federal Fluminense University, where she co-directed, with Martha Abreu, a collection of four documentary films about the memory of slavery among Black peasant communities, entitled *Present Pasts* (2012). With Keila Grinberg and Martha Abreu, she is currently directing the public digital history project "Pasts Present: Memories of Slavery in Brazil."

**Robin D. Moore** is Professor of Ethnomusicology at the University of Texas at Austin. His publications include *Nationalizing Blackness* (1997), *Music and Revolution* (2006), *Music of the Hispanic Caribbean* (2010), *Musics of Latin America* (2012), *Danzón: Circum-Caribbean Dialogues in Music and Dance* (2013, co-written with Alejandro Madrid), *College Music Curricula for a New Century* (2017), and articles on Cuban music in *Cuban Studies, Ethnomusicology, Encuentro de la cultura cubana*, the *Latin American Music Review*, and other journals and book anthologies. Since 2005 he has served as editor of the *Latin American Music Review*.

His most recent project involves a translation into English of a selection of Fernando Ortiz's writings on Cuban music and dance (2018).

**Karl Offen** is Professor of Environmental Studies at Oberlin College and conducts historical-environmental research in the Caribbean Basin and Latin America. He is the coeditor of two books, *Mapping Latin America* (with Jordana Dym, 2011) and *The Awakening Coast* (with Terry Rugeley, 2014), and the author of over a dozen articles concerning political ecology, the history of cartography, Afro-Amerindian relations, and colonial bio-prospecting in Central America and the far western Caribbean.

**Stephan Palmié** is Professor of Anthropology at the University of Chicago. He is the author of *Das Exil der Götter: Geschichte und Vorstellungswelt einer afrokubanischen Religion* (1991), *Wizards and Scientists: Explorations in Afro-Cuban Modernity and Tradition* (2002), and *The Cooking of History: How Not to Study Afro-Cuban Religion* (2013), as well as the editor of *Slave Culture and the Culture of Slavery* (1995), and *Africas of the Americas: Beyond the Search for Origins in the Study of Afro-Atlantic Religions* (2008). He has coedited a four-volume critical edition of the original manuscripts of C. G. A. Oldendorp's eighteenth-century *History of the Moravian Missions on the Caribbean Islands of St. Thomas, St. Corix, and St. John* (with Gudrun Meier, Peter Stein, and Horst Ulbricht, 2000–2002), a volume of essays entitled *Empirical Futures: Anthropologists and Historians Engage the Work of Sidney Mintz* (with George Baca and Aisha Khan, 2009), a compendium on *The Caribbean: A History of the Region and Its Peoples* (with Francisco Scarano, 2011), and a special section of *HAU: Journal of Ethnographic Theory* entitled "The Anthropology of History" (with Charles Stewart, 2016).

**Tianna S. Paschel** is Assistant Professor of African American Studies at the University of California–Berkeley. She is the author of *Becoming Black Political Subjects: Movements and Ethno-Racial Rights in Colombia and Brazil* (2016), which has received numerous book awards including the Herbert Jacob Book Award (Law and Society Association) and the Barrington Moore Award (American Sociological Association). She is also coeditor, with Petra Rivera-Rideau and Jennifer Jones, of *Afro-Latin@s in Movement: Critical Approaches to the Study of Blackness and Transnationalism in the Americas* (2016) and has published in *American Journal of Sociology*, *Du Bois Review*, *SOULS: A Critical Journal of Black Politics, Culture and Society*, and *Ethnic and Racial Studies*.

**Lara Putnam** is UCIS Research Professor of Latin American and Caribbean history at the University of Pittsburgh. She writes on theories and methods of transnational history as well as researching migration, kinship, and gender in the Greater Caribbean. Publications include *The Company They Kept: Migrants and the Politics of Gender in Caribbean Costa Rica, 1870–1960* (2002), *Radical Moves: Caribbean Migrants and the Politics of Race in the Jazz Age* (2013), and more than two dozen chapters and articles. Putnam is President of the Conference on Latin American History and a member of the Board of Editors of the *American Historical Review.*

**Tatiana Seijas** is Associate Professor of History at Pennsylvania State University. Her first monograph, *Asian Slaves in Colonial Mexico: From Chinos to Indians* (2014), won the Berkshire Conference Book Prize. She is also co-author (with Jake Frederick) of *Spanish Dollars and Sister Republics: The Money That Made Mexico and the United States* (2017) and coeditor (with Stuart B. Schwartz) of *Victors and Vanquished: Spanish and Nahua Views of the Fall of the Mexica Empire* (2nd edition, 2017). Her current monograph project is tentatively titled "First Routes: Indigenous Commerce in Early North America."

**Doris Sommer** is Ira and Jewell Williams Professor of Romance Languages and Literatures and of African and African American Studies at Harvard University and the founder of Cultural Agents, an NGO dedicated to reviving the civic mission of the humanities. Among her books are *Foundational Fictions: The National Romances of Latin America* (1991), *Proceed with Caution when Engaged by Minority Literature* (1999), *Bilingual Aesthetics: A New Sentimental Education* (2004), and *The Work of Art in the World: Civic Agency and Public Humanities* (2014). Sommer benefited from, and is dedicated to developing, good public-school education.

**Peter Wade** is Professor of Social Anthropology at the University of Manchester and recently held a British Academy Wolfson Research Professorship (2013–2016). His publications include *Blackness and Race Mixture* (1993), *Race and Ethnicity in Latin America* (2010), *Race, Nature and Culture: An Anthropological Perspective* (2002), and *Race and Sex in Latin America* (2009). He recently directed a project, funded by the Economic and Social Research Council and the Leverhulme Trust, on "Race, genomics and *mestizaje* (mixture) in Latin America." An edited book from the project is *Mestizo Genomics: Race Mixture, Nation, and Science in Latin America* (2014). His most recent books are *Race: An Introduction* (2015) and *Degrees of Mixture, Degrees of Freedom: Genomics, Multiculturalism and Race in Latin America* (2017). With Mónica Moreno Figueroa, he is currently co-directing a project on "Latin American Antiracism in a 'Post-Racial' Age."

# Acknowledgments

The publication of this book marks a quarter-century of our professional collaboration and deep friendship, which began with Alejandro's arrival in the United States from Cuba in 1992. The volume had its origins in a dinner conversation in Charlotte, North Carolina, in 2015. The two of us were reflecting on the astonishing growth that the field of Afro-Latin American studies has experienced over the last twenty to thirty years, and about the need for a systematic survey of those advances in all the many subfields that address Latin America's Black past, present, and future. This volume is our reply to that need and our contribution to the further consolidation and expansion of this field.

In May of 2015 we convened an "exploratory seminar" on Afro-Latin American Studies with the generous support of the Radcliffe Institute for Advanced Studies at Harvard University. Over a period of two days, a stellar group of scholars presented their ideas on what such a volume might cover. In addition to those colleagues who contributed essays to the volume, we thank Rose-Marie Belle Antoine, Jaime Arocha, Aisha Beliso-de Jesús, Sidney Chalhoub, Henry Louis Gates, Jr., Michael Hanchard, Marial Iglesias Utset, Márcia Lima, Bárbaro Martínez-Ruiz, Judith Morrison, Rafael Guerreiro Osório, Rebecca Scott, and Edward Telles for lending us their expertise and helping us think through the agenda for the volume.

Over the next year and a half, contributors to the volume wrote initial drafts of their essays and extensively revised those drafts. The group then met in December 2016 in Cartagena, Colombia, to discuss final revisions, taking advantage of our participation in the symposium, "Después de Santiago 2000: El movimiento afrodescendiente y los

xix

estudios afrolatinoamericanos," sponsored and organized by the Afro-Latin American Research Institute at Harvard University and the University of Cartagena.

From the very beginning of our work on this volume, and on the Afro-Latin America Series of which the volume forms part, Deborah Gershenowitz, our editor at Cambridge University Press, has been consistently supportive in smoothing the way for a big and complex undertaking. We hope that the final result repays her confidence in this project.

Although we did not know this at the outset, we could not possibly have convened, and gone on to work with, a more knowledgeable, conscientious, and thoroughly enjoyable group of contributors. Our profound gratitude to you all, and let's try to think of another project to do together!

# The Making of a Field

## *Afro-Latin American Studies*

### Alejandro de la Fuente and George Reid Andrews

This volume seeks to introduce readers to the dynamic and growing field of Afro-Latin American studies. We define that field, first, as the study of people of African ancestry in Latin America, and second, as the study of the larger societies in which those people live. Under the first heading, scholars study Black histories, cultures, strategies, and struggles in the region. Under the second, they study blackness, and race more generally, as a category of difference, as an engine of stratification and inequality, and as a key variable in processes of national formation.

There are sound historical reasons for both approaches. Of the 10.7 million enslaved Africans who arrived in the New World between 1500 and 1870, almost two-thirds came to colonies controlled by Spain or Portugal (Borucki, Eltis, and Wheat 2015, 440; see also Chapter 2). It was in those territories that slavery lasted for the longest periods of time in the Western Hemisphere, spanning over 350 years. Africans began arriving at the islands of the Caribbean in the early sixteenth century, and slavery was not finally abolished in those islands until 1886, when the last slaves were emancipated in Cuba. Two years later, Brazil became the last country in the Americas to abolish slavery; today it is home to the second-largest Afrodescendant population in the world, exceeded in size only by Nigeria. Close to a million Africans arrived in Cuba during the nineteenth century and over two million in Brazil, a process that helps explain the profound influence that African-based cultural practices have exercised in the formation of national cultures in those two countries and around the region more generally.

Yet it was not until quite recently that the scholarship on race, inequality, and racial stratification in Latin America had grown enough to develop the sorts of questions and debates that sustain and constitute a field of study. Writing in 1992, Thomas Skidmore, at that time the leading scholar of Brazil in the United States, noted that one could "count on the fingers of one hand the ... authors who have done serious research on post-abolition race relations." Skidmore was talking specifically about Brazil, but his observation could be applied to Spanish America as well. Throughout Latin America, scholars interested in Afro-descendant peoples had focused almost entirely on the period of slavery, "as if the topic of race ceased to have any relevance ... after slavery ended" (Skidmore 1992, 8).

During most of the 1900s, the idea that race was not an important dimension of Latin American societies was widespread in the region. National ideologies of racial inclusion, discussed in depth in Paulina L. Alberto and Jesse Hoffnung-Garskof's contribution to this volume (Chapter 8), argued that Latin American societies had transcended their colonial histories of state-mandated racial inequality to become, in the 1800s and 1900s, "racial democracies" governed by social norms of racial harmony and equality. National politics in the region were driven not by racial tensions and divisions, it was argued, but by conflicts and negotiations among competing social classes. For most observers of the region, the central questions of the twentieth century were how to achieve self-sustaining economic growth and development, and how to allocate power and resources among elites, middle classes, workers, and peasants.

As we write in 2017, that panorama has shifted dramatically. Formerly considered "irrelevant," race is now at the center of research on Latin American societies (see, e.g., Wade 2009, 2010, 2017; Gotkowitz 2011; Hernández 2013; Loveman 2014; Telles and PERLA 2014). This has been especially the case with Afro-Latin American topics. As the chapters in this volume abundantly show, over the last thirty years scholars have produced a rich outpouring of research and writing on time frames ranging from the period of colonial slavery to the present day. This shift occurred partly in response to the realization, articulated by postcolonial scholars, that race is central to historic and contemporary processes of coloniality (Quijano 2000; Mignolo 2005). Just as important, however, were the political and social changes taking place in the region.

The field of Afro-Latin American studies has developed in tandem with, and to a large degree in response to, a wave of racially defined social, cultural, and political movements that, taking advantage of democratization processes since the 1980s, have transformed how Latin Americans think about their region, culture, and history. Building on social sciences research that has documented persistent racial inequality across time, these movements have challenged traditional discourses on race and nation that depict the region as racially egalitarian and harmonious. They have also demanded legislation and specific policies to address discrimination and inequality, and their efforts have produced results. Starting with the Nicaraguan constitutional reform of 1987, which recognized the existence of minority communities on the Atlantic coast, legal instruments that ban discrimination and acknowledge the multiracial character of Latin American societies have proliferated. In 1988 the Brazilian constitution banned discrimination and recognized the rights of former runaway slave communities (*quilombos*) to their ancestral lands. Other countries (e.g., Bolivia, Colombia, Ecuador, Guatemala, Honduras) followed suit and now recognize collective rights for the population of African descent, while others (Argentina, Colombia, Cuba, Panama, Uruguay) explicitly condemn discrimination because of race (see Chapters 5, 7, and 13). Activists also targeted the national censuses and demanded the inclusion of ethno-racial categories to counter the traditional invisibility of these groups. While in the 1980s only Cuba and Brazil collected information concerning individuals of African descent, by the 2010s Afrodescendants were counted in seventeen of the nineteen countries in the region (Loveman 2014).

International organizations and agencies have acknowledged the importance and scope of these movements and taken concrete institutional steps to address issues of racial justice in their activities. Examples include the Rapporteurship on the Rights of Persons of African Descent and against Racial Discrimination created by the Organization of American States in 2005, and the Gender and Diversity Division created by the Inter-American Development Bank in 2007. The Division's mission is to "promote gender equality and support development with identity for African descendants and indigenous peoples in the Latin America and the Caribbean region" (IADB 2017). The United Nations Development Program sponsors a project on the Afrodescendant Population of Latin America and monitors racial discrimination in the region through its Committee on the Elimination of Racial Discrimination (CERD). In 2010 the US State Department created the Race, Ethnicity, and Social Inclusion Unit, which coordinates US diplomacy on social inclusion and racial equality issues in the Western Hemisphere. Three years later the United Nations approved resolution 68/237, which proclaims 2015–24 as the International Decade for People of African Descent. International development agencies have also included metrics of racial inequality in their development benchmarks, giving additional visibility and support to race justice agendas.

All of these actors – activists, government officials, representatives and employees of international agencies and organizations – have contributed to the growth and development of Afro-Latin American studies as a field. Their programs and demands have shaped how scholars study Afrodescendants in the region. The chapters in this volume illustrate the richness and disciplinary variety of this scholarly production.

## THE ORIGINS OF AFRO-LATIN AMERICAN STUDIES

Early studies of the history, behavior, and culture of Afrodescendants in Latin America were very much attuned to the voluminous scientific literature that, in the second half of the nineteenth century, sought to demonstrate and document the biological foundations of black inferiority. The combination of anthropometric measurements feeding a variety of indices of human worth, evolutionary theories, and the social Darwinist belief that human history was centrally about the inevitable competition of racial groups, some of which were destined to perish and live under the control of the fittest – all of these turned Latin America into an area of special interest for "scientific" studies of race. The region's high degree of miscegenation or racial mixture was seen as a clear indicator of racial degeneration and social decadence, a point emphasized by the pioneering scientific racists Arthur de Gobineau and Louis Agassiz when they (independently) visited Brazil in the 1860s (Skidmore 1974).

In an effort to better understand that degeneration and decadence, a handful of Latin American scholars and writers – for example, Raimundo Nina Rodrigues (1900) in Brazil, Fernando Ortiz (1906, 1916) and Israel Castellanos (1916) in Cuba – carried out research on what they viewed as black "pathologies," gathering information on turn-of-the-century Afro-Latin American religious life, criminality, and family structure. Much of the information reported by those writers is still useful to scholars today, but the racial attitudes embodied in their work, and widely diffused among the region's elites, left little room for black participation in national life.

This was very much in keeping with the oligarchical political and social structures in force in most of Latin America at that time – indeed, scientific racism was a primary support of elite arguments that the racially mixed masses were incapable of playing a responsible role in national life (Figueras 1907; Ingenieros 1913; Valenilla Lanz 1919; Viana 1922).

During the 1910s and 1920s, however, workers' movements and middle-class reformist movements began to demand a greater role in national politics; at the same time, nationalist pressures grew for the construction of new national identities based not on ideas and models imported from Europe, but on the actual historical and present-day experiences of Latin Americans as a people. These political developments set the stage for a major revision of racial thought in the region, in the form of the concept of "racial democracy" (see Chapter 8). Where the scientific racists had either rejected the notion of black contributions to national life, or had treated those contributions as almost entirely negative, writers and intellectuals associated with new ideologies of racial inclusion – Gilberto Freyre in Brazil, Fernando Ortiz in Cuba, José Vasconcelos in Mexico, Juan Pablo Sojo in Venezuela – acknowledged the role of Africans and their descendants in creating new, distinctly Latin American national cultures, societies, and identities. Those cultures and societies were neither African nor European in form or content. Rather, they were a mixture of African, European, and Amerindian elements, combined in a centuries-long process of cultural and racial mixture that had produced something completely new in world historical experience: a "New World in the tropics," in Freyre's formulation, or a new "cosmic race," in the language of Vasconcelos.

The willingness of the proponents of racial democracy to acknowledge black contributions to national life opened the door to greatly expanded research on Afro-Latin American topics. This was most notably the case in Brazil, where Freyre (1933, 1936), Arthur Ramos (1937, 1940), and Edison Carneiro (1936, 1937), to mention only the most prominent names, spearheaded a wave of research on Afro-Brazilian history and culture in the plantation zones of the Northeast. Some of their findings were presented at two Afro-Brazilian Congresses held during the 1930s (Congresso Afro-Brasileiro 1937, 1940), which in turn stimulated more such work; a small core of scholars started working on racial questions in the southeastern state of São Paulo in the 1940s (Nogueira 1942; Bicudo 1947; Bastide and Fernandes 1953). In Cuba, the Sociedad de Folklore Cubano and the Sociedad de Estudios Afrocubanos, both founded by Fernando Ortiz during the 1920s and 1930s, respectively, carried out research on black contributions to Cuban culture and national identity, much of it published in Ortiz's journal, *Estudios Afrocubanos*. Similar institutions were created in Venezuela (the Servicio de Investigaciones Folklóricas, established in 1946), Colombia (the Instituto Etnológico Nacional, 1943), and Brazil (the Comissão Nacional de Folclore, 1947).

In other countries, individual scholars – Gonzalo Aguirre Beltrán (1946, 1958) in Mexico, Aquiles Escalante (1964) in Colombia, Armando Fortune (Maloney 1994) in Panama, Ildefonso Pereda Valdés (Carvalho Neto 1955) in Uruguay – carried out pioneering research.

These early efforts tended to focus on black religion, dance, linguistics, and other cultural forms, or on community studies. For the most part they left aside questions of racial inequality or discrimination, largely accepting the argument that Latin America's historical experience of racial and cultural mixture had eliminated racism and prejudice and produced societies that offered equal opportunity to all. There were some dissenting voices, however, particularly in the black newspapers of the region, which noted sharp disparities between semi-official ideologies of racial equality and the empirical realities of discrimination, prejudice, and black poverty (de la Fuente 2001; Andrews 2010; Geler 2010; Guridy 2010; Alberto 2011; see also Chapter 6). Those voices in the black press were joined in the 1930s and 1940s by Communist activists in Brazil, Cuba, Venezuela, and other countries, who made anti-racism a central plank of their party programs, and then in the 1940s and 1950s by a handful of intellectuals and scholars who increasingly questioned whether Latin American societies were in fact racial democracies. Most of these critics were Afrodescendant: in Brazil, Edison Carneiro, Clóvis Moura (1959, 1977), Abdias do Nascimento (1968; *Quilombo* 2003), and Alberto Guerreiro Ramos (1957); in Cuba, Gustavo Urrutia, Alberto Arredondo (1939), Juan René Betancourt (1945, 1954, 1959), Serafín Portuondo Linares (1950), and Walterio Carbonell (1961); and in Colombia, Aquiles Escalante (1964), and Manuel Zapata Olivella (1967).

In Brazil, some of the racial democracy critics were white, particularly in São Paulo, where French sociologist Roger Bastide had encouraged his students Florestan Fernandes, Oracy Nogueira, and others to study Brazilian race relations, and Fernandes had gone on to train his own students, Fernando Henrique Cardoso and Octávio Ianni, to do the same. These white intellectuals enjoyed much greater legitimacy and received far greater public and scholarly attention than their black colleagues. Black critics of racial democracy were more likely to occupy marginal positions in academic and intellectual life, both because of their racial status and because of their questioning of one of the core components of national identity. They were also more easily dismissed as poorly adjusted malcontents with personal axes to grind. White critics, by contrast, acted from seemingly disinterested motives; the previously mentioned white Brazilians, far from being socially or professionally marginal, were affiliated with the most prestigious institution of higher education in the country, the University of São Paulo.

Still, even if white critics of racial democracy received more attention than black ones, neither group had much immediate impact on mainstream scholarly institutions in the region, which remained for the most part indifferent to Afro-related themes. Despite the undeniable progress that had been made since the 1930s in studying black history and culture, by the 1970s the quantity of scholarly literature available was still miniscule, in relation either to studies of black history and culture in the United States or to studies of Amerindian populations in Latin America. During the last forty years, however, the situation has changed dramatically, as the chapters in this volume make clear.

Why this explosion of work on Afro-Latin America? One reason is undoubtedly the growth in Latin American higher education more generally. Since 1960, Brazil, Colombia, Mexico, Venezuela, and other countries have invested enormous sums in expanding their university systems; inevitably this expanded those countries' research capacity as well (Balán 2013). But after years of relative indifference to Afro-Latin American topics, why did researchers start turning toward black history and culture as an area of study?

That turn took place in part because of thickening scholarly networks and dialogues between Latin America and the United States, particularly around questions of slavery and race. In response to the rise of the civil rights and Black Power movements, scholars in the United States were paying increasing attention to questions of race, producing classic works that are still obligatory reading today (Woodward 1955; Stampp 1956; Davis 1966, 1975; Franklin 1967; Wilson 1978). As US scholars thought about their country's racial past and present, many pushed on to ask how the US experience of slavery, or of the post-emancipation period, or of present-day race relations, compared to similar experiences in Brazil, Cuba, and the British Caribbean. At the same time, newly trained US historians of Latin America wrestled with the other end of the comparison: how did the racial experiences of Latin America compare to those of the United States? A few undertook research comparing the two regions (Tannenbaum 1946; Elkins 1959; Harris 1964; Klein 1967; Degler 1971; Hoetink 1973). Most, while motivated by comparative interests, focused on Latin America, and usually on the experience of slavery. The result was a surge of scholarship during the 1970s that, while small in relation to the amount of work being done on the United States, nevertheless represented a marked increase in scholarly attention to Afro-Latin

America (e.g., Knight 1970; Hall 1971; Conrad 1972; Bowser 1974; Skidmore 1974; Toplin 1974; Whitten 1974; Dean 1976; Rout 1976).

Those early comparative studies were based on the belief that race relations in Latin America were more harmonious than in the United States and that this difference was the product of dissimilar histories of race and slavery. Scholars such as Frank Tannenbaum and Stanley Elkins had fully absorbed the racial democracy arguments that Latin American intellectuals had articulated in the 1920s and 1930s. They studied Latin America, but they did so in order to understand and find solutions to race problems in the United States. The same belief animated some of the first studies about racial inequality in Latin America, sponsored by UNESCO in the 1950s. In a world besieged by racial conflicts, these studies sought to understand how Brazil had succeeded in creating a functioning racial democracy. In the process, they made two key contributions to the field. First, they highlighted the need to study contemporary race relations (not just slavery) in the region. Second, their findings generated a healthy skepticism concerning some of the central claims of the proponents of racial democracy.

This skepticism informed the work of a new generation of Latin American scholars, some of whom had studied in US universities. In the 1960s, 1970s, and 1980s, these scholars produced their own readings of the Afro-Latin American past and present (Fernandes 1965; Costa 1966; Carvalho Neto 1971; Moreno Fraginals 1978; Silva 1978; Hasenbalg 1979; Colmenares 1979; Deive 1980; Nistal-Moret 1984; Friedemann and Arocha 1986; Reis 1986; Machado 1987). As they did so, they engaged not just with their North American counterparts but also with the black political movements that were forming in various countries of the region during the 1970s and 1980s. Those movements, discussed in depth in Chapter 7, had major impacts not just on the politics of the region but on its intellectual and scholarly life as well.

## BLACK MOBILIZATION AND THE PRODUCTION OF KNOWLEDGE

On December 5–7, 2000, more than 1,700 activists and government representatives from all over the Americas convened in Santiago de Chile. They were attending the Regional Conference of the Americas, in preparation for the World Conference against Racism, Racial Discrimination, Xenophobia and Related Intolerance that would take place in Durban, South Africa, a year later. It was a landmark event. On the one hand, the widespread participation of activists and community leaders illustrated how much the movement for civil rights and racial justice had advanced in Latin America since the collapse of most authoritarian regimes in the 1970s and 1980s (Andrews 2004, 2016; Yashar 2005; Hernández 2013). On the other hand, the event marked the public acknowledgment by state authorities that racism is a major problem in the region, demanding a serious policy response. As the conference's concluding declaration stated, "ignoring the existence of discrimination and racism, at both the State and the society level, contributes directly and indirectly to perpetuating the practices of racism, racial discrimination, xenophobia and related intolerance." Racism and discrimination were characterized as historical products of "conquest, colonialism, slavery and other forms of servitude" but, taking a cue from scholarship on contemporary engines of racial stratification, the declaration noted that the effects of these processes persisted and "are" – in present tense – "a source of systemic discrimination that still affects large sectors of the population" (UN General Assembly 2001).

In order to combat the effects of racism, discrimination and racial injustice in the region, the Conference approved an ambitious "Plan of Action" (UN General Assembly 2001). This plan had deep implications for the field of Afro-Latin American studies, for several of its measures were linked to the production and dissemination of knowledge concerning people of African descent in the region. The plan "urged" states to compile and disseminate statistical data on racialized groups. This information would serve as the basis for programs of inclusion and access to basic social services and economic opportunities, including policies of affirmative action. Some of the items in the plan concerned education in fairly concrete ways. The parties agreed on the need to create educational and research programs about Africa's contributions to history and civilization, as well as to disseminate information against racial stereotypes and myths. The plan asked states to include the study of racism in university curricula and to organize courses on racism and discrimination "for prosecutors, law enforcement officials, members of the judiciary and other public employees." Attention was also given to the media, to its role in disseminating racial images and information and to the need "to ensure the fair and balanced presence of people of African descent" in it.

One of the key contributions of the Santiago Conference is that it sanctioned and normalized the category of "Afrodescendants" as a group with legal, cultural, and ethical implications in the arenas of international justice and human rights (Laó-Montes 2009; Campos García 2015).

It also helped consolidate and make visible a transnational network of race-justice activists that was able to exercise pressure on national governments for the adoption of specific policies against racism and discrimination. As part of these efforts, activists not only deployed knowledge produced by academics, as was notably the case in Brazil during the 1980s and 1990s (Htun 2004), but they also produced, systematized, and disseminated important new knowledge concerning their communities. As activists formulated demands in the areas of health care, education, environmental justice, job training, gender violence, poverty eradication, and police brutality, among others, they were compelled to gather and produce valuable information concerning Afrodescendants and their cultures and living conditions across the region. On top of that, the movement itself has become a subject of intense study, prompting numerous studies about race and mobilization in contemporary Latin America (Escobar 2008; de la Fuente 2012; Martínez 2012; Pisano 2012; Rahier 2012; Pereira 2013; Valero and Campos García 2015; Paschel 2016).

This volume constitutes yet another example of the impact of activists from the Afrodescendant movement on the field of Afro-Latin American Studies. Our book has been conceived and executed in conversations between academics and activists. These exchanges took place in two landmark events sponsored by the Afro-Latin American Research Institute at Harvard University, in collaboration with the University of Cartagena, in 2015 and 2016. The events gathered prominent figures of the Afrodescendant movement, many of whom had attended the 2000 meeting in Santiago, to assess the implementation of the Plan of Action, its successes and failures. Part of the agenda, however, was also to analyze the impact of the movement on the field of Afro-Latin American studies, in order to articulate new research questions and agendas. Just as we attempted to evaluate the outcomes of the Santiago meeting, we sought also to evaluate the trajectory of this field of study that, not coincidentally, has come of age along with the consolidation and expansion of the Afrodescendant movement. The field has grown enough to sustain specialized journals such as *Estudos Afro-Asiáticos*, *Afro-Hispanic Review*, *Revista Áfro-Asia*, *América Negra* (published in Colombia from 1991 to 1998), and *Latin American and Caribbean Ethnic Studies*; to allow for the publication of several synthetic overviews (Andrews 2004; Wade 2010; Gates 2011); to sustain specialized research units such as the Afro-Latin American Research Institute (ALARI) at Harvard University; and to populate the *Afro-Latin America* book series at Cambridge

University Press. It is precisely because the field has grown so much, both thematically and in terms of disciplinary approaches, that we felt the need to assess its current state, recent achievements, and possible future directions. That is the purpose of the chapters in this volume.

## THE CHAPTERS

In thinking about how to organize the volume, we faced a series of questions. What topics were essential to include? And how should those topics be presented: as literature reviews tracing the development of a field or subfield (how have scholars thought and written about, for example, Afro-Latin American religions over time?); as historical narratives based on syntheses of past and current literature (how have Afro-Latin American religious forms evolved and developed over time?); or as some combination of those two? Meanwhile, what about the challenges of achieving full regional and chronological coverage? All of the topics in this volume have long historical trajectories, and most of them appear, in one form or another, in all or most of the countries in the region. How could we effectively compress 500-year continent-wide experiences into relatively short synthetic articles?

On both fronts – mode of presentation, and temporal and geographical coverage – we ultimately decided that authors would be free to decide how best to present their topic. Concerning mode of presentation, most opted for some combination of literature review and historical narrative. In terms of geographical coverage, the volume ended up leaning heavily on Brazil, with Cuba and Colombia in second and third place. Those emphases reflect both the size of Afrodescendant populations in those countries – Brazil alone accounts for over 70 percent of Latin America's Afrodescendants (Telles and PERLA 2014, 26) – and, not coincidentally, the relative state of development of Afro-Latin American studies in those countries. In an effort to ensure adequate coverage of Spanish America, we invited contributors who have worked on Argentina, Central America, the Dominican Republic, Mexico, Uruguay, and Venezuela. One of our hopes for the volume is that setting the Brazilian literature in dialogue with its Spanish American counterparts will spark new research questions on both sides of that exchange, leading to further development and enrichment of the field.

From the beginning of the volume to the end, a focus on the voices, actions, strategies, and decisions of Africans and their descendants drives every one of the chapters. In direct response to earlier generations of scholarship, recent work on Afro-Latin American studies privileges the concept of black agency. The scientific racists had seen black people as hapless victims of their genetic inferiority. The proponents of racial democracy did not completely escape the heritage of scientific racism, assuming that blacks and mulattoes would progress in Latin American societies only to the degree that they were able to whiten themselves, either genetically or culturally. The Marxist-influenced writers of the 1950s and 1960s (e.g., Fernandes 1965; Costa 1966; Rama 1967; Moreno Fraginals 1978) forcefully rejected any hint of racism but viewed Afro-Latin America and its inhabitants as being very much at the mercy of the needs and "imperatives" of capitalist development.

A focus on black agency is most obvious in chapters by Frank A. Guridy and Juliet Hooker on black political thinkers (Chapter 6); by Doris Sommer on black writers (Chapter 9); by Tianna Paschel on black political movements (Chapter 7); by Alejandro de la Fuente on black visual artists (Chapter 10); and by Karl Offen (Chapter 13) on the cultural geographies of black settlement in the New World. But the other chapters follow this approach as well. In Chapter 2, Roquinaldo Ferreira and Tatiana Seijas trace the multiple roles of Africans in the Atlantic slave trade, not least their role in introducing African understandings of the world to colonial societies in the Americas. Offen focuses in Chapter 13 on the environmental knowledge that Africans brought with them, and how they and their descendants applied that knowledge first to understand and then to modify the landscapes that were their new homes. Brodwyn Fischer, Keila Grinberg, and Hebe Mattos apply a similar perspective in Chapter 5 to the legal landscapes that enslaved Africans encountered in the New World, showing how Africans and their descendants learned those landscapes and then, through quiet lobbying and legal action, gradually transformed them. Lara Putnam considers Afrodescendants' decisions on how, when, and whether to move from one place to another, and the evolving migratory streams and experiences that those decisions produced in Chapter 14. George Reid Andrews discusses the broad range of strategies that Afrodescendants used to move upward in colonial and post-independence societies in Chapter 3.

All of the chapters grapple as well with the notorious methodological difficulties of researching the Afro-Latin American past and present. For example, in order to recover the ideas and voices of black political thinkers, Guridy and Hooker push well beyond traditional canons of political thought in the region to include black newspapers, poetry, and song lyrics. In Chapter 10, de la Fuente cautions that most of the artistic production that he is writing about no longer exists, and most of its creators are now forgotten. In almost all of the subfields addressed by the chapters, scholarly reconstructions of that past and present are very much still in progress, and in some cases just beginning.

The volume begins with a section of chapters on the deeply embedded inequalities that have shaped the development of Afro-Latin American societies over time. Ferreira and Seijas present the starting point of those inequalities, the Atlantic slave trade, in Chapter 2. Noting how scholarly research on the trade began in the 1950s and 1960s with questions that were primarily quantitative (how many people were involved? from what parts of Africa? traveling to what parts of the Americas?), they discuss how recent research has sought to supplement quantitative interpretations with approaches drawn from social, cultural, and Atlantic history. Those approaches are more likely to focus on the lived experiences of those caught up in the slave trade and on the reciprocal impacts of long-term ties between Africa and the Americas.

Chapters by Andrews (Chapter 3) and Peter Wade (Chapter 4) also begin with slavery and then go on to trace the long-term historical impacts of colonial institutions and practices. Andrews surveys the evolving intersections of racial, class, and gender inequality in the region over the last 500 years. Wade takes as his starting point the colonial ideologies and regulations governing African and indigenous peoples. While those practices assigned Africans and indigenous peoples different places in colonial racial hierarchies, they did not prevent frequent cross-racial contacts and interaction and the creation, in much of Afro-Latin America, of large Afro-indigenous populations. Black and indigenous peoples continue to interact up to the present, helping to shape the contours of present-day multicultural movements and state policies in the region.

Focusing specifically on Brazil, Fischer, Grinberg, and Mattos (Chapter 5) examine the legal structures through which inequality was established and maintained during the colonial period, followed by the "racial silence" of the post-slavery period, in which Brazilian (and Spanish American) law dropped almost all references to race and any formal pretense to maintaining racial inequality. They find that "racial silence" did little to reverse inequalities inherited from the colonial period and in some ways worked to reinforce them. The chapter concludes with a review of recent (post-1985) policies that seek to combat racial inequality.

A second section of chapters considers the realm of politics. In Chapter 6, Guridy and Hooker examine the broad spectrum of Afro-Latin American political thought during the 1800s and 1900s. They demonstrate the multivocality and intellectual richness of the debates among those thinkers. Especially valuable is the chapter's discussion of black feminist thinkers and, as suggested earlier, its efforts to recover ideas that were expressed in venues other than canonical political writing. Paschel's chapter on black political movements pays equally close attention to black feminism, and to Afrodescendant participation in key moments of the region's history: independence and nation-building in the 1800s, the rise of populism and mass-based political movements in the 1900s, and the multicultural turn of the late 1900s and early 2000s (Chapter 7).

One of the central demands of the most recent (post-1980) generation of black movements and thinkers has been that Latin American societies reconsider the idea that they were, to use the Brazilian term, "racial democracies." In Chapter 8, Alberto and Hoffnung-Garskof carefully trace the origins of that term and concept and identify its national variants in Puerto Rico, the Dominican Republic, and other Spanish American countries. In so doing, they document a lively hemispheric conversation on ideas of racial inclusion and exclusion that continues to the present.

A third section of chapters examines black thought and action in various cultural fields: literature (Chapter 9), visual arts (Chapter 10), music (Chapter 11), religion (Chapter 12), and cultural geographies (Chapter 13). While exploring those topics, the chapters grapple with several common questions, beginning with what we mean when we talk about Afro-Latin American cultural artifacts. Do we mean works produced by Afrodescendants, works on Afrodescendant themes or topics, works incorporating African or African-derived cultural elements, or something else entirely? Sommer responds to that question by focusing on formal literary strategies, and in particular on black authors' use of an "unrelenting ... doubling of codes, of systems, beliefs, meanings, languages, personae." De la Fuente adopts a three-part definition incorporating works produced by Afrodescendant artists, works that include (or claim to include) African-derived cultural elements, and works that comment in some way on race and blackness. Paul Christopher Johnson and Stephan Palmié focus in Chapter 12 on the second part of that definition, examining religious beliefs and practices that claim descent from Africa. They explore the content and meaning of such claims and how they have evolved over time to produce, since 2000, a transnational religious "superform" drawing elements from across the region and from Africa. They also consider the question of what we mean when we talk about a "religion," as distinct from spiritual beliefs and practices.

Religion figures as well in Robin Moore's chapter on music (Chapter 11) and Offen's on African and Afro-Latin American cultural geographies (Chapter 13). Music was intimately connected to African religious observance, and many nineteenth- and twentieth-century musical forms – Cuban rumba, Brazilian samba, Uruguayan candombe – trace their antecedents to African ritual musics. As those forms were commercialized and "nationalized" (Moore 1997) in the 1900s, becoming core symbols of national identity, how did that change their relationship to blackness and to the African-derived traditions on which they were based? Offen explores both the spiritual meanings that Africans and their descendants read in New World landscapes and the scientific understandings that they applied to those landscapes. Both sets of understandings were critical to slave survival on plantations and to the establishment of independent quilombo and free black communities in the countryside. They also continue to inform current debates on rural black communities and their claims to land and cultural rights.

Reflecting an important recent trend in social scientific and humanistic scholarship, a final set of chapters considers the role of transnational connections and spaces in Afro-Latin American life. Beginning with the Atlantic slave trade and continuing up to the present, Putnam surveys the many different migratory streams that developed both within Latin America, and from the region to destinations in North America and Europe (Chapter 14). In keeping with the volume's emphasis on agency, she discusses how, why, and when individuals, families, and entire communities made strategic decisions to leave specific places to move to others, producing an evolving panorama of movement that indelibly shaped the societies of the region. The volume's concluding chapter, by Jennifer A. Jones, focuses specifically on Afro-Latin American migration to the United States and the recent emergence of a new scholarly subfield, Afro-Latino studies (Chapter 15). Reflecting on the challenges that that migration has posed to racial understandings both in this country and in Latin America, Jones calls for the further development of Afro-Latino studies as a field that can mediate among African diaspora studies, African-American studies, and Afro-Latin American studies.

## FUTURE DIRECTIONS

Our volume highlights the complexity and richness of this growing field, but by no means exhausts it. There are many themes that have resulted in the production of significant bodies of scholarship – gender and

patriarchy, slave emancipation, marronage and slave resistance, the rise of
legal human rights regimes concerning blackness – that could have been
considered for possible chapters. These themes do appear in the chapters
in this volume, but we readily concede that there are alternative ways to
organize an exploration of the field.

Many of the chapters are chronologically ambitious and encompass
the colonial and the national periods. By adopting this temporal frame,
they explore the long-term impact of slavery on post-emancipation
societies. This is one of the research questions that has guided the field
since the comparative studies of the mid-twentieth century, which
posited that the explanation for differences in modern race relations
was to be found in the evolution of different slave systems. In the 1970s
and 1980s, scholars became critical of what they perceived as teleo-
logical narratives connecting slave systems and post-emancipation race
relations. Carl Degler (1971, 92) for instance, concluded that slavery
did not shape race relations in "fundamental" ways. In his comparative
study of racist regimes in the United States and South Africa, John
Cell (1982, xii) offered a similar formulation, arguing that slavery had
"relatively little to do" with subsequent racial dynamics. Anthony
Marx (1998, 8–9) agreed that slave systems "cannot directly explain"
the shape of later racial orders. None of these authors disputed that
some connection exists between slavery and race relations after emancipation, but they did not explore the nature and possible importance of
these links.

Recent scholars dealing with this problem have noted the need to pay
serious attention to the contradictory expectations and goals informing
emancipation processes everywhere. Rebecca Scott emphasized the unpre-
dictability of these processes in her landmark comparative study of Louisiana and Cuba, arguing that it is unlikely that we will be able to create
"any simple global explanation" that accounts for different outcomes in
how slave societies evolved after emancipation. "Neither structures nor
struggles could fully determine the outcome," she notes, thus the need
to study how conflicts over rights, standing, and resources produced
different results in each case (Scott 2005, 263, 264). These conflicts were
framed by preexistent practices, understandings, and expectations, however, so it remains necessary to research them under slavery in order to
establish possible continuities and innovations. Andrews (2004, 8) offers
a possible analytical path forward by suggesting patterns that could
become the subject of specific future research: "forms of behavior that
originated under slavery... proved unexpectedly durable and long lasting,

and continued to shape the course of Afro-Latin American history... in the nineteenth and twentieth centuries."

Among those behaviors that proved to be remarkably resilient are African-based cultural practices. There is a growing literature concerning the reproduction and longevity of African cultures in colonial societies, provoked by longstanding debates concerning creolization (Mintz and Price 1992; Thornton 1998; Sweet 2003; Bennett 2003, 2009). As discussed in several of the chapters in this volume, some of these cultural practices came to be identified as foundational elements of national identity in the twentieth century, although it is not always clear why some were selected while others were not. Processes of cultural nationalization were invariably mediated by stylization, appropriation, and filtering efforts that made popular cultures legible and acceptable to the middle classes. Are we to interpret this primarily as an expression of the endurance and creativity of Afro-Latin Americans, or as successful elite cooptation strategies that deprive Afrodescendants of their own culture? What are the social and political implications of transforming Afro-diasporic symbols and artifacts into national symbols? Do these processes lead to the commodification and depoliticization of such symbols (Hanchard 1994), or do they create opportunities for political action, empowerment, and community formation, not to mention sustenance, visibility, and mobility for practitioners (Moore 1997; Alberto 2011; Hertzman 2013; Putnam 2013; Abreu 2015)? These debates are not strictly academic, as activists have frequently pondered the effectiveness of cultural spaces to make demands for racial justice. For example, in countries where open discussions of racism and discrimination have not been welcomed, such as in Cuba or in Brazil during the dictatorship, art became a platform to discuss issues of racial justice (Fernandes 2006; de la Fuente 2008, 2010, 2013, 2017; Alberto 2011; Gaiter 2015).

The long-term impact of colonial processes also points to another important area of research: comparisons with indigenous populations. Years ago, Peter Wade (1997, 39) called for the need to integrate "blacks and indians into the same theoretical frame of reference, while recognizing the historical differences between them." As he details in his chapter in this volume, significant scholarship has been produced on Afro-indigenous relations in the last few years, including work on communities of mixed African and indigenous origins, such as the Garifuna of Central America. But taking seriously Wade's (1997, 35) insight about the "different location of blacks and indians in the political and imagined space of the nation" means that we are faced with contrasting histories of inclusion and citizenship that merit further attention. The dissimilar location of so-called Indians and blacks in colonial societies is well known. To what degree did these configurations create dissimilar platforms for citizenship and belonging after independence (Larson 2004; Sanders 2004; Gotkowitz 2011)? Why have ideologies of mestizaje and racial harmony been produced in some countries but not others? Scholars interested in those ideologies would benefit by crossing the traditional divide between indigenous peoples and Afrodescendants. Furthermore, as Andrews notes in his discussion of inequality, indigenous poverty rates are consistently higher than Afrodescendant rates in the region (with the exception of Uruguay). Why? "Colonial tracings," to use Florencia Mallon's (2011, 281) expression, can be found in the histories of both indigenous and Afrodescendant peoples, but they seem to operate in different ways.

These questions and agendas are not just about reconstructing the past. The field of Afro-Latin American studies is deeply implicated in current struggles for racial justice and its existence is inseparable from past mobilization efforts. A richer understanding of these histories of race, culture, nation, and mobilization is indispensable for envisioning futures of equality, respect, coexistence, and belonging.

### BIBLIOGRAPHY

Abreu, Christina D. 2015. *Rhythms of Race: Cuban Musicians and the Making of Latino New York City and Miami, 1940–1960.* Chapel Hill, NC: University of North Carolina Press.

Aguirre Beltrán, Gonzalo. 1946. *La poblacíon negra de México.* Mexico City: Fondo de Cultura Económica.

1958. *Cuijla: Esbozo etnográfico de un pueblo negro.* Mexico City: Fondo de Cultura Económica.

Alberto, Paulina L. 2011. *Terms of Inclusion: Black Intellectuals in Twentieth-Century Brazil.* Chapel Hill, NC: University of North Carolina Press.

Andrews, George Reid. 2004. *Afro-Latin America, 1800–2000.* New York, NY: Oxford University Press.

2010. *Blackness in the White Nation: A History of Afro-Uruguay.* Chapel Hill, NC: University of North Carolina Press.

2016. *Afro-Latin America: Black Lives, 1600–2000.* Cambridge, MA: Harvard University Press.

Arredondo, Alberto. 1939. *El negro en Cuba.* Havana: Editorial Alfa.

Balán, Jorge. 2013. "Latin American Higher Education Systems in a Historical and Comparative Perspective." In *Latin America's New Knowledge Economy,* edited by Jorge Balán, vii–xx. New York, NY: Institute of International Education.

Bastide, Roger, and Florestan Fernandes, eds. 1953. *Relações raciais entre brancos e negros em São Paulo*. São Paulo: Anhembi.

Bennett, Herman. 2003. *Africans in Colonial Mexico: Absolutism, Christianity and Creole Consciousness*. Bloomington, IN: Indiana University Press.

2009. *Colonial Blackness: A History of Afro-Mexico*. Bloomington, IN: Indiana University Press.

Betancourt, Juan René. 1945. *Prejuicio, ensayo polémico*. Camagüey, n.p.

1959. *El negro: Ciudadano del futuro*. Havana: Cárdenas y Cía.

Bicudo, Virgínia. 1947. "Atitudes raciais de pretos e mulatos em São Paulo." *Sociologia* 9, 3: 196–219.

Borucki, Alex, David Eltis, and David Wheat. 2015. "Atlantic History and the Slave Trade to Spanish America." *American Historical Review* 120, 2: 433–461.

Bowser, Frederick. 1974. *The African Slave in Colonial Peru, 1524–1650*. Stanford, CA: Stanford University Press.

Carbonell, Walterio. 1961. *Crítica, cómo surgió la cultura nacional*. Havana: Editorial Yaka.

Campos García, Alejandro. 2015. "Normalización y formación del modelo de justicia social de los derechos humanos: El tema afrodescendiente y la contribución del sistema interamericano (2005–2011)." In *Identidades políticas en tiempos de afrodescendencia: Auto-identificación, ancestralidad, visibilidad y derechos*, edited by Silvia Valero and Alejandro Campos García, 579–627. Buenos Aires: Corregidor.

Carneiro, Edison. 1936. *Religiões negras: Notas de ethnografia religiosa*. Rio de Janeiro: Civilização Brasileira.

1937. *Negros bantus: Notas de etnografia religiosa e de folk-lore*. Rio de Janeiro: Civilização Brasileira.

Carvalho Neto, Paulo de. 1955. *La obra afro-uruguaya de Ildefonso Pereda Valdés*. Montevideo: Centro de Estudios Folklóricos del Uruguay.

1971. *Estudios afros: Brasil, Paraguay, Uruguay, Ecuador*. Caracas: Universidad Central de Venezuela.

Castellanos, Israel. 1916. *La brujería y el ñañiguismo en Cuba desde el punto de vista médico-legal*. Havana: Imprenta de Lloredo y Cía.

Cell, John W. 1982. *The Highest Stage of White Supremacy: The Origins of Segregation in South Africa and the American South*. New York, NY: Cambridge University Press.

Colmenares, Germán. 1979. *Popayán: Una sociedad esclavista*. Bogotá: La Carreta.

Congresso Afro-Brasileiro (Recife), ed. 1937. *Novos estudos afro-brasileiros*. Rio de Janeiro: Civilização Brasileira.

Congresso Afro-Brasileiro (Salvador), ed. 1940. *O negro no Brasil: Trabalhos apresentados ao 2º Congresso Afro-Brasileiro*. Rio de Janeiro: Civilização Brasileira.

Conrad, Robert. 1972. *The Destruction of Brazilian Slavery, 1850–1888*. Berkeley, CA: University of California Press.

Costa, Emília Viotti da. 1966. *Da senzala à colônia*. São Paulo: Difusão Européia do Livro.

Davis, David Brion. 1966. *The Problem of Slavery in Western Culture*. Ithaca, NY: Cornell University Press.

1975. *The Problem of Slavery in the Age of Revolution, 1770–1823*. Ithaca, NY: Cornell University Press.

Dean, Warren. 1976. *Rio Claro: A Brazilian Plantation System, 1820–1920*. Stanford, CA: Stanford University Press.

Degler, Carl. 1971. *Neither Black Nor White: Slavery and Race Relations in Brazil and the United States*. New York, NY: Macmillan.

Deive, Carlos Esteban. 1980. *La esclavitud del negro en Santo Domingo, 1492–1844*. Santo Domingo: Museo del Hombre Dominicano.

De la Fuente, Alejandro. 2001. *A Nation for All: Race, Inequality, and Politics in Twentieth-Century Cuba*. Chapel Hill, NC: University of North Carolina Press.

2008. "The New Afro-Cuban Cultural Movement and the Debate on Race in Contemporary Cuba." *Journal of Latin American Studies* 40, 4: 697–720.

2011. *Queloides: Race and Racism in Cuban Contemporary Art*. Pittsburgh, PA: Mattress Factory.

2012. "'Tengo una raza oscura y discriminada ...' El movimiento afrocubano: hacia un programa consensuado." *Nueva Sociedad* 242: 92–105.

2013. *Grupo Antillano: The Art of Afro-Cuba*. Pittsburgh, PA: University of Pittsburgh Press.

2017. *Diago: The Pasts of This Afro-Cuban Present*. Cambridge, MA: Cooper Gallery and Harvard University Press.

Elkins, Stanley. 1959. *Slavery*. Chicago, IL: University of Chicago Press.

Escalante, Aquiles. 1964. *El negro en Colombia*. Bogotá: Universidad Nacional de Colombia.

Escobar, Arturo. 2008. *Territories of Difference: Place, Movements, Life, Redes*. Durham, NC: Duke University Press.

Fernandes, Florestan. 1965. *A integração do negro na sociedade de classes*. São Paulo: Dominus.

Fernandes, Sujatha. 2006. *Cuba Represent! Cuban Arts, State Power, and the Making of New Revolutionary Cultures*. Durham, NC: Duke University Press.

Figueras, Francisco. 1907. *Cuba y su evolución colonial*. Havana: Imprenta Avisador Comercial.

Franklin, John Hope. 1967. *From Slavery to Freedom: A History of Negro Americans*. New York, NY: Knopf.

Freyre, Gilberto. 1933. *Casa-grande e senzala: Formação da família brasileira sob o regime de economia patriarcal*. Rio de Janeiro: J. Olympio.

1936. *Sobrados e mucambos, decadência do patriarcado rural no Brasil*. São Paulo: Companhia Editora Nacional.

Friedemann, Nina S. de, and Jaime Arocha. 1986. *De sol a sol: Génesis, transformación y presencia de los negros en Colombia*. Bogotá: Planeta.

Gaiter, Colette. 2015. "Introspection and Projection in Cuban Art." In *African Diaspora in the Cultures of Latin America, the Caribbean, and the United States*, edited by Persephone Braham, 113–26. Newark, DE: University of Delaware Press.

Gates, Henry Louis. 2011. *Black in Latin America*. New York, NY: New York University Press.

Geler, Lea. 2010. *Andares negros, caminos blancos: Afroporteños, estado y nación: Argentina a fines del siglo XIX*. Rosario: Prohistoria/TEIAA.

Gotkowitz, Laura, ed. 2011. *Histories of Race and Racism: The Andes and Mesoamerica from Colonial Times to the Present*. Durham, NC: Duke University Press.

Gould, Stephen Jay. 1996. *The Mismeasure of Man*. 2nd edition. New York, NY: W. W. Norton.

Guridy, Frank. 2010. *Forging Diaspora: Afro-Cubans and African Americans in a World of Empire and Jim Crow*. Chapel Hill, NC: University of North Carolina Press.

Hall, Gwendolyn Midlo. 1971. *Social Control in Slave Plantation Societies: A Comparison of St. Domingue and Cuba*. Baltimore, MD: Johns Hopkins University Press.

Hanchard, Michael George. 1994. *Orpheus and Power: The Movimento Negro of Rio de Janeiro and São Paulo, Brazil, 1945–1988*. Princeton, NJ: Princeton University Press.

Harris, Marvin. 1964. *Patterns of Race in the Americas*. New York, NY: Walker.

Hasenbalg, Carlos. 1979. *Discriminação e desigualdades raciais no Brasil*. Rio de Janeiro: Graal.

Hellwig, David. 1990. "Racial Paradise or Run-around? Afro-North American Views of Race Relations in Brazil." *American Studies* 31, 2: 43–60.

Hernández, Tanya Katerí. 2013. *Racial Subordination in Latin America: The Role of the State, Customary Law, and the New Civil Rights Response*. New York, NY: Cambridge University Press.

Hertzman, Marc A. 2013. *Making Samba: A New History of Race and Music in Brazil*. Durham, NC: Duke University Press.

Hoetink, H. 1973. *Slavery and Race Relations in the Americas: Comparative Notes on Their Nature and Nexus*. New York, NY: Harper and Row.

Htun, Mala. 2004. "From 'Racial Democracy' to Affirmative Action: Changing State Policy on Race in Brazil." *Latin American Research Review* 39, 1: 60–89.

IADB (Inter-American Development Bank). 2017. *Gender and Diversity*, www .iadb.org/en/topics/gender-indigenous-peoples-and-african-descendants/what-we-do,9601.html.

Ingenieros, José. 1913. *Sociología argentina*. Madrid: D. Jorro.

Klein, Herbert S. 1967. *Slavery in the Americas: A Comparative Study of Virginia and Cuba*. Chicago, IL: University of Chicago Press.

Knight, Franklin W. 1970. *Slave Society in Cuba during the Nineteenth Century*. Madison, WI: University of Wisconsin Press.

Laó-Montes, Agustín. 2009. "Cartografías del campo político afrodescendiente en América Latina." *Universitas Humanística* 68: 207–245.

Larson, Brooke. 2004. *Trials of Nation Making: Liberalism, Race, and Ethnicity in the Andes, 1810–1910*. New York, NY: Cambridge University Press.

Loveman, Mara. 2014. *National Colors: Racial Classification and the State in Latin America*. New York, NY: Oxford University Press.

Machado, Maria Helena P.T. 1987. *Crime e escravidão: Trabalho, luta, e resistência nas lavouras paulistas, 1830–1888*. São Paulo: Brasiliense.

Mallon, Florencia. 2011. "Indigenous Peoples and Nation States in Latin America." In *Oxford Handbook of Latin American History*, edited by Jose C. Moya, 282–308. New York, NY: Oxford University Press.

Maloney, Gerardo, ed. 1994. *Obra selecta: Armando Fortune*. Panama: Instituto Nacional de Cultura.

Martínez, María Inés, ed. 2012. *El despertar de las comunidades afrocolombianas*. Houston, TX: Editorial LACASA.

Marx, Anthony W. 1998. *Making Race and Nation: A Comparison of South Africa, the United States, and Brazil*. New York, NY: Cambridge University Press.

Mignolo, Walter. 2005. *The Idea of Latin America*. Malden, MA: Blackwell.

Mintz, Sidney W., and Richard Price. 1992. *The Birth of African-American Culture: An Anthropological Perspective*. Boston, MA: Beacon Press.

Moore, Robin. 1997. *Nationalizing Blackness: Afrocubanismo and Artistic Revolution in Havana, 1920–1940*. Pittsburgh, PA: University of Pittsburgh Press.

Moreno Fraginals, Manuel. 1978. *El ingenio: El complejo económico social cubano del azúcar*. Havana: Editorial de Ciencias Sociales.

Moura, Clóvis. 1959. *Rebeliões de senzala: Quilombos, insurreições, guerrilhas*. São Paulo: Edições Zumbi.

1977. *O negro, de bom escravo a mau cidadão?* Rio de Janeiro: Conquista.

Nascimento, Abdias do, ed. 1968. *O negro revoltado*. Rio de Janeiro: GRD.

Nistal Moret, Benjamín. 1984. *Esclavos prófugos y cimarrones: Puerto Rico, 1770–1870*. Río Piedras: Editorial de la Universidad de Puerto Rico.

Nogueira, Oracy. 1942. "Atitude desfavorável de alguns anunciantes de São Paulo em relação a seus empregados de cor." *Sociologia* 4, 4: 324–358.

Ortiz, Fernando. 1906. *Los negros brujos: Apuntes para un estudio de etnologia criminal*. Madrid: Editorial América.

1916. *Hampa afro-cubana: Los negros esclavos. Estudio sociológico y de derecho público*. Havana: Revista Bimestre Cubana.

Paschel, Tianna S. 2016. *Becoming Black Political Subjects: Movements and Ethno-Racial Rights in Colombia and Brazil*. Princeton, NJ: Princeton University Press.

Pereira, Amilcar Araujo. 2013. *O mundo negro: Relações raciais e a constituição do movimento negro contemporâneo no Brasil*. Rio de Janeiro: Pallas/FAPERJ.

Pisano, Pietro. 2012. *Liderazgo político "negro" en Colombia, 1943–1964*. Bogotá: Universidad Nacional de Colombia.

Portuondo Linares, Serafín. 1950. *Los independientes de color: Historia del Partido Independiente de Color*. Havana: Ministerio de Educación.

Putnam, Lara. 2013. *Radical Moves: Caribbean Migrants and the Politics of Race in the Jazz Age*. Chapel Hill, NC: University of North Carolina Press.

Quijano, Anibal. 2000. "Coloniality of Power, Eurocentrism and Latin America." *Nepantla: Views from South* 1, 3: 533–580.

*Quilombo: Vida, problemas, e aspirações do negro*. 2003. São Paulo: FAPESP/ Editora 34.

Rahier, Jean Muteba, ed. 2012. *Black Social Movements in Latin America: From Monocultural Mestizaje to Multiculturalism.* New York, NY: Palgrave Macmillan.

Rama, Carlos M. 1967. *Los afro-uruguayos.* Montevideo: El Siglo Ilustrado.

Ramos, Alberto Guerreiro. 1957. *Introdução crítica à sociologia brasileira.* Rio de Janeiro: Editorial Andes.

Ramos, Arthur. 1937. *As culturas negras no Novo Mundo.* Rio de Janeiro: Civilização Brasileira.

   1940. *O negro brasileiro.* São Paulo: Companhia Editora Nacional.

Reis, João José. 1986. *Rebelião escravo no Brasil: História do levante dos malês.* São Paulo: Brasiliense.

Rodrigues, Raimundo Nina. 1900. *L'animisme fétichiste des nègres de Bahia.* Bahia: Reis.

Rout, Leslie B. 1976. *The African Experience in Spanish America, from 1502 to the Present Day.* New York, NY: Cambridge University Press.

Sanders, James E. 2004. *Contentious Republicans: Popular Politics, Race, and Class in Nineteenth-Century Colombia.* Durham, NC: Duke University Press.

Scott, Rebecca J. 2005. *Degrees of Freedom: Louisiana and Cuba after Slavery.* Cambridge, MA: Harvard University Press.

Silva, Nelson do Valle. 1978. "Black-White Income Differentials: Brazil, 1960." PhD dissertation, University of Michigan.

Skidmore, Thomas E. 1974. *Black into White: Race and Nationality in Brazilian Thought.* New York, NY: Oxford University Press.

   1992. "Fact and Myth: Discovering a Racial Problem in Brazil." Working Paper #173, Kellogg Institute for International Affairs, University of Notre Dame.

Stampp, Kenneth M. 1956. *The Peculiar Institution: Slavery in the Ante-Bellum South.* New York, NY: Knopf.

Sweet, James H. 2003. *Recreating Africa: Culture, Kinship, and Religion in the African-Portuguese World, 1441–1770.* Chapel Hill, NC: University of North Carolina Press.

Tannenbaum, Frank. 1946. *Slave and Citizen: The Negro in the Americas.* New York: Alfred A. Knopf.

Telles, Edward, and the Project on Ethnicity and Race in Latin America (PERLA). 2014. *Pigmentocracies: Ethnicity, Race, and Color in Latin America.* Chapel Hill, NC: University of North Carolina Press.

Thornton, John K. 1998. *Africa and Africans in the Making of the Atlantic World, 1400–1800.* New York, NY: Cambridge University Press.

Toplin, Robert Brent, ed. 1974. *Slavery and Race Relations in Latin America.* Westport, CT: Greenwood.

UN General Assembly. 2001. *Report of the Regional Conference of the Americas Santiago, Chile, 5–7 December 2000.* Accessed at http://dag.un.org/bitstream/handle/11176/234584/A_CONF.189_PC.2_7-EN.pdf?sequence=3&isAllowed=y.

Valenilla Lanz, Laureano. 1919. *Cesarismo democrático: Estudios sobre las bases efectivas de la Constitución de Venezuela.* Caracas: El Cojo.

Valero, Silvia, and Alejandro Campos García, eds. 2015. *Identidades políticas en tiempos de afrodescendencia: Auto-identificación, ancestralidad, visibilidad y derechos*. Buenos Aires: Corregidor.

Viana, Francisco José Oliveira. 1922. *Populações meridionais no Brasil*. São Paulo: Monteiro Lobato e Cia.

Wade, Peter. 1997. *Race and Ethnicity in Latin America*. London: Pluto Press.

2009. *Race and Sex in Latin America*. London: Pluto Press.

2010. *Race and Ethnicity in Latin America*. 2nd edition. London: Pluto Press.

2017. *Degrees of Mixture, Degrees of Freedom: Genomics, Multiculturalism, and Race in Latin America*. Durham, NC: Duke University Press.

Whitten, Norman. 1974. *Black Frontiersmen: A South American Case*. New York, NY: Wiley.

Wilson, William J. 1978. *The Declining Significance of Race: Blacks and Changing American Institutions*. Chicago, IL: University of Chicago Press.

Woodward, C. Vann. 1955. *The Strange Career of Jim Crow*. New York, NY: Oxford University Press.

Yashar, Deborah. 2005. *Contesting Citizenship in Latin America: The Rise of Indigenous Movements and the Postliberal Challenge*. New York, NY: Cambridge University Press.

Zapata Olivella, Manuel. 1967. *Chambacú, corral de negros*. Medellín: Editorial Bedout.

# PART I

# INEQUALITIES

# 2

# The Slave Trade to Latin America

## A Historiographical Assessment

### Roquinaldo Ferreira and Tatiana Seijas

#### INTRODUCTION

Two interpretive streams have marked the historiography of the slave trade to Latin America. The first stream involves quantitative scholarship that seeks to estimate the number of enslaved Africans taken to the Americas (Curtin 1969). The contributions of the quantitative paradigm are legion, and it is currently epitomized by the multi-authored Trans-Atlantic Slave Trade Database (TSTD) – a powerful tool that has captured the imagination of scholars of the largest forced migration in history.[1] It provides detailed information about the orientation of the trade and has served to illustrate the magnitude of Latin America – particularly Brazil – in the making of the African diaspora.

The enormous contribution of the slave trade dataset has come with a price to a certain degree. Firstly, large-scale trends and dry numerical analyses are not always the best window into histories that are ultimately composed of individual experiences. By writing from a viewpoint that overemphasizes the structural dimensions of the slave trade, quantitative scholars have sometimes failed to account for its human dimension. Secondly, the quantitative paradigm has operated within a perhaps inflated sense of certainty about the reliability of official data, which is an imperfect representation of the multilayered nature of the trade. Thirdly, the TSTD's emphasis on shipping and accounting records ignores the realities of contraband, which, in the Iberian context, will

[1] The TSTD or Voyages database includes more than 34,000 slaving expeditions between 1514 and 1866; it can be publicly accessed at www.slavevoyages.org.

require scholars to comb local archives for evidence of this activity, in order to then produce numbers that better approximate the reality of slave trading on the ground. The few studies that do account for illegal traffic through local sources like notarial documentation testify to the potential of this methodology, both to alter traditional periodizations of the slave trade to certain regions and to magnify the volume of the trade overall (Stark 2009; Seijas and Sierra Silva 2016).

Overall, social historians who embrace a quantitative approach are beginning to examine the domestic or trans-Americas trade, as well as accounting for specific slave markets in Latin America. These new efforts join pathbreaking works by social scientists who have analyzed the impact of slavery in the social and economic fabrics of colonial and postcolonial societies (Klein, Moreno Fraginals, and Engerman 1983; Bergad, Iglesias García, and Barcia 1995; Klein and Luna 2010).

The second paradigm, inspired by cultural anthropologists, investigates the cultural and social implications of the slave trade. This historiographical stream has undergone significant changes in the past decades, moving beyond debates about cultural retention and creolization, to studying strategies of community building and cultural reinvention in Africa and the Americas. This newer diasporic/Atlantic perspective has been particularly useful for analyzing polycultural dynamics around the Atlantic basin (Hawthorne 2010; Sweet 2011; Thornton 2015). As social historians have demonstrated, the rise of the slave trade had important ramifications for commercial relations, as well as for social identities across the Atlantic world (Green 2012; Thornton 2016). By relying on a micro-historical approach, scholars have sought to accentuate the human dimension of the slave trade, underlining the multiple ways Africans successfully resisted and negotiated space against the backdrop of growing Atlantic slavery (Ferreira Furtado 2012; Candido 2013).

This chapter follows a linear chronology, with special attention to the interconnectedness of Iberian trade. A short overview of the Iberian Union period (1580–1640) serves as a reminder for why Spanish and Portuguese America have long been joined, especially in terms of the slave trade. This combined history, in fact, has enabled scholars to employ Latin America as a category of analysis and to investigate topics such as the African diaspora under a larger geographic framework that appropriately includes Africa.

The quantification of the slave trade remains an ongoing project, but the most widely accepted numbers are that ten to eleven million people forcibly migrated to the Americas from Africa. From fifty to sixty percent of these individuals were forced to disembark in Latin America, in ports as geographically distant as Salvador and Veracruz (Klein 2010; Borucki, Eltis, and Wheat 2015).[2] This chapter traces the rise of the slave trade to Latin America from the sixteenth through the eighteenth centuries, as Portuguese and Spanish colonialism advanced to different corners of the Americas. The trade's impact on sociocultural shifts and identity formation are central to this history. The persistence of the slave trade in spite of abolitionist forces underlines the degree to which slavery sustained colonial and newly independent societies across the Americas.

## THE EARLY PHASE: FROM PORTUGUESE FACTORIES IN AFRICA TO IBERIAN COLONIES IN THE AMERICAS

Several factors explain the preponderance of Latin America in the transatlantic slave trade. First, the region witnessed a demographic catastrophe in the wake of European colonialism that decimated millions of indigenous people, forcing colonists to look elsewhere for productive labor. Second, Portugal had a preexisting slave trade to Europe and other African regions, which enabled Portuguese traders to deliver enslaved Africans to the Americas (Almeida Mendes 2008). Third, the slave trade to Latin America reflected the region's place in the early modern global economy, which was largely defined by the massive production of agricultural commodities for export to Europe (Menard and Schwartz 1993). The rise of the plantation complex, defined as an economic and political order dependent on slave plantations in the New World tropics, was contingent on the slave trade.

The preponderance of Portuguese traders in the slave trade to Latin America as a whole had to do with early patterns in Atlantic colonialism. The Portuguese crown prioritized controlling the export trade out of West Africa, while the Spanish crown focused on territorial settlement in the Americas. Portuguese merchants during the fifteenth century turned coastal West Africa into a zone of Portuguese commercial and cultural influence and positioned themselves to control the transatlantic trade.

---

[2] The TSDT database on recorded voyages accounts for 4,523,748 individuals disembarking in the Spanish Caribbean, Spanish mainland, and Brazil between 1514 and 1866; the database shows 9,180,918 individuals disembarked in the Americas overall. The percentage to Latin America is 49.27 percent. The TSDT estimates data set (www.slavevoyages .org/assessment/estimates) suggests greater numbers, with 6,157,289 (58 percent) people arriving in Latin America. Accessed November 15, 2016.

Portuguese networks in Africa, with bases in Senegambia, the Gold Coast, and Central Africa, enabled slave traders to meet the growing demand for labor in Spanish America and Brazil. The trade to Europe from the mid-1400s had already given rise to sizable African and African-descent communities in cities like Lisbon, Seville, and Valencia (Saunders 1982; Blumenthal 2009; Garofalo 2012). This trade had also been geared toward the Atlantic, delivering enslaved Africans, for example, to the sugar plantations of Madeira (Phillips 2011; Almeida Mendes 2012; Seibert 2013). The slave trade to Spanish America and Brazil was an outgrowth of these highly effective trading networks, first to Spanish America from the early 1500s and then to Brazil from the 1570s (Green 2012).

Sugar, more than any other product, embodies the close connection between the rise of an international labor market (based on slavery) and the development of plantation economies that tied together Europe, Africa, and the Americas (Schwartz 2004). The first large-scale production of sugar in tropical lands occurred in the Portuguese colony of São Tomé and Príncipe, but the plantation complex was perfected in the Americas, first in Brazil and later in the Caribbean (Schwartz 1985; Galloway 1989). In these regions, high mortality rates fueled an insatiable thirst for enslaved labor. Such was the value of sugar that its slave-based production sustained Cuba's economy in the nineteenth century, driving the slave trade upwards at a time when anti-slave trade efforts had succeeded in most of the Atlantic basin (Graden 2014).

The production of sugar required the construction of a transatlantic machinery of labor procurement. In the sixteenth century, enslaved Africans working alongside Indians in sugar mills in Hispaniola sometimes numbered up to one hundred, signaling the importance of slavery in the earliest phase of Spanish colonization in the Caribbean (Cassá 1978; Rodríguez Morel 2012). Although estimates of the number of captives taken to the region vary significantly, approximately 16,500 enslaved Africans may have entered the Caribbean prior to 1581 (Green 2012). African slaves also played an important role in Cuba's sixteenth-century economy, and they labored in sugar plantations in Central Mexico (Barrett 1970; Brockington 1989; de la Fuente, García del Pino, and Iglesias Delgado 2008). Later, dependence on African slaves gained further momentum due primarily to the demographic collapse of indigenous peoples and legal constraints on Indian slavery.

### IBERIAN UNION (1580–1640): RECONSIDERING THE PORTUGUESE ASIENTO AND THE SOCIOECONOMIC IMPACT OF SLAVERY IN SPANISH AMERICA

The slave trade to Spanish America functioned under a semi-monopoly system, in which the crown entered into contracts or *asientos* with foreign merchants, who were given licenses for the delivery of a specified number of slaves to particular ports (Cartagena de Indias, Veracruz, and Buenos Aires) (Scelle 1906). The asiento developed in the late sixteenth century as a way to expand the volume of the trade in response to colonists' urgent call for more laborers. The increase also profited the royal treasury, as asiento holders had to pay fees and rents for the privilege of trading large numbers of slaves. The asiento system existed alongside an earlier practice, in which the crown issued permits to certain officials and favored people to travel with a set number of slaves for their personal service, with the understanding that they had license to sell their property in Spanish America (Seijas 2014).

Asiento agreements and individual permits, along with other required paperwork, such as ship registries and official inspections at ports of disembarkation, were meant to control the trade and ensure that it profited the crown. The asiento contracts, however, should only be regarded as a partial source for the trade, as merchants often did not complete the trips allowed in their licensing contracts, while others blatantly misrepresented the number of captives they brought into port. Traders, who acquired their asiento contracts in Spain, worked with port officials to undercount the number of slaves boarded on arrival in Africa, and again upon delivery in Spanish America. Once slaves left the ship, local traders found eager buyers for the merchandise, even without the necessary legal papers. The crown's flawed accounting measures, along with the immensity of the mostly unguarded coastline everywhere in Spanish America, enabled contraband to flourish (Navarrete Peláez 2007; Eagle 2014).

Until recently, most studies on the slave trade to Spanish America have employed the periodization of the Iberian Union (1580–1640), when the Spanish crown wielded political control over the Portuguese empire (Vila Vilar 1977). The trade during these decades has commonly been called the Portuguese asiento period because the crown tended to favor Portuguese slave traders with contracts (Studnicki-Gizbert 2007). Nearly 400,000 African slaves disembarked in Spanish America during the period of Iberian Union, marking the first zenith of the trade, which was only superseded in the nineteenth century.[3] Newer analyses, however, recognize that Spaniards were equally rewarded with trading contracts to deliver enslaved Africans to Spanish America during this period and afterwards. After 1640, the crown also awarded asiento contracts to Dutch, Genoese, and later English merchants, who continued to bring enslaved Africans to Spain's colonies (Vega Franco 1984; García de León 2001; Anes 2007; Ribeiro da Silva 2011).

Scholars must take a longer view of the slave trade in order to challenge the idea that slavery in Spanish America diminished in economic importance after 1640. Pioneering social historians may have acknowledged that the trade to Spanish America continued after Iberian Union, but most quantitative studies have continued to use the 1580–1640 timeframe, which serves, in part, to hinder examination of the social and economic consequences of ongoing African arrivals (Curtin 1969; Canabrava 1984; Studer 1984). The endurance of this periodization has also served to discourage scholars from weighing late seventeenth- and eighteenth-century markets, which sold captives born in Africa and the Americas. Quantitative studies on Mexico and Río de la Plata that extend beyond 1580–1640 demonstrate the potential of transcending outdated timeframes (Moutoukias 1988; Schultz 2016; Seijas and Sierra Silva 2016). This work supports the argument that slavery remained integral to the economy of Spanish colonies throughout the colonial period (Borucki, Eltis, and Wheat 2015). Enslaved Africans and their descendants labored in agriculture, textile industries, mining, and other productive sectors for domestic and export markets. Most slaves in Spanish America, in fact, worked to produce food and goods for local consumption, and to provide services for the same.

The demand for slaves during the second half of the seventeenth and eighteenth centuries remained constant from the so-called Portuguese asiento period, and it was increasingly met through intra-American trade. According to a recent estimate, this regional and transimperial trade began in the sixteenth century and steadily grew over the next two hundred years, peaking in the 1760s and 1770s, when over 200,000 enslaved people

---

[3] The TSDT accounts for 386,092 individuals disembarking in the "Spanish Caribbean and Mainland" (principal places of landing) between 1580 and 1640; 163,447 of these people disembarked from Portuguese ships. Accessed November 15, 2016. Another estimate accounts for 444,900 captives disembarking in the Spanish Americas between the same dates (Borucki, Eltis, and Wheat 2015, 442).

arrived in Spanish America, primarily from Brazil but also from the British and Dutch Caribbean (Rupert 2009; Borucki, Eltis, and Wheat 2015).

The case of Mexico exemplifies the necessity of expanding the traditional periodization of the slave trade in order to evaluate the socioeconomic impact of African slavery in this region. Quantitative studies based on metropolitan sources, like asiento contracts and shipping registries, reveal that a minimum of 32,000 African captives entered Mexico during the first half of the seventeenth century. Africans, however, forcibly migrated to Mexico throughout the 1600s and into the 1700s. Further research in local archives, especially notaries, is required to adequately assess the dynamics of the transatlantic and transcolonial slave trades to Mexico, the fluctuations of its slave markets, and slavery's impact on regional labor dynamics (Seijas and Sierra Silva 2016).

Scholars have made estimates on the periodization and volume of the trade according to established narratives about the labor supply in Mexico, assuming that the rise and fall of the trade was directly correlated to the demographic collapse and recovery of the indigenous population, which experienced devastating epidemic diseases in the sixteenth century (Valdés 1987; Ngou-Mvé 1994; Bennett 2003). The driving idea behind these studies is that individuals who needed workers after 1640 turned away from slave labor and embraced wage labor, hiring indigenous and mixed-race people to do the work once done by African slaves. Such a line of reasoning obfuscates the harrowing fact that the indigenous population only recovered to its 1580s levels at the start of the nineteenth century (Gerhard 1972). There was no apparent recovery during the mid-seventeenth century. Yet sugar plantations in Oaxaca, Puebla, Veracruz, and other provinces continued to require large numbers of laborers into the eighteenth century; *ingenio* owners acquired their workforce at regional slave markets (Naveda Chávez-Hita 1987; Motta Sánchez and Meza Peñaloza 2001). Textile mills or *obrajes* also remained dependent on slave labor (Super 1976; Salvucci 1987; Miño Grijalva 1989; Motta Sánchez 2005; Proctor 2010; Reynoso Medina 2010). Much quantitative and qualitative work remains to be done to articulate this history, which must be founded on the acknowledgment of the vital role of enslaved labor in rural and urban Mexico throughout the colonial period (Sierra Silva 2018).

Scholars of the slave trade to Cartagena de Indias have mainly worked within the traditional Iberian Union periodization and examined the inflow vis-à-vis the Peruvian mining and urban industries (Bowser 1974). The private records of individual Portuguese traders, for example, have been used to elucidate the Iberian commercial networks that enabled slavers to take people from the coasts of Upper Guinea and Angola to Cartagena, and hence to Lima and beyond (Bühnen 1993; Newson and Minchin 2007). This documentation from traders has also revealed the traumatic reality of multitiered journeys, which made surviving the Middle Passage all the more terrifying. The slave trade to Cartagena was a highly risky business, but sufficiently cost-effective to account for nearly 80,000 arrivals between 1570 and 1640 (Wheat 2011).

Apart from supporting the Peruvian mining and agricultural economy, slave trade disembarkations at Cartagena also supplied Ecuador. In this region, enslaved Africans labored in gold mining, plantations, and urban industries. Enslaved Africans were a minority population, but the institution of slavery was central to how local elites exercised power and conceived of labor more broadly (Lane 2002; Bryant 2014). New understandings of the racialization of social relations in cities like Quito and Trujillo point to the importance of the sociocultural paradigm in studies of slavery in Andean South America (O'Toole 2012). Scholars employing gender as an analytical category have also highlighted the centrality of slavery in Lima (Walker 2015; McKinley 2016).

Slavery also upheld the economy of Costa Rica, even though it existed at the margins of the Atlantic slave trade. African captives arrived legally in this region by way of Panama and sometimes Nicaragua, while the illegal influx depended on British and Dutch smugglers, primarily from Jamaica and Curaçao. The irregularity of the trade to this market makes estimating the volume nearly impossible, but records of slave sales suggest that no more than 1,000 Africans arrived during the entire colonial period (Lohse 2014). These individuals joined enslaved Creoles in cacao haciendas, livestock ranches, and domestic service. Together, they played an integral part in shaping Costa Rican society. Scholars working on other parts of Central America, such as sixteenth-century Honduras, are equally bringing to the fore the economic importance of local slave markets (Velásquez Lambur 2015). The social and cultural significance of Africans and their descendants in Central America is undisputable (Tardieu 2009; Gudmundson and Wolfe 2010).

The slave trade to the Río de la Plata spanned three centuries and reveals long-standing South Atlantic connections (Ortega and Guariglia Zás 2005). Buenos Aires developed connections with Central Africa starting in the mid-1580s, when it became a key port in the South Atlantic. Contraband traders dominated this network, which was primarily oriented toward delivering enslaved Africans to the silver mines in Potosí but also catered to local labor needs (such as the sale of children for domestic service). The illegal nature of this trade only allows for approximations of the volume, but surviving documentation accounts for over 34,000 individuals arriving during the Portuguese asiento period, many on ships from Angola, but mainly from Brazil (Andrews 1980; Schultz 2015). The actual numbers were much higher, but this sample underlines the profitability of the Río de la Plata slave market and the complexity of the network. The slave trade to Chile is another topic awaiting further research (Arre Marfull 2011).

The same patterns prevailed in the Río de la Plata region during the first half of the eighteenth century, when British and French companies officially delivered some 14,000 slaves, who made their way inland along with people who arrived via contraband. Due to the demand from mines and plantations in the interior, Buenos Aires remained a city with a free wage-earning majority, where enslaved Africans labored mainly as servants and workshop artisans (Johnson 2011). Slaves living in the city during the second half of the century primarily came from West Africa (via Rio de Janeiro as part of the transimperial slave trade). Many of the enslaved were also from East Africa, who arrived near death after enduring the extraordinarily long Middle Passage from Mozambique.

Building on the sociocultural paradigm, recent work on the Río de la Plata region has shown that enslaved Africans in Buenos Aires and Montevideo created resilient social identities based on their common experiences, ranging from their forced passages on slave vessels, to serving as soldiers in independence-era black battalions (Borucki 2015). Individuals' shared memories and experiences, especially those that confirmed their ties to Angola, become visible in African-based cultural celebrations. Africans, for example, congregated and celebrated in places first called *tambos* (a funeral ritual of Portuguese Angola) and then *candombes* (referring to black celebrations in both Rio de Janeiro and Minas Gerais). These kinds of connections confirm the need for slave trade scholars to combine their quantitative and qualitative findings to write new histories of the African diaspora in the South Atlantic.

## BRAZIL AND SUGAR: RETHINKING THE TRADE TO PORTUGUESE AMERICA

The end of Iberian Union in 1640 coincided with an extension of European control over coastal Africa that shifted the slave trade. Portuguese dominance in the trade to the Spanish mainland and the Caribbean came to an end when European states like England and the Dutch Republic infiltrated Portuguese trading networks, initially along Senegambia and later along the Gold Coast, in order to make their newly acquired Caribbean colonies economically viable (Pestana 2004). Portugal's role in the slave trade to the Americas thus waned, except for Brazil, which became the most important colony in the Portuguese empire in the seventeenth century.

This development provided a stark contrast to the early phase of the Portuguese slave trade, when Brazil lacked a strategic value for Portugal. At that time, the crown's energies were mostly devoted to the *Estado da India*, a region that stretched from ports in East Africa to Japan and centered on Portuguese India. The status quo changed slowly as Portugal decided to increase its footprint in Brazil to fend off European challenges to its claim to the *Terra de Santa Cruz*, especially by the French. The slave trade then gained decisive momentum as colonists staked their claim to Brazil by introducing sugar production, which required the deployment of enslaved labor (Alencastro 2000).

As in Spanish America, the slave trade to Brazil stemmed mostly from the devastating impact of disease on the indigenous populations. The availability of indigenous labor was critical to making sugar production a viable enterprise in its early phase, but the pool of potential laborers declined dramatically by the end of the sixteenth century (Schwartz 1978). There were also debates about the legitimacy of enslaving indigenous people, with disputes that pitted Portuguese settlers against Jesuit missionaries (Metcalf 2005). As such, by the mid-1600s the majority of captives in Brazil hailed from Africa or were descendants of Africans, despite the continuing existence of indigenous slavery.

The increase of sugar production in Brazil in the seventeenth century brought the slave trade to a new level of intensity and built a truly distinct economy that fully integrated the South Atlantic and advanced Portuguese colonialism (Schwartz 1985). The economic growth of Brazil, for example, provided the necessary capital for military forces from Rio de Janeiro to restore Portuguese control of the slave trade out of Angola from Dutch interlopers after 1648. Angola henceforth remained a key source of labor in the South Atlantic (Miller 1988; Candido 2013). Portugal's close relationship with African allies (the kingdom of Casanje resulted from this alliance) led to the development of an internal network of enslavement in Angola that significantly escalated the slave trade to Brazil. The slave trade from Africa to Brazil strengthened bilateral connections between the two colonies and turned Rio de Janeiro into the coastal epicenter of the eighteenth-century gold-mining economy.

The slave trade to Brazil benefited greatly from Portuguese presence in Central Africa, which centered on the coastal cities of Luanda and Benguela – focal points of polycultural societies that held tight and multifaceted ties with Brazil. This trade was fueled by the extensive use of commodities from Brazil such as rum, tobacco, and gold. Portuguese involvement in the global trade of Indian textiles also contributed to ties between Brazil and Africa, particularly Angola. As in other African societies, most of the slave trade in Angola was fueled by high demand for textiles, which served as currency and to highlight social hierarchies (Larson 2013). For decades, the *Carreira da India* (India trade) – the underlining infrastructure of the Portuguese commercial empire – enabled Lisbon-based merchants to procure highly valued textiles from Portuguese India for sale in Africa. By the mid-seventeenth century, however, Brazil's sugar economy had bolstered the profile of Salvador-based merchants, who came to dominate the India trade, as well as the slave trade, by using Indian cloth to purchase slaves in Angola for the Brazilian market.

Gold mining and coffee production in the eighteenth century upheld the demand for slaves, and ultimately resulted in Brazil receiving nearly 45 percent of the total number of enslaved Africans who arrived in the Americas (Klein and Luna 2010). The discovery of gold and diamonds in Minas Gerais transformed the economy of the Portuguese empire and increased the slave trade (Miller 1988). Commercial ties between Brazil and the Mina Coast (Gold Coast and Bight of Benin) revived through intricate networks of gold contraband that gave Portuguese merchants an edge in the competition for slaves with British, Dutch, and French merchants (Verger 1976). Between 1700 and 1750, Portuguese vessels outmatched vessels from all other European nations trading in the Bight of Benin, taking almost 600,000 enslaved Africans to Brazil – more than the combined number of slaves taken by the British, French, and Dutch to their colonies in the Americas. Due to its connection to Salvador, the Bight of Benin became the largest supplier of enslaved labor to the Americas, temporarily toppling Angola from the dubious status of largest supplier of labor. The rise of gold production in Brazil also affected the slave trade from Angola, which remained a key source of labor due to increased trading out of the southern city of Benguela. This port provided a safe haven for merchants seeking to avoid high taxes and corruption by metropolitan administrators in Luanda, the capital city of Angola. Portuguese presence in Angola had by then morphed into a set of complex relations between Angola and Brazil maintained by the frequent transit of administrators, soldiers, and merchants (Candido 2013).

By the eighteenth century, the slave trade was firmly entrenched in Angola and the Bight of Benin, with these two regions accounting for almost 70 percent of the overall number of enslaved Africans taken to Brazil. Angola functioned mostly as Brazil's colony – an unusual situation that led to intense political instability after Brazil became independent of Portugal in 1822 (Birmingham 2015). Unlike the slave trade elsewhere in Africa, most of the Angolan slave trade took place within a Portuguese-influenced framework, with Portugal stationing a sizable military and civilian bureaucracy in Luanda. The colonial presence was not restricted to the coast; an internal network of trading and administrative outposts in Luanda's hinterlands contributed to the growth of slavery in the interior. Individuals who claimed a Portuguese identity, although they were culturally Africans, manned the interior's outposts (Heywood and Thornton 2007).

The bilateral links that developed between Salvador and the Bight of Benin during the eighteenth century escalated the slave trade to Salvador. From there, enslaved Africans traveled to sugar fields in the hinterland or made their way to the mining regions (Ferreira Furtado 2012). Many stayed in Salvador itself, which was a booming commercial center with connections to cities in Europe, Africa, and Asia. The Portuguese fort in Whydah, founded in 1721, for example, was mostly financed and managed from Salvador, largely bypassing Portuguese control in Lisbon. Metropolitan Portugal, in fact, did little to upset the structures of the South Atlantic slave trade until the end of the eighteenth century. Once Brazil became independent, the South Atlantic slave trade became entangled with the politics of nation-building and Britain's global campaign against the slave trade. Brazil ended imports of enslaved Africans in the 1850s.

In Central Africa, the escalation of the slave trade in the eighteenth century exacted a heavy toll on the social fabric of African communities, as internal networks drew on African communities to produce captives for the ships bound to the Americas (Candido 2013). In West Africa, especially the Bight of Benin, the slave trade was both a byproduct and an engine of systemic warfare pitting African kingdoms against each other. The production of slaves in West and Central Africa also took on a multiplicity of forms ranging from warfare-induced enslavement, to judicial enslavement, to kidnappings. The growing demand for labor in the Americas broadened the definition of crime, and enslavement became a sentence dispensed to a wider range of transgressions.

From the viewpoint of the enslaved, the fact that the slave trade to Brazil drew mostly on the Bight of Benin and Central Africa had a direct impact on how they built lives under slavery in Brazil, since the existence of a relatively common set of cultural traits shaped slave resistance and religiosity. In the seventeenth century, the *Quilombo dos Palmares*, a maroon society in the northeast of Brazil, was built on elements of Central Africa societies (Reis and Gomes 1996). In the nineteenth century, the provenance of the enslaved played a critical role in a series of revolts in Bahia, contributing to widespread fear of slave revolts that led to the passing of a law to end the slave trade in 1850 (Reis 1993). Free and unfree Africans also drew on African culture and religion and elements of colonial culture to form composite social identities (Reis 2015). By charting the simultaneity of continuity and change, scholars have demonstrated that these cultural strategies were by no means necessarily at odds with each other, with European Christianity and African cultures and religion mingling in religious brotherhoods and Candomblé temples (Soares 2011; Sweet 2011; Parés 2013; see also Chapter 12).

### THE LAST PHASE: CUBA AND BRAZIL

Two major developments shaped the last century of the slave trade to Latin America: the growth of the slave trade to Cuba and the protracted process of ending the forced migration of Africans across the Atlantic. These two developments played out in the aftermath of the Haitian Revolution and amid an increasing number of slave revolts in Cuba and Brazil, which both catalyzed and complicated efforts to end the slave trade (Barcia 1987; Ferrer 2014).

The development of the slave trade to Cuba had challenged Brazilian domination of the slave trade by the end of the eighteenth century. Geopolitics was central to this change, as British occupation of Havana in 1762 suddenly secured a continuing flow of slaves from Africa to Cuba. Later, the rise of sugar production on the island in the wake of the Haitian Revolution escalated the flow of enslaved labor to Cuba. There, Creole elites saw an opportunity to develop sugar production and profit from high international prices brought on by the collapse of sugar production in Haiti. Cuban planters saw this turn of events as an opening to be fully explored, boldly sending envoys to Madrid to lobby for the deregulation of the slave trade to Cuba, thus ushering in a new and unprecedented era of connection with Africa (Tomich 2003; Ferrer 2014).

The staggering growth of African slavery in Cuba was driven by the production of agricultural commodities for the European and North American markets. Cuba's agricultural landscape included the cultivation of tobacco and coffee, but it would be difficult to deny the level of dominance of sugar production by the 1840s (Van Norman 2013). Cuba's mid-century status as the largest producer of sugar in the world depended on enslaved and forced labor by Africans and Asians. As quantifiable evidence, Cuba exported 16,731 metric tons of sugar in 1791; exports reached 728,250 metric tons in 1868 (Tomich 2014). The island's proximity to the United States clearly played a key role in this process, as the United States was the primary market for Cuban sugar and fostered sugar production (Moreno Fraginals 1978; Barcia, García, and Torres-Cuevas 1994).

Sugar production resulted in great technological innovations, such as the establishment of a railroad system (the first in Latin America) that spread sugar production to regions beyond Havana and Matanzas (Funes Monzote 2008; Curry-Machado 2011). This complex economy drew extensively on capital derived from the slave trade with Central Africa (Laviña and Zeuske 2014; Perera Díaz and Meriño Fuentes 2015). Against this backdrop, an estimated 715,000 enslaved Africans arrived in Cuba during the nineteenth century. As in Brazil, the provenance of the enslaved played a central role in a succession of slave revolts that were further catalyzed by the geographic proximity between Cuba and Haiti. Free and unfree Africans and people of African descent drew on the example of the Haitian Revolution to fight slavery, as well as on elements of African culture and religion (Barcia 2014; Ferrer 2014).

The growth of abolitionism was a central factor in the history of the nineteenth-century slave trade to Latin America. Portugal and Spain both experienced increasing diplomatic pressure to end the slave trade in the late eighteenth century. Each crown responded to the abolitionist cause according to their different geopolitical contexts. The Portuguese crown had colonies in Africa and resided in Brazil from 1808 to 1821 – two realities that made abolition of the slave trade follow a slightly different path than in the Spanish empire. Spain prohibited the trade in 1817, and Portugal agreed to end the slave trade above the equator that same year. With this concession, the Portuguese succeeded in sparing Central Africa from abolitionist pressures in the short term, thus shielding the region that supplied the largest number of enslaved laborers to Brazil and Cuba. It was not until 1836 that Portugal passed a law that criminalized the slave trade in its African colonies. Official complicity with the slave trade and weak colonial government in Angola, however, hindered its implementation (Marques 2006).

The historiography on the abolition of the slave trade in the Spanish and Portuguese empires has mainly emphasized the role of the British in suppressing the trade and the empires' diverging reactions to this campaign (Murray 2002). New scholarship, however, has begun to question this top-down diplomatic perspective by emphasizing the role of antislavery grassroots movements within the colonies in bringing about abolition. The Spanish empire had a significant abolitionist faction starting in the late eighteenth century, which successfully lobbied for the end of the trade after the restoration of Ferdinand VII (Berquist 2010). Recent studies have also revisited the established narrative about the abolition of slavery in Spanish America, which has emphasized the liberating rhetoric of the Wars of Independence and the central role of the nation-state. The abolition of slavery was not, in fact, an automatic outcome of independence, but rather a protracted process opposed by Creole elites who feared black citizenship (Andrews 2004; Lasso 2007). Spain's loss of most of its American colonies, moreover, led to the hardening of slavery in Cuba and Puerto Rico and the shift to the so-called coolie trade (Meagher 2008). Slave emancipation in this arena remained a dream until 1873 in Puerto Rico and 1886 in Cuba (Ferrer 1999; Schmidt-Nowara 1999).

Brazil's ties (involving multicentury family and social connections) to Central Africa, particularly Angola and the Bight of Benin, significantly complicated the suppression of the slave trade (Reis, Gomes, and Carvalho 2010). Portugal's opposition to ending the slave trade was primarily related to the fact that there was simply more at stake; its colonies were the most important sources of enslaved labor in the nineteenth century (Marques 2006). After Brazil became independent from Portugal in 1822, the Portuguese government sought to prevent exports of slaves to the former colony, but they lacked resources on the ground to implement a law passed in 1836. The Portuguese feared that the British campaign was nothing more than a façade to stake out a claim over commerce and territory in Africa. Several other nations in the Atlantic, including the United States, held variations of the same concerns (Bergad 2007).

In Brazil, the abolition of the slave trade dragged on for decades due to the central place of slavery in the rising economy of coffee production in the Paraíba Valley. Anti-slave trade laws had relative success in terms of suppressing the slave trade from the Bight of Benin, but were much less consequential in affecting the slave trade from Central and East Africa. In Central Africa, the rise of abolitionism led to the decentralization of the structure of the trade along the African coast, preventing an effective suppression of the trade. The trade also increased out of East Africa, which had become an important source of slaves in the late eighteenth century as a function of Brazil's increasing demand for labor. Brazilian dependence on the slave trade deeply shaped the country's political fabric in the wake of independence from Portugal (Chalhoub 2012). Supporters of the slave trade held key positions in government and displayed lukewarm commitment to implementing a law passed in 1831 to end the slave trade (Parron 2011).

By the mid-nineteenth century, the abolition of the slave trade had become a major geopolitical conundrum, pitting the British government against the Portuguese government due to the countries' competing agendas in Africa. British diplomatic and military pressures did eventually impel the Portuguese crown to abolish the slave trade, but Portugal did so as part of a wider process of revamping the Portuguese empire after the loss of Brazil in 1822. Portugal, in other words, saw Angola as a new Brazil – a colony that required laborers – which is why the crown passed laws against the exportation of slaves out of Africa. The rise of abolitionism wound up indirectly bolstering Portuguese political control over slave-exporting regions near the River Congo and Cabinda.

Suppressionist efforts significantly changed the operation and financial underpinnings of the slave trade to the Americas. To hinder efforts to halt the trade, slavers decentralized the shipments of captives to different locales along the African coast and increased the number of disembarkation points. They also developed new trading networks run out of multiple financial hubs across the Atlantic, including New York City (Marques 2016). At the same time, formerly enslaved Africans (known as liberated or emancipated Africans) continued to toil under working conditions very similar to slavery (Mamigonian 2009). Despite the movement to end the slave trade, shipments of slaves to Cuba continued into the 1860s, frustrating those who expected that the slave trade would come to an end with the shutdown of the slave trade to Brazil in 1850.

CONCLUSION

Latin America absorbed the majority of Africans who forcibly migrated across the Atlantic. This demographic impact meant that slavery played a key role in shaping the social, cultural, and political fabrics of this vast region. The slave trade also made Latin America a zone with deep cultural and social connections to Africa (Wheat 2016). Much of the trade's corollaries, however, are unquantifiable. In Africa, the trade led to the blurring or collapse of distinctions between different forms of social dependence, dramatically increasing the number of potential victims of the slave trade. The end of the slave trade in the nineteenth century, moreover, ushered in a new era of increased European presence that set the stage for the rise of colonialism. Slavery survived these transformations, morphing into new slaveries or practices of forced labor that closely resembled slavery.

In Latin America, Africans and people of African descent succeeded in building social communities by drawing on African culture, while also adjusting to colonial societies in myriad ways. At the same time, the slave trade also encouraged constant and ongoing resistance to slavery. Liberty from chattel slavery was a primary goal from the moment enslaved peoples set foot in the American continents, and everywhere runaway communities testified to this aim (Lockley 2015). In urban settings from Mexico City to Rio de Janeiro, a shared sense of cultural commonality fostered African participation in brotherhoods and fraternities (Germeten 2006; Soares 2011). The history of the trade is therefore necessarily conjoined with the fight for freedom and community.

The slave trade intertwined with the political fabric of Latin America in complex ways, paving the way for the rise of powerful elite groups that seized on the economic leverage of slaving to enhance their standing in colonial society. In Cuba, these commercial groups played a critical role in the deregulation of slave imports that catapulted Cuba into the second largest destination of the nineteenth-century slave trade. At the same time, the politics of the slave trade shaped nascent nation-state formation in Brazil, hindered the execution of anti-slave trade laws, and strengthened conservative forces. The end of the slave trade to Latin America only took place in 1867. While slavery in Brazil and Cuba survived the end of the slave trade by several decades, other countries in Latin America tapped into new forms of forced labor provided by laborers brought from places as far away as India and China.

While quantitative, economic, and social historians have contributed groundbreaking analyses on the aggregated features and social and cultural impacts of the slave trade, the longevity and scope of trade dictates that many themes still deserve scholarly scrutiny. More research is needed, for instance, to understand the intersection of the slave trade and gender relations in Africa and Latin America. Another area that deserves attention relates to the public memory of slavery and the slave trade, a theme that has been analyzed by scholars of Africa but remains relatively underexplored by scholars of Latin America (Araujo 2014).

Another glaring lacuna is studies that take a comparative approach, drawing parallels and distinctions between different African or Latin American regions.

Interdisciplinary analyses and collaborative scholarship provide yet another potential venue for future research. Groundbreaking archeological studies, for instance, have shed critical light into the inner workings of the slave trade, be it on the Island of Santa Helena, home to 30,000 enslaved Africans in the nineteenth century, or in downtown Rio de Janeiro, one of the most important points of disembarkation in the Americas (Lima 2016; Pearson 2016). Historians have already begun to collaborate closely with archeologists, anthropologists, and geneticists (Symanscki and Gomes 2013; Schroeder et al. 2015). These interdisciplinary partnerships have the potential of bearing fruitful results for advancing our knowledge about the multifaceted slave trade.

### BIBLIOGRAPHY

Alencastro, Luiz Felipe de. 2000. *O trato dos viventes: formação do Brasil no Atlântico Sul, séculos XVI e XVII*. São Paulo: Companhia das Letras.
Almeida Mendes, Antonio de. 2008. "The Foundations of the System: A Reassessment of the Slave Trade to the Spanish Americas in the Sixteenth and Seventeenth Centuries." In *Extending the Frontiers: Essays on the New Transatlantic Slave Trade Database*, edited by David Eltis and David Richardon, 63–94. New Haven, CT: Yale University Press.
2012. "Slavery, Society and the First Steps Towards an Atlantic Revolution in Senegambia Western Africa (XV–XVI Centuries)." In *Brokers of Change: Atlantic Commerce and Cultures in Precolonial Western Africa*, edited by Toby Green, 239–59. Oxford: Oxford University Press.
Andrews, George Reid. 1980. *The Afro-Argentines of Buenos Aires, 1800–1900*. Madison, WI: University of Wisconsin Press.
2004. *Afro-Latin America, 1800–2000*. New York, NY: Oxford University Press.
Anes, Rafael Donoso. 2007. "Un análisis sucinto del Asiento de esclavos con Inglaterra (1713–1750) y el papel desempeñado por la contabilidad en su desarrollo." *Anuario de Estudios Americanos* 64, 2: 105–43.
Araujo, Ana Lucia. 2014. *Shadows of the Slave Past: Memory, Heritage, and Slavery*. New York, NY: Routledge.
Arre Marfull, Montserrat. 2011. "Comercio de esclavos: Mulatos criollos en coquimbo o circulación de esclavos de 'reproducción' local, siglos xviii–xix. Una propuesta de investigación." *Cuadernos de Historia* 35: 61–91.
Barcia, Manuel. 2014. *West African Warfare in Bahia and Cuba: Soldier Slaves in the Atlantic World, 1807–1844*. New York, NY: Oxford University Press.
Barcia, María del Carmen. 1987. *Burguesía esclavista y abolición*. La Habana: Editorial de Ciencias Sociales.

Barcia, María del Carmen, Gloria García, and Eduardo Torres-Cuevas. 1994. *Historia de Cuba: La colonia, evolución socioeconómica y formación nacional de los origenes hasta 1867*. La Habana: Editora Política.

Barrett, Ward J. 1970. *The Sugar Hacienda of the Marqueses del Valle*. Minneapolis, MN: University of Minnesota Press.

Bennett, Herman L. 2003. *Africans in Colonial Mexico: Absolutism, Christianity, and Afro-Creole Consciousness, 1570–1640*. Bloomington, IN: Indiana University Press.

Bergad, Laird W. 2007. *The Comparative Histories of Slavery in Brazil, Cuba, and the United States*. New York, NY: Cambridge University Press.

Bergad, Laird W., Fe Iglesias García, and María del Carmen Barcia. 1995. *The Cuban Slave Market, 1790–1880*. New York, NY: Cambridge University Press.

Berquist, Emily. 2010. "Early Anti-Slavery Sentiment in the Spanish Atlantic World, 1765–1817." *Slavery & Abolition: A Journal of Slave and Post-Slave Studies* 31, 2: 181–205.

Birmingham, David. 2015. *A Short History of Modern Angola*. New York, NY: Oxford University Press.

Blumenthal, Debra. 2009. *Enemies & Familiars: Slavery and Mastery in Fifteenth-Century Valencia*. Ithaca, NY: Cornell University Press.

Borucki, Alex. 2015. *From Shipmates to Soldiers: Emerging Black Identities in the Río de la Plata*. Albuquerque, NM: University of New Mexico Press.

Borucki, Alex, David Eltis, and David Wheat. 2015. "Atlantic History and the Slave Trade to Spanish America." *American Historical Review* 120, 2: 433–61.

Bowser, Frederick P. 1974. *The African Slave in Colonial Peru, 1524–1650*. Stanford, CA: Stanford University Press.

Brockington, Lolita Gutiérrez. 1989. *The Leverage of Labor: Managing the Cortés Haciendas in Tehuantepec, 1588–1688*. Durham, NC: Duke University Press.

Bryant, Sherwin K. 2014. *Rivers of Gold, Lives of Bondage: Governing Through Slavery in Colonial Quito*. Chapel Hill, NC: University of North Carolina Press.

Bühnen, Stephan. 1993. "Ethnic Origins of Peruvian Slaves (1548–1650): Figures for Upper Guinea." *Paideuma* 39: 57–110.

Canabrava, A. P. 1984. *O comércio português no Rio da Prata (1580–1640)*. São Paulo: Editora da Universidade de São Paulo.

Candido, Mariana P. 2013. *An African Slaving Port and the Atlantic World: Benguela and Its Hinterland*. New York, NY: Cambridge University Press.

Cassá, Roberto. 1978. *Historia social y económica de la República Dominicana: introducción a su estudio*. 2nd edition. Santo Domingo: Editora Alfa y Omega.

Chalhoub, Sidney. 2012. *A força da escravidão: ilegalidade e costume no Brasil oitocentista*. São Paulo: Companhia das Letras.

Curry-Machado, Jonathan. 2011. *Cuban Sugar Industry: Transnational Networks and Engineering Migrants in Mid-Nineteenth Century Cuba*. New York, NY: Palgrave Macmillan.

Curtin, Philip D. 1969. *The Atlantic Slave Trade: A Census.* Madison, WI: University of Wisconsin Press.

de la Fuente, Alejandro, César García del Pino, and Bernardo Iglesias Delgado. 2008. *Havana and the Atlantic in the Sixteenth Century.* Chapel Hill, NC: University of North Carolina Press.

Eagle, Marc. 2014. "Chasing the Avença: An Investigation of Illicit Slave Trading in Santo Domingo at the End of the Portuguese Asiento Period." *Slavery & Abolition: A Journal of Slave and Post-Slave Studies* 35, 1: 99–120.

Eltis, David, Stephen D. Behrendt, Manolo Florentino, and David Richardson. 2013. *Voyages: The Trans-Atlantic Slave Trade Database.* Emory University. www.slavevoyages.org.

Ferreira Furtado, Junia. 2012. "From Brazil's Central Highlands to Africa's Ports: Trans-Atlantic and Continental Trade Connections in Goods and Slaves." *Colonial Latin American Review* 21, 1: 127–60.

Ferrer, Ada. 1999. *Insurgent Cuba: Race, Nation, and Revolution, 1868–1898.* Chapel Hill, NC: University of North Carolina Press.

2014. *Freedom's Mirror: Cuba and Haiti in the Age of Revolution.* New York, NY: Cambridge University Press.

Funes Monzote, Reinaldo. 2008. *From Rainforest to Cane Field in Cuba: An Environmental History since 1492.* Chapel Hill, NC: University of North Carolina Press.

Galloway, J.H. 1989. *The Sugar Cane Industry: An Historical Geography from Its Origins to 1914.* Cambridge: Cambridge University Press.

García de León, Antonio. 2001. "La real compañía de inglaterra y el tráfico negrero en el veracruz del siglo XVIII, 1713–1748." *Investigación Económica* 61, 237: 153–82.

Garofalo, Leo J. 2012. "The Shape of a Diaspora: The Movement of Afro-Iberians to Colonial Spanish America." In *Africans to Spanish America: Expanding the Diaspora,* edited by Sherwin K. Bryant, Rachel Sarah O'Toole and Ben Vinson, 27–49. Urbana, IL: University of Illinois Press.

Gerhard, Peter. 1972. *A Guide to the Historical Geography of New Spain.* Cambridge: Cambridge University Press.

Germeten, Nicole von. 2006. *Black Blood Brothers: Confraternities and Social Mobility for Afro-Mexicans.* Gainesville, FL: University Press of Florida.

Graden, Dale T. 2014. *Disease, Resistance, and Lies: The Demise of the Transatlantic Slave Trade to Brazil and Cuba.* Baton Rouge, LA: Louisiana State University Press.

Green, Toby, ed. 2012. *Brokers of Change: Atlantic Commerce and Cultures in Precolonial Western Africa.* Oxford: Oxford University Press.

Gudmundson, Lowell, and Justin Wolfe, eds. 2010. *Blacks and Blackness in Central America: Between Race and Place.* Durham, NC: Duke University Press.

Hawthorne, Walter. 2010. *From Africa to Brazil: Culture, Identity, and an Atlantic Slave Trade, 1600–1830.* Cambridge: Cambridge University Press.

Heywood, Linda M., and John Kelly Thornton. 2007. *Central Africans, Atlantic Creoles, and The Making of the Foundation of the Americas, 1585–1660.* New York, NY: Cambridge University Press.

Johnson, Lyman L. 2011. *Workshop of Revolution: Plebeian Buenos Aires and the Atlantic World, 1776–1810*. Durham, NC: Duke University Press.

Klein, Herbert S. 2010. *The Atlantic Slave Trade*. 2nd edition. New York, NY: Cambridge University Press.

Klein, Herbert S., and Francisco Vidal Luna. 2010. *Slavery in Brazil*. New York, NY: Cambridge University Press.

Klein, Herbert S., Manuel Moreno Fraginals, and Stanley L. Engerman. 1983. "Nineteenth Century Cuban Slave Prices in Comparative Perspective." *American Historical Review* 88, 4: 1201–18.

Lane, Kris. 2002. *Quito 1599: City and Colony in Transition*. Albuquerque, NM: University of New Mexico Press.

Larson, Pier M. 2013. "African Slave Trades in Global Perspective." In *The Oxford Handbook of Modern African History*, edited by John Parker and Richard J. Reid, 54–76. Oxford: Oxford University Press.

Lasso, Marixa. 2007. *Myths of Harmony: Race and Republicanism during the Age of Revolution, Colombia 1795–1831*. Pittsburgh, PA: University of Pittsburgh Press.

Laviña, Javier, and Michael Zeuske, eds. 2014. *The Second Slavery: Mass Slaveries and Modernity in the Americas and in the Atlantic Basin*. Zürich: Lit Verlag.

Lima, Tania Andrade. 2016. "A Meeting Place for Urban Slaves in Eighteenth-Century Rio de Janeiro." *Journal of African Diaspora Archaeology and Heritage* 5, 2: 102–46.

Lockley, Tim. 2015. "Runaway Slave Colonies in the Atlantic World." *Latin American History: Oxford Research Encyclopedias*. Accessed May 6, 2016. doi: 10.1093/acrefore/9780199366439.013.5.

Lohse, Russell. 2014. *Africans into Creoles: Slavery, Ethnicity, and Identity in Colonial Costa Rica*. Albuquerque, NM: University of New Mexico Press.

Mamigonian, Beatriz G. 2009. "In the Name of Freedom: Slave Trade Abolition, the Law and the Brazilian Branch of the African Emigration Scheme (Brazil–British West Indies, 1830s–1850s)." *Slavery & Abolition: A Journal of Slave and Post-Slave Studies* 30, 1: 41–66.

Marques, João Pedro. 2006. *The Sounds of Silence: Nineteenth-Century Portugal and the Abolition of the Slave Trade*. Translated by Richard Wall. 2nd edition. New York, NY: Berghahn Books.

Marques, Leonardo. 2016. *United States and the Transatlantic Slave Trade to the Americas, 1776–1867*. New Haven, CT: Yale University Press.

McKinley, Michelle A. 2016. *Fractional Freedoms: Slavery, Intimacy, and Legal Mobilization in Colonial Lima, 1600–1700*. New York, NY: Cambridge University Press.

Meagher, Arnold J. 2008. *The Coolie Trade: The Traffic in Chinese Laborers to Latin America, 1847–1874*. Philadelphia, PA: Xlibris Corporation. First published 1975.

Menard, Russell R., and Stuart B. Schwartz. 1993. "Why African Slavery? Labor Force Transitions in Brazil, Mexico, and the Carolina Lowcountry." In *Slavery in the Americas*, edited by Wolfgang Binder, 89–114. Würzburg: Königshausen & Neumann.

Metcalf, Alida C. 2005. *Go-Betweens and the Colonization of Brazil, 1500–1600.* Austin, TX: University of Texas Press.

Miller, Joseph C. 1988. *Way of Death: Merchant Capitalism and the Angolan Slave Trade, 1730–1830.* Madison, WI: University of Wisconsin Press.

Miño Grijalva, Manuel. 1989. "El Obraje Colonial." *European Review of Latin American and Caribbean Studies* 47: 3–19.

Montoya, Ramón Alejandro. 2016. *El esclavo africano en San Luis Potosí durante los siglos xvii y xviii.* San Luis Potosí: Universidad Autónoma de San Luis Potosí.

Moreno Fraginals, Manuel. 1978. *El ingenio: complejo económico social cubano del azúcar.* 3 vols. La Habana: Editorial de Ciencias Sociales.

Motta Sánchez, J. Arturo. 2005. "La población negra y sus orígenes en el estado de Oaxaca. Siglos XVI y XVII." In *Pautas de convivencia étnica en la América Latina colonial (indios, negros, mulatos, pardos y esclavos)*, edited by Juan Manuel Serna Herrera. México: UNAM.

Motta Sánchez, J. Arturo, and A. Meza Peñaloza. 2001. "La reproducción de la población esclava del ingenio de San Nicolás Ayotla, Oaxaca, siglo XVIII." *Estudios de Antropologla Biológica* 10, 2: 429–44.

Moutoukias, Zacarías. 1988. *Contrabando y control colonial en el siglo XVII: Buenos Aires, el Atlántico y el espacio peruano.* Buenos Aires: Centro Editor de América Latina.

Murray, David R. 2002. *Odious Commerce: Britain, Spain, and the Abolition of the Cuban Slave Trade.* 2nd edition. Cambridge: Cambridge University Press. First published 1980.

Navarrete Peláez, María C. 2007. "De las 'malas entradas' y las estrategias del "buen pasaje": el contrabando de esclavos en el Caribe neogranadino, 1550–1690." *Historia Crítica* 34: 160–83.

Naveda Chávez-Hita, Adriana. 1987. *Esclavos negros en las haciendas azucareras de Cordoba, Veracruz, 1690–1830.* Xalapa: Universidad Veracruzana.

Newson, Linda A., and Susie Minchin. 2007. *From Capture to Sale: The Portuguese Slave Trade to Spanish South America in the Early Seventeenth Century.* Leiden: Brill.

Ngou-Mvé, Nicolás. 1994. *El África bantú en la colonización de México (1595–1640).* Madrid: CSIC.

O'Toole, Rachel Sarah. 2012. *Bound Lives: Africans, Indians, and the Making of Race in Colonial Peru.* Pittsburgh, PA: University of Pittsburgh Press.

Ortega, Álvaro, and Melba Guariglia Zás, eds. 2005. *La ruta del esclavo en el Río de la Plata: su historia y sus consecuencias.* Montevideo, Uruguay: UNESCO, Organización de las Naciones Unidas para la Educación, la Ciencia y la Cultura.

Parés, Luis Nicolau. 2013. *The Formation of Candomblé: Vodun History and Ritual in Brazil.* Chapel Hill, NC: The University of North Carolina Press.

Parron, Tâmis. 2011. *A política da escravidão no Império do Brasil, 1826–1865.* Rio de Janeiro: Civilização Brasileira.

Pearson, Andrew. 2016. *Distant Freedom: St Helena and the Abolition of the Slave Trade, 1840–1872.* Liverpool: Liverpool University Press.

Perera Díaz, Aisnara, and María de los Ángeles Meriño Fuentes. 2015. *Estrategias de libertad: Un acercamiento a las acciones legales de los esclavos en Cuba (1762–1872)*. 2 vols. La Habana: Editorial de Ciencias Sociales.

Pestana, Carla G. 2004. *The English Atlantic in an Age of Revolution, 1640–1661*. Cambridge, MA: Harvard University Press.

Phillips, William D. 2011. "Slavery in the Atlantic Islands and the Early Modern Spanish Atlantic World." In *The Cambridge World History of Slavery*, edited by David Eltis and Stanley L. Engerman, vol. 3, 325–49. Cambridge: Cambridge University Press.

Proctor, Frank T., III. 2010. *"Damned Notions of Liberty": Slavery, Culture, and Power in Colonial Mexico*. Albuquerque, NM: University of New Mexico.

Reis, João José. 1993. *Slave Rebellion in Brazil: The Muslim Uprising of 1835 in Bahia*. Baltimore, MD: Johns Hopkins University Press.

    2015. *Divining Slavery and Freedom: The Story of Domingos Sodré, an African Priest in Nineteenth-Century Brazil*. New York, NY: Cambridge University Press.

Reis, João José, and Flávio dos Santos Gomes. 1996. *Liberdade por um fio: história dos quilombos no Brasil*. São Paulo: Companhia das Letras.

Reis, João José, Flávio dos Santos Gomes, and Marcus J. M. de Carvalho, eds. 2010. *O alufá Rufino: tráfico, escravidão e liberdade no Atlântico Negro (c. 1822–1853)*. São Paulo, Brazil: Companhia das Letras.

Reynoso Medina, Araceli. 2010. *Esclavitud y trabajo en los obrajes de Coyoacán siglo XVII*. Mexico City: Ediciones INDAASEL.

Ribeiro da Silva, Filipa. 2011. "Crossing Empires: Portuguese, Sephardic, and Dutch Business Networks in the Atlantic Slave Trade, 1580–1674." *The Americas* 68, 1: 7–32.

Rodríguez Morel, Genaro. 2012. *Orígenes de la economía de plantación de La Española*. Santo Domingo, República Dominicana: Editora Nacional.

Rupert, Linda M. 2009. "Marronage, Manumission and Maritime Trade in the Early Modern Caribbean." *Slavery & Abolition: A Journal of Slave and Post-Slave Studies* 30, 3: 361–82.

Salvucci, Richard J. 1987. *Textiles and Capitalism in Mexico: An Economic History of the Obrajes, 1539–1840*. Princeton, NJ: Princeton University Press.

Saunders, A.C. de C.M. 1982. *A Social History of Black Slaves and Freedmen in Portugal, 1441–1555*. Cambridge: Cambridge University Press.

Scelle, Georges. 1906. *La traite négrière aux Indes de Castile, contrats et traités d'assiento*. 2 vols. Paris: L. Larose & L. Tenin.

Schmidt-Nowara, Christopher. 1999. *Empire and Antislavery: Spain, Cuba, and Puerto Rico, 1833–1874*. Pittsburgh, PA: University of Pittsburgh Press.

Schroeder, Hannes, María C. Ávila-Arcos, Anna-Sapfo Malaspinas, G. David Poznik, Marcela Sandoval-Velasco, Meredith L. Carpenter, José Víctor Moreno-Mayar, Martin Sikora, Philip L. F. Johnson, Morten Erik Allentoft, José Alfredo Samaniego, Jay B. Haviser, Michael W. Dee, Thomas W. Stafford, Antonio Salas, Ludovic Orlando, Eske Willerslev, Carlos D. Bustamante, and M. Thomas P. Gilbert. 2015. "Genome-Wide Ancestry of 17th-century Enslaved Africans from the Caribbean." *Proceedings of the National Academy of Sciences* 112, 12: 3669–73.

Schultz, Kara D. 2015. "'The Kingdom of Angola Is Not Very Far from Here': The South Atlantic Slave Port of Buenos Aires, 1585–1640." *Slavery & Abolition: A Journal of Slave and Post-Slave Studies* 36, 3: 424–44.

2016. "'The Kingdom of Angola Is Not Very Far from Here': The Río de la Plata, Brazil, and Angola, 1580–1680." PhD diss., Vanderbilt University.

Schwartz, Stuart B. 1978. "Indian Labor and New World Plantations: European Demands and Indian Responses in Northeastern Brazil." *American Historical Review* 83, 1: 43–79.

1985. *Sugar Plantations in the Formation of Brazilian Society: Bahia, 1550–1835*. New York, NY: Cambridge University Press.

Schwartz, Stuart B., ed. 2004. *Tropical Babylons: Sugar and the Making of the Atlantic World, 1450–1680*. Chapel Hill, NC: University of North Carolina Press.

Seibert, Gerhard. 2013. "São Tomé and Príncipe: The First Plantation Economy in the Tropics." In *Commercial Agriculture, the Slave Trade and Slavery in Atlantic Africa*, edited by Robin Law, Suzanne Schwarz and Silke Strickrodt, 54–79. Woodbridge: James Currey.

Seijas, Tatiana. 2014. *Asian Slaves in Colonial Mexico: From Chinos to Indians*. New York, NY: Cambridge University Press.

Seijas, Tatiana, and Pablo Miguel Sierra Silva. 2016. "The Persistence of the Slave Market in Seventeenth-Century Central Mexico." *Slavery & Abolition: A Journal of Slave and Post-Slave Studies* 37, 2: 307–33.

Sierra Silva, Pablo Miguel. 2018. *Urban Slavery in Colonial Mexico: Puebla de los Ángeles, 1531–1706*. New York, NY: Cambridge University Press.

Soares, Mariza de Carvalho. 2011. *People of Faith: Slavery and African Catholics in Eighteenth-Century Rio de Janeiro*. Durham, NC: Duke University Press.

Stark, David M. 2009. "A New Look at the African Slave Trade in Puerto Rico Through the Use of Parish Registers: 1660–1815." *Slavery & Abolition: Journal of Slave and Post-Slave Studies* 30, 4: 491–520.

Studer, Elena F. S. de. 1984. *La trata de negros en el Río de la Plata durante el siglo XVIII*. Buenos Aires: Libros de Hispanoamérica.

Studnicki-Gizbert, Daviken. 2007. *A Nation upon the Ocean Sea: Portugal's Atlantic Diaspora and the Crisis of the Spanish Empire, 1492–1640*. New York, NY: Oxford University Press.

Super, John C. 1976. "Querétaro Obrajes: Industry and Society in Provincial Mexico, 1600–1810." *Hispanic American Historical Review* 56, 2: 197–216.

Sweet, James H. 2011. *Domingos Álvares, African Healing, and the Intellectual History of the Atlantic World*. Chapel Hill, NC: University of North Carolina Press.

Symanscki, Luís Cláudio, and Flávio Gomes. 2013. "Da Cultura Material da Escravidao e do Pós-Abolição: Perspectivas Comparadas em Arqueologia e História." *Revista de História Comparada* 7: 293–338.

Tardieu, Jean-Pierre. 2009. *Cimarrones de Panamá: la forja de una identidad afroamericana en el siglo XVI*. Madrid: Iberoamericana; Vervuert.

Thornton, John. 2015. "The Slave Trade and the African Diaspora." In *The Cambridge World History*, edited by Jerry H. Bentley, Sanjay Subrahmanyam, and Merry E. Wiesner-Hanks, 135–59. Cambridge: Cambridge University Press.

2016. "The Kingdom of Kongo and Palo Mayombe: Reflections on an African-American Religion." *Slavery & Abolition: A Journal of Slave and Post-Slave Studies* 37, 1: 1–22.

Tomich, Dale. 2003. "The Wealth of Empire: Francisco Arango y Parreño, Political Economy, and the Second Slavery in Cuba." *Comparative Studies in Society and History* 45, 1: 4–28.

2014. "Commodity Frontiers, Conjuncture and Crisis: The Remaking of the Caribbean Sugar Industry, 1783–1866." In *The Second Slavery: Mass Slaveries and Modernity in the Americas and in the Atlantic Basin*, edited by Javier Laviña and Michael Zeuske, 143–64. Zürich: Lit Verlag.

Valdés, Dennis N. 1987. "The Decline of Slavery in Mexico." *The Americas* 44, 2: 167–94.

Van Norman, William C. 2013. *Shade-Grown Slavery: The Lives of Slaves on Coffee Plantations in Cuba*. Nashville, TN: Vanderbilt University Press.

Vega Franco, Marisa. 1984. *El tráfico de esclavos con América: asientos de Grillo y Lomelín, 1663–1674*. Sevilla: Escuela de Estudios Hispano-Americanos.

Velásquez Lambur, Rosa Melida. 2015. "Una interpretación de la esclavitud africana en honduras siglos xvi–xviii." PhD diss., Iniversitat Pompeu Fabra.

Verger, Pierre. 1976. *Trade Relations between the Bight of Benin and Bahia from the 17th to 19th Century*. Translated by Evelyn Crawford. Ibadan, Nigeria: Ibadan University Press.

Vila Vilar, Enriqueta. 1977. *Hispanoamérica y el comercio de esclavos: los asientos portugueses*. Sevilla: Escuela de Estudios Hispano-Americanos.

Walker, Tamara J. 2015. "The Queen of *los Congos*: Slavery, Gender, and Confraternity Life in Late-Colonial Lima, Peru." *Journal of Family History* 40, 3: 305–22.

2017. *Exquisite Slaves: Race, Clothing, and Status in Colonial Lima*. New York, NY: Cambridge University Press.

Wheat, David. 2011. "The First Great Waves: African Provenance Zones for the Transatlantic Slave Trade to Cartagena de Indias, 1570–1640." *Journal of African History* 52, 1: 1–22.

2016. *Atlantic Africa and the Spanish Caribbean, 1570–1640*. Published for the Omohundro Institute of Early American History and Culture, Williamsburg, Virginia. Chapel Hill: University of North Carolina Press.

# 3

# Inequality

## *Race, Class, Gender*

## George Reid Andrews

In the present-day social sciences, few issues are more hotly debated than those of social and economic inequality. In the United States, scholarly and policy discussions of the transition from a relatively egalitarian distribution of income in the 1960s and 1970s to an increasingly unequal distribution in the 1990s and early 2000s; of the growing concentration of wealth and income in the hands of the top one-tenth of one percent of the US population; of the political consequences of that extreme concentration of wealth; and of possible policy responses to growing inequality: all of these debates evidence inequality's status as a core topic of academic and political concern (Stiglitz 2013; Piketty 2014; Atkinson 2015; Manning 2017).

In Latin America, which has long been recognized as the world region with the highest levels of social and economic exclusion, inequality is an even more pressing topic. In the last two decades, policy experiments in various countries aimed at reducing disparities in wealth, education, income, and other important social goods have produced promising early results (de Ferranti et al. 2004; Blofeld 2011; Huber and Stephens 2012). Despite those successes, however, patterns of inequality remain deeply entrenched and continue to form a bedrock feature of Latin American social structure (Hoffman and Centeno 2003; Márquez et al. 2007; Frankema 2009; Gootenburg and Reygadas 2010).

What do we mean when we talk about "inequality"? On the simplest and most literal level, "inequality" refers to any relationship in which the numerical (or other) values attached to the items being compared are not the same. If country A's land area is larger than country B's, then those two countries are unequal in size. If I have less money than you, or fewer rights, or less public esteem, then you and I are in an unequal relationship, at least as measured by those indicators. If I have far fewer of those goods than you do, then we are in an extremely unequal relationship. When entire societies are described as extremely unequal, it means that important social goods – wealth, education, health, life expectancy, political representation – are distributed across that society in very unequal ways, with small elite groups receiving much more than their proportional share, and large groups of non-elites receiving much less than their proportional share.

Of those social goods just mentioned, some are customarily expressed in numerical terms: most obviously wealth and income, but also education (How many years of education does one person have as compared to another? How did they score, comparatively, on their qualifying exams?), health (How long on average do the members of one group live, as compared to another?), housing (What is the value of your home as compared to mine? What percentage of houses and apartments in town A are connected to public sewer systems, as compared to town B?), and others.

The concept of inequality also applies to qualities and relationships that can be harder to measure in quantitative terms. How do we quantify differential levels of public respect and esteem, for example, or the different places that groups and individuals hold in national imaginaries and public symbolism? What about unequal access to legal rights and protections (see Chapter 5), to space and mobility, to honor and dignity? And what about the ideological and attitudinal dimensions of inequality: the intellectual work that societies do to justify inequality and explain why it makes sense and is appropriate, or alternatively, to criticize and oppose it?

While acknowledging the importance of all those forms and dimensions of inequality, this chapter will focus most of its effort on the unequal distribution over time of quantifiable material resources: property, wealth, income, education, housing, and life expectancy. Those goods form the baseline determinants, I would argue, of any individual's, group's, or society's well-being. And while statistical measures of those resources are either lacking or very fragmentary for most of the region's history, recent advances by researchers in recovering and piecing together such data provide some starting points for constructing a long-term narrative of social and economic inequality in the region.

During the region's colonial period, there was little if any public debate over the appropriateness and even the social necessity of extreme inequality.

Independence introduced new concepts of civic and legal equality into public life, leading to discussions of how best to prepare citizens for participation in new republican societies. By the late 1800s and early 1900s, social progressives and state reformers were calling for increased investment in education and public health. In the decades following World War II, debates over the causes and consequences of extreme inequality became even more pointed and intense. Dependency theorists identified patterns of "unequal exchange" between developed and underdeveloped countries as the principal barrier to Latin American economic development. Liberation theologists condemned widespread poverty as immoral and unethical and demanded that the Catholic Church adopt a "preferential option for the poor." Beginning in 1959, Cuba's Marxist government undertook radical social and economic reforms that dramatically redistributed wealth and opportunity in that country.

For most of the twentieth century, national doctrines of racial democracy and racial inclusion (see Chapter 8), developmentalist and modernization theory, and radical critiques based in Marxism all sought to explain social and economic inequality in Latin America primarily in terms of social class. In the 1970s and 1980s, however, and responding in part to the rise of new social movements, sociologists and economists began to pay increasing attention to the roles of race and of gender in producing and maintaining social inequality. By the beginning of this century, their research had made clear that racial and gender discrimination are integral dimensions of class-based inequality. Indeed, for most students of inequality, it is impossible to separate the effects of race, gender, and class. Researchers studying those effects developed the concept of "intersectionality": the idea that patterns of racial, gender, and class inequality intersect and interact in complex ways to produce "durable, categorical inequalities" that are very difficult to untangle and uproot (Crenshaw 1991; Tilly 1998; Massey 2007; Greenman and Xie 2008; Cho, Crenshaw, and McCall 2013).

This chapter seeks to identify some of those intersections and to briefly review how they have evolved in Latin America over the last five hundred years. In keeping with this volume's focus on people of African ancestry, it discusses how structures of class and gender inequality interacted with structures of racial inequality and how Africans and Afrodescendants took part in and were affected by those interactions. It also considers how people of color in the region responded to inequality, both by pursuing individual and family-based strategies of advancement and by mobilizing to combat social and racial exclusion through social movements.

Summarizing the findings of recent scholarship, the chapter argues that structures of inequality imposed by colonial rule sank very deep roots that continued to affect the societies of the region into the 1800s and 1900s. Industrialization, urbanization, and the rise of populist political movements in the mid-1900s brought important transformations that reduced measures of class inequality somewhat. But owing partly to structural factors, partly to barriers of prejudice and discrimination, Afrodescendants remained significantly disadvantaged in the competition for admission to growing middle classes and heavily over-represented among the region's poor. Barriers obstructing upward mobility were even greater for Afrodescendant women than for Afrodescendant men. Beginning around 1990, governments in the region increasingly acknowledged poverty and inequality as major obstacles obstructing national progress and undertook social and economic programs aimed at reducing both. But inequality remains a baseline characteristic of Afro-Latin American societies and will continue to demand policy responses well into the current century.

As will become clear in the following pages, the study of racial inequality is considerably more developed in Brazil than in the Spanish American nations. Most of the literature cited in this chapter will therefore deal with that country. When we consider, however, that Brazil received more than two-thirds of the enslaved Africans brought to Latin America, and that today three-quarters of all Afro-Latin Americans live in that country, that level of attention does not seem excessive (Borucki, Eltis, and Wheat 2015, 440; Andrews 2016, 42–44). I also hope that, by suggesting some lines of dialogue between research findings on Brazil and on the Spanish American countries, this chapter may serve to stimulate more work on the latter.

## COLONIAL FOUNDATIONS

How much of present-day inequality in Latin America can be traced back to the region's colonial experience, and in particular to its experience with racially defined forced labor, taxation, and social exclusion? Several foundational texts written during the 1960s and 1970s sought the roots of present-day underdevelopment and inequality in colonial-period institutions and practices (Harris 1964; Frank 1967; Stein and Stein 1970; Stern 1982). Other scholars acknowledged the importance of the colonial experience while insisting on the equal or even greater importance of subsequent developments in the 1800s and 1900s (Cardoso and Faletto 1979 [1969]; Halperín-Donghi 1993 [1969]; Adelman 1999).

In recent years economic historians and historical sociologists have returned to the question of the long-term consequences of colonial institutions for present-day inequality, again arguing, as in earlier decades, the importance of colonial policies and practices for inscribing "indelible inequalities" in the societies of the region (Gootenburg and Reygadas 2010). In an influential series of essays, Engerman and Sokoloff argued that "the great majority of European colonies in the New World," including Brazil and most of Spanish America, experienced "extreme inequality in the distributions of wealth, human capital, and political influence ... These initial differences in inequality were of major import, because societies that began with great inequality tended ... to evolve institutions that contributed to the persistence of substantial inequality" into the 19th and 20th centuries (Engerman and Sokoloff 2012, 297–98). Mahoney concurs, assigning particular importance (for understanding long-term patterns of social and economic development) to "the ways in which colonial institutions constitute particular elite economic actors and define societal ethnic cleavages." In most former European colonies, and certainly those of Spain and Portugal, "ethnic polarization carried over from colonialism and meant intense inequality, with all of the attendant negative consequences" (Mahoney 2010, 20, 266). Analyzing patterns of inequality at the global level, Korzeniewicz and Moran found that countries that have "low and high levels of inequality [today] are for the most part the very same areas that had relatively low and high levels of inequality during or even before the eighteenth century" (Korzeniewicz and Moran 2009, 23).

From the very beginning of European colonization in Latin America, inequality based on inherited difference lay at the heart of colonial rule. Those differences were conceptualized in terms of "blood" rather than "race," the latter a concept that at that time was applied to animals rather than to humans. Nevertheless, imputed differences between "clean" and "unclean" blood and ancestry functioned very much like later racial distinctions, making the Spanish and Portuguese caste laws the first systematic body of racial law in the Atlantic world. By the second half of the 1400s, the Iberian kingdoms were legislating state-mandated distinctions among people of Christian, Jewish, Moorish, Roma, and African ancestry and assigning varying combinations of privileges and obligations to each group (Bethencourt 2013, 144–56). Following the acquisition of Spanish and Portuguese possessions in the Americas, those laws were extended to the colonies and broadened to include indigenous Amerindians and, over time, new racially mixed groups referred to collectively as "the castes" (Sweet 1997; Martínez

2008; O'Toole 2012). When combined with other laws and administrative practices that favored the interests of mercantile, landowning, and mine-owning elites, "colonial society embodied all of the elements required to perpetuate an inequality prone social structure" (Bértola and Ocampo 2012, 53)

The purpose of the caste laws was to define and enforce conditions of inequality among groups identified by their cultural and racial inheritance. Indigenous people were required to pay tribute taxes of money, goods, or labor. In the early years after the conquest, those taxes were paid to individual Spaniards who had received grants of *encomienda* from the Spanish monarch. Beginning in the second half of the 1500s, those taxes were reassigned to the Crown and collected by Spanish officials.

During the first half of the 1500s, indigenous people were also subject to enslavement by Spanish and Portuguese conquerors. Indigenous slavery was outlawed in both empires in the mid-1500s, though with the significant loophole that groups and individuals who resisted Spanish or Portuguese conquest remained liable to enslavement. Under that provision indigenous people continued to be captured in slaving raids on Spanish American and Brazilian frontiers and trafficked to other locales. Van Deusen estimates that in the 1500s alone, at least 650,000 indigenous people were enslaved in the Spanish colonies and sent to other parts of the empire or back to Europe. This was almost four times as many captives as the 170,000 enslaved Africans brought to Spanish America during those years (Eltis, et al. 2013; Borucki, Eltis, and Wheat 2015; Van Deusen 2015, 2).

Over the colonial period as a whole, however, the weight of enslavement fell much more heavily on Africans and their descendants than on indigenous people. While indigenous people under Spanish rule retained legal freedom, collective land rights, and limited powers of self-government, enslaved Africans and Afrodescendants formed the bottom-most level of colonial caste societies. In both Brazil and Spanish America, the word "negro" became synonymous with "slave," and this equation of black racial status with slavery had momentous long-term consequences. In material terms, slavery systematically transferred the wealth produced by Africans and their descendants to slaveowners, producing a centuries-long legacy of expropriation and poverty that continued to affect Afrodescendants long after slavery had ended.

Historians have amply demonstrated that conditions of slavery varied enormously depending on time period, where slaves lived, the kinds of work they did, and other factors (Bergad 2007; Klein and Vinson 2007). Even on sugar plantations, probably the sites of the most brutal exploitation of slave labor, some slaves held positions that required technical skills or managerial abilities, occasionally earning wages or other concessions for their work (Schwartz 1985, 152–59). Vocational diversity was even greater in towns and cities, where slaves worked at positions at all skill levels, often earning wages that were close to those of free workers in the same trades (Karasch 1987, 185–213; Johnson 2011, 216–48).

Did that relative parity of wages represent opportunities for slaves to improve their economic position? Or, conversely, did it reflect the downward pressure exerted by slavery on the wages of free workers? Certainly the former, as evidenced by the many slaves who capitalized on wage-earning opportunities to accumulate the funds with which to buy their freedom. Though we must note that, when slaves did earn wages, they were required to hand over most of their earnings to their owners. Then, in the act of buying their freedom, they handed over much or all of what they had managed to save along the way. Here are two egregious, and highly visible in historical sources, forms of masters' appropriation of the wealth produced by their slaves.

In theory, the widespread use of slave labor would drive down wages for free workers. Yet the (fairly meager) historical evidence presented thus far does not tend to support that assertion. In Buenos Aires during the late 1700s and Rio de Janeiro during the first half of the 1800s, wages rose for free workers even during periods of intense importation of African slaves. The same economic growth that created demand for slaves created demand for free workers as well, driving up wages (including, in some cases, for slaves). In both cities, "slaves were the most evenly distributed form of wealth, and the most important for the middle sectors" of artisans and small businessmen. During periods of heavy slave importation and, therefore, lower slave prices, "inequality [of wealth] diminished among the free population and social mobility was relatively high." (Frank 2004, 10, 44; Johnson 2011, 232–33).

Yet even if on balance the free population benefited economically from the importation of slaves, slavery as an institution inevitably translated into extreme overall inequality. The same study that finds slaves to be a vehicle of middle-class upward mobility in Rio de Janeiro finds the Gini coefficient of wealth distribution among the city's households to have been 0.84 in 1820 and 0.85 in 1850.[1] And those coefficients "would rise

---

[1] The Gini coefficient, a commonly used measure of inequality, varies from 0, a condition of perfect equality in which everyone owns the same amount of wealth, to 1.0, a condition of perfect inequality in which one person owns all wealth and the rest of the population owns nothing. A Gini coefficient of 0.85 indicates a very high level of inequality.

even higher if slaves were considered as potential heads of households" rather than simply as property (Frank 2004, 77).

Just as powerful as the material consequences of slavery were its symbolic and ideological impacts. Though slavery was often justified as an effective means for Christianizing Africans, the cruelty and abuses of the system contradicted the core messages of Christianity in almost every way. The earliest abolitionist tracts in the Iberian Atlantic world were written by priests who had witnessed the brutalities of slavery and were appalled by them (Bethencourt 2013, 231–33). For most colonists, however, the contradictions between slavery and Christianity could be resolved by explanations focused on alleged character defects that were presented as inherent aspects of blackness: laziness, criminality, sexual and other forms of immorality, lower intellectual capacity, and other deficiencies. These negative stereotypes became widely diffused in colonial society, providing powerful ideological and cultural justifications both for African slavery and for the discriminatory treatment of free Africans and Afrodescendants.

Thus state policy, systematic material deprivation, and deeply embedded racial stereotypes combined to enforce racial inequality in the Spanish and Portuguese colonies. That inequality began with slavery and continued with restrictions on free black opportunity and upward mobility. While rigorously enforcing the terms of slavery, Spanish and Portuguese law also recognized slaves' right to pursue freedom and to negotiate with owners for the purchase of their freedom. By 1800, most black and brown people in Latin America had either been born free or had won their freedom from slavery; as a result, the free black and brown populations outnumbered slaves. Only in Brazil and Cuba, the sites of intense importation of enslaved Africans, did slaves continue to outnumber free people of color. Even in those two colonies, however, free black and brown people formed a large minority of the population (30 percent of the total population in Brazil, 19 percent in Cuba) (Andrews 2004, 40–44).

In the face of the colonial racial laws, free black and brown people pursued a variety of strategies for social advancement. Some of these strategies were collective and involved free black participation in institutions that legitimated their position in the colonial social order. Probably the most important such institutions were Catholic religious brotherhoods and colonial militia units. Both entities offered free blacks access to institutions that wielded great authority in colonial society: the Catholic Church and the royal military establishment. Membership in those institutions simultaneously contradicted racist stereotypes while enabling free blacks to negotiate directly with royal officials. Black militiamen in Mexico, for example, were able to win exemption from racial tribute taxes not just for themselves but for the free black population more generally: a major step toward breaching the caste distinctions between free blacks and whites (Vinson 2001, 132–72; Russell-Wood 2002, 83–94, 128–60; Germeten 2006; Soares 2011; Borucki 2015).

While pursuing strategies of collective advancement, free blacks pursued individual strategies as well. One of the principal such strategies focused on accumulating wealth through hard work and investment. Throughout the Spanish and Portuguese empires, visiting European travelers commented on the presence of free black artisans and small-business owners, including both male and female entrepreneurs. One of the consequences of slavery had been the development of a strong association between two socially degrading conditions: nonwhite racial status and manual labor. In response to that association, many white people were reluctant to jeopardize their social standing by taking up the manual trades. That reluctance opened the doors to widespread black entry into the trades. And successful artisans, especially those who owned workshops employing slave or free laborers, generated incomes sufficient to support their families and invest in urban real estate or small businesses (Frank 2004; Rosal 2009, 71–103; Klein and Luna 2010, 283–92; Reid-Vazquez 2013, 17–41).

Successful members of these small black middle classes were those most directly affected by the strictures of the colonial caste laws. Restrictions on Afrodescendants' ability to enter the university, the professions, the priesthood, the civilian and military bureaucracy, and even some of the higher-status skilled trades, set the upper limits to free black advancement, further defining and enforcing inequality. Here again, free black strivers sought to circumvent those strictures. Some married white spouses, with the goal of producing lighter-skinned offspring who might escape the caste restrictions. Others petitioned the Crown to pardon them from their black or brown racial status and accord them the privileges of whiteness. Those petitions, and the Crown's acceptance of some of them, provided the legal precedents for the *Gracias al sacar* decree of 1795, which formalized the procedures and fees for requesting royal dispensations of nonwhite racial status (Twinam 2014).

Still, the number of people who obtained such dispensations was vanishingly small: of the estimated 1.7 million free black and brown people living in Spanish America in 1800, only twenty-one individuals are known to have petitioned for whiteness. For the vast majority of free

Africans and Afrodescendants, the strictures of the caste laws, of poverty, and of racism continued to set them at major disadvantage to their white compatriots.

## SINCE INDEPENDENCE: RACE AND CLASS

In every Spanish American country, independence meant the end of the caste laws and, eventually, the abolition of slavery. Massive slave and free black participation in the independence armies combined with liberal republican ideologies to produce official declarations of civic and legal equality for all citizens, regardless of race. These declarations, and the eventual abolition of slavery and the slave trade, were major steps toward the overturning of differences between whites and nonwhites. Yet the long-term impacts of colonial racial thought and practice remained visible in the nineteenth-century politics of the newly independent republics and in fact formed one of the axes around which those politics revolved.

In most of Spanish America, ex-slaves and free blacks saw Liberal parties as the more reliable (as compared to Conservative parties) defenders of their rights and freedoms. Those parties actively pursued black support, both as voters and as soldiers in inter-party civil wars, by formally pledging themselves to principles of racial equality. Surveying nineteenth-century Liberal parties, James Sanders found that they placed anti-racism at the heart of their political program and took "pride in their societies having advanced, at least institutionally, beyond racism." Yet in their private writings, "many Liberals could never escape the racism that considered civilization the provenance of white Europeans, while 'blacks' and Indians would remain 'barbarous' until educated and disciplined... Race would be the aspect of [Latin American liberalism] that often hewed most closely to the colonialist past and the racial currents of Europe and North America that celebrated whiteness" (Sanders 2014, 36, 102, 158). Jason McGraw concurs that "the flip side of Colombians' eschewing race in public relationships was their general acceptance of antiblack racism in private ... [where they] reproduce[d] racism even as they upheld democratic forms of nondiscrimination in the street and in the press" (McGraw 2014, 10; for more on racial tensions in Latin American liberalism, see Ferrer 1999; Sanders 2004; Lasso 2007; Gobat 2013).

While following a different and less violent path to independence than the Spanish American countries, Brazil joined them in abolishing the caste laws and state-mandated racial inequalities. As many historians have noted, it is precisely the removal of racial labels and categories from official records and documents – the "racial silence" analyzed by Brod-wyn Fischer, Keila Grinberg, and Hebe Mattos in Chapter 5 – that makes it so difficult to study racial inequality in the 1800s and to document patterns of racial difference at that time. Yet as historians Martha Abreu and Mattos have cogently noted, the disappearance of race from official sources did not mean that it disappeared from daily life, in which "color prejudice was clearly evident at all levels of society" and continued to impede black upward mobility (Grinberg 2002; Mattos 2009, 366; Klein and Luna 2010, 275).

Partly as a result of the continuation of racial attitudes and practices from the colonial period, indicators of black vocational achievement in the newly independent nations did not initially show much change. In Argentina, the Buenos Aires census of 1827 found free blacks working mainly in manual labor and almost completely absent from the ranks of property owners, merchants, or professionals (categories that accounted for almost half of those white respondents who listed an occupation). Free blacks did somewhat better in Rio de Janeiro, where, of free black and pardo males listing occupations in the census of 1834, 20 percent worked in high- or middle-status occupations. Among whites, however, the proportion working in high- or middle-status jobs was 75 percent, a striking disparity. In San Juan, Puerto Rico, rates of home ownership in the 1823–46 period were four to ten times higher (depending on the neighborhood) for white heads of household than free black. And since black-owned homes were concentrated in the poorer neighborhoods of the city, those numbers understate racial differentials in the value of urban property holding (Andrews 1980, 40; Karasch 1987, 69; Kinsbruner 1996, 68–73; Rosal 2009, 85, documented 577 black property owners in Buenos Aires between 1811 and 1830 but did not compare that number to rates of property ownership in the white population).

Further obstructing black economic advancement in the 1800s was the economic stagnation that afflicted much of the region. Between 1820 and 1870, annual growth in per capita GDP was very close to 0 for Latin America as a whole (Bértola and Ocampo 2012, 62–67). One of the exceptions to the region's economic stagnation was Cuba, where the expanding sugar economy produced per capita GDP growth rates of 0.9 percent per year. As a continuing Spanish colony, however, slavery and the caste laws both remained very much in effect throughout the island, and the slave and free black populations both suffered brutal repression in the wake of the Escalera conspiracy in 1844. The black middle class continued to expand even in the wake of that repression, but under legal strictures that still enforced racial difference (Reid-Vazquez 2013). Under those conditions, when the first independence war erupted in 1868, slaves and free blacks flocked to the rebel cause (Ferrer 1999; on those Afro-Cubans who remained loyal to Spain, see Sartorius 2014). Following the defeat of the first (1868–78) and second (1879–80) insurrections, Afro-Cubans formed a civil rights movement to contest the provisions of the caste laws. That movement obtained several court rulings overturning racially discriminatory laws and practices and an 1893 decree by the governor-general banning all legal "distinctions based on color." Following independence in 1898, efforts by the US occupation government to enact racially discriminatory suffrage requirements similar to those in effect in the southern United States were rejected by the Cuban constitutional convention of 1901 (de la Fuente 2001, 54–60; Scott 2005, 200–07).

In Cuba, however, as in Brazil and other Spanish American republics, anti-racist political ideals ran up against deeply rooted racist beliefs. And by the late 1800s, everyday, "common-sense" racism was being powerfully reinforced by the "scientific" racism that permeated Western thought at that time. The new academic disciplines of psychology, anthropology, criminology, and history all promoted the concept of a human species divided into clearly defined racial groups, each characterized by specific combinations of strengths and debilities. Europeans, and "white" people descended from Europeans, occupied the top of the racial hierarchy, with Asians, Africans, and indigenous Amerindians and Pacific Ocean peoples at lower levels. Scientific racism not only justified social and economic inequality; it insisted on it as inevitably determined by the racial inheritance of individuals and societies (Bethencourt 2013, 271–306; Sussman 2014, 31–63).

According to the dictates of scientific racism, the majority-nonwhite character of most Latin American societies destined them for second- or even third-tier status in the community of nations, which would be dominated by the "white" republics of Europe, North America, Australia, and New Zealand. In an effort to escape this fate, every Latin American nation sought to modify its racial composition by attracting European immigration. That effort was primarily successful in Argentina, Uruguay, the southern states of Brazil, and in Cuba, which continued to receive large numbers of Spanish immigrants even after independence in 1898.

In each of those countries, European immigrants received clear employment preferences over Afrodescendants. De la Fuente (2001, 115–28) has argued that in Cuba Spanish immigrants tended to displace native-born white workers as well. That does not appear to have been the case in Rio de Janeiro, where native-born whites worked at higher skill levels and earned higher average wages than immigrants, or in Buenos Aires, where Argentines "outranked the European born not only on the top tiers of the occupational structure but in the intermediate ones as well" (Adamo 1983, 50–74; Moya 1998, 213). In all four countries, black and mulatto workers were the clear losers in the economic competition with the immigrants, being relegated to informal occupations in domestic service and construction or to lower-paying positions in industry. This in turn placed their descendants in a very weak position to compete in the 1930s, 1940s, and 1950s for entry into the expanding urban middle class (Andrews 1991; de la Fuente 2001, 138–71; Andrews 2010, 85–111; Monsma 2016).

While European workers do appear to have benefited from racial preferences, those preferences were not strong enough to provide markedly better living conditions for immigrants than for native-born families. In Havana, Rio de Janeiro, São Paulo, Montevideo, Buenos Aires, and smaller cities, black and white families shared tenement slums and informal shanty communities (Fischer 2008; Andrews 2010; Horst 2016). Those poor and working-class neighborhoods were the incubators in which the African-inflected musical forms of the early 1900s – tango in Argentina, rumba and son in Cuba, candombe in Uruguay, samba in Brazil – took form (Chasteen 2004; see also Chapter 11). They were also the breeding grounds for the cross-racial labor movements that by the 1930s and the 1940s were joining newly formed populist coalitions and governments. Beginning in those decades and continuing through the 1960s and 1970s, those governments instituted social and economic policies that had profound impacts on structures of inequality in the region.

During the colonial period and through the 1800s, land had been the principal form of wealth in Latin America and thus the leading source of social and economic inequality. Colonial land policies had favored the formation of large landed estates over medium- and small-holdings. While the statistical data that we have on the distribution of land during those years is quite limited, the few studies that we do have make clear that, in most of the region, ownership of land was very unequally distributed. Between 1880 and 1930, as the Second Industrial Revolution in Europe and North America intensified demand for Latin American agricultural and mineral exports, land values increased in much of the region. This led to massive dispossessions of peasant and subsistence farmers and further increases in inequality as those lands were transferred to large landowners (Frankema 2009, 75–84; Bértola and Ocampo 2012, 116–23).

The economic crisis of the 1930s persuaded many Latin American governments that basing their economies on export commodities made those economies excessively vulnerable to external conditions of supply and demand over which they had little or no control. The time had come, they decided, to declare national economic independence by undertaking state-sponsored national industrialization. In addition to industrialization, governments in Argentina, Brazil, Cuba, Mexico, and other countries also expanded social programs in education, health, and housing. And seeking the support of organized labor, a key participant in any program of national industrialization, governments guaranteed labor rights, enacted social security programs and set federally-mandated minimum wages.

Throughout the region, these policies produced a "golden age of economic growth" that lasted from the mid-1940s through the mid-1970s (Bértola and Ocampo 2012, 175; Thorp 1998, 155–200). Increases in industrial and urban employment made wages a larger percentage of GDP than was the case earlier in the century and also produced lower levels of income inequality than was the case either in the earlier or the later decades of the 1900s (Frankema 2009, 147–75). Even in the face of these advances, however, structures of extreme social inequality persisted. Populist governments were seeking not so much to eliminate disparities among social classes as to mediate and "harmonize" class relations through corporatist political institutions. Most governments also took no action against the concentration of landownership, which remained very high: in 1960 Gini indices of inequality in landholdings averaged .80 for South America as a whole and even higher in Venezuela (.86), Chile (.84), and Colombia (.81). (Frankema 2009, 53–54)

Populist governments' reluctance to confront the rural sector extended to labor reforms as well, which focused almost entirely on industrial workplaces. Workers in agriculture, domestic service, and informal urban occupations were pointedly excluded from national labor legislation, which set them at marked disadvantage to their industrial counterparts (Collier and Collier 2002; French 2004). The profound differences between formality and informality in employment were then reproduced in urban housing. By the early 1900s, rural-to-urban migration had already outstripped the housing resources of major Latin American cities, producing the beginnings of shantytown settlements in Rio de Janeiro, São Paulo, Havana, Mexico City, and other urban areas. As migration intensified in the second half of the century, informal settlements continued to swell, accounting for ever-increasing percentages of the urban population. These settlements occupied a liminal, insecure urban space, with no clear rights to the land on which they were built or to the urban services – water, electricity, garbage and sanitation, and education – that they so desperately needed. Neighborhood associations representing shantytown residents sought alliances with political parties, labor unions, the Catholic Church, and other potential allies. But throughout the region, their rights to property, livelihood, and political representation remained insecure and uncertain (Fischer 2008; Fischer, McCann, and Auyero 2014; Horst 2016; and Chapter 5).

The Afro-Brazilian *favelada* Carolina Maria de Jesus gave memorable voice to the inhabitants of those settlements in her diary-cum-memoir, *Child of the Dark*, in which she roundly condemned Brazilian politicians and state institutions for their indifference to the poor. Describing the offices of "that so-called State Social Service" as "a branch of Purgatory," Jesus insisted that "Brazil needs to be led by a person who has known hunger." Until that day came, she lamented, she and her family would struggle on, nursing their dream to someday be able to move to "a house of bricks" to which they could hold clear and legal title (Jesus 1962, 22, 25, 46, 129; on state social services to the poor, see Auyero 2012).

## 1960 TO THE PRESENT

Despite the shortcomings of the populist years, economic growth and expanding social services unquestionably opened new opportunities for black advancement. Observing at first hand the transformations taking place in Brazil during the 1950s and 1960s, sociologist Florestan Fernandes famously argued that Afro-Brazilians were seizing those opportunities and would soon become fully integrated into the urban working and middle classes (Fernandes 1965). Writing some fifteen years later, sociologist Carlos Hasenbalg found that Afro-Brazilians had indeed moved purposefully to exploit the openings created by industrialization and state-sponsored social programs. That movement began with massive migration from rural areas to cities and from the economically stagnant Northeast to the more dynamic Southeast (see Chapter 14). As they actively pursued employment and education, however, Afro-Brazilians found themselves consistently coming up short. Using census and survey data, Hasenbalg documented clear racial differentials in education and employment (Hasenbalg 1979).

Noting that those differentials increased as blacks and whites moved up the educational and vocational ladder, Hasenbalg suggested that "there is good reason to believe that the higher the educational level achieved by a person of color, the greater the discrimination they will experience in the labor market" (Hasenbalg 1979, 181). That hypothesis was confirmed by economist Nelson do Valle Silva, who used data from the Brazilian census of 1960 to show that "not only [do] whites have higher initial returns to schooling, that is, higher average income for no formal schooling, but the white-nonwhite relative difference actually increase[s] as schooling level increases." Silva attributed that increasing differential to racial discrimination, which accounts for "a very substantial proportion of the income difference between the racial groups in Brazil" (Silva 1978: 204, 215; see also Silva 1985; Hasenbalg, Silva, and Lima 1999).

Hasenbalg's and Silva's research, based on data gathered in Brazil's censuses and national household surveys, prompted a wave of studies on various dimensions of racial inequality in Brazil: vocational inequality (Oliveira et al. 1983), wage inequality (Lovell 1989), educational inequality (Rosemberg 1986), and the racial attitudes and stereotypes that undergird racism and discrimination (Turra and Venturi 1995). (For updates of those early findings, see Telles 2004; Paixão and Carvano 2008; Paixão et al. 2010.) That research in turn contributed to policy debates in Brazil over how to reduce the high levels of inequality that the country has historically suffered. From 1970 to 2000, Brazil had the highest levels of income inequality in Latin America, a region which itself had the highest levels of income inequality in the world. Upon taking office in 1995, President Fernando Henrique Cardoso committed his government to reducing poverty and inequality in Brazil, which he described as "no longer an underdeveloped country. [Rather,] it is an unjust country," which he proposed to transform through a comprehensive program of social and economic reform (Nobles 2000, 123). Having already reduced hyper-inflation – a major driver of inequality through its devastating impact on wages – through the Real Plan, Cardoso undertook a series of other programs, including conditional cash transfer payments to poor families, investments in primary and secondary education, and gradual increases in the value of the minimum wage. These programs, further expanded and deepened by Presidents Luiz Inácio Lula da Silva (2003–10) and Dilma Rousseff (2011–16), lowered Gini indices of income inequality in Brazil from .60 in 1995 to .52 in 2014 (IPEA 2010; IPEADATA 2016).

In addition to lowering overall inequality, the social programs of the last twenty years lowered racial inequality as well. Cash transfers to poor families and increased federal expenditure on education eliminated racial differentials in elementary-school enrollment (though not in academic performance or graduation). Cash transfer programs and increases in the minimum wage reduced the white/nonwhite household income ratio from 2.4 in 1990 (i.e., average income for households headed by a white person was 2.4 times greater than the average income for households headed by a black or brown person) to 2.0 in 2009. Black-white differentials in life expectancy fell from 6.6 years in 1990 to 3.2 years in 2005, by which point they were smaller than black-white differentials in the United States (5.1 years in 2005) (Andrews 2014).

Brazil's achievements in reducing overall socioeconomic inequality, and racial inequality specifically, were somewhat of a bellwether in a region where already high levels of inequality had increased further during the 1980s. The economic slowdown of that decade, combined with reductions in government spending, reversed the gains of the 1950s and 1960s and led to widening income gaps between rich and poor (Frankema 2009, 1–5). Those increases in poverty and inequality injected new urgency into longstanding debates over the most appropriate social and economic policies for the region. While national governments had to face the social and political pressures engendered by rising poverty, international agencies like the World Bank and the Inter-American Development Bank had come to see extreme inequality as one of the principal impediments to the region's immediate economic recovery and long-term development. Those agencies produced a series of reports acknowledging the severity of inequality in the region and proposing measures to combat it (IDB 1998; de Ferranti et al. 2004; Márquez et al. 2007).

As they considered the various factors promoting inequality, international agencies sought to include race in their analyses but were greatly hindered in doing so by the lack of census data on race for most countries. Of the independent Latin American nations, only Brazil and Cuba had consistently gathered data on race during the 1900s. Most of the other countries dropped racial categories from their population counts entirely or included them only for indigenous people. Under pressure both from national black movements and from international agencies (including the UN), first Colombia and then Uruguay included race either in the census (Colombia, 1993) or the national household survey (Uruguay 1996). By 2010, every Latin American country except Chile, the Dominican Republic, and Mexico was gathering data on its Afrodescendant population (Loveman 2014, 250–300).

TABLE 3.1 *Poverty Rates by Race in Selected Countries, in Percentages, 2003–2011*

| | Indigenous | Blacks and mulattos | Whites | B-W |
|---|---|---|---|---|
| *Measured by household earnings* | | | | |
| Uruguay (2006) | 31.8 | 50.1 | 24.4 | 25.7 |
| Ecuador (2006) | 55.8 | 52.1 | 31.2[a] | 20.9 |
| Brazil (2009) | – | 33.8 | 16.7 | 17.1 |
| Colombia (2003) | – | 61.0 | 54.1[a] | 6.9 |
| *Measured by unmet basic needs* | | | | |
| Uruguay (2011) | – | 51.3 | 32.1 | 19.2 |
| Colombia (2003) | – | 34.5 | 22.7[a] | 11.8 |
| Costa Rica (2011) | 54.2 | 34.1 | 25.5[a] | 8.6 |
| Venezuela (2011) | 69.7 | 31.1 | 22.6 | 8.5 |

[a] Whites and mestizos.
*Source:* Andrews 2016, 38

Those data formed the basis for a wave of reports on racial inequality throughout the region, many of them published by the World Bank (Stubbs and Reyes 2006) or the United Nations (Scuro Somma 2008; Cruces, Gasparini, and Carbajal 2010a; Cruces, Gasparini, and Carbajal 2010b; Díaz and Madalengoitia 2012; López Ruiz and Delgado Montaldo 2013). Those reports, and the census data on which they were based, provide the starting point for a systematic comparison of present-day patterns of inequality across the region. Such a comparison is beyond the scope of this chapter, but let us look briefly at two basic indicators of social well-being: poverty and education. Table 3.1 tabulates poverty rates by race, as measured either by household earnings or by a household's having one or more "unmet basic needs" (adequate housing, sanitation, or education). For all racial groups, poverty rates are high: with only a couple of exceptions (Brazilian whites and Uruguayan indigenous people), over 50 percent for indigenous people, from one-third to one-half for Afrodescendants, and from one-quarter to one-third for whites. Except in Uruguay, indigenous poverty rates are higher than Afrodescendant poverty rates, and in Costa Rica and Venezuela much higher. And while black poverty rates are higher than white rates in every country, those differentials tend to cluster in two groups: a high-inequality group of countries with differentials of 17–26 percent points (Uruguay, Ecuador, Brazil), and a somewhat lower-inequality group with differentials of 7–12 percentage points (Colombia, Costa Rica, Venezuela).

TABLE 3.2 *Literacy Rates by Race in Selected Countries, in Percentages,* ca. 2010

|  | Indigenous | Blacks and mulattos | Whites | W-B |
|---|---|---|---|---|
| Brazil | 73.7 | 85.7 | 92.8 | 7.1 |
| Colombia | 70.8 | 88.3 | 92.4[a] | 4.1 |
| Ecuador | 79.6 | 92.4 | 96.3 | 3.9 |
| Venezuela | 70.8 | 94.4 | 96.5 | 2.1 |
| Uruguay | 98.6 | 97.3 | 98.6 | 1.3 |
| Costa Rica | 88.9 | 96.9 | 97.6[a] | 0.7 |

[a] Whites and mestizos.
*Source:* Andrews 2016, 40

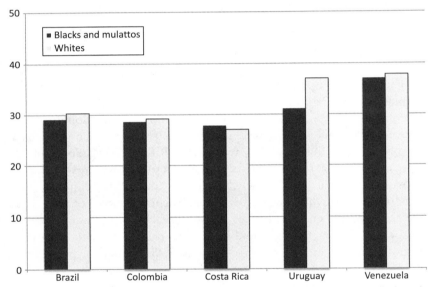

FIGURE 3.1 Percentage of Population Age 15 and Over That Had Attended High School, by Race, Selected Countries, ca. 2010

Educational opportunity is also unequally distributed among racial groups, though not to the same degree as income. Table 3.2 shows smaller racial differentials in literacy rates than in poverty rates. Again with the exception of Uruguay, the indigenous population lags far behind the Afrodescendant population. Black/white differentials are then highest in Brazil, lower in Colombia and Ecuador, and lowest of all, and fairly close to parity, in Venezuela, Uruguay, and Costa Rica. Figure 3.1 also shows

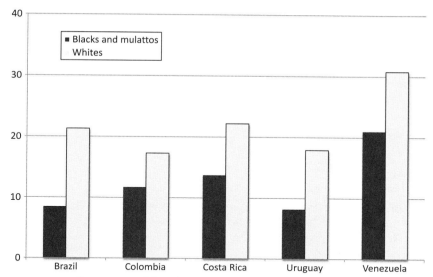

FIGURE 3.2 Percentage of Population Age 15 and Over That Had Attended Post-Secondary Education, by Race, Selected Countries, ca. 2010
*Source:* Andrews 2016, 42–43

relative racial parity in high-school enrollment for every country except Uruguay; Figure 3.2, however, shows marked racial differentials in university enrollment.

That differential was largest in Brazil (the country that, in this brief comparison, consistently ranks at or near the top of black/white inequality in Latin America). During the first decade of the 2000s, over forty Brazilian universities adopted affirmative action policies aimed at increasing black representation in their student bodies. Lawsuits challenging the constitutionality of those policies were rejected by the Brazilian Supreme Court in 2012, and later that year the Brazilian Congress approved an affirmative action policy for the country's system of federal universities. That policy combined class and racial affirmative action by reserving 50 percent of places in each year's freshman class for graduates of the country's public high schools; within that fifty percent, the policy mandated racial quotas for Afrodescendants and indigenous people and an income-based quota for families earning 150 percent or less of the federal minimum wage. The results of this policy will be evaluated by a congressional commission in 2022; for now, the initial indications are that the law has succeeded in dramatically increasing nonwhite enrollment in the

federal universities and that students benefiting from the law are performing at a level comparable to, or in some cases better than, non-quota
students (Santos 2013; Peria and Bailey 2014). Activists and policymakers
in Colombia, Uruguay, and other countries are following this Brazilian
experiment with great interest and considering its potential applicability
to their own societies.[2]

## GENDER

Okezi Otovo's observation that "black Brazilian women, either historical
or present-day, remain grossly understudied" applies to all the countries
of the region (Otovo 2016, 205). Yet even the limited work that has been
done to date makes clear that profound gender differentials shaped the
development of Afro-Latin American societies from their very beginnings.
Those differentials began with the gender composition of African and
European migration to the New World. Over the course of the Atlantic
slave trade, enslaved males outnumbered enslaved females by a ratio of
2:1 (Eltis et al. 2013). Among European migrants, males outnumbered
females to an even greater degree, though by ratios that varied over time.
Women accounted for about 15 percent of Spanish migrants during the
mid-1500s, 30–40 percent by the early 1600s, and 15 percent during the
1700s. The proportion of women migrating from Portugal to Brazil was
even lower (Socolow 2015, 63).

The relative scarcity of African and Iberian women in the colonies had
major social and economic consequences. First, while Iberian laws and
Catholic beliefs both guaranteed enslaved people's right to marry and
form families, most African males were denied that right because of a
lack of potential partners. Partly in response to that shortage, partly
in order to guarantee freedom for their children, many enslaved males
sought out indigenous women, in the process producing a growing Afroindigenous population (Twinam 2014, 90–96; Restall 2009, 257–65;
see also Chapter 4).

Despite their relative under-representation in the enslaved population,
females were strikingly over-represented among those slaves who received
grants of freedom from their owners. Females accounted for 60 percent or
more of slave manumissions in Brazil and Cuba in the 1800s, in Buenos

---

[2] The impeachment of President Rousseff in 2016, however, has created major uncertainties
about future governments' commitment to the policies enacted under her administration
and those of her predecessors.

Aires in the late 1700s, and in Mexico City and Lima in the first half of the 1600s (Bergad 2007, 199; Klein and Luna 2010, 257–58). This was owing partly to females' ability to earn cash wages in petty commerce and domestic service, renting out their skills as cooks, laundresses, or wet nurses. It may also have reflected decisions by slave families to buy the freedom of female members before male members, so that future children born to those women would be born free.

A final contributing factor to the predominance of women among freed people was emotional ties between female slaves and their owners. As they cooked, cleaned, and cared for slaveowners and their families, ties of mutual affection often developed. Especially when combined with offers of cash purchase and other forms of negotiation, those ties could tip the balance between continued enslavement and grants of freedom, both for enslaved women and, in many cases, for their children (Higgins 1999; Proctor 2006; Cowling 2013).

Still, those ties of affection developed within a context of extreme inequality that corrupted everything it touched. One of the darkest dimensions of that inequality was the sexual abuse to which enslaved women were subject. While it is impossible to quantify the frequency or nature of sexual contacts between masters and slaves, cases of sexual abuse occasionally appear in court records. Sexual relationships between enslaved women and their owners were also occasionally cited as a motive for manumission, both of the women themselves and sometimes their children. However, given the low incidence of manumission – on average about one percent or less per year, across the region – it seems likely that most children of such unions continued enslaved, reflecting yet another aspect of profound gender difference under slavery: that free and slave legal status was inherited from the mother, and not from the father.

Higher rates of manumission for enslaved women, as compared to enslaved men, translated into high rates of natural increase for the free black and racially mixed population. By the end of the colonial period, free blacks and pardos were the most rapidly growing racial group in most of the colonies. As indicated previously in this chapter, this made them critically important actors in the independence struggles of the 1810s and 1820s (or, in Cuba, the second half of the century) and in the civil wars and electoral contests that followed. In theory women took no part in those struggles, but in practice, they were deeply involved, and in various roles. Many joined their husbands and partners on campaign; a few even served as soldiers in the independence armies (Blanchard 2008, 141–59; see also the case of María Remedios del Valle, recently acknowledged by the Argentine government as a national heroine of independence [Guzmán 2016]).

Most enslaved and free black women, however, remained at home while their men campaigned, taking charge of children and families. As the independence wars and post-independence civil violence wore on, removing men for years at a time or in many cases permanently, women became increasingly prominent in black community life. In Buenos Aires, gender ratios in the black population (number of men per 100 women) fell from 108 in 1810 to 59 in 1827; in Montevideo, ratios fell from 119 in 1805 to 78 in 1819 (Andrews 2004, 62). Under these conditions, women became responsible for sustaining not just their own families but the corporate institutions of community life. In Montevideo, at least three women served as monarchs of African national associations during the first half of the 1800s; in Buenos Aires, women took over the administration of several African associations and then went to court to avoid handing the organizations back to returning male veterans (Andrews 1980, 148; Borucki 2015, 166–67).

In Brazil, black Catholic religious brotherhoods differed from white brotherhoods in according fuller membership rights to women. While white women joined the brotherhoods as dependents of male members and held no voting powers, black women joined the brotherhoods as dues-paying members able "to meet the men on equal financial grounds." Nevertheless, "their presence was contested all along the way," leading to a case in Rio de Janeiro in the 1780s in which male officers of the brotherhood of Santo Elesbão and Santa Efigênia, constituted by members of the Mina Mahi nation, appealed to the Tribunal da Relação (High Court) to regain control of the organization from its female regent (Soares 2011, 183–221, quotations from 166, 214). In the northeastern city of Salvador, African women founded two of the earliest Candomblé congregations, Casa Branca (ca. 1830) and Gantois (1849). Women constituted the majority of Candomblé congregations' membership over the course of the 1800s and 30–40 percent of their leadership (Parés 2013, 91–97; Alonso 2014, 56–59).

At the same time that African and Afrodescendant women were playing significant roles in community organizations, they were a focus of elite attention as well, especially in the symbolic realm. Writers and intellectuals trying to imagine the new nations that they were building returned repeatedly to images of black women, who contradicted in almost every way the concepts of white male civilization that the new republics sought to emulate. Esteban Echeverría's famous short story,

"El matadero" (The Slaughter Yard), evoked the image of the black *achuradoras,* African and Afro-Argentine women who worked in the slaughter yards scavenging intestines and other organ meats, as a symbol of the brutality and violence of the Rosas dictatorship (Echeverría 2010 [1871]). In Rio de Janeiro, Luis Edmundo da Costa contrasted the elegance of bourgeois couples parading on the Rua do Ouvidor to, "on the sidewalk, a young mulata exposing a shiny, jelly-like breast outside of a ragged blouse" (Needell 1987, 165). That young mulata was immortalized as Rita Baiana, the sensual temptress of Aluísio Azevedo's *O cortiço* (The Slum), who lures the honest, hard-working Portuguese immigrant Jerónimo to abandon his wife and child. "Little by little, all the sober habits of a Portuguese peasant were transformed, and Jerónimo became a Brazilian" (Azevedo 2000 [1890], 76; see also the Cuban figure of Cecilia Valdés [Villaverde 2005 (1882)] or the twentieth-century Brazilian, Gabriela da Silva [Amado 2006 (1958)]).

By 1900, in much of Afro-Latin America representations of Afrodescendant women had coalesced into the cultural figure of the Mulata or Morena, a highly sexualized dark-skinned woman embodying – literally – essential qualities of Latin American nationhood. Her image was propagated through a variety of media: the tangos, sambas, rumbas, candombes, and other popular musical forms that proclaimed her sensuality; poetry and novels; plays and theatrical reviews; and increasingly, as the 1900s wore on, Carnival celebrations, regulated and overseen by the state, that placed dark-skinned women at the center of the festivities (Kutzinski 1993, 163–98; Chasteen 2004, 197–204; Wade 2009, 142–55; Adamovsky 2016).

At the same time that mulatas and morenas were being exalted as core symbols of national identity, they continued to labor at the lowest levels of local and national economies. While most Latin American nations, including Brazil, did not gather racial data in the censuses of the early 1900s, the Cuban census of 1899 did include vocational data differentiated by race and gender. For the population aged ten and over, rates of labor force participation were quite similar for white males (87 percent) and black and mulatto males (88 percent). But while fewer than 5 percent of white females reported paid occupations, 23 percent of black females did so. That rate of black female participation in the labor force pushed total black labor force participation (54 percent) significantly higher than white labor force participation (49 percent) (War Department 1900, 438–39).

Of those Afro-Cuban women who reported an occupation, three-quarters worked in domestic service, with the rest equally divided between agriculture and industry. Black women's concentration in domestic work declined somewhat during the first half of the century but remained their most frequent occupation: of those Afro-Cuban women who reported a profession in the census of 1943, 42 percent worked as domestic servants (República de Cuba 1945, 1042–43). In Bahia during the first half of the 1900s, "the majority of domestics were black and brown women, and the majority of wage-earning black and brown women worked as domestics" (Otovo 2016, 26). At the national level, of those Afro-Brazilian women who reported an occupation in the census of 1950, 49 percent worked as domestics. (Another 31 percent worked in agriculture, a similarly low-paying area of the labor market.) As late as the 1980s, Peter Wade found 60 percent of black female migrants to the Colombian city of Medellín working as domestics, a "striking concentration" that was disproportionate both to the role of domestic service in the local economy and to Afro-Colombian women's educational levels, which exceeded those of white female domestics. A 1997 survey of Afro-Uruguayan women in Montevideo found 50 percent of them working in domestic service (IBGE 1956, 30–31; Wade 1993, 187, 205; *Diagnóstico socioeconómico* 1997, 31).

Being disproportionately concentrated in domestic service places Afro-Latin American women at severe social, economic, and even emotional disadvantage. Wages are low, hours are long and unpredictable, and most domestics work (and in many cases, live) in isolated conditions under the direct and immediate control of their employers. Under these conditions, black women's ability to see and care for their own families can be greatly compromised. And as we have seen, when mid-century populist regimes created new social security systems and bodies of labor legislation, those systems of benefits and protection were designed with factories and industrial workers in mind. They pointedly excluded domestic work and, in most countries, agriculture as well (Chaney and Castro 1989; Goldstein 2013, 58–101; Otovo 2016; Hicks 2017).

Autobiographical narratives of black women's lives in Latin America consistently stress their authors' efforts to find work that, even if poorly paid, offered more autonomy and independence than domestic service. María de los Reyes Castillo Bueno (1902–97) ran a small diner in her house, worked as a spiritual medium, and took in laundry to support herself and her family. Benedita da Silva (b. 1942), later to become a prominent politician, alternated stints of domestic service with working as a street vendor and delivery person in Rio de Janeiro's public markets. Carolina Maria de Jesus (1914–1977) walked miles through the streets of

São Paulo, gathering waste paper and other items to recycle and sell. Martha Gularte (1919–2002) became a cabaret and Carnival dancer in large part to escape the indignities and low pay of domestic service (Jesus 1962; Benjamin and Mendonça 1997; Castillo Bueno 2000; Porzecanski and Santos 2006, 27–43).

The over-representation of black females at the lowest levels of the labor force is particularly striking in relation to their educational levels, which tend to be higher than those of black males. Despite that educational disparity, in those countries for which salary data are available, black female earnings lag significantly behind those of their black male counterparts, even further behind those of white women, and disastrously far behind those of white men. By the 1980s and 1990s, black female activists were insistently denouncing the "triple discrimination" to which they were subject: class discrimination, racial discrimination, and gender discrimination.

In a series of path-breaking studies using salary data from Brazil, sociologist Peggy Lovell (1994, 2000, 2006) confirmed the devastating impacts of those intersecting forms of inequality. She found that, as measured by the differential between the salaries predicted by their levels of education and work experience and the salaries that women actually received, gender discrimination was an even more potent force than racial discrimination. "White women were the most discriminated against of all groups," in the sense that their educational achievement (which exceeded that of white men), previous work experience, and other qualifications should have earned them salaries equal to or higher than those of their white male counterparts. Instead, in 2000, white women in São Paulo earned on average only 68 percent of white male salaries. Afro-Brazilian men, whose levels of education were far below those of white women, earned on average 58 percent of the salaries received by white men. Meanwhile, Afro-Brazilian women, whose levels of education exceeded those of Afro-Brazilian men but who suffered the combined effects of racial and gender discrimination, earned on average only 41 percent of the salaries received by white males (Lovell 2006; for similar findings for Latin America as a whole, and including indigenous people, see Atal, Ñopo, and Winder 2009).

In the face of these inequalities, Afro-Latin American women experimented with a variety of social movements, including neighborhood associations, labor unions, feminist movements, religious organizations ranging from Protestant and Catholic churches to Candomblé and other African-inspired congregations, political parties, peasant movements, and racially defined black movements. Concluding that black movements were paying insufficient attention to questions of gender, while feminist movements were paying insufficient attention to questions of race, in the 1980s and 1990s activists founded new organizations and movements devoted specifically to the needs of black women: Geledés, Criola, Nzinga, and Fala Preta in Brazil, the Grupo de Apoyo a la Mujer Afrouruguaya in Uruguay, the Unión de Mujeres Negras de Venezuela, and others. In 1992 some 300 black female activists from various countries convened an international meeting in the Dominican Republic; after several subsequent meetings, in 2001 they constituted the Red de Mujeres Afrolatinoamericanas, Afrocaribeñas y de la Diáspora (RMAAD), a transnational NGO that seeks to coordinate strategies and communication among various national-level movements (Red de Mujeres 2016; González Zambrano 2017; see also Chapter 7).

Still, as Kia Caldwell suggests in her study of black women's activism in Brazil, "it is important to note that the vast majority of black women are not involved in the movement." Facing innumerable and exhausting challenges in their daily lives, they see little point in devoting time to causes that are unlikely to produce immediate benefits. As one woman commented to her, "the cause has to motivate me a lot to run after it" (Caldwell 2007, 169; for similar conclusions, see Scheper-Hughes 1993, 505–33; Sheriff 2001, 191–94; Goldstein 2013, 14; for a counter-view, see Perry 2013).

## FUTURE RESEARCH

As we think about possible directions of future research on inequality in Afro-Latin America, and especially on racial inequality, four principal areas suggest themselves:

(a) Continued statistical research aimed at documenting degrees of inequality along various social dimensions, and the causes of those inequalities.

(b) Expanded attention to forms of inequality that are harder to quantify but have equally concrete and damaging impacts on groups and individuals.

(c) Ethnographic research, both historical and present-day, on how inequality is lived in the flesh, on a daily basis: how people experience inequality, and how people think, talk, or remain silent about inequality.

(d) Analysis of how state policies have worked to either promote or combat inequality over time, with particular attention to present-day policy experiments.

As we have seen over the course of this chapter, the relative absence of statistical data on race has made it difficult to specify levels of social and economic inequality during the colonial period and the nineteenth and twentieth centuries. In response to those lacunae, historians have sifted patiently through census manuscript returns, wills and testaments, parish records, notarial archives, employment records, and other sources in order to generate data on wages, property-owning, and other dimensions of economic life, and how those assets were distributed across class, racial, and gender groups (Adamo 1983; Andrews 1991; Frank 2004; Restall 2009; Rosal 2009; Johnson 2011; Gelman and Santilli 2013; Morrison 2015; Stark 2015).

Research of that sort is likely to continue and deepen, supplemented now by the rich statistical data on race contained in post-2000 censuses and national household surveys. Those newly available sources are enabling economists, demographers, and sociologists, in most cases for the first time ever in their nations' histories, to systematically analyze patterns of class, gender, and racial inequality and how those dimensions of social difference interact with each other. That research is most advanced in Brazil, where the magnitude of class, racial, and gender inequities is by now quite clear. In coming years similar research will surely be extended to Colombia, Costa Rica, Uruguay, and other Spanish American countries. (For initial efforts in this direction, see Urrea Giraldo and Viáfara López 2007; Bucheli and Cabella 2007; Cabella et al. 2013; López Ruiz and Delgado Montaldo 2013.)

One of the key questions motivating such research will be the degree to which racial differences in access to desirable social goods is determined by structural factors – by, for example, the concentration of black populations in more rural, less developed parts of the country – and the degree to which access is constrained by discrimination and prejudice. Again, this research is most advanced in Brazil, where a series of studies has demonstrated clear increases in the incidence and effects of wage discrimination from 1960 to 2000 (Lovell 1989, 1994, 2000, 2006). The absence of data from earlier years prevents that longer-term perspective for most of Spanish America, but it will still be valuable to have a picture of the situation in different countries as of the early 2000s (Atal, Ñopo, and Winder 2009; Bucheli and Porzecanski 2011).

Still, for all its value, statistical analysis is only a starting point toward the understanding of inequality in all its dimensions. In recent years, scholars have broadened their attention to forms of inequality that are not so easily quantifiable and convertible into numerical measures. Examples include research on unequal access to legal rights and to full, effective citizenship (Holston 2008); on racial differentials in police treatment of citizens, and obstacles to people's movement through urban neighborhoods and public spaces (Caldeira 2000; Soares 2016); on racially differentiated levels of membership and inclusion in national, regional, or local communities (Appelbaum 2003; Weinstein 2015); on unequal access to the right to "authorship," the ability to write, both literally and metaphorically, the story of one's own life (Alberto 2011; Alberto 2016); racial inequalities within families (Fernandez 2010; Hordge-Freeman 2015); and other forms of social and racial difference.

How do people think (or not) about race, and incorporate it (or not) into their daily lives? How are racial boundaries enforced and maintained at the level of the individual, the family, the neighborhood, the community, the nation? How does discrimination, both conscious and unconscious, operate in practice? In addition to the economic costs of racial exclusion, what are its emotional and psychic costs? Answering these questions requires close ethnographic investigation, on the ground (Scheper-Hughes 1993; Twine 1998; Sheriff 2001; Golash-Boza 2011; Goldstein 2013; Perry 2013; Sue 2013). The first-person narratives referred to earlier in this chapter can also provide valuable insight into the lived experience of inequality (in addition to texts cited earlier, see interviews collected in Pérez Sarduy and Stubbs 2000; Porzecanski and Santos 2006; Costa 2009; Brown 2013).

Lying somewhere between national censuses and ethnographies as a source of information are surveys, which can be designed to focus on specific aspects of lived experience. Here the most important recent contribution is the Project on Ethnicity and Race in Latin America (PERLA), directed by sociologist Edward Telles (Telles and PERLA 2014). Using surveys administered by the Latin American Public Opinion Project (and available at LAPOP 2016), PERLA researchers gathered data not just on race, earnings, education, and attitudes, but also on what is perhaps the principal marker of race: skin color. Administering questionnaires in Brazil, Colombia, Mexico, and Peru, the researchers found even stronger correlations between socioeconomic inequality and skin color than between socioeconomic inequality and the standard census racial categories. In other words, Latin American societies assign social goods and opportunities, thus enforcing and reinforcing racial inequality, to individuals more systematically by skin color than by their "official" racial identities.

The PERLA project also established that most citizens of Latin American nations are well aware of the differential treatment accorded darker-skinned members of their societies and are in sympathy with black and indigenous political movements aimed at redressing those inequalities (for similar findings, see Bailey 2009). This leads us to a final focus of future research: the impacts of state policies aimed at reducing inequality. Such research might well begin with closer looks at the populist policies of the 1950s and 1960s, which claimed to redistribute wealth and opportunity to middle and working classes but varied greatly in the extent to which they actually did so. Meanwhile, to what degree did those policies open opportunities for black (and indigenous) advancement? Research on Brazil has suggested that Afrodescendants were more or less fully integrated into the industrial working class but found it much more difficult to move into the expanding middle class. We may hypothesize similar processes in effect in the Spanish American countries as well; but research definitively confirming (or refuting, or modifying) those hypotheses remains to be done.

Meanwhile, what about the one Latin American country that moved beyond populism to full-fledged socialism? In a pathbreaking article published in 1995, Alejandro de la Fuente used data from the Cuban census of 1981 to document the dramatic reduction in the 1960s and 1970s of racial differentials in health, education, marriage, and vocational achievement. Policies that were conceived in terms of social class, with the goal of improving the position of poor and working-class people, had enormous impacts on racial inequality as well, and for obvious reasons: since Afro-Cubans were heavily over-represented among the poor and working classes, policies that targeted those social groups would disproportionately benefit people of color, thus reducing the disparities between them and the white population.

Subsequent research by de la Fuente and others has suggested that the crisis of the "special period," following the cut-off of Soviet aid to the island in the 1990s, may have reversed some of those reductions, particularly in the area of earnings (de la Fuente 2001, 317–34; Sawyer 2006; Blue 2007; de la Fuente 2011). Recently-released public-use samples of the Cuban census of 2002 will enable researchers to look more closely at the developments of the 1990s (IPUMS 2016). For now, the apparent resurgence of racial inequality in the island during that decade further confirms, in a negative sense, the role of class-based "universalist" social policies in combating racial inequality. When those policies are applied effectively, they reduce not only class inequality but racial inequality as well; when those policies are withdrawn or undermined by fiscal crisis, class and racial inequality both tend to increase.

National experiments in the relationship between class and racial inequality, and state policy concerning both, are currently playing out in countries across the region. In reaction to the social and economic setbacks of the 1980s, when rates of poverty and inequality rose in most countries, during the 1990s and early 2000s many Latin American governments significantly increased their investments in education, health and other social programs (Bértola and Ocampo 2012, 213–21, 245–57; Huber and Stephens 2012, 177–207). Research in Brazil indicates that those policies had significant impacts on reducing racial inequality in earnings, education, and health (Paixão and Carvano 2008; Andrews 2014); might the same be true in other countries as well? The census rounds of 2000, 2010, and 2020 should furnish data to answer this question; and again, ethnographic research could document the effects of those policies on the ground.

Finally, future researchers will surely be investigating the impacts of the racial affirmative action programs adopted in Brazil, Uruguay, and Colombia during the early 2000s. Initial research on the trajectories of students admitted to Brazilian universities under those programs suggests that, given the disparities in preparation and cultural capital between the "quota" students and those admitted through traditional channels, the performance of the former group has been considerably better than expected, in many cases on a par with that of the non-quota students (Santos 2013). Will those results continue with future cohorts? And how will those students fare as they leave the university and compete for jobs and advancement? Will their university credentials win them the employment opportunities, incomes, and other benefits that they have prepared for? Or will racial and skin-color barriers continue to impede their advancement?

These questions and others will keep inequality at the top of the research agenda in the field of Afro-Latin American studies.

## BIBLIOGRAPHY

Adamo, Sam. 1983. "The Broken Promise: Race, Health, and Justice in Rio de Janeiro, 1890–1940." PhD diss., University of New Mexico.

Adamovsky, Ezequiel. 2016. "A Strange Emblem for a (Not So) White Nation: *La Morocha Argentina* in the Latin American Racial Context, c. 1900–2015." *Journal of Social History* 50, 2: 386–410.

Adelman, Jeremy, ed. 1999. *Colonial Legacies: The Problem of Persistence in Latin American History*. New York, NY: Routledge.

Alberto, Paulina. 2011. *Terms of Inclusion: Black Intellectuals in Twentieth-Century Brazil*. Chapel Hill, NC: University of North Carolina Press.

2016. "El Negro Raúl: Lives and Afterlives of an Afro-Argentine Celebrity, 1886 to the Present." *Hispanic American Historical Review* 96, 4: 669–710.

Alonso, Miguel C. 2014. *The Development of Yoruba Candomblé Communities in Salvador, Brazil, 1835–1986*. New York, NY: Palgrave Macmillan.

Amado, Jorge. 2006. *Gabriela, Clove and Cinnamon*. Translated by James L. Taylor and William L. Grossman. New York, NY: Vintage.

Andrews, George Reid. 1980. *The Afro-Argentines of Buenos Aires, 1800–1900*. Madison, WI: University of Wisconsin Press.

1991. *Blacks and Whites in São Paulo, Brazil, 1888–1988*. Madison, WI: University of Wisconsin Press.

2004. *Afro-Latin America, 1800–2000*. New York, NY: Oxford University Press.

2010. *Blacks in the White Nation: A History of Afro-Uruguay*. Chapel Hill, NC: University of North Carolina Press.

2014. "Racial Inequality in Brazil and the United States, 1990–2010." *Journal of Social History* 47, 4: 829–54.

2016. *Afro-Latin America: Black Lives, 1600–2000*. Cambridge, MA: Harvard University Press.

Appelbaum, Nancy. 2003. *Muddied Waters: Race, Region, and Local History in Colombia, 1846–1948*. Durham, NC: Duke University Press.

Atal, Juan Pablo, Hugo Ñopo, and Natalia Winder. 2009. "New Century, Old Disparities: Gender and Ethnic Wage Gaps in Latin America." Washington, DC: IDB Working Paper Series 109.

Atkinson, Anthony B. 2015. *Inequality: What Can Be Done?* Cambridge, MA: Harvard University Press.

Auyero, Javier. 2012. *Patients of the State: The Politics of Waiting in Argentina*. Durham, NC: Duke University Press.

Azevedo, Aluísio. 2000. *The Slum*. Translated by David H. Rosenthal. New York, NY: Oxford University Press.

Bailey, Stanley R. 2009. *Legacies of Race: Identities, Attitudes, and Politics in Brazil*. Stanford, CA: Stanford University Press.

Benjamin, Medea, and Maisa Mendonça. 1997. *Benedita da Silva: An Afro-Brazilian Woman's Story of Politics and Love*. Oakland, CA: Institute for Food and Development Policy.

Bergad, Laird W. 2007. *The Comparative Histories of Slavery in Brazil, Cuba, and the United States*. New York, NY: Cambridge University Press.

Bértola, Luis, and José Antonio Ocampo. 2012. *The Economic Development of Latin America since Independence*. New York, NY: Oxford University Press.

Bethencourt, Francisco. 2013. *Racisms: From the Crusades to the Twentieth Century*. Princeton, NJ: Princeton University Press.

Blanchard, Peter. 2008. *Under the Flags of Freedom: Slave Soldiers and the Wars of Independence in Spanish South America.* Pittsburgh, PA: University of Pittsburgh Press.

Blofeld, Merike, ed. 2011. *The Great Gap: Inequality and the Politics of Redistribution in Latin America.* University Park, PA: Pennsylvania State University Press.

Blue, Sarah. 2007. "The Erosion of Racial Equality in Post-Soviet Cuba." *Latin American Politics and Society* 49, 3: 35–68.

Borucki, Alex. 2015. *From Shipmates to Soldiers: Emerging Black Identities in the Río de la Plata.* Albuquerque, NM: University of New Mexico Press.

Borucki, Alex, David Eltis, and David Wheat. 2015. "Atlantic History and the Slave Trade to Spanish America." *American Historical Review* 120, 2: 433–61.

Brown, Danielle, ed. 2013. *Memoria viva: Historias de mujeres afrodescendientes en el Cono Sur.* Montevideo: Linardi y Risso.

Bucheli, Marisa, and Wanda Cabella. 2007. *Perfil demográfico y socioeconómico de la población uruguaya según su ascendencia racial.* Montevideo: Instituto Nacional de Estadística.

Bucheli, Marisa, and Rafael Porzecanski. 2011. "Racial Inequality in the Uruguayan Labor Market: An Analysis of Wage Differentials between Afro-Descendants and Whites." *Latin American Politics and Society* 53, 2: 113–150.

Cabella, Wanda et al. 2013. *La población afrouruguaya en el Censo 2011.* Montevideo: Ediciones Trilce.

Caldeira, Teresa P.R. 2000. *City of Walls: Crime, Segregation, and Citizenship in São Paulo.* Berkeley, CA: University of California Press.

Caldwell, Kia Lilly. 2007. *Negras in Brazil: Re-Envisioning Black Women, Citizenship, and the Politics of Identity.* New Brunswick, NJ: Rutgers University Press.

Cardoso, Fernando Henrique, and Enzo Faletto. 1979. *Dependency and Development in Latin America.* Translated by Marjorie Mattingly Urquidi. Berkeley, CA: University of California Press. First published in 1969.

Castillo Bueno, María de los Reyes. 2000. *Reyita: The Life of a Black Woman in the Twentieth Century.* Edited by Daisy Rubiera Castillo, translated by Anne McLean. Durham, NC: Duke University Press.

Chaney, Elsa, and Mary Garcia Castro, eds. 1989. *Muchachas No More: Household Workers in Latin America and the Caribbean.* Philadelphia, PA: Temple University Press.

Chasteen, John Charles. 2004. *National Rhythms, African Roots: The Deep History of Latin American Popular Dance.* Albuquerque, NM: University of New Mexico Press.

Cho, Sumi, Kimberlé Williams Crenshaw, and Leslie McCall. 2013. "Toward a Field of Intersectionality Studies: Theory, Applications, and Praxis," *Signs* 38, 4: 785–810.

Collier, Ruth Berins, and David Collier. 2002. *Shaping the Political Arena: Critical Junctures, the Labor Movement, and Regime Dynamics in Latin America.* 2nd edition. Notre Dame, IN: University of Notre Dame Press.

Crenshaw, Kimberlé. 1991. "Mapping the Margins: Intersectionality, Identity Politics, and Violence against Women of Color," *Stanford Law Review* 43, 6, 1241–99.

Costa, Haroldo, ed. 2009. *Fala crioulo: O que é ser negro no Brasil.* 2nd edition. Rio de Janeiro: Record.

Cowling, Camillia. 2013. *Conceiving Freedom: Women of Color, Gender, and the Abolition of Slavery in Havana and Rio de Janeiro.* Chapel Hill, NC: University of North Carolina Press.

Cruces, Guillermo, Leonardo Gasparini, and Fedora Carbajal. 2010a. *Situación socioeconómica de la población afrocolombiana en el marco de los Objetivos de Desarrollo del Milenio.* Panama City: Programa de las Naciones Unidas para el Desarrollo.

2010b. *Situación socioeconómica de la población afroecuatoriana en el marco de los Objetivos de Desarrollo del Milenio.* Panama City: Programa de las Naciones Unidas para el Desarrollo.

De Ferranti, David et al. 2004. *Inequality in Latin America: Breaking with History?* Washington, DC: World Bank.

De la Fuente, Alejandro. 1995. "Race and Inequality in Cuba, 1899–1981." *Journal of Contemporary History* 30: 131–168.

2001. *A Nation for All: Race, Inequality, and Politics in Twentieth-Century Cuba.* Chapel Hill, NC: University of North Carolina Press.

2011. "Race and Income Inequality in Contemporary Cuba." *NACLA Report on the Americas* 44, 4: 30–33, 43.

*Diagnóstico socioeconómico y cultural de la mujer afrouruguaya.* Montevideo: Mundo Afro, 1997.

Díaz, Ramón, and Oscar Madalengoitia. 2012. *Análisis de la situación socioeconómica de la población afroperuana y de la población afrocostarricense y su comparación con la situación de las poblaciones afrocolombiana y afroecuatoriana.* Panama City: Programa de las Naciones Unidas para el Desarrollo.

Echeverría, Esteban. 2010. *The Slaughteryard.* Translated by Norman Thomas di Giovanni and Susan Ashe. London: The Friday Project. First published in 1871.

Eltis, David, Stephen D. Behrendt, Manolo Florentino, and David Richardson. 2013. *Voyages: The Trans-Atlantic Slave Trade Database.* Emory University. www.slavevoyages.org/assessment/estimates.

Engerman, Stanley L., and Kenneth L. Sokoloff. 2012. *Economic Development in the Americas since 1500: Endowments and Institutions.* New York, NY: Cambridge University Press.

Fernandes, Florestan. 1965. *A integração do negro na sociedade de classes.* 2 vols. São Paulo: Dominus.

Fernandez, Nadine T. 2010. *Revolutionizing Romance: Interracial Couples in Contemporary Cuba.* New Brunswick, NJ: Rutgers University Press.

Ferrer, Ada. 1999. *Insurgent Cuba: Race, Nation, and Revolution, 1868–1898.* Chapel Hill, NC: University of North Carolina Press.

Fischer, Brodwyn. 2008. *A Poverty of Rights: Citizenship and Inequality in Twentieth-Century Rio de Janeiro.* Stanford, CA: Stanford University Press.

Fischer, Brodwyn, Bryan McCann, and Javier Auyero, eds. 2014. *Cities from Scratch: Poverty and Informality in Urban Latin America.* Durham, NC: Duke University Press.

Frank, Andre Gunder. 1967. *Capitalism and Underdevelopment in Latin America.* New York: Monthly Review Press.

Frank, Zephyr L. 2004. *Dutra's World: Wealth and Family in Nineteenth-Century Rio de Janeiro*. Albuquerque, NM: University of New Mexico Press.

French, John D. 2004. *Drowning in Laws: Labor Law and Brazilian Political Culture*. Chapel Hill, NC: University of North Carolina Press.

Frankema, Ewout. 2009. *Has Latin America Always Been Unequal? A Comparative Study of Asset and Income Inequality in the Long Twentieth Century*. Leiden: Brill.

Gelman, Jorge, and Daniel Santilli. 2013. "Movilidad social y desigualdad en el Buenos Aires del siglo XIX: El acceso a la propiedad de la tierra entre el rosismo y el orden liberal." *Hispanic American Historical Review* 93, 4: 659–84.

Germeten, Nicole von. 2006. *Black Blood Brothers: Confraternities and Social Mobility for Afro-Mexicans*. Gainesville, FL: University Press of Florida.

Gobat, Michel. 2013. "The Invention of Latin America: A Transnational History of Anti-Imperialism, Democracy and Race." *American Historical Review* 118, 5: 1345–75.

Golash-Boza, Tanya Maria. 2011. *Yo Soy Negro: Blackness in Peru*. Gainesville, FL: University Press of Florida.

Goldstein, Donna. 2013. *Laughter Out of Place: Race, Class, Violence, and Sexuality in a Rio Shantytown*. 2nd edition. Berkeley, CA: University of California Press.

González Zambrano, Catalina. 2017. "Mulheres negras em movimento: Ativismo transnacional na América Latina (1980–1995)." PhD diss., University of São Paulo.

Gootenburg, Paul, and Luis Reygadas, eds. 2010. *Indelible Inequalities in Latin America: Insights from History, Politics, and Culture*. Durham, NC: Duke University Press.

Greenman, Emily, and Yu Xie. 2008. "Double Jeopardy? The Interaction of Gender and Race on Earnings in the United States." *Social Forces* 86, 3: 1217–44.

Grinberg, Keila. 2002. *O fiador dos brasileiros: Cidadania, escravidão e direito civil no tempo de Antonio Pereira Rebouças*. Rio de Janeiro: Civilização Brasileira.

Guzmán, Florencia. 2016. "María Remedios del Valle: 'Capitana,' 'Madre de la Patria' e 'Niña de Ayohuma.' Um percurso interpretativo da sua figura singular." In *Afrolatinoamérica: Estudos comparados*, edited by Viviana Gelado and María Victoria Secreto: 59–86. Niterói: Mauad.

Halperín-Donghi, Tulio. 1993 (1969). *The Contemporary History of Latin America*. Edited and translated by John Charles Chasteen. Durham, NC: Duke University Press.

Harris, Marvin. 1964. *Patterns of Race in the Americas*. New York, NY: Walker and Company.

Hasenbalg, Carlos. 1979. *Discriminação e desigualdades raciais no Brasil*. Rio de Janeiro: Graal.

Hasenbalg, Carlos, Nelson do Valle Silva, and Márcia Lima. 1999. *Cor e estratificação social*. Rio de Janeiro: Contra Capa.

Helg, Aline. 1995. *Our Rightful Share: The Afro-Cuban Struggle for Equality, 1886–1912*. Chapel Hill, NC: University of North Carolina Press.

Hicks, Anasa. 2017. "Hierarchies at Home: A Twentieth-Century History of Domestic Service in Cuba." PhD diss., New York University.

Higgins, Kathleen J. 1999. *"Licentious Liberty" in a Brazilian Gold-Mining Region: Slavery, Gender, and Social Control in Eighteenth-Century Sabará, Minas Gerais.* University Park, PA: Pennsylvania State University Press.

Hoffman, Kelly, and Miguel Angel Centeno. 2003. "The Lopsided Continent: Inequality in Latin America." *Annual Review of Sociology* 29: 363–90.

Holloway, Thomas H. 1980. *Immigrants on the Land: Coffee and Society in São Paulo, 1886–1930.* Chapel Hill, NC: University of North Carolina Press.

Holston, James. 2008. *Insurgent Citizenship: Disjunctions of Democracy and Modernity in Brazil.* Princeton, NJ: Princeton University Press.

Hordge-Freeman, Elizabeth. 2015. *The Color of Love: Racial Features, Stigma, and Socialization in Black Brazilian Families.* Austin, TX: University of Texas Press.

Horst, Jesse. 2016. "Sleeping on the Ashes: Slum Clearance in Havana in an Age of Revolution, 1930–1965." PhD diss., University of Pittsburgh.

Huber, Evelyne, and John D. Stephens, eds. 2012. *Democracy and the Left: Social Policy and Inequality in Latin America.* Chicago, IL: University of Chicago Press.

IBGE (Instituto Brasileiro de Geografia e Estatística). 1956. *Brasil: Censo demográfico, 1950. Série nacional.* Rio de Janeiro: IBGE.

IDB (Inter-American Development Bank). 1998. *Facing Up to Inequality in Latin America.* Washington, DC: IDB.

IPEA (Instituto de Pesquisa Econômica Aplicada). 2010. *Perspectivas da política social no Brasil.* Brasília: IPEA.

IPEADATA. 2016. Accessed May 13, 2016. www.ipeadata.gov.br.

IPUMS (International Public Use Microdata Series). 2016. Accessed August 12, 2016. https://international.ipums.org/international-action/samples.

Jesus, Carolina Maria de. 1962. *Child of the Dark: The Diary of Carolina Maria de Jesus.* Translated by David St. Clair. New York, NY: E. P. Dutton.

Johnson, Lyman L. 2011. *Workshop of Revolution: Plebeian Buenos Aires and the Atlantic World, 1776–1810.* Durham, NC: Duke University Press.

Karasch, Mary C. 1987. *Slave Life in Rio de Janeiro, 1850–1888.* Princeton, NJ: Princeton University Press.

Kinsbruner, Jay. 1996. *Not of Pure Blood: The Free People of Color and Racial Prejudice in Nineteenth-Century Puerto Rico.* Durham, NC: Duke University Press.

Klein, Herbert S., and Ben Vinson III. 2007. *African Slavery in Latin America and the Caribbean.* New York, NY: Oxford University Press.

Klein, Herbert S., and Francisco Vidal Luna. 2010. *Slavery in Brazil.* New York, NY: Cambridge University Press.

Korzeniewicz, Roberto Patricio, and Timothy Patrick Moran. 2009. *Unveiling Inequality: A World-Historical Perspective.* New York, NY: Russell Sage Foundation.

Kutzinski, Vera M. 1993. *Sugar's Secrets: Race and the Erotics of Cuban Nationalism.* Charlottesville, VA: University Press of Virginia.

LAPOP (Latin American Public Opinion Project). 2016. Accessed Dec. 22, 2016. www.vanderbilt.edu/lapop/.

Lasso, Marixa. 2007. *Myths of Harmony: Race and Republicanism during the Age of Revolution, Colombia, 1795–1831*. Pittsburgh, PA: University of Pittsburgh Press.

Lesser, Jeffrey. 2013. *Immigration, Ethnicity, and National Identity in Brazil, 1808 to the Present*. New York, NY: Cambridge University Press.

López Ruiz, Luis Ángel, and David Delgado Montaldo. 2013. *Situación socio-económica de la población afrodescendiente de Costa Rica según datos del X Censo Nacional de Población y VI de Vivienda 2011*. Panama City: Programa de las Naciones Unidas para el Desarrollo.

Lovell, Peggy A. 1989. "Racial Inequality in the Brazilian Labor Market." PhD diss., University of Florida.

——— 1994. "Race, Gender and Development in Brazil." *Latin American Research Review* 29, 3: 7–35.

——— 2000. "Gender, Race and the Struggle for Social Justice in Brazil." *Latin American Perspectives* 27, 6: 85–103.

——— 2006. "Race, Gender, and Work in São Paulo, Brazil, 1960–2000." *Latin American Research Review* 41, 3: 63–87.

Loveman, Mara. 2014. *National Colors: Racial Classification and the State in Latin America*. New York, NY: Oxford University Press.

Mahoney, James. 2010. *Colonialism and Postcolonial Development: Spanish America in Comparative Perspective*. New York, NY: Cambridge University Press.

Manning, Patrick. 2017. "Inequality: Historical and Disciplinary Approaches." *American Historical Review* 122, 1: 1–22.

Márquez, Gustavo et al. 2007. *Outsiders? The Changing Patterns of Exclusion in Latin America and the Caribbean*. Washington, DC: Inter-American Development Bank.

Martínez, María Elena. 2008. *Genealogical Fictions: Limpieza de Sangre, Religion, and Gender in Colonial Mexico*. Stanford, CA: Stanford University Press.

Massey, Douglas. 2007. *Categorically Unequal: The American Stratification System*. New York, NY: Russell Sage Foundation.

Mattos, Hebe. 2013. *Das cores de silêncio: Os significados da liberdade no Sudeste escravista (Brasil, século XIX)*. 3rd edition. Campinas: Editora da UNICAMP.

McGraw, Jason. 2014. *The Work of Recognition: Caribbean Colombia and the Postemancipation Struggle for Citizenship*. Chapel Hill, NC: University of North Carolina Press.

Monsma, Karl. 2016. *A reprodução do racismo: Fazendeiros, negros e imigrantes no oeste paulista, 1880–1914*. São Carlos: EdUFSCar.

Morrison, Karen Y. 2015. *Cuba's Racial Crucible: The Sexual Economy of Social Identities, 1750–2000*. Bloomington, IN: Indiana University Press.

Moya, José C. 1998. *Cousins and Strangers: Spanish Immigrants to Buenos Aires, 1850–1930*. Berkeley, CA: University of California Press.

Needell, Jeffrey D. 1987. *A Tropical Belle Epoque: Elite Culture and Society in Turn-of-the-Century Rio de Janeiro*. New York, NY: Cambridge University Press.

Nobles, Melissa. 2000. *Shades of Citizenship: Race and the Census in Modern Politics*. Stanford, CA: Stanford University Press.

Oliveira, Lúcia Helena Garcia de et al. 1983. *O lugar do negro na força de trabalho*. Rio de Janeiro: Fundação IBGE.

O'Toole, Rachel Sarah. 2012. *Bound Lives: Africans, Indians, and the Making of Race in Colonial Peru*. Pittsburgh, PA: University of Pittsburgh Press.

Otovo, Okezi. 2016. *Progressive Mothers, Better Babies: Race, Public Health, and the State in Brazil, 1850–1945*. Austin, TX: University of Texas Press.

Paixão, Marcelo, and Luiz M. Carvano, eds. 2008. *Relatório anual das desigualdades raciais no Brasil, 2007–2008*. Rio de Janeiro: Garamond.

Paixão, Marcelo et al. 2010. *Relatório anual das desigualdades raciais no Brasil, 2009–2010*. Rio de Janeiro: Garamond.

Parés, Luis Nicolau. 2013. *The Formation of Candomblé: Vodun History and Ritual in Brazil*. Translated by Richard Vernon. Chapel Hill, NC: University of North Carolina Press.

Peria, Michelle, and Stanley R. Bailey. 2014. "Rethinking Racial Inclusion: Combining Race and Class in Brazil's New Affirmative Action." *Latin American and Caribbean Ethnic Studies* 9, 2: 156–76.

Pérez-Sarduy, Pedro, and Jean Stubbs, eds. 2000. *Afro-Cuban Voices: On Race and Identity in Contemporary Cuba*. Gainesville, FL: University Press of Florida.

Perry, Keisha-Khan Y. 2013. *Black Women against the Land Grab: The Fight for Racial Justice in Brazil*. Minneapolis, MN: University of Minnesota Press.

Piketty, Thomas. 2014. *Capital in the Twenty-First Century*. Translated by Arthur Goldhammer. Cambridge, MA: Harvard University Press.

Porzecanski, Teresa, and Beatriz Santos. 2006. *Historias de exclusión: Afrodescendientes en el Uruguay*. Montevideo: Linardi y Risso.

Proctor III, Frank "Trey." 2006. "Gender and the Manumission of Slaves in New Spain." *Hispanic American Historical Review* 86, 2: 309–336.

Red de Mujeres Afrolatinoamericanas, Afrocaribeñas y de la Diáspora. 2016. Accessed May 17, 2016. www.mujeresafro.org.

Reid-Vazquez, Michelle. 2013. *Year of the Lash: Free People of Color in Cuba and the Nineteenth-Century Atlantic World*. Athens, GA: University of Georgia Press.

República de Cuba. 1945. *Informe general del censo de 1943*. Havana: P. Fernández y Cía.

Restall, Matthew. 2009. *The Black Middle: Africans, Mayas, and Spaniards in Colonial Yucatan*. Stanford, CA: Stanford University Press.

Rosal, Miguel Angel. 2009. *Africanos y afrodescendientes en el Río de la Plata. Siglos XVIII-XIX*. Buenos Aires: Editorial Dunken.

Rosemberg, Fúlvia. 1986. *Situação educacional de negros (pretos e pardos)*. São Paulo: Fundação Carlos Chagas.

Russell-Wood, A.J.R. 2002. *Slavery and Freedom in Colonial Brazil*. 2nd edition. Oxford: Oneworld Publications.

Sanders, James E. 2004. *Contentious Republicans: Popular Politics, Race, and Class in Nineteenth-Century Colombia*. Durham, NC: Duke University Press.

2014. *The Vanguard of the Atlantic World: Creating Modernity, Nation, and Democracy in Nineteenth-Century Latin America*. Durham, NC: Duke University Press.

Santos, Jocélio Teles dos, ed. 2013. *O impacto das cotas nas universidades brasileiras (2004–2012)*. Salvador: Centro de Estudos Afro-Orientais.

Sartorius, David. 2014. *Ever Faithful: Race, Loyalty, and the Ends of Empire in Spanish Cuba*. Durham, NC: Duke University Press.

Sawyer, Mark Q. 2006. *Racial Politics in Post-Revolutionary Cuba*. New York, NY: Cambridge University Press.

Scheper-Hughes, Nancy. 1993. *Death without Weeping: The Violence of Everyday Life in Brazil*. Berkeley, CA: University of California Press.

Schwartz, Stuart B. 1985. *Sugar Plantations in the Formation of Brazilian Society, 1550–1835*. New York, NY: Cambridge University Press.

Scott, Rebecca J. 2005. *Degrees of Freedom: Louisiana and Cuba after Slavery*. Cambridge: Harvard University Press.

Scuro Somma, Lucía, ed. 2008. *Población afrodescendiente y desigualdades étnico-raciales en Uruguay*. Montevideo: Programa de las Naciones Unidas para el Desarrollo.

Sen, Amartya. 1992. *Inequality Reexamined*. Cambridge, MA: Harvard University Press.

1997. *On Economic Inequality*. 2nd edition. Oxford: Clarendon Press.

Sheriff, Robin. 2001. *Dreaming Equality: Color, Race, and Racism in Urban Brazil*. New Brunswick, NJ: Rutgers University Press.

Silva, Nelson do Valle. 1978. "Black-White Income Differentials: Brazil, 1960." PhD diss., University of Michigan.

1985. "Updating the Cost of Not Being White in Brazil." In *Race, Class and Power in Brazil*, edited by Pierre-Michel Fontaine, 42–55. Los Angeles, CA: Center for Afro-American Studies, University of California-Los Angeles.

Soares, Luiz Eduardo. 2016. *Rio de Janeiro: Extreme City*. Translated by Anthony Doyle. New York, NY: Penguin.

Soares, Mariza de Carvalho. 2011. *People of Faith: Slavery and African Catholics in Eighteenth-Century Rio de Janeiro*. Translated by Jerry D. Metz. Durham, NC: Duke University Press.

Socolow, Susan Migden. 2015. *The Women of Colonial Latin America*. 2nd edition. New York, NY: Cambridge University Press.

Stark, David M. 2015. *Slave Families and the Hato Economy in Puerto Rico*. Gainesville, FL: University Press of Florida.

Stein, Stanley J., and Barbara Stein. 1970. *The Colonial Heritage of Latin America*. New York, NY: Oxford University Press.

Stern. Steve J. 1982. *Peru's Indian Peoples and the Challenge of Spanish Conquest: Huamanga to 1640*. Madison, WI: University of Wisconsin Press.

Stiglitz, Joseph E. 2013. *The Price of Inequality: How Today's Divided Society Endangers Our Future*. New York, NY: W. W. Norton.

Stubbs, Josefina, and Hiska N. Reyes, eds. 2006. *Más allá de los promedios: Afrodescendientes en América Latina*. 4 vols. Washington, DC: World Bank.

Sue, Christina A. 2013. *Land of the Cosmic Race: Race Mixture, Racism, and Blackness in Mexico*. New York, NY: Oxford University Press.

Sussman, Robert Wald. 2014. *The Myth of Race: The Troubling Persistence of an Unscientific Idea*. Cambridge, MA: Harvard University Press.

Sweet, James H. 1997. "The Iberian Roots of American Racist Thought." *William and Mary Quarterly* 54, 1: 143–166.

Telles, Edward. 2004. *Race in Another America: The Significance of Skin Color in Brazil*. Princeton, NJ: Princeton University Press.

Telles, Edward and PERLA (Project on Ethnicity and Race in Latin America). 2014. *Pigmentocracies: Ethnicity, Race, and Color in Latin America*. Chapel Hill, NC: University of North Carolina Press.

Thorp, Rosemary. 1998. *Progress, Poverty and Exclusion: An Economic History of Latin America in the Twentieth Century*. Washington, DC: Inter-American Development Bank.

Tilly, Charles. 1998. *Durable Inequality*. Berkeley, CA: University of California Press.

Turra, Cleusa, and Gustavo Venturi. 1995. *Racismo cordial: A mais completa análise sobre preconceito de cor no Brasil*. São Paulo: Ática.

Twinam, Ann. 2014. *Purchasing Whiteness: Pardos, Mulattos, and the Quest for Social Mobility in the Spanish Indies*. Stanford, CA: Stanford University Press.

Twine, France Winddance. 1998. *Racism in a Racial Democracy: The Maintenance of White Supremacy in Brazil*. New Brunswick, NJ: Rutgers University Press.

Urrea Giraldo, Fernando, and Carlos Viáfara López. 2007. *Pobreza y grupos étnicos en Colombia: Análisis de sus factores determinantes y lineamientos de políticas para su reducción*. Bogotá: Departamento Nacional de Planeación.

Van Deusen, Nancy E. 2015. *Global Indios: The Indigenous Struggle for Justice in Sixteenth-Century Spain*. Durham, NC: Duke University Press.

Villaverde, Cirilo. 2005. *Cecilia Valdés, or El Angel Hill*. Translated by Helen Lane. New York, NY: Oxford University Press.

Vinson III, Ben. 2001. *Bearing Arms for His Majesty: The Free-Colored Militia in Colonial Mexico*. Stanford, CA: Stanford University Press.

Wade, Peter. 1993. *Blackness and Race Mixture: The Dynamics of Racial Identity in Colombia*. Baltimore, MD: Johns Hopkins University Press.

2009. *Race and Sex in Latin America*. London: Pluto Press.

War Department [US]. 1900. *Report on the Census of Cuba, 1899*. Washington, DC: Government Printing Office.

Weinstein, Barbara. 2015. *The Color of Modernity: São Paulo and the Making of Race and Nation in Brazil*. Durham, NC: Duke University Press.

# 4

## Afro-Indigenous Interactions, Relations, and Comparisons

### Peter Wade

#### INTRODUCTION

In history and anthropology, there has traditionally been a strong tendency to deal with Latin American indigenous and Afrodescendant people as separate categories. The separation has been structured by conceptual distinctions between rural and urban, ethnicity and race, anthropology and sociology, and more and less "other." This academic tendency has deep roots in colonial and postcolonial governance practices, which treated indigenous Americans and Africans as very distinct – in terms of their places in the legal system and in the political-economic divisions of labor, and in terms of their moral-physical constitution – and posited a basic antagonism between them. The practice of colonial authorities tended to assume the separation of the two categories, and this was reproduced in the historical archive, fragmenting and masking evidence of exchanges and interactions. The same separation continued in different ways in regimes of governance after independence and into the present day. This divergence influenced the shape of anthropology in Latin America, when, during the twentieth century, it was institutionalized as a discipline that focused almost entirely on indigenous peoples, often seen as under threat not only from whites and mestizos, but also blacks. The study of Afrodescendants was undertaken by historians and sociologists, but they too obeyed a conceptual distinction that kept apart black and indigenous.

In the colonial and republican eras, the separation of indigenous and black was founded on an enduring conceptualization of *mestizaje* (roughly, mixture) as organized around three polar categories: white/Spanish, indigenous, and black/slave/African. Interactions among these three poles were seen to produce mixed people, who were often labeled by capacious terms, such as *castas* (types or breeds) or *libres de todos los colores* (free people of all colors). However, some key subcategories emerged as conceptual anchors that structured the shifting, complex variety of people and labels: *mulatos* resulted from a black-white mix, while *mestizos* derived from an indigenous-white mix. Of course, a third mixture of indigenous with black was possible – indeed, inevitable – and *zambo* was one term that eventually emerged for this mix. However, the dominance of whiteness meant that mixtures tended to be reckoned in terms of their relation to the white pole. Hence mestizo and mulato were common categories, while *zambaje* was marginalized by colonial and republican observers, who saw it as a particularly troublesome form of mixture that could foment intransigence. Zambo as a term did not emerge at first and black-indigenous mixtures were included in the category mulato; later in the colonial period, in some areas, such mixtures might be labeled mestizos. Also, while racialized terms in general showed great regional variations, the terminology for Afroindigenous mixture was from the start particularly variable, suggesting the unconventional character of the category: *cafuso* was typical of Brazil, *lobo* could be used in Mexico, and so on (Forbes 1988). In short, the idea of black-indigenous mixture has been seen as abnormal and "discomforting" (Whitten and Whitten 2011, 35) because it challenges the dominance of the white pole in the triadic structure of mestizaje, which requires that all mixtures be directed toward itself.

Recently this separatist tendency has been challenged by historians who look at indigenous-black interactions: despite colonial divide-and-rule policies, the two sets of people interacted and lived together in harmony as well as conflict; they mixed together to produce important zambo populations, in what historians now see as a widespread process. Anthropologists have likewise revised the categorical separation by increasingly including Afro-Latins in the purview of their discipline, by exploring interactions between them and indigenous peoples, by revealing the ambiguity of the classificatory boundary, and by casting both categories as similar in their subordinate status in national hierarchies of race and class (Greene 2007a). In terms of politics, too, there have been some black-indigenous alliances in social mobilizations around land, rights, and identity; governance regimes have also created some convergences between black and indigenous minorities in legal terms.

In this chapter, I will discuss the reasons behind the powerful conceptual divide between indigenous and Afro-Latin people, before exploring their interactions and exchanges, first in the colonial and republican periods, and then in the present day. I will show how Afroindigenous interactions highlight the flexibility and ambiguity of "racial" categories in Latin America. My overall argument is that the conceptual divide between Afro and indigenous has an enduring power, which has left traces even in the processes that seem to overcome the divide, and which means that recent processes of political mobilization and multiculturalist reform actually tend to reinstate the divide. Revisionist attention to Afroindigenous interactions helps us to see how the conceptual divide operates in practice, rather than taking it for granted as an historical fact.

## CONCEPTUAL ORIGINS

In Latin America, the differences in how Africans and indigenous Americans were seen to fit into dominant "structures of alterity" had several aspects (Wade 2010, ch. 2). First, blacks were seen principally as slaves; they were already known in Iberia, where they had been brought as slaves from the 1440s. The very first blacks in Latin America included freed men, but the vast majority of blacks were brought to Latin America to work as slaves and, although individual enslaved blacks were, from the start, set free or purchased their own freedom, the moral propriety of enslaving blacks was only questioned when the institution of slavery itself was challenged in the late eighteenth century. In contrast, the moral appropriateness of slavery for indigenous Americans – a previously unknown kind of human and society – was questioned early on and legally rejected in 1542 by Spain and in 1570 by Portugal. Slavery for indigenous Americans was seen as unjustified because they were defined as vassals of the Crown (as long as they did not rebel) and as inappropriate because they were perceived as unsuited to the rigors of forced servitude compared to Africans, who were perceived as robust. Second, slavery for Africans was seen as morally justified because they originated from a region identified as mainly infidel in the European imagination. In contrast, indigenous Americans were variously considered to be both cannibals and prelapsarian innocents (Pagden 1982), but they were not seen as tainted by Islam. Third, Africans were thought to have unclean blood – fifteenth-century Iberian statutes of *limpieza de sangre* (purity of blood), enacted during the final stages of the Christian re-conquest of the Iberian peninsula, defined social exclusions for people with *raza de judío o moro* (Jewish or Moorish ancestry). Africans could be perceived as *moros*, and anyway, in the New World, ideas of impurity rapidly expanded to include all black people. In contrast, indigenous Americans were initially defined as pure of blood, although this definition lost traction during the sixteenth century (Martínez 2008, 121, 146). These ideas about purity influenced marriage regulations, which obstructed unions between blacks and non-blacks more strictly than those between indigenous Americans and whites.

Fourth, these differences were reflected in legislation defining a – frankly utopian – *república de indios*, supposedly separate and protected from the so-called *república de españoles*, which was the world of whites, but which by default ambivalently included mestizos, and, even more ambivalently, enslaved and free blacks. Colonial governance was ideally based on three separate categories: (a) Spanish/whites, who lived in towns and cities, and directed law, governance, religion, and other "civilized" pursuits; (b) indigenous people, who lived in their communities and paid tribute to their Spanish rulers, via labor or goods; (c) Africans/blacks, who were enslaved workers on plantations, in mines, and in their owners' domestic spaces. In practice, this neat schema was undermined by three processes: slave manumission, self-purchase, and escape, which gave rise to a free black population; indigenous migration and urbanization, and the usurpation of indigenous lands by nonindigenous settlers; and the social recognition of mestizos of all kinds. But *indio* remained an institutionalized category of fiscal, legal, and religious governance. Although "slave" was a specific legal and administrative status, "black" was usually not, instead forming part of intermediate categories – such as libres de todos los colores, *pardos* (browns), castas, or mestizos – which by the eighteenth century actually formed a majority in some areas.

Fifth, after independence, although the category indio lost some of its institutional and legal scaffolding, partially dismantled by liberal ideologies of common citizenship, it persisted in many nation-building projects, where it acted as a symbolic resource for elites trying to define and nurture national identities on an international stage. Indios appeared most obviously in *indigenismo*, an intellectual ideology and state policy that constructed indigenous people both as glorious ancestors of the nation and as communities to be protected with the assistance of government agencies and legal provisions, informed by academic and applied anthropology – though the ultimate aim was assimilation. In contrast, post-abolition Afro-Latins were rarely seen as a specific category of "other" that might have a special role in defining the nation's heritage or be in need of particular attention. The emergence in the twentieth century – particularly in Brazil, Cuba, and Colombia – of what might be called *negrismo* was a contrary trend that was mostly artistic, musical, and literary, and it did not enjoy the same state-backed institutional support as indigenismo.

These are key factors that have created a conceptual division between blackness and indigeneity in the Latin American context, a division that has shaped academic enquiry, such that historians and social scientists have traditionally tended to deal with indigenous people and Afro-Latins as distinct categories – with Afro-Latins often taking the back seat in terms of the amount of attention they have received. Many studies deal *either* with indigenous Americans *or* with enslaved and free black people. A long-standing exception to this trend is the historical study of mestizaje, broadly conceived, and of the hierarchies of colonial society as a whole, which perforce included inputs from both subaltern slots as well as the dominant white classes (see, e.g., Chambers 1999; Cope 1994; Jaramillo Uribe 1968; Martínez 2008; Mörner 1967; Silverblatt 2004; Twinam 1999). But even these studies have rarely considered mixtures *between* indigenous and black people.

### COLONIAL PERIOD

Until recently, the dominant historiographical paradigm suggested that Afro-Latins and indigenous Americans tended to have antagonistic and hostile relations, kept at daggers drawn by colonial legislation and divide-and-rule tactics. This version of events was indeed often deployed by indigenous people themselves in tactical claims made to the authorities, which sought to depict them and their communities as victims in need of protection and assistance: the depredations of free or even enslaved blacks, albeit doing the bidding of their Spanish masters, were often cited in this respect (Restall 2005b). Guamán de Poma's early seventeenth-century text, *El primer nueva corónica y buen gobierno*, includes a drawing of a Spanish official ordering an enslaved black man to flog an indigenous magistrate (O'Toole 2012, 158–59). For northern Peru, O'Toole (2012) shows that indigenous people, in order to bring out conflicts that would bolster their complaints and allow them to make use of the legal protections attached to the category of indio, would gloss over the everyday processes of cohabitation and interaction with Afro-Andeans that constituted what Gilroy might call "conviviality."[1] These native accounts tallied with the ideas of colonial authorities in Spanish America and Brazil about the need to keep black and indigenous people separate to prevent a form of mixture perceived as troublesome because it was thought to taint the indios with the inferior blood and dangerous moral influences of blacks, and also foment rebellion. On the other hand, Carroll (2005) contends that the co-residence of black and indigenous people in colonial Mexico was often ignored by the authorities, if it was peaceable and did not attract their attention.

Revisionist "red-black" studies indicate that matters were rarely quite so simple. Restall (2005b) argues that a "hostility-harmony dialectic" is characteristic of black-indigenous relations in Latin America (for an early example of this dialectic, see Schwartz [1970]). Indigenous and black people did come into conflict, which tends to jump out of the archival records in the form of complaints, fights, and disagreements. As noted previously, indigenous and black people occupied different slots in the colonial economic and political order. Even if the ideal slots of tributary and slave did not conform completely to reality – especially for free blacks – the governance of colonial society meant that opportunities and constraints were often structured in divergent ways: indigenous people could seek protection in ways that black people could not. Colonial authorities also organized indigenous and Afro-Latin soldiers into separate militias where it was possible. But indigenous and black people also shared spaces, cooperated, worked and lived together, and had children together. In the eighteenth century, it also became more common to find indigenous troops in black and mixed-race militias, although this was partly due to "indigenous" individuals claiming to be "black" or vice versa for personal tactical reasons (Vinson III and Restall 2005). When conflicts did occur, it was often as a result of everyday disagreements, rather than categorical enmities, although, as noted previously, indigenous Americans might present a disagreement in categorical terms to enhance its traction with the authorities. But "harmonious" interactions have frequently been neglected, due in part to the nature of the historical record and the biases therein due to the perceptions of the authorities and the indigenous Americans (Forbes 1988; O'Toole 2012; Restall 2005a, 2009).

A first step in grasping the complexities of indigenous-black interactions is to understand the indeterminate and highly variable terminology

---

[1] Gilroy (2004, xi) defines conviviality as "the processes of cohabitation and interaction that have made multiculture an ordinary feature of urban life in Britain."

used to label social diversity at the time. As noted previously, it is commonplace to understand colonial society as organized around three polar categories – white/Spanish, indigenous, and black/slave/African – and their three sub-categories – mulato, mestizo, and zambo. This schematic provides a useful shorthand (Whitten and Corr 1999, 226) but needs to be understood in context. Forbes (1988, 266) shows that the "modern European and North American tendency to be obsessed with 'black-white' relations" has obscured the fact that many terms (colored, black, *negro*, mulato, pardo, *loro*, etc.) were applied, in their diverse European-language variants, to indigenous Americans in the colonial period. Therefore, the appearance of these words (especially negro and black) in the archival sources on the Americas cannot be taken unequivocally as referring to Africans. He shows that the term mulato often referred to mixed people who had some African ancestry, but not necessarily combined with European; in fact, in Spanish America in the sixteenth and seventeenth centuries most mulatos were people of African-indigenous ancestry (see also Lutz and Restall 2005, 193; Schwaller 2011). In addition, Forbes says, indigenous Americans were often referred to as people of color (pardos, loros, etc.). All of this implies that an overly schematic grasp of racialized terminology will inevitably underestimate the extent of black-indigenous mixture.

Such mixture was certainly more frequent than traditionally thought. Particular cases of black-indigenous mixture have long been recognized, such as the "black Caribs" – now known as Garifuna – of the coastal strip and offshore islands stretching from northern Nicaragua, through Honduras and Guatemala to southern Belize. This population emerged on the eastern Caribbean island of St. Vincent before European settlement began in the early eighteenth century. From the late seventeenth century, shipwrecked Africans and other escapees from enslavement from nearby islands had been socially and linguistically integrated by local Caribs. This process that continued through the eighteenth century, during the second half of which the Garifuna fought a series of wars with the British, often with French support. These wars ended with British victory in 1793, after which about five thousand Garifuna were deported to the island of Roatán off the coast of Honduras; they then spread along the Caribbean coast. The deportees were those the British deemed "black," rather than "yellow," which suggests the power of the Afro/indigenous conceptual divide to reappear in contexts that seem to transcend it (Gonzalez 1988). I will explore the present-day situation of this group later.

The Garifuna are a well-recognized case. Perhaps less so are the Miskitu people, who live in the coastal region of eastern Honduras and along the northern half of Nicaragua's coast (Gabbert 2007; Gordon 1998; Hale 1994; Hooker 2009). The story of this mixture also begins with an early seventeenth-century shipwreck and progressive increments of escapees from enslavement, who settled mainly in the northern, Honduran part of the territory. A long-standing distinction developed between the so-called Sambo Miskito – more "Afro" and more northerly – and the Tawira Miskito – more "indigenous" and more southerly – which became entangled with British-Spanish colonial rivalries. Later, although Miskito people in Nicaragua mixed further with English-speaking black Creoles, the latter nevertheless retained their social distance, asserting superior status, thereby helping to create an image of the Miskitu as basically "indigenous" (Hale 1994, 40, 267; Offen 2002).

This illustrates my overall argument about the enduring power of the Afro/indigenous divide, which in the cases of the Garifuna and the Miskitu can be seen in the tendency to refigure Afroindigenous people as leaning toward *either* indigenous *or* black. While all racialized categories are inherently unstable, zambo is rendered particularly protean by the dominance of the white pole in the triangle of mestizaje, which tends to force all mixture to relate to whiteness. This refiguring is not just imposed from above in a simple fashion: Miskitu people tend to see themselves as "indigenous" – language plays an important role here – and some of them devalue phenotypical traits seen as African (Dennis 2010, 63; Hale 1994, 230).

Other contexts for indigenous-black mixture have been less visible. In colonial Guatemala and Yucatán, interactions varied considerably by urban or rural location, illustrating the hostility-harmony dialectic in different ways (Lutz and Restall 2005). In rural areas, Maya people were often distrustful of blacks, fearing they might be bandits liable to attack them on roads into the cities of Santiago, Campeche, and Mérida. Blacks and mulatos (a term that included people of black-Maya ancestry) also acted as middlemen traders who intercepted city-bound Maya on the roads and coerced them into selling their market goods at low prices. In rural areas too, Maya laborers tended to have black and mulato overseers, leading to complaints of ill treatment. But even in rural areas, there was everyday co-residence and mixture, mostly through informal unions but also through marriage: half of the married enslaved black men in a late seventeenth-century small Guatemalan town had Maya wives

(Lutz and Restall 2005, 198). In urban areas, there was much more interaction and mestizaje, which also included some formal marriage: 30 percent of married black or pardo men in Campeche between 1688 and 1700 had Maya wives (Restall 2009, 263). Mestizaje also occurred in rural areas, albeit not as much as in urban centers: in urban Campeche in 1779, the proportion of blacks and mulatos to the total population was 17 percent, and in Yucatán as a whole the proportion was only 12 percent by 1791. Still, by the late colonial period "the Mayas of Yucatán had in a sense become Afro-Mayas," implying that still today they "must be viewed" as such (Restall 2009, 5, 285).

This kind of racial conviviality flourished in areas that, while reasonably close to colonial economic centers, were beyond the close control of the authorities. The northern coastal region of Nueva Granada (Colombia) was dominated by Cartagena, a major city and slaving port; Santa Marta, another important colonial port city; and Mompox, a city on the Magdalena River, Nueva Granada's main fluvial artery. In the extensive hinterland, with its hacienda economy, the authorities struggled to impose order beyond the estates themselves. This led to the formation of *palenques*, generally defined as communities founded by escapees from enslavement. In this region, however, enslaved, indigenous, and free colored people not only worked together on the haciendas, but lived together outside them in settlements. Some of these settlements were, in the eyes of the Spanish, little different from palenques – that is, they were composed of escapees from enslavement, renegades of all types, indigenous people, zambos, mestizos, and even some poor whites. In the late 1700s, the Spanish authorities encouraged further mixture by herding scattered and diverse people into villages and towns *a son de campana* (within range of the church bell), with the aim of creating a controllable work force (Fals Borda 1979, 62A, 71A; Wade 1993, 82–87). The result was that the free mixed population that formed almost two-thirds of the region's total population by 1778 had been shaped powerfully by a process of zambaje. The famous *bogas* (boatmen), who poled rafts transporting travelers up the Magdalena toward Bogotá, were the object of many colorful (and often derisive) descriptions that usually characterized them as black (negros), but many were very likely zambos (Nieto and Riaño 2011; Peñas Galindo 1988; Villegas 2014).

A similar situation existed in the northeast of Brazil, where sugar plantations dominated the regional economy but were confined to relatively small areas on the coast in Bahia, Pernambuco, and Sergipe. Initially slavery created a space for Afroindigenous interactions because the plantations used enslaved indigenous people and, by 1600, these so-called *negros da terra* (blacks of the land) outnumbered enslaved Africans by three to one. At this time, records show some intermarriage between the two groups (Schwartz 1970, 325). Thereafter, enslaved Africans quickly took over, but indigenous enslavement persisted through the seventeenth century and indeed thereafter in some regions; for example, the southern region of Paraná had more indigenous than African enslaved people until the 1740s (Sokolow 2003, 108–09). Moreover, Miki (2014) argues that, in the area around the border between Bahia and Espírito Santo provinces, indigenous enslavement actually expanded in the nineteenth century, as this frontier zone was colonized by coffee planters dependent on the proportionally dominant enslaved African population.

During the colonial period, the indigenous presence remained strong in the hinterlands of the northeast (the *sertão*), which was seen as hostile territory. In fact, fighters from "domesticated" indigenous groups were consistently used – often commanded by free blacks or mulatos – as slave-catchers, as soldiers in campaigns against *quilombos* and *mocambos* (settlements of escapees from enslavement), and as a defense against slave revolts (Schwartz and Langfur 2005, 91). Partly because of indigenous hostility, while mocambos were always located in inaccessible areas, the majority were not far from the urban centers that they depended on economically. But, in a clear illustration of the hostility-harmony dialectic, "there are also many references [in the archives] to the incorporation of escaped enslaved Africans and Afro-Brazilians into Indian villages" even in the apparently hostile sertão and indeed, "Afro-Indian cooperation against the Europeans and slavery was common" (Schwartz 1970, 324; Schwartz and Langfur 2005, 99). A study of northern Brazil also found evidence of intermarriage and cooperation, alongside "strife" (Roller 2014). These processes fomented African-indigenous mixture to the extent that a plebeian population of mixed-race people formed, many of whom looked rather "black" in Brazilian terms, but some of whom continued to identify as indigenous and do so in increasing numbers today, as I will discuss later (Warren 2001, 28–29).

In contrast to these cases, the Pacific coastal region of Nueva Granada, with its slavery-driven, frontier-zone mining economy, does not seem to have generated the same kind of Afroindigenous mixture, despite huge areas of it being basically outside colonial control (Sharp 1976; Wade 1993, 98–103). The southernmost portion of this region, Esmeraldas (in today's Ecuador), has long claimed an original history of zambaje, based on the story – known from other locations in Latin America – about a slave ship running aground in the mid-sixteenth century, leaving the enslaved Africans to liberate themselves and mix with the local indigenous people (Whitten 1986, 40; Whitten and Whitten 2011, 40). It seems likely that, further north, in the Colombian part of this Pacific region, some indigenous-black mixture was also taking place (Lane 2005, 171). Enslaved people were 40 percent of the late eighteenth-century population of the northerly Chocó province, where there was an almost equal number of indigenous people, while whites made up a tiny 2 percent, and 22 percent were free blacks (including mulatos and, doubtless, zambos). By 1808, the free black population had increased to 61 percent, while the indigenous population had decreased to 18 percent. Some of the free blacks remained attached to the mining centers, which were also supplied with food by local indigenous groups, creating a social space for interaction. Other free blacks lived outside direct colonial control (which was very restricted) and hence, in principle, shared territory with indigenous people. But overall, black and indigenous people occupied rather different spaces, as free black settlement tended to displace indigenous communities, rather than mixing with them (Losonczy 2006, 60–65). Data are thin, but the situation here was clearly distinct from the Caribbean coast region, for reasons that should be the subject of further research. It may be that the intensive mining economy initially discouraged interaction by creating distinct niches for black and indigenous people and that this pattern persisted even when the majority of blacks were no longer just miners.

In the gold mines of Colombia, black workers, free and enslaved, predominated, living and sometimes also working alongside indigenous people. In the silver mines of Potosí (Upper Peru) and Zacatecas (Mexico), indigenous workers predominated but were accompanied by enslaved Africans. By 1600, 6,000 Andean indigenous men shared the city of Potosí with about 5,000 African and black men and women. Most Africans did not work in the mines – contemporary views held that they were not constitutionally suited to hard labor at very high altitudes – but in Mexico enslaved blacks were about 14 percent of the mining workforce in the same period. While blacks and indigenous Americans clearly lived side by side in these mining sites, it is not certain how much mixture actually occurred between them. Lane observes that in the silver mines of late colonial Guanajuato (Mexico), mulatos (mostly free) were over 40 percent of the mine workers and that "no doubt" many of these were of Afroindigenous ancestry (Lane 2005, 174–77).

Colonial authorities feared that interactions between blacks and indigenous Americans would foment rebellions, and indeed several uprisings involved such alliances in the Andes (see, e.g., Lane 2005, 171–72) and in Brazil, where in one Bahian case a millenarian religious cult helped bind together indigenous and black rebels (Schwartz and Langfur 2005, 100). The authorities also feared the more everyday power of magic (Wade 2009, 100–07). In this realm, indigenous people and blacks drew on their own and each other's reputed sorcery skills. A 1700 case from Barbacoas, a gold mining district in Nueva Granada's Pacific coastal region, demonstrates that enslaved blacks and indigenous Americans collaborated in sorcery to exact revenge on a predatory master who had sexually assaulted an indigenous worker (Lane 2005, 171). White and mixed-race women accused of witchcraft – often involving love magic – in the seventeenth-century Andes revealed that they were helped by indigenous and black accomplices, who in fact took a leading role in their activities. One Spanish woman was accused of working with a mulata woman (of African-Portuguese parentage) who was famous as a witch, but who herself made recourse to an *indio hechicero* (an indigenous sorcerer) to augment her powers (Silverblatt 2004, 172–73). In seventeenth-century Yucatán, the same pattern emerged of Spanish women featuring as clients (and denouncers) of mainly mulato but also Maya women selling their magical services. The witches used a common repertory of folk healing and love magic, drawing eclectically on indigenous, African, and European knowledge (Restall 2009, 265–76).

In sum, the hostility-harmony dynamic that sums up interactions between blacks and indigenous people also led to – more so in some contexts than in others – the emergence of mixed Afroindigenous populations. An underlying conceptual Afro/indigenous divide could be transcended through historical interactions, but the divide was rarely erased and even could resurface, whether prompted from above or from below.

### FROM INDEPENDENCE TO THE TWENTIETH CENTURY

Nation-building is the key frame for grasping Afroindigenous interactions during this period. Elites and intellectuals across Latin America were bent on defining identities to distinguish their nations, regionally and globally. Whether they liked it or not, the symbolic and material resources at their disposal included whiteness, indigeneity, and blackness, and, although this triad was configured in different ways across the region, it almost never lost its tripartite structure. Even in "white" Argentina, "los negros" has been a resilient category, and even in Puerto Rico, Taino culture, reputedly wiped out by the mid-1500s, is still venerated.

Post-independence liberal-inspired attempts to dismantle indigenous communities and juridical identity ran out of steam and, although the category indio lost some of its institutional underpinning, it persisted and indeed gained ground in many countries as an object of attention for nation-builders, politicians, and state policy-makers (Appelbaum, Macpherson, and Rosemblatt 2003; Gotkowitz 2011; Graham 1990; Larson 2004). This interest crystallized in indigenismo, which constructed indigenous people both as glorious ancestors of the nation and as communities in need of protection and ultimately assimilation. Although it was more powerful in countries such as Mexico, indigenismo was widespread in Latin America in its diverse variants of ideology and policy, and it was also found in countries with tiny indigenous populations, such as Brazil. Indigenismo existed in Argentina, where indigenous populations had largely been exterminated, while in mid-nineteenth-century Cuba, the literary current of *siboneyismo* glorified the Edenic innocence of Cuba's extinct Siboney indigenous culture (Alberto and Elena 2016; Earle 2007; Menocal 1964; Ramos 1998).

This was part of the context in which Latin American anthropology was institutionalized with an infrastructure of state-backed indigenous institutes, beginning with the overarching Inter-American Indigenist Institute (founded in Mexico in 1940, with the participation of most Latin American governments), and followed by national bodies such as Colombia's National Ethnological Institute (1941), the National Indigenist Institute of Guatemala (1945), and Mexico's National Indigenist Institute (1948). Earlier government initiatives, such as Brazil's Indian Protection Service (1910) or Mexico's Department of Indigenous Affairs (1934), made extensive use of anthropologists.

In contrast to the concern with the indigenous population – albeit sometimes just the *idea* of the indio/*indígena* – black people as a category were, once slavery had been abolished, rather less an object of special attention by the state, policy-makers, or even nation-building intellectuals. Afro-Latins were rarely seen as a category of "other" that was in need of protection and special programs of assimilation, and they were only occasionally seen as having a special role in defining the nation's heritage. In the context of eugenics, which burgeoned in Latin America in the early decades of the 1900s, physicians and other scientists often remarked on the presence of black populations, as they did on indigenous people and mestizos, but black populations were not accorded a special role, even if they were sometimes seen as the least valuable eugenic resource the nation could count on (Hochman, Lima, and Maio 2010; Schell 2010; Stepan 1991; Stern 2009). Blackness was never completely out of the frame as a relational counterpoint in the national imaginary, but it was only in a few countries – such as Brazil, Cuba, and Colombia – that blackness achieved some institutional status as a result of positive re-evaluations by artists and intellectuals in the twentieth century (see Chapter 6 and Chapter 10). However, this did not result in the levels of state backing and institutional infrastructure supporting indigenismo. Gilberto Freyre's *Casa-grande e senzala* (1933) famously re-evaluated in positive terms the African input into Brazilian society, while samba became enshrined as a national music and Afro-Brazilian religions and practices such as Candomblé and Capoeira became emblems of identity in some regions (Burke and Pallares-Burke 2008; Vianna 1999; see also Chapter 12). In Brazil too, anthropology took an early if minor interest in Afro-Brazilian culture, via the writings of anthropologist and psychiatrist Arthur Ramos and ethnologist Edison Carneiro. In Cuba *afrocubanismo* made an impact in literary and artistic circles beginning in the 1920s (Moore 1997). In Colombia, an incipient literary, artistic, and musical negrismo developed in the 1940s (Gilard 1994; Wade 2000).

This sketch outlines the frame within which indigenous and black people lived in the nineteenth and twentieth centuries: the divisions between them bequeathed by the colonial past continued and if anything were reinforced by the new context. The processes of mixture and conviviality that were also a part of the colonial heritage continued to operate in similar ways, albeit in a new legislative and institutional framework. A few examples will serve to illustrate this.

In the Colombian Chocó, abolition meant that enslaved blacks who had once worked in *cuadrillas* (mining crews) moved into the forest. Indigenous people were gradually displaced into the headwaters of the rivers, as black people occupied the lower and middle reaches in a dispersed pattern of settlement. As the black population grew, they cleared lands notionally belonging to indigenous people, who ceded usufruct on the expectation of a reciprocal return. But because the black people thought the work of clearing the land gave them sole rights to its use, a certain underlying antipathy developed, which was mediated by ties of *compadrazgo* (godparenthood), trade, and exchange of services (Losonczy 2006, 65–73). Some intergroup unions doubtless occurred – it is not unusual to hear individual black people today claiming indigenous parentage – but it has not been common and has not blurred a relatively clear boundary. Whitten and Whitten (2011, 40) argue that the black Esmeraldans who had a colonial history of zambaje were "blackened" in the late twentieth century, subsuming their zambo history into a politicized black identity, but in the national frame of Colombia, Afrodescendant Pacific coast dwellers have long figured as unequivocally black and clearly distinct from the *cholos*, as indigenous people are known locally (Wade 1993).[2] In the 1970s, Friedemann (1975) observed the Fiesta del Indio in Quibdó, provincial capital of the Chocó, which had been going for forty years. The Emberá indigenous people came down from the headwaters of the rivers to the city, bringing their trade goods to market. They were given old clothes to dress up with, plied with food and alcohol, and subjected to ridicule and paternalism, while also staying with black *compadres* (godparents of their children) and participating in street parades with the black populace. Friedemann interpreted the festival as a means of enacting dominant relations between the Emberá and the local black residents – who ran the local institutions of the state (police, fire service, schools, and city administration) – and also a means of integrating the Emberá into the commercial networks of the city. Although the study hints at more complex relations of conviviality, the festival clearly marked black-indigenous difference.

In the Cauca valley region of Colombia, once a colonial center of power and wealth, old colonial divisions persisted, now in relation to a different political conjuncture. Sanders (2004) shows how indigenous people in this region in the late nineteenth century based their claims to land partly on ideas of universal citizenship and partly on familiar stereotypes of indios as weak, dim-witted, and defenseless – and therefore warranting the special treatment they had been accorded under colonial rule. Meanwhile, black people in the region did not identify themselves as negros or mulatos in land claims, although there were occasional petitions in which individuals identified as slaves or ex-slaves. This illustrates differences in the ways in which indigenous and black people understood that their claims might be recognized as appropriate or even possible by people in power, which was a product of how black and indigenous identities fitted into dominant structures of alterity. (In addition to the general difference, this case reminds us to attend to specific regional factors: indigenous identities worked as a bargaining chip due to the political power struggles between Liberals and Conservatives going on

---

[2] In the Andes, *cholo* usually means an urbanized indigenous person.

at the time, the fact that indigenous communities had some electoral weight, and the structure of patron-client relationships in the region.)

In the Mosquitia region of Nicaragua in the nineteenth century, with the white planter class mostly gone, black Creoles gained a dominant position in relation to the Miskitu people: they monopolized local trade in mahogany and controlled local politics. When the British established a protectorate over the region in 1844, they resurrected the old "Kingdom of Mosquitia," first recognized by them in 1638, which was ruled over by a native (and now puppet) "king" who supposedly protected the rights of his Miskitu indigenous subjects. In 1860, Britain and United States recognized Nicaraguan sovereignty over the Atlantic region and the Kingdom was replaced by the Mosquito Reserve, in which "Mosquito Indians" had the right to autonomy. In fact, in both the Kingdom and the Reserve, black Creoles dominated the institutions of governance. The ethnic and racial lines separating Miskitu "Indians" from blacks were reinforced. When the Nicaraguan state dismantled the Reserve government in 1894, the Creole elite lost much of its power to US companies, which were investing in banana production, but they had access to middle-management, commercial, and professional occupations, which allowed them to maintain a superior status locally, until this was challenged by the Miskitu elite in the 1970s (Gabbert 2007, 48–49, 52–53).

Overall, then, the picture is one of distinct indigenous and black identities, rather than the transcendence of this difference. This may be in part because of a lack of historical data. It is clear that in places such as the Caribbean coast of Colombia and the northeast of Brazil, the extensive colonial black-indigenous mixture that had resulted in the predominance of a rural, heterogeneous mixed-race population prior to independence was not undone during the nineteenth and most of the twentieth centuries.

### PRESENT-DAY CONTEXTS

The dominant context for grasping changing Afroindigenous relations over the last few decades has been political mobilization and reform around ethnicity, race, and multiculturalism. We saw previously that, historically, black and indigenous people collaborated on occasion in rebellion, resistance, and self-liberation, even if the bulk of such processes followed separate trajectories for each category. During the twentieth century, the pattern of separation was dominant in overt political mobilization. For obvious reasons, Cuba's short-lived Independent Coloured

Party (Partido Independiente de Color, 1908–12) did not address indigeneity (Helg 1995). Equally focused only on blackness were Brazil's black press, based in São Paulo in the 1920s and 1930s, the Brazilian Black Front (Frente Negra Brasileira, 1931–36), the Experimental Black Theatre (Teatro Negro Experimental, Rio de Janeiro, 1944–1961), and other postwar black movements in Brazil (Andrews 1991; Hanchard 1994; Mitchell 1992). Meanwhile, indigenous political mobilization proceeded down its own path, whether it was indigenous leaders promoting literacy campaigns in Peru in the 1920s (De la Cadena 2000, ch. 2), K'iche' leaders in early twentieth-century Guatemala struggling to maintain a place for indigenous people within a modernizing nation that saw them as obstinate resistors of progress (Grandin 2000), or the Paéz leader Manuel Quintín Lame, who headed a resistance movement in early twentieth-century Colombia based on recuperating land for indigenous people (Castillo-Cárdenas 1987). It is worth noting that because the latter movement was based in the northern Cauca province, an area where black and indigenous people lived side by side, an early leader of the movement was Luis Ángel Monroy, an Afrodescendant (Rappaport 2005, 71). This relates to the general point that, in the Andes in the first half of the twentieth century, popular struggles for land and justice were often seen as class-based, peasant movements, even if in practice they had powerful indigenous roots (Gotkowitz 2007); future research could explore further the extent to which such struggles formed a space for Afroindigenous cooperation (see also later in the chapter).

The wave of ethnic political mobilizations that began in the 1960s formed part of the "new social movements," which made ethnic and racial identities a strong focus of mobilization, overshadowing class. These mobilizations were mostly indigenous at first, followed by dispersed black initiatives in the 1970s, with Brazil in the vanguard (Hanchard 1994; Warren and Jackson 2003; see also Chapter 7). Almost always, indigenous and black people organized separately around different agendas: although both sets of people were concerned with citizenship and exclusion, the indigenous movements focused on land, language, and culture – what Greene (2007c, 345) calls the "holy trinity" of *pueblo* (people) status. Their claims rested on a concept of cultural otherness and authenticity, and on their original native status and pre-conquest relationship to the land (Torres 2008). Black movements made little recourse to similar rationales and, at this time, focused on racism and identity linked to diasporic blackness – drawing inspiration from race-based civil rights struggles in the United States and South Africa. In many areas, such as the Andean countries and   Mexico, an additional focus was on the "invisibility" of black people in nations that rested on ideologies of white-indigenous mestizaje (Andrews 2004, 182–90; Fontaine 1981, 1985; Rahier 2012; Wade 1993, 325–33, 1995). After Durban (2001), the focus of black movements expanded to include the idea of reparations for slavery and racial discrimination (e.g., Mosquera Rosero-Labbé and Barcelos 2007).

## Multiculturalist Reform, Continuing Asymmetry, and the Indigenization of Blackness

The widespread process of "multiculturalist" political and legislative reform that emerged in the 1990s followed in many ways the existing asymmetry between black and indigenous identities, already deeply inscribed into the institutions of the state, the academy, and international organizations such as the International Labor Organization (e.g., in its Indigenous and Tribal Populations Conventions, 1957 and 1989). Nearly all countries either already had or now created legislation that defined varying degrees of rights for indigenous peoples. Of these, only Brazil, Colombia, Ecuador, Guatemala, Honduras, and Nicaragua now have laws giving some collective rights to Afro-Latins.

Even within these countries, asymmetry exists. For example, in Colombia, which has some of the region's most comprehensive provision for Afrodescendants, Law 70 of 1993 allows "black communities" to elect two delegates to the House of Representatives by special electoral circumscription, while indigenous communities can elect one representative and two senators. In the 2005 census, Afro-Colombians made up 10.5 percent of the population, and indigenous people 3.5 percent. Black communities in the Pacific coast region could apply for land titles and in 2013 the number approved was 181, encompassing over 5 million hectares or about 4 percent of the national territory. In comparison, by 2013, legally constituted indigenous *resguardos* (land reserves) numbered 715 (some of them predating the 1991 political reform), with an area of about 32 million hectares, representing 30 percent of the national territory (Salinas Abdala 2014). These reserves receive fiscal transfers from the state, giving them some financial autonomy. In Brazil, indigenous people comprise about 0.4 percent of the population and have about seven hundred demarcated territories (covering over 117 million hectares or 14 percent of the country's land mass), almost all in the Amazon region (Instituto Socioambiental 2016). In contrast, by 2014 the state had officially recognized 2,500 settlements as "remnants" of quilombos whose residents can, under the law, claim collective land title (Fundação Cultural Palmares 2014); by the same date, only 129 of these settlements had had land actually titled, covering just over 1 million hectares (INCRA 2014).

The overall effect of legislative reforms on Afroindigenous relations and identifications has been uneven. On the one hand, the reforms started with differential frameworks for Afrodescendant and indigenous people, obeying traditional differences in the structures of alterity. Indigenous people were understood as rural ethnic groups, ancestrally rooted in the land, with their own languages and cultures that were clearly distinct from mainstream national society. They were still seen as in need of protection; they were victims or at least victim-like. Black people, on the other hand, were understood as more urban, more assimilated and not so culturally different; while black lifeways were distinctive in some ways, black people were Spanish- or Portuguese-speaking, with a few telling exceptions where they had adopted indigenous languages such as Aymara, spoken by some Afro-Bolivians (Lipski 2008), or Carib, spoken by the Garifuna. Mostly they were Catholic, too; even some followers of Afro-Brazilian religions, such as Candomblé, claim to be simultaneously Catholic. Black people were distinct more by virtue of their "race" (mostly defined, in this context, by their phenotype) than their culture. These were all reasons for many Latin American governments not to recognize legal rights for Afrodescendants or to do so reluctantly.

On the other hand, to the extent that the laws did confer rights on black people, they tended to impose an "ethnic," indigenous-looking definition of blackness, which shifted the emphasis away from color and toward cultural difference, focusing on "black communities" and land rights. The main way Afro-Latins could claim rights was by looking similar to indigenous groups (Hooker 2005; Ng'weno 2007a; Wade 1995). A review of cases brought by Afrodescendant communities before the International Court of Human Rights shows that they based their claims on some combination of collective possession and/or ancestral ownership, and/or special relationship to land, and did not mention racial discrimination (Torres 2008, 125–37). A major exception to this indigenization of blackness was Brazil's affirmative actions in higher education and health, which targeted the "black" population at large (i.e., those self-identifying with the political label negro or the census categories of pardo and *preto*). But overall when legislation recognized Afrodescendant rights, it mainly put black and indigenous people on the same "ethnic" footing in relation to the state, and thus put them into potential competition.

In sum, the effect of post-1990 reforms has been to consolidate the existing mode of legal and political institutionalization of indigenous identities, while creating a powerful drive toward ethnic indigenization for black identities vis-à-vis the state and international agencies, based on concepts of community territory and land rights. Such an indigenist, culturalist mold risks sidelining racial inequality and injustice (Hooker 2009). However not all black mobilization took this route; a different option focused on racial identities, anti-racism, and urban markets.

## Colombia and Brazil

Colombia is a rich example of these processes (see also Chapter 7). In the run-up to the 1991 constitutional reform, black and indigenous communities in the Pacific coastal region, which had a history of "hostility-harmony," began to collaborate in local peasant organizations. The common aim was to defend land and livelihoods against increasing encroachment by outsiders, which was driven by overall processes often glossed as "neo-liberalization" (i.e., opening up markets to international capitalist interests) (Escobar 2008; Pardo 1996; Wade 1995). This common aim overrode to some extent existing occasional conflicts over land, caused by the state's tendency to give priority to indigenous land claims (Arocha 1987; Arocha Rodríguez 1998). When the Constitutional Assembly was formed, no black delegates were elected, but indigenous delegates from the region supported black demands, leading to the inclusion of a transitory article that recognized Afro-Colombians as an "ethnic group" and led to Law 70 of 1993. Its provision for land-title claims applied only to rural, riverine "black communities" in the Pacific coast region, strongly reinforcing the regionalized imaginary of blackness that associated it with the Pacific coastal region and effecting an "ethnicization" – and indigenization – of blackness in Colombia (Restrepo 2013; Wade 1995). In light of the forced displacement disproportionately suffered by both indigenous and black communities – especially in the Pacific coast region, which has been wracked by violence since the early 1990s (Oslender 2016) – it has also been argued that black communities are staking a claim to the status of "victim," a role traditionally occupied by indigenous peoples (Cárdenas 2012; Jaramillo Salazar 2014). Further linking black and indigenous communities, when making a land title claim black communities sometimes defined their membership to include the occasional indigenous person who was already attached to the community via kinship or conviviality (Hoffmann 2002). On the other hand, Law 70 sometimes led to an increase in conflicting claims from contiguous indigenous and black communities in the region, which had historically rubbed along together but also kept each other at arm's length, and had collaborated politically in the 1980s (Arocha 1996).

The generation of conflicting claims is evident from a location technically outside the Pacific coast region targeted by Law 70, but which is nevertheless a zone of traditional black settlement. In northern Cauca province, indigenous and black people have lived side by side for a long time; in the indigenous resguardos, Afrodescendants have long held office in local *cabildos* (governing councils) and have collaborated with local Nasa indigenous people, and other peasant farmers in land occupations and cabildo-led development plans in the 1980s (Rappaport 2005, 17, 35). In the municipality of Buenos Aires, for example, they had worked together over a number of decades to oppose an outsider's attempt to claim mining rights to a hill, known as Cerro Teta; they collectively channeled their challenge through the vehicle of the local indigenous resguardo. Indigenous and black people together confronted what might be seen as only a class-based land dispute, but it was experienced simultaneously as a conflict with a racist and slavery-like regime (Ng'weno 2007b, ch. 2). In the wake of 1991 reforms, the indigenous people decided to claim sole rights to the hill, provoking a counterclaim by local Afro-Colombians to the land as a "collective territory of black communities" under the provisions of Law 70. The Afro-Colombian claim was very problematic because it lay outside the Pacific coastal region recognized by Law 70. Against a history of intercultural cooperation and ethnic pluralism, Law 70 created more clearly opposed identities and potential conflict in a context of increasing economic and political vulnerability caused by capitalist expansion and paramilitary activity.

Overall, Law 70 in Colombia resulted in a reinscription of the traditional dividing line that had previously been bridged through collective mobilization in the face of a common threat. Black and indigenous communities are now both "ethnic groups," but they claim land and rights as separate constituencies and relate to the state through separate agencies – the Directorate of Afro-Colombian Affairs and the Directorate of Indigenous Affairs. On the other hand, from the point of view of Afro-Colombian movements, the ethnicization imposed by Law 70 has not proved to be an immutable straitjacket. It has offered a foothold from which to return to the wider agendas of anti-racism, which had inspired Afro-Colombian mobilizations in the 1970s that have endured. Racial hierarchy and discrimination were evermore urgent realities for the growing black urban population seeking education, jobs, and political power (Wade 2010, 38–39, 2012). Interestingly, such concerns may be having repercussions in indigenous movements that traditionally have had little truck with the concept of racism, preferring to mobilize around culture, despite suffering the effects of racism (Hooker 2009, 71). This may reflect the increasing trend toward indigenous urbanization: a future avenue for research is Afroindigenous urban interactions.

The paradoxical effects of recent legislation can be seen in a different way in rural northeastern Brazil, where long-standing mixture had created a mainly peasant population of Afroindigenous ancestry, who identified as "rural workers" and *caboclos* (a term applied to people of white-indigenous ancestry or to assimilated indigenous people) (Arruti 2003). In the state of Sergipe, for example, new identities have emerged in parallel, first indigenous (from the 1970s) and later *quilombola* (from the 1990s), as neighboring communities decided to make land claims in different directions under legal provisions that allow the possibility of ethnogenesis – the emergence of new ethnic communities – as well as the recognition of existing ones. In both cases, local syncretic cultural forms, such as music and dance, took on renewed symbolic significance as markers of indigenous and quilombola identity (Arruti 2003; French 2009). The collective decisions of communities were guided by factors that may seem, to the outside eye, rather contingent: particular bits of historical information, stories, and memories; the role of outside mediators, such as priests, who had their own ideas about local history; and anthropologists contracted by the state to assess communities' claims. The decision to become a quilombo was not always agreed on within the community itself (French 2009, ch. 4) and some individuals in Sergipe and Ceará identify as both indigenous and black (French 2009, 90; Pinheiro 2009, 2011).

Northeast Brazil is an example of how multiculturalist legislation around land titling can both build on existing differences between indigenous and black peoples (indigenous land claims in the area started in the 1960s, before the 1988 constitutional reform that kick-started quilombo claims) and also reinstitute those differences in a context in which they had become blurred as a result of long-standing mixtures. The legislation seems to discourage Afroindigenous mixture, but it has not resulted in a complete separation of black from indigenous: some individuals claim to be both at the same time.

The same tendency can perhaps be observed in the Guajira province of northeastern Colombia, where a population made up largely of Afroindigenous mixtures coexists with Wayúu indigenous people. Here, rural communities attempting to claim land and rights (to clean water, for example) as Afrodescendants have had little luck in their struggles with the Cerrejón mining company, whose lawyers deny that these are "black communities" in the legal sense of the term (Chomsky and Forster 2006). The lawyers also contest claims by Wayúu communities made in zones that the company considers outside Wayúu ancestral lands. But there are already over two dozen Wayúu resguardos occupying over 1 million hectares of the province, so this puts indigenous people on a very different footing from the Afrodescendant communities handicapped by the fact that Law 70 applies principally to the Pacific coast region (cf. Engle 2010, 254–73, on claims made by black island communities near Cartagena). Nevertheless, in the mainly black community of Chancleta, some resident Wayúu families were included in the community's successful claim against Cerrejón for the provision of clean water and the right to prior consultations about relocation plans (Corte Constitucional 2015). Such individual instances suggest the operation of an interethnic conviviality – based, like in northern Cauca, on a shared sense of class-race injustice – which escapes the segregationist tendencies of the law. It is tempting to speculate that this draws on the region's long history of zambaje.

## Central America, Mexico, and Peru

The way recent political mobilizations and associated legislative reforms have shaped Afroindigenous relations is illustrated in a different way by the Garifuna. They have long occupied that anomalous slot of "black Indians": some anthropologists have contended that the Garifuna insisted on their indigenous ancestry and denied Africa; others argue that they always carved out a specific space between black and indigenous, with variations over time. From the 1920s to the 1940s, for example, despite being racialized as black in the Honduran nation and acknowledging that identity, they tended to distance themselves from other black groups and a history of slavery; then, from the 1950s, they began to make stronger links to diasporic blackness and anti-racism (Anderson 2009, ch. 2). From the 1980s, Garifuna activists adopted a model of indigenous rights and actively allied with indigenous activism – partly challenging shared problems of land dispossession, as in the Colombian case. They thus shaped multiculturalist reform by obliging it to accommodate people racialized as "indigenous" and as "black." The indigenization of blackness for the Garifuna was reinforced by their classification as "autochthonous," because they had settled as free people on their lands prior to Honduran independence and because of their linguistic difference – and this stance underwrote claims to land titles. At the same time, they identified and were identified as black – and later, "Afro-Honduran" – along with non-Garifuna Afrodescendants. A key organization was named Black Fraternal Organization of Honduras (OFRANEH, Organización Fraternal Negra Hondureña), which used Afro-diasporic symbols and icons, and promoted an anti-racist agenda (which, however, fell on deaf ears in the 1990s).

While Garifuna and other Afro-Hondurans were recognized by the state and some Garifuna lands titled, progress was tenuous in the context of neoliberal development, driven in part by tourism, which particularly affected Garifuna coastal settlements. In addition, some indigenous activists, while not denying Garifuna status as an autochthonous pueblo, questioned the viability of interethnic unity: they competed with Garifuna organizations over access to funding, they disagreed with them over political tactics, and they saw them as historically and culturally different (Anderson 2007, 400, 2009, 147). Within Garifuna activism there is a distinction between OFRANEH (which, notwithstanding its name, insists on a simultaneously Afroindigenous identity and privileges land rights) and the Organization for Ethnic Community Development (ODECO, Organización de Desarrollo Étnico Comunitario), which privileges blackness and anti-racism). This divergence is reinforced by the fact that OFRANEH takes a radical anti-neoliberal stance, thus putting it in a critical relationship with the state, while ODECO tends to be more "participatory" and less critical (Anderson 2009). The residual power of the underlying conceptual divergence between blackness and indigeneity is once again evident in this Garifuna history.

This kind of interethnic cooperation can also be seen further south on Nicaragua's Caribbean coast, with its mix of indigenous peoples (including the Afroindigenous Miskitu), Garifuna, and black Creoles (Hooker 2009, ch. 4). A land-mapping project carried out there in 1997 took place in a context in which the near unanimity of the common struggle of *costeños* (coastal dwellers) against the Sandinista government (1979–90) for some measure of regional autonomy had faded away (Gordon, Gurdián, and Hale 2003). The project worked with 130 communities, which by the end had formulated twenty-nine land-title claims, with 116 communities involved in seventeen multi-community claims, some involving only Garifuna or Miskitu communities while others were multiethnic. This was both for strategic reasons of achieving strength in numbers for particular claims and in order to present a united (black and indigenous) costeño front to the state. A common historical sense of shared ownership over the coastal territory to some extent overrode ethnic divisions. Such political solidarity can perhaps be seen as deriving from shared interests defined by history and social structure, rather than from some primordial sense of belonging (Hooker 2009).

These Central American cases indicate the possibilities of overcoming simple ethnic-racial divisions in particular conjunctures, despite the potential of multiculturalist policies for institutionalizing differences in ways that might suit a state pursuing governance tactics of divide-and-rule and co-optation. As with the Guajira example, it is tempting to infer that the history of Afroindigenous mixing in these regions set the scene for collaborative ethnic pluralism and intercultural cooperation. At the same time, these cases show us that the elements of a conceptual divide between blackness and indigeneity can be rearticulated and reassembled, remerging in new contexts, rather than being erased.

A local history of Afroindigenous mixture in Mexico's Costa Chica region of the southern Pacific coast also seems to operate in a way that short-circuits the pigeonholing tendencies of institutional multiculturalism and ethnic politics. In these coastal regions of the states of Guerrero and Oaxaca, organized around agricultural and livestock haciendas and peasant smallholdings, people identify as *morenos* (moreno means brown and, euphemistically, black). In the village of San Nicolás, Guerrero, according to Lewis (2012), people see their history as one of indigenous-African mixture resulting in a local population of *negros indios* ("black Indians"). They also anchor themselves to the notion of the indio because they know it figures as authentically Mexican, given the importance of indigenismo, whereas negros are often seen as foreigners in Mexico. Despite this, they do not identify with hegemonic discourses about Mexicans as mestizos (indigenous-white mixture) because in the local context mestizos are economically and politically dominant over morenos. Relations with present-day indigenous people are ambivalent: morenos disparage them as backward, but also identify with them as disadvantaged.

On the other hand, some villagers recognize that anthropologists and cultural workers pursuing the state's "Third Root" project (dedicated since the 1980s to visibilizing Mexico's African heritage) sometimes come looking for blackness in this corner of Mexico, first studied by Mexican anthropologist Gonzalo Aguirre Beltrán (1958). So some among them perform blackness for these audiences. Yet supposed material evidence of African origins in the village – a *casa redonda* (a traditional type of round thatched hut) and an *artesa* (a wooden trough used as a platform for traditional wedding dances) – were made in the 1980s for the explicit purpose of catering to seekers of blackness, and by the early 1990s the evidence had been left untended. For morenos, real blackness belongs in the past. Likewise, the Museum of Afromestizo Cultures, founded in 1999 in Cuijinicuilapa, about twenty kilometers away, excites little interest among the villagers. According to Lewis, then, the insistence of morenos on their mixed origins is part of their recalcitrance to being interpellated as politically "black": initiatives such as the museum, which have been driven by a segment of the local elite and funded by the local and federal state, have not succeeded in restructuring the local racial order in a fully multiculturalist mode.

Another anthropologist takes a different view, which denies a history of Afroindigenous mixture for the people of Collantes, 100 kilometers away in the neighboring state of Oaxaca. Vaughn (2005) argues that local blacks identify primarily as Mexicans but see themselves as different from both indigenous people and mestizos/whites. They dissociate themselves from the indigenous heritage that is so central to Mexican nationalism, but which they see as a mark of inferiority. Despite seeing themselves as distinctive, blackness is an ambivalent node of personal identification and does not function well as a channel for a political identity. But this is not because of their ideas about their Afroindigenous mixture: instead it is a result of the low status of blackness in Mexico.

This difference of opinion between Lewis and Vaughn may be due in part to the different epistemological positions of the authors – in terms of their desire to challenge the Afro/indigenous conceptual divide in academic research – but it may also be explained by the different locations in which they worked. The point is less that two anthropologists can interpret neighboring contexts so differently and more so that the way Afroindigenous relations play out on the ground is shaped by minor differences in economic and political organization – for example, the fact that local state multiculturalism has been more developed in Oaxaca (Hoffmann 2007).

In Peru, the indigenous-black division is mostly well established (Greene 2007b), but in the northern lowland coastal plains, there is a context that bears comparison with Mexico's Costa Chica – and again, two anthropologists interpret neighboring communities in divergent ways. In the rural village of Yapatera, built around an abandoned sugarcane plantation, many people identify as zambos or morenos (Hale 2014, 2015). These terms are principally descriptors of physical appearance – especially skin color and hair type – but there is also acknowledgment of historical mixture between blacks and indigenous people, especially those who formed the plantation workforce. Locals do use the term "negro," but as a descriptor of someone with very dark skin, or someone who is the darkest in a given context, such as a sibling group, rather than as a collective identity term. Indeed, people insist on being mixed and reject the idea – often imposed by outsiders and by black activists and ethnic entrepreneurs (a handful of whom are residents) – that Yapatera is a "black village" and that the villagers belong to a group of "black people" or "Afro-Peruvians" with ancestral connections to Africa or to slavery. For example, a local "Afro-Peruvian" leader, who obtained international NGO funding to run an Afro-Peruvian Women's Pottery Project, was dismayed to find the villagers producing pottery that did not, in his eyes, represent Afro-Peruvian culture: a set of predefined pottery molds was then imposed on the producers.

These features of identification are not unique to Yapatera or even Peru and can be found in Mexico and Colombia, among other countries. Of interest in Yapatera is the explicit acknowledgment of black-indigenous mixture as the basis on which to reject or avoid a politicized and multiculturalist definition of ethnicity or race, seen as imposed from outside (although the state was less involved in Peru than in Mexico). On the other hand, an Afro/indigenous divide is reproduced because people also draw a distinction between morenos/zambos and cholos, with the latter being more associated with migrants from the highlands, who have more indigenous physical features, such as straight hair. The distinction is reflected in a spatial subdivision of the village into La Hacienda and Cruz Pampa, based on the different original residential locations of the plantation employees and the field hands. As such, in people's memories, La Hacienda was more cholo, while Cruz Pampa was more moreno/zambo, and this racial (or color) inflection, while said to have been blurred over time by intermarriage, persists as a trace (Hale 2014, 240). In other words, while zambaje might give a basis for evading multiculturalist pigeonholing and identity politics around blackness, the underlying distinction between black and indigenous still operates as a residual force.

An interesting contrast is the rural village of Ingenio, a mere fifty kilometers from Yapatera. Here (and among migrants from Ingenio to Lima), according to Golash-Boza (2010, 2011), most people identify quite clearly with the category black, not just as a color term, but as a racial category, implying collective descent and identity, and opposed to white in a bipolar fashion. This phenomenon was more marked in Lima and among those who had participated in an Afro-Peruvian social movement, but it also existed in the village. In some ways, Golash-Boza's findings resonate with Hale's for Yapatera (e.g., the denial of African and slave connections, the use of color terms as descriptors), but (a) she reveals a much clearer identification with blackness as a category and the existence of "black consciousness" (Sue and Golash-Boza 2008–2009, 49), and (b) she barely mentions mixture between black and indigenous people, except in specific cases (e.g., a black woman whose father was from the highlands). We can only speculate whether the apparent absence of zambaje (or recognition of it by locals) relates to the stronger identification with blackness.

## Mutual Enactments of Identity

A very different expression of the Afro/indigenous conceptual divide – which reiterates its power, while also destabilizing and fragmenting its structure – is in the area of performative representations, specifically the festival contexts in which indios mask as negros (and, to a lesser extent, vice versa). In Bolivia, the *morenada* involves indigenous people dressing up and parading as caricatured versions of enslaved black people, reputedly those who worked in the mining industry of colonial Potosí (Guss 2006). In the Peruvian Andes, indigenous and mestizo dancers parade as *qhapaq negros* (elegant blacks), again wearing grotesque masks (Mendoza 2000). In Latacunga, Ecuador, a local man dresses up as La Mama Negra, a horse-mounted, black female figure of exaggerated proportions, who parades the streets in September, sponsored by local *chola* market women (Weismantel 2001). In festivals in Salasaca, Ecuador, indigenous actors play the late nineteenth-century black soldiers who both harassed indigenous women and protected the Liberal leader, Eloy Alfaro, revered as a liberator of the oppressed, both indigenous and Afrodescendant (Whitten and Corr 1999). In Pasto in the Colombian Andes, people color themselves black for the Día de los Negros, the penultimate day of the Carnaval de Negros y Blancos. In the reverse direction, less frequently found, Afro-Colombians perform the Danza de los Indios in the carnival of the Caribbean port of Barranquilla, while Afro-Ecuadorians also disguise themselves as indios on January 7, the day of the *raza india* in the Festival of the Kings (Rahier 2013).

These examples are all instances of wider patterns of racial and sexual cross-dressing, often in festive and carnival contexts, in which white, black, and indigenous figures are dramatized in a play of mimesis and alterity, partaking of each other's perceived qualities, meanings, and powers by dint of the magic of playacting in an imaginative hall of mirrors (Taussig 1993). Two things stand out in these cases. First, the performances evoke an "original" time when only the "three races" existed in pure form as indios, negros, and blancos, before mestizos emerged. The performances often refer to the colonial period: the black people are often said to represent enslaved Africans, for example, and one version of the Barranquilla carnival's Danza de los Indios is said to enact indigenous Faroto men, disguised as women, taking revenge on the Spaniards who had abused indigenous women. Going back in time like this distills the essence of the social categories involved and turns each racialized figure into a potent symbol of power relations. Second, a common theme is oppression and liberation, which figure as elements of a history shared by indigenous and Afrodescendant peoples. Whitten and Corr (1999) recount many cases of indigenous people who do not see black people as reduced to a history of slavery; instead they see blackness as linked to self-liberation, creativity, adaptability, and a knowledge of the past. In La Paz, "native campesinos on the way to becoming middle class mestizos dress up as African slaves who in turn are parodying their white masters"; this "racial displacement is at the heart of the Morenada" (Guss 2006, 319). The enslaved African – not just as a symbol of oppression, but also satirical intransigence – is a good figure with which to express awkward aspirations to overcome constraints of class and race. Likewise, the Mama Negra – an indigenous man playing a sexually assertive, sensually exuberant black woman – expresses in contradictory ways the aspirations and self-image of the chola market women, successful entrepreneurs whose race and gender also challenge Andean social hierarchies (Weismantel 2001, 230). These mutual enactments of identity play upon the difference between blackness and indigeneity, but in ways that highlight their relational interoperability in contexts of race-class hierarchy.

## CONCLUSION

Afrodescendant and indigenous people in Latin America have traditionally been treated in history and social science as separate categories, specified by their different relations to the dominant white category – schematically understood as rooted in the difference between "native other" and "slave" – and also by their different mixtures with whiteness (schematically, "mestizo" and "mulato"). As we have seen, more recent scholarship has challenged this tendency, (a) by exploring interactions between categories and communities of people who identify themselves and others as black or indigenous (or variants of these labels), and (b) by examining contexts in which such interactions have given rise to intermediate, mixed categories of people, who do not fit into either term nor into the dominant conception of mestizaje specified in relation to whiteness.

The resulting materials show two things. First, they highlight the flexibility and ambiguity of racial categories in Latin America, but also in general. These categories change over time – witness the fact that "zambos" were called "mulatos" for much of the colonial period, hiding Afroindigenous mixture behind a label later associated with white-black mixture. They also change over space – witness the different meanings of cholo in the Colombian Pacific, where it means rural indigenous person, and Ecuador or Peru, where it means urbanized indigenous person. They also vary according to people's strategies – witness the way the same peasant "caboclo" people in northeastern Brazil can become either "indigenous" or "quilombola," depending on a variety of factors. If scholars already knew not to take racial labels and terms for granted, the material on Afroindigenous mixtures reinforces this lesson with great clarity.

Second, on this shifting terrain, certain nodes retain a relational structuring role – black, indigenous, and white, with the latter in a clearly dominant position. The nodes are not fully fixed: each only gains meaning and force from its relation to the others and from its mode of operation in a given context (and we have seen how important local contexts are in defining the meanings of categories such as negro and moreno in Peru and Mexico). But the triad works in topological fashion: the underlying relations of power and hierarchy between the nodes retain their structure through multiple and successive distortions of the terrain on which they are mapped. Like a subway map, it does not matter if the surface on which the structure lies is in the form of a donut or a square – it is still readable as a guide. Unlike a subway map, the network connecting the three nodes is, in principle, unbounded and unfixed in the potentiality of its connections: black, white, and indigenous can acquire new connections with other nodes – people, institutions, and knowledge – which change their meanings and their relationships within a network that is nevertheless persistently shaped by racial hierarchy. Thus, on the one hand, Afroindigenous mixtures show a tendency to be structured by a persistent conceptual divergence between negro and indio, which can be interpreted as a continuing result of the dominance of whiteness. On the other hand, the meaning and effects of that divergence vary across time and space. In the Colombian Pacific, the divergence feeds into a network that includes state multiculturalism, which defines legal blackness as parallel to legal indigeneity – an indigenization of blackness that is a striking feature of much multiculturalist legislation. In the Costa Chica, the divergence is backgrounded in relation to a local identity as moreno, which by some accounts is rooted in an explicitly Afroindigenous history, and which sits awkwardly, almost recalcitrantly, in the negro box defined by multiculturalist identity politics.

The materials in this chapter suggest that the space for a *sui generis* Afroindigenous slot has a tenuous existence with little traction on the terrain of today's political landscape. For scholars, this implies the need to continue to give focused attention to Afroindigenous interactions and mixtures, despite their orthogonal fit with dominant identity slots. The past may perhaps act as a guide to the present in this respect. We have seen how in colonial Colombia the trajectory of Afroindigenous interactions was very different in the Pacific and Caribbean regions; what, then, are the factors that shaped these differences? We have also seen how in the first half of the 1900s, many Andean struggles for land that in practice were strongly indigenous could make room for a broader ethnic constituency, a tendency that still has occasional parallels today, albeit besieged by multiculturalist politics. Do we need to reconceptualize what counts as an effective "ethnic" mobilization and embrace forms that are less identity-based and more coalitional, based, in Hooker's words (2009, 170), on "contingent solidarities" derived from sharing geographical, social, and political spaces?

## BIBLIOGRAPHY

Aguirre Beltrán, Gonzalo. 1958. *Cuijla: Esbozo etnográfico de un pueblo negro*. México, D. F.: Fondo de Cultura Económica.
Alberto, Paulina, and Eduardo Elena, eds. 2016. *Rethinking Race in Modern Argentina*. New York, NY: Cambridge University Press.
Anderson, Mark. 2007. "When Afro Becomes (Like) Indigenous: Garifuna and Afro-Indigenous Politics in Honduras." *Journal of Latin American and Caribbean Anthropology* 12, 2: 384–413.
  2009. *Black and Indigenous: Garifuna Activism and Consumer Culture in Honduras*. Minneapolis, MN: University of Minnesota Press.

Andrews, George Reid. 1991. *Blacks and Whites in São Paulo, Brazil, 1888–1988*. Madison, WI: University of Wisconsin Press.

2004. *Afro-Latin America, 1800–2000*. Oxford: Oxford University Press.

Appelbaum, Nancy P., Anne S. Macpherson, and Karin A. Rosemblatt, eds. 2003. *Race and Nation in Modern Latin America*. Chapel Hill, NC: University of North Carolina Press.

Arocha, Jaime. 1987. "Violencia Contra Minorías Étnicas en Colombia." In *Colombia: Violencia y Democracia*, edited by Comisión de Estudios sobre la Violencia en Colombia, 105–33. Bogotá: Universidad Nacional.

1996. "Afrogénesis, eurogénesis y convivencia interétnica." In *Pacífico: ¿Desarrollo o biodiversidad? estado, capital y movimientos sociales en el Pacífico colombiano*, edited by Arturo Escobar and Alvaro Pedrosa, 316–28. Bogotá: CEREC.

Arocha Rodríguez, Jaime. 1998. "Etnia y guerra: relación ausente en los estudios sobre las violencias colombianas." In *Las violencias: inclusión creciente*, edited by Jaime Arocha, Fernando Cubides and Myriam Jimeno, 205–35. Bogotá: Centro de Estudios Sociales, Universidad Nacional de Colombia.

Arruti, José Mauricio Andion. 2003. De como a cultura se faz política e vice-versa: Sobre religiões, festas, negritudes e indianidades no nordeste contemporâneo. *Comunidade Virtual de Antropologia* 10, http://www.antropologia.com.br/arti/colab/a10-jmauricio.PDF.

Burke, Peter, and Maria Lúcia G. Pallares-Burke. 2008. *Gilberto Freyre: Social Theory in the Tropics*. Oxford: Peter Lang.

Cárdenas, Roosbelinda. 2012. "Multicultural Politics for Afro-Colombians: An Articulation 'without Guarantees.'" In *Black Social Movements in Latin America: From Monocultural Mestizaje to Multiculturalism*, edited by Jean Muteba Rahier, 113–34. New York, NY: Palgrave Macmillan.

Carroll, Patrick J. 2005. "Black-indigenous Relations and the Historical Record in Colonial Mexico." In *Beyond Black and Red: African-indigenous Relations in Colonial Latin America*, edited by Matthew Restall, 245–68. Albuquerque, NM: University of New Mexico Press.

Castillo-Cárdenas, Gonzalo. 1987. *Liberation Theology from Below: The Life and Thought of Manuel Quintín Lame*. Maryknoll, NY: Orbis Books.

Chambers, Sarah C. 1999. *From Subjects to Citizens: Honor, Gender, and Politics in Arequipa, Peru, 1780–1854*. University Park, PA: Pennsylvania State University Press.

Chomsky, Avi, and Cindy Forster. 2006. "Who Is Indigenous? Who Is Afro-Colombian? Who Decides?" *Cultural Survival Quarterly* 30, 4, https://www.culturalsurvival.org/publications/cultural-survival-quarterly/colombia/who-indigenous-who-afro-colombian-who-decides.

Cope, R. Douglas. 1994. *The Limits of Racial Domination: Plebeian Society in Colonial Mexico City, 1660–1720*. Madison, WI: University of Wisconsin Press.

Corte Constitucional. 2015. Sentencia T-256/15, acción de tutela instaurada por miembros de la comunidad ancestral de negros afrodescendientes de los corregimientos de Patilla y Chancleta del municipio de Barrancas, La Guajira, contra la empresa "Carbones del Cerrejón Limited." Bogotá: Corte Constitucional de la República de Colombia.

De la Cadena, Marisol. 2000. *Indigenous Mestizos: The Politics of Race and Culture in Cuzco, 1919–1991*. Durham, NC: Duke University Press.

Dennis, Philip A. 2010. *The Miskitu People of Awastara*. Austin, TX: University of Texas Press.

Earle, Rebecca. 2007. *The Return of the Indigenous: Indians and Myth-Making in Spanish America, 1810–1930*. Durham, NC: Duke University Press.

Engle, Karen. 2010. *The Elusive Promise of Indigenous Development: Rights, Culture, Strategy*. Durham, NC: Duke University Press.

Escobar, Arturo. 2008. *Territories of Difference: Place, Movements, Life*, Redes. Durham, NC: Duke University Press.

Fals Borda, Orlando. 1979. *Mompox y Loba*. 4 vols. Vol. 1, *Historia doble de la costa*. Bogotá: Carlos Valencia Editores.

Fontaine, Pierre-Michel. 1981. "Transnational Relations and Racial Mobilization: Emerging Black Movements in Brazil." In *Ethnic Identities in a Transnational World*, edited by John F. Stack, 141–62. Westport, CT: Greenwood Press.

    ed. 1985. *Race, Class, and Power in Brazil*. Los Angeles, CA: Centre of Afro-American Studies, University of California.

Forbes, Jack D. 1988. *Africans and Indigenous Americans: The Language of Race and the Evolution of Red-Black Peoples*. 2nd ed. Oxford: Basil Blackwell.

French, Jan Hoffman. 2009. *Legalizing Identities: Becoming Black or Indian in Brazil's Northeast*. Chapel Hill, NC: University of North Carolina Press.

Freyre, Gilberto. 1933. *Casa-grande & senzala: Formação da familia brasileira sob o regime de economia patriarcal*. Rio de Janeiro: Maia & Schmidt.

Friedemann, Nina de. 1975. "La Fiesta del Indio en Quibdó: Un caso de relaciones inter-étnicas en Colombia." *Revista Colombiana de Antropología* 19, 2: 65–78.

Fundação Cultural Palmares. 2014. *Comunidades quilombolas*. http://www.palmares.gov.br/?page_id=88.

Gabbert, Wolfgang. 2007. "In the Shadow of the Empire – The Emergence of Afro-Creole Societies in Belize and Nicaragua." *Indiana* 42: 39–66.

Gilard, Jacques. 1994. "Le débat identitaire dans la Colombie des années 1940 et 1950." *Cahiers du Monde Hispanique et Luso-Brésilien, Caravelle* 62: 11–26.

Gilroy, Paul. 2004. *After Empire: Melancholia or Convivial Culture*. London: Routledge.

Golash-Boza, Tanya. 2010. "Does Whitening Happen? Distinguishing between Race and Color Labels in an African-Descended Community in Peru." *Social Problems* 57, 1: 138–56.

    2011. *Yo Soy Negro: Blackness in Peru*. Gainesville, FL: University Press of Florida.

Gonzalez, Nancie. 1988. *Sojourners of the Caribbean: Ethnogenesis and Ethnohistory of the Garifuna*. Urbana, IL: University of Illinois Press.

Gordon, Edmund T. 1998. *Disparate Diasporas: Identity and Politics in an African-Nicaraguan Community*. Austin, TX: University of Texas Press.

Gordon, Edmund T., Galio C. Gurdián, and Charles R. Hale. 2003. "Rights, Resources and the Social Memory of Struggle: Reflections on a Study of

Indigenous and Black Community Land Rights on Nicaragua's Atlantic Coast." *Human Organization* 62, 4: 369–81.

Gotkowitz, Laura. 2007. *A Revolution for Our Rights: Indigenous Struggles for Land and Justice in Bolivia, 1880–1952.* Durham, NC: Duke University Press.

ed. 2011. *Histories of Race and Racism: The Andes and Mesoamerica from Colonial Times to the Present.* Durham, NC: Duke University Press.

Graham, Richard, ed. 1990. *The Idea of Race in Latin America, 1870–1940.* Austin, TX: University of Texas Press.

Grandin, Greg. 2000. *The Blood of Guatemala: A History of Race and Nation.* Durham, NC: Duke University Press.

Greene, Shane. 2007a. "Entre 'lo indio' y 'lo negro': Interrogating the Effects of Latin America's New Afro-Indigenous Multiculturalisms" (Special Issue guest edited by Shane Greene). *Journal of Latin American and Caribbean Anthropology* 12, 2.

2007b. "Entre lo indio, lo negro, y lo incaico: The Spatial Hierarchies of Difference in Multicultural Peru." *Journal of Latin American and Caribbean Anthropology* 12, 2: 441–74.

2007c. "Introduction: On Race, Roots/Routes, and Sovereignty in Latin America's Afro-Indigenous Multiculturalisms." *Journal of Latin American and Caribbean Anthropology* 12, 2: 329–55.

Guss, David M. 2006. "The Gran Poder and the Reconquest of La Paz." *Journal of Latin American Anthropology* 11, 2: 294–328.

Hale, Charles R. 1994. *Resistance and Contradiction: Miskitu Indians and the Nicaraguan State, 1894–1987.* Stanford, CA: Stanford University Press.

Hale, Tamara. 2014. *Mixing and Its Challenges: An Ethnography of Race, Kinship, and History in a Village of Afro-Indigenous Descent in Coastal Peru.* PhD thesis, Anthropology, London School of Economics, London, UK.

2015. "A Non-essentialist Theory of Race: The Case of an Afro-Indigenous Village in Northern Peru." *Social Anthropology* 23, 2: 135–51.

Hanchard, Michael. 1994. *Orpheus and Power: The Movimento Negro of Rio De Janeiro and São Paulo, Brazil, 1945–1988.* Princeton, NJ: Princeton University Press.

Helg, Aline. 1995. *Our Rightful Share: The Afro-Cuban Struggle for Equality, 1886–1912.* Chapel Hill, NC: University of North Carolina Press.

Hochman, Gilberto, Nísia Trindade Lima, and Marcos Chor Maio. 2010. "The Path of Eugenics in Brazil: Dilemmas of Miscegenation." In *The Oxford Handbook of the History of Eugenics*, edited by Alison Bashford and Philippa Levine, 493–510. Oxford: Oxford University Press.

Hoffmann, Odile. 2002. "Collective Memory and Ethnic Identities in the Colombian Pacific." *Journal of Latin American Anthropology* 7, 2: 118–38.

2007. "De las 'tres razas' al mestizaje: Diversidad de las representaciones colectivas acerca de lo 'negro' en México (Veracruz y Costa Chica)." Diario de Campo *Suplemento* 42: 98–109.

Hooker, Juliet. 2005. "Indigenous Inclusion/Black Exclusion: Race, Ethnicity and Multicultural Citizenship in Contemporary Latin America." *Journal of Latin American Studies* 37, 2: 285–310.

2009. *Race and the Politics of Solidarity.* Oxford: Oxford University Press.

INCRA. 2014. *Títulos expedidos às comunidades quilombolas.* Instituto Nacional de Colonização e Reforma Agrária. Accessed January 29, 2015. www .incra.gov.br/sites/default/files/uploads/estrutura-fundiaria/quilombolas/titulos_ expedidos.pdf.

Instituto Socioambiental. 2016. *Povos indígenas no Brasil: terras indígenas.* Accessed January 7, 2017. https://povosindigenas.org.br/pt/c/terras-indi genas/introducao/o-que-sao-terras-indigenas.

Jaramillo Salazar, Pablo. 2014. *Etnicidad y victimización. Genealogías de la violencia y la indigenidad en el norte de Colombia.* Bogotá: Ediciones Uniandes.

Jaramillo Uribe, Jaime. 1968. *La sociedad neogranadina.* Vol. 1, *Ensayos sobre historia social colombiana.* Bogotá: Universidad Nacional de Colombia.

Lane, Kris. 2005. "Africans and indigenouss in the Mines of Spanish America." In *Beyond Black and Red: African-indigenous Relations in Colonial Latin America*, edited by Matthew Restall, 159–84. Albuquerque, NM: University of New Mexico Press.

Larson, Brooke. 2004. *Trials of Nation Making: Liberalism, Race, and Ethnicity in the Andes, 1810–1910.* Cambridge: Cambridge University Press.

Lewis, Laura A. 2012. *Chocolate and Corn Flour: History, Race, and Place in the Making of "Black" Mexico.* Durham, NC: Duke University Press.

Lipski, John M. 2008. *Afro-Bolivian Spanish.* Frankfurt, Germany, and Madrid, Spain: Vervuert, Iberoamericana.

Losonczy, Anne-Marie. 2006. *La trama interétnica: Ritual, sociedad y figuras de intercambio entre los grupos negros y emberá del Chocó.* Bogotá: Instituto Colombiano de Antropología e Historia, Instituto Francés de Estudios Andinos.

Lutz, Christopher, and Matthew Restall. 2005. "Wolves and Sheep?: Black-Maya Relations in Colonial Guatemala and Yucatan." In *Beyond Black and Red: African-indigenous Relations in Colonial Latin America*, edited by Matthew Restall, 185–222. Albuquerque, NM: University of New Mexico Press.

Martínez, María Elena. 2008. *Genealogical Fictions: Limpieza De Sangre, Religion, and Gender in Colonial Mexico.* Stanford, CA: Stanford University Press.

Mendoza, Zoila S. 2000. *Shaping Society through Dance: Mestizo Ritual Performance in the Peruvian Andes.* Chicago, IL: University of Chicago Press.

Menocal, Feliciana. 1964. "*La Piragua y* el siboneyismo." *Revista de la Biblioteca Nacional de Cuba José Martí* 2: 1–13.

Miki, Yuko. 2014. "Slave and Citizen in Black and Red: Reconsidering the Intersection of African and Indigenous Slavery in Postcolonial Brazil." *Slavery & Abolition* 35, 1: 1–22.

Mitchell, Michael. 1992. "Racial Identity and Political Vision in the Black Press of Sao Paulo, Brazil, 1930–1947." *Contributions in Black Studies* 9, 1: 17–29.

Moore, Robin. 1997. *Nationalizing Blackness: Afrocubanismo and Artistic Revolution in Havana, 1920–1940.* Pittsburgh, PA: University of Pittsburgh Press.

Mörner, Magnus. 1967. *Race Mixture in the History of Latin America*. Boston, MA: Little, Brown.

Mosquera Rosero-Labbé, Claudia, and Luiz Claudio Barcelos, eds. 2007. *Afro-reparaciones: Memorias de la esclavitud y justicia reparativa para negros, afrocolombianos y raizales*. Bogotá: Universidad Nacional de Colombia.

Ng'weno, Bettina. 2007a. "Can Ethnicity Replace Race? Afro-Colombians, Indigeneity and the Colombian Multicultural State." *Journal of Latin American and Caribbean Anthropology* 12, 2: 414–40.

2007b. *Turf Wars: Territory and Citizenship in the Contemporary State*. Stanford, CA: Stanford University Press.

Nieto, María Camila, and María Riaño. 2011. *Esclavos, negros libres y bogas en la literatura del siglo XIX*. Bogotá: Universidad de los Andes.

O'Toole, Rachel Sarah. 2012. *Bound Lives: Africans, Indians, and the Making of Race in Colonial Peru*. Pittsburgh, PA: University of Pittsburgh Press.

Offen, Karl H. 2002. "The Sambo and Tawira Miskitu: The Colonial Origins and Geography of Intra-Miskitu Differentiation in Eastern Nicaragua and Honduras." *Ethnohistory* 49, 2: 319–72.

Oslender, Ulrich. 2016. *The Geographies of Social Movements: Afro-Colombian Mobilization and the Aquatic Space*. Durham, NC: Duke University Press.

Pagden, Anthony. 1982. *The Fall of Natural Man: The American Indian and the Origins of Comparative Ethnology*. Cambridge: Cambridge University Press.

Pardo, Mauricio. 1996. "Movimientos sociales y relaciones inter-étnicas." In *Pacífico: ¿Desarrollo o biodiversidad? Estado, capital y movimientos sociales en el Pacífico colombiano*, edited by Arturo Escobar and Alvaro Pedrosa, 299–315. Bogotá: CEREC.

Peñas Galindo, David. 1988. *Los bogas de Mompox: Historia del zambaje*. Bogotá: Tercer Mundo Editores.

Pinheiro, Joceny. 2009. "Authors of Authenticity: Indigenous Leadership and the Politics of Identity in the Brazilian Northeast." PhD thesis, University of Manchester.

2011. Identificação indígena e mestiçagem no Ceará. *Cadernos do Leme* 3, 2: 21–49.

Rahier, Jean, ed. 2012. *Black Social Movements in Latin America: From Monocultural Mestizaje to Multiculturalism*. New York, NY: Palgrave Macmillan.

2013. *Kings for Three Days: The Play of Race and Gender in an Afro-Ecuadorian Festival*. Urbana, IL: University of Illinois Press.

Ramos, Alcida. 1998. *Indigenism: Ethnic Politics in Brazil*. Madison, WI: University of Wisconsin Press.

Rappaport, Joanne. 2005. *Intercultural Utopias: Public Intellectuals, Cultural Experimentation, and Ethnic Pluralism in Colombia*. Durham, NC: Duke University Press.

Restall, Matthew, ed. 2005a. *Beyond Black and Red: African-indigenous Relations in Colonial Latin America*. Albuquerque, NM: University of New Mexico Press.

2005b. "Introduction: Black Slaves, Red Paint." In *Beyond Black and Red: African-indigenous Relations in Colonial Latin America*, edited by Matthew Restall, 1–14. Albuquerque, NM: University of New Mexico Press.

2009. *The Black Middle: Africans, Mayas, and Spaniards in Colonial Yucatan.* Stanford, CA: Stanford University Press.

Restrepo, Eduardo. 2013. *Etnización de la negridad: La invención de las 'comunidades negras' como grupo étnico en Colombia.* Popayán: Universidad del Cauca.

Roller, Heather. 2014. *Amazonian Routes: Indigenous Mobility and Colonial Communities in Northern Brazil.* Stanford, CA: Stanford University Press.

Salinas Abdala, Yamile. 2014. "Los derechos territoriales de los grupos étnicos: ¿Un compromiso social, una obligación constitucional o una tarea hecha a medias?" *Punto de Encuentro* 67: 1–39.

Sanders, James. 2004. *Contentious Republicans: Popular Politics, Race, and Class in Nineteenth-Century Colombia.* Durham, NC: Duke University Press.

Schell, Patience A. 2010. "Eugenics Policy and Practice in Cuba, Puerto Rico, and Mexico." In *The Oxford Handbook of the History of Eugenics*, edited by Alison Bashford and Philippa Levine, 477–92. Oxford: Oxford University Press.

Schwaller, Robert C. 2011. "'Mulata, hija de negro y india': Afro-Indigenous Mulatos in Early Colonial Mexico." *Journal of Social History* 44, 3: 889–914.

Schwartz, Stuart B. 1970. "The 'Mocambo': Slave Resistance in Colonial Bahia." *Journal of Social History* 3, 4: 313–33.

Schwartz, Stuart B., and Hal Langfur. 2005. "Tapanhuns, negros da terra, and curibocas: Common Cause and Confrontation between Blacks and indigenouss in Colonial Brazil." In *Beyond Black and Red: African-indigenous Relations in Colonial Latin America*, edited by Matthew Restall, 81–114. Albuquerque, NM: University of New Mexico Press.

Sharp, William. 1976. *Slavery on the Spanish Frontier: The Colombian Chocó, 1680–1810.* Norman, OK: University of Oklahoma Press.

Silverblatt, Irene. 2004. *Modern Inquisitions: Peru and the Colonial Origins of the Civilized World.* Durham, NC: Duke University Press.

Sokolow, Jayme A. 2003. *The Great Encounter: Indigenous Peoples and European Settlers in the Americas, 1492–1800.* Armonk, NY: M. E. Sharpe.

Stepan, Nancy Leys. 1991. *"The Hour of Eugenics": Race, Gender, and Nation in Latin America.* Ithaca, NY: Cornell University Press.

Stern, Alexandra Minna. 2009. "Eugenics and Racial Classification in Modern Mexican America." In *Race and Classification: The Case of Mexican America*, edited by Ilona Katzew and Susan Deans-Smith, 151–73. Stanford, CA: Stanford University Press.

Sue, Christina A., and Tanya Golash-Boza. 2008–9. "Blackness in Mestizo America: The Cases of Mexico and Peru." *Latino(a) Research Review* 7 (1–2): 30–58.

Taussig, Michael. 1993. *Mimesis and Alterity: A Particular History of the Senses.* London: Routledge.

Torres, Gerald. 2008. "Indigenous Peoples, Afro-Indigenous Peoples, and Reparations." In *Reparations for Indigenous Peoples: International and*

*Comparative Perspectives*, edited by Federico Lenzerini. Oxford: University of Oxford Press.

Twinam, Ann. 1999. *Public Lives, Private Secrets: Gender, Honor, Sexuality and Illegitimacy in Colonial Spanish America*. Stanford, CA: Stanford University Press.

Vaughn, Bobby. 2005. "Afro-Mexico: Blacks, Indígenas, Politics, and the Greater Diaspora." In *Neither Enemies nor Friends: Latinos, Blacks, Afro-Latinos*, edited by Anani Dzidzienyo and Suzanne Oboler, 117–36. New York, NY: Palgrave Macmillan.

Vianna, Hermano. 1999. *The Mystery of Samba: Popular Music and National Identity in Brazil*. Translated by John Charles Chasteen. Chapel Hill, NC: University of North Carolina Press.

Villegas, Álvaro. 2014. "El valle del río Magdalena en los discursos letrados de la segunda mitad del siglo XIX: Territorio, enfermedad y trabajo." *Folios* 39: 149–59.

Vinson III, Ben, and Matthew Restall. 2005. "Black Soldiers, indigenous Soldiers: Meanings of Military Service in the Spanish American Colonies." In *Beyond Black and Red: African-indigenous Relations in Colonial Latin America*, edited by Matthew Restall, 15–52. Albuquerque, NM: University of New Mexico Press.

Wade, Peter. 1993. *Blackness and Race Mixture: The Dynamics of Racial Identity in Colombia*. Baltimore, MD: Johns Hopkins University Press.

1995. "The Cultural Politics of Blackness in Colombia." *American Ethnologist* 22, 2: 342–58.

2000. *Music, Race, and Nation: Música Tropical in Colombia*. Chicago, IL: University of Chicago Press.

2009. *Race and Sex in Latin America*. London: Pluto Press.

2010. *Race and Ethnicity in Latin America*. 2nd ed. London: Pluto Press.

2012. "Afro-Colombian Social Movements." In *Comparative Perspectives on Afro-Latin America*, edited by Kwame Dixon and John Burdick, 135–55. Gainesville, FL: University Press of Florida.

Warren, Jonathan W. 2001. *Racial Revolutions: Antiracism and Indian Resurgence in Brazil*. Durham, NC: Duke University Press.

Warren, Kay B., and Jean E. Jackson, eds. 2003. *Indigenous Movements, Self-Representation, and the State in Latin America*. Austin, TX: University of Texas Press.

Weismantel, Mary. 2001. *Cholas and Pishtacos: Stories of Race and Sex in the Andes*. Chicago, IL: University of Chicago Press.

Whitten, Norman. 1986. *Black Frontiersmen: A South American Case*. 2nd ed. Prospect Heights, IL: Waveland Press.

Whitten, Norman E., and Dorothea S. Whitten. 2011. *Histories of the Present: People and Power in Ecuador*. Urbana, IL: University of Illinois Press.

Whitten, Norman E., and Rachel Corr. 1999. "Imagery of 'Blackness' in Indigenous Myth, Discourse, and Ritual." In *Representations of Blackness and the Performance of Identities*, edited by Jean Muteba Rahier, 213–34. Westport, CT: Greenwood Press.

# 5

# Law, Silence, and Racialized Inequalities in the History of Afro-Brazil

## Brodwyn Fischer, Keila Grinberg, and Hebe Mattos

### INTRODUCTION

The relationship between Afrodescendants and the law in Latin America is highly complex; it is rooted in the violence of slavery, muddled by the legal system's importance in unraveling enslavement's dominion, and darkened by the law's modern entanglement with durable racialized inequalities. This chapter will explore that history through a Brazilian lens, taking advantage of a rich tradition of inquiry into the legal underpinnings of racial oppression, inequality, and emancipation. The Brazilian experience should not be mistaken for Latin America's. Both legal and racial practices are intensely localized historical phenomena that cannot be easily generalized to an entire diverse region. But Brazilian scholarship has emphasized the legal dimensions of the Afrodescendant experience over many generations and from multiple perspectives. This dense scholarly tradition in matters of race and the law offers a unique opportunity to emphasize depth over breadth, thus exposing histories that can only be illuminated through intensive, multigenerational, and polyphonic scholarship. We hope that the Brazilian case will illuminate both the law's emancipatory potential and the entanglements of violence, silence, and institutional inequity that have helped to perpetuate racialized injustice across Latin America.

Brazil was the New World's first, largest, and most enduring slave society. The fact and fear of bondage shaped Afrodescendants' place in Brazil's legal order until emancipation in 1888. For a century thereafter, legally institutionalized racial inequalities persisted, both produced and cloaked by racial silence. That silence was largely shattered in the late twentieth century. As racism was named and denounced more clearly, the legal legacies of slavery became increasingly apparent, and for the first time legal remedies to racialized injustice and inequality assumed tangible form. Politicians enacted laws elevating racism to a crime and recognizing Afrodescendant rights to memory, cultural heritage, and landed property; affirmative action opened new doors to education and governmental employment; slavery came to be characterized as a crime against humanity with victims in need of reparation. Still, 130 years after slavery's abolition, its deepest legal inheritances endure in the form of state violence, racialized bias, differential access to the guarantees of citizenship, and social and economic policies with tangibly disparate racial impacts. As we trace the complex history of race and the law in Afro-Brazilian history, we hope to expose the historical roots of that fraught modern reality.

## THE LAWS OF SLAVERY

The history of race and the law in Brazil began in the Ancient Mediterranean, with the Roman and Islamic legal precepts that lay the basis for modern slavery across the Atlantic world. During the expansion of European empires, slavery's legal structures varied greatly across both regions and nations. Slave societies posed very different legal challenges than societies with slaves, slavery's racialized underpinnings varied across time and space, and the laws of slavery were often transformed by the enslaved through legal challenges, systematic resistance, or outright rebellion (Berlin 1988). This section will explore these variations. It begins with a brief history of laws of slavery in the Iberian Peninsula and the Atlantic world, and then traces the legal history of Brazil's slave regime and its significance for the broader history of slavery and race.

### From Iberia to Empire

Europeans often held common attitudes regarding slavery, but Iberian juridical traditions diverged significantly from those of France or England. To begin with, domestic slavery held a continuous place in daily life across the Iberian Peninsula; even throughout the Islamic and Medieval periods, a small but significant number of people remained enslaved. By the end of the middle ages, both the Mediterranean and Slavic slave trades impacted the Iberian Peninsula with particular force (Stanziani 2013). Between the sixteenth and eighteenth centuries, more than a million people – Slavs, Moors, "Ethiopians" – lived as slaves in the Iberian Peninsula, comprising nearly 10 percent of the population (Vincent 2000). More important, both the Portuguese and the Spanish empires constructed unified legal codes based on Roman law. This legislation – later transplanted and adapted to suit the needs of the American colonial context – had two especially important features: it regulated slaves both as property and as people, and it created ample legal space for manumission.

In the Spanish case, the legal framework could be found in the *Siete Partidas* (1265). The Siete Partidas represented Castilian King Alfonso X's attempt to implement a centralized juridical system. After the second half of the fifteenth century, when Castile and Aragon initiated Spanish unification, the *Siete Partidas* became the legal framework for Spain and its overseas empire. In Portugal, slavery's legal framework would be found in the *Ordenações Afonsinas*, a fifteenth-century legal codification derived from Roman and Canon law that sought to unify legal practice within the Portuguese Kingdom. The *Ordenações Afonsinas* (1446–1448) defined civil, fiscal, administrative, military, and penal law. That compilation was twice revised and renamed for reigning monarchs, resulting in the *Ordenações Manuelinas* (1521) and the *Ordenações Filipinas* (1603). These eventually regulated the entire Portuguese empire, including not only Brazil but also São Tomé/Príncipe, Madeira, Angola, and Mozambique in Africa, Goa in India, and Macau in China. Many of the *Ordenações*' provisions fell into disuse across the centuries, yielding incrementally to more modern laws. But in Brazil they would remain in force until the implementation of modern civil codes in Portugal (1867) and Brazil (1916).

Both the Siete Partidas and the Ordenações Filipinas mentioned slaves frequently, and both reflected significant ambivalence over the nature of enslavement. The Siete Partidas were based on the principle that slavery was a regime counter to Natural Law: "by nature, all creatures are free, especially humans." Not by chance, one of the best known and widely cited of its references to slave labor was the stipulation that "many things that go against the general regulations can be authorized in favor of freedom" (book 4, title 11, paragraph 4). This did not impede slaves from being considered beings without juridical personality, incapable of holding goods separate from their masters and subject to re-enslavement even as freedmen. All the same, the legislation did place various limits on seigniorial power. Title 22 of the Fourth Partida permitted manumission against a master's will if a slave married a free person, became a cleric, or paid for freedom. The same title prevented masters from inflicting exaggerated punishment: if, for example, a master killed his slave, even without meaning to, he could be subject to five years of banishment. Spanish legislation thus resembled Roman law in its restrictions on seigniorial power. With the incorporation of New World territories into the kingdom of Castile, Spanish law – including that which regulated slavery – became valid throughout Spanish America. It is difficult to establish to what extent the Siete Partidas were literally applied in the New World, but it is clear that at least some of their dispositions came to regulate the lives of the 2.1 million Africans brought to the Spanish colonies between 1493 and 1866. (Borucki, Eltis, and Wheat 2015, 440. During the same period, 4.7 million enslaved Africans were brought to Brazil.) The fact that many of those enslaved people and their descendants came to comprise a large free population can largely be attributed to the Siete Partidas.

The Ordenações Manuelinas shared the Siete Partidas' allowances for limited movement toward freedom, but they were centrally concerned with the delineation of the juridical principles that would undergird relations between masters and slaves. These mostly asserted the dominion of the former, even after manumission. Beyond this, the Ordenações Filipinas – unlike its antecedents – conceived slavery as a commercial practice in need of governmental control; the code in fact first mentioned African slavery *per se* in relation to commerce. Previously, laws related to slavery appeared in Ecclesiastical portions of the Ordenações, with reference to the enslavement of Moors defeated in the Christian-Muslim wars. In the Ordenações Filipinas, laws relating to slavery were mostly incorporated into sections governing goods and commerce, an indication of the importance the Atlantic slave trade had attained in the Portuguese economy. The Ordenações Filipinas governed relations between masters and slaves through Brazilian independence in 1822. Even thereafter, despite the gradual imposition of new national laws, many of the Ordenações Filipinas' regulations governing slavery remained in force.

By the end of the fifteenth century, Portuguese Atlantic expansion opened a new slave-trading frontier in Africa. Initially the trade was fed partially through prisoners taken in the Moorish wars, and partially through Portuguese participation in the prosperous North African slave market. In 1455, the Papal Bull *Romanus Pontifex* amplified religious sanction for these practices, justifying the Portuguese Crown's commerce of enslaved Africans by their possible conversion and evangelization in Christian Europe. Considered the "charter of Portuguese imperialism," the bull conceded to the Kings of Portugal powers to invade and conquer any kingdom ruled by non-Christians and to reduce their inhabitants to slavery. From that point on, captivity became the form *par excellence* through which the Portuguese empire and the Catholic faith incorporated individuals "saved" from paganism (Mattos 2001a, 143–45). The source of such captivity could be the slave trade or "just war"; in practice the two concepts often overlapped (Alencastro 2000, 168–80). The "justice" of war was determined by the king, and was generally linked to legitimate defense, to the guarantee of freedom to preach and evangelize, and for some to the guarantee of free commerce (Hespanha and Santos 1993, 396). By the end of the fifteenth century, African slavery was an integral part of Iberian societies, especially in the Portuguese Empire (Peabody and Grinberg, 2007).

The notions of just capture and just war thus held a central place in the theological-juridical thought of the Iberian empires, and were in turn extended to the New World. In Brazil, a favorable orientation toward the natural liberty of Amerindians did not prevent their enslavement, which was legitimated as just war against pagan or hostile Indians and considered legal in Portuguese America at least until the eighteenth-century Pombaline reforms (Perrone-Moises 1992). Seventeenth-century moral theologians defended a similar (and controversial) perspective in relation to Africans: legally, only just war legitimated slavery. Jesuits had often confronted sixteenth-century American colonists over issues of enslavement and mistreatment, and Catholic voices also emerged denouncing excesses committed in the context of African tribal wars or mercantile aggression of the slave traders (Gray 1987; Hespanha and Santos 1993, 409). But in practice it proved difficult to mark such moral frontiers, and "just war" continued to justify the hereditary enslavement of African "barbarians."

In both Catholic empires, slavery's legitimacy was thus built on religious and bellicose principles rather than on an explicitly racial basis. Yet stigmas and distinctions based on descent and race were certainly present. In Portugal, the Ordenações Afonsinas re-codified previous statutes regarding purity of blood, restricting access to public offices and honorific titles to "Old" Christians (families that had been Catholic for at least four generations) and excluding the descendants of Moors and Jews. The Ordenações Manuelinas extended the same restrictions to gypsies and indigenous peoples, and the Ordenações Filipinas added *negros* and *mulatos* to the list. The eighteenth-century Pombaline reforms explicitly revoked restrictions for Jews, Moors, and indigenous peoples but they remained in place for Afrodescendants, only finally shattered in Brazil by the 1824 Constitution (Carneiro 1988, 57).

These racialized stigmas had especially important implications for free Afrodescendants. Manumission was a relatively frequent phenomenon throughout the Luso-Brazilian world, the result both of Roman legal traditions and the complex mechanisms of discipline and legitimation that sustained the slave system. But manumission did not signify full freedom. Throughout the Portuguese Empire, following the tradition of Roman law, ex-slaves remained bound to their masters even after manumission, which could be revoked for ingratitude. Only those who had never been enslaved could consider themselves fully free subjects. And even among the fully free, restrictions on high offices and honorific titles would persist for four generations. The descendants of slaves would bear the mark of their ancestry, in this case inscribed in their skin and stigmatized through the explicit hierarchies of color that were created and consolidated from that time forth (Lara 2000, 103–04; Lahon 2001, 519 n82).

The religious conviction that a propensity to heresy could be propagated through "infected" blood of "Moors and Jews" also tended to extend itself to free African and Amerindian descendants over the course of the seventeenth century. In Portugal, the Archbishop of Lisbon's Constituições Sinodaes (1640) banned membership in the sacred orders to those who were "part of the Hebrew or other infected Nation, or *mulato*, or *negro*." The Archbishop of Bahia's Constituições Primeiras of 1707 reproduced that restriction, and the Portuguese state officially incorporated it with a law on August 16, 1671.

In Portugal, and especially in Brazil, colonial documentation often repeated the formulaic phrase "without a trace of the Moorish, Jewish, or Mulato race" (Carneiro 1988; Lahon 2001; Viana 2007). This repetition, ironically, is probably a signal that restrictive formulas were most often honored in the breach. In the military orders, despite a virtual obsession with Jewish blood, many men from New Christian families managed to achieve high commendations and honors, including the coveted Order of Christ (Olival 2001). In Brazil, "mulatismo" came to be seen as a problem that had to be confronted by those who wished to monopolize posts of prestige and power. As John Russell-Wood has emphasized, the repeated reiteration of rules was itself an indication that free Afrodescendants had a significant presence in prestigious colonial positions (1982).

During the same period, another type of legislation approached the presence of a free Afrodescendant population with a distinct variant of racial language. The *Pragmática* of 1749 banned "*negros* and *mulatos* of conquest" from using clothing and material symbols that indicated prestige and distinction. In this case, mixed race Afrodescendants – who could pose a threat to the seignorial class with their expectations of social ascension – were classified together with *negros*, without any distinction between the free and the enslaved. Whenever they sought to occupy public office or positions of prestige in the colonial order, their mere classification as free *pardos* or *mulatos* could serve as an impediment (Lara 2007, 329–42).

In both Portuguese and Spanish America, the large number of free and liberated Afrodescendants presented a challenge of governance for colonial officials. What was the legal difference between a freed person and an enslaved one, if physical characteristics alone were not an adequate marker and the borders between slave and free were porous? Regulation was especially difficult when it involved practices such as coartación, or self-purchase in installments, which opened ambiguous spaces between slavery and freedom across Spanish America (de la Fuente 2007). But other examples abounded as slavery hardened into an integral institution and increasing numbers of freedpersons and their descendants engendered new challenges to the socio-racial hierarchy even where their presence did not threaten slavery's institutional strength. Even before independence, racial descent began to emerge as a convenient form of legal differentiation among otherwise equivalent subjects.

## Brazil's Slaveholding Monarchy

After Brazilian independence in 1822, slavery remained fundamental, and Brazil's conservative order was in some ways reinforced by fears of revolutionary upheaval. All the same, Brazilian independence did incorporate legal reform. The 1824 Constitution negated all rights to those born in Africa, but it recognized the basic citizenship of free Afrodescendants born in Brazil. It also made merit the only valid criteria for filling civil, military, and political posts, thus granting – at least formally – equal access to all citizens and finally abolishing already weakened colonial distinctions.

Constitutional equality was belied, however, by the massive illegal slave trade. In 1831, Brazil ceded to years of British pressure and formally outlawed the slave trade as a condition of national recognition. Yet in open defiance of British pressure, Brazilians continued to illegally traffic slaves for two decades thereafter. Fueled by the coffee economy, slave traders imported more captives in the first half of the nineteenth century than ever before, and some one million enslaved people were brought illegally to newly independent Brazil.

The final extinction of slave trafficking after 1850 brought enormous transformations in Brazil's juridical, demographic, political, social, and economic structures. Slave prices rose, and internal trafficking intensified, with massive displacement of enslaved people from the stagnant Northeast to the booming coffee regions of the Center-South. These changes, as well as a general push toward intensified labor exploitation in the coffee regions, represented a fundamental break in the customary expectations of enslaved people throughout Brazil. In a country where slaves worked in disparate settings and often outnumbered their masters, a wide variety of customary privileges had evolved, rooted in the ambiguities of slave law and the need to balance carrots and sticks in order to uphold the slave system. In many settings, enslaved people came to expect familial integrity, limited economic autonomy (including the right to maintain their own savings), the opportunity for self-purchase, and some degree of occupational mobility within slavery. When these and other rights were denied, in violation of customary expectations, slaves' struggles became increasingly public and oppositional.

These forms of resistance varied greatly. Some were classified as criminality, from petty thefts and small acts of violence to intentional murder of owners and overseers or mass insurrections. Punishment for these acts was particularly harsh: Brazil's first Criminal Code (1830) considered slaves a special class of juridical persons, responsible for their acts and subject to uniquely harsh penalties, including death. Other forms of resistance involved work slowdowns or even proto-strikes. And still others concentrated on the transition to freedom, as slaves fled their masters, established maroon communities (*quilombos*) on a greater scale, and did everything in their power to obtain manumission. This resulted in the proliferation and politicization of judicial suits that used the courts, sometimes successfully, to question illegal enslavement, enforce informal promises of manumission, and demand the right to purchase freedom even against a master's wishes (Chalhoub 1990; Gomes 2006; Grinberg 1994, 2002; Mattos 1995; Pirola 2015; Reis 1993a, 1993b).

In partial reaction to this wave of resistance and in an effort to centrally control what many had come to see as slavery's inevitable demise, the Brazilian government took the first formal step toward abolition: the so-called Law of the Free Womb of 1871. In addition to freeing all children born of enslaved mothers, the law recognized numerous customary rights, including those to accumulate savings and self-purchase. In recognizing enslaved people's right to rights and limiting seignorial authority, and in placing the imperial government at the forefront of the emancipation process, the Free Womb law had an enormous symbolic impact. With the slave trade ended, and every Brazilian born on national territory from that point forward considered free, the Free Womb law firmly established that slavery's days were numbered. An 1885 law freed all enslaved persons over the age of sixty (but also freed their masters of any responsibility for their maintenance), and a wave of mass flights, rebellions, and conditional manumission removed many others from bondage. By the time of final abolition of slavery in 1888, only around 600,000 people remained enslaved (Conrad 1972; Costa 1966; Machado 1994; Mattos 1995; Toplin 1975).

## The Historiography of Law and Slavery

Historiographical controversy long obscured the deeper legal dynamics and implications of these developments. In 1947, Frank Tannenbaum published *Slave and Citizen*, a pioneering comparative study of divergent race relations in the United States and Latin America. For Tannenbaum, Brazil served as a historical counterpoint (and foil) to the United States' harshly racialized legal regime. During Brazil's era of slavery, the Iberian legal corpus, Catholic religious recognition, high manumission rates, and liberal racial mixture had laid the basis for a society in which racial discrimination was supposedly mostly devoid of legal sanction. In the United States, by contrast, manumission was tightly restricted, racial mixture was condemned, and the "one drop rule" denied social ascendance even to free Afrodescendants, resulting in widespread legalized racism.

Tannenbaum's work inspired a generation of comparative studies, including a wave of polarizing debates that eventually produced a comprehensive portrait of the inherent and indisputable violence of American slave societies (Elkins 1959; Genovese 1969). Few of these studies contested the legal differences between Brazil and the United States, but the critique of Tannenbaum's comparative conclusions was devastating: in its wake, most historians shied away from analyses that emphasized the importance of legal structures in shaping slavery and post-abolition societies (de la Fuente 2004; Grinberg 2001).

It was only in the mid-1980s, with the advent of the new social history, that this began to change. Working with judicial sources that opened rich windows into the social and political dynamics of slave societies, historians began to open new analytical terrain in relation to both criminal and civil law (Chalhoub 2001; Machado 1988, 1994; Scott 1985; Wissenbach 1988). Beyond elucidating structural and formal dimensions of Brazilian law that Tannenbaum had largely ignored, these studies sought above all to break the static coherence of structuralist analysis by highlighting agency, questioning the unity of blunt social categories, and focusing on the complexities of everyday legal practice. We now understand much more clearly the ways in which Brazil's nineteenth-century codes and policing practices created the foundations for racialized patterns of criminal justice, as well as the degree to which enslaved people worked within the legal system to delegitimize and escape slavery. We can also see much more clearly the fragmentation of the seigneurial class, and the degree to which laws and state institutions became the instruments of slavery's demise. At the same time, we can also see the limits of the law's hegemony and the many fragilities of freedom, both of which would leave important legacies for race and law in the post-abolition period.

Studies of criminal law and policing in nineteenth-century Brazil have been especially fertile in deconstructing the racial dynamics of public authority, personhood and citizenship. Criminal codes and court practices laid the bases for racially differential treatment of accused criminals. (Ferreira 2005; Flory 1981; Holloway 1993; Jesus 2007; Pires 2003; Rosemberg 2006, 2010). The ambiguous status of the enslaved (at once people and things) long vexed Brazilian jurists in the realm of civil law (Grinberg 2002). But the authors of Brazil's 1830 Criminal Code, following Book 5 of the Ordenações Filipinas, classified slaves as juridical persons, both autonomous and fully responsible for their actions. At the same time, both the 1830 code and an important criminal law of June 10, 1835, made it clear that some persons were more culpable than others. The 1830 code contained a range of punishments and penalties that applied only to slaves. The 1835 law subjected slaves to the death penalty for a range of crimes deemed insurrectionary, a provision that remained in place even after the death penalty was abolished for other Brazilians in 1870. In the words of Ricardo Pirola, the 1835 law thus "became a symbol of slavery itself in Brazil" (2015). Police practices followed suit. While the growth of urban police forces could often offer surprising paths for Afro-Brazilian mobility and formal incorporation (Rosemberg 2010), it is also clear that racialized notions of order influenced the early genesis of those forces in Rio de Janeiro and elsewhere. Police often collaborated with slave owners and local elites to enforce slave discipline, pursue vendettas, and suppress challenges to hierarchical and racialized patterns of culture, behavior, and social mobilization (Holloway 1993).

In the field of civil law, it is now clear that slaves and freedpersons pursued struggles for freedom and legal rights throughout the nineteenth century. And to a significant degree, those struggles reflected intensive engagement with the state. This emerged most clearly in the so-called *ações de liberdade* (freedom lawsuits), in which thousands of slaves sought judicial recourse – sometimes successfully – for illegal enslavement or broken manumission agreements. Plaintiffs in these suits (and the lawyers who represented them) expressed faith in the court system's power to guarantee their right to freedom, even if those rights had only been conferred informally. The sheer number of judgments that favored liberation point to the state's concrete role in emancipation. But the state's mediating role can also be seen in extrajudicial appeals made by Africans and their descendants, who wrote directly to the Emperor asking that he exercise compassion with his subjects, freeing them from punishments, conceding them special favors, or deciding in favor of appeals for liberty when all other channels had been exhausted. In relation to the state and its laws, many enslaved people acted with enormous creativity and resourcefulness, seeking to shape their own destinies in ways that clearly escaped the false dichotomy of passivity and rebellion. Collectively, it is highly likely that these actions had structural as well as individual impact, playing an important role in delegitimizing slavery over the course of the nineteenth century (Chalhoub 1990; Grinberg 1994; Mattos 1995; Russell-Wood 1982).

Freedom lawsuits called established customs into question, reshuffled relationships between slaves and masters, exposed the beliefs that enslaved people had about the judicial system, and were an important tool in the hands of slaves and lawyers seeking manumission. But they also revealed complexities within the state and among the seigneurial classes. Judges and lawyers, in particular, were driven by a wide range of beliefs about race, slavery, and their implications for codification, citizenship and the rule of law (Azevedo 1999; Grinberg 2002; Mendonça 1999; Pena 1999). In the 1870s and 1880s, as Brazilian abolitionism emerged as a full-fledged social movement and the rhythm of emancipation rapidly accelerated, slaves, lawyers, judges and politicians engaged in increasingly coordinated efforts to elaborate, interpret, apply, and claim Brazilian law in favor of freedom. The continuity and subversive power of those actions have forced a reevaluation of older historical arguments that broke Brazilian abolitionism neatly into two phases, one reformist and characterized the search for liberation within the system, and a second more radical and characterized by more extreme measures such as mass flight (Azevedo 2010; Machado and Castilho 2015). It is now clear that in Brazil, as in Spanish America, the final decades of slavery were marked by a deepening discussion of the legitimacy of property rights over living persons; legal actions took on new political significance in the context of abolitionism.

All in all, the reconsideration of law and judicial practice has resulted in a new understanding of freedom within Brazil's slave society. We now appreciate the possible forms of liberation that existed within slavery, including diverse forms of manumission (conditional, unconditional, paid), long-term contracts (*coartação*) that allowed freedom to be bought in installments, or judicial suits for freedom. We also see more clearly the web of legal strategies that bound diverse actors together in the judicial abolitionist project, and the connections between legal arguments and more radical social movements.

Yet in the early twenty-first century, a powerful wave of new historiography – also based largely in judicial sources – has begun to question the very premise that late slavery and early abolition could be understood mainly through the lens of freedom and emancipation. Every step toward manumission was countered by practices of illegal enslavement, strategies to preserve seigniorial domination, and the extension of the internal and Atlantic slave trades; legal routes to freedom were blocked by the weak reach of the law, or by its embeddedness in patriarchal systems of power. Freedmen struggled to maintain their liberty and establish a firm social status, and hundreds of thousands of Africans illegally imported after the official abolition of the slave trade found themselves in an especially vulnerable liminal space between slavery and freedom (Chalhoub 2012; Mamigonian 2017).

In all of these ways, the universe composed of slaves, the illegally re-enslaved, freedmen and free blacks was united by what Sidney Chalhoub has called "the precariousness of freedom" (Chalhoub 2011). That precariousness limited freedom's meaning for Africans and Afrodescendants before 1888, and aptly describes the everyday conditions in which they lived in the post-abolition period. In emphasizing the violence of social relations under and beyond slavery, and in returning to the long tradition of thinking about the durability and historical malleability of paternalism, this new scholarship balances the possibilities of liberty with the realities of illegal slaving, re-enslavement, and diverse forms of forced labor.

The precariousness of nineteenth-century freedom was intimately tied to one of slavery's most significant legal legacies: formal racial silence. Official silence about racial matters emerged early in Brazil as a form of quieting potential Afrodescendant mobilization (Albuquerque 2009; Chalhoub 2006; Mattos 2001b). More than fifty years after the Haitian Revolution, shaken by the US Civil War, residents of majority Afrodescendant societies were well attuned to the possibility that formal racial distinction could catalyze violent strife (Ferrer 2014). Accordingly, in the latter decades of the nineteenth century, the vast majority of imperial documentation came gradually but systematically to avoid specifying the race of free people. As abolitionist pressure mounted in the 1870s and 80s, an "ethic of silence" developed in relation to free Afrodescendants, operating in situations of formal equality even as racial language continued to stigmatize slaves and freedpersons (Mattos 2004, 25). This ethic of silence responded to the demands of people of color who sought spaces for social respectability, yet it perpetuated the association of terms of color with the stigma of slavery. Silence allowed the presumption of equality even as it rendered fragile the liberty of free people of color (Mattos 1995, 2015). After abolition, it would become the unwritten law of the land.

## A HUNDRED YEARS OF SILENCE

When slavery ended, so too did the most obvious source of Afrodescendant legal inequality: after bondage, few traces of clear racial differentiation persisted in Latin America's national laws. Such formal equality was still relatively unusual in multiracial societies. For those living under Jim Crow or apartheid, it was scarcely conceivable. Yet in Latin America, formal equality did little to attenuate racial inequality or eliminate prejudice. For scholars of the law, this has long posed a conundrum: did deep racial injustice persist because of the law, or despite it? It now seems clear that institutionalized legal prejudice had a far greater impact on patterns of racial injustice in the century after Brazilian abolition than early generations of scholars believed. Overtly *disparate treatment* was frequent; more important still was the *disparate impact* of the incomplete and fragmentary reach of Latin American law. Scholars have traditionally defined legal discrimination by North Atlantic standards, seeking out clear instances of purposeful racial prejudice as evidence of institutionalized inequalities. But in Brazil, as in much of the rest of Latin America, phenomena such as widespread informality, weak civil rights protections, and incomplete access to public rights and benefits had a radically disparate impact on Afrodescendants in the century after abolition, effectively blocking full legal equality.

## Abolition and the Bureaucratic Construction of Racial Silence

Brazil's Lei Áurea, signed by Princess Regent Isabel on May 13, 1888, disintegrated the legal foundation of Brazilian racial inequality with deceptive simplicity: "Slavery is declared abolished in Brazil: All legislation to the contrary is revoked." The decree angered former slave owners with its terse refusal to provide indemnification or legally mandate forced labor; it disappointed abolitionists such as Joaquim Nabuco and André Rebouças by failing to fortify abolition with "rural democracy," educational commitments, or vocational training (Alonso 2015). But the law's terseness was also its essence. Decreed when most of Brazil's Afrodescendant population was already free, the Abolition Law gave continuity to a fundamental feature of Brazil's multi-secular process of liberation. The state clipped the cord of bondage, but no more: once emancipated, freedpeople and their children would be mere persons, neither marked nor aided by special legal status.

Subsequent legal measures taken after the advent of the Brazilian Republic in 1889 reinforced the state's reluctance to legally differentiate liberated slaves. In 1890, slavery's densest logbooks burned, rendering former slave status less plain (Chazkel 2015). In 1891, the republican constitution consecrated legal equality and welcomed all residents and children of Brazilian parents as citizens, regardless of racial or geographic origin (1891 Constitution, articles 69 and 72). As noted previously, the terms "preto" and "negro" gradually faded from official documentation in the decades after abolition: without them, the formal mark of slavery lost bureaucratic legibility. Enslavement retreated from the written record: Brazil, like much of Latin America, would construct a highly unequal liberal order without overt legal distinction.

Documentary omission matters to the history of law and race because it has often been mistaken for incipient racial equality. But it represented instead a deeply rooted and strategic commitment to the ethic of racial silence, capacious enough to encompass both dreams of equality and affirmations of prejudice. After abolition, in the context of radicalized republican demands for civic equality, racial silence became a zone of compromise wherein deep prejudice could exist without provoking political resistance.

Silence was also central to the ideologies and policies of whitening, Brazil and Latin America's *sui generis* solution to the dilemmas posed by scientific racism in societies peopled overwhelmingly by non-European populations (Andrews 2004; Azevedo 1987; Schwarcz 1993; Skidmore

1993; Wade 2014). Without denying the validity of Spencerian racial hierarchies, Latin America's nineteenth-century intellectual elite argued that the key to the racial dilemma was not separation or expulsion, but rather "whitening"; a flood of European immigrants would gradually absorb Afrodescendant traces. Although whitening policies were justified with racist language and often involved racially exclusive immigration legislation, their eventual success in fact – and somewhat paradoxically – depended on formal racial silence: as generations merged across the color line, they could not be separated by bureaucratic distinction.

Whitening and silence both reflected deep racial prejudice. But they were effective precisely because they resonated paradoxically with many grassroots strategies for emancipation and social mobility. Everyday politics among Afrodescendants sought to incarnate visions of freedom and citizenship centered on mobility, family, land, work, or urban permanence (Chalhoub 1992; Fraga 2016; Mattos 1995). Such visions were intensely emancipatory. But their racial meaning was subterranean, at once too obvious to require articulation and too subversive to risk proclamation. In a context where racialization was almost inevitably associated with discrimination and the fear of re-enslavement, Afrodescendants across Brazil often – though certainly not always – chose to embrace a silent, sinuous pursuit of full freedom.

Whitening, racial depoliticization, and quiet pursuits of full freedom spurred powerful bureaucratic logics. Echoing the mid-nineteenth century and anticipating a Latin American trend, Brazil's 1920 census deliberately omitted Brazil's racial demographics (Loveman 2014; Nobles 2000). Many civil registries and government agencies erased racial queries from their stock forms and police records formally (if not actually) eliminated racial identification for witnesses and many crime victims. Even Brazil's nascent eugenics movement began to de-emphasize racial heredity as a factor in the analysis of national backwardness, emphasizing instead hygiene, nutrition, and education (Hochman 1998; Hochman and Lima 1996; Stepan 1991). By the 1930s, when Brazilian law entered a period of rapid expansion, formal racial silence had largely enveloped the realms of policy and governance.

## Transnationalism, Institutions, and "Racial Democracy"

For more than a century, this legacy of racial silence obscured the law's role in structuring post-abolition racial injustice. Numerous scholars have wrestled with the ambiguous legacies of Brazil and Latin America's myths of racial democracy, especially in comparison with the United States and South Africa (Alberto 2011; Andrews 1996; de la Fuente 2001; Fry 1996; Seigel 2009; Telles 2004; Wade 1997 see also Chapter 8). Yet few have considered the constitutive role of racial silence in constructing that myth. For most twentieth-century observers, steeped in forms of racialized violence and discrimination that required explicit labeling and crudely disparate treatment, it was difficult to conceptualize institutional or legal discrimination within a legal framework where race so rarely spoke its name. If racial categories were not strictly defined or fixed, and if no law sanctioned disparate treatment, was it not logical to think of Latin America as a pioneer in color-blind governance, where apparent racial disparities would eventually melt away because they lacked formal sanction or enforcement?

Such views undergirded the transnational exchange that projected Brazil as a "racial paradise" worthy of emulation (Hellwig 1990). Theodore Roosevelt found silence an intriguing solution to the racial problem (1914). Black activists and scholars from W. E. B. DuBois to Robert Abbott to E. Franklin Frazier constructed Brazil's race-blind law as an idealized foil to Jim Crow (Du Bois 1914; Frazier 1942; Hellwig 1992). White scholars from the US and elsewhere largely followed this comparative logic, noting instances of racial prejudice but affirming the lack of legal distinction.

Within Brazil, visions of race relations were considerably more complex (Guimarães 2001). White scholars such as Gilberto Freyre and Arthur Ramos had been mentored by scientific racists, and they extensively documented Brazilian racial prejudice (Freyre 1959a, 1959b, 1951; Ramos 1939, 74). Yet they also staked international careers on Brazil's racial cordiality and lack of institutionalized racial difference. For Afro-Brazilian activists and scholars, the picture was more fraught still. They felt racial prejudice keenly, both in Brazilian society and in the attitudes of white researchers (Alberto 2011, 217–19). They sought to expose the shortcomings of "theoretical" legal equality, calling for a "second abolition" that could close the gap between "*o negro legal*" and "*o negro real*" and allow black men to struggle for their "right to rights" (Alberto 2011, 171–72). They successfully pursued the criminalization of racial prejudice with the pioneering Afonso Arinos law in 1951 (Andrews 2004, 178, 180; Grin and Maio 2013; Telles 2004, 37–38). Yet black intellectuals were critically aware of legal neutrality's value, and of what Paulina Alberto terms the "emancipatory, claims making potential" of a doctrine that promised to model race relations for a world in which racial justice was newly elevated to a human right (Alberto 2011, 179, 176).

The ideal of racial democracy, like the ethic of racial silence, thus proved an accommodating space for both conservative paternalism and emancipatory racial mobilization (Chapter 8). And it was rooted in the deceptive reign of formal legal equality: what separated Brazil from the United States was not a lack of discrimination, but rather a lack of legal sanction for it, which left ample room for Frank Tannenbaum's idealistic prediction:

Physical proximity, slow cultural intertwining, the growth of a middle group ... and the slow process of moral identification work their way against all seemingly absolute systems of values and prejudices ... while the mills of God grind slow, they grind exceedingly sure. Time ... will draw a veil over the white and black in this hemisphere, and future generations will look back upon the record of strife ... with wonder and incredulity.

(1946, 128)

## Legal History and the Unveiling of Brazilian Racial Prejudice

Tannenbaum's optimism proved misplaced. Racial democracy was always a fragile edifice, undone even as it was constructed. A generation of UNESCO-funded studies exposed widespread racial inequality in the 1940s and 50s (Azevedo 1955; Bastide and Fernandes 1955; Costa Pinto 1953; Guimarães 1999, 2004; Maio 1999; Wagley 1952). The military government's crass brandishing of racial democracy as a weapon against black organizing restricted its pliability, and the US civil rights movement and global anti-colonial currents transformed the comparative context (Alberto 2011, 245, 249; Dávila 2010). Formal legal equality was no longer distinctive, and as attention shifted to subtler lived realities of racism, Brazil's stubborn racial injustices emerged in sharp relief. Modernizing narratives that posited that a society of classes would subsume racial inequality proved historically sterile (Chakrabarty 2000; Fernandes 1965). By the 1990s, both Brazilian and international scholars had produced overwhelming evidence of historically rooted discrimination in employment, education, policing, and everyday social interactions, and few would argue that racial cordiality or silence had produced racial justice (Adorno 1999; Alberto 2012; Andrews 2004; Fernandes 1965; Guimarães 2006; Hasenbalg 1979; Ianni 1966; Lovell 1991; Reichman 1999; Sheriff 2000; Silva and Hasenbalg 1988, 1992; Telles 2004).

This generation of critiques of racial democracy focused overwhelmingly on discriminatory practice rather than legal structure. Yet some also directly contested the notion that Brazilian law had no explicit role in perpetuating racial inequality, particularly in the areas of immigration and criminal law. Florestan Fernandes and Roger Bastide first noted the role of openly discriminatory immigration policies in structuring Afrodescendant opportunities (Bastide and Fernandes 1955; Fernandes 1972). Subsequent research documented an elaborate legal structure that served to restrict non-European migration until the 1940s and provided disproportionate access to state assistance and property acquisition for white laborers (Azevedo 1987; Hernández 2013; Seyferth 2002, 2007; Skidmore 1993). Immigration and colonization policies were the legal backbone of whitening, and did much to explain the racially patterned economic inequalities that characterized the Brazilian Southeast, as well as the regional disparities that cemented Brazilian racial inequalities on a national scale.

The historical study of criminal law and procedure has likewise produced ample evidence of direct legal racial discrimination. A curious divergence between Brazil's formal criminal codes and the body of jurisprudence that guided judicial practice long obscured the racial assumptions undergirding republican law. The 1890 Brazilian Criminal Code adhered mostly to the so-called classical school of criminology, wherein all persons were considered equal individuals, invested with free will and subject to repression and punishment only on the basis of their criminal acts. But post-abolition Brazilian jurisprudence and practice were deeply influenced by the Italian "positivist" school of criminology, which held that individuals had different inherent proclivities to crime and ought to receive differential treatment (and even preventative discipline) based on their racial, cultural, or psycho-social characteristics (Álvarez 2003; Fischer 2008; Fry 1985; Fry and Carrara 1986; Ribeiro Filho 1994). Given this duality, evidence of entrenched racist practice in criminal law resides well below the surface of Brazil's official legal codes, deep in the treatises that shaped jurisprudence and the juridical rationales that shaped case law and police practice.

For many decades, scholars of Brazilian race relations ignored these sources, in part because so many early advocates of racial democracy emerged from the tradition of racist criminal anthropology, and in part because the tropes of African primitivism and Afro-Brazilian cultural marginality endured far longer than biological determinism (Fernandes 1965; Ramos 1939). Beginning in the 1970s, this changed, and scholars began to highlight three areas in which Brazilian criminal law and practice sanctioned explicit racial inequity. The first involved the criminalization and persecution of Afro-Brazilian cultural and political practices, not only capoeira but also Afro-Brazilian religion, music, and healing (Borges 2001; Butler 1998; Guillen 2008; Holloway 1989, 1993; Líbano Soares 1994; Maggie 1992; Ozanam 2013; Ozanam and Guillen 2015; Pires 2004). The second involved the racialization of certain seemingly neutral criminal categories such as vagrancy or arms possession (Chalhoub 1996, 2001; Cunha 2002; Fausto 1984; Fraga 1996; Holloway 1993; Huggins 1984; Kowarick 1987). And the last involved discriminatory practices within the Brazilian police and judicial system, which were rooted in positivist criminology and resulted in higher rates of arrest and conviction among Afrodescendants, as well as decreased protection for Afrodescendant victims of crime (Adorno 1999; Carrara 1990, 1998; Caulfield 2000; Cunha 2002; Fry 1999; Ribeiro Filho 1994).

Together, these discriminatory criminal laws and practices had a powerful impact on Brazilian racial inequalities in the century after 1888, hampering Afro-Brazilian cultural organization, stigmatizing Afrodescendants as "marginals" and "criminals," denying them civil rights and full freedom, and depriving them of equal protection. The gulf thus opened mattered doubly because Brazil's few twentieth-century anti-discrimination laws were conceived in the criminal realm. The 1951 Afonso Arinos law was one of the earliest in Latin America to define racial discrimination as a punishable (if minor) crime, and was an important predecessor to several provisions of the 1988 Constitution and the Lei Caó of 1989. Yet it gave initial jurisdiction to the investigative police and public prosecutors, whose quotidian practice often incorporated racist assumptions and whose case overload precluded energetic pursuit of most claims. The few cases that advanced to trial often received short shrift from a judiciary that incorporated few Afrodescendants and frankly questioned the possibility of racial bias in a society without clear racial demarcations (Hensler 2006–2007, 273–74, 337). Given this, and the mistrust it generated, it comes as no surprise that the 1951 law resulted in few convictions (Hensler 2006–2007; Silva Jr, 2000). Just as importantly, a biased criminal justice system imposed upon Afrodescendants a permanent vulnerability that exacerbated incentives to enter into clientelist and neo-clientelist relationships capable of protecting them from the police abuses and providing adjudication for disputes (Fischer 2008; Santos 1977).

Racialized thought influenced numerous other institutions and structures at the heart of Brazilian governance. Certain public entities – the diplomatic corps, the navy and the air force – made whiteness a requirement for high-level employment (Maio 2015, 78; Skidmore 1993). Racism also partially inspired the most important limitation of Brazilian political citizenship; the literacy requirement for voting (decreed in the Saraiva law of 1881 and imposed constitutionally until a 1985 amendment) emerged in partial response to the prospect of politically empowered free Afrodescendant voters (Alencastro 2014; Costa 2013; Graham 1990; Moreira 2003).[1] Racist thought impregnated public health and urban reform policies beginning in the belle-époque, explaining why yellow fever was combated so much more vigorously than tuberculosis, and why Afro-Brazilian residents disproportionately bore the costs of urban sanitation campaigns and slum removal (Benchimol 1990; Carvalho 1987; Chalhoub 1996; Fischer 2008; Meade 1997; Needell 1987). In all of these ways, it is now difficult to sustain any serious argument that Brazilian law or institutions were racially neutral in the century following abolition.

## Disparate Impact, Informality, and Institutional Structure: New Critical Perspectives

All the same, Tannenbaum's ghosts persist. Brazil's patterns of overt racialization still pale in comparison to those found in South Africa or the Jim Crow South (Cottrol 2013; Marx 1998). Absent the familiar signals of specifically racial discrimination—clear legal delineation of racial categories, segregationist laws, bans on intermarriage, red-lining, voting obstruction, political and civil rights blatantly limited along racial lines –the questions still remains: if Brazil's institutions were so much less explicitly racialized than those of the US, why were Brazil's Afrodescendant peoples still so much worse off their white counterparts in Brazil, and even their black counterparts in the US, a hundred years after slavery disintegrated (Andrews 1992)?

Part of the answer can be found in the durability of Brazil's "vertical" inequalities, deep socioeconomic gulfs that entwine with racism to perpetuate unbridgeable divides (Telles, 2004; see also Chapter 3). But other

---

[1] Murilo (2002) adds the insight that the 1891 constitution relieved the state of the obligation to provide primary education even as it reaffirmed the literacy requirement for political citizenship.

explanations contest the very assumption that Brazilian law harbored relatively weak racial bias. Here, the key analytical leap involves racialized legal biases that are formally inscribed – comprising structure as well as practice – yet never explicitly articulated in racial terms. This logic here resembles that of the "disparate impact" strategies that have deeply influenced civil rights struggles across the globe for the past half-century. In both cases, the point is to dismantle the artifices of racial silence, exposing the ways in which institutions perpetuate racial inequality behind a veil of linguistic or conceptual neutrality (Carle 2011; Hensler 2006–2007; Hunter and Shoben 1998; Tushnet, Fleiner and Saunders 2013, 319–22).

This is an especially significant argument for Brazilian law because of the coincidence of racial silence and social distinction in the construction of Brazil's post-abolition racial order. Racial terminology was often deliberately absent from Brazilian law, but the silence was filled with a cacophony of other distinctions. Despite constitutional affirmations of equality, Brazil's legal system in fact functions on the basis of seemingly infinite bureaucratic and categorical inequalities. Theoretically universal rights and public benefits are unequally apportioned – by law – depending on factors such as bureaucratic agility, education, employment sector, employment status, regional origin, family status, and place of residence (Fischer 2008). The categories of distinction that regulate these inequalities are apparently racially neutral. Yet they correlate highly with skin color, so much so that their disproportionate racial impacts are easily predictable. Lawmakers know this when writing such laws, and policemen and bureaucrats know this in enforcing them. The logic of disparate impact can thus be applied to Brazil's twentieth-century legal history: regardless of intent, laws or practices with clearly disproportionate impacts upon members of disparate racial groups must be understood as part of the institutional structure of racial inequality.

Brazilian labor and social welfare law furnish a prime example of racially disparate impact. Brazil came relatively late to social and economic rights, even within Latin America (Carvalho 2002; Gomes 1979; Hochman 2003). But after 1930, under President Getúlio Vargas, Brazil's labor and social welfare legislation sprinted forward. By the 1940s, constitutional and statutory law entitled Brazilians to labor protections and social welfare entitlements as generous as any in the western hemisphere. Yet the devil was in the details: Brazil's labyrinthine legal structure effectively restricted theoretically universal rights to a small subset of the population (Cardoso 2010; Fischer 2008; Gomes 1988; Santos 1979). This occurred partially through categorical distinction: the group of "workers" endowed with rights consisted not of all laboring people, but rather of formal-sector workers who were not employed in domestic or rural labor; and only members of legally constituted families could claim most pension, housing, welfare, and death benefits. Bureaucratic obstacles further narrowed the path to rights: no benefit could be claimed without official documentation of birth, marriage, and work status, and complex procedures mediated full entitlement. As in other countries (including the US), the sphere of inclusion gradually expanded, even under military rule between 1964 and 1985. But expansion coincided with significant devaluation of rights' real value, and the gradient structure that allowed certain classes of privileged workers disproportionate claim to public resources remained firmly in place.

The racial consequences of this were not entirely straightforward; disparate impact could work both ways. For Afrodescendant men in urban areas, industrialization opened significant opportunities for formal-sector work, particularly after Getúlio Vargas signed a 1932 decree mandating that two-thirds of all formal employees be Brazilian-born (Andrews 1991, and 2004, 160–64). With formal-sector jobs came formal-sector benefits; Brazilian labor law's well-known failure to fulfill its promises notwithstanding, the expansion of public regulation and welfare contributed mightily to both the reality and perception of social mobility among formal-sector workers in the mid-twentieth century (Fischer 2008; Fontes 2016; French 2004; Gomes 1988). Even those formally excluded from labor and social welfare legislation gained hope of a legible publicly sanctioned pathway to richer forms of citizenship that did not exist before the 1930s (Cardoso 2010, ch. 4; Rios and Mattos 2005).

At the same time, Afrodescendant workers, and especially Afrodescendant women, disproportionately labored in sectors explicitly excluded from economic citizenship. Although racially specific statistics are scarce before the 1970s, we know that Afrodescendant women comprised the overwhelming majority of urban female domestic employees from the 1940s through the 1980s, and that Afrodescendant men composed the majority in occupations typically performed off the books (Costa Pinto 1952; Lovell 1994, 17–18, 2000, 2006; Pierson 1942). Analysis of census statistics from 1940 forward indicates that Afrodescendant men counted disproportionately among agricultural workers; just as important, some longitudinal studies suggest that rates of inter-generational mobility may have been considerably lower among non-white populations (Telles 2004, 143–44). By the 1990s, the percentage of black and brown workers engaged in unskilled rural manual labor was twice as large as that of white workers, and the average income earned by those workers was also much less (Lovell 1994, 17–21, and 1999, 407; Telles 2004, 118–119). Rates of formal marriage also tended to be lower among Afrodescendant populations, which meant that common-law spouses and widows had considerably reduced access to public welfare before the legal incorporation of concubinage in the mid-twentieth century (Caulfield 2012). While deeper research is necessary to document the extent and impact of differential access to Brazilian social and economic citizenship, particularly across generations, it seems clear that both categorical and procedural obstacles had at least some role to play in the persistence of racialized inequality through the 1980s.

Disparate impact analysis can also be applied to the laws that fostered divergent regional development patterns in Brazil, both through economic federalism and through uneven state support for economic infrastructure and modernization. From the very beginning of the Republic in 1889, federalism favored the wealthy South. States controlled export revenues from their booming coffee economies, and São Paulo was particularly effective in converting both export revenues and untaxed profits into backward linkages that would facilitate subsequent industrial development, which in turn undergirded claims to regional superiority (Klein and Vidal Luna 2014, 73; Love 1980; Weinstein 2015). The South also enjoyed enhanced access to public-private infrastructural partnerships; while liberal mythology held that private initiative and state-level subsidies fueled the South's economic growth, in fact federal law at various points facilitated immigration, guaranteed international loans to stabilize coffee prices, and ensured returns on the private transportation networks that created most of Brazil's wealth and early industrial investment (Dean 1969; Klein et al. 2014; Summerhill 2003). At mid-century, when the federal government assumed a larger role in fostering industrial development and infrastructure, the regional bias only deepened: federal roads, power plants, and subsidies concentrated in the South, and the few initiatives that prioritized the Northeast were notoriously corrupt and ineffective. The Northeast's share of industrial income actually dropped from 12.1 percent in 1940 to 6.2 percent in 1970 (Merrick and Graham 1979, 139); in that year its leading industrial center (Recife) employed only 1.9 percent of the Brazil's industrial workforce and accounted for only 1.4 percent of industrial production (Melo 1978, 189–90). Measures promoting human capital showed a similar imbalance, especially with regard to public health and education. In 1980, the Southeast greatly outpaced the Northeast in literacy (79.3%/47.7%), high school enrollment

(26%/17%), piped water (65.9%/30.1%), sewage service (56.2%/16.4%), electricity (81.3%/42%) and life expectancy (56.4 years/47 years) (Merrick and Graham 1979, 261; Wood and Carvalho 1988, 73).

The net impact was extreme regional disparity that closely mirrored Brazil's racial demography (and regional racial ideology) (Lovell 2000; Telles 2004; Weinstein 2015). Brazil's most Afrodescendant region (the Northeast) became the "capital of underdevelopment" while its whitest major city (São Paulo) became Latin America's leading industrial center. Even within regions, the rural areas where Afrodescendant populations concentrated lagged far behind urban infrastructural and industrial advances. This disequilibrium produced massive regional and rural-to-urban migration, but it did not eliminate racialized disequilibria. The Northeast remained home to the largest proportion of Afrodescendant Brazilians (Lovell 1994, 16). And urban geographies mirrored national ones, concentrating public resources in the whitest formal neighborhoods and imposing the heaviest costs of development on peripheries and favelas. While it is clear that Brazil is not as racially segregated as the United States (Telles 2004), Afrodescendant populations are most heavily represented in the poorest and least-well serviced urban regions, and blackness has historically correlated with poor access to urban public resources (Abreu 1988; E. Pinheiro 2002; Fischer 2007, 2008; Holston 2008, ch. 5; Marques 2013; Rolnik 1989). While scholars rarely explain these geographically distorted patterns as specifically legal phenomena, they were clearly rooted in the legal structures that regulated property, tax policy and the allocation of public goods, and their disproportionate impact on Afrodescendant populations should be understood as part of the legal infrastructure of racial inequality.

A final area of disparate impact analysis involves not the distribution of public resources, but rather distribution of the rule of law itself. Legal scholars have substantially understudied the impact of law's weak reach, in Brazil and the Global South but also in the North Atlantic. The law's absence or inaccessibility rarely emerges as a structural feature of the legal system, and analysts often accept a modernizing narrative in which the legalized sphere gradually encompasses an ever-greater proportion of public social relations. It is evident, however, that in Brazil this pattern did not hold. In the twentieth century, three dimensions of weak legal protection or jurisdiction became especially significant permanent features of the Brazilian legal system: the public violation and inaccessibility of civil rights guarantees; the overwhelming inaccessibility of the law's positive protections; and the tacit acceptance of extensive informal housing and employment. We often lack direct evidence that these features were conceived with racial intent easily separable from other social biases, but they disproportionately impacted Afrodescendant populations and thus served to further entrench the racial inequalities inherited from slavery.

The weakness of civil law protections is a perennial theme in recent analyses of Brazilian democracy. José Murilo de Carvalho has highlighted Brazil's ordinal inversion of North Atlantic patterns of rights extension, whereby social rights were granted by a state still unwilling to guarantee personal freedom and the rule of law (Carvalho 2002). Paulo Sérgio Pinheiro has argued forcefully for the corroding impact of weak civil and human rights on the possibilities of real democracy in Brazil (Pinheiro 2000, 2002); James Holston and Teresa Caldeira have likewise posited that the stunted development of civil citizenship has created "disjunctive" and incomplete forms of democracy (Caldeira 2000; Caldeira and Holston 1999; Holston 2008). Numerous analysts have made more specific arguments about civil rights violations by police, especially in the escalating cycles of violence that have seized Brazilian cities since the 1980s (Cano 2010b; Feltran 2011; Zaluar 1985, 1994).

We still lack adequate historical analysis of the trajectory of Brazilian civil rights, and relatively few scholars have rigorously considered the specific impact of racial bias on their disregard. Still, extant studies suggest that Afrodescendant populations have suffered disproportionate impact from abuse of public power and weak civil rights guarantees: they have been more often killed by police, they have spent longer periods illegally imprisoned, they have been more likely to be harassed and abused, and they have had weaker access to legal protections against private violence (Adorno 1999; Cano 2010a, 2010b; Fry 1999; Telles 2004). More subtly, it seems clear that civil rights abuses and loose public guarantees are historically rooted in notions of private jurisdiction over subordinates that were directly inherited from slavery (Albuquerque 2009; Carvalho 2002; Holston 2008), and that the construction of seemingly neutral categories of "worker" and "marginal" that mediate civil rights violations has a strong racial dimension (Fischer 2008; Zaluar 1985). Even in the absence of the explicitly racialized lynchings and beatings that made racial injustice so palpable in the Jim Crow South, Brazil's Afrodescendant populations have suffered disproportionately from both direct state abuse and unwillingness to guarantee bodily integrity, security, and freedom of expression.

The racialized impact of weak enforcement of positive legal rights and guarantees has been considerably less well studied than that of direct civil rights abuses. Brazilian scholars, when conceiving the relationship between law and society, frequently resort to the old adage, "for my friends, everything; for my enemies, the law!" (da Matta 1991; Holston 2008) Along those lines, many activists and academics have argued that Brazilian law works systematically to oppress its poorest citizens. The point is valid but incomplete. Brazilian law has often served historically to preserve hierarchy and perpetuate violence. But paradoxically it has also opened terrains of opportunity. For populations emerging from slavery, equality under the law signified one of the only conceivable routes to fuller freedom; and as law has proliferated, the rights that it upholds have become ever more expansive (Fischer 2008). The obstacle to equality was not law; it was rather a legal system that made it nearly impossible to access public rights and guarantees.

The problem of legal access involves both structure and practice. As in many civil law systems, ordinary Brazilian citizens have had historical difficulty making claims based on constitutional provisions. Without specific legislation, individuals can only claim constitutional guarantees when an agent of the state violates them. Binding precedent (*súmula vinculante*) did not exist before 2004, which meant that constitutional claims had to be tried on a case-by-case basis, clogging courts and imposing high costs. Class action suits were virtually unknown in Brazil before 1985, further limiting the repercussions of judicial decisions involving constitutional law (Gidi 2003). Although claims of racial bias have recently achieved some success in labor courts (Hensler 2006–2007), for most of the twentieth century the lack of precedent and class action has also weighed heavily in other realms of civil law, even without taking into account the backlog, bureaucracy, and high costs that also impede access. And in the arena of criminal law – that most accessed by common citizens, and also one of the only places where instances of racism can be directly denounced – all of those problems have been compounded by judicial bias, police abuse, and overload that has led most common complaints to be ignored (Hensler 2006–2007; Racusen 2002). The net result is that positive legal rights have served as aspirational tools but not as universal guarantees. Even laying aside the question of racial bias in judicial decision making, the structure of Brazil's legal system has made it difficult for the people who most need the equalizing power of the law to make full use of it. Afrodescendants have thus not generally benefited from specific protections against racism, and have suffered disproportionately from the inaccessibility of civil, political, and economic guarantees.

A final area where the law's weak reach has had a disparate impact on Afrodescendant Brazilians involves the overwhelming centrality of informality to Brazilian political and economic systems (Cardoso 2016; Fischer 2008; Gonçalves 2013; Holston 2008). As in much of Latin America, informality in Brazil has long been widespread, rooted largely in the unrealistic aspirations of the legal structure. Many of the laws governing employment, housing, public health, and safety have required resources that poor Brazilians do not have and wealthier Brazilians do not expend on their behalf; they have also often implied levels of public authority over private life that many Brazilians find intolerable. In that context, informality emerged historically as an attractive alternative to the legal sphere, yet another zone of compromise where popular aspirations converge with elite exploitation. For the poor, informal housing and employment have facilitated rural-to-urban migration and social mobility, allowing them footholds in geographies of opportunity that would otherwise have been inaccessible. For the economic elite, informality has offered opportunities for greater profit and the skirting of labor and safety regulations; at the same time, it has allowed them to claim ownership of the most sophisticated legal and regulatory structures even when the required resources are too scarce to ensure their enforcement. For politicians, informal housing has created forms of vulnerability that amount to a political goldmine, reducing the costs of urbanization and allowing protection from the law to become a valuable commodity at election time. In Brazil and in most of Latin America, informality came to symptomize the disjunctures of idealistic legal ideologies and the pragmatic and hierarchical realities of everyday practice (Fischer 2008, 2014).

Informality has never been strictly racialized, or even classed: it has existed at every level of the Brazilian economy and in every neighborhood of every Brazilian city. It has also not necessarily been prejudicial: legality was expensive, and most of the Brazilian poor preferred the opportunities and vulnerabilities of informality to the exclusions of legal enforcement. But in the century after abolition, Afrodescendants disproportionately inhabited the informal sphere, and they thus also disproportionately endured its long-term costs. In the transition from slavery to freedom, Afrodescendants were more likely to gain access to land through squatting or informal clientelistic agreement; European migrants, conversely, often enjoyed contractual rights (Andrews 2004, 131–35). In cities, Afrodescendant workers (and especially women) disproportionately staffed informal occupations, and they most often lived informally in favelas, peripheries, and tenements. All of these informal options facilitated daily life and even social mobility, but they also left Afrodescendants especially vulnerable to informality's significant costs: brutal expulsion from homes and fields, political and economic dependency, vulnerability to abuse, reduced profits from ownership and reduced benefits from work. Informality stemmed from too many sources and served too many interests to be understood only as a source of enduring racial inequality. But informality was deeply racialized in the Brazilian imagination, and it has perpetuated subtle and powerful patterns of socio-political differentiation that can go far in explaining Brazil's ingrained racial inequalities.

## ENDING A CENTURY OF DISPARATE FREEDOMS

These were the legacies confronted by Brazilian activists and lawmakers in the mid-1980s as they set out to reconstruct Brazilian democracy nearly a century after abolition. After more than two decades of military rule (1964–1985), and in the midst of far-reaching constitutional and institutional reform, activists for racial justice were keenly aware of two especially urgent challenges. The first was to shatter the racial silence that had infused Brazilian institutional life since the nineteenth century and been a national mantra under military rule (Alberto 2011; Dávila 2003; Guimarães 2002). The second was to transform Brazil's legal structures to render racial inequalities visible, actionable and incompatible with democratic governance.

Forty years later, much has changed. Beginning with the 1988 constitution, and especially after 2001's International Conference against Racism in Durban (2001), denunciations of the myth of racial democracy proliferated across governmental agencies. Activists and politicians developed affirmative action policies that sanctioned the importance of racial identity and broke Brazil's institutional silence regarding the legacies of slavery and racism. Legislators have strengthened criminal laws against racism, and lawyers have championed successful civil and labor suits against employment discrimination. Other activists have gone further still, calling for reparations for systematic historical injustices such as the slave trade and indigenous ethnocide. By 2006, when Tianna Paschel began her research on the politics of race in Colombia and Brazil, she "did not find the silencing of racial critique" noted by previous scholars, and "black identity was considered a legitimate political category." (Paschel 2016, 4; see also Chapter 7).

But it has proved easier to expose racial inequality than to institutionally diminish it. Even as racism has come to be recognized and racial violence officially condemned, police killings and other forms of systematic lethal violence have escalated in areas marked by drug trafficking and land conflicts, disproportionately impacting Afrodescendants and indigenous peoples (Americas Watch 1987; Cano 2010; Human Rights Watch (Americas) 1997; Human Rights Watch 2009, 2016a, 2016b, 2017). Informality remains entrenched both as a strategy for survival and as a source of power. Many of the deep structures in Brazilian law and social welfare policy that perpetuate disparate racial impacts have remained stubbornly intact. Well into the twenty-first century, the challenge of creating a legal infrastructure that might promote a more genuinely democratic racial order remains daunting.

## Breaking Institutional Silence

The debates leading up to Brazil's 1988 Constitution, which institutionalized democratization after the end of Brazil's military dictatorship, were crucial in cracking the facade of racial democracy. The constitution not only legally ended more than two decades of military rule; it also emerged amidst an enormous wave of celebration of and mobilization around the hundred-year anniversary of slavery's abolition. The constitution adopted as a guiding principle the valorization of ethnic and cultural difference, thus encouraging the elaboration of laws in which explicit reference to race and ethnicity became a necessary condition for the pursuit of equality.

The impact of black and Indigenous political activism in the constitutional process still awaits deeper study (Pereira 2013). But activists' work left an indelible mark on constitutional law. For the first time, the 1988 Constitution specifically mandated racial equality. Article five declared racial discrimination a crime. Articles 215 and 216 protected all expressions of Afrodescendant and indigenous popular cultures, and extended the notion of rights to the arena of cultural practice. As in neighboring Colombia three years later, the Brazilian constitution also linked land claims to racial reparation (Gnecco and Zambrano 2000; Paschel 2016; Rosero-Labblé and Barcelos 2007). It guaranteed territorial rights to indigenous populations and promised through Article 68 of the Transitory Dispositions that "the definitive property rights of the remnants of quilombo communities still occupying their lands are legally recognized, and the State must emit the respective titles."

It took seven years for the Brazilian government to begin to articulate a legal structure to enforce Article 68's quilombo guarantees; even then, regulation proved mostly restrictive, limiting quilombo status to communities proven in juridical terms to be descendants of slaves. Over the course of the 1990s and early 2000s, activists worked with anthropologists, historians and legal experts to considerably broaden that definition, moving toward a broader ethnic interpretation that denoted virtually any self-identified black rural community (French 2009; Mattos 2008). By 2005, after more than ten years of intensifying political pressure and incremental legal wrangling, President Luiz Inácio Lula da Silva's government finally issued regulatory legislation capable of transforming quilombo self-identification into concrete land rights for thousands of black rural communities. As a result, by 2016 more than 2600 quilombola remnant communities had been recognized by the Fundação Palmares, although only a small fraction of those had received any land title.[2] 2003 legislation also established a series of social and educational programs for quilombos. One of the most significant impacts of this legislation has been a remarkable process of ethno-genesis; scholars have identified numerous processes of identity formation rooted in new public policies, providing convincing proof of ties between legal incentives and the weakening of racial silence (Arruti 2006; French 2009; O'Dwyer 2001; Oliveira 1998).

The 1988 Constitution oriented discussions about racial identity and racism that would expand and strengthen throughout the 1990s. They eventually resulted in a robust body of twenty-first-century policy initiatives that placed race and racial voice at the center of national debates about social justice, equality, and citizenship. Legal steps accelerated after 2000, first in the last years of Fernando Henrique Cardoso's government (1995–2002) and then especially under Luiz Inácio Lula da Silva (2003–10).

In direct response to the demands of a growing black movement, many of these laws mandated official recognition of Afro-Brazilian cultural forms and historical contributions. Decree 3551/2000 facilitated the institution of Afro-Brazilian cultural forms as cultural patrimony, a move that led to official recognition of musical traditions such as *samba de roda* and *jongo* and even culinary heritage such as *acarajé*. In January of 2003, Law 10639 made the teaching of Afro-Brazilian history and

---

[2] For an updated list of quilombo certifications and land titles, see www.incra.gov.br/estrutura-fundiaria/quilombolas.

culture mandatory throughout public and private school curricula, establishing a set of "National Cultural Directives for Education about Ethno-Racial Relations and the Teaching of Afro-Brazilian History and Culture." In 2008, law 11,645 extended the multicultural educational mandate to the history and culture of Indigenous Brazil (Abreu and Mattos, 2008; Lima 2013).

In realizing the hopes of these laws, the lines between scholarship and activism have often blurred, especially as Afrodescendant scholars have assumed a more central role in Brazilian universities. Some have written new textbooks that highlight Afro-Brazilian history and culture (Albuquerque and Fraga Filho 2006), and many more have produced monographs (Abreu, Mattos, and Vianna 2010). In partnership with quilombola and black movements, scholars also worked with communities to create documentary films chronicling Afro-Brazilians' collective impact on Brazilian national life, with a particular focus on cultural practices such as jongo, capoeira and maracatu (Cicalo 2012, 2015; Saillant 2010; Mattos and Abreu 2012). In all of these cases, scholars have helped to channel institutional resources that might once have promoted only erudite North Atlantic forms of learning toward the rescue and legal recognition of Afro-Brazilian historical memory. They have also helped to spark processes of ethnic visibility and identity formation much like those documented in the case of quilombos (Arruti 2006; Mattos 2006, 2008).

This new legal language of race reached far beyond symbolism in encouraging Brazilians to affirm Afro-Brazilian descent. In 1996, Fernando Henrique Cardoso responded to intense Afro-Brazilian mobilization by becaming the first Brazilian president to recognize the historical significance of Brazilian racism and to suggest affirmative action initiatives as a remedy. Though little initially materialized at the federal level, the 1990s did witness a flurry of affirmative action experiments in both private and public settings (Andrews 2004; Telles 2004). After the Durban conference, during Lula da Silva's presidency, federal action accelerated. Decree 4228/2002 instituted the National Program for Affirmative Action in the federal bureaucracy and set off a long string of progressive federal legislation. In 2003, Decree 4886 created the Special Secretariat of Policies to Promote Racial Equality (SEPPIR) to coordinate new federal initiatives. In 2010, after much controversy, the government approved the Statute of Racial Equality, which used racial self-identification as the basis for a series of anti-discriminatory policies and required that information about race and skin color be included in all public documents so as to facilitate reparation and affirmative action (Hernández 2013).[3]

In 2012, following a decade of experimentation, ethno-racial quotas became law in all federal universities (Telles and Paixão 2013). Pilot programs, beginning at the State University of Rio de Janeiro in 2000 and expanding to forty-nine federal and state universities by 2010, had already tripled black representation in Brazilian higher education between 2001 and 2011 from 10.2 percent to 35.8 percent (Corbucci 2014). But after the 2012 law, 50 percent of all spaces in federal universities would gradually come to be reserved for students who were either black or public-school alumni. According to data from Brazil's National Secretariat of Racial Equality (SEPPIR), this new policy granted approximately 150,000 black students access to universities between 2013 and 2015, and officials hoped to meet half of the full quota by 2016 (SEPPIR 2016). Though reparations have not received equivalent legal support (Saillant 2010), the National Brazilian Lawyers Association's 2015 decision to form a Truth Commission on Black Slavery may yet yield recommendations in that direction.

Affirmative action, by its very definition, forced racial language and racial identity into the socio-political mainstream. Afrodescendant self-identification is central to the implementation of those policies, serving as a prerequisite for access to new rights and opportunities. This requirement collapsed Brazil's traditional spectrum of color identities to a black-white dichotomy, and worked in conjunction with Afro-Brazilian mobilization to produce a clear increase in Afrodescendant identification (Loveman 2014; Nobles 2000). In the 2010 census, Brazil officially became a majority black nation, with 43.1 percent of the population (82 million) identifying as pardo (brown) and 7.6 percent (15 million) identifying as preto (black). The self-declared white population fell from 53.7 percent in 2000 to 47.7 percent (91 million) in 2010. These numbers have continued to grow; in 2013, 8.6 percent of the population declared themselves pretos and 45.0 percent declared themselves pardos (IBGE 2014). Public policy and grassroots mobilization have clearly converged to create a Brazilian population ever more willing to assume Afro-descent.

---

[3] The Statute of Racial Equality was the object of great controversy among Brazilian scholars. Some believed that the statute would be a great step forward in breaking racial silence (Abreu and Mattos, 2008; Saillant 2010), while others believed it would exacerbate racial division (Fry et al. 2007; Maggie and Barcelos 2002). The conflict in the National Congress over the final approval of the law in 2010 is presented in the documentary *Raça*, directed by Joel Zito Araújo and Meg Mylan (2013).

### The Institutional Limits of Racial Voice

Since the mid-1980s, the combination of activism and progressive governance has driven many obvious forms of institutionalized racism from Brazilian public life. Illiterates have voted for three decades, and their political participation has had a decisive impact in promoting racial and social inclusion. Immigration policy has long ceased to be an obvious tool of whitening, and affirmative action is the only race-based hiring policy with legal standing. Practitioners of Candomblé and Maracatu continue to be threatened by religious intolerance (Saillant 2010), but the notion that Afro-Brazilian cultural practices would be criminally prosecuted by the state seems almost inconceivable.

Many initiatives have also sought to eliminate subtler forms of institutional bias. Procedures for gaining access to public rights became simpler, public institutions expanded their presence in poor urban neighborhoods and remote regions, and rural and domestic workers gained unprecedented access to labor benefits and protections. The legal realm also began – glacially – to work more consistently to provide remedy for and protection from discrimination. Disparate racial treatment is now considered both unconstitutional and criminal, and the new visibility of race in official statistics has made it easier to expose racial discrimination. Class action suits and the extension of binding precedent have increased the impact of racially progressive decisions. Afrodescendants have gradually (if still far too slowly) increased their representation among lawmakers and legal professionals, civil and labor courts have proved responsive to complaints of racial bias, and high court judges have provided strong support for affirmative action.

Economic measures have also wrought significant progress. Because of the tight correlation between race and class, legal initiatives targeting poverty and social exclusion have disproportionately improved the lot of Brazil's Afrodescendant populations. For a brief period in the early 2000s, rapid economic expansion went hand in hand with regional pump priming, expanded welfare for the very poor, higher minimum wages, and increased access to housing, healthcare, urban services, and education. As a result, Brazil fell from its long reign as the most unequal country in the world: extreme hunger and illiteracy nearly disappeared, infant mortality plummeted, tens of millions emerged from poverty, school attendance skyrocketed, the formal job market expanded, and the poorest sectors of the population began to enjoy new access to consumer consumption. Even taking into account regressive political tendencies and the severe economic crisis of the mid-2010s, most Afro-Brazilians have better access to public resources than ever before. They also suffer less severely from the devastating inter-generational impacts of social exclusion and extreme inequality.

Yet such gains rest on fragile foundations. The 2016 political crisis, in which Dilma Rousseff was impeached amidst enormous controversy, marked a dramatic conservative shift in Brazil's political landscape. Since then, politicians who oppose much of the progressive legislation that helped to diminish racial inequality after 2000 have assumed the helm of agencies charged with enforcing it (Bessone, Mamigonian, and Mattos 2016). This, along with the general delegitimization of a state awash in accusations of corruption and patrimonialism, has placed affirmative action as well as laws promoting cultural and social equality at risk.

Even beyond the immediate political conjuncture, there are many reasons to believe that some of the deepest forms of legal-racial exclusion stubbornly persisted even through the best of times. One of the knottiest problems resides in Brazil's legal infrastructure. Access to rights and positive legal guarantees remains limited in ways that disproportionately impact Afro-Brazilians. Courts are clogged, lawyers are expensive, and individuals often lack standing to challenge unconstitutional laws or claim constitutional benefits. Judicial bias and resistance to claims of disparate impact remain an issue, along with access to adequate legal knowledge and representation. The people most in need of legal rights and protections still often have the least access to them.

A graver problem involves inadequate, discriminatory, and abusive policing (Telles, 2004, 166–69). Afrodescendant populations continue to have disproportionately weak access to police protection, and their communities continue to suffer disproportionately from drug violence and militia extortion. Long after the 1988 Constitution banned racial discrimination, police still (and even increasingly) subject poor Afro-Brazilians to disproportionate harassment, civil rights abuses, and killings. In 2015, without even counting the killings of private militias, police officers in Rio and São Paulo admitted two deaths per day in each city, and 3,320 people were killed by police across Brazil. The vast majority of victims were Afrodescendant men (Fórum Brasileira de Segurança Pública 2016, 19). In an average year, Brazilian police forces kill many times more people than those murdered during Brazil's entire twenty-one year dictatorship, and their lethality rate is far higher than that of countries with higher incidence of violent crime (Americas Watch, 1987, 1993; Brinks 2003, 2005; Caldeira 2000; Human Rights Watch (Americas)

1997; Human Rights Watch 2009, 2016, 2017). The fact that we can identify the racial injustice inherent in these murders is a consequence of the rupture of racial silence in Brazilian statistical practices (Waiselfisz, 2016). But that is scant comfort as racialized state violence continues apace. Mistrust of police makes it nearly impossible for poor Afro-Brazilian populations to fully claim their everyday protections, and may do much to explain relatively low rates of prosecution for the crime of racism as defined in 1989's Lei Caó.

It has proved equally challenging to transform the elusive role of informality in (dis)ordering Brazilian citizenship and perpetuating racial hierarchies. Subsidized housing and innovative land regularization schemes have in most places failed to end residential informality among the poor, and strict mandates for the formalization of domestic and other workers have met with mixed success. While the economic boom decreased informality's share in the labor and housing markets, there are indications that this was merely cyclical variation; in the crisis of the mid-2010s, as historically, informality provides a refuge for those who cannot afford the formal realm, exposing them to private exploitation in exchange for viable channels of work and residence. There is still a tight correlation between race and informality: the vast majority of favela residents are Afrodescendant, and those who are not are *quase pretos de tão pobres* – racialized as black because they are so poor. Indeed, the condition of the favela or the urban periphery serves as a metaphor for modern Afro-Brazil; dynamic, visible, mobilized, in some ways nationally emblematic – yet still not equally or fully integrated into the legal realm. Nearly 500 years after slavery took root on Brazilian soil, racial justice has a voice and a legal toolkit, but those have yet to alter the deep institutional structures that promote disparate racial outcomes at every level of Brazilian society.

## BIBLIOGRAPHY

Abreu, Mauricio. 1988. *Evolução urbana do Rio de Janeiro.* 2nd edition. Rio de Janeiro: IPPUR/ Jorge Zahar.
Abreu, Martha, and Hebe Mattos. 2008. "Em torno das diretrizes curriculares nacionais para a educação das relações étnico-raciais e para o ensino de história e cultura afro-brasileira e africana: Uma conversa com historiadores." *Estudos Históricos*, 21: 5–20.
Abreu, Martha, Hebe Mattos, and Carolina Vianna Dantas. 2010. "Em torno do passado escravista: As ações afirmativas e os historiadores." *Antíteses* 3, 5: 21–37.

Adorno, Sérgio. 1999. "Racial Discrimination and Criminal Justice in São Paulo." In *Race in Contemporary Brazil*, edited by Rebecca Reichman, 123–38. University Park: Pennsylvania State University Press.

Alberto, Paulina. 2011. *Terms of Inclusion: Black Intellectuals in 20th Century Brazil*. Chapel Hill, NC: University of North Carolina Press.

2012. "Of Sentiment, Science and Myth: Shifting Metaphors of Racial Inclusion in Twentieth-Century Brazil." *Journal of Social History* 37, 3: 261–96.

Albuquerque, Wlamyra de, and Walter Fraga Filho. 2006. *Uma história do negro no Brasil*. Salvador: CEAO/Fundação Palmares.

Albuquerque, Wlamyra de. 2009. *O jogo da dissimulação: Abolição e cidadania negra no Brasil*. São Paulo: Companhia das Letras.

Alencastro, Luiz Fernando de. 2000. *O trato dos viventes: Formação do Brasil no Atlântico Sul*. São Paulo: Companhia das Letras.

2014. "As cotas raciais na UNB: Um parecer apresentado ao Supremo Tribunal Federal contra a ADPF 186." In *Políticas da Raça*, edited by Flávio Gomes and Petrônio Domingues, 403–10. Rio de Janeiro: Selo Negro.

Alonso, Angela. 2015. *Flores, votos e balas: O movimento abolicionista brasileiro (1868–1888)*. São Paulo: Companhia das Letras.

Álvarez, Marcos C. 2003. *Bacharéis, criminologistas e juristas: Saber jurídico e nova escola penal no Brasil*. São Paulo: Método.

Americas Watch. 1987. *Police Abuse in Brazil: Summary Executions and Torture in São Paulo and Rio de Janeiro*. New York, NY: Human Rights Watch.

Americas Watch. 1993. "Urban Police Violence in Brazil: Torture and Police Killings in São Paulo and Rio after Five Years." *News from Americas Watch* 5, 5: 1–30.

Andrews, George Reid. 1991. *Blacks and Whites in São Paulo, Brazil, 1888–1988*. Madison, WI: University of Wisconsin Press.

1992. "Racial Inequality in Brazil and the United States: A Statistical Comparison." *Journal of Social History* 26, 2: 229–64.

1996. "Brazilian Racial Democracy, 1900–90: An American Counterpoint." *Journal of Contemporary History* 31, 3: 483–507.

2004. *Afro-Latin America, 1800–2000*. New York, NY: Oxford University Press.

Araújo, Joel Z., and Megan M. 2013. *Raça: Um filme sobre a igualdade*. Brasil/United States: Princípe Productions & Casa da Criação.

Arruti, José M. 2006. *Mocambo: Antropologia e história do processo de formação quilombola*. Bauru: EDUSC.

Azevedo, Célia M. M. 1987. *Onda negra, medo branco: O negro no imaginário das elites – século XIX*. São Paulo: Paz e Terra.

Azevedo, Elciene. 1999. *Orfeu de Carapinha: A trajetória de Luiz Gama na imperial cidade de São Paulo*. Campinas: Editora da Unicamp.

2010. *O direito dos escravos*. Campinas: Editora da Unicamp.

Azevedo, Thales. 1955. *As elites de cor numa cidade brasileira: Um estudo de ascenção social*. São Paulo: Companhia Editora Nacional.

Bastide, Roger, and Florestan Fernandes. 1955. *Relações raciais entre negros e brancos em São Paulo*. São Paulo: Anhembi.

Beattie, Peter. 2001. *The Tribute of Blood: Army, Honor, Race and Nation in Brazil*. Durham, NC: Duke University Press.

Benchimol, Jaime L. 1990. *Pereira Passos: Um Haussmann tropical*. Rio de Janeiro: Biblioteca Carioca (Prefeitura da Cidade do Rio de Janeiro).

Berlin, Ira. 1988. *Many Thousands Gone: The First Two Centuries of Slavery in North America*. Cambridge, MA: Harvard University Press.

Bessone, Tânia, Beatriz Mamigonian, and Hebe Mattos. 2016. *Historiadores pela democracia: O golpe de 2016 e a força do passado*. São Paulo: Alameda.

Borges, Dain. 2001. "Healing and Mischief: Witchcraft in Brazilian Law and Literature, 1890–1922." In *Crime and Punishment in Latin America*, edited by Carlos Aguirre, Gilbert Joseph, and Ricardo Salvatore, 181–2010. Durham, NC: Duke University Press.

Borucki, Alex, David Eltis, and David Wheat. 2015. "Atlantic History and the Slave Trade to Spanish America." *American Historical Review*, 120, 2: 433–61.

Brinks, Daniel. 2003. "Informal Institutions and the Rule of Law: The Judicial Response to State Killings in Buenos Aires and São Paulo in the 1990s." *Comparative Politics* 36, 1: 1–19.

      2008. "Inequality, Institutions and the Rule of Law: The Social and Institutional Bases of Rights." Kellogg Institute Working Paper 351. Notre Dame, IN: Kellogg Institute Working Paper Series.

Butler, Kim. 1998. *Freedoms Given, Freedoms Won: Afro-Brazilians in Post-Abolition São Paulo and Salvador*. New Brunswick, NJ: Rutgers University Press.

Caldeira, Teresa P. R. and James Holston. 1999. "Democracy and Violence in Brazil." *Comparative Studies in Society and History* 41, 4: 691–729.

Caldeira, Teresa. 2000. *City of Walls: Crime, Segregation and Citizenship in São Paulo*. Berkeley, CA: University of California Press.

Cano, Ignacio. 2010a. "Racial Bias in Police Use of Lethal Force in Brazil." *Police Practice and Research* 11, 1: 31–43.

Cano, Ignacio, Ludmila Ribeiro, and Elisabet Meireles. 2010b. "Race Crime and Criminal Justice in Brazil." In *Race Crime and Criminal Justice: International Perspectives*, edited by Anita Kalunta-Crumpton, 207–41. New York, NY: Palgrave-MacMillan.

Cardoso, Adalberto. 2010. *A construção da sociedade do trabalho no Brasil*. Rio de Janeiro: FGV/Faperj.

      2016. "Informality and Public Policies to Overcome it: The Case of Brazil." *Sociologia e Antropologia* 6, 2: 321–49.

Carle, Susan. 2011. "A Social Movement History of Title VII Disparate Impact Analysis." *Florida Law Review* 63, 1: 251–300.

Carneiro, Maria Luiza T. 1988. *Preconceito racial no Brasil Colônia*. São Paulo: Brasiliense.

Carrara, Sérgio L. 1990. "A sciência e doutrina da identificação no Brasil." *Religião e Sociedade* 15,1: 83–105.

      1998. *Crime e loucura: O aparecimento do manicômio judiciário na passagem do século*. Rio de Janeiro: UERJ.

Carvalho, José M. 1987. *Os bestializados: O Rio de Janeiro e a República que não foi*. São Paulo: Companhia das Letras.

      2002. *Cidadania no Brasil. O longo caminho*. 3rd edition. Rio de Janeiro: Civilização Brasileira.

Caulfield, Sueann. 2000. *In Defense of Honor: Sexual Morality, Modernity, and Nation in Early-Twentieth-Century Brazil*. Durham, NC: Duke University Press.

    2012. "The Right to a Father's Name: A Historical Perspective on State Efforts to Combat the Stigma of Illegitimate Birth in Brazil." *Law and History Review* 30, 1: 1–36.

Chakrabarty, Dipesh. 2000. *Provincializing Europe: Postcolonial Thought and Historical Difference*. Princeton, NJ: Princeton University Press.

Chalhoub, Sidney. 1990. *Visões da liberdade: Uma história das últimas décadas da escravidão na Corte*. São Paulo: Companhia das Letras.

    1996. *Cidade febril: Cortiços e epidemias na corte Imperial*. São Paulo: Companhia das Letras.

    2001. *Trabalho, lar e botequim: O cotidiano dos trabalhadores no Rio de Janeiro da Belle Époque*. 2nd edition. Campinas: Editora da Unicamp.

    2006. "The Politics of Silence: Race and Citizenship in Nineteenth-Century Brazil." *Slavery and Abolition* 27, 1: 73–87.

    2011. "The Precariousness of Freedom in a Slave Society (Brazil in the Nineteenth Century)." *International Review of Social History* 56, 3: 405–39.

    2012. *A força da escravidão: Ilegalidade e costume no Brasil escravista*. São Paulo: Companhia das Letras.

Chazkel, Amy. 2015. "History Out of the Ashes: Remembering Brazilian Slavery after Rui Barbosa's Burning of the Documents." In *From the Ashes of History: Loss and Recovery of Archives and Libraries in Modern Latin America*, edited by Carlos Aguirre and Javier Villa-Flores. Raleigh, NC: Editorial A Contracorriente.

Cicalo, André. 2012. *Urban Encounters: Affirmative Action and Black Identities in Brazil*. New York, NY: Palgrave Macmillan.

    2015. "From Public Amnesia to Public Memory: Re-Discovering Slavery Heritage in Rio de Janeiro." In *African Heritage and Memory of Slavery in the South Atlantic World*. Edited by Ana Lucia Araujo, 180–211. Amherst, NY: Cambria Press.

Conrad, Robert E. 1972. *The Destruction of Brazilian Slavery (1850–1888)*. Berkeley, CA: University of California Press.

Corbucci, Paulo R. 2014. *Evolução do acesso de jovens à educação superior no Brasil*. Brasília: Instituto de Pesquisa Economica Aplicada (IPEA).

Costa, Emilia V. da. 1966. *Da senzala à colônia*. São Paulo: DIFEL.

Costa, Hilton. 2013. "Era junho de 1880: Notas acerca da discussão da reforma eleitoral e os libertos." *Anais do 6o Encontro Escravidão e Liberdade no Brasil Meridional*. Florianópolis: Universidade Federal de Santa Catarina.

Costa Pinto, Luiz de A. 1953. *O negro no Rio de Janeiro: Relações raciais numa sociedade em mudança*. São Paulo: Companhia Editora Nacional.

Cottrol, Robert J. 2013. *The Long, Lingering Shadow: Slavery, Race, and Law in the American Hemisphere*. Athens, GA: University of Georgia Press.

Cunha, Olivia G. 2002. *Intenção e gesto: Pessoa, cor e a produção cotidiana da (in)diferença no Rio de Janeiro, 1927–1942*. Rio de Janeiro: Arquivo Nacional.

Da Matta, Roberto. 1991. "Do You Know Who You Are Talking To? The Distinction between Individual and Person in Brazil." In Roberto da Matta,

    *Carnivals, Rogues and Heroes*, 137–97. Notre Dame, IN: University of Notre Dame Press.
Dávila, Jerry. 2003. *Diploma of Whiteness: Race and Social Policy in Brazil.* Durham, NC: Duke University Press.
    2010. *Hotel Trópico: Brazil and the Challenge of African Decolonization, 1950–1980.* Durham, NC: Duke University Press.
De la Fuente, Alejandro. 2001. *A Nation for All: Race, Inequality, and Politics in Twentieth-century Cuba.* Chapel Hill, NC: University of North Carolina Press.
    2004. "Slave Law and Claims-Making in Cuba: The Tannenbaum Debate Revisited." *Law and History Review* 22, 2: 339–69.
    2007. "Slaves and the Creation of Legal Rights in Cuba: *Coartación* and *Papel.*" *Hispanic American Historical Review* 87, 4: 652–92.
Dean, Warren. 1969. *The Industrialization of São Paulo, 1880–1945.* Austin, TX and London: University of Texas Press.
Du Bois, W. E. B. 1914. "Brazil." *The Crisis* 7 (April 1914): 286–87. .
Elkins, Stanley. 1959. *Slavery: A Problem in American Institutional and Intellectual Life.* Chicago, IL: University of Chicago Press.
Feltran, Gabriel. 2013. "Sobre anjos e irmãos." *Revista do Instituto de Estudos Brasileiros* 56: 43–72.
    2011. *Fronteiras de tensão: política e violência nas periferias de São Paulo.* São Paulo: Editora Unesp/CEM.
Fernandes, Florestan. 1965. *A integração do negro na sociedade de classes.* São Paulo: Dominus.
    1972. *O negro no mundo dos brancos.* São Paulo: DIFEL.
Ferreira, Ricardo A. 2005. *Senhores de poucos escravos: Cativeiro e criminalidade num ambiente rural, 1830–1888.* São Paulo: Editora da UNESP.
Ferrer, Ada. 2014. *Freedom's Mirror: Cuba and Haiti in the Age of Revolution.* Cambridge, MA: Cambridge University Press.
Fischer, Brodwyn. 2007. "Partindo a cidade maravilhosa." In *Quase cidadão: Histórias e antropologias da pós-emancipação no Brasil*, edited by Flávio Gomes and Olivia G. da Cunha, 419–50. Rio de Janeiro: Editora da Fundação Getúlio Vargas.
    2008. *A Poverty of Rights: Citizenship and Inequality in Twentieth-Century Rio de Janeiro.* Stanford, CA: Stanford University Press.
    2014. "A Century in the Present Tense: Crisis, Politics and the Intellectual History of Brazil's Informal Cities." In *Cities from Scratch*, edited by Brodwyn Fischer, Bryann McCann, and Javier Auyero, 9–67. Durham, NC: Duke University Press.
Flory, Thomas. 1981. *Judge and Jury in Imperial Brazil, 1808–1871: Social Control and Political Stability in the New State.* Austin, TX: University of Texas Press.
Fontes, Paulo. 2016. *Migration and the Making of Industrial São Paulo.* Durham, NC: Duke University Press.
Fórum Brasileiro de Segurança Pública. 2016. *100 Anuário Brasileira de Segurança Publica.* São Paulo: FBSP.
Fraga, Walter. 1996. *Mendigos, moleques e vadios na Bahia do século XIX.* Salvador: EDUFBA.

2016. *Crossroads of Freedom: Slavery and Post-Emancipation in Bahia, Brazil (1870–1910)*. Durham, NC: Duke University Press.

Frazier, E. Franklin. 1942. "Brazil Has No Race Problem." *Common Sense* 11: 363–65.

French, Jan. 2009. *Legalizing Identities: Becoming Black or Indian in Brazil's Northaeast*. Chapel Hill, NC: University of North Carolina Press.

French, John. 2004. *Drowning in Laws*. Chapel Hill, NC: University of North Carolina Press.

Freyre, Gilberto. 1951. *Sobrados e mucambos*. 2nd edition. Rio de Janeiro: J. Olympio.

1959a. *Ordem e progresso*. Rio de Janeiro: J. Olympio.

1959b. *New World in the Tropics*. New York, NY: Random House.

Fry, Peter. 1985. "Direito positivo versus direito clássico: A psicologização do crime no Brasil no pensamento de Heitor Carrilho." In *Cultura e psicanálise*, edited by Sérvulo A. Figueira, 117–41. São Paulo: Brasiliense.

1996. "O que a Cinderela negra tem a dizer sobre a política racial no Brasil." *Revista USP* 28: 122–35.

1999. "Color and the Rule of Law in Brazil." In *The (Un)rule of Law and the Underprivileged in Latin America*, edited by Juan Méndez, Guillermo O'Donnell, and Paulo Sérgio Pinheiro, 186–210. Notre Dame, IN: Notre Dame University Press.

Fry, Peter and Sérgio Carrara. 1986. "As vicissitudes do liberalismo no direito penal brasileiro." *Revista Brasileira de Ciências Sociais* 1, 2: 48–54.

Fry, Peter, Yvonne Maggi, Marcos Chor Maio, Simone Monteiro, and Ricardo V. Santos, eds. 2007. *Divisões perigosas: Políticas raciais no Brasil contemporâneo*. Rio de Janeiro: Civilização Brasileira.

Genovese, Eugene. 1969. *The World the Slaveholders Made: Two Essays in Interpretation*. New York: Pantheon.

Gidi, Antonio. 2003. "Class Actions in Brazil: A Model for Civil Law Countries." *American Journal of Comparative Law* 51, 2: 311–408.

Gnecco, Cristóbal, and Marta Zambrano. 2000. *Memorias hegemónicas, memórias dissidentes: El passado como política de la historia*. Bogotá: Universidad del Cauca/Afro Editores Ltda.

Gomes, Angela M. C. 1979. *Burguesia e trabalho: Política e legislação social no Brasil, 1917–1937*. Rio de Janeiro: Campus.

1988. *A invenção do trabalhismo*. São Paulo: Vértice.

Gomes, Flávio S. 2006. *Histórias de quilombolas: Mocambos e comunidades de senzalas no Rio de Janeiro, século XIX*. São Paulo: Companhia das Letras.

Gomes, Flávio S., and Olivia Gomes da Cunha, eds. 2007. *Quase-cidadão: Histórias e antropologias da pó- emancipação no Brasil*. Rio de Janeiro: FGV.

Gomes, Flávio S., and Petrônio Domingues. 2014. *Políticas de raça: Experiências e legados da abolição e da pós-abolição*. São Paulo: Selo Negro.

Gonçalves, Rafael S. 2013. *Favelas do Rio de Janeiro: História e Direito*. Rio de Janeiro: Pallas/PUC-Rio.

Graham, Richard. 1990. *Patronage and Politics in Nineteenth-Century Brazil*. Stanford, CA: Stanford University Press.

Gray, Richard. 1987. "The Papacy and the Atlantic Slave Trade: Lourenço da Silva, the Capuchins and the Decisions of the Holly Office." *Past and Present* 115, 1: 52–68.

Grin, Mônica, and Marcos Chor Maio. 2013. "O antirracismo da ordem no pensamento de Afonso Arinos de Melo Franco." *Topoi* 14, 26: 33–45.

Grinberg, Keila. 1994. *Liberata, a lei da ambigüidade: As ações de liberdade da Corte de Apelação do Rio de Janeiro no século XIX.* Rio de Janeiro: Relume Dumará.

————. 2001. "Freedom Suits and Civil Law in Brazil and the United States." *Slavery and Abolition* 22, 3: 66–82.

————. 2002. *O fiador dos brasileiros: Cidadania, escravidão e direito civil no tempo de Antonio Pereira Rebouças.* Rio de Janeiro: Civilização Brasileira.

Guillen, Isabel C. M. 2008. "Maracatus-Nação, uma história entre a tradição e o espetáculo." In *Tradições e traducções: A cultura imaterial em Pernambuco,* edited by Isabel Guillen, 183–99. Recife: Editora da UFPE.

Guimarães, Antônio Sérgio. 1999. "Baianos e paulistas: Duas 'escolas' de relações raciais?" *Tempo Social* 11, 1: 75–95.

————. 2001. "Democracia racial: O ideal, o pacto e o mito." *Novos Estudos* 61: 147–62.

————. 2002. *Classe, raças e democracia.* São Paulo: Editora 34.

————. 2004. "Preconceito de cor e racismo no Brasil." *Revista de Antropologia* 47, 1: 9–43.

————. 2006. "Depois da democracia racial." *Tempo Social* 18, 2: 269–87.

Hasenbalg, Carlos. 1979. *Discriminação e desigualdades raciais no Brasil.* Rio de Janeiro: Graal.

Hellwig, David. 1990. "Racial Paradise or Run Around? Afro-North American Views of Race Relations in Brazil." *American Studies* 31, 2: 43–60.

————. 1992. *African American Reflections on Brazil's Racial Paradise.* Philadelphia, PA: Temple University Press.

Hensler, Benjamin. 2006–2007. "Não vale a pena? (Not Worth the Trouble?) Afro-Brazilian Workers and Brazilian Anti-Discrimination Law." *Hastings International and Comparative Law Review* 30, 3: 267–346.

Hernandez, Tanya K. 2013. *Racial Subordination in Latin America.* New York, NY: Cambridge University Press.

Hespanha, António M., and Maria C. Santos. 1993. "Os poderes num Império oceânico." In *História de Portugal,* edited by António M. Hespanha, vol. 4. Lisbon: Editoria Estampa.

Hochman, Gilberto. 1998. *A era do saneamento: As bases da política de saúde pública no Brasil.* São Paulo: Hucitec/ANPOCS.

————. 2003. "Previdência e assistência social nos anuários estatísticos do Brasil." In *Estatísticas do século XX,* edited by Wanderley Guilherme dos Santos and Marcelo de Paiva Abreu, 167–190. Rio de Janeiro: IBGE.

Hochman, Gilberto, and Nísia T. Lima. 1996. "Condenado pela raça, absolvido pela medicina: O Brasil descoberto pelo movimento sanitarista da Primeira República." In *Raça, ciência e sociedade,* edited by Marcos Chor Maio and Ricardo V. Santos, 23–40. Rio de Janeiro: FIOCRUZ/CCBB.

Holloway, Thomas. 1989. "A Healthy Terror: Police Repression of Capoeiras in Nineteenth Century Rio de Janeiro." *Hispanic American Historical Review* 69, 4: 637–76.

1993. *Policing Rio de Janeiro: Repression and Resistance in a 19th-Century City*. Stanford, CA: Stanford University Press.

Holston, James. 2008. *Insurgent Citizenship*, Princeton, NJ: Princeton University Press.

Huggins, Martha. 1984. *From Slavery to Vagrancy in Brazil*, New Brunswick, NJ: Rutgers University Press.

Human Rights Watch/Americas. 1997. *Police Brutality in Urban Brazil*. New York: Human Rights Watch.

Human Rights Watch. 2009. *Lethal Force: Police Violence and Public Security in Rio de Janeiro and São Paulo*. New York: Human Rights Watch. Accessed April 9, 2017. www.refworld.org/docid/4b1fc9322.html.

Human Rights Watch. 2016a. Good Cops are Afraid: The Toll of Unchecked Police Violence in Rio de Janeiro. Accessed April 9, 2017. www.refworld .org/docid/577fc5304.html.

Human Rights Watch. 2016b. World Report 2016: Brazil. Accessed April 9, 2017. www.hrw.org/world-report/2016/country-chapters/brazil.

Human Rights Watch. 2017. World Report 2017: Brazil. Accessed April 9, 2017. www.hrw.org/world-report/2017/country-chapters/brazil.

Hunter, Rosemary, and Elaine W. Shoben, E. 1998. "Disparate Impact Discrimination: American Oddity or Internationally Accepted Concept?" *Berkeley Journal of Employment and Labor Law* 19, 1: 108–52.

Ianni, Octavio. 1987. *Raças e classes sociais no Brasil*. São Paulo: Brasiliense, 3rd edition. First published 1966.

IBGE. 2014. *Pesquisa Nacional por Amostra de Domicílios (PNAD)*. Accessed April 9, 2017. https://ww2.ibge.gov.br/home/estatistica/populacao/trabal hoerendimento/pnad2014/default.shtm.

Jesus, Alysson. L. Freitas de. 2007. *No sertão das Minas: Escravidão, violência e liberdade no norte de Minas – 1830–1888*. São Paulo: Editora Annablume.

Klein, Herbert, and Francisco Vidal Luna. 2014. *The Economic and Social History of Brazil since 1889*. New York, NY: Cambridge University Press.

Kowarick, Lucio. 1987. *Trabalho e vadiagem: A origem do trabalho livre no Brasil*. São Paulo: Brasiliense.

Lahon, Didier. 2001. *O negro no coração do Império. Uma memória a resgatar. Séculos XV-XIX*. Lisbon: Casa do Brasil.

Lara, Silvia. 2000. *Legislação sobre escravos africanos na América Portuguesa*. Madrid: Fundación Historica Tavera/Digibis.

2007. *Fragmentos setecentistas. Escravidão, cultura e poder na América Portuguesa*. São Paulo: Companhia das Letras.

Líbano Soares, Carlos Eugênio. 1994. *A negregada instituição: Os capoeiras no Rio de Janeiro*. Rio de Janeiro: Biblioteca Carioca (Prefeitura da Cidade do Rio de Janeiro).

Lima, Monica. 2013. "The Sound of Drums: Teaching and Learning African History and the History of Africans in Brazil." In *The Transatlantic Slave Trade and Slavery: New Directions in Teaching and Learning*, edited by Paul Lovejoy and Benjamin Bowser. Trenton, NJ: Africa World Press.

Love, Joseph. 1980. *São Paulo in the Brazilian Federation*. Stanford, CA: Stanford University Press.

Lovell, Peggy A., ed. 1991. *Desigualdade racial no Brasil contemporâneo.* Belo Horizonte: CEDEPLAR/FACE/UFMG.

Lovell, Peggy A. 1994. "Race, Gender and Development in Brazil." *Latin American Research Review* 29, 3: 7–35.

1999. "Persistence of Racial Inequality in Brazil." *Journal of Developing Areas* 33: 395–418.

2000. "Race, Gender and Regional Labor Market Inequalities in Brazil." *Review of Social Economy* 58, 3: 277–93.

2006. "Race, Gender, and Work in São Paulo, Brazil, 1960–2000." *Latin American Research Review* 41. 3: 63–87.

Loveman, Mara. 2014. *National Colors: Racial Classification and the State in Latin America.* New York, NY: Oxford University Press.

Machado, Maria Helena. 1988. *Crime e escravidão.* São Paulo: Brasiliense.

1994. *O plano e o pânico: Os movimentos sociais na década da abolição.* São Paulo: EDUSP.

Machado, Maria Helena, and Celso Castilho, eds. 2015. *Tornando-se livre: Agentes históricos e lutas sociais no processo de abolição.* São Paulo: EDUSP.

Maggie, Yvonne. 1992. *Medo do feitiço: Relações entre magia e poder no Brasil.* Rio de Janeiro: Arquivo Nacional.

Maggie, Yvonne, and Claudia Barcellos Rezende, eds. 2002. *Raça como retórica.* Rio de Janeiro: Civilização Brasileira.

Maio, Marcos Chor. 1999. "O projeto UNESCO e a agenda das ciências sociais no Brasil dos anos 40 e 50." *Revista Brasileira de Ciências Sociais* 14: 41, 141–45

2015. "Guerreiro Ramos interpela a Unesco: Ciências sociais, militância e antirracismo." *Cadernos CRH* 28: 73, 77–89.

Mamigonian, Beatriz Galotti. 2017. *Africanos livres: A abolição do tráfico de escravos no Brasil.* São Paulo: Companhia das Letras.

Marques, Eduardo. 2013. "Governing São Paulo: Governance Patterns in a Highly Unequal Metropolis." Unpublished paper presented at the Lemann Dialogue.

Marx, Anthony W. 1998. *Making Race and Nation: A Comparison of the United States, South Africa, and Brazil.* New York, NY: Cambridge University Press.

Mattos, Hebe. 1995. *Das cores do silêncio: Os significados da liberdade no sudeste escravista—Brasil século XIX.* Rio de Janeiro: Arquivo Nacional.

2001a. "A escravidão moderna nos quadros do Império português: O Antigo Regime em pespectiva atlântica." In *O Antigo Regime nos trópicos: A dinâmica imperial portuguesa (séculos XVI-XVIII)*, edited by João Fragoso, Maria Fernanda Bicalho, and Maria de Fatima Gouvêa. Rio de Janeiro: Civilização Brasileira.

2001b. *Escravidão e cidadania no Brasil monárquico.* Rio de Janeiro: Jorge Zahar.

2004. "Prefácio." In *Frederick Cooper, Thomas Holt and Rebecca Scott, Além da escravidão: Investigações sobre raça, trabalho e cidadania em sociedades pós-emancipação.* Rio de Janeiro: Civilização Brasileira.

2006. "Remanescentes das comunidades dos quilombos: Memórias do cativeiro e políticas de reparação no Brasil." *Revista USP* 68: 104–11.

2008. "Terras de Quilombo: Land Rights, Memory of Slavery, and Ethnic Identification in Contemporary Brazil." In *Africa, Brazil, and the Construction* of *Trans-Atlantic Black Identities*, edited by Livio Sansone, Elisé Soumoni, and Boubacar Barry, 293–318. Trenton, NJ: Africa World Press.

2015. "The Madness of Justina and Januário Mina: Rethinking Boundaries between Free and Enslaved Labor in Nineteenth-Century Brazil." *Quaderni Storici* 1: 175–200.

Mattos, Hebe, and Martha Abreu. 2012. "Stories of Jongos: Hidden Memories and Public History in Brazil." In *Remembering Africa and Its Diasporas: Memory, Public History and Representation of the Past*, edited by Audra Diptee and David Trotman, 119–36. Trenton, NJ: Africa World Press.

Meade Teresa. 1997. *Civilizing Rio: Reform and Resistance in a Brazilian City, 1889–1930*. University Park, PA: Pennsylvania State University Press.

Melo, Mario Lacerda de. 1978. *Metropolização e subdesenvolvimento: O caso de Recife*. Recife: UFPE.

Mendonça, Joseli. 1999. *Entre a mão e os anéis: A lei dos sexagenários e os caminhos da abolição no Brasil*. Campinas: Editora da Unicamp.

Merrick, Thomas W., and Douglas Graham. 1979. *Population and Economic Development in Brazil*. Baltimore, MD: Johns Hopkins University Press.

Moreira, Paulo Roberto Staudt. 2003. *Os cativos e os homens de bem*. Porto Alegre: EST Edições.

Needell, Jeffrey. 1987. "The Revolta Contra Vacina of 1904: The Revolt Against 'Modernization' in Belle-Époque Rio de Janeiro." *Hispanic American Historical Review* 67, 2: 233–69.

Nobles, Melissa, 2000. *Shades of Citizenship: Race and the Census in Modern Politics*. Stanford, CA: Stanford University Press.

O'Dwyer, Eliane Cantarino. 2001. *Quilombos: Identidade étnica e territorialidade*. Rio de Janeiro: Fundação Getúlio Vargas.

Olival, Fernanda. 2001. *As Ordens Militares e o Estado Moderno: Honra, mercê e venalidade em Portugal (1641–1789)*. Lisbon: Estar Editora Ltda.

Oliveira, João Pacheco. 1998. *Indigenismo e territorialização: Poderes, rotinas e saberes coloniais no Brasil contemporâneo*. Rio de Janeiro: Contracapa.

Ozanam, Israel de Souza Cunha 2013. *Capoeira e capoeiras entre a guarda negra e a educação física no Recife*. Recife: Universidade Federal de Pernambuco.

Ozanam, Israel de Souza Cunha, and Isabel Guillen. 2014. "Com a licença da polícia: Maracatu e capoeira no Recife no primeiro carnaval do século XX." In *Políticas da raça: Experiências e legados da abolição e da pós-emancipação no Brasil*, edited by Flávio Gomes and Petrônio Domingues, 307–28. São Paulo: Selo Negro.

Paschel, Tianna. 2016. *Becoming Black Political Subjects: Movements and Ethno-Racial Rights in Colombia and Brazil*. Princeton, NJ: Princeton University Press.

Peabody, Susan, and Keila Grinberg. 2007. *Slavery, Freedom and the Law in the Atlantic World*. Boston, MA: Bedford/St Martin's.

Pena, Eduardo Spiller. 1999. *Pajens da Casa Imperial: Jurisconsultos e escravidão no Brasil do século XIX*. Campinas, Editora da Unicamp.

Pereira, Amílcar Araújo. 2013. *O mundo negro: Relações raciais e a constituição do movimento negro contemporâneo no Brasil*. Rio de Janeiro: Pallas/ FAPERJ.

Perrone-Moises, Beatriz. 1992. "Índios livres e índios escravos: Os princípios da legislação indigenista do período colonial (séculos XVI a XVIII)." In *História dos índios no Brasil*, edited by Manuela Carneiro da Cunha. São Paulo: Companhia da Letras.

Pierson, Donald. 1942. *Negroes in Brazil*. Chicago, IL: University of Chicago Press.

Pinheiro, Eloísa Petit. 2002. *Europa, França e Bahia: Difusão e adaptação de modelos urbanos*. Salvador: UFBA, 2nd edition.

Pinheiro, Paulo Sérgio. 2000. "Democratic Governance, Violence, and the (Un)Rule of Law." *Daedalus* 129, 2; 119–43.

2002. "The Paradox of Democracy in Brazil." *Brown Journal of World Affairs* 7, 2: 113–22.

Pires, Antonio Liberac Cardoso Simões. 2004. *A capoeira na Bahia de Todos os Santos*. Porto Nacional: Fundação Federal de Tocantins/NEAB.

Pires, Maria de Fatima Novaes. 2003. *O crime na cor: Escravos e forros no alto sertão da Bahia (1830–1888)*. São Paulo: Annablume/FAPESP.

Pirola, Ricardo. 2015. *Escravos e rebeldes nos tribunais do Império: Uma história social da lei de 10 de junho de 1835*. Rio de Janeiro: Arquivo Nacional.

Racusen, Seth., 2002. "A Mulatto Cannot be Prejudiced: The Legal Construction of Racial Discrimination in Contemporary Brazil." PhD diss., Massachusetts Institute of Technology.

Ramos, Arthur. 1939. *The Negro in Brazil*. Washington, DC: Associated Publishers.

Reichman, Rebecca, ed. 1999. *Race in Contemporary Brazil*. University Park, PA: Pennsylvania State University Press.

Reis, João José. 1993a. "A greve negra de 1857 na Bahia." *Revista USP* 18: 6–29.

1993b. *Slave Rebellion in Brazil: The Muslim Uprising of 1835 in Bahia*. Translated by Arthur Brakel. Baltimore, MD: Johns Hopkins University Press.

Ribeiro Filho, Carlos A. Costa 1994. "Clássicos e positivistas no moderno direito penal brasileiro." In *A invenção do Brasil Moderno*, edited by Michael Herschman and Carlos A. Pereira, 130–46. Rio de Janeiro: Rocco.

Rios, Ana Lugão, and Hebe Mattos. 2005. *Memórias do cativeiro: Família, trabalho e cidadania no pós-abolição*. Rio de Janeiro: Civilização Brasileira.

Rolnik, Raquel. 1989. "Territórios negros nas cidades brasileiras." *Estudos Afro-Asiáticos* 17: 29–41.

Roosevelt, Theodore. 1914. "Brazil and the Negro." *The Outlook* 21: 409–11.

Rosemberg, André. 2006. *Ordem e burla: Processos sociais, escravidão e justiça em Santos, década de 1880*. São Paulo: Alameda.

2010. *De chumbo e festim: Uma história da polícia paulista no final do Império*. São Paulo: EDUSP/Fapesp.

Rosero-Labbé, Claudia M., and Luiz Claudio Barcelos, eds. 2007. *Afro-reparaciones: Memorias de la esclavitud y justicia reparativa para negros, afrocolombianos y raizales*. Bogotá: Universidad Nacional de Colombia.

Russell-Wood, A. J. R. 1982. *The Black Man in Slavery and Freedom in Colonial Brazil*. New York, NY: St. Martin's.

Saillant, Francine. 2010. *Le mouvement noir au Brésil (2000–2010): Réparations, droits et citoyenneté.* Paris: L'Harmattan.

Santos, Boaventura de Sousa. 1977. "The Law of the Oppressed: The Construction and Reproduction of Legality in Pasargada." *Law and Society Review* 12, 1: 5–126.

Santos, Wanderley Guilherme dos. 1979. *Cidadania e justiça.* Rio de Janeiro: Campus.

Schwarcz, Lilia Moritz. 1993. *O espetáculo das raças: cientistas, instituições e questão racial no Brasil, 1870–1930.* São Paulo: Companhia das Letras.

Scott, Rebecca. 1985. *Slave Emancipation in Cuba.* Princeton, NJ: Princeton University Press.

Seigel, Micol. 2016. "Uneven Encounters: Making Race and Nation in Brazil and the United States." Em 3 anos, 150 mil negros ingressaram em universidades por meio de cotas. Brasilia: SEPPIR. Accessed November 29, 2017. www .seppir.gov.br/central-de-conteudos/noticias/2016/03-marco/em-3-anos-150-mil-negros-ingressaram-em-universidades-por-meio-de-cotas.

Seyferth, Giralda. 2002. "Colonização, imigração e a questão racial no Brasil." *Revista USP* 53: 117–49.

2007. "Imigração, ocupação territorial e cidadania." In *Quase cidadão: Histórias e antropologias da pós-emancipação no Brasil*, edited by Flávio Gomes and Olivia G. da Cunha, 79–118. Rio de Janeiro: Editora da Fundação Getúlio Vargas.

Sheriff, Robin. 2000. "Exposing Silence as Cultural Censorship: A Brazilian Case." *American Anthropologist* 102, 1: 114–32.

Silva Jr., Hédio. 2000. "Do racismo legal ao princípio da ação afirmativa." In *Tirando a máscara: Ensaios sobre o racismo no Brasil*, edited by Antonio Sérgio A. Guimarães and Lynn W. Huntley, 359–88. Rio de Janeiro: Paz e Terra.

Silva, Nelson do Valle, and Carlos Alfredo Hasenbalg. 1988. *Estrutura social, mobilidade e raça.* Rio de Janeiro: Vértice.

1992. *Relações raciais no Brasil contemporâneo.* Rio de Janeiro: Rio Fundo.

Skidmore, Thomas. 1993. *Black into White: Race and Nationality in Brazilian Thought.* 2nd edition. Durham, NC: Duke University Press.

Stanziani, Alessandro. 2013. "Slavery, Debt and Bondage: The Mediterranean and the Eurasia Connection from the Fifteenth to the Eighteen Century." In *Debt and Slavery in the Mediterranean and Atlantic World*, edited by Gwyn Campbell and Alessandro Stanziani. London: Pickering & Chatto.

Stepan Nancy. L. 1991. *The Hour of Eugenics: Race, Gender, and Nation in Latin America.* Ithaca: Cornell University Press.

Summerhill, William R. 2003 *Order Against Progress: Government, Foreign Investment, and Railroads in Brazil, 1854–1913.* Stanford, CA: Stanford University Press.

Tannenbaum, Frank. 1946. *Slave and Citizen.* Boston, MA: Beacon Press.

Telles, Edward. 2004. *Race in Another America: The Significance of Skin Color in Brazil.* Princeton: Princeton University Press.

Telles, Edward, and Marcelo Paixão. 2013. "Affirmative Action in Brazil." *LASA Forum* 14, 2: 10–11.

Toplin, Robert. 1975. *The Abolition of Slavery in Brazil*. Cambridge, MA: Athenaeum.

Tushnet, Mark, Thomas Fleisner, and Cheryl Saunders, eds. 2013. *Routledge Handbook of Constitutional Law*. New York: Routledge.

Viana, Larissa. 2007. *O idioma da mestiçagem: As irmandades de pardos na América portuguesa*. Campinas: Editora da Unicamp.

Vincent, Bernard. 2000. "Les Confréries de Noirs dans La Péninsule Ibérique (XVe. XVIIIe Siècles)." In *Religiosidad y costumbres populares en Iberoamérica*, edited by David Gonzales Cruz. Huelva: Universidad de Huelva y Centro de Estudios Rocieros.

Wade, Peter. 1997. *Race and Ethnicity in Latin America*. London: Pluto Press.

——— 2014. "Race, Multiculturalism and Genomics in Latin America." In *Mestizo Genomics: Race Mixture, Nation, and Science in Latin America*, edited by Peter Wade, Carlos Lopez Beltrán, Eduardo Restrepo, and Ricardo Ventura Santos. Durham, NC: Duke University Press.

Wagley, Charles. 1952. *Race and Class in Rural Brazil*. Paris: UNESCO.

Waiselfisz, Julio. J. 2016. *Mapa da violência 2016: Homicídios por armas de fogo no Brasil*. Rio de Janeiro: FLACSO.

Weinstein, Barbara. 2015. *The Color of Modernity: São Paulo and the Making of Race and Nation in Brazil*. Durham, NC: Duke University Press.

Wissenbach, Maria Cristina Cortez. 1998. *Sonhos africanos, vivências ladinas: Escravos e forros em São Paulo (1850–1880)*. São Paulo: Hucitec.

Wood, Charles. H., and José Alberto Magno de Carvalho. 1988. *The Demography of Inequality in Brazil*. New York, NY: Cambridge University Press.

Zaluar, Alba. 1985. *A máquina e a revolta: As organizações populares e o significado da pobreza*. São Paulo: Brasiliense.

# PART II

# POLITICS

# 6

## Currents in Afro-Latin American Political and Social Thought

### Frank A. Guridy and Juliet Hooker

In 1909 Cuba's *Partido Independiente de Color*, founded by dissatisfied Afro-Cuban veterans of the war of independence who continued to face racial discrimination in everyday life and unequal access to better paying government positions in the new republic, stated: "we do not long for black supremacy over whites; but neither do we accept, and never will, white supremacy over blacks" (cited in Helg 1991, 110). The *Partido Independiente de Color* was brutally repressed by the Cuban state, but its existence and the policy positions it adopted exemplify key themes in Afro-Latin American political thought, particularly the challenge of how to mobilize against racism in political and social systems in which racial discrimination exists, but whose official ideology is one of color-blindness, such that separate black organizing is often viewed as racist and anti-patriotic. Afro-Latin American thinkers have thus long had to contend with the predicament of color-blind racism: how to expose practices of racial exclusion when the national state denies the existence of racism (Bonilla-Silva 2009). While the *Partido Independiente de Color* was ahead of its time in advocating for racial equality and critiquing the predominant scientific racism of the era that justified white supremacy, it was also committed to what would today be called a politics of black respectability, including the subordination of women and full Afro-Cuban integration into Cuban society as well as adoption of European cultural norms. Like most Black movements of the day, it certainly "did not advocate a separate Afro-Cuban culture" (Helg 1991, 109). Moreover, some of the most prominent Afro-Cuban legislators and intellectuals of the time, fearing that it would lead to greater repression against Afro-Cubans, rejected the party and were complicit in its banning and the persecution of its members.

We begin our exploration of Afro-Latin American thinkers with the *Partido Independiente de Color* because it is an apt example of two key features of Afro-Latin American political thought that we wish to emphasize in this chapter. Afro-Latin American thought is not monolithic, and it has been insufficiently acknowledged within most accounts of Latin American intellectual history. Afro-Latin American thinkers disagreed about how best to mobilize to contest the social and political inequalities they and other people of African descent faced within Latin American societies; they also had different analyses of the cause of these disparities and whether blacks should mobilize as a distinct group in Cuba and other countries in the region. Yet, despite the richness and complexity of Afro-Latin American thought, and despite the growing attention it has received by scholars (particularly intellectual historians), it remains an understudied tradition. The *Partido Independiente de Color*, for instance, was one of the first organized black political parties in the Americas. It was founded in 1908, a year before W. E. B. Du Bois and other African American intellectuals founded the National Association for the Advancement of Colored People (NAACP) in the United States in 1909. Despite its short-lived existence, the *Partido Independiente de Color* is an important example of early twentieth-century black political organizing in the Americas. Indeed, along with the *Partido Autóctono Negro* (1936–44) in Uruguay and the *Frente Negra Brasileira* (1931–37) in Brazil, Afro-Latin Americans founded some of the earliest examples of separate black political institutions in the hemisphere. Part of the work that remains to be done in the field is thus to recover the contributions of Afro-Latin American thinkers and to expand the canon of Latin American and African-American (understood hemispherically) political thought to include them. The aim of this chapter is thus to redress the exclusion of Afro-Latin American thinkers from the canons of both Latin American thought and black political thought (in which certain Caribbean intellectuals, such as Frantz Fanon and C. L. R. James, are regularly included).

Because of the vexed relationship black thinkers have had with the nation-state in Latin America, Afro-Latin American thought offers a distinctive vision of Latin American societies and grapples directly with otherwise under-explored questions in Latin American political thought writ large. Since independence, black thinkers (like their indigenous counterparts) have challenged the official nationalisms of the region that claimed to be racially inclusive (see Chapter 8). Likewise, in the post-independence period of the early nineteenth century, Afro-Latin American thinkers struggled to negotiate their place in the new nations of which they were now a part and had in many cases actively helped to found. Operating in a space of what Jossianna Arroyo (2013, 23) has described as "subjugated freedom" after emancipation, Afro-Latin American thinkers nevertheless participated in, and made significant contributions to, central intellectual debates in Latin America in the nineteenth and twentieth centuries about the character of postcolonial nationhood, the validity of scientific racism, the threat of US imperialism, how to achieve genuine social and political democracy, etc. Afro-Latin American intellectuals thus both participated in the construction of, and contestation of, discourses of inclusion and color-blindness that existed alongside ongoing practices of racial exclusion and informal and extralegal forms of segregation and exploitation.

Afro-Latin American intellectuals have engaged with, rejected, and adapted a variety of sources and ideas. They engaged in central debates in Latin American politics: struggles over the meaning of freedom and citizenship as well as the forms of political community that best served new nations in the postcolonial period. Most, though not all, tended to gravitate toward political movements that championed racially inclusive visions of community. Others advocated various iterations of more conservative strands of racial thought, some of which even replicated colonial hierarchies. Still others, particularly in the twentieth century, influenced and were influenced by radical anti-imperial, Marxist thought that pushed for forms of community that rejected liberal nationalist frameworks.

Drawing on Michael Dawson's typology of different currents within black political thought, we situate the ideas formulated by Afro-Latin American thinkers as radical egalitarian, black liberal, black Marxist, black nationalist, black feminist, and black conservative political projects (Dawson 2001). Black conservative political thinkers, for example, have tended to emphasize self-help as well as individual economic or social uplift and often rejected the idea of separate organizing on the basis of race or black identity. Black liberals, meanwhile, have critiqued racism but also promoted assimilation into existing national states, which they have generally viewed as capable of living up to their official ideologies of racial inclusion. Radical egalitarians have supported the ideal of multiracial democracy while also highlighting the need for vocal and visible black political organizing to pressure the state to actively pursue racial justice and racial repair. Black nationalists have eschewed assimilation into existing nation-states in favor of emphasizing diasporic alliances with black people globally and advocating for various forms of black autonomy. Finally, black Marxists have foregrounded a critique of capitalism and sought to address the lack of attention to race in much of the Latin American left, while black feminists have formulated an intersectional analysis in contrast to the lack of attention to gender in black movements and to race in mainstream Latin American feminism. While these strands of thought often overlapped and converged even in the work of individual intellectuals, we nevertheless find Dawson's framework useful in highlighting dominant tendencies in Afro-Latin American thought.[1]

The ideological and political orientations of Afro-Latin American thinkers thus varied widely. Black conservatives such as the Afro-Brazilian independence activist, lawyer, and politician Antonio Pereira Rebouças (1798–1880) sought to distance themselves from any kind of black identity and embraced assimilation, while black liberals such as the Afro-Cuban independence leader, journalist, and politician Juan Gualberto Gómez (1854–1933) contributed to the formulation of a national discourse of racial inclusion in Cuba.[2] Others embraced more radical political projects, such as the Afro-Brazilian intellectual Abdias do Nascimento, who shifted from adherent of Brazilian *mestiçagem* to proponent of Negritude to Pan-African thinker and critic of racial democracy. The evolution of Nascimento's political ideas over time demonstrates the fluidity of these labels and the ideological diversity of Afro-Latin American thought.

Grappling with black political thought in Latin America raises various methodological questions. One of these is who counts as a thinker, an issue that is closely related to the locations in which political ideas are

---

[1] Dawson's understanding of each of these strands of black political thought is grounded almost exclusively in African-American history and politics in the United States. We therefore adapt his categories to describe each of the variants as they have developed specifically in a Latin American context.

[2] Rebouças was the son of a freed slave who sought to distance himself as far as possible from Africa and slavery; he was committed to a radically deracialized version of liberalism that rejected any identifications of citizens by skin color. For these reasons, we identify him as a black conservative. For more on Rebouças see Grinberg (2002) and Spitzer (1989). Gomez, meanwhile, forged a more complicated position, which is why we classify him as a black liberal. He presided over the *Directorio Central de Sociedades de la Raza de Color* in the 1890s, which fought for the extension of civil rights to Afro-Cubans and won important victories from the Spanish colonial authorities outlawing restrictions on inter-racial marriage and ending government segregation in schools and other public spaces; yet after independence he was also an opponent of the *Partido Independiente de Color*.

produced. We have chosen to focus in this chapter on individual thinkers who left behind a sufficiently substantial corpus of published work such that their political ideas can be analyzed in some detail. There are gendered implications of the choice to focus on persons who left behind a substantial written corpus, however, as black women faced even greater challenges to accessing traditional sites of intellectual production than black men. This choice might also give the misleading impression that Afro-Latin American thought is a far less substantial corpus than is actually the case. This is in part because Afro-Latin American political ideas were formulated in unusual locations. Historically, black thinkers tended to be marginalized by mainstream academic, literary, and cultural institutions in Latin America.[3] In the colonial and early postcolonial periods, many Afro-Latin American thinkers emerged from the urban artisan classes, a middle and somewhat marginalized sector of the political economy due to their manual laboring status. As historians and literary critics have shown, religious brotherhoods, masonic temples, literary, social, and recreation societies, and an active black press were the warehouses of Afro-Latin American thought (Alberto 2011; Andrews 2010; Arroyo 2013; de la Fuente 2001; Geler 2010).[4] Afrodescended communities throughout the hemisphere created their own robust cultural and intellectual institutions that became sites of debate and political mobilization. We thus use an expansive definition of political thought in this chapter. We do not restrict ourselves to philosophical essays or explicitly political texts such as constitutions or party platforms, but instead include a wide variety of texts written by non-elite intellectuals in different genres, such as poetry, memoir, fiction, etc., because these are sites in which Afro-Latin American thinkers formulated their political

---

[3] The novelist, poet, playwright, and short story writer Joaquim Maria Machado de Assis in Brazil appears to have been an important exception to this pattern, as he was one of the founders of the Brazilian Academy of Letters and its first president. Yet Machado, who was the son of a mulatto and a grandson of freed slaves, in fact, exemplifies how black inclusion was indexed to the kinds of political ideas espoused by intellectuals of African descent. Machado, for example, was identified at the beginning of his career as a mulatto but "whitened" as he grew in prominence. During his lifetime he never publicly advocated for abolition. Yet he is now seen as unambiguously black. His racial identification thus changed over time.

[4] The historical marginalization of Afro-Latin American thinkers continues to be reproduced today in the politics of translation, i.e., in decisions about which texts and thinkers are available outside their original language. One of the challenges that non-Spanish and non-Portuguese readers face when trying to engage with Afro-Latin American thought is that the vast majority of these texts have not been translated into English.

ideas. We also do not limit our analysis only to written texts; we also include film, for example, as a medium in which political thinking has been articulated.

Grappling with Afro-Latin American thought not only requires that we expand understandings of who is a thinker, it also means that we need to be explicit about how "black" is being understood. Our contribution explores the topic of Afro-Latin American thought from the perspective of thinkers (mostly men and some women) who self-identified as, were, or are now considered persons of African descent. This is not to deny the importance of non-black thinkers to the evolution of Afro-Latin American thought. Figures such as Gilberto Freyre in Brazil, Fernando Ortiz in Cuba, and Gonzalo Aguirre Beltrán in Mexico were foundational to twentieth-century understandings of the black experience in Latin America. These elite "founding fathers" of Afro-Latin American studies have already received extensive attention, however (Arroyo 2003; Burke and Pallares-Burke 2008; de la Fuente 2010). Afro-Latin American thinkers necessarily approached the subject from a different perspective than the elite intellectuals who are credited with first celebrating the African sources of Brazilian, Cuban, and Mexican national cultures and societies.

Given the much more limited attention paid to black thinkers, we want to emphasize their contributions, which have tended to be overlooked. We acknowledge the robust debates about racial identity and self-identification in Latin America, particularly as they relate to blackness (see Bourdieu and Wacquant 1999; Hanchard 2003). Yet most of the thinkers analyzed in this chapter grappled directly with the question of what it meant to be black and Latin American, even as they utilized different conceptions of blackness. This is reflected in the diverse nomenclature of blackness found in their work, such as mulatto, negro, afro, etc. Indeed, the richness of this corpus is precisely that it helps us to understand the complexity of black thought because Afro-Latin American thinkers grappled directly with how to define blackness as they moved between the different categories of mulatto, negro, etc.

Our chapter also underscores the masculinist nature of much of the corpus of Afro-Latin American thought. In contexts where literacy was a relative privilege for most Afro-Latin Americans, men of African descent went to great lengths to forge a self-identification as "lettered *men* of the colored race," to showcase their masteries of the knowledges that often subjugated them. In this regard, Afro-Latin American intellectual traditions reflect the masculinist tendencies of Latin American thought more generally. We address this gap by paying special attention to gender and sexuality in our analysis of thinkers and movements, and by highlighting the contributions of Afro-Latin American feminists.

Our conception of Latin America is also an expansive one, and it is especially attuned to transnational flows of ideas and people across the hemisphere. As with any overview, ours is not fully comprehensive in its geographical reach, and some countries inevitably receive more attention than others, reflecting the significant national disparities in preserving the archive of Afro-Latin American thought. Although we focus primarily on thinkers from Spanish America and Brazil, we also consider connections among black thinkers in different parts of the Americas. The impact of transnational encounters and connections on the work of black intellectuals throughout the hemisphere is evident in the development of anti-imperial attempts to foster Caribbean unity (as in Puerto Rican nationalist Ramón Emeterio Betances' idea of a *Confederación Antillana* in the second half of the nineteenth century), and in the relationship between Pan-African movements in the English-speaking Caribbean, Negritude in the French-speaking Caribbean, and black movements in the United States and mainland Latin America in the early twentieth century (Davis 2007). Indeed, recent scholarship has underscored the centrality of diasporic dialogues and cross-national linkages in the making of Afro-Latin American thought (Andrews 2010; Guridy 2010; Landers 2010; Seigel 2009), as well as the far less-recognized route of intellectual influence whereby US African-American intellectuals drew on Latin American sources and ideas (Hooker 2017; Pereira Araujo 2013).

The complicated roots and routes of Afro-Latin American thought are exemplified by Afro-diasporic figures such as Maymie de Mena, the New Orleans-born activist who married into an Afro-Nicaraguan community and became a prominent UNIA leader (Morris 2016) and Arturo Schomburg, the Afro-Puerto Rican intellectual turned African-American bibliophile, who spent much of his life in New York City (Hoffnung-Garskof 2001). De Mena and Schomburg have been recuperated by present-day scholars as pioneering Afro-Latin@s or Afro-Latin Americans living in the US (see Jiménez Román and Flores 2010 and Chapter 15). The trajectories and movement across black diasporic spaces of these figures suggest not only that the boundaries between US and Latin American blackness were porous, but also that ideas and bodies traveled complicated hemispheric routes (Rivera-Rideau, Jones, and Paschel 2016; Seigel 2009). Charting the contours of Afro-Latin American thought thus requires that we be attuned to the complexities of location, translation, and dislocation.

## SLAVERY AND THE STRUGGLE FOR FREEDOM

Enslavement functioned as a mode of racial governance that subjugated people of African descent in Latin America, which they simultaneously resisted through multiple, creative strategies of self-emancipation. The struggles for freedom of enslaved men and women in Latin America took a variety of forms, including everyday forms of resistance (slowdowns, faking illness, sabotage, etc.), taking legal action against abusive masters, mass flights from slavery, and slave revolutions and uprisings against colonial states. As Bryant (2004, 10) has argued, rather than viewing legal action (which is often seen as passive accommodation) and supposedly more radical resistance methods aimed at dismantling the system as dichotomous, there were continuities between the two because "even when 'working the system,' slaves were, in fact, questioning and challenging the very foundation upon which it rested."

The self-emancipation strategies of the enslaved have been a generative site for conceiving the meaning of black liberation in Afro-Latin American thought. Black political and cultural movements of the twentieth century, for example, drew inspiration from the history of slave flight and resistance, as is reflected in the nomenclature of the *Quilombhoje* group, founded in 1980 in Brazil, and the Afro-Colombian organization *Movimiento Nacional Cimarrón*, founded in 1982.[5] We focus in this section on some key themes that emerge from the protracted struggle to abolish slavery in Latin America, including the difficulties of interpreting the historical record that remains to trace the political ideas of the enslaved, the impact of the Haitian revolution, the influence of maroon communities on slave societies, and the relationship between slavery and republicanism.

Depictions of slavery in Latin America generally have not included the perspective of enslaved Afro-Latin Americans. Analyses of slavery and abolition in Latin America have only relatively recently begun to focus on recuperating the experiences and ideas of enslaved people. Pioneering early- to mid-twentieth-century scholars who highlighted

---

[5] Comparable to the Black Arts Movement of the 1960s and 1970s in the United States, the *Quilombhoje* group is best known for its publication of the *Cadernos Negros* (Black Notebooks), which brought together poetry, fiction, and essays by Afro-Brazilian writers, artists, and intellectuals to refute stereotypical images of blackness and to formulate a counter-discourse informed by Black pride and Pan-Africanism. For a discussion of the emergence and activism of *Cimarrón* in Colombia, see Chapter 7.

African contributions to national cultures and identities, such as Gilberto Freyre in Brazil and Fernando Ortiz in Cuba, tended to present slavery as a site of contact, where national syncretism was forged. Freyre did not deny the violence of slavery, but he also attributed the ostensibly more harmonious race relations developed in Latin America to the widespread *mestiçagem* resulting from sexual encounters between masters and slaves (Freyre 1946). There has been a shift in the historiography of slavery and abolition since these early texts, however, as Chapter 5 shows. Contemporary scholars are much more attuned to the "living memory of slavery" and contending visions of freedom (Chalhoub 1990; Machado 1988; Mattos 1995; Peabody and Grinberg 2007), as well as to the question of how to use the archive creatively to trace the political ideas of the enslaved (see Ferrer 2009).

In contrast to the United States, where there were numerous slave narratives published by fugitive slaves, there are only two known autobiographies published by enslaved persons in Latin America, both written by men who had an unusual level of access to education. Mahommah Gardo Baquaqua's autobiography recounts the two years he spent enslaved in Brazil after being captured in Africa as a young man, where he was raised a Muslim. Baquaqua escaped slavery in 1847 in New York with the aid of black and white abolitionists, and he subsequently lived in Haiti, Canada, and the northern United States. His autobiography (Baquaqua 2006) was written in English and published in the US in 1854; it was only subsequently translated into Portuguese and published in Brazil. The only other Latin American slave narrative is the poet Juan Francisco Manzano's *Autobiografía de un esclavo* (1996), which details the brutality of slavery in nineteenth-century Cuba.[6] Manzano's text is a devastating account of the psychological effects of enslavement and of the way the enslaved were forced to adapt to white cultural hegemony in their quest for freedom. Manzano described the physical abuse he endured as a slave: "For the least childish mischief, I was locked up for twenty-four hours in a coal cellar without floorboards and nothing to cover myself . . . after suffering brutal lashes . . . This penance was so frequent that a week did not go by in which I did not suffer this kind of punishment two or three times" (Manzano 1996, 57, 59).

Manzano and Baquaqua's autobiographies share a number of common themes. Both texts are subject to questions about authorship and the degree

---

[6] Manzano gained renown as a poet while still enslaved; his poetry is collected in Mullen (2014).

of autonomy in the authorial voice that bedevil the slave narrative genre as a whole (but see the discussion of the meaning of Manzano's strategic use of silence in Chapter 9). Manzano's autobiography was written at the request of his Cuban patron Domingo del Monte and was originally published in England with the assistance of the British abolitionist Richard R. Madden; Baquaqua's was dictated to a Unitarian minister and abolitionist, Samuel Downing Moore. In Baquaqua's text in particular there are passages where clearly the person speaking is Moore rather than Baquaqua. More centrally, the conception of freedom that emerges from both their texts is individualist and integrationist in the sense that Manzano aspires to assimilate into Cuban society and Baquaqua to return to Africa as a Christian missionary; theirs are not accounts of collective black liberation. Moreover, neither Manzano nor Baquaqua contest Eurocentric assumptions about the superiority of European culture, and in both texts Christianity plays a central role while African religious traditions are deemed superstitious; the latter is a striking contrast to the role of African-derived religious traditions in enabling and sustaining black political mobilization in the diaspora. With the exception of their mothers, enslaved women also rarely appear in Manzano and Baquaqua's texts, an omission that obscures the central role enslaved women played in the resistance efforts of enslaved people (see Finch 2015). Manzano's text does offer an interesting depiction of masculinity, however. He continually describes being overwhelmed by emotion, breaking down in tears, feeling fear, etc. While this representation of vulnerability is consistent with a portrayal of enslaved blacks as pitiable nonthreatening victims that could appeal to white liberal sympathy, it is also a contrast to standard accounts of heroic black masculinity.

In addition to narratives documenting the horrors of slavery, Afro-Latin American thought includes important accounts of the struggle for freedom. Perhaps the single most important event in the canon of black resistance to enslavement in Latin America is the Haitian Revolution, the only anti-colonial revolution carried out by the actually enslaved to gain their freedom (as opposed to the use of slavery as a metaphor for political disenfranchisement by elite Creole revolutionaries in the US and Latin America). Although the question of abolition was raised in the context of many independence wars throughout the Americas, it was only in Haiti where emancipation was not postponed until after the establishment of political independence from European colonialism. Though Haiti has been historically peripheralized in Latin American studies, it has profoundly influenced Afro-Latin American thinkers in a variety of ways. Building on the foundational work of Julius Scott and others, historian Ada Ferrer has shown how Haiti helped catalyze Afro-Cuban insurgents, such as José Antonio Aponte, to envision a "black kingdom of this world" which he sketched in his famous "libro de pinturas" that was confiscated and disappeared by Spanish colonial officials (Ferrer 2014).

The profound impact of the Haitian Revolution cannot be underestimated. Latin American independence leaders incorporated black soldiers into their armies and promised freedom in exchange for their service motivated in part by the fear of a similar slave uprising in their own countries. Beyond its influence as an example that had to be disavowed (Fischer 2004), the legacy of the Haitian Revolution endures in the thought that emerged from it, such as the novel aspects of the Haitian constitution of 1805, which instituted a notion of political blackness and banned most whites from citizenship and from owning land in Haiti (Roberts 2015). In an effort to overcome distinctions based on mixture and skin color, it declared that "Haytians shall hence forward be known only by the generic appellation of Blacks" (Dubois and Garrigus 2006, 193). The revolution was also the most radical manifestation of liberal democracy during the Age of Revolution, expanding the boundaries of citizenship beyond the racial limits envisaged by most political thinkers at the time (Dubois 2006).

The Haitian Revolution was a living argument for the political capacities of black people and a model of revolutionary transformation. The figure of Toussaint Louverture, for example, became a symbol of successful violent resistance to slavery and colonialism, as well as of black aspirations to leadership. Louverture's iconic stature as a skillful military leader who defeated European armies became a powerful symbol of antislavery martial masculinity that other black male freedom seekers throughout the hemisphere would adopt and celebrate in subsequent decades (Scott 2005). For subsequent black intellectuals in the Americas, such as W. E. B. Du Bois and the Trinidadian-born Marxist intellectual C. L. R. James, Louverture and other Haitian slave rebels provided models of revolutionary change for the twentieth-century Pan-African liberation struggle (James 1963).

The Haitian Revolution was a source of inspiration not just for Anglophone Pan-African intellectuals, but also for Afrodescendants in the former colonies of Iberian America, as is evident in rhetorical appeals to it in Gran Colombia in the course of local conflicts with post-independence elites (Lasso 2001). It is also evident in accusations against Afro-Cuban independence leader Antonio Maceo of seeking to emulate or being in league with Haiti, and against Afro-Brazilian intellectual Antonio Rebou-ças of fomenting hostility against whites for having noted that blacks and mulattoes could become generals (Geggus 2007, 26).

Enslaved and free Afro-Latin Americans did not need to turn to Haiti to find examples of violent resistance to slavery, however. The abolition of slavery in Latin America was a slow, protracted process in much of the region that required the active agency of the enslaved. Afro-Latin Americans engaged in their own struggles for self-emancipation, including legal actions as well as escape and flight. During both the colonial and post-independence eras in what is today Ecuador, for example, "the enslaved were active agents in seeking to end slavery," not simply trying to gain their own individual freedom (Townsend 2007, 39). The existence of maroon communities of fugitive slaves throughout the region were incentives for better treatment of those who remained enslaved in order to prevent further flights. They were also centers of active, armed Afro-Latin American resistance to slavery. Fugitive Africans and Afrodescendants in many parts of Latin America forged maroon communities outside of (but co-existing with) colonial and postcolonial slave societies in the Americas. The existence of *palenques* in Colombia and *quilombos* in Brazil, afforded people of African descent the oppor-tunity to exercise political agency and develop political orders based on their own conceptions of freedom and political governance, such as the elected chiefdom in the Palmares *quilombo*, the largest and most enduring maroon community in the Americas (Cheney 2014; Kent 1979; Reis and Dos Santos Gomes 1996). Eduardo Silva has also noted the existence of what he calls abolitionist *quilombos* (to differentiate them from break-away *quilombos*), such as the *quilombo* of Leblon, which served as an important symbol and site of the radical abolitionist movement in Brazil (Silva 2007).

Afro-Latin Americans were also prominent leaders and activists in abolitionist movements, such as the escaped slave and poet Luiz Gama (1830–82) in Brazil, the last country to abolish slavery in the hemi-sphere in 1888. Gama has been called the Brazilian Frederick Douglass. He was born the son of a free African mother in Bahia but was illegally sold as a slave by his Portuguese father as a child. After learning to read and write, Gama escaped, studied law, and later became a journalist in São Paulo, where he wrote for various newspapers and founded a satirical magazine. Gama was also a fervent republican (he was one of the founders of the Republican Party of São Paulo) and had firm anti-clerical views. In 1859 he published a collection of poems, *Primeiras trovas burlescas* [Burlesque Ballads] (Gama and Ferreira 2011). The poems include condemnations of slavery, celebrations of black women and of Africa, and commemorations of African cultural practices Gama experienced growing up in Bahia; they also mocked mixed-race Brazilians who aspired to whiteness and denied their African ancestry in order to join the elite. Gama believed that the use of violence was justified in order to resist slavery, but he was also extremely effective in using the law to free hundreds of enslaved persons. As "the lawyer of the slaves," Gama convinced the courts to enforce the often-ignored 1831 decree that Africans entering the country after that date would be free (Ferreira 2007, 273). Gama was one among a number of prominent black abolitionists in Brazil, including André Rebouças (son of Antonio), José Carlos do Patrocínio, and Maria Firmina dos Reis, who published an abolitionist novel, *Ursula*, in 1859 (Reis 1859). Whether it was through the condemnation of slavery in Manzano's and Baquaqua's autobiographies, the legal cases brought by enslaved women in the courts (Bryant 2004), Toussaint and other Haitian generals' enactment of antislavery martial masculinity, or the legal and political activism of black abolitionists such as Gama, Rebouças (the son), and Patrocínio, Afro-Latin Americans played fundamental roles in dismantling slavery in Latin America.

## AFRO-LATIN AMERICAN CONCEPTIONS OF CITIZENSHIP IN THE EARLY REPUBLICAN ERA

The abolition of slavery was a part of a broader problematic that free Afro-Latin Americans were dealing with in the nineteenth century: the question of their relationship to the colonial, and eventually the new republican, polities that emerged in many parts of Latin America. Free persons of African descent during the era of slavery were active participants in colonial and Republican-era debates on the nature of political community. Some participated in the wars of independence and became heroes of the Creole revolutions against Spain in South America and Cuba, even in areas with smaller Afrodescendant populations, such as Mexico, exemplified by the Afro-mestizo leaders José María Morelos and Vicente Guerrero (Vincent 2001). In Nueva Granada (Colombia), *pardos* (free persons of African descent) were attracted to republican ideals in the wars for independence. Despite fears of "*pardocracia*" (rule by free populations of color) by elite Creole leaders of the wars of independence, such as Simón Bolívar, *pardo* generals such as José Prudencio Padilla insisted on equal representation in the new republican polities that were emerging. Padilla, who was executed for purportedly attempting to assassinate Bolívar, found, like many Afrodescendants, that they could be accused of fomenting "race war" if they threatened Creole elite power (Lasso 2007). For Afro-Latin Americans abolition and emancipation did not necessarily equal freedom; newly freed slaves had to contend with what their position would be in post-slave societies. For many of the formerly enslaved, this meant finding themselves at the bottom of an economic system in which their labor continued to be exploited as "free" laborers.

Over the course of the nineteenth century, Afro-Latin Americans continued to craft understandings of freedom and equality under the umbrella of republicanism. A period that was previously viewed by historians as one marked by political instability and *caudillismo* is now seen by many scholars as one when competing visions of nationhood and political community were articulated by subaltern populations. Afro-Latin American thinkers were very much engaged in these struggles. Historians have carefully documented efforts by plebeian Afro and indigenous intellectuals and activists to insist on an expansive suffrage beyond the landed elite classes. This "popular" and even "black" liberalism widened the parameters of republican visions of citizenship in the decades after independence (Andrews 2004; Sanders 2004, 2014). In Colombia, from the wars for independence into the national period, organic intellectuals crafted their own visions of liberalism. One such figure was another poet, Candelario Obeso, whose writings succinctly articulated Afro-Colombian conceptions of popular liberalism. In *Cantos populares de mi tierra*, Obeso wrote:

> In return for my friendship
> I ask only a single thing of you ...
> You should say how citizens
> Are black, white, Indian ...
> If someone wants
> To climb to the top,
> He should look for a ladder
> Somewhere else; ...
> The time of the slaves
> Is over;
> Today we are as free
> As the white...
>                     (McGraw 2014, 1)

To historian Jason McGraw, Obeso's conception of "a multihued citizenry" was rooted in a broader discourse and practice of "vernacular citizenship" in post-emancipation Caribbean Colombia (McGraw 2014, 1). In equating citizenship with friendship, Obeso was also elucidating a vision of egalitarian democracy in which wealth and status could no longer be built on exploited and unremunerated black and Indian labor. Obeso's conception of emancipation and multiracial belonging in the language of the popular sectors in the region, namely the *bogas* [black boatmen], presages subsequent attempts by black poets in the Americas to express black experiences and aspirations in vernacular idioms in the 1920s and 1930s.

Another prominent black *letrado* of the nineteenth century was Jacinto Ventura de Molina, a free black shoemaker who was a prolific writer in the early years of the Uruguayan republic. Molina eventually became a lawyer and his writings often involved crafting petitions on behalf of the poor and vulnerable local black population. Unlike many of his contemporaries, who tended to valorize Western-oriented models of black organizational life, he was a passionate advocate for local African-based societies. Though the state sanctioned these organizations, semi-autonomous black organizations were often treated cautiously by elites and political authorities. As in other parts of Latin America, religious and recreational societies were incubators of Afro-Latin American thought. Molina's activities make this quite clear, playing the role of a "humble black" before Uruguayan authorities, while taking his role as defender of Afro-Uruguayan associations seriously. "Through my association with the Uruguayan state, I have been charged with the defense of the blacks," he wrote in a petition on behalf of the Congos de Gunga, a local African "nation" which was petitioning for a meeting space in Montevideo. "Sir Minister," he continued "you will be most gracious and dignified in permitting the nation Congos de Gunga to have their house to dance to their drums on Sundays and holidays." In these petitions, Ventura sought to legitimate the civic and cultural value of Afro-Uruguayan organizations (Acree 2009, 50; Andrews 2010, 30). Still, as an Afrodescendant who dared to fashion himself as a writer, he was greeted with disdain and scorn. One anonymous responder to one of his petitions expressed his distaste for Ventura in no uncertain terms:

> Be gone, crazy, disgusting black man,
> Stop your foolish impertinence.
> Follow your profession of shoemaker
> And don't be a lazy idler
> Stop writing foolishness
> That makes everyone laugh out loud
> (Andrews 2010, 30).

As the process of slave emancipation and national independence unfolded in the nineteenth century, Afro-Latin American intellectuals imagined political communities that were both smaller (*quilombos*, *palenques*, etc.) and larger than the nation-state. As in other parts of the Americas, black and mulatto intellectuals have explored many supra-national political projects, from Pan-Africanism to Pan-Americanism. Pan-Caribbean *antillanismo* was one approach crafted by black and mulatto intellectuals as they sought to create anti-colonial, post-slave societies. Ramón Emeterio Betances, the Puerto Rican-born intellectual, was one of the more eloquent pan-regional thinkers in the nineteenth-century Caribbean. Betances was a light-skinned mulatto whose father proved *limpieza de sangre* in order to marry his daughter into a white Creole family; he has been read as a black thinker but he only calls himself black in a private letter, and was never attacked by his contemporaries as a mulatto (Baerga Santini 2009, 82). Still, in his writings, Betances developed a concept of transracial community that foregrounded the region's enslaved and free populations of color. If the notion of American freedom from colonial rule tended to be dominated by elite Creole interests in the 1820s, by the 1870s anti-colonial insurgent ideas were firmly linked to the liberation of slaves in the writings and speeches of the period. Betances became perhaps the foremost exponent of the Antillian Confederation. His Pan-Caribbean politics were clear in his *nom de plume*, "El Antillano," which he used in many of his articles. In the revealingly titled, "A Cuba libre, Ensayo sobre Alexandre Petión," Betances praised the Haitian leader's efforts to make the Haitian nation-state a model of political leadership that could inform a broader Pan-Caribbean identification. This vision of *antillanismo*, as Arroyo has shown, was a gendered conception of community informed by the brotherhoods forged in the Freemason movement, which was populated by a number of prominent Afro (and Euro)-descended intellectuals:

The Antilles are facing a moment they have never faced before in history; they now have to decide whether "to be, or not to be." We reject this troubling proposal. Now is the precise moment for us to present a united defensive front . . . Let us unite. Let us love one another. Together let us build a society of true Freemasons, and only then will we be able to build a temple with foundations so solid that not even the united force of the Saxon and Spanish races will be able to shake them; a temple that we will consecrate to independence, and on those frontpiece, we will engrave this inscription, as imperishable as the Motherland itself; "The Antilles for the Antilleans"

(Arroyo 2013, 96).

As we know, however, this vision of *antillanismo* did not come to pass, and Afro-Latin American intellectuals participated in the crafting of new national discourses that claimed to transcend the racial divisions of slavery.

In Cuba, where the abolition of slavery was also prompted by the struggle for independence from Spain, Afro-Cuban activists and intellectuals linked abolition of slavery and racial equality to the cause of national liberation. Along with José Martí, who championed the notion of Cuba *con todos y para todos* (with all and for all), Antonio Maceo, the iconic mulatto general, was one of the more eloquent proponents of emancipation and national independence. Though usually known for his military prowess (like Toussaint) and steadfast commitment to Cuban patriotism, Maceo, even as a free man of color who was never a slave, saw Cuban independence as inextricably linked to the abolition of slavery. In a letter written to Haitian General Joseph Lamothe while in exile in 1879, Maceo explained the need to free Cuba's enslaved population:

> Those slaves, General, worn out from the whip and chains, are too weak to break their own bonds, and looking around they see us, men of color, who have had the good fortune of not being born into slavery, or of having freed ourselves from it, and they seek our help. Our duty is to concede to them, to deny it would be a crime ... I am an emissary of an enslaved people who struggle to gain their independence near another people of the same origin who enjoy an independent existence, and who are too generous not to continue to extend a protective hand to their brothers
>
> (Foner 1977, 99).

While other Afro-Cuban separatists went to great lengths to disavow any connection to Haiti for fears of being accused of engaging in a race war, Maceo embraced a connection between the black republic and the Cuban nation in formation (Zacaïr 2005). But transracial nationalism, as Maceo and his contemporaries came to realize, could be perilous terrain. This was particularly true for the Afro-Cuban intellectuals who survived the wars of independence and lived in the early years of the Cuban Republic.

Ricardo Batrell was one of the few Cubans of African descent who wrote about the transition from the wars of independence to the neocolonial republic under US supervision. Born poor in Sabanilla, Matanzas, the heart of Cuba's nineteenth-century sugar plantation economy, Batrell wrote about his experiences as a black soldier in the Liberation Army. His *Para la historia: Apuntes autobiográficos de la vida de Ricardo Batrell Oviedo*, recently translated and published in English, underscored both the triumphs of Cuba's transracial liberation army and the unfulfilled promises of the early years of the republic. "There were no worries or any races," Batrell writes of the Cuba he encountered at the end of the war. "Everyone was truly joyful and full of brotherly love" (Batrell 2010, 193). Yet a few years later, Batrell was among a number of Afro-Cuban insurgent intellectuals who criticized the marginalization of blacks in the early Republic. With Martí's mantra of "Cuba with all and for all" now the dominant ideology of the Cuban Republic, some Afro-Cuban intellectuals found their protests against ongoing racial discrimination delegitimized by white elites and their Afro-Cuban allies, who claimed that black and white men had conquered the hierarchies of slavery on the battlefields of the war. This is clear in the case of the short history of the *Partido Independiente de Color* (1908–12). The party was outlawed by the Morúa Law, an amendment that banned race-based political parties and that was sponsored by a black senator named Martín Morúa Delgado, a member of the ruling party's governing coalition. In 1912, the government violently repressed the *Partido* by executing its leadership and thousands of Afro-Cubans. In independent Cuba, as in other Latin American republics, race-based mobilization was often unable to challenge the power of multiracial patronage networks and ideologies of racial inclusion under the banner of de-racialized liberalism (de la Fuente 2001; Helg 1995; on a similar dynamic in Brazil, see Alberto 2011, 196–244).

## EMPIRE, RACE SCIENCE, AND TRANSNATIONAL BLACK NETWORKS

In the late nineteenth and early twentieth centuries, Afro-Latin Americans confronted a context in which the dominant scientific view was that blacks and other non-whites were "inferior races" whose presence detracted from (or at least did not contribute to) the region's ability to develop and match European civilization or US progress. These currents were facilitated by the triumph of elite liberalism in Latin America, which, by the latter decades of the century, had generally eclipsed the popular brands of liberalism of previous decades. Euro-Creole thinkers drew upon Eurocentric positivist thought to forge state policies that would exclude the region's Afro and indigenous-descended populations. This is clear in Republican Brazil, where elites sought to exclude former slaves from employment and political participation through European immigration (Andrews 1988). Some Afro-Brazilian thinkers, such as the well-known case of Nina Raimundo Rodrigues, were unabashed proponents of scientific theories of racial inferiority, even though he was a person of African descent. Writing in a period when racially informed theories of criminality predominated among Atlantic world thinkers, Rodrigues argued that "Aryan civilization is represented in Brazil by a small minority of the white race, which in turn has the task of defending it, not only against anti-social – crimes – by its own members, but also against the anti-social acts of inferior races" (Rodrigues 1957 [1894], 161; see also the case of Francisco José Oliveira Viana [Needell 1995]).

Other black intellectuals, such as the Haitian diplomat Anténor Firmin (1850–1911), who was a contemporary of Betances, confronted these ideas head-on and challenged the dominant scientific racism of the time. A lawyer who was born and educated in Haiti, Firmin studied law and held several political offices before being posted as a diplomat to France, where he was admitted to the *Societé d'Anthropologie de Paris*; he has been recovered as a pioneer black anthropologist (Fluehr-Lobban 2000). While in Paris Firmin wrote and published a radical text challenging Count Joseph Arthur de Gobineau's *The Inequality of the Races*, which coupled a historically determinist account of Aryan supremacy with a condemnation of miscegenation (de Gobineau 1967 [1915]. Firmin's text, *The Equality of the Human Races*, was originally published in French in 1855; the first English translation only became available in 2002. Firmin made a number of arguments that were revolutionary for the time: for example, that all races were equal and that racial mixture did not lead to degeneration. He also emphasized the arbitrary nature of scientific racism. "Classifications of race are confusing because their authors mix all sorts of criteria together instead of limiting themselves to a single one. Most often they devise arbitrary and fanciful designation[s] ... Thus they speak of an *Aryan* race and of an *Indo-European* race. This artificial nomenclature is particularly specious as its scientific veneer impresses the general public" (Firmin 2002, 116).

Firmin refuted all the supposed measures purporting to show that whites were superior to other races, including brain size, as well as the claim that blacks had never achieved a high degree of civilization (by pointing to the African influence on Egypt). He repeatedly pointed to the Haitian Revolution of 1804 as an example of black capacity, and argued that all of the achievements of "the small Haitian Republic, a shining buoy in the small Antilles archipelago, will provide sufficient evidence in support of the idea of the equality of the races in all its ramifications" (Firmin 2002, 295). Firmin also cited the famous US black abolitionist, orator, and ex-slave Frederick Douglass as an example of a "remarkable" mulatto and quoted passages from Douglass' first autobiography,

*Narrative of the Life of Frederick Douglass* (1845) in which Douglass claimed that he had inherited his abilities from his enslaved black mother, not his white father.

Douglass was a great admirer of Haiti, and he lauded it as "the only self-made black republic in the world" (Douglass 1893, 4). Douglass was US ambassador to Haiti in the 1890s, at a time when Firmin was serving as Haiti's Foreign Relations Minister. They were interlocutors in a series of tense diplomatic negotiations over US attempts to lease a Haitian port, an episode that would lead the US press to accuse Douglass of being too sympathetic to Haiti because of his race, but which also highlights how US imperial ambitions toward Latin America divided black intellectuals across the hemisphere during this era. In addition to having produced one of the few texts by a black intellectual to directly challenge nineteenth-century scientific racism, Firmin was also an early advocate of Pan-Africanism and was one of two Haitian delegates to the first Pan-African Conference in London in 1900. Nevertheless, in *The Equality of the Human Races* Firmin accepted the idea that Europeans at the time had reached a higher level of civilization, and repeatedly portrayed Africa as less developed than diasporic black populations in the Americas.

As they contested the influence of scientific racism and ideas of *blanqueamiento*, black male writers sought to project themselves as worthy of equality by foregrounding their mastery of letters and Eurocentric culture. Like black aspiring classes and elites in the United States, black male intellectuals in Latin America championed various iterations of racial uplift, the notion that the educated elite had a responsibility to lift the "race" out of the vestiges of slavery. Various iterations of uplift ideologies similar to W. E. B. Du Bois's "Talented Tenth" were articulated by black thinkers throughout the hemisphere. In São Paulo, Brazil, a region where black activists tended to espouse race-based mobilization, Afro-Brazilian male intellectuals sought to contest *blanqueamiento* and newly formed practices of racial exclusion by cultivating an image of "men of worth." Like black and mulatto freemasons in the Caribbean, these men aimed to show white Brazilians that it was "not just the One-Steps, the Ragtime, and *Picadinhos* [popular dance] that we know how to cultivate, but that we also feel love and goodwill toward instructive things, good books of literature and morals." In a period when only literate males were eligible for the franchise, these black Paulista writers wanted to place themselves alongside white men so that they could "solidify the fraternity that makes us indistinguishable from whites born under the gold and green flag" (Alberto 2011, 34, 41).

In the Caribbean, Afrodescendant thinkers were profoundly influenced by the emergence of US imperialism in the region after the War of 1898. Black thinkers found themselves struggling for national and racial self-definition in a moment of intensifying imperial encounters with a nation increasingly defined by legalized racial segregation. One Caribbean "lettered man of the colored race" who attempted to craft a wider (and also elitist) sense of political community in this context was José Celso Barbosa, an Afro-Puerto Rican intellectual of the late nineteenth and early twentieth centuries. Barbosa represented a strand of black conservative thought which posited the United States as a model for equality and citizenship. In the midst of the summer of 1919, known in US history as the "Red Summer" – a moment of racial terror and repression of radical movements – Barbosa wrote several revealing pieces on "the race problem in the United States." An 1880 graduate of the University of Michigan and, like Rodrigues, a doctor, Barbosa's experience in the United States during the country's transition from slavery to wage labor brought him into direct contact with the question of race in the United States. As Miriam Jiménez Román has pointed out, this period had a lasting influence on Barbosa and led him to conclude that integration into the United States, rather than political independence, was not only the best option for Puerto Ricans in general but also for "the colored race" in Puerto Rico in particular. Unlike Betances, who was wary of US incursion into the Caribbean, Barbosa welcomed it, even in the moment when Jim Crow segregation was consolidating itself in the US South. "All men of the colored race owe gratitude to the American people," Barbosa wrote, "not only because this noble nation shed its blood of its children to liberate the Negro, but also because after redeeming him from servitude, did not abandon him to his own luck, but has invested its money for millions of dollars to educate the black race" (Barbosa 1937, 91).

As in other parts of Latin America, news of US racist practices were well known in Puerto Rico. Nevertheless, Barbosa worked out his own understanding of the United States and its history of mistreatment of African Americans, one that did not run counter to his dream of US statehood for Puerto Rico. To Barbosa, the United States federal government was not responsible for the continuing oppression of people of African descent within its borders. Rather, he laid the blame on the southern state governments for passing laws designed to disenfranchise and terrorize African Americans. He argued that it was at the state level that the problem of racial oppression needed to be rectified. According to this schema of statehood, Puerto Ricans, like the racist southerners who implemented the Jim Crow laws, would be in full control of the Puerto Rican state legislature, and thus racism could not simply be imposed on the island by the US federal government. "The problem can only emerge," he argued, "by the will of the Puerto Rican people" (Barbosa 1937, 55). Thus, from Barbosa's perspective, the US presence in Puerto Rico was actually a way to check Puerto Rican racism, an argument that may perplex the twenty-first-century observer, and no doubt would have confounded many in Barbosa's day. However puzzling his position may seem, Barbosa's arguments demonstrate the ways that Afrodescendant intellectuals could refashion US understandings of political community in different national contexts.[7]

By the 1920s and 1930s, Barbosa's generation of Afro-Latin American "race men" were eclipsed by a younger cohort of writers, activists, and artists whose identities were profoundly impacted by black nationalist ideologies that emphasized diasporic solidarities and black autonomy. The spread of these ideas was facilitated by mass black migration throughout the hemisphere. Diasporic organizations such as the Universal Negro Improvement Association (UNIA) crafted a vision of Pan-African nationalism that skillfully harmonized the seemingly contradictory ideas of imperialism, black entrepreneurship, and race pride. The association, founded by Marcus Garvey and Amy Ashwood in Kingston, Jamaica, in 1914, had by the 1920s turned into a mass movement that was made up of Afro-diasporic people from a vast array of cultural, linguistic, and national backgrounds, primarily in the United States and the circum-Caribbean. By the middle part of the decade, Cuba had the largest number of UNIA branches outside of the United States (Guridy 2010). In Central America, the UNIA's Pan-Africanist message of black pride and self-determination resonated among West Indians employed by the United Fruit Company in Costa Rica and in the Panama Canal, as well as among Afrodescendant Creoles in Nicaragua. In the 1920s there were ninety active UNIA chapters in Central America, which represented one-third of all UNIA branches outside the United States (there were twenty-three UNIA chapters in Costa Rica, eighteen in Guatemala, Nicaragua, and Honduras, and forty-nine in Panama and the Canal Zone). The impact of the UNIA on local black populations was significant.

---

[7] Barbosa was part of a larger movement of black Puerto Rican annexationists in this period. See Findlay (2000).

In Nicaragua, for example, there were five UNIA chapters on the Caribbean coast, two of them in Bluefields (Liberty Hall and the Union Club). The two Bluefields divisions had 500–1,000 active members at their peak, nearly a quarter of the city's black population at the time (Harpelle 2003). These divisions were linked together by the *Negro World*, the organization's newspaper, along with an impressive assemblage of UNIA paraphernalia and performance practices that enabled members to forge a commonality and embody a black transnational nation in the making.

Although the UNIA tended to be most popular among Anglophone black Caribbean migrants, it also had some influence among Spanish-speaking Afrodescendant activists. One of Garveyism's most loyal adherents was the still understudied Eduardo Morales. Morales was born in Cuba, but raised in Panama, where he developed his racial awareness and his political activism. In the early 1920s, Morales was one of the more visible leaders of the UNIA in the United States-controlled Panama Canal Zone. Along with William Preston Stoute, the Barbadian-born leader of the United Brotherhood labor union, Morales led the famous canal workers strike of 1920. For Morales, the strike was an opportunity for the divided black population to overcome the cultural differences that had stifled racial organizing. Morales's rousing speeches never failed to extol the virtues of Garvey's black nationalist philosophy, themes that he would continue to preach a short while later as a UNIA leader in Cuba. In a meeting in Panama reported in the *Negro World*, Morales asked his fellow male Canal workers: "Do you want to prevent, when you get up in the morning and go one way in search of work [that] your wife is compelled to go to those white people and beg them for permission to scrub their floors? You will prevent that if you join the union." For Morales, unionism was the first step on the road to Pan-African nationhood. Rejecting national identities, Morales declared: "I am a Panamanian but I do not call myself one." Morales insisted, "we should all be one and call ourselves negroes." In another speech, the UNIA leader attacked skin colorism among the local Afro-diasporic population: "our direct object is Racial Success; physically, morally, intellectually and financially. In order to achieve Racial Success, we must first realize that however fair our complexion may be, however straight our hair may be, as long as we possess the minimum amount of Negro blood in our veins, we are considered Negroes." Morales's explicit racial/diasporic consciousness, which was informed by his travels throughout the circum-Caribbean, disrupt prevailing understandings of comparative race relations models that have tended to differentiate the Anglophone race-conscious black person from the unconscious Latin American Afrodescendant (Burnett 2004, 68).[8]

## REFASHIONING NATION AND *MESTIZAJE*

Along with Garveyism, another transnational intellectual current that had an even more profound impact on Afro-Latin American thinkers and artists during the 1920s and 1930s was the work of the poets and writers associated with the Harlem Renaissance, Afrocubanismo, Negritude, and other black-identified cultural movements. These movements were part of the larger cultural revolution that enveloped the Americas and the Atlantic World during the 1920s and 1930s. The popularity of tango, jazz, and "Negro" literature, as well as the "enormous vogue of things Mexican" were in part products of white fascination with "folk" and "primitive" cultures (Delpar 1992).

While the movements in Paris, Havana, and Mexico City all contributed to this broader cultural transformation, the Harlem Renaissance became in many ways the most influential. African American intellectuals touted the emergence of a "New Negro" whose art and literature would work in the service of the goal of racial equality. US imperial hegemony and the hegemonic position of African Americans in the African Diaspora made the Harlem Renaissance central to the Atlantic and American-hemispheric fascination with Afro-diasporic cultural production (Baldwin and Makalani 2013).

Afrocubanismo, unlike the Harlem Renaissance, was a more thoroughly cross-racial movement that featured not only the participation of Afro-Cuban poets and musicians Nicolás Guillén, Regino Pedroso, Teodoro Ramos Blanco, but also many white poets and artists, including José Tallet, Emilio Ballagas, Alejandro García Caturla, and Ernesto Lecuona. While the movement was clearly shaped by white primitivist fantasies about black culture, it nevertheless resulted in greater recognition of the African roots of Cuban culture. The new *mestizaje*-infused nationalism was epitomized by Guillén's prologue to *Sóngoro Cosongo*, in which he argued that the intermixture of Cuba's European and African roots led to the creation of "Cuban color." Although Guillén was at times critical of the vogue of blackness, he himself benefited, even

---

[8] Another Afro-Latin American thinker who was profoundly influenced by Garveyism was Carlos Cooks, the Afro-Dominican activist (Rivera 2012).

if indirectly, from the heightened attention Afro-diasporic writers received in this period (Kutzinski 1993; Moore 1997).

The relationships among Langston Hughes, Nicolás Guillén, and Jacques Roumain illustrate the profound influence of cross-national intellectual and artistic exchange on Afrodescendant writers in this period. The impact of these relations spread throughout Latin America, as the older comparative literature scholarship and recent historical work has shown (Andrews 2010; Flórez Bolívar 2015; Mullen 1977). Guillén as much as any other Afrodescendant intellectual, powerfully re-envisioned transracial nationalism in this period. While nineteenth-century black separatists saw transracialism emerging from fraternal bonds forged in battle, Guillén, like Freyre, saw transracialism forged through *mestizaje* (race mixture). The new *mestizaje*-infused national-ism was epitomized by Guillén's prologue to his groundbreaking volume of poems, entitled *Sóngoro Cosongo*, published in 1931, in which he argued that the intermixture of Cuba's European and African roots led to the creation of "Cuban color." "The spirit of Cuba is mestizo and our true color will come from the spirit to the skin. One day it will be called 'Cuban color.'" (Guillén 2004: 91–92). Guillén's writing at this time represents attempts by an Afrodescended thinker to envision a *mestizaje* from "below," that explicitly used the language of mixture and Afro-Cuban vernacular language to celebrate black cultural contributions to national culture.

A key interlocutor for both Hughes and Guillén was the radical Haitian poet, essayist, and activist, Jacques Roumain. Roumain's ascendance and his relations with Guillén, Hughes, and other writers in the Atlantic World highlights the influence of Marxism on Afrodescendant thinkers in the 1930s. His posthumously published novel, *Gouverneurs de la rosée* (Masters of the Dew), traces the experiences of Manuel, a Haitian peasant who returns to his homeland after working in the sugar fields of neighboring Cuba. Here again one notes the theme of the radic-alizing effect of cross-national migration. Manuel's story exemplifies the struggles of black migrant workers and peasants in the era of the Great Depression. After he returns to Haiti from Cuba, the fictional character responds to a question, "what are we?" by bluntly saying:

We're this country, and it wouldn't be a thing without us, nothing at all. Who does the planting? Who does the watering? Who does the harvesting? Coffee, cotton, rice, sugar cane, cacao, corn, bananas, vegetables, and all the fruits, who's going to grow them if we don't?

(Roumain 2008, 80)

The world of Manuel, not unlike the worlds of Roumain, Guillén, and Hughes, was shaped by Jim Crow segregation, US imperial rule, and the catastrophic effects of the Great Depression. After the onset of the Depression, Afrodescendant poets and writers looked to black laboring majorities, not only for sources of cultural inspiration, but to highlight their exploitation by capitalist imperialism. Hughes, like Roumain, made this point clear in his essay, "People Without Shoes," which highlighted the conditions of exploitation in US-occupied Haiti.

Haiti is a land of people without shoes – black people, whose bare feet tread the dusty roads to market in the early morning, or pat softly on the bare floors of hotels, serving foreign guests. These barefooted ones care for the rice and cane fields under the hot sun. They climb high mountains picking coffee beans, and wade through surf to fishing boats in the blue sea. All of the work that keeps Haiti alive, pays for the American Occupation, and enriches foreign traders – that vast and basic work – is done there by Negroes without shoes.

(Hughes 1931, 12)

Hughes, a "mulatico" as Guillén once playfully called him, critiques the light-skinned elite (the people with shoes) when he asks his reader: "What then, pray, have the dignified native citizens with shoes been doing all the while – those Haitians, mulattoes largely, who have dominated the politics of the country for decades, and who have drawn almost as sharp a class line between themselves and their shoeless black brothers as have the Americans with their imported color line dividing the Occupation from all Haitians?" (Hughes 1931, 12). Here Hughes links his critique of class and color hierarchies with US imperialism. The theme of imperialist domination emerges in Guillén's poem from the same year, "Caña."

> The Negro
> in the cane fields
> The Yankee
> above the cane fields
> The earth
> beneath the cane fields
> Blood that flows from us!
> (Guillén 2004, 104)

The writings and political trajectories of Hughes, Guillén, and Roumain in the 1930s highlight the growing influence of the international Communist movement and anti-imperialism on Afrodescendant (and many Latin American) writers in this period. Indeed, it was not merely the "vogue" for the primitive that propelled the themes and artistic choices of these cultural producers. As US interventionism and the economic crisis of the Great Depression exposed the fragilities of Latin American political economies, these writers joined with writers and artists in Mexico and other parts of Latin America to challenge both the prevailing scientific racism of the early part of the century and elite nationalisms of previous decades and to formulate forms of black Marxism and critiques of capitalist imperialism. The ongoing tensions engendered by the US presence in Latin America continued to shape the thinking of Afro-Latin American writers, especially as the Cold War further polarized politics in the region.

BLACK CONSCIOUSNESS, BLACK MARXISM, BLACK FEMINISM

Afro-Latin American thought in the mid- to late-twentieth century was diverse and complex. Prominent black intellectuals across the region grappled with the content of black culture in the Americas, the forms and goals of black politics, the situation of black women, and the kinds of transnational relationships that Afro-Latin Americans could establish with Africa and with African-Americans in the United States. We have chosen to focus on three important strands of Afro-Latin American thought during this period.

First, we explore evolving conceptions of black consciousness that can be traced from movements influenced by *negritude* in the 1930s and 1940s to writings on black identity associated with the wave of Afro-Latin American cultural and political mobilization from the 1970s to the present. In contrast to nineteenth-century attempts by black *letrados* to demonstrate their mastery of European culture, twentieth-century black consciousness movements in Latin America rejected assimilationist strategies and instead sought to trace the African roots and diasporic routes of Afro-Latin America in order to ground a specific black identity distinct from dominant national imaginaries of nationhood.

Second, we highlight the important interventions of black intellectuals and artists in the Marxist revolutions of the second half of the twentieth century, particularly in Cuba and Nicaragua, that challenged the Latin American Left's history of silence about racism and sexism.

Finally, we trace the emergence of Afro-Latin American feminisms that foreground the intersectional struggles of black women in Latin America and that chart new avenues for Afro-Latin American thought. Afro-Latin American feminists have formulated a powerful critique of the lack of a gender analysis in previous strands of black political thought in Latin America, as well as of mainstream Latin American feminism's inattention to race. Gendering Afro-Latin American thought is "necessary to draw a more complex and concrete picture of black humanity that not only includes women as agents and cocreators of

Afro-diasporic life and thought but sees issues of gender and sexuality as constitutive of black identity, black life, and black liberation" (Laó-Montes and Buggs 2014, 385).

Given the existence of *mestizaje* and the hegemony of deracialized liberalisms that militated against race-based identification and organizing in Latin America, the question of who was black and what it meant to be black has been a central concern for Afro-Latin American thinkers. In the 1930s and 1940s, various cultural and artistic movements emerged in the Caribbean and mainland Latin America that rejected Eurocentrism, celebrated blackness, and promoted various forms of black nationalism. In the Francophone Caribbean, black intellectuals such as the Martinican poet and decolonial theorist Aimé Césaire and the Haitian intellectual and politician Jean Price-Mars formulated the idea of Negritude. This cultural and political movement embraced the African roots of New World societies, celebrated blackness, championed African-derived religions and spiritual practices, and leveled a fierce critique of European and US imperialism. While it did not produce a mass following, "Negritude became one of the most important cultural revolutions of black intellectuals in the twentieth century" (Davis and Williams 2007, 148). Negritude thinkers were deeply in dialogue with Marxism; in his *Discours sur le colonialisme* (1955), for example, Césaire connected colonialism to economic exploitation and racism. Yet, as one can note in the Harlem Renaissance and Afrocubanismo, there was a tension inherent in Negritude's celebration of black contributions to Western civilization, as a focus on black cultural production could easily overshadow the political and economic causes of black oppression.

In Brazil, the Teatro Experimental do Negro (TEN) founded by Abdias do Nascimento (1914–2011), drew inspiration from Negritude as it sought to contest dominant Brazilian representations of blackness that promoted whitening. Emerging after the dismantling of the Frente Negra Brasilerira, TEN, which was active from 1944 to 1961, engaged in various forms of cultural activism, including organizing the First Congress of Brazilian Blacks, to counter the invisibility of blacks in Brazilian society and give them a voice. TEN sought to contest the hegemony of white intellectuals who researched African contributions to Brazilian culture without making space for black intellectuals to speak for themselves. Nascimento explained that "while the black [man] continues as 'a mere object of verses in whose elaboration he does not participate,' Negritude will stay alive and active" (Davis and Williams 2007, 160). Like Negritude, the TEN did not produce an organized political movement, but it had a profound impact on racial thought in Brazil and paved the way for the emergence of organizations such as the Movimento Negro Unificado (MNU) a conglomeration of intellectuals and activists who came together in 1978 to reinvigorate the movement for racial equality. Mobilized by the global de-colonization movement and the Black Freedom Struggle in the United States, the MNU challenged the Brazilian military dictatorship's attempts to suppress critiques of ongoing racism in Brazil.

The evolution of twentieth-century Afro-Latin American thought is perhaps best exemplified by the shifts in the political ideas of Nascimento, from adherent of Brazilian *mestiçagem* to proponent of Negritude to Pan-African thinker and critic of racial democracy. Nascimento was originally an advocate of Brazilian racial inclusion. In 1950, for example, he argued that Brazil's "widespread miscegenation" produced a "well-delineated doctrine of racial democracy, that will serve as a lesson and model to other nations of complex ethnic formation" (quoted in Alberto 2011, 12). By the 1970s, he had largely rejected this vision, arguing that "racial democracy" was a spurious myth that obscured the reality of a state-sponsored project of "whitening" and "black genocide" in Brazil. Nascimento formulated the definitive statement rejecting the official ideology of racial democracy that had prevailed in Brazil for decades. "Brazil as a nation proclaims itself to be the only racial democracy in the world," he wrote, "yet a close examination of its historical development reveals the true nature of its social, cultural and political structures: they are essentially racist and vitally threatening to blacks" (Nascimento 1979, 59).

Nascimento also formulated a notion of "Quilombismo" influenced by Pan-Africanism and Marxism. He argued that *quilombos* should serve as a model for Afro-Brazilian political mobilization because they represented "an authentic, broad and permanent sociopolitical movement ... Quilombos were ... the methodical and constant life form of the African masses who refused to submit to the exploitation and violence of the slave system" (Nascimento 1980, 151). The essay reflects the Pan-African and Marxist influences on his political ideas; in it he argues that "as an economic system, Quilombismo has meant the adaptation of African traditions of communitarianism and/or Ujamaa to the Brazilian environment" (161). Nascimento used an expansive definition of quilombo that encompassed a broad variety of Afro-Brazilian cultural, religious, and political organizations. "This web of associations, brotherhoods, clubs, *terreiros* (houses of worship of Afro-Brazilian religion), *tendas*, *afochés*, samba schools, *gafieiras, grêmios, confrarias*, were and are Quilombos." Together, these various sites of black collective resistance enacted "a practice of liberation" (152). Nascimento thus identified the experience of slave flight as an original model of black political organizing in Latin America. "Quilombismo and its various equivalents throughout the Americas, expressed in the legacy of *cumbes, palenques, cimarrones*, and maroons, constitute an international alternative for popular Black political organization" (152).

Nascimento was part of a generation of Afro-Latin American intellectuals, artists, writers, and filmmakers who widened and, in some cases, actively challenged prevailing conceptions of race and national identities during the 1970s. This was a period when black rights movements found inspiration in the global national liberation and US-based Black freedom struggle, the mobilization against military dictatorships in Latin America, and previous moments of black resistance (e.g., *quilombos*). The promotion of black consciousness that was a hallmark of Negritude and other black cultural movements in the first half of the twentieth century laid the groundwork for the emergence of a robust wave of black political organizing in the late twentieth century. These new black movements coupled assertions of black identity with demands that Latin American states recognize racism and proactively implement race-conscious public policy to overcome racial discrimination (see Chapter 7).

One of the characteristics of Afro-Latin American thought has thus been the symbiotic relationship between the cultural and the political. In Colombia, for example, which now has some of the most visible black movements in the region, the groundwork for Afro-Colombian political mobilization can be traced back to the consolidation of notions of black consciousness in the 1970s. International events, such as the Congresses of Black Culture (in Colombia in 1977, Panama in 1980, and Brazil in 1982), which brought together activists and thinkers from throughout Latin America, played an important role in this process. The first Congress was organized by the Afro-Colombian medical doctor, novelist, and researcher Manuel Zapata Olivella (1920–2004), whose most famous work, *Changó el Gran Putas* (1983) or *Changó the Biggest Badass*, is an epic account of the Afro-American experience (see Chapter 9). Beginning with Africa and the transatlantic slave trade, Zapata Olivella highlights the history of maroon communities in Cartagena, Haitian independence, Simón Bolívar's fears of pardocracia, and the heroism of *pardo* general José Prudencio Padilla. The book ends with the struggle against Jim Crow racial segregation in the United States. Zapata Olivella's work inspired later activists such as Juan de Dios Mosquera, one of the founders of the urban Afro-Colombian organization *Cimarrón*, which was modeled on the black civil rights movement in the United States. Together with Afro-Colombian organizations in the Pacific coast region focused on questions of land and territory, these organizations have pushed the Colombian state to adopt race-conscious laws and policies since the 1990s (Paschel 2016).

The ideas of the earlier generation of thinkers who formulated strong conceptions of black consciousness that translated from culture to politics were thus crucial to the emergence of late twentieth-century black movements that pushed Latin American states to enact unprecedented constitutional recognition of racial and cultural diversity as well as policies to redress racial discrimination (Hooker 2008; Paschel 2016). Late twentieth-century black movements posed radical challenges to official state ideologies of racial harmony that denied racism and the legitimacy of a separate black consciousness and political organizing by people of African descent. In Panama, for example, Afro-Panamanian intellectuals of West Indian descent who were also political activists – such as Gerardo Maloney, George Priestley, and Alberto Barrow – traced the development of twentieth-century black consciousness in Panama, the formation of various Afro-Panamanian organizations, and the successes and failures of the black movement in their writings (Barrow 2001; Barrow and Priestley 2003). Similarly, in Venezuela, black movement-affiliated writings such as those of Jesús "Chucho" García (1990, 1992) and Ligia Montañez (1993) sketched the African presence in the country and the "hidden racism" of a society that had been officially color-blind since independence.

The same pattern can be observed in many other countries in the region. Yet it is important to note that the explicitly black (or Afro) social movements that began to emerge in Latin America in the 1970s are not monolithic. Agustín Laó-Montes, for example, has argued that rather than seeing all contemporary black movements as the heirs of a black radical tradition, there are identifiable "afro-izquierda" and "afro-derecha" currents in the field of black politics in Latin America. This is because "the very partial successes of the Afro-Latin American movements facilitated the conditions for the emergence of conservative black elites and also for the integration to the state and the NGOization of some of its key leaders and organizations" (Laó-Montes 2008/2009, 253).

A second important strand of Afro-Latin American thought in the twentieth century is the work of black intellectuals involved in Marxist-inspired revolutions and leftist movements. Among the more influential were those Afro-Cuban thinkers who emerged with, and were sometimes thwarted by, the Cuban Revolution of the 1950s and 60s. In this period, Afro-Cuban intellectuals such as Walterio Carbonell, Juan René Betancourt and Carlos Moore crafted radical visions of racial inclusion, though each was eventually silenced by Fidel Castro's government (Guerra 2012, 273–77; Moore 2008). But it was in the realm of cultural production and aesthetics where interventions around questions of race, gender, revolution, and social justice were often most effectively made by black artists within leftist movements in Cuba and other parts of Latin America.

Afro-Latin American women in particular made important cultural interventions as part of revolutionary movements in Cuba and Nicaragua that highlighted the raced and gendered dimensions of leftist politics in the region. In Revolutionary Cuba, this was risky business in an era when intellectuals had to work with and against Fidel Castro's ambiguous mandate, "dentro la revolución todo; contra la Revolución, nada." While historians of the Revolution have highlighted the repression experienced by Afro-Cuban male intellectuals, such as Carbonell and Moore, few have examined closely the work of Sara Gómez, the innovative filmmaker who died prematurely at age 31 in 1974.

Born of a middle-class black family in 1943, Gómez abandoned a musical career to take up filmmaking. Though her work is usually situated in Latin American cinema studies, her style and techniques also resemble those of Charles Burnett, Haile Gerima, and other members of the "LA Rebellion," the black filmmaker movement in 1970s Los Angeles (Field, Horak, and Stewart 2015). In eleven short films, and one full-length feature film, Gómez innovatively presented the desires and struggles of the black working classes and poor in 1960s and 1970s Cuba. Like the Afrocubanist poets and writers of the 1930s, Gómez centralized the experiences of the black working classes in her films, many of which remained unseen for decades after her death.

Her best-known film, *De Cierta Manera* (One Way or Another), was released posthumously in 1977. It explores a love story between a man and a woman living in a poor and predominantly black Havana neighborhood. Using a black and white realist style, the film blurs the boundaries between "documentary" and fictional film. Throughout the movie, Gómez deploys a notion of "marginalism" to describe the black urban poor in Cuba, even as the plot and archival footage undermine the very notion of a black underclass. Gómez was unafraid to question the patriarchal structure of the Abakuá, the Calabar-based all-male secret society that, for her, represented the lingering manifestation of "male chauvinism" in Revolutionary Cuba.

And yet, the film humanizes her subjects in their daily struggles for revolutionary citizenship, juxtaposing the fictional characters with an objective-sounding social science narrator who describes the revolutionary government's plans to modernize the community. Finally, the film foregrounds the struggles of the main protagonists (Mario and Yolanda) to overcome their patriarchal and class-based biases in a new revolutionary context.

By skillfully portraying these issues in *De Cierta Manera* and in her other films, Gómez's work can be seen as offering "intersectional" analyses of everyday life in 1960s and 1970s Cuba. While the films seemingly foreground gender and class dynamics, her casting of Afro-Cuban actors and non-actors makes her films necessarily about race and the limits of the Revolution's ability to uproot racism and sexism. In this way, Gómez was a path-breaking intellectual who created a space for intersectional analyses of black life in Cuba that Gloria Rolando and others have taken up in recent decades (Chanan 2004; Ebrahim 2007; Lesage 1978).

In Nicaragua, the poet and painter June Beer (1931–86) symbolically made the black and indigenous inhabitants of the country's Caribbean Coast a part of a revolutionary movement that otherwise had little to say about them. Two vivid examples of Beer's marrying of race, gender, and revolution are her paintings, whose subjects were most often black women, and "Love Poem" (Beer 2006):

> Oscar, yuh surprise me,
> assin far a love poem.
> Ah sing a song a love fa meh contry
> small contry, big lite
> hope fa de po,' big headache fa de rich.
> Mo' po' dan rich in de worl
> mo' peeple love fa meh contry.
> Fa meh contry name Nicaragua
> Fa meh people ah love dem all.
> Black, Miskito, Sumu, Rama, Mestizo.
> So yuh see fa me, love poem complete
> 'cause ah love you too.
> Dat no mek me erase de moon
> and de star fran de firmament.
> Only somehow wen ah remnba
> how you bussing yo ass
> to defend this sunrise, an keep back
> de night fran fallin,
> ah know dat tomara we will have time
> fa walk unda de moon an stars.
> Dignify an free, sovereign
> children a Sandino.

Beer's poetry was subversive because it is written in Creole, which was suppressed both by Nicaraguan governments that wished to Hispanicize the region and by US Moravian missionaries who wanted Creoles to speak standard English. It also placed the black and indigenous peoples of the Caribbean Coast at the center of the revolutionary project. In a country where blackness had long been denied or relegated to the marginalized Caribbean coast, Beer's art presciently suggested that racism could be an Achilles heel of the revolutionary project.

The examples of Gómez and Beer demonstrate the important contributions that Afro-Latin American women have made to a variety of political struggles in the region, as well as the important interventions they have made as thinkers in their own right. Yet Afro-Latin American thought (like Latin American philosophy and black political thought) has been a male-dominated field, at least in terms of those intellectuals whose contributions have been most recognized. If Afro-Latin American thinkers were seen as marginal to the region's intellectual production, the contributions of Afro-Latin American women have been doubly invisibilized. In response, Afro-Latin American feminists have developed an intersectional analysis that challenges the silence on race in mainstream feminist movements and the lack of attention to gender from within black movements.

Afro-Latin American feminism thus envisions a radical decolonization of black political thought by challenging its longstanding masculinist presuppositions. As Sonia Alvarez and Kia Caldwell have argued in a recent journal special issue on the subject, "Afro-descendant feminisms have advanced radical re-imaginings of not only 'mainstream' or hegemonic Latin American feminisms, but also of race, gender, sexuality, democracy, health, development, cultural production, generation, citizenship, and other issues and ideas that are central to feminist theory" (Alvarez and Caldwell 2016, vi). Afro-Brazilian women activists in particular have been at the forefront of the development of Afro-Latin American feminism (Caldwell 2007). Two important black Brazilian feminists who made important early contributions to the theorization of Afro-Latin American feminism are Lélia Gonzalez and Beatriz Nascimento.

The intellectual, activist, and poet Beatriz Nascimento (1942–95) was one of the early theoreticians of the significance of *quilombos* as a model of political praxis for twentieth-century black movements (Nascimento 1982, 1985); she also formulated an intersectional analysis of the situation of black women in Brazil. She argued that, "As it served before as a manifestation of resistance to literal colonialization, in

1970 the quilombo becomes a code that responds to cultural colonialism, reaffirms African heritage and seeks a Brazilian model able to strengthen ethnic identity" (Ratts 2007, 124). Yet compared to her male counterparts, Nascimento's work has not received much scholarly attention to date, despite the profound influence of the theoretical insights she elicited from ethnographic work in *quilombo* communities on the recuperation of the *quilombo* by other black intellectuals and activists in Brazil (for example, the essay by Abdias do Nascimento discussed previously draws on her pioneering work). She rejected the idea of quilombos as only rural spaces, arguing that favelas could be considered *quilombos* insofar as they constituted autonomous spaces of black liberation defined by migration and escape. She also developed an analysis of Brazilian racism amidst the myth of racial democracy, calling it *"um emaranhado de sutilezas "* or a tangle of deceit (Ratts 2007, 47). Nascimento critiqued the lack of research on Afro-Brazilians (as well as their near-total absence from Brazilian universities), arguing that they were only discussed in conventional studies of slavery that depicted them as forced laborers with no agency. In contrast, she argued that slavery was a living past and that studies of the history of black Brazilians had to be connected to contemporary discrimination. "The slave quarters are still present," she wrote (Ratts 2007, 97).

Another important Afro-Brazilian feminist is Lélia Gonzalez, a pioneer in explicitly theorizing Afro-Latin American feminism. Gonzalez put forward an important critique of the way mainstream Latin American feminists ignored questions of race and marginalized the concerns and experiences of black and indigenous women. She pointed to "the internal contradictions of Latin American feminism," where "black and Indian women are living testimony to their exclusion from" the feminist movement (Gonzalez 1988, 95). She argued that the Latin American feminist movement was weakened by its lack of an intersectional analysis that connected racism and sexism. "Latin American feminism loses much of its force ... [when it] speaks, for example, of the sexual division of labor without articulating the corresponding racial division of work" (Gonzalez 1988, 97). Gonzalez pointed to black and indigenous women's participation in struggles for racial equality and liberation in Latin America as key to their political praxis, but she also criticized the way these movements "reproduce patriarchal sexist practices and try to exclude us from the decision-making process. And it is precisely for that reason that we seek to participate in a women's movement" (Gonzalez 1988, 99–100). Gonzalez thus articulated the double-bind that required the formulation of Afro-

Latin American feminism: sexism within black movements and racism within mainstream feminism. Gonzalez also centered the experiences of black women in Brazil in spaces of enslavement and fugitivity such as the *quilombos* (Gonzalez 1983).

Following in the footsteps of Nascimento and Gonzalez, contemporary Afro-Latin American feminists such as Yuderkys Espinosa Miñoso and Ochy Curiel have posited a decolonial feminism that can challenge the Eurocentric underpinnings of mainstream feminisms and the patriarchal and masculinist tendencies of black political thought (Espinosa Miñoso, Gómez Correal, and Ochoa Muñoz 2014). Espinosa has argued that "decolonial feminism" is "nourished by popular, communal knowledge, long-term memories, and from there it is constructing a critique of the way in which [traditional] feminism has envisioned the emancipation of women or sexualities or non-binary genders" (Barroso 2014, 23). Decolonial feminists have thus made an analysis of sexuality integral to Afro-Latin feminism (Curiel 2013). Rather than using decolonial thought to reconceive Afro-Latin American feminism, however, contemporary black feminists in Latin America have posited Afro-Latin American feminisms (and black feminism in the United States, and indigenous feminism) as forms of postcolonial theory (Curiel 2007). Afro-Latin American feminisms thus point to new and exciting avenues in black political thought.

## CONCLUSION

Today in Latin America vibrant black movements in many countries have spurred interest in the study of Afro-Latin American thinkers and in recovering the intellectual contributions of peoples of African descent in the region. In the academy, the consolidation of Afro-Latin American Studies and the impact of calls to decolonize Latin American political thought and abandon Eurocentric epistemologies that marginalize the knowledge produced by black and indigenous sources (Walsh 2007) have also contributed to the growing interest in Afro-Latin American thought. Indeed, much of what we sketch in this chapter about the contours of nineteenth- and twentieth-century Afro-Latin American thought is only possible because scholars have begun to do the work of uncovering the non-traditional spaces in which Afro-Latin American thinkers did their work and to creatively re-imagine the archive to uncover missing black voices and experiences.

We hope this chapter has demonstrated the complexity and richness of Afro-Latin American thought. Black thinkers in the region have been anything but monolithic: they have disagreed about what it means to be Afro-Latin American; they have crafted multiple visions of inclusion into existing states or of how to forge autonomous spaces for black liberation; they have debated whether black freedom can be achieved without decolonizing Latin American political thought, and indeed black political thought itself, in the case of Afro-Latin American feminists. There is still much work to be done, however, to recuperate the work of black thinkers in Latin America. Future avenues of research will include: centering the voices and experiences of Afro-Latin American women in struggles over slavery and citizenship in the republican era; tracing the links between black intellectuals across the Americas, especially those that disrupt easy narratives of North-South influence; and exploring the work of black cultural producers as sources of political and social thought. We need to continue to excavate Afro-Latin American freedom dreams, in all their complexity; their efforts, in the words of June Beer, to "walk unda de moon an stars. Dignify an free, sovereign."

## BIBLIOGRAPHY

Acree, Jr., William. 2009. "Jacinto Ventura de Molina: A Black Letrado in a White World of Letters." *Latin American Research Review* 44, 2: 37–58.

Alberto, Paulina, L. 2011. *Terms of Inclusion: Black Intellectuals in Twentieth Century Brazil.* Chapel Hill, NC: University of North Carolina Press.

Alvarez, Sonia, and Kia Caldwell. 2016. "Introduction." *Meridians* 14, 1: v–xi.

Andrews, George Reid. 1988. "Black and White Workers: São Paulo, Brazil, 1888–1928." *Hispanic American Historical Review* 68, 3: 491–524.

1991. *Blacks and Whites in São Paulo, 1888–1988.* Madison, WI: University of Wisconsin Press.

2004. *Afro-Latin America, 1800–2000.* New York, NY: Oxford University Press.

2010. "Afro World: Afro-Diasporic Thought and Practice in Montevideo, Uruguay, 1830–2000," *Americas* : 83–107.

Arroyo, Jossianna. 2003. *Travestismos culturales: Literatura y etnografía en Cuba y Brasil.* Pittsburgh, PA: Instituto Internacional de Literatura Iberoamericana, 2003.

2013. *Writing Secrecy in Caribbean Freemasonry.* New York, NY: Palgrave Macmillan.

Baerga Santini, María del Carmen. 2009. "Transgresiones corporales: El mejoramiento de la raza y los discursos eugenésicos en el Puerto Rico de finales del siglo XIX y principios del XX." *Op.Cit* 19: 79–106.

Baldwin, Davarian, and Minkah Makalani, eds. 2013. *Escape from New York The New Negro Renaissance beyond Harlem.* Minneapolis, MN: University of Minnesota Press.

Baquaqua, Mahommah Gardo. 2006. *The Biography of Mahommah Gardo Baquaqua: His Passage from Slavery to Freedom in Africa and America,* edited by Robin Law and Paul Lovejoy. Princeton, NJ: Markus Wiener.

Barbosa, José. 1937. "Problema de razas." In *La obra de José Celso Barbosa,* edited by Pilar Barbosa de Rosario, vol. 3, 63–186. San Juan: Imprenta Venezuela.

Barroso, J. M. 2014. "Feminismo decolonial: Una ruptura con la visión hegemónica eurocéntrica, racista y burguesa. Entrevista con Yuderkys Espinosa Miñoso." *Iberoamérica Social: Revista-Red de Estudios Sociales* 2, 3: 22–33.

Barrow, Alberto. 2001. *No me pidas una foto: Develando el racismo en Panamá.* Panamá: Universal Books.

Barrow, Alberto, and George Priestley. 2003. *Piel oscura Panamá: Ensayos y reflexiones al filo del centenario.* Panamá: Editorial Universitaria.

Battrell, Ricardo. 2010. *A Black Soldier's Story: The Narrative of Ricardo Batrell and the Cuban War of Independence.* Edited and translated by Mark A. Sanders. Minneapolis, MN: University of Minnesota Press.

Beer, June. 2006. "Love poem." *ANIDE: Asociación Nicaragüense de Escritoras* 5, 12: 5–6.

Betances, Ramón Emeterio. 1871. *A Cuba libre: Ensayo sobre Alexandre Petión.* New York, NY: M. M. Zarzamendi.

Bonilla-Silva, Eduardo, 2009. *Racism without Racists: Color Blind Racism and the Persistence of Racial Inequality in America,* 3rd edition. Lanham, MD: Rowman and Littlefield.

Bourdieu, Pierre, and Loic Wacquant. 1999. "On the Cunning of Imperialist Reason." *Theory, Culture & Society* 16, 1: 41–58.

Bryant, Sherwin K. 2004. "Enslaved Rebels, Fugitives, and Litigants: The Resistance Continuum in Colonial Quito." *Colonial Latin American Review* 13, 1: 7–46.

Burke, Peter, and Maria Lúcia G. Pallares-Burke. 2008. *Gilberto Freyre: Social Theory in the Tropics.* Oxford: Peter Lang.

Burnett, Carla. 2004. "'Are We Slaves or Free Men?': Labor, Race, Garveyism and the 1920 Panama Canal Strike." PhD diss., University of Illinois at Chicago.

Caldwell, Kia. 2007. *Negras in Brazil: Re-Visioning Black Women, Citizenship, and the Politics of Identity.* New Brunswick, NJ: Rutgers University Press.

Chalhoub, Sidney. 1990. *Visões da liberdade: Uma história das últimas décadas da escravidão na corte.* São Paulo: Companhia. das Letras.

Chanan, Michael. 2004. *Cuban Cinema.* Minneapolis, MN: University of Minnesota Press.

Cheney, Glenn Alan. 2014. *Quilombo dos Palmares: Brazil's Lost Nation of Fugitive Slaves.* Hanover, NH: New London Librarium.

Curiel, Ochy. 2007. "Crítica poscolonial desde las prácticas políticas del feminismo antirracista." *Nómadas* 26: 92–101.

———. 2013. *La nación heterosexual: Análisis del discurso jurídico y el régimen heterosexual desde la antropología de la dominación.* Bogotá: Brecha Lésbica.

Davis, Darién J., and Judith Michelle Williams. 2007. "Pan-Africanism, Negritude, and the Currency of Blackness: Cuba, the Francophone Caribbean, and

Brazil in Comparative Perspective, 1930–1950s." In *Beyond Slavery: The Multilayered Legacy of Africans in Latin America and the Caribbean*, edited by Darién J. Davis, 143–67. Lanham, MD: Rowman and Littlefield.

Dawson, Michael. 2001. *Black Visions: The Roots of Contemporary African-American Political Ideologies*. Chicago, IL: University of Chicago Press.

De Gobineau, Arthur Comte de. 1967 [1915]. The Inequality of Human Races. New York: H. Fertig.

De la Fuente, Alejandro. 2001. *A Nation for All: Race, Inequality, and Politics in Twentieth Century Cuba*. Chapel Hill, NC: University of North Carolina Press

2010. "From Slaves to Citizens? Tannenbaum and the Debates on Slavery, Emancipation, and Race Relations in Latin America." *International Labor and Working-Class History* 77: 154–73.

Delpar, Helen. 1992. *The Enormous Vogue of Things Mexican: Cultural Relations between the United States and Mexico, 1920–1935*. Tuscaloosa, AL: University of Alabama Press.

Deschamps Chapeaux, Pedro. 1963. *El negro en el periodismo cubano del siglo XIX*. Havana: Ediciones R.

Douglass, Frederick. 1893. *Lecture on Haiti*. Chicago: Violet Agents Supply Co.

Dubois, Laurent. 2006. *Avengers of the New World: The Story of the Haitian Revolution*. Cambridge; MA: Harvard University Press.

Dubois, Laurent, and John D. Garrigus, eds. 2006. *Slave Revolution in the Caribbean, 1789–1804: A Brief History with Documents*. New York, NY: Bedford/St. Martins.

Ebrahim, Haseenah. 2007. "Sarita and the Revolution: Race and Cuban Cinema." *European Review of Latin American and Caribbean Studies* 82: 107–18.

Espinosa Miñoso, Yuderkys, Diana Gómez Correal, and Karina Ochoa Muñoz, eds. 2014. *Tejiendo de otro modo: Feminismo, epistemología y apuestas descoloniales en Abya Yala*. Popayán: Editorial Universidad del Cauca.

Ferreira, Lígia Fonseca. 2007. "Luiz Gama: Um abolicionista leitor de Renan." *Estudos Avançados* 21, 60: 271–88.

Ferrer, Ada. 2009. "Speaking of Haiti: Slavery, Revolution, and Freedom in Cuban Slave Testimony." In *The World of the Haitian Revolution*, edited by David Patrick Geggus and Norman Fiering, 223–47. Bloomington, IN: Indiana University Press.

2014. *Freedom's Mirror: Cuba and Haiti in the Age of Revolution*. New York, NY: Cambridge University Press.

Field, Allyson, Jan-Christopher Horak, and Jacquelin Najuma Stewart, eds. 2015. *LA Rebellion: Creating a New Black Cinema*. Berkeley, CA: University of California Press.

Finch, Aisha K. 2015. *Insurgency at the Crossroads: Cuban Slaves and the Conspiracy of La Escalera, 1841–1844*. Chapel Hill, NC: University of North Carolina Press.

Findlay, Eileen Suarez. 2000. *Imposing Decency: The Politics of Sexuality and Race in Puerto Rico, 1870–1920*. Durham, NC: Duke University Press.

Firmin, Anténor. 2002. *The Equality of the Human Races*, translated by Asselin Charles. Urbana, IL: University of Illinois Press.

Fischer, Sibylle. 2004. *Modernity Disavowed: Haiti and the Cultures of Slavery in the Age of Revolution*. Durham, NC: Duke University Press.

Flórez Bolívar, Francisco, 2015. "Un diálogo diaspórico: El lugar del Harlem Renaissance en el pensamiento racial e intellectual afrocolombiano (1920–1948)." *Historia Crítica* (enero-marzo): 101–24.

Fluehr-Lobban, Carolyn. 2000. "Antenor Firmin: Haitian Pioneer of Anthropology." *American Anthropologist* 102, 3: 449–66.

Foner, Philip, S. 1977. *Antonio Maceo: The Bronze Titan of Cuban Independence*. New York, NY: Monthly Review Press.

Freyre, Gilberto. 1946. *The Masters and the Slaves: A Study in the Development of Brazilian Civilization*, translated by Samuel Putnam. New York, NY: Alford A. Knopf.

Gama, Luiz, and Lígia F. Ferreira. 2011. *Com a palavra Luiz Gama: Poemas, artigos, cartas, máximas*. São Paulo: Imprensa Oficial do Estado de São Paulo.

García, Jesús. 1990. *Africa en Venezuela: Pieza de Indias*. Caracas: Lagoven.

1992. *Afrovenezuela: Una vision desde adentro*. Caracas: APICUM.

Geggus, David. 2007. "The Sounds and Echoes of Freedom: The Impact of the Haitian Revolution on Latin America." In *Beyond Slavery: The Multilayered Legacy of Africans in Latin America and the Caribbean*, edited by Darién J. Davis, 19–36. Lanham, MD: Rowman and Littlefield.

Geler, Lea. 2010. *Andares negros, caminos blancos: Afroporteños, estado y nación: Argentina a fines del siglo XIX*. Rosario: Prohistoria Ediciones.

Gonzalez, Lélia. 1983. "Racismo e sexismo na cultura brasileira." In *Movimentos sociais, minorias etnicas e outros estudios*. Brasilia: ANPOCS.

1988. "For an Afro Latin American Feminism." In *Confronting the Crisis in Latin America: Women Organizing for Change*, 95–101. Santiago: Isis International.

Grinberg, Keila. 2002. *O fiador dos brasileiros: Cidadania, escravidão e direito civil no tempo de Antonio Pereira Rebouças*. Rio de Janeiro: Civilização Brasileira.

Guerra, Lillian. 2012. *Visions of Power in Cuba: Revolution, Redemption, and Resistance, 1959–1971*. Chapel Hill, NC: University of North Carolina Press.

Guillén, Nicolás. 2004. *Obra Poética*. Vol. 1. Havana: *Letras Cubanas*.

Guridy, Frank Andre. 2010. *Forging Diaspora: Afro-Cubans and African Americans in a World of Empire and Jim Crow*. Chapel Hill, NC: University of North Carolina Press.

Hanchard, Michael. 2003. "Acts of Misrecognition: Transnational Black Politics, Anti-Imperialism and the Ethnocentrisms of Pierre Bourdieu and Loic Wacquant." *Theory, Culture & Society* 20, 4: 5–29.

Harpelle, Ronald. 2003. "Cross Currents in the Western Caribbean: Marcus Garvey and the UNIA in Central America." *Caribbean Studies* 31, 1: 35–73.

Helg, Aline. 1991. "Afro-Cuban Protest: The Partido Independiente de Color, 1908–1912." *Cuban Studies* 21: 101–21.

1995. *Our Rightful Share: The Afro-Cuban Struggle for Equality, 1886–1912*. Chapel Hill, NC: University of North Carolina Press.

Hoffnung-Garskof, Jesse. 2002. "The Migrations of Arturo Schomburg: On Being Antillano, Negro, and Puerto Rican in New York, 1891–1938." *Journal of American Ethnic History* 21: 3–49.

Hooker, Juliet. 2008. "Afro-Descendant Struggles for Collective Rights in Latin America." *Souls: A Critical Journal of Black Politics, Culture and Society* 10, 3: 279–91.

2015. "'A Black Sister to Massachusetts': Latin America and the Fugitive Democratic Ethos of Frederick Douglass." *American Political Science Review* 109, 4: 690–702.

2017. *Theorizing Race in the Americas: Douglass, Sarmiento, Du Bois, and Vasconcelos*. New York, NY: Oxford University Press.

Hughes, Langston. 1931. "People Without Shoes." *New Masses* 12: 11–12.

James, C. L. R. 1963. *The Black Jacobins: Toussaint Louverture and the San Domingo Revolution*. 2nd edition. New York, NY: Vintage.

Jiménez Román, Miriam. 1996. "Un hombre (negro) del pueblo: José Celso Barbosa and the Puerto Rican 'Race' Toward Whiteness." *Centro* 8: 8–29.

Jiménez Román, Miriam, and Juan Flores, eds. 2010. *The Afro-Latin@ Reader: History and Culture in the United States*. Durham, NC: Duke University Press.

Kent, Raymond, K. 1979. "Palmares: An African State in Brazil." In *Maroon Societies: Rebel Slave Communities in the Americas*, edited by Richard Price. Baltimore, MD: Johns Hopkins University Press.

Kutzinski, Vera, M. 1993. *Sugar's Secrets: Race and the Erotics of Cuban Nationalism*. Charlottesville, VA: University Press of Virginia.

Landers, Jane. 2010. *Atlantic Creoles in the Age of Revolutions*. Cambridge, MA: Harvard University Press.

Laó-Montes, Agustín. 2008. "Cartographies of Afro-Latina/o Politics: Political Contests and Historical Challenges." *Negritud: Revista de Estudios Afro-Latinoamericanos* 2, 2: 237–62.

Laó-Montes, Agustín, and Mirangela Buggs. 2014. "Translocal Space of Afro-Latinidad/Critical Feminist Visions for Diasporic Bridge Building." In *Translocalities/Translocalidades: Feminist Politics of Translation in the Latin/a Américas*, edited by Sonia Alvarez, et al., 380–400. Durham, NC: Duke University Press.

Lasso, Marixa. 2001. "Haiti as an Image of Popular Republicanism in Caribbean Colombia: Cartagena Province (1811–1828)." In *The Impact of the Haitian Revolution in the Atlantic World*, edited by David P. Geggus. Columbia, SC: University Press of South Carolina.

2007. *Myths of Harmony: Race and Republicanism During the Age of Republicanism*. Pittsburgh, PA: University of Pittsburgh Press.

Lesage, Julia. 1978. "One Way or Another, Dialectical, Revolutionary, Feminist." *Jump Cut* 20: 20–23.

Machado, Maria Helena. 1988. *Crime e escravidão*. São Paulo: Brasiliense.

Manzano, Juan F. 1996. *Autobiography of a Slave/Autobiografía de un esclavo*. Detroit, MI: Wayne State University Press.

Mattos Hebe. 1995. *Das cores do silêncio: Os significados da liberdade no sudeste escravista – Brasil século XIX*. Rio de Janeiro: Arquivo Nacional.

McGraw, Jason. 2014. *The Work of Recognition: Caribbean Colombia and the Postemancipation Struggle for Citizenship*. Chapel Hill, NC: University of North Carolina Press.

Mena, William, ed. 2016. *Manuel Zapata Olivella: Un legado intercultural.* Bogotá: Desde Abajo.

Montañez, Ligia. 1993. *El racismo oculto de una sociedad no racista.* Caracas: Fondo Editorial Tropykos.

Moore, Carlos. 2008. *Pichón: A Memoir of Race and Revolution in Castro's Cuba.* Chicago, IL: Lawrence Hill Books.

Moore, Robin, D. 1997. *Nationalizing Blackness: Afrocubanismo and Artistic Revolution in Havana, 1920–1940.* Pittsburgh, PA: University of Pittsburgh Press.

Morris, Courtney Desiree. 2016. "Becoming Creole, Becoming Black: Migration, Diasporic Self-Making, and the Many Lives of Madame Maymie Leona Turpeau de Mena." *Women, Gender, and Families of Color* 4, 2: 171–95.

Mullen, Edward, J. 1977. *Langston Hughes in the Hispanic World and Haiti.* Hamden, CT: Archon Books.

Mullen, Edward, J., ed. 2014. *The Life and Poems of a Cuban Slave, Juan Francisco Manzano, 1797–1854.* New York, NY: Palgrave Macmillan.

Nascimento, Abdias do. 1979. *Brazil, Mixture of Massacre: Essays in the Genocide of a Black People,* translated by Elisa Larkin Nascimento. Dover, MA: The Majority Press.

1980. "Quilombismo: An Afro-Brazilian Political Alternative." *Journal of Black Studies* 11, 2: 141–78.

Nascimento, Beatriz. 1982. "Kilombo e memória comunitária: um estudo de caso." *Estudos Afro-Asiáticos* 6–7: 259–65.

1985. "O conceito de quilombo e a resistência cultural negra." *Afrodiáspora* 6–7: 41–49.

Needell, Jeffrey D. 1995. "History, Race, and the State in the Thought of Oliveira Viana." *Hispanic American Historical Review* 75, 1: 1–30.

Paschel, Tianna, 2016. *Becoming Black Political Subjects: Movements and Ethno-Racial Rights in Colombia and Brazil.* Princeton, NJ: Princeton University Press.

Peabody, Sue, and Keila Grinberg. 2007. *Slavery, Freedom, and the Law in the Atlantic World: A Brief History with Documents.* New York, NY: Palgrave Macmillan.

Pereira Araujo, Amilcar. 2013. *O mundo negro: Relações raciais e a constituição do movimento negro contemporâneo no Brasil.* Rio de Janeiro: Pallas.

Ratts, Alex. 2007. *Eu sou Atlântica: Sobre a trajetória de vida de Beatriz Nascimento.* São Paulo: Imprensa Oficial/Instituto Kuanza.

Reis, João Jose, and Flávio dos Santos Gomes, eds. 1996. *Liberdade por um fio: História dos quilombos no Brazil.* São Paulo: Companhia das Letras.

Reis, Maria Firmina dos. 1859. *Úrsula: Romance original brasileiro.* São Luis: Typographia Progresso.

Rivera-Rideau, Petra, Jennifer Jones, and Tianna Paschel, eds. 2016. *Afro-Latin@s in Movement: Critical Approaches to Blackness and Transnationalism in the Americas.* New York, NY: Palgrave Macmillan.

Rivera, Pedro R. 2012. "Carlos Cooks and Garveyism: Bridging Two Eras of Black Nationalism," PhD diss., Howard University.

Roberts, Neil. 2015. *Freedom as Marronage.* Chicago, IL: University of Chicago Press.

Rodrigues, Nina Raymundo. 1957. *As raças humanas a e responsabilidade penal no Brasil.* Salvador: Livararia Progresso. First published in 1894.

Roumain, Jacques. 2008. *Gouverneurs de la rosée.* Alexandria, VA: Alexander Street Press.

Sanders, James E. 2004. *Contentious Republicans: Popular Politics, Race, and Class in Nineteenth-Century Colombia.* Durham, NC: Duke University Press.

2014. *The Vanguard of the Atlantic World: Creating Modernity, Nation, and Democracy in Nineteenth-Century Latin America.* Durham, NC: Duke University Press.

Scott, Rebecca, J. 2005. *Degrees of Freedom: Louisiana and Cuba After Slavery.* Cambridge, MA: Harvard University Press.

Seigel, Micol. 2009. *Uneven Encounters: Making Race and Nation in Brazil and the United States.* Durham, NC: Duke University Press.

Silva, Eduardo. 2007. "Black Abolitionists in the *Quilombo* of Leblon, Rio de Janeiro: Symbols, Organizers, and Revolutionaries." In *Beyond Slavery: The Multilayered Legacy of Africans in Latin America and the Caribbean,* edited by Darién J. Davis, 109–22. Lanham, MD: Rowman and Littlefield.

Spitzer, Leo. 1989. *Lives in Between: Assimilation and Marginality in Austria, Brazil, and West Africa, 1780–1945.* New York, NY: Cambridge University Press.

Townsend, Camilla. 2007. "In Search of Liberty: The Efforts of the Enslaved to Attain Abolition in Ecuador, 1822–1852." In *Beyond Slavery: The Multilayered Legacy of Africans in Latin America and the Caribbean,* edited by Darién J. Davis, 37–56. Lanham, MD: Rowman and Littlefield.

Vincent, Theodore G. 2001. *The Legacy of Vicente Guerrero: Mexico's First Black Indian President.* Gainesville, FL: University Press of Florida.

Walsh, Catherine. 2007. "Shifting the Geopolitics of Critical Knowledge." *Cultural Studies* 21, 2–3: 224–39.

Zacaïr, Philippe. 2005. "Haiti on his Mind: Antonio Maceo and Caribbeanness." *Caribbean Studies* 33: 47–78.

Zapata Olivella, Manuel. 1983. *Changó el Gran Putas.* Bogotá: Ministerio de Cultura.

# 7

# Rethinking Black Mobilization in Latin America

## Tianna S. Paschel[1]

Black mobilization in Latin America has long been cast as a story of absence. Both scholars who saw the region as a kind of racial paradise and those who challenged such characterizations agreed that effective black mobilization was not likely. For the former group, Latin American countries had overcome histories of racialized slavery and colonization to construct inclusive nationalist projects. The absence or relatively low levels of race-based mobilization signaled the lack of salience of race in the everyday realities of Latin Americans. For critics, it was precisely the illusion of inclusion that proved most challenging for the prospect of true equality. According to these accounts, the relatively low levels of black mobilization were not because race did not profoundly structure these societies, but rather that nationalist ideologies had made the development of oppositional consciousness difficult, and the emergence of large-scale, effective black movements unlikely (Hanchard 1994; Marx 1998; Telles 1999; Winant 2001; Goldberg 2002; Appelbaum 2003).

In much of this work, Brazil has been used as a contrasting case of black mobilization compared to the United States or South Africa. In some ways, it makes sense that the latter two would serve as an entrée into understanding black resistance elsewhere. Movements in those two countries have not only become canonical examples of anti-racist struggle in the social movement literature, but also in the world. Nevertheless, we know that the ideological and legal context of Latin American countries was very different from that of apartheid or Jim Crow, and this difference

---

[1] I would like to thank the editors of this volume, as well as all of the contributors, for the thoughtful feedback on previous drafts of this chapter.

may have necessitated a different kind of response. Thus while scholars like Hanchard (1994) and Marx (1998) offered brilliant analyses of the ideological impediments to black organizing in Brazil, their attention to these challenges did not always translate into a reimagining of what black mobilization might look like in that context. As Andrews (2010) aptly notes, "it was overt, state-mandated segregation that had provoked black mobilization in the United States; in the absence of such conditions in Uruguay, why would one expect civil rights movements comparable to those of the United States?" (103). Indeed, reading black mobilization in Latin America through a US civil rights or anti-apartheid movement lens has arguably created a specific benchmark for what counts as substantial black mobilization, just as it may have also narrowed the wide range of activities that we might include under that category.

Over the last two decades, the scholarship on black mobilization in Latin America has shifted from asking why people of African descent have *not* organized, to asking new questions about the dynamics, trajectories, and often-ambiguous outcomes of black mobilization in this region. In so doing, these scholars have expanded our understandings in several ways. First, historians of Latin America have uncovered lesser-known histories of black mobilization in earlier periods (Andrews 2010; Priestley and Barrow 2008), while still others have deepened our understanding of black mobilization in more-well-known cases in the region (Helg 1995; de la Fuente 2001; Bronfman 2005; Ferrer 2005; Pires 2006; Alberti and Pereira 2007; Guridy 2010; Alberto 2011; Brunson 2011; Pereira 2013).

Second, the literature has expanded temporally to analyze the recent upsurge in black mobilization over the last decades, including the activism that brought about multicultural reforms beginning in the 1980s (Wade 1998; Arruti 2000; Van Cott 2000; Oslender 2001; Restrepo 2004; Agudelo 2005; Hooker 2005; Covin 2006; Anderson 2007; Asher 2007; Caldwell 2007; Greene 2007; Ng'weno 2007; Escobar 2008; Hooker 2008; Paschel and Sawyer 2008; Sánchez 2008; Asher 2009; French 2009; Cristiano and Prado 2010; Paschel 2010; Cárdenas 2012; Rahier 2012; Paschel 2016). Finally, academics have looked to other articulations of black mobilization that had previously been dismissed or ignored in the literature. This included re-reading certain kinds of political articulations as black mobilization, as Keisha-Khan Perry does in her study of black women–led, anti-racist neighborhood associations in Bahia (Perry 2013). Additionally, scholars have recently made the case that the politicization of blackness in popular culture should be understood as a form of black mobilization (Fernandes 2006; de la Fuente 2008; Rivera-Rideau 2015). All of this work has uncovered important insights into the dynamics of black politicization in this region, while also expanding the definition of black mobilization itself.

In this chapter, I draw on this growing literature to give an overview of the nature and impact of black mobilization in late twentieth-century Latin America. By black mobilization, I am referring to the collective action of activists and organizations that organize primarily, though not always exclusively, *as* black. This definition contrasts with what I have called in my previous work "mobilizing while black," by which I meant the instances in which black people organize primarily around other social and political categories (Paschel 2016). Making the decision to focus on black mobilization – as opposed to anti-racist movements more generally – was an intentional one. It allows me to narrow in on the more specific moments in which blackness becomes politicized in Latin American countries, as well as examine the consequences of such articulation.

Focusing on black mobilization does present some possible pitfalls. First, it runs the risk of reading all racial silence as a case of black denial or false consciousness, when in fact, people of African descent have often made strategic decisions about when to emphasize racial identity and when not to. Second, looking specifically at movements in which black identity is the central category of politicization means leaving some important instances of mobilization out of the analysis. This includes movements primarily organized around other political categories and platforms, but for which anti-racism is one aspect of their work. Some examples of this include labor movements throughout the region, and the Cordobismo movement in Colombia, a socialist movement emerging in the 1930s and named after Afro-Colombian political leader Diego Córdoba. In this vein and in this same period, Brazil also saw labor movements made up of self-identified blacks with a critique of racial inequality (Alberto 2011). While more analyses of these anti-racist efforts will give us a fuller picture of the limits and possibilities of contesting ethno-racial inequality and racism in these countries, they are outside the scope of this chapter.

I have also chosen to zoom in on black mobilization in a particular historical period, the 1970s and forward. And while I offer an overview of black mobilization throughout the region, many of my examples are drawn from the cases of Colombia and Brazil, both because of their regional importance, and because they are the countries I know best. I start by situating these more recent instances of black politics into a longer trajectory of mobilization, first analyzing the important role that people of African descent played in resisting slavery and in bringing about independence. I then give an overview of the increasing politicization of black identity in the early twentieth century in the form of black social clubs, black newspapers, and black political parties throughout the region, arguing that these articulations laid the foundation for more recent ones. Finally, I move to an analysis of more contemporary black mobilization. I argue that while the political and economic contexts vary widely from country to country, there has been an overall convergence in the form that black movements have taken in this period. While the black social movements of the 1910s–1930s tended to be urban and integrationist, the field of black mobilization expanded both geographically and ideologically in the latter part of the century. More specifically, I examine three branches of black mobilization, each with its own genealogy, ideology, and organizational form: ethno-territorial movements, urban black movements, and black feminist/women's movements. I show how each of these branches has engaged in transnational politics, and how each has also been effective at bringing about both policy and social change.

## THE ROOTS OF CONTEMPORARY BLACK MOBILIZATION

Contemporary Afro–Latin American movements often trace their roots back to resistance to slavery and colonial rule. Enslaved Africans and their descendants concealed and blended their own cultural traditions with European cultures in order to preserve them; they also appropriated colonial law and formed mutual aid societies that, among other things, helped in the manumission of many people. Enslaved people and their descendants also engaged in more overt forms of resistance to slavery, including slave rebellions. Though these revolts occurred throughout the Western Hemisphere, the scale and sheer number of such rebellions in present-day Latin America was striking, especially when compared to the Anglophone colonies (Andrews 2004). While many of these rebellions were extinguished before they were fully realized, they still often shook colonial authorities, especially in the aftermath of the successful slave revolt we know today as the Haitian Revolution (Davidson 1966; de la Fuente 2001; Andrews 2004; Ferrer 2014).

Another important form of resistance to slavery and colonial rule was maroonage, a practice that also was particularly widespread in Latin America (Price 1996). Maroon communities, which were known by many names including *quilombos, palenques, mocambos, cumbes*, and *ladeiras*, ranged from small groups of people that sometimes only survived for months to "powerful states encompassing thousands of members and surviving for generations or even centuries" (Price 1996, 1). In the latter category were the iconic cases of Colombia's Palenque de San Basílio, which was founded some time in the sixteenth century and whose descendants still maintain strong African-based cultural traditions and language, and the Palmares *quilombo* founded in 1605 in Brazil's northeastern region, which lasted nearly a century (Price 1996). These practices of maroonage became especially important for black activists in recent decades, as they have often claimed them as precedents to their own mobilization. For contemporary black movements, the images of maroon communities came to represent utopian projects far removed from the racial ordering, exploitation, and inequality characteristic of present-day societies. Maroons also provided ideological inspiration for these activists as they developed political philosophies based in ideas of *cimmaronaje* and *quilombismo* (Arruti 2000; see also Chapter 6).

As the nineteenth century dawned, and the prospect of independence became a more viable political option for Creole elites throughout the region, African descendants became crucial actors in the rebel forces that brought about independence in much of the region. They were well represented among the foot soldiers of rebel armies and were also among the high-ranking military officers; as such, they devised military strategy and began to articulate their own visions of postindependence nations (Vincent 1994; Andrews 2004; Ferrer 2005). Beyond their military contributions, the participation of blacks and *mulatos* in rebel militaries throughout the region also profoundly shaped the nature and discourse of nationalism (Vincent 1994; de la Fuente 2001; Andrews 2004; Borucki 2015). The participation of free people of color and, in many cases, of enslaved people posed deep questions about the nature of freedom, independence, and equality. Additionally, as people of African descent from Mexico to Cuba to Argentina fought for independence from Spain, they often articulated more inclusive and anti-racist nationalist projects than their white/*mestizo* counterparts.

Yet while Afro–Latin Americans played a crucial role in the wars that led to independence, they found that national sovereignty had not fully resolved the many racial tensions and hierarchies of the colonial period. While independence did bring about the manumission of those who fought in the wars, typically it did not bring with it complete abolition of slavery (Andrews 2004). What is more, freedom itself became a much more elusive concept as free people of color continued to experience racism and marginalization in the political, economic, and social spheres in postindependence Latin America. This all foreshadowed the entanglements and ambivalences that people of African descent would have to confront for decades to come. This included navigating ambivalent inclusion in nationalist projects.

## Whitening and the Problem of "Self-Identification" in Latin America

By the turn of the twentieth century; many countries in Latin America had already invested decades in whitening projects that entailed offering incentives to European immigrants with the goal of whitening the nation (Stepan 1991; Loveman 2014). The idea was that an infusion of white immigrants would inject the right kind of culture and gene pool into the nation, eventually moving it closer to whiteness and to European ideals. It was only after whitening policies failed that Latin American elites began to celebrate race mixture as the foundation of their nations (see Chapter 8). Yet the shift to racial mixture did not mean leaving behind whitening all together. *Mestizaje* ideologies often relegated blackness and indigeneity to inferior spheres of society, such as dance, food, folklore, and often to the past (Wade 1997). In contrast, political and intellectual elites in Latin America often attributed their nations' intellectual accomplishments, work ethic, and innovation, to their European ancestry (Stepan 1991; Loveman 2014).

It is important to note that while *mestizaje* characterized much of the region, in some countries it never quite took hold. When their neighboring countries embraced mixture as national ideology, Uruguay, Argentina, and Costa Rica continued to fashion themselves as white nations (Andrews 1980, 1988, 2010; Purcell 1993; Leeds 2010). Nevertheless, these "white nations" still shared a key feature with their neighbors that embraced *mestizaje*: they sought to transcend race through what were ultimately deeply racialized, and arguably racist, nationalist projects. At the center of these projects was not only a privileging of whiteness but also inherent anti-blackness, albeit of a more complex version than that found in the United States.

Indeed, racial regimes in Latin America did not require the same kind of legal exclusion or military might that proved so central to racial exclusion in the US South under Jim Crow or South Africa under apartheid. Some scholars have argued that discourses of race mixture and egalitarianism created a more durable form of racial domination by creating a racial ideological apparatus that was often internalized, producing a kind of consent to the racial order (Hanchard 1994; Marx 1998; Winant 2001; Goldberg 2002). Hanchard (1994) developed the idea of what he called "racial hegemony"; Sawyer (2005) argued that in the context of Cuba, state discourses of racial egalitarianism, alongside deeply inegalitarian practices, amounted to a kind of "inclusionary discrimination."

If not consent, nationalist narratives did make it more difficult for racial critique and oppositional consciousness to develop. By the 1940s, *mestizaje* had permeated the discourse of state officials in many Latin American countries, just as it had become institutionalized into the state apparatus, mainly through social policy (Dávila 2003; Sue 2013; Loveman 2014). Education became a particularly important vehicle for the diffusion of such ideologies. A whitening logic also became embedded in gendered social practices in this region, shaping the most intimate aspects of people's lives, from decisions about whom to marry to individuals' sense of self-worth (Wade 1993, 2009; Burdick 1998; Twine 1998; Telles 2004; Hordge-Freeman 2015; Viveros Vigoya 2016). If the nation was thought to be collectively moving toward whiteness, it was also the responsibility of individuals to '*mejorar la raza.*' By marrying lighter, Latin Americans could presumably whiten themselves and their families, and in so doing, contribute to the collective whitening of the nation (Wade 1998). Social mobility was another vehicle through which whitening often occurred, as whiteness was imbricated with material wealth and higher status (Degler 1971; Wade 1993; Telles 2004). Escaping blackness proved an attractive ambition in societies in which blackness continued to be associated with inferiority, hypersexuality, ugliness, ignorance, and criminality, as it was in the colonial period. Yet while challenges to black mobilization in Latin America were significant, they were not insurmountable.

## Black Social Clubs, Newspapers, and Political Parties

As historians have begun to study black mobilization in the 1800s and early 1900s, they have found that it was much more widespread and varied than previously recognized. African-based religious brotherhoods and mutual-aid societies existed during the colonial period in some Latin American countries and continued into the postindependence period. During the late 1800s and early 1900s, people of African descent in Montevideo, Havana, São Paulo, and elsewhere faced barriers to achieving political power, exclusion from explicit and de facto white social spaces, and discrimination in labor markets that often privileged recently arrived European immigrants over black citizens (Andrews 2004; Alberto 2011). In response, they created black social clubs and mutual-aid societies that engaged in a number of activities including social events and educational programming around literacy and sports (de la Fuente 2001; Guridy 2010; Brunson 2011). More importantly, black social clubs served as sites for people of African descent to articulate their own visions of race, nation, and culture just as they also underscored the profound limitations of their respective nationalist projects.

There is also a long history of a vibrant black press dating back to the nineteenth century. It was in that period that Buenos Aires saw the creation of a number of black newspapers, including *La Igualdad, El Tambor,* and *La Broma* (Quijada 2000; Geler 2010). In Brazil the periodical *O Homem de Cor* (1833) was created by free people of color (Pereira 2013), and after abolition in 1888, a number of other black newspapers sprung up in cities throughout the country, including *O Exemplo* in Porto Alegre, *A Patria* in São Paulo, and *Treze de Maio* in Rio de Janeiro. These newspapers constituted what Michael Hanchard has called "the Afro-Brazilian public sphere," or what Alberto (2011) refers to as an "alternate public consciousness." Alberto adds that this public consciousness "would oppose scientific racism, whitening ideologies, racist immigration policies, and the racism of immigrants themselves" (69). While the overwhelming majority of the descendants of enslaved people in these countries were illiterate, black newspapers were often successful at reaching audiences much broader than their official subscriber base (Helg 1995; Pires 2006).

Black social clubs and newspapers in Latin America served as a refuge for middle-class and upwardly mobile black people who had experienced direct exclusion from de facto white spaces. Nevertheless, there were still tensions inherent to these early instances of black mobilization. First was the complex and sometimes vexed relationship with mainstream politics. While some black social clubs were truly independent, others served as the black arms of white-dominated political parties or were funded by mainstream political parties interested in courting the votes of people of color (Geler 2010, 339–82). Second were internal tensions around class and culture. Black social clubs throughout the region were attempting to assert their own value to and visions of the nation during the height of scientific racism. As such, they had to navigate and contest hegemonic ideas of black women's hypersexuality, just as they worked incessantly to dislink the experience of slavery from the moral degeneracy with which it was increasingly associated (Guridy 2010; Brunson 2011). One of the main goals of black social clubs of this time was to prove to white elites that their members were in fact upstanding, moral citizens. Indeed, shaking the moral degradation associated with blackness was perhaps a necessary strategy for making claims to inclusion and equality within their respective nations. This meant that black newspapers often came with a fair dose of cultural disciplining of African-based religion, and the performance of upper-class values (Andrews 2010; Guridy 2010; Brunson 2011).

While black social clubs were ostensibly social, they were also fundamentally political institutions. Their very presence signaled the hypocrisy and limits of nationalism in their respected countries; additionally, they often took positions on elections, lobbying mainstream political parties and holding them accountable for promises they had made (de la Fuente 2001; Andrews 2010; Brunson 2011). Both directly and indirectly, black social clubs and newspapers also laid the foundations for official black political parties to form in this period. In Cuba in 1887, twelve black social clubs formed the Central Directorate of the Societies of the Colored Race; by 1893, the organization included some one hundred clubs spread across the island (de la Fuente 2001, 38). The organization established its own newspaper, *La Igualdad*, developed a unified political platform, and successfully brought about the end of legal segregation in public office, schools, and marriage (de la Fuente 2001). De facto segregation continued, however, and the organization became defunct in 1895 when Cuba's final war of independence began and many of the Directorate's leaders and members took up arms.

After independence, Cuba became the first country in the hemisphere to see the emergence of a black political party: the Partido Independiente de Color (PIC), founded in 1908 by Evaristo Estenoz, a veteran of Cuba's wars of independence. The party formed at a time in which the place of blacks and *mulatos* in Cuban society, and in the newly independent Cuban government, was far from certain. While the leadership of the PIC was made up of professionals – many of them war veterans like Estenoz – the majority of the party's membership was drawn from the popular classes, including tobacco workers, unskilled workers, day laborers, and carpenters (Helg 1991).

Two decades later, South America saw the emergence of two black political parties. In 1931, one of Brazil's most formidable black political organizations – the Frente Negra Brasileira (FNB) – was born; in 1936 it became an official political party, and the first attempt to build a black political organization nationally (Pereira 2013). The same year, the

Afro-Uruguayan Partido Autóctono Negro (PAN) was founded in Montevideo, a city with a long history of black newspapers and social clubs (Andrews 2010). The FNB, PAN, and PIC emerged out of similar experiences of political and social exclusion, and as such, developed explicit critiques of racism and constructed political platforms that sought to move their countries in the direction of true racial egalitarianism and inclusion. Though they did attract some support and succeeded in expanding geographically beyond the cities in which they were founded, none of them enjoyed much electoral success and they were all short-lived. The PAN disbanded in 1944 (Andrews 2010) and the FNB was dissolved in 1937 along with all political parties in Brazil under President Getúlio Vargas's Estado Novo government (Alberto 2011).

Despite the black parties' limited electoral appeal, white political elites saw them as a potential threat to their own control of the political process (Helg 1995; Andrews 2010; Alberto 2011). This was especially the case in Cuba, where the PIC was developing an alliance with the Conservative Party (de la Fuente 2001). Members of the PIC, along with thousands of other presumed sympathizers, were massacred in what is now known as the 1912 Massacre or the Guerrita de las Razas, aimed at ridding the country of antipatriotic forces. Perhaps ironically, many of the members of the PIC had been soldiers and officers in the majority-black and *mulato* Mambi Army that had fought Spain in the wars of independence (Ferrer 2005). For them, forming the PIC was a way to fully realize the Cuba for which they had fought; it was a way to build a truly racially egalitarian Cuba and to demand their "rightful share" of the nation (Helg 1995). However, their actions were interpreted as precisely the opposite, as a threat to the nation, and as an act of civil war.

While the 1912 Massacre was an especially devastating case of overt repression against explicit black organizing, it is important to note that it was not the only one. President Vargas' Estado Novo government closed down the Frente Negra Brasileira in 1937, and some decades later, the military dictatorship engaged in surveillance of black political organizations (Alberti and Pereira 2007; Alberto 2011). Additionally, Latin America saw some of the most severe authoritarian regimes in the world in the late 1900s. So while some scholars have tended to locate the limits to black mobilization in nationalist ideologies that impede the development of oppositional consciousness, it is also true that state repression, or the threat of it, presented a serious impediment to black mobilization.

These earlier instances of black mobilization were important to the trajectory of contemporary black movements, exposing many of the issues that would continue to plague later movements. However, while the earlier instances of black mobilization tended to be urban, integrationist, and male-dominated, their post-1970 successors would be more varied in geographic and ideological terms; gender would also become a key site of contestation within these movements. What is more, while the black organizations that emerged in the early part of the twentieth century were to some degree outward-looking (Hellwig 1992; Alberto 2011; Guridy 2012; Pereira 2013), they were decidedly nationalist in their ideology, organization, and strategies. For the black movements that emerged in the latter part of the century, transnationalism would be central to their articulation and success.

## BLACK MOBILIZATION IN LATIN AMERICA, 1970S–2000S

The late 1970s and early 1980s marked a boom in black mobilization throughout Latin America. Here I focus on three principal arms of that mobilization: black urban movements, black peasant or ethno-territorial movements, and black women's or feminist movements. Rather than paint a picture of a singular black movement, I suggest that this was a movement of movements. These different sectors developed different conceptualizations of blackness, articulated distinct political ideologies, and engaged in different styles of political mobilization, even if they also overlapped to some degree. Together these movements catalyzed the adoption of ethno-racial policies, while they reshaped Latin American societies in substantial ways (Hanchard 2000; Hooker 2008; Paschel and Sawyer 2008; Davis, Paschel, and Morrison 2011; Loveman 2014).

### Contemporary Urban Black Movements

Beginning in the late 1970s, a large number of black political organizations were being formed and consolidated in Latin America and the Caribbean. This renaissance of political organizing came in part because of a unique and changing political context both nationally and globally. At home, activists were taking initial steps toward democratization after decades of authoritarian rule. Black activists had also watched from afar the unfolding of black mobilization throughout the world, from civil rights and Black Power in the United States to struggles against apartheid in South Africa. Both of these political shifts helped catalyze the creation and solidification of Latin America's contemporary black movements, especially black urban leftist organizations.

The upsurge in black mobilization was also directly linked to the emergence of a black cultural scene that borrowed heavily from soul music and black power aesthetics from the United States. The best-documented case of this is in Brazil, where black power scenes developed in Rio de Janeiro and São Paulo, based on black soul parties organized by racially conscious DJs (Hanchard 1994; Vianna 1998; Alberto 2011; Pereira 2013). On a typical weekend in Rio de Janeiro in 1976, these "bailes black" amassed over a million young people, many of whom did identify as black (Palombini 2009). Similarly, in Lima, black soul parties emerged alongside the advent of a hybrid Afro-Peruvian music inspired by funk and soul from the United States (Thomas 2009). In Cuba, groups like Los Van Van and Irakere were also born in this period, playing music that blended Afro-Cuban sacred drums with classic Cuban music, funk, and soul (Vaughan 2012).

While we might think of these as purely cultural movements, these social events were often directly connected to the political organizations that were also being developed at the time (Dias 2005; Thomas 2009). In Brazil, some of the most important militants of the contemporary black movement would meet up with like-minded young people at these events (Dias 2005; Alberti and Pereira 2007; Paschel 2016). These cultural movements and localized political activities culminated in the creation of Brazil's Unified Black Movement (MNU).

In July of 1978, activists from a number of Brazilian cities organized a public demonstration in São Paulo in response to two disturbing incidents: the case of Robson Silveira da Luz, a black worker accused of stealing fruit from a market and later murdered by the police; and discrimination against four black men who were not allowed to play volleyball at the Clube de Regatas Tietê in São Paulo. The demonstration led to the founding of the Unified Black Movement against Racial Discrimination (Covin 2006; Alberti and Pereira 2007). The organizational and ideological base for the MNU included the Rio-based Institute for Research on Black Cultures (IPCN), founded in 1974 from the Society for Brazil-Africa Exchange (SINBA). Because the IPCN had developed organizational and physical infrastructure, it served as an important nexus in the construction of this new national black movement.

Activists like Amauri Mendes and Yêdo Ferreira of IPCN joined Lélia Gonzalez, Milton Barbosa, and many other leftist black activists organizing around anti-racism in São Paulo and around the country to eventually create the MNU. The MNU was different from previous black mobilization in several ways. First, it was arguably the first attempt at consolidating all black organizations throughout the country into a national movement. Previously, aside from local grassroots groups, organizations based in São Paulo or Rio tended simply to expand to the rest of the country, with varying levels of success. Second, while the ultimate goal of the Black Brazilian Front of the 1930s and the Black Experimental Theatre of the 1940s had been full integration into the political and sociocultural life of the country, MNU founders had a much more vexed relationship with the nation. While the MNU's stated goal was to fight for a "real racial democracy," many of its founding members had a more separatist political orientation and were skeptical of political integration and formal politics (Covin 2006).

While still far from a large-scale movement, the organization had become by the mid-1980s the most important black political organization in the country (Covin 2006), and arguably in Latin America. Much of the MNU's work around the country sought to build a strong collective identity among marginalized black Brazilians and to denounce systematic racism in every part of Brazilian society. For many of these black Brazilian activists – most of whom hailed from lower-class neighborhoods in the suburbs or peripheries of Brazil's major cities – finding the MNU was the beginning of their own racial consciousness (Covin 2006; Pereira 2013; Paschel 2016). As former MNU militant Hamilton Borges put it, members were "obligated to mobilize within communities, to mobilize in the places where the majority of us were" (Paschel 2016). Through these "grassroots nucleuses" – which met in community centers, local work sites, schools, and members' homes – the organization sought to build a strong collective identity among young and marginalized black Brazilians while at the same time denouncing structural and everyday racism in Brazilian society.

Similar organizations also began to form in other Latin American cities. Such was the case with the creation of the Center for Afro-Ecuadorian Studies by Juan García in the late 1970s, which was followed by the founding of the Movimiento Afroecuatoriano Conciencia (1983) in Quito to combat discrimination and racism. It was also in this period that a contemporary black movement emerged in Colombia. In the 1970s, Afro-Colombian writer, doctor, and anthropologist Manuel Zapata Olivella organized alongside Delia Zapata a theater group that worked to affirm the contributions of Afro-Colombians to the history of the country. Zapata Olivella later founded the Colombian Foundation for Folkloric

Research, Manuel Zapata Olivella, which organized and hosted the first Congress of Black Culture in Cali in 1977.[2]

In 1976, Juan de Dios Mosquera and other young black Colombians created the Soweto study group, named after the South African township that was at the center of the anti-apartheid uprisings. The group, which consisted mostly of young students, became more politicized through reading works by Malcolm X, Fanon, Cabral, and Martin Luther King (Wade 1998). In 1982, Soweto's leaders decided to move beyond a study group and become a more overtly political organization, Cimarrón. As they did so, they did not leave behind the intellectual aspect of their project. In many ways, the organization served as a school of black consciousness, and many of the most important black activists in the country received their political education there (Paschel 2016). From its inception, the organization was largely an urban, intellectual movement highly influenced by the civil rights movement in the United States and the anti-apartheid struggles in South Africa. While some of the founders were originally from the Pacific coast of Colombia, Cimarrón's activities were mainly in Medellín, Pereira, and Bogotá, with some activities in rural communities (Wade 1998).

Like black urban organizations throughout the region, Cimarrón's main objective was to recapture the history of the African presence and contributions to Colombian society as a way of developing a common identity among black Colombians. Its founder, Juan de Dios Mosquera Mosquera, was a teacher, and most of its activities reflected his interests. Members read and produced material on the importance of blacks in the making of the Colombian nation and tried to raise consciousness among black Colombians and the general population alike around this heritage. In this sense, Cimarrón's approach was not targeted at the state but rather at society. It organized events around African history and black history in Colombia, attempted to educate people about racism in the country, and worked to develop black consciousness in the grassroots. This was not unlike the work of Brazil's MNU in the same period.

The nature of Cimarrón's platform against racial discrimination mirrored that of other urban black organizations emerging elsewhere in the region. This period also saw the birth of Grupo Antillano in Cuba, a

---

[2] The second congress happened in 1980 in Panama and the third in Brazil.

collective of visual artists, whose work challenged dominant portrayals of African culture as folklore and constructed a vision that centered the African and Caribbean foundations of the modern Cuban nation (de la Fuente 2013). While these urban movements varied substantially from city to city and from country to country, their similarities are nonetheless remarkable. Many of the organizations that began in this period, even the ostensibly cultural ones, began in response to systemic racism not only in economic and political spaces, but also in the social spheres of these countries. From Ilê Aiyê in Brazil to Mundo Afro in Uruguay, activists created cultural spaces that valorized African-based traditions, affirmed the experiences of black people, and in many cases offered educational and social services to local communities. These ostensibly cultural organizations also called out discrimination, sometimes taking public stances against racism. As Andrews (2010) notes in the case of Mundo Afro, the organization "set out to unmask that discrimination by denouncing it whenever and wherever it occurred and by holding public events to discuss its cultural, historical, and even psychological roots and frequency" (149).

Latin American states' responses to the increasing politicization of blackness in this period ranged from ridicule to repression. In Brazil, black activists were themselves accused of being racists (Hanchard 1994; Alberto 2011), both by the state and by their fellow citizens. In Colombia, for example, explicit discussions about racial inequality were seen as racist. Ivan Sinisterra of Cimarrón said that "everyone would tell us that we were the racists, even our own people! They would compare and say 'in the United States, they hit you, they kill you, not here! Here, we are equal'" (interview, Ivan Sinisterra, March 2009).[3] The idea that critiquing racism was incompatible with, and even an act against, the nation had deep historical roots. In her work on the independence wars in Colombia, Lasso (2007) argues that any "explicit expression of racial grievances" by nonwhite patriots "became a mark of unpatriotic divisiveness" (13). Yet despite that uneasiness, by the 1990s and early 2000s black movements were starting to significantly shift state policy and public discourse around race, nation, and inequality (Paschel 2016).

---

[3] Interviews and translations were done by the author.

## Black Peasants and the Rise of Ethno-Territorial Movements

As black organizations were being consolidated in cities throughout Latin America, organized black struggles were also brewing in the countryside and forests of the region. There were a number of things that distinguished rural movements from urban. First was the question of what kinds of claims black rural movements sought to articulate. Whereas black urban movements tended to focus on the fight against racial discrimination and for social, economic, and political equality, black rural movements were often making claims to difference and autonomy. Second, many of these communities had more direct ties to the legacy of maroonage. While urban activists held up historical maroon figures as their inspiration and developed political philosophies based on ideas of *cimarronaje/quilombismo*, black rural communities were constructing a political platform as lineal descendants (*renascientes/remanescentes*) of those same maroon communities, and as heirs to those communities' claims to collective territory.

These ethno-territorial movements also had a different genealogy and different transnational linkages than their urban counterparts. While urban black movements were heavily influenced by anti-apartheid in South Africa and the US civil rights and black power movements, rural black movements often found their political philosophies in politicized peasant struggles based in liberation theology. By the 1970s, a radical arm of the Catholic Church had emerged and proliferated throughout Latin America, organizing grassroots communities to fight against authoritarianism, inequality, and capitalist development. For missionaries and others working within the liberation theology tradition in Latin America, the *bases* or grassroots were peasants; they were seen as an important social actor in the making of more just, and egalitarian, futures in these countries (Restrepo 2004). In so doing, they articulated struggles not only at the intersection of the political categories of "peasant," "indigenous," and "black" but also in the language of territoriality and ethnic rights.

Colombia is the quintessential case of this kind of political articulation (Grueso et al. 2003; Restrepo 2004; Hooker 2005; Castillo 2007). The movement based in black identity that emerged in the mid-1980s in the Chocó region set the pattern that other Colombian regions followed. In this period, missionary groups helped start a number of peasant associations along the rivers that run through the Chocó, including the Río Atrato, Río San Juan, and Río Baudó. The first of these was the Peasant Association of Atrato (ACIA), created amid deep concerns about and contestation over land. The intensification of capitalist expansion served as the main catalyst for organizing peasants in this region. Communities held no land titles and they were afraid they would be forcibly displaced; with the help of missionary groups, they began to try to stave off these market forces (Grueso, Rosero, and Escobar 2003. Nearly all the organizations that emerged in the Chocó in this period – the Peasant Association of the Lower Atrato (OCABA), the Peasant Association of the Lower and Middle San Juan (ACADESAN), and the Peasant Association of the Higher Baudó (ACABA), among others – initially talked about their struggle in terms of defending "the traditional territory of the Pacific."

The Catholic Church was extremely important in the emergence of this peasant movement not just in Colombia but also in Ecuador and in Brazil through its "Pastoral da Terra" (Wade 1998; Mattos 2004; Restrepo 2004). As Restrepo (2004) highlights, by the 1980s, the core mission of the church in Colombia and around the world was to organize the people through grassroots mobilization. This was particularly the case in the Chocó, where Claretian missionaries in the tradition of liberation theology began to develop political consciousness around land and a critique of capitalism. These peasant organizations would eventually become what we now understand as the black rural or ethno-territorial movement in Colombia. Initially, however, these organizations were not always explicitly ethno-racial. They were instead a nascent movement based in regional and class-based identities, even while they were made up almost entirely of black peasants. Indeed, in the early years, these movements were first and foremost about defending the territory of the Pacific coast, even if they were aware that they were also black and living in a black region.

It was only later that these implicitly black peasant organizations from Colombia's Pacific coast underwent a laborious process of ethnicization and coalition-building with other movements: civic strikes in Tumaco and the north of Cauca, organizing in Palenque on the Atlantic Coast. (Restrepo 2004). Together, these efforts would ultimately constitute Colombia's black ethno-territorial movement, which made claims to collective lands and life, rather than individual property, and defended rural, traditional, self-sustaining life, rather than the kind of social mobility and inclusion in capitalist development more prominent in the discourse of urban organizations (Paschel 2016).

Similar movements, with similar claims to ethnic difference, were also developing in other Latin American countries, though sometimes with different genealogies. In Honduras, Garífuna populations had begun consolidating a movement based on claims to collective ethnic identity and territory, starting with the founding of the Fraternal Black Organization (OFRANEH) in 1977. The organization initially came out of earlier struggles against racial discrimination, particularly movements against labor market discrimination. It was only as serious land conflicts emerged on the country's northern coast that OFRANEH and other organizations began to focus on questions of territoriality (Anderson 2007; on the somewhat comparable case of Nicaragua, see Hooker 2009). In Ecuador, it was the Organización de la Familia Negra – which emerged in 1983 in the Chota Valley, a region of the country associated with strong African roots – that led such ethno-territorial struggles.

In Brazil, a black rural movement emerged first in the Northeast, the part of the country with the highest concentration of poverty, rurality, and people who identify as Afrodescendant. In 1986, just as the country was embarking upon an intense process of democratization and the rewriting of its constitution, the Center for Black Culture (CCN) of Maranhão organized the first National Encounter of Rural Blacks. The meeting took place in São Luis and had as its main theme "blacks and the new constitution" (Alberti and Pereira 2007). It was at this meeting that the concept of *terra de pretos* (black territories) – which had been used by CCN for some time – became part of the lexicon of the black movement more generally. That same year, the MNU organized the Brasília Convention, which convened black activists and allies from around the country to compose a list of demands to present to the Constituent Assembly preparing to write the country's new constitution. At the Brasília gathering, CCN members argued strenuously that the platform of demands had to include collective land rights for *quilombolas*.

In places like Maranhão, the dominant organizations that emerged were hybrids of both rural and urban organizing, speaking in a language both of anti-racism and of territoriality. In other countries, the relationship between these two sectors and kinds of claims making was more complex. In both Colombia and Honduras, some of the main activists and organizations of the ethno-territorial struggle began their political activism by fighting against racial discrimination in urban areas (Anderson 2007; Paschel 2016). In Colombia, Chocoano activists eventually decided to split off from Cimarrón and dedicate their efforts toward building the struggle for territory in rural areas (Paschel 2016). These divisions between urban and rural black movements were further exacerbated by the fact that it was ethno-territorial organizations – not the urban ones that emerged in the same period, or arguably earlier – that ultimately gained the most political traction. It was the black farmers' demands that were ultimately institutionalized in Colombia's 1991 constitution in the form of rights to collective territory in rural areas on the Pacific coast, alternative development, and differentiated citizenship. However, this success further aggravated already sharp tensions between urban and rural activists, ones that mapped onto historic divisions and hierarchies. For the former – many of whom were believers in a certain kind of social and economic integration and capitalist development – the 1991 constitution institutionalized an anachronistic idea of blackness as outside of modernity. Moreover, the fact that black peasants were the ones rising to national prominence and achieving unprecedented access to the state was disturbing to black urban activists who had fought for such political integration for decades (Paschel 2016).

These distinctions were often as much about the language of claims-making as they were about the ideological position and material realities of these different sectors of the movement. Activist nun Hermana Aida, who was involved in the founding of the Black Peasant Association of the San Juan River (ACADESAN), explained in an interview: "There was always a kind of distrust of blacks from the city, who rural folks see as making fun of them. The blacks from the city think that the people from the countryside don't know anything, that because they haven't ever worn shoes, that they don't know how to walk right or speak properly" (interview, Hermana Aida, February 2009). Similar divides between the material realities and political ideologies of Colombia's urban and rural black movements were visible in Bolivia, Ecuador, and Honduras (Anderson 2007; Busdiecker 2010; de la Torre and Sánchez 2012). Those divides not only represented differences in the way that each of these sectors diagnosed the problems facing black communities, but more fundamentally, different solutions to those very problems. If for urban activists it was a lack of integration into national social, economic, and political life that plagued black populations, for many rural activists it was precisely that kind of integration that worried them. In Colombia, the project proposed by black urban activists, of racial uplift and integration, left intact a particular idea of development that implied radical changes to peasant livelihoods that threatened to remove them from rural territories (Escobar 2008). Once collective land rights were recognized for black rural populations throughout Latin America, collective memory and academic expertise would both play a critical role in legitimating the rights claims of specific communities (Mattos 2008; French 2009).

## Patriarchy and the Articulation of Black Women's Struggles

Black women, alongside black men, engaged in various forms of resistance to the colonial order, just as they were also crucial to the black social clubs that emerged in the late nineteenth and early twentieth centuries (Butler 1998; de la Fuente 2001; Andrews 2010). As historian Kim Butler notes, "[black] women played significant roles as leaders and organizers whereas white Brazilian women had yet to overcome the weight of traditional stereotypes" (1999, 87). Black social clubs in this period often included a specific arm, or "auxiliary" for women (Butler 1998; Brunson 2011). These women's groups were extremely important to the functioning of the clubs as they often collected membership and subscription dues, organized social events, carried out the social work mandate of these organizations, and did a great part of the fundraising (Andrews 2010; Brunson 2011). These activities were crucial to keeping black organizations afloat, just as they also created the infrastructure upon which these organizations would transform into official political parties (Andrews 2010).

Nevertheless, the black social clubs were profoundly gendered projects (Carneiro 2003; Caldwell 2007; Brunson 2011). As Brunson (2011) argues in her work on Afro-Cuban *sociedades,* these organizations "articulated a gendered agenda for racial progress as they socialized, pursued education, and sought political influence" (36). She shows how black women were themselves invested in upholding these deeply patriarchal projects of racial uplift (Brunson 2011). Additionally, black women were in this period typically organized in less visible ways than their male counterparts. Thus, we still know very little about the many contributions that black women made to these organizations, especially their contributions to what might be called black political thought in the region (Grueso and Arroyo 2002; Caldwell 2007; Caldwell 2009; Prado and Rodrigues 2010; see also Chapter 6).

While the gendered language of black mobilization would change over the following decades, black organizations in the mid- and late twentieth century continued to be profoundly patriarchal and masculinist (Carneiro 2003; Caldwell 2007; Hernandez 2011; Paschel 2016). Black women were much more visible figures in the black organizations that were founded in the 1970s in Latin America, including figures like Delia Zapata and Lélia Gonzalez. However, the fissures around gender within these movements became more apparent in the 1980s as black women in Latin America began to make public critiques of patriarchy within black movements and within their societies at large (Alvarez 1990; Caldwell 2007). Some did so from within mixed-gender black organizations; others, fed up with overt and subtler forms of sexism within male-dominated black organizations, began to form autonomous black women's and black feminist organizations (Caldwell 2007; Paschel and Sawyer 2008; Andrews 2010). Organizing separately meant that women could take leadership positions in ways that they could not in male-dominated organizations. Black feminist activists had also fought for years to make the case that black movements should pay more attention to the unique ways that racism and gendered hierarchies differentially affected black women. In so doing, they raised intersectional issues, including violence against black women, sterilization campaigns, the exploitation of domestic workers, and the negative portrayals of black women within popular culture (Safá 2002; Morrison 2003; Caldwell 2007; Rodrigues and Prado 2010; see also Chapter 3). If male-dominated black organizations addressed these issues at all, they often relegated them to the margins. This marginalization mirrored the ways in which women's movements dominated by white, middle-class women treated issues affecting black women (Alvarez 1990; Carneiro 2003).

In response to what Cathy Cohen (1999) calls secondary marginalization, black women in cities throughout Latin America began to create their own organizations in the 1980s. The first significant group of this kind in Brazil was Maria Mulher, founded in 1987 in Porto Alegre by some thirty women active in the black movement, the women's movement, and the labor movement. These women were originally a chapter of the S.O.S. Racism campaign, which provided legal and psychosocial services for victims of racism as well as other services aimed at "ensuring the rights and dignity of human life" (Paschel 2016). A year later, in 1988 – amid the constitutional-reform process and celebrations of the centennial of the abolition of slavery in Brazil – black women activists from throughout the country met in Valença, for the First Meeting of Black Women. That same year, Geledés: The Institute of Black Women – one of the most important black political organizations in Latin America– was founded in São Paulo by black women with professional degrees and active in the women's movement. Over the next decade, dozens of other organizations would follow (Caldwell 2007). Today, Brazil's black feminist movement could be said to be in its second or third generation, with regular national meetings of young black feminists, black women university students, and black lesbian feminists. These different generations of black women activists came together in the historic March of

Black Women, which congregated thousands of black women in Brasília in November of 2015 (de Oliveira Rocha, forthcoming).

While Brazil is unique in its large number of black feminist and black women's organizations, the 1980s–1990s did see the emergence of similar organizations, especially black women's NGOs, throughout Latin America and the Caribbean. Solange Pierre in Santo Domingo developed the Movement for Dominican Women of Haitian Descent (MUDHA, founded in 1983), Cecilia Moreno created the Center for the Panamanian Woman (1990), and Epsy Campbell Barr founded the Center for Afro–Costa Rican Women in Limón (1992). Two years later the Enlace de Mujeres Negras de Honduras was created, as were similar women's organizations in Peru and Ecuador.

These black women's organizations shared a number of characteristics. First, they often operated with one foot in the male-dominated black movement and one in the white/*mestiza*-dominated women's movement. Their experiences within the latter, though also difficult, gave these black women activists what they often referred to as "*acúmulo político*" (Paschel 2016). Their involvement in the broader women's movement positioned them better to form NGOs and develop transnational strategies (Caldwell 2009). It also gave black women's organizations access to funding that mixed-gender black-movement organizations could not successfully obtain. As Jurema Werneck of Criola explained, women working in organizations like Maria Mulher, Geledés, and Criola also tended to have the "kind of labor market skills" that middle-class white Brazilians commanded (Paschel 2016). Black women activists from the Dominican Republic, Costa Rica, Colombia, and elsewhere had a similar profile, which mirrored a general trend toward the NGO-ization of the women's movement throughout Latin America (Alvarez 1990).

Also like their Brazilian counterparts, black women at the helm of black women's organizations throughout the region had participated in international conferences like the Fourth World Conference on Women (held in 1995 in Beijing), even before they participated in similar meetings on anti-racism like the 2001 Durban conference. As such, they had developed national and transnational repertoires of political action around engaging with state officials and effecting policy change. At home, they also typically engaged in legal advocacy and provided educational, legal, and health services to communities. MUDHA, in the Dominican Republic, for example, was founded in 1983 "to combat anti-Haitian prejudice and sexism." It did this through developing "primary healthcare, family planning services and educational programs in the chronically impoverished and State-neglected bateys" (MUDHA 2017). This kind of work was also central to the programs of organizations like Geledés and Maria Mulher in Brazil and the Center for Afro–Costa Rican Women.

In Colombia, the black women's movement was slower to develop, despite the fact that women were always central to the black movement in that country (Grueso and Arroyo 2002). The Association of Afro-Colombian Women was created in 1990; however, it was not until a decade later that the network would actually take shape. During the First National Assembly of Afro-Colombian Women, held in Tolima in 2000 and which convened hundreds of participants, the association became the Kambirí National Network of Afro-Colombian Women. Unlike Brazil's Articulation of Black Women's Organizations (AMNB), which was made up of organizations, Kambirí was created as a network of individual women, many of them professionals and community leaders. Another key difference was that Kambirí was an outgrowth of the mixed-gender organization Cimarrón, whereas in Brazil the black women's and black feminist movement largely emerged either out of rupture with male-dominated mainstream black organizations or out of complete autonomy from those organizations (Caldwell 2007).

Meanwhile, another dynamic was emerging in the countryside with the founding of rural black women's groups and networks within the ethno-territorial movement (Grueso and Arroyo 2002; Asher 2004). Like their counterparts in urban black organizations, black rural women had also been central to the intellectual, political, and everyday administrative functioning of black peasant organizations. Nevertheless, and with few exceptions, it was men who became the most visible protagonists of these movements (Arroyo and Grueso 2002, Escobar 2008). In ethno-territorial movements on Colombia's Pacific Coast, this internal contradiction became increasingly pronounced, and it was at the center of the rise of black women's groups and networks (Escobar 2008). Unlike their urban counterparts, these black women's groups were less likely to understand themselves as feminists, even though they were radically challenging gender hierarchies within the movement (Asher 2004; Escobar 2008; on similar dynamics in Brazil, see Francisco 2015).

At the center of this organizing by black rural women were not just debates about what role black women should play in the movements, but more fundamental questions about their role within communities. These two spaces are, of course, deeply imbricated. This is especially so when we consider that one of the principal goals of ethno-territorial movements in Colombia and elsewhere is the right to cultural difference and tradition.

Much like indigenous communities, some women involved in Colombia's ethno-territorial movement have argued that, in contrast to the opposition and hierarchy that characterized western gender relations, traditional black communities are best understood through a lens of gender complementarity (Escobar 2008; Grueso 2011). Yet while complementarity may be prevalent in the social life of these communities, this kind of symbiosis has proven difficult to translate into the political sphere. Some activists argued that the trope of "traditional culture" was actually used as a justification for the submission of black women, and for their relegation to secondary, less visible roles within these movements (Hernandez 2011). More fundamentally, patriarchy and traditional ideas of politics being a "cosa de hombre" or a man's thing, presented many challenges to black women activists at home and in the movement. Ultimately, the experiences of black women active in Colombia's male-dominated ethno-territorial movement sound strikingly like those of black women in both urban and rural areas throughout the hemisphere. Nevertheless, women active in these movements typically chose a different *camino* than urban black women. Rather than create autonomous black women's organizations, many black women peasants have decided to work within mixed-gender black organizations, sometimes in black women's groups within these organizations.

### From Diasporic Imaginings to Transnational Articulations

These different sectors of contemporary black movements – urban movements, ethno-territorial movements, and black women's movements – overlap at the same time that they reflect distinct geographies, conceptions of blackness, political claims, and ideologies. But one feature that they all have in common is their embeddedness in transnational networks. In the 1980s and 1990s, as the black movement was consolidating throughout the region and winning constitutional and legal recognition, organizations became more involved in building transnational networks and organizations. This includes networks like the Pastoral Afro, the Organization of Africans in the Americas, the Network of Afro-Latin American and Caribbean Women, Afro-America XXI, the Central American Black Organization (ONECA), and the Strategic Afro-Latin American Alliance (Alianza) (Davis, Paschel, and Morrison 2008).

The development of transnational networks was also directly linked to the trajectories of individual activists. Andrews (2010), for example, tells the story of Romero Rodríguez, an Afro-Uruguayan activist who lived in exile in Brazil, and who, after meeting Afro-Brazilian activists like Abdias do Nascimento, returned home determined to build a similar movement in Uruguay. Rodríguez was also central to the founding of transnational networks, including Alianza. Another critical transnational figure was Afro–Costa Rican activist-turned-congresswoman Epsy Campbell Barr, who founded the Center for Afro–Costa Rican Women. From its beginning in 1992, the organization's language has been transnational: "from its inception and due to the nature of Afrodescendant identity – which transcends national borders – the women of the Center proposed the need to work at the local, national and regional level" (Centro de Mujeres Afrocostarricenses 2017).

Precisely because of this vision, in 1992 activists from the Centro joined women from twenty-three other countries at the First Meeting of Afro-Caribbean and Afro–Latin American Women, held in Santo Domingo. It was there that the Network of Afro–Latin American and Caribbean Women, which includes many of the black women's and black feminist organizations, was formed. A decade later, they were instrumental in the preparations for the Third World Conference against Racism, held in Durban, South Africa, in 2001 (Martins et al. 2004; Telles 2004). Afro–Latin American activists from throughout the region decided early on that they would mobilize not only around Durban but also the regional preparatory Conference of the Americas, held in 2000 in Santiago de Chile.

In preparation for the Santiago and Durban conferences, activists came together to form the Strategic Afro–Latin American Alliance (Alianza), founded in San José, Costa Rica, in September 2000. The Alianza held a number of international meetings and consultations in the months leading up to the conferences, developed a regional strategy for leveraging the Durban conference, and secured international funding to ensure a strong activist presence at both the Santiago and Durban conferences (Telles 2004). Made up mostly of black activists representing organizations in various Latin American and Caribbean countries, the network's main goal was to pressure Latin American states to collect data on ethnoracial inequality and to adopt specific policies for black populations (Martins et al. 2004; Telles 2004). Alianza also lobbied national governments to support the inclusion of specific policies in the official Santiago document and later the Durban Plan of Action.

At the nexus of this transnational Afro–Latin American mobilization were Afro-Brazilian feminist organizations, which had attended and organized around the 1994 Population and Development Conference in

Cairo and the Fourth World Conference on Women in Beijing in 1995. Those organizations now mobilized at the local and national levels in the months preceding Durban. In 2000, they founded the Articulation of Black Brazilian Women's Organizations (AMNB), which was made up of twenty-four organizations from around the country with the goal of "establishing the adequate conditions for the participation of this segment [black women] in the process of mobilization and development of the Third World Conference Against Racism, Xenophobia and Related Intolerances" (Articulação 2007). Geledés and Criola were critical to the establishment of AMNB and oversaw international funding for Alianza members to participate in both the Santiago and Durban conferences. Ultimately, they secured a grant from the Ford Foundation and consequently managed the participation of the Latin American black organizations in Durban (interview, Jurema Werneck, October 2009).

The impulse of Afro–Latin American activists to look outward and see connections between their struggle and those of other people of African descent in Latin America or elsewhere was not new. In the early twentieth century, Garveyism and other strands of Pan-African movements gained sway in places like Cuba, Central America, and Brazil (Guridy 2010; Pereira 2013); the FNB and black Brazilian newspapers often sustained dialogue with the black press in the United States (Leite 1992; Hanchard 2003; Pereira 2013). As Hanchard (2003) rightfully argues, these movements should be seen as constructing an "imagined community" that is at once "multinational, multilingual, ideologically and culturally plural" (22). For many activists, this solidarity with black people around the globe came from a belief not only that they had a shared history but also that they continued to face some of the same problems.[4]

While many of these linkages were symbolic in nature – an imagined community, the appropriation of US black power aesthetics, the naming of organizations like Colombia's Soweto Study Group and the neighborhood of Nelson Mandela – there were also key moments of tangible exchange (Paschel 2016). This was the case with the 1977 First Congress of Black Culture of the Americas in Cali, Colombia, as well as the first meetings of the Pastoral Afroamericana held in Buenaventura, Colombia (1980), and Esmeraldas, Ecuador (1983). While these events did not translate into sustained networks, they were the foundation upon which later exchanges would take place.

---

[4] This resembles Dawson's (1994) idea of linked fate among African Americans across class and other cleavages, only on a global scale.

Transnationalism was thus a longstanding feature of Afro–Latin American activism. But what made Durban unprecedented was the degree to which Afro–Latin American activists – across ideological, regional, and language divides – consolidated a unified platform and strategic plan of action. This was a crucial moment in the history of black mobilization in the region, which has continued to shape how black organizations engage with their respective states and to hold them accountable. While their efforts were met in their home countries with uneven success, in most countries mobilization around Durban raised the national visibility of racial issues. This was part of a larger shift catalyzed by black movements, not only toward specific legislation and policies for black populations, but toward a change in the national consciousness around questions of race and nation.

## THE POLITICAL AND SOCIAL IMPACT OF BLACK MOBILIZATION

In August of 2013, then Colombian vice president Angelino Garzón addressed an auditorium of some 900 Afro-Colombian grassroots leaders. It was an historic national black-movement congress marking the twenty-year anniversary of the 1993 Law of Black Communities and held in the majority-black city of Quibdó on the country's Pacific coast. The vice president started his speech by saying, "I'm so happy to be in the folkloric city of Quibdó!" to which he received no applause. However, he began to win over the crowd with his discussion of Afro-Colombians' contributions to the nation. In the charismatic, populist oratorical style he is known for, he said: "Comrades, I've said this before and I think this congress should discuss this. Of course, the law prohibits discrimination and racism in Colombia, but in Colombia culturally, we are discriminators, we are racists!" The auditorium was overwhelmed with emotion and applause. He continued: "Everyone that governs Colombia has a duty. They have a duty to fight for a politics of social inclusion, to fight against racism, to fight against discrimination!" (Paschel 2016, 144). Similarly, some years before, Fernando Henrique Cardoso became the first Brazilian president to recognize the existence of racism and racial inequality in Brazilian society. In a speech in December 2001 he stated: "We lived boxed into the illusion that this was a perfect racial democracy, when it wasn't, and it still isn't today. Our democracy does have some elements that allow for greater malleability and flexibility, but if those elements aren't worked on, if there isn't a conscious fight for equality and against discrimination, we're not going to advance" (Cardoso 2001). He also vowed to take "affirmative actions" to address the ongoing consequences of slavery in the country.

These statements by the highest level of government officials in these countries stood in stark contrast with those of previous decades, which emphasized these countries' race mixture, cultural homogeneity, and lack of race problems. These discourses that had effectively shut down any critique of the de facto racial order in these countries. But more than symbolic change, these statements signaled a much more profound change in Latin American states' approach to questions of race, nation, and citizenship. In that same speech in December 2001 and right after the Third World Conference against Racism, Cardoso also vowed that he, and the state more generally, would "continue with the task of repairing such damage through policies that promote equal opportunity." He added that the best way to address racial discrimination was through both "universal and affirmative action policies for Afro-descendants" (Cardoso 2001).

## The Shift in State Discourse and Policy

Over the last three decades there has been a significant change in many Latin American states' orientation on racial issues from denying racism to adopting ethno-racial policies including affirmative action. In doing so, states moved from citizenship regimes based on a universal unmarked citizen to a more differentiated model, from repressing or ignoring black movements to coopting them (Rahier 2012). These changes often came as the result of overlapping political articulations, domestic and global, but ones where black political organizations were at the center (Hooker 2005; Van Cott 2006; Hooker 2008; Paschel and Sawyer 2008). Beginning in the late 1980s governments throughout the region adopted multicultural constitutions that recognized the collective rights of indigenous communities and in some cases also for certain sectors of these countries' black populations (Hooker 2005). These constitutional reforms, which included the recognition of collective land rights, the right to alternative development, local political autonomy, ethnic education, and other rights, were the direct result of mobilization by the territorial arm of the black movement in countries like Brazil, Ecuador, and Honduras.

Such reforms came with great promise. If fully implemented, they would not only assure that black rural communities could remain on the land that they had inhabited since the colonial era, but they would also challenge the dominant economic development model. Granting black and indigenous communities the right to collective, unalienable territory; political autonomy; natural resources; and the right to be consulted on development projects before they began meant putting a brake on previously unregulated capitalist expansion, particularly extractive industries (Oslender 2001; Escobar 2008). Precisely because of these stakes, these multicultural reforms brought with them nearly insurmountable challenges. In recent decades, black rural activists from Honduras to Colombia to Brazil have spent much of their time engaged in legal struggles and transnational activism to realize and access those rights, and they are also in deep internal debates over the limits and possibilities of being institutionalized into the state apparatus (Rahier 2012; Paschel 2016). They have also had to fight against the criminalization of black activists and of protest more generally.

It was about a decade after this initial wave of reforms, and in the context of Durban, that some Latin American governments initiated a new round of ethno-racial reforms that seemed to reconcile some of the contradictions inherent to multicultural policies. They created national holidays around black history, identity, and culture; included questions in their national census to count their Afrodescendant populations, sometimes for the first time since the colonial period; and in some cases passed anti-racism legislation. Some states also created national-level state entities with the mandate of combating racial and other forms of discrimination. While the impact of Durban is most clear in the Brazilian case, it also impacted policy and political discourse throughout the region. As John Anton argues in the case of Ecuador, in the wake of Durban, and because of the efforts of a unified Afro-Ecuadorian movement, "the principle of 'no discrimination' was included in the new constitution [2008], declaring any manifestation of racism unacceptable and asserting the obligation of the state to guarantee affirmative action to victims of racism and to stimulate positive public policy through National Councils of Equity" (Antón Sánchez 2009, 43).

In Panama, once-fragmented black organizations came together to organize the First Afro-Panamanian Forum in 1999, which Priestley argues "was evidence of the unprecedented level of cohesion and strength within the black movement" (Priestley and Barrow 2010, 63). In 2002, in response to demands from the black movement, and after the Panamanian government participated in Durban, it approved a federal antidiscrimination law. Similarly, in response to black-movement pressure, in the late 2000s the Colombian government began to adopt antidiscrimination laws and policies aimed at bringing about racial equality. Unlike the cultural and territorial rights granted to subsets of the black populations in the 1990s, these new racial equality polices of the 2000s were broader and wrapped in the language of racial equality and inclusion (Paschel 2016).

Like the previous round of reforms, these new racial equality policies still fell short in many senses. First, they were far from meeting all of the historic demands of black movement organizations in each country. For example, in Brazil, black activists had long fought against the criminalization of black people; however, nowhere in Brazil's expansive discourse of racial equality was there space for reforms to the country's infamous military police and death squads (Smith 2015). Second, the anti-racist discourse of government officials was often much stronger than the policies themselves, and the quantity of state agencies charged with bringing about racial equality was often greater than their quality. Finally, the adoption of specific legislation for black populations also engendered new politics in the region that arguably undermined black movements, including the cooptation of movements in some cases as well as the development of reactionary movements committed to undermining the gains of black movements (Anderson 2007; Rahier 2012; Paschel 2016). At the center of the literature on contemporary black mobilization are attempts to make sense of these new political articulations that have happened in the aftermath of ethno-racial reforms. Moreover, scholars have also begun to look at the impact of black mobilization beyond the sphere of formal politics in part because confining change to the precarious realm of policy runs the risk of missing the myriad ways that black activists and organizations have reshaped their societies in recent years.

## Reshaping Identities, Transforming Societies

Perhaps the greatest achievement of black mobilization over the last few decades has been to break the taboo around racial critique, to bring once-marginalized and ignored critiques of racial inequality into the mainstream. This was both the direct and indirect result of black mobilization. Black activists shifted the terms of these debates through direct action, just as their work to change state discourse and policy also reshaped these societies in important ways. For example, the adoption of affirmative action policies in Brazilian universities not only slowly chipped away at racial gaps in education but also led to the proliferation of public discussions around race in Brazilian media (Feres Júnior 2008).

Beyond public discourse, black mobilization is fundamentally changing identities on the ground in Latin America. One of the spaces through which this is happening is education. Black movements through-out Latin America had historically sought to educate communities about the history of the African diaspora in the Americas and the African continent, through informal educational projects and through cultural production (Covin 2006; Alberti and Pereira 2007; Andrews 2010; Smith 2015). In Brazil and Colombia, this kind of education became a central political demand. Rather than the MNU or Cimarrón providing this kind of education to communities, activists came to see it as a state responsibility. This obligation of the state was institutionalized through legislation like Colombia's ethno-education laws, and Brazil's law 10.639, which mandates the history of Afro-Brazilians and Africa in all schools, public and private, and at all levels.

There was also a palpable sense among scholars and activists alike that black mobilization has shifted identities on the ground (Telles 2004; Caldwell 2007; Schwartzman 2007; Telles and Paschel 2014). Giovani Sobrevivente of the MNU, for example, noted that "today, as we arrive in the twenty-first century, children are *assumindo*[5] their blackness, wearing their afros, *assumindo* their clothes, *assumindo* their culture. That was the work of the black movement" (interview, Giovanni Sobrevivente, December 2009). Thus, while the adage "money whitens" may still hold true in some contexts, there is growing evidence that this may no longer be the case (Schwartzman 2007; Telles and Paschel 2014). This is less surprising when we consider that the black organizations in Latin America sought to simultaneously reshape state institutions and social practices.

One of the places where this link between political and social transformations is perhaps most clear is in the mobilization around national censuses. Between 1980 and 2000, the number of Latin American states that included an ethno-racial question on their national census nearly doubled (del Popolo 2008). Between 1900 and 2000, Cuba and Brazil were the only two countries in the region that systematically collected data on Afrodescendants; by the 2010 round of censuses, the Dominican Republic was the only Latin American country that did not include an ethno-racial question (Loveman 2014). Black movements pressured their respective states to collect ethno-racial statistics on the black population and to influence the actual wording of the question(s) included (Telles 2007). One of the first census-related mobilizations was the Don't Let Your Color Pass for White campaign, organized around the 1991

---

[5] "Assuming" in the sense of accepting, acknowledging, taking on.

Brazilian census (Nobles 2000). In addition to affirming black identity, such campaigns have sought to persuade people of visible African ancestry (including mixed-race people) to identify as black/Afrodescendant on the census. As Latin American states geared up for the 2010 census rounds, black organizations in Bolivia, Chile, Colombia, Costa Rica, Honduras, Panama, and Uruguay – and even Afro-Latino organizations in the United States – organized similar campaigns. These mobilizations led to an unprecedented collection of ethno-racial statistics in most of the region (Loveman 2014). These campaigns, as well as the broader mobilization efforts of black activists, were arguably behind the rise in people who self-identified as nonwhite in the recent censuses.

Even while black movements did, in many cases, change the ethno-racial language of official statistics, the census is ultimately a blunt instrument for measuring socially complex realities, racial identity not excepted. This is why many scholars have also analyzed the link between black mobilization and the transformation of identities on the ground in other spaces, charting, for example, the changing representations of blackness in television, radio, and print media (Caldwell 2007; Gillam 2016). They have argued that black mobilization has been central to these changing representations of blackness in popular culture by launching campaigns against racist expressions, filing court cases, and creating alternative media. While most of this scholarship tends to focus on Brazil, similar dynamics are underway throughout the region. In 2013, the Afro-Peruvian organization LUNDU launched a successful media and legal campaign against the El Negro Mama blackface character on the TV show *El Especial del Humor*. After a drawn-out battle, Peru's Ethics Tribunal for Radio and Television found the character to be discriminatory, charged the TV channel a fine of about US $24,000, and mandated that it follow the Unified Code of Ethics. While not as successful, Afro-Colombians launched a similar campaign in Colombia against the US TV show *Grey's Anatomy*, which when translated into the Colombian version omitted all of the black characters for which the show had originally been famous.

Music has been another important site of the increasing politicization of black identity in Latin America. Like salsa a generation before, musical forms from hip hop to currulao to reggaetón have become critical spaces both for critiques of racism and for the construction and circulation of alternative ideas of blackness (Fernandes 2006; Quintero 2006; Rivera-Rideau 2015). While the production of these alternative representations is not typically understood as black mobilization, increasingly scholars have argued that artists like Kafu Banton in Panama, Obsesión and Las Krudas in Cuba, and Tego Calderón in Puerto Rico can be seen as working in tandem with more formalized black political organizations, and that they even could be understood as activist-artists in their own right (Fernandes 2006; de la Fuente 2008; Rivera-Rideau 2015). Like black activists throughout the region over the twentieth century, figures like Tego Calderón have unburied pervasive practices of racial discrimination, just as his critiques "make evident the slippages and contradictions within dominant discourses of racial democracy" (Rivera-Rideau 2015). In other cases, like Colombia, the link between such cultural production and political mobilization was even more direct. Ethnomusicologist Birembaum Quintero (2006), for example, shows how important currulao music was to the solidification of the politicized black identity and demands of Colombia's ethno-territorial movement in the 1990s.

It is this combination of explicit black political mobilization and the consolidation of a kind of cultural politics of blackness that has arguably led to the explosion of new, more popular forms of black mobilization in places like Brazil. The React or Die movement (Reaja o Será Morto/a), a network of community-based organizations that emerged to politicize the deaths of black people and to expose police brutality and inequality in Brazil's criminal justice system, first emerged in 2005. Nearly a decade later, in 2014, it gained national and international media attention with a number of marches against the genocide of black people (Smith 2016). While the trend within Brazil's larger black movement at the time had been to work within state bureaucracies and in more professionalized black NGOs, Reaja was amassing thousands of protestors in the streets. As anthropologist Christen Smith, and co-founder of Reaja, argues, such organizing was directly linked to Bahia's hip hop and popular theater movement, with groups like Etnia Negra and Culture Shock acting as a cultural backbone to the organization (119).

The combination of historic forms of black mobilization and politicized cultural production has created new forms of mobilization that are arguably more grassroots than their previous incarnations. In some cases, the cultural workers within the larger panorama of black organizing have been those most likely to be targeted by the state. As late as the 2000s, the Afro-Cuban artists that critiqued racism on the island were heavily repressed by the state. One of the responses to these practices of censorship, containment, and co-optation of hip hop artists by the Cuban state was to flee to the United States and Europe (Fernandes 2006). All of this suggests the need to re-center cultural politics and the politics of culture in our analyses of black mobilization in Latin America.

## CONCLUSION

The politicization of blackness is not a new phenomenon in Latin America. While previous scholarship underscored the lack of racial consciousness in this region and the many impediments to this type of organizing, more recent work has uncovered a long history of people of African descent organizing as such. They have uncovered lesser-known histories of black mobilization in the late nineteenth and early twentieth century and examined the upsurge of black mobilization in recent decades. In this chapter, I build on that work by situating black mobilization in a long history. I argue that, depending on how one defines it, we might trace black mobilization back to the struggles against slavery and colonial rule, as Afro–Latin American activists often do. In the late nineteenth and early twentieth centuries, Afrodescendants constructed public spaces built on black newspapers, social clubs, and political parties. All of these forms of black mobilization are remarkable given the political contexts in which they emerged. They also complicate dominant narratives of Latin America either as a racial paradise, or as a region offering insurmountable ideological obstacles to black consciousness and mobilization.

Despite much within- and between-country variation, I argue that contemporary black movements in Latin America share a number of important features. First, rather than a singular, cohesive movement, black movements today are best understood as intersectional and multi-faceted movements. Rather than see divisions within these movements as a sign that they are pathologically fragmented – a claim often made by state officials and international donors – this chapter highlights the material and ideological foundations for different articulations of black politics within and between countries in the region. Moreover, in contrast to the black organizations of the earlier part of the twentieth century, many contemporary black movements operate at the intersection of a number of political categories. From Honduras to Colombia to Brazil, the organizations that have been the chief protagonists of the story of political and social change in recent years have been black peasant organizations and black women's organizations (Caldwell 2007; Rodrigues and Prado 2010; Perry 2013).

Second, much like other social movements in Latin America and around the world, black movements today are embedded in transnational networks in unprecedented ways. Black activists have moved beyond the kind of symbolic diasporic imaginings of the 1900s to construct tangible transnational umbrella organizations, solidarity networks, and strategies aimed at effecting change at home. Deeply grassroots Pan-African organizations like Reaja in Brazil have found themselves working in solidarity with the Black Lives Matter movement in the United States; Afro-Colombian activists have intensified transnational activism around peace negotiations. These transnational networks are crucial to understanding the articulation, and success, of contemporary black movements in Latin America.

Finally, in recent decades black political organizations in Latin America have been effective in reconfiguring the terms of mainstream debates around questions of race, equality, and difference, and in some cases they have also achieved unprecedented legal recognition. These policy changes catalyzed by black mobilization were at once significant and limited. In recent decades, black activists' efforts, and the resultant policy changes, have arguably shaken up politics as usual in many Latin American countries (Sawyer and Paschel 2008). Yet rather than resolve the deep-seated inequalities upon which these countries were built, racial and otherwise, their efforts have unearthed an entirely new set of empirical and political questions. Among them is the extent to which these reforms represent a break with these countries' racial pasts, or simply a re-articulation. This question, and others, will continue to drive the future work of activists and the scholars who study black movements.

## BIBLIOGRAPHY

Agudelo, Carlos. 2005. *Retos del multiculturalismo en Colombia: Política y poblaciones negras*. Medellín: La Carreta.

Alberti, Verena, and Amilcar Pereira. 2007. *Histórias do movimento negro no Brasil: Depoimentos ao CPDOC*. Rio de Janeiro: Fundação Getulio Vargas.

Alberto, Paulina. 2011. *Terms of Inclusion: Black Intellectuals in Twentieth-Century Brazil*. Chapel Hill, NC: University of North Carolina Press.

Alvarez, Sonia E. 1990. *Engendering Democracy in Brazil: Women's Movements in Politics*. Princeton, NJ: Princeton University Press.

Anderson, Mark. 2007. "When Afro Becomes (like) Indigenous: Garifuna and Afro-Indigenous Politics in Honduras." *Journal of Latin American and Caribbean Anthropology* 12, 2: 384–413.

Andrews, George Reid. 1980. *The Afro-Argentines of Buenos Aires, 1800–1900*. Madison, WI: University of Wisconsin Press.

   1988. "Black and White Workers: São Paulo, Brazil, 1888–1928." *Hispanic American Historical Review* 68, 3: 491–524.

2004. *Afro-Latin America, 1800–2000.* New York, NY: Oxford University Press.

2010. *Blackness in the White Nation: A History of Afro-Uruguay.* Chapel Hill, NC: University of North Carolina Press.

Antón Sánchez, Jhon. 2009. "Multiethnic Nations and Cultural Citizenship: Proposals from the Afro-Descendant Movement in Ecuador." In *New Social Movements in the African Diaspora: Challenging Global Apartheid*, edited by Leith Mullings, 33–48. New York, NY: Palgrave Macmillan.

Appelbaum, Nancy P. 2003. *Muddied Waters: Race, Region, and Local History in Colombia, 1846–1948.* Durham, NC: Duke University Press.

Articulação de Organizações de Mulheres Negras Brasileiras (AMNB). 2007. "*Construindo a equidade: Estratégia para implementação de políticas públicas para a superação das desigualdades de gênero e raça para as mulheres negras.*" Rio de Janeiro: AMNB.

Arruti, José Maurício Andion. 2000. "Direitos étnicos no Brasil e na Colômbia: Notas comparativas sobre hibridização, segmentação e mobilização política de índios e negros." *Horizontes Antropológicos* 6, 14: 93–123.

Asher, Kiran. 2004. "Texts in Context: Afro-Colombian Women's Activism in the Pacific Lowlands of Colombia." *Feminist Review* 78, 1: 38–55.

2009. *Black and Green: Afro-Colombians, Development, and Nature in the Pacific Lowlands.* Durham, NC: Duke University Press.

Birenbaum Quintero, Michael. 2006. "La música pacífica al Pacífico violento: Música, multiculturalismo y marginalización en el Pacífico negro colombiano." *Revista Transcultural de Música* 10 (2006).

Borucki, Alex. 2015. *From Shipmates to Soldiers: Emerging Black Identities in the Río de la Plata.* Albuquerque, NM: University of New Mexico Press.

Bronfman, Alejandra. 2005. *Measures of Equality: Social Science, Citizenship, and Race in Cuba, 1902–1940.* Chapel Hill, NC: University of North Carolina Press.

Brunson, Takkara Keosha. 2011. "Constructing Afro-Cuban Womanhood: Race, Gender, and Citizenship in Republican-Era Cuba, 1902–1958." PhD diss., University of Texas at Austin.

Burdick, John. 1998. *Blessed Anastácia: Women, Race, and Popular Christianity in Brazil.* New York, NY: Routledge.

Busdiecker, Sara. 2009. "The Emergence and Evolving Character of Contemporary Afro-Bolivian Mobilization." In *New Social Movements in the African Diaspora: Challenging Global Apartheid*, edited by Leith Mullings, 121–37. New York, NY: Palgrave Macmillan.

Butler, Kim. 1998. *Freedoms Given, Freedoms Won: Afro-Brazilians in Post-Abolition São Paulo and Salvador.* New Brunswick, NJ: Rutgers University Press.

Caldwell, Kia. 2007. *Negras in Brazil: Re-Envisioning Black Women, Citizenship, and the Politics of Identity.* New Brunswick, NJ: Rutgers University Press.

2009. "Transnational Black Feminism in the Twenty-first Century." In *New Social Movements in the African Diaspora: Challenging Global Apartheid*, edited by Leith Mullings, 105–20. New York, NY: Palgrave Macmillan.

Cárdenas, Roosbelinda. 2012. "Green Multiculturalism: Articulations of Ethnic and Environmental Politics in a Colombian 'Black Community.'" *Journal of Peasant Studies* 39, 2: 309–33.

Cardoso, Fernando Henrique. 2001. "Discurso na cerimônia de entrega do Prémio Nacional dos Direitos Humanos." Accessed on March 12, 2017 at http://www.biblioteca.presidencia.gov.br/presidencia/ex-presidentes/fernando-henrique-cardoso/discursos/20-mandato/2001/85.pdf/view.

Carneiro, Sueli. 2003. "Enegrecer o feminismo: A situação da mulher negra na América Latina a partir de uma perspectiva de gênero." In *Racismos contemporâneos*, edited by Ashoka Empreendimentos Sociais, 49–58. Rio de Janeiro: Takano Editora.

Castillo, Luis Carlos. 2007. *Etnicidad y nación: El desafío de la diversidad en Colombia*. Cali: Universidad del Valle.

Castro-Gómez, Santiago, and Eduardo Restrepo. 2008. "Introducción: Colombianidad, población y diferencia." *Genealogías de la colombianidad: Formaciones discursivas y tecnologías de gobierno en los siglos XIX y XX*, edited by Santiago Castro-Gómez and Eduardo Restrepo, 11–40. Bogotá: Editorial Pontificia Universidad Javeriana.

Centeno, Miguel Angel. 2003. *Blood and Debt: War and the Nation-State in Latin America*. University Park, PA: Pennsylvania State University Press.

Centro de Mujeres Afrocostarricenses. 2017. Accessed on February 20, 2017 at http://mujeresafrocostarricenses.blogspot.com/.

Cohen, Cathy J. 1999. *The Boundaries of Blackness: AIDS and the Breakdown of Black Politics*. Chicago, IL: University of Chicago Press.

Covin, David. 2006. *The Unified Black Movement in Brazil, 1978–2002*. Jefferson, NC: McFarland.

Davidson, David M. 1966. "Negro Slave Control and Resistance in Colonial Mexico, 1519–1650." *Hispanic American Historical Review* 46, 3: 235–53.

Dávila, Jerry. 2003. *Diploma of Whiteness: Race and Social Policy in Brazil, 1917–1945*. Durham, NC: Duke University Press.

Davis, Darién, Tianna Paschel, and Judith Morrison. 2012. "Pan-Afro-Latin African Americanism Revisited: Legacies and Lessons for Transnational Alliances in the New Millennium." In *Re-examining the Black Atlantic: Afro-Descendants and Development*, edited by Bernd Reiter. East Lansing, MI: Michigan State University Press.

de la Fuente, Alejandro. 2001. *A Nation for All: Race, Inequality, and Politics in Twentieth-Century Cuba*. Chapel Hill, NC: University of North Carolina Press.

2008. "The New Afro-Cuban Cultural Movement and the Debate on Race in Contemporary Cuba." *Journal of Latin American Studies* 40, 4: 697–720.

2013. *Grupo Antillano: The Art of Afro-Cuba*. Pittsburgh, PA: University of Pittsburgh Press.

De la Torre, Carlos, and Jhon Antón Sánchez. 2012. "The Afro-Ecuadorian Social Movement Between Empowerment and Co-optation." In *Black Social Movements in Latin America: From Monocultural Mestizaje to Multiculturalism*, edited by Jean Rahier, 135–50. New York, NY: Palgrave Macmillan.

De Oliveira, Luciane Rocha. Forthcoming. "The Black Women's March in Brazil." In *When Rights Ring Hollow*, edited by Charles Hale and Juliet Hooker.

Degler, Carl. 1986. *Neither Black nor White: Slavery and Race Relations in the United States and Brazil*. Madison, WI: University of Wisconsin Press. First published in 1971.

Del Popolo, Fabiana. 2008. *Los pueblos indígenas y afrodescendientes en las fuentes de datos: Experiencias en América Latina*. Santiago de Chile: Comisión Económica para América Latina y el Caribe (CEPAL).

Dias, Cláudia Marcia Coutinho de. 2005. *Lideranças negras*. São Paulo, Brasil: Aeroplano.

Fernandes, Sujatha. 2006. *Cuba Represent! Cuban Arts, State Power, and the Making of New Revolutionary Cultures*. Durham, NC: Duke University Press.

Escobar, Arturo. 2008. Territories of Difference: Place, Movements, Life, *Redes*. Durham, NC: Duke University Press.

Ferrer, Ada. 1999. *Insurgent Cuba: Race, Nation, and Revolution, 1868–1898*. Chapel Hill, NC: University of North Carolina Press.

   2014. *Freedom's Mirror: Cuba and Haiti in the Age of Revolution*. New York, NY: Cambridge University Press.

Francisco, Marilda de Souza. 2015. Interviewed by Sueann Caulfield. Accessed at https://globalfeminisms.umich.edu/sites/default/files//GFP-Brazil-deSouza-English.pdf.

French, Jan Hoffman. 2009. *Legalizing Identities: Becoming Black or Indian in Brazil's Northeast*. Chapel Hill, NC: University of North Carolina Press.

Geler, Lea. 2010. *Andares negros, caminos blancos: Afroporteños, estado y nación: Argentina a fines del siglo XIX*. Rosario: Prohistoria Ediciones.

Gillam, Reighan. 2016. "The Help, Unscripted: Constructing the Black Revolutionary Domestic in Afro-Brazilian Media." *Feminist Media Studies* 16, 6: 1043–56.

Goldberg, David Theo. 2002. *The Racial State*. London: Blackwell.

Greene, Shane. 2007. "Introduction: On Race, Roots/Routes, and Sovereignty in Latin America's Afro-Indigenous Multiculturalisms." *Journal of Latin American and Caribbean Anthropology* 12, 2: 329–55.

Grueso, Libia, Carlos Rosero, and Arturo Escobar. 2003. "The Process of Black Community Organizing in the Southern Pacific Coast Region of Colombia." In *Perspectives on Las Américas: A Reader in Culture, History, and Representation*, edited by Matthew C. Gutmann et al., 430–77. Malden, MA: Wiley-Blackwell.

Grueso, Libia, and Leyla Arroyo. 2002. "Mujeres y defensa del lugar en las luchas del Movimiento Negro colombiano." In *Desarrollo, lugar, política y justicia: Las mujeres frente a la globalización*, edited by Wendy Harcourt and Arturo Escobar, 68–76. Roma: Society for International Development.

Guridy, Frank Andre. 2010. *Forging Diaspora: Afro-Cubans and African Americans in a World of Empire and Jim Crow*. Chapel Hill, NC: University of North Carolina Press.

Hanchard, Michael. 2003. "Acts of Misrecognition: Transnational Black Politics, Anti-Imperialism and the Ethnocentrisms of Pierre Bourdieu and Loïc Wacquant." *Theory, Culture & Society* 20, 4: 5–29.

Hanchard, George Michael. 1994. *Orpheus and Power: The Movimento Negro of Rio de Janeiro and São Paulo, Brazil, 1945–1988*. Princeton, NJ: Princeton University Press.

Helg, Aline. 1991. "Afro-Cuban Protest: The Partido Independiente de Color, 1908–1912." *Cuban Studies* 21: 101–21.

1995. *Our Rightful Share: The Afro-Cuban Struggle for Equality, 1886–1912*. Chapel Hill, NC: University of North Carolina Press.

Hellwig, David J., ed. 1992. *African-American Reflections on Brazil's Racial Paradise*. Philadelphia, PA: Temple University Press.

Hernández, Dorina. 2011. "Dorina Hernández." In *El despertar de las comunidades afrocolombianas*, edited by María Inés Martínez. Río Piedras: Centro de Investigaciones Sociales, Universidad de Puerto Rico.

Hooker, Juliet. 2005. "Indigenous Inclusion/Black Exclusion: Race, Ethnicity and Multicultural Citizenship in Latin America." *Journal of Latin American Studies*. 37, 2: 285–310.

2008. "Afro-Descendant Struggles for Collective Rights in Latin America." *Souls* 10, 3: 279–91.

2009. *Race and the Politics of Solidarity*. New York, NY: Oxford University Press.

Hordge-Freeman, Elizabeth. 2015. *The Color of Love: Racial Features, Stigma, and Socialization in Black Brazilian Families*. Austin, TX: University of Texas Press.

Lasso, Marixa. 2007. *Myths of Harmony: Race and Republicanism during the Age of Revolution, Colombia, 1795–1831*. Pittsburgh, PA: University of Pittsburgh Press.

Leeds, Asia. 2010. "Representations of Race, Entanglements of Power: Whiteness, Garveyism, and Redemptive Geographies in Costa Rica, 1921–1950." PhD diss., University of California, Berkeley.

Leite, José Correia. 1992. *E disse o velho militante José Correia Leite*. São Paulo: Secretaria Municipal de Cultura.

Loveman, Mara. 2014. *National Colors: Racial Classification and the State in Latin America*. New York, NY: Oxford University Press.

Martins, Sergio da Silva, Carlos Alberto Medeiros, and Elisa Larkin Nascimento. 2004. "Paving Paradise: The Road from 'Racial Democracy' to Affirmative Action in Brazil." *Journal of Black Studies* 34, 6: 787–816.

Marx, Anthony W. 1998. *Making Race and Nation: A Comparison of South Africa, the United States, and Brazil*. New York, NY: Cambridge University Press.

Mattos, Hebe. 2008. "'Terras de Quilombo': Land Rights, Memory of Slavery, and Ethnic Identification." In *Africa, Brazil, and the Construction of Trans-Atlantic Black Identities*, edited by Livio Sansone, Elisée Soumoni, and Boubacar Barry, 293–318. Trenton, NJ: Africa World Press.

2004. "Marcas da escravidão: Biografia, racialização e memória do cativeiro na história do Brasil." Tese apresentada como requisito para concurso de professor titular, Universidade Federal Fluminense.

MUDHA (Movimiento de Mujeres Dominico-Haitianas). 2017. Accessed on February 19, 2017 at www.mudhaong.org.

Ng'weno, Bettina. 2007. *Turf Wars: Territory and Citizenship in the Contemporary State.* Stanford, CA: Stanford University Press.

Nobles, Melissa. 2000. *Shades of Citizenship: Race and the Census in Modern Politics.* Stanford, CA: Stanford University Press.

Oslender, Ulrich. 2002. "'The Logic of the River': A Spatial Approach to Ethnic-Territorial Mobilization in the Colombian Pacific Region." *Journal of Latin American Anthropology* 7, 2: 86–117.

Palombini, Carlos. 2009. "Soul brasileiro e funk carioca." *OPUS-Revista Eletrônica da ANPPOM* 15, 1: 37–61.

Paschel, Tianna S. 2010. "The Right to Difference: Explaining Colombia's Shift from Color Blindness to the Law of Black Communities." *American Journal of Sociology* 116, 3: 729–69.

2016. *Becoming Black Political Subjects: Movements and Ethno-Racial Rights in Colombia and Brazil.* Princeton, NJ: Princeton University Press.

Paschel, Tianna S., and Mark Q. Sawyer. 2008. "Contesting Politics as Usual: Black Social Movements, Globalization, and Race Policy in Latin America." *Souls* 10, 3: 197–214.

Pereira, Amilcar. 2013. *O mundo negro: Relações raciais e a constituição do Movimento Negro contemporâneo no Brasil.* Rio de Janeiro: Pallas.

Perry, Keisha-Khan Y. 2013. *Black Women against the Land Grab.* Minneapolis, MN: University of Minnesota Press.

Pires, Antônio Liberac Cardoso Simões. 2006. *As associações dos homens de cor e a imprensa negra paulista: Movimientos negros, cultura e política no Brasil republicano (1915–1945).* Palmas: Fundação Universidade Federal do Tocantins.

Price, Richard, ed. 1996. *Maroon Societies: Rebel Slave Communities in the Americas.* Baltimore, MD: John Hopkins University Press. First published in 1973.

Priestley, George. 2004. "Antillean-Panamanians or Afro-Panamanians? Political Participation and the Politics of Identity During the Carter-Torrijos Treaty Negotiations." *Transforming Anthropology* 12, 1–2: 50–67.

Priestley, George, and Alberto Barrow. 2008. "The Black Movement in Panama: A Historical and Political Interpretation, 1994–2004." *Souls* 10, 3: 227–55.

Purcell, Trevor W. 1993. *Banana Fallout: Class, Color, and Culture Among West Indians In Costa Rica.* Center for Afro-American Studies, University of California, Los Angeles.

Quijada, Mónica. 2000. "Nación y territorio: La dimensión simbólica del espacio en la construcción nacional argentina. Siglo XIX." *Revista de Indias* 60, 219: 373–94.

Rahier, Jean Muteba, ed. 2012. *Black Social Movements in Latin America: From Monocultural Mestizaje to Multiculturalism.* New York, NY: Palgrave Macmillan.

Red Nacional de Mujeres Afrocolombianas-Kambirí. 2017. Accessed on February 20, 2017 at www.facebook.com/Red-Nacional-de-Mujeres-Afrocolombianas-kambir%C3%AD-504584149586245/.

Restrepo, Eduardo. 2004. "Ethnicization of Blackness in Colombia: Toward De-Racializing Theoretical and Political Imagination." *Cultural Studies* 18: 698–715.

Rivera-Rideau, Petra R. 2015. *Remixing Reggaetón: The Cultural Politics of Race in Puerto Rico.* Durham, NC: Duke University Press.

Rodrigues, Cristiano Santos, and Marco Aurélio Maximo Prado. 2010. "Movimento de mulheres negras: Trajetória política, práticas mobilizatórias e articulações com o Estado brasileiro." *Psicologia & Sociedade* 22, 3: 445–56.

Sawyer, Mark. 2006. *Racial Politics in Post-Revolutionary Cuba.* New York, NY: Cambridge University Press.

Schwartzman, Luisa Farah. 2007. "Does Money Whiten? Intergenerational Changes In Racial Classification in Brazil." *American Sociological Review* 72, 6 : 940–63.

Smith, Christen A. 2016. *Afro-Paradise: Blackness, Violence, and Performance in Brazil.* Urbana, IL: University of Illinois Press.

Sue, Christina A. 2013. *Land of the Cosmic Race: Race Mixture, Racism, and Blackness in Mexico.* New York, NY: Oxford University Press.

Telles, Edward. 1999. "Ethnic Boundaries and Political Mobilization among African Brazilians: Comparisons with the U.S. Case." In *Racial Politics in Contemporary Brazil*, edited by Michael Hanchard, 82–97. Durham, NC: Duke University Press.

2004. *Race in Another America: The Significance of Skin Color in Brazil.* Princeton, NJ: Princeton University Press.

2007. "Race and Ethnicity and Latin America's United Nations Millennium Development Goals." *Latin American and Caribbean Ethnic Studies* 2, 2: 185–200.

Telles, Edward, and Tianna Paschel. 2014. "Who Is Black, White, or Mixed Race? How Skin Color, Status, and Nation Shape Racial Classification in Latin America." *American Journal of Sociology* 120, 3: 864–907.

Thomas III, John. 2009. "Theorizing Afro-Latino Social Movements: The Peruvian Case." Master's thesis, University of Chicago.

Twine, France Winddance. 1998. *Racism in a Racial Democracy: The Maintenance of White Supremacy in Brazil.* New Brunswick, NJ: Rutgers University Press.

Van Cott, Donna Lee. 2000. *The Friendly Liquidation of the Past: The Politics of Diversity in Latin America.* Pittsburgh, PA: University of Pittsburgh Press.

2006. "Multiculturalism versus Neoliberalism in Latin America." In *Multiculturalism and the Welfare State: Recognition and Redistribution in Contemporary Democracies*, edited by Keith Banting and Will Kymlicka, 272–96. New York, NY: Oxford University Press.

Vaughan, Umi. 2012. *Rebel Dance, Renegade Stance: Timba Music and Black Identity in Cuba.* Ann Arbor, MI: University of Michigan Press.

Vincent, Ted. 1994. "The Blacks Who Freed Mexico." *Journal of Negro History* 79, 3: 257–76.

Viveros Vigoya, Mara. 2016. "La interseccionalidad: Una aproximación situada a la dominación." *Debate Feminista* 52: 1–17.

Wade, Peter. 1993. *Blackness and Race Mixture: The Dynamics of Racial Identity in Colombia*. Baltimore, MD: Johns Hopkins University Press.

1997. *Race and Ethnicity in Latin America*. London: Pluto Press.

1998. "The Cultural Politics of Blackness in Colombia." In *Blackness in Latin America and the Caribbean: Social Dynamics and Cultural Transformations*, edited by Norman E. Whitten Jr. and Arlene Torres, vol. 1, 311–34. Bloomington, IN: Indiana University Press.

2009. *Race and Sex in Latin America*. London: Pluto Press.

Winant, Howard. 2001. *The World Is a Ghetto: Race and Democracy since World War II*. New York, NY: Basic Books.

# 8

# "Racial Democracy" and Racial Inclusion

## Hemispheric Histories

### Paulina L. Alberto and Jesse Hoffnung-Garskof

Until not so long ago, the story of the Latin American ideologies that have come to be known as "racial democracy" was told in one of two ways. In one optimistic narrative, Iberian colonial practices bequeathed the region a relatively benign form of slavery, fluid racial identification, and widespread intermixture. The independent nations of Latin America abolished racial strictures and included people of African descent as citizens, concretely and symbolically. To the extent that Afrodescendant people tended to be clustered in the lowest rungs of local social hierarchies, this was the result of extreme class divisions and the lack of economic development rather than racial discrimination. This rosy vision of racial democracy was eventually codified as a contrast with the United States and, despite deeper historical precedents, came to be associated mainly with the mid-twentieth-century writings of Brazilian sociologist Gilberto Freyre and North American sociologist Frank Tannenbaum.

A second narrative about racial democracy was far more critical. The appearance of flexibility and inclusion in Latin America, according to this view, was overstated, and the idea of a gentler Iberian form of slavery was unsustainable. Claims of racial democracy obscured the extent to which people of African descent (regardless of skin tone) were victims of anti-black racism and of discrimination that severely limited their citizenship

The authors would like to express their thanks to colleagues who generously read and offered comments on earlier drafts of this essay: Sueann Caulfield, Eduardo Elena, the editors and contributors to this volume, the participants in a workshop hosted by the Grupo de Estudios Afro-Latinoamericanos in Buenos Aires, especially Lea Geler, Florencia Guzmán, Alejandro Frigerio, and Nicolás Fernández Bravo, and participants at the Brazil Seminar at Columbia University, especially John Collins.

and life chances. In some versions of this narrative, the idea that Latin America was a racial democracy was not only factually wrong – it was destructive. The main difference between Latin America and explicitly racist societies like the United States or South Africa was the existence of deceitful "myths" of racial democracy themselves, which not only masked inequality but actively inhibited the race-based movements necessary to counteract it. This critical vision of racial democracy is most commonly associated with the work of Afro-Brazilian thinkers and activists since the 1970s, especially Abdias do Nascimento, and with a group of sympathetic scholars in Brazil and the United States.

How has it been possible to tell two such diametrically opposed stories about the same thing? Part of the answer lies in different narrative choices: when to begin the story of race and racism in the Americas and where to set it; whom to include as main or supporting characters, heroes, or foils; who is doing the narrating and for what audiences; and above all, what is at stake in the telling. Indeed, one person could, and can, emphasize one or the other interpretation – "reality" or "myth" – over a lifetime or even in the course of a single conversation. But the other part of the answer is that the many people who engaged in telling those divergent stories about "racial democracy" were often *not* actually talking about the same thing. As we see it, "racial democracy" is best understood as the result of multiple stories, about different dynamics, periods, places, and people, that have become tangled together in a wooly conceptual knot. This knot can give us something to hold on to in analyses of extremely unstable and complex ideas. But it can also create the illusion of coherence, of a unified and readily identifiable object at the center of a single debate. In what follows, we attempt to lay a framework for a geographically, temporally, and conceptually diverse history of Latin American ideas of racial inclusion by teasing apart two main strands of this knot.

One strand – the narrower one – is the history of the term "racial democracy" itself, which looms large in comparative discussions about racial inclusion in the Americas and carries considerable historical and conceptual baggage. In both its English and Portuguese variants, the term has been strongly identified with Brazil. From the mid-twentieth century onward, Brazil gained unparalleled international fame as a "racial democracy," a seemingly harmonious multiracial society that appeared to offer hope for a world traumatized by the horrors of World War II. Yet as the term gained traction in Brazil and abroad – even, at times, as a way of talking about race in Latin America more broadly – critics in Brazil and elsewhere decried it as a deleterious "myth," an elite ideology of social control. In many ways, their view ultimately prevailed.

This history of the rise and fall of "racial democracy" as a supposed descriptor of Brazil's social realities will be familiar to some readers. In retelling it here, however, we look beyond the term's better-known Brazilian genealogy to reveal its intersections with other inter-American conversations, especially among African American and Caribbean writers for whom the term had its own history. In particular, we find another history of "racial democracy" that unfolded in the 1940s and 1950s in relation to Puerto Rico, a Latin American society that was a US colony and was also the source of the first mass migration of Afrodescendant Latin Americans into spaces governed by US-style race relations. The island therefore plays an important role in the evolution of the concepts used to compare the "Negro question" in the United States and Latin America. Along with African Americans, Afro-Brazilians, and other Afro-Caribbeans, Puerto Ricans of various backgrounds contributed to comparative inter-American conversations about race and democracy that, from their very beginning, oscillated between celebrating the existence of racial democracy in the region and denouncing its shameful absence.

The second, thicker strand we seek to pull from the "racial democracy" tangle is the much deeper history of ideas, ideals, and negotiations about racial inclusion that emerged across Latin America at least since the wars of independence, well before the advent, in the 1940s, of the now-classic term. In much of the US- and Brazilian-based scholarship, these diverse ideas have become subsumed into discussions of "racial democracy," even when historical actors did not use that language. By contrast, the term has had relatively little incidence in the scholarly literature on race produced in many parts of Spanish America, where scholars tend to analyze ideas of racial inclusiveness through various local vocabularies like "mestizaje" or the racially unmarked nation. These ideas share important features with "racial democracy," both in their impact on the lives and politics of Afrodescendants and in the ways that they have been taken up, analyzed, or rejected by scholars and activists. But they are not interchangeable. Most obviously, expressions of mestizaje that emphasize mixture between Europeans and indigenous peoples or that stress whiteness created very different obstacles and opportunities for people of African descent than did the mid-century Brazilian idea of racial democracy, which included indigenous people but primarily emphasized relations along a black-white axis. Although we recognize that "racial democracy," as a generic term, has allowed for comparison across often insular local and national analyses of race, in this chapter we seek to attend to differences between that term (and its many regional and temporal variants) and the various terms of racialized nationhood that emerged in other contexts.

We therefore open our account with an overview of the diverse ways that Latin Americans of different social and racial backgrounds conceived of the relationship between race and belonging, as applied to Afrodescendant people, since the late colonial period. While by the twentieth century such formulations almost always relied on contrasts between Latin America and the United States, in the nineteenth century they sought rather to distinguish Latin America from Spain or Haiti (or both). In sketching this deeper history of ideologies of racial inclusion, we build on recent works that increasingly espouse the idea of coexistent myths *and* realities and that highlight the struggles of Afrodescendants, in different times and places, to accentuate the concept's more inclusionary meanings.

The next two sections of the chapter trace the rise and fall of the racial democracy thesis as well as recent scholarly attempts to reconcile or transcend debates about whether racial democracy is myth or reality. Throughout those sections, we pay close attention to where and when the trajectories of the term "racial democracy" – our narrower strand – intersected with broader discussions of national ideologies of racial inclusion across time and place – our thicker strand. We examine how, why, and with what effects "racial democracy" came to name a field larger than itself – to stand in, especially in the US scholarship, for patterns of racial formation and interaction across Latin America that were imagined to work similarly to Brazil's. By placing those processes at the center of our story, we hope to contribute to that comparative project even as we seek to expand the terms of the conversation beyond "racial democracy" itself. Finally, we consider the future of that term, and of broader ideas of racial inclusion, in light of recent transformations in both scholarship and activism.

## LATIN AMERICAN IDEAS OF RACIAL INCLUSION: A HISTORICAL OVERVIEW TO THE 1930S

Without conceding to the rosiest pictures of Iberian colonialism associated with Freyre and Tannenbaum, it is important to note that their accounts acquired some of their resonance because they relied on historical portraits that, though highly selective, were not wholly imagined (de la Fuente 2004, 2010). From the earliest days of conquest, some

Afrodescendant people found spaces for social advancement within the extremely hierarchical social order established by Iberian colonists. Despite high rates of mortality among enslaved populations in the region, many parts of Latin America saw the emergence and growth of significant free brown and black populations through manumission, self-purchase, and natural reproduction. Many free African-descended persons became peasants, ranch hands, or agricultural workers. Some escaped slavery and created maroon communities. But even in the heart of colonial cities, free people were able to move out of the lowest ranks of the social hierarchy through military service, as artisans, as midwives and peddlers, and in religious brotherhoods (Andrews 2004; Klein and Vinson 2007). At the same time, Spanish and Portuguese Americans employed systems of racial classification that, while aiming to create fixed and stratified categories, allowed for some flexibility in practice. "Race" itself was often embedded in other forms of social distinction, including gender, legitimacy, honor, place of origin, and occupation, meaning not only that persons of African ancestry could move up in the social order despite their color, but that this mobility could attenuate, and in some cases overturn, their status as non-white (Cope 1994; Soares 2000; Martínez 2008; Baerga 2014; Twinam 2015).

To call these opportunities to participate in colonial society "citizenship" or "democracy" would be anachronistic. Ideas about racial difference still provided the ideological backbone for the systematic enslavement and brutalization of people of African descent and for widespread sexual violence against Afrodescendant women. Free black and brown people lived in the fearsome shadow of this brutality. Moreover, the fact that colonial society recognized the personhood of people of African descent and made possible certain kinds of legal protections and opportunities for mobility did not imply any notion of political or social equality, because equality was not a meaningful feature of early modern political and social systems. It was only much later that the opportunity for mobility within these colonial societies would be recast, retrospectively, in terms of "democracy." Nor, in this early moment, did Latin American experiences of mobility and ambiguity for free persons of African descent stand in stark contrast to the British colonies of North America. Only after the middle of the eighteenth century did North American planters and their allies succeed in reshaping the law to erode the membership and legal personhood of free people of color, creating a narrow definition of whiteness and a close association between whiteness and freedom (Berlin 2003; Gross 2008; Cottrol 2013; Gross and de la Fuente 2013; de la Fuente and Gross 2015). The growth of plantations in both Portuguese and Spanish America in this period also put pressure on existing social arrangements. But in many parts of Brazil and Spanish America, these negotiations had a different outcome, with lines drawn between enslaved and free people (including large free African-descended populations) rather than between white and non-white. The Spanish crown even made a number of concessions to free blacks and "castas" (mixed-race people) in the colonies in the hopes of recruiting them to counterbalance the rising power of Creole planters and traders or to guard against the threat of indigenous revolt (Andrews 2004, 47–49; Lasso 2007, 16–33; Cottrol 2013, 60–67).

Latin Americans began to frame this complex historical experience in positive terms – describing peaceful race relations and a lack of racism as unique features of their American identities – in the context of the wars of independence that unfolded in the first decades of the nineteenth century. During the Napoleonic invasion of the Iberian Peninsula (1808–14), Spanish liberals, including representatives from the American provinces, met in Cádiz to govern in the king's name and to write a constitution. The assembly established broad suffrage in the Spanish empire but excluded African-descended people from the right to vote, a strategy for limiting the number of representatives from the Americas. The move set the terms for a new, tentative alliance between white Creoles and urban, Afro-descended militias. King Ferdinand VII returned to the throne in 1814, abrogated the liberal constitution, and dissolved local juntas in the Americas. This touched off civil wars, primarily in Gran Colombia and the Río de la Plata area, between loyalists and independence forces. As the independence movements sought to recruit *pardo* (brown) and *moreno* (black) militias and to mobilize the population more generally, they created the first nationalist myths of racial integration and equality (Helg 2004; Lasso 2007; L. Johnson 2011; Guzmán 2016).

While later celebrations of the racially tolerant nature of Creole or Latin American society took the United States as their principal foil and traced the region's apparent lack of racial divisions back to Iberian colonization, early Spanish American nationalists framed these celebrations, together with assertions of the harmonizing power of republicanism, in contrast to Spain. They repudiated slavery and racial oppression as key elements of Spanish absolutism and cruelty, creating their own variant of the centuries-old "Black Legend" (Adelman 1999). Early republican societies in Spanish America did not, of course, do away with systems of social distinction built around honor, class, and race. They preserved, and frequently expanded, entrenched systems of exploitation of indigenous communities and only eliminated slavery gradually. But across the region, the languages of liberty and universalism, as well as trajectories of military service, created opportunities for the inclusion and mobility of free Afrodescendants that provided the social bases for continuing discourses of racial harmony in the early independent republics (Di Meglio 2006; Lasso 2007; Blanchard 2008; Sanders 2014).

The architects of the state that emerged from the Haitian Revolution also created an ideal of racial harmony. But rather than deploying this idea in distinction to French rule, Haitian leaders proposed a vision of national unity in contrast to whiteness. In order for color to cease to be a source of division in the national family, the 1805 constitution decreed, "the Haytians shall henceforth be known by the generic appellation of blacks." This was a political rather than a biological definition of "black" – an ideology of racial harmony in which Haitian citizenship conferred blackness to a range of ethnic groups from Africa as well as to French, Germans, and Poles, while eliminating colonial racial categories from public discussion. By the 1820s, Haitian leaders expanded this ideal of harmony to manage the incorporation of white residents of Spanish Santo Domingo into a multiracial Haitian nation bonded by the shared soil of Hispaniola and a common African heritage (René 2014; Walker 2016).

Spanish- and Portuguese-speaking Americans who identified as white did not generally share this view of Haiti as racially harmonious, to say the least. Indeed, in parts of Latin America where local planters worked to preserve and expand slavery in the wake of the Haitian Revolution, Haiti, rather than Spain, emerged as the crucial point of comparison against which to fashion discussions of racial harmony. Not coincidentally, these were also the parts of Latin America that had not experienced independence wars in the first decades of the nineteenth century: Puerto Rico and Cuba (which remained Spanish colonies) and Brazil (where the transition to independence from Portugal took place with far less upheaval than in most of Spanish America). In these societies, discussions of racial harmony skewed more heavily toward order, management, and quiescence than toward its potentially more radical or egalitarian connotations. Proponents of slavery argued that under the right conditions – an increase in white immigration, restraints on the cruelty of masters, the proper management of free people of color, annexation to the United States (in the case of Cuba and Puerto Rico), and strict prohibitions on the flow of people and information from Haiti – planters and political authorities could maintain control even as slavery expanded (Moreno Fraginals 1978; Scarano 1984; Figueroa 2005; Ferrer 2014). During the 1820s and 1830s in Brazil, as in Spanish America, many free people of color embraced the racially egalitarian potentials of liberalism and universalism (C. M. M. de Azevedo 2005). Yet state concessions to black and mulatto middle sectors and their firm integration into systems of patronage, as well as the state's ability to suppress the most radical (and blackest) expressions of republicanism, helped produce apparent harmony among Brazil's free population in the decades after independence while maintaining the stability of the slave system (Lara 1988; Andrews 2004, 109–12; R. Graham 1999).

By the middle of the nineteenth century, debates about racial harmony in these societies had shifted to a concern with managing the end of slavery. Opponents of slavery frequently argued that slavery itself was a threat to social harmony, public security, racial equilibrium, hygiene, and stability, or that the preservation of harmony under conditions of slavery required unacceptable compromises such as, in the case of Puerto Rico and Cuba, dependence on external powers (Chalhoub 1993; Graden 1996; Schmidt-Nowara 1999; Figueroa 2005). In both Brazil and Puerto Rico, as thinkers and politicians considered the prospects for abolition and as planters struggled with free black workers over the outlines of new systems of dependent rural labor, they put forth conservative accounts of racial harmony. Many of these elites represented slavery in their territories as uniquely benign and paternalistic, continued to uphold the achievements of prominent mulattos as evidence of the absence of racism, celebrated traditions of harmonious cultural and racial mixture, and emphasized the enlightened generosity of elites in emancipating slaves without warfare or rebellion, in contrast to Haiti, the United States, and Cuba (C. M. M. de Azevedo 1987; Andrews 1991; Schmidt-Nowara 1999; M. Abreu 2000; Chalhoub 2006; Rodríguez-Silva 2012).

Yet abolitionism in Brazil and colonial reform movements in Puerto Rico were also successful alliances among free blacks, mulattos, whites, and (in Brazil) slaves; as such, like Spanish American independence struggles, these movements are also examples of the rights-oriented, affirmatively inclusionary potentials of ideas of racial harmony (Andrews 2004, 80–84; Hoffnung-Garskof 2011). This was even more clearly the case in Cuba, where the liberal reform movement – long preoccupied with the dangers of "Africanization," eager to whiten the island, and reluctant to move quickly on abolition – took on new contours in the context of an armed struggle for independence (1868–78). As in early independence movements in South America, Cuban insurgents emphasized a contrast between the racial fraternity that had emerged among independence fighters on the battlefield and the long history of racial oppression under Spanish rule. Separatists in Cuba continued also to emphasize the racial harmony of their movement in explicit contrast to Haiti. There could never be a war between the races in Cuba, José Martí explained seven years after the abolition of slavery, because the revolution, by working for emancipation, had "redeemed" both the Afrodescendant former slaves and the white former slave owners, and the Cuban Republic would make no distinctions based on race (Martí 1893).

By the end of the century, Martí and other Cuban nationalists also increasingly framed their claims of racial fraternity and "equilibrium" in contrast to the United States, where the brief experiment in interracial democracy following the Civil War had given way to extreme racial violence and the exclusion of African Americans from most of the protections of citizenship (Martí [1891] 2012). The emergence of scientific racism in the United States and Europe, moreover, posited a relationship between white racial purity and the capacity for self-government, providing a justification for both the exclusion of African Americans from citizenship and the assertion of US power over large parts of the Caribbean and Central America (Kennedy 1971; Santiago-Valles 1994; Erman 2008; Pérez 2008).

In the early decades of the twentieth century, Latin American elites broadly shared the view that nonwhites were ill-suited to civilization and democracy. They often worked to perform their own "civilization" and insisted on their own whiteness in their interactions with representatives of Europe and the United States (Ferrer 1999, 186–201; Caulfield 2000, 48–78). Governments across the region sought to attract immigrants from Europe and to promote other eugenic policies aimed at "whitening" their nations (R. Graham 1990; Stepan 1991). Yet in their engagement with European and North American race science, Latin American elites were also frequently constrained by local demographics. Some, though certainly not all, began to dissent from reigning North Atlantic race theories that read mixture exclusively as racial degeneration, arguing that mixture could be a means to "improve" racial stock (through the gradual prevalence of superior white "blood" over generations) as well as to achieve racial harmony. The rejection of the ideal of racial purity, therefore, did not imply a wholesale rejection of whitening ideals or of the notion of white superiority itself (Skidmore 1974; de la Fuente 2001, 39–52; Bronfman 2005, 117–34).

Thus, by the early twentieth century, Latin Americans increasingly drew contrasts, as Martí and other Cubans had begun to do decades earlier, between the supposed racial harmony that existed in the region and the racial disharmony in the United States. In 1912, for example, the Brazilian historian and diplomat Manoel de Oliveira e Lima lectured audiences in the United States that "the rule of love followed by the Latin peoples of America" had led to "a fusion in which the inferior elements will shortly disappear," whereas the United States, securing a temporary superiority through the purity of its white race, "will some day have to have its dénouement, and the dénouement brought about by love is always preferable to that which is the result of hate" (Lima 1914, 40). The racial violence directed against Mexicans in the United States provoked Mexican intellectuals to make similar contrasts between what they depicted as the peaceful fusion of the races in Mexico, or "mestizaje," and the racial hatred present in the United States (Gamio 1929; Vasconcelos [1935] 1976).

As the century unfolded, literary and essayistic celebrations of racial and cultural hybridity and harmony emerged from Argentina to Mexico (Ugarte 1920; Morais 1922; Bomfim 1929; Freyre [1933] 1943; Rojas [1924] 1951; Ortiz [1940] 1978; Vasconcelos [1925] 1979). In these contexts, the contrast with the United States proved especially useful to Latin American thinkers in minimizing the possibility or legitimacy of racial divisions within their societies. The Puerto Rican author Tomás Blanco offers an exceptionally clear view of how this worked: "Prejudice, as it exists in the United States, will serve us as a point of comparison, as a specimen for contrast and reference, as we try to determine if authentic racial prejudice exists in our island." This system of measurement, which identified only the types of prejudice at work in the United States as "authentic," allowed him to conclude that, by comparison, any prejudice in Puerto Rico was "innocent child's play" (Blanco 1942, 10). Afrodescendant thinkers in the region, including the prominent Puerto Rican politician José Celso Barbosa, also frequently claimed that their national communities were marked by a relative absence of racial prejudice and racial conflict in contrast to the United States, a factor that provided the potential, if not the guarantee, of fair treatment. This comparison was also useful in combating racism and whitening projects by making the case to local elites that Brazil, Puerto Rico, or Cuba was at moral risk of becoming like their much-maligned Anglo-Saxon neighbor (Serra y Montalvo 1907; Morais 1922; Barbosa 1937, 31–57; de la Fuente 2001, 61; Alberto 2011, 42–67).

One of the most famous expressions of mestizo nationalism is *Casa-grande e senzala*, published to great acclaim in 1933 by the white Brazilian sociologist Gilberto Freyre. Freyre described the unequal but intimate and often affectionate relationships between masters and slaves on plantations as the basis for what he saw as Brazil's peaceful race relations in the present. Though he acknowledged the violence and hierarchy of Brazilian slavery, he nonetheless believed that interpersonal relationships between residents of the *casas grandes* ("big houses") and the *senzalas* ("slave quarters") – from sex between white masters and enslaved women, to the rearing of white babies by African nursemaids, to the friendships between white and black children in extended households – created an overarching organic inclusiveness that tempered social hierarchies. This social intimacy, rooted in the supposed predisposition of Portuguese colonizers toward mixture, eventually gave rise to a society not only schooled in attitudes of racial or ethnic brotherhood but whose members were themselves, each and every one, partly African in their bodies or souls. Stark segregation and institutionalized racism – of the kind that Freyre himself had witnessed as a student in the United States – were thus inconceivable in Brazil (Freyre [1933] 1943). Notably, though he is commonly credited with coining the term "racial democracy," Freyre did not use it in this foundational tract; rather, like many black thinkers and other public figures in the 1920s and 1930s, he spoke primarily of Brazil's singular interracial "fraternity" (Guimarães 2002; Alberto 2011).

Despite their anti-US stance, the accounts of race relations in Latin America produced by writers like Vasconcelos, Blanco, and Freyre served the cause of a group of academics in the United States. These were scholars who, already by the 1920s, began to build the field of Latin American Studies as an alternative to the "dreary waste of ... interest-ridden propaganda" that dominated English-language accounts of the region (Simpson 1927; see also Hoffnung-Garskof 2012) and who wished to challenge the mainstream of race science, with its emphasis on racial purity. In this vein, Rüdiger Bilden, a German scholar pursuing advanced studies in the United States, wrote an article for *The Nation* in 1929 that criticized the "intellectual atrocities" that North Americans frequently committed against Latin Americans, especially in their presumptions of Latin American racial inferiority. Instead, he argued, Brazil in particular presented a unique "laboratory" where the "fundamental problems of civilization," the coexistence and integration of "supposedly incompatible ethnic elements," were being resolved peacefully. Likewise, Rayford Logan, an African American historian, argued in 1933 that Cuba's Oriente region "has solved the race problem with more fairness than any other region of which I know except possibly Brazil." The point, for writers like Logan and Bilden, was not to pick apart the weaknesses of the Cuban or Brazilian racial systems or the region's nationalist accounts of racial harmony, but to draw a useful contrast in order to highlight failings in the United States. For Bilden, Brazil's experience was a "humane" counterpoint to the United States, where racism was a "cancerous growth in the social body." Logan thought that Cuba had something to show the United States about what "real democracy means" (Bilden 1929; R. Logan 1933; see also Hellwig 1992). In pursuit of their anti-racist goals, these scholars inadvertently helped solidify the image of racially "democratic" Latin American nations that subsequent generations of Afrodescendant thinkers and activists would struggle to dismantle.

Logan's phrase "real democracy" highlights a final shift in the nature of these comparisons as they evolved throughout the 1930s. Negotiations over how to interpret the supposed absence of racism and racial tension in Latin America gained new significance in light of the populist politics that emerged across the region after the collapse of export economies. As politicians began to incorporate poor urban and rural citizens into their coalitions, they frequently adopted and promoted variants of mestizo or raceless nationalism while also celebrating racial inclusion as a nationalist value against older, or foreign, projects of scientific racism or whitening (Andrews 2004, 153–90). At the same time, in both the United States and Latin America, a wide range of social critics, including Communists and Fascists, pointed to the limitations of liberal democracy for resolving fundamental questions of economic and racial inequality. Many on the left and the right began to argue that non-democratic regimes could produce more meaningfully egalitarian outcomes. Others, including many within the newly elected Roosevelt administration in Washington, argued that the defense of democratic political forms required expanding labor and social rights and eliminating racial discrimination. All sides in these debates adopted the terms "social democracy," "economic democracy," or "industrial democracy," though they differed on whether these amounted to expansions of political democracy or alternatives to it. It was in this context that Gilberto Freyre – a vocal opponent of European fascism and its Brazilian manifestations – began to argue that "social democracy though the mixture of races" was a deeper expression of democratic values than mere political democracy. He later added the term "ethnic democracy" (cited in Guimarães 2007).

Freyre's logic proved extremely useful to the nationalist regime of Getúlio Vargas (1930–45), which had overthrown an oligarchic republic and which now adopted the idea that Brazil was a society free of racial injustice – a mark of true democracy – to help justify its increasingly authoritarian rule (Guimarães 2002; J. L. Graham 2010). Such claims to have eliminated racism can hardly be taken literally for Brazil or for the other populist regimes that adopted forms of mixed-race or racially inclusive nationalism in this period. The effects of Vargas's policies, rather, exemplify the contradictions that marked the racial politics of populist movements across the region. Some people of African descent benefited from access to industrial labor and to new social rights and benefits, but many rural, domestic, and informal workers did not. Brazilians and other Latin Americans continued to produce racist cultural expressions and to practice racial discrimination in employment or education (see Chapters 3 and 5). Governments in much of the region also, in the name of mestizo or whitened nationalism, created or revived restrictions on black migrants and perpetrated new forms of violence against black "foreigners" in these years. The massacre of ethnic Haitians in the border region of the Dominican Republic in 1937 was only the most extreme case (Turits 2002; Putnam 2013).

Thus, by the end of the 1930s, white and black intellectuals and national governments in both Latin America and the United States had begun a new conversation that substantially reframed earlier ideas of Latin American racial inclusion and harmony. Narratives that had originally emerged to distinguish the region from Spain and Haiti now worked principally to distinguish Latin America from the domineering and racially repressive United States. This contrast, which arose first in those parts of the region most deeply influenced by US imperialism, was now embedded in a broader surge of nationalism across the region, in the negotiation of populist politics, and in debates over the meanings of democracy itself. It was in the context of a series of diplomatic efforts by the Roosevelt administration under the banner of Pan-Americanism, aimed at uniting the hemisphere in defense of "democracy," that long-standing narratives about racial harmony in Latin America would become the basic currency of a new inter-American politics of race and democracy – of "racial democracy." It is here that we shift from the broad strand of our story to the narrow one, to see how participants in this inter-American conversation adopted, debated, and debunked the term, and in the process gave it such staying power.

## RISE AND FALL OF "RACIAL DEMOCRACY"

During World War II, Brazilian and international scholars glossed the story that Freyre and others had told about Brazil's uniquely fraternal interracial relations with a new term: "racial democracy." As best we can reconstruct, Brazilian psychologist and anthropologist Arthur Ramos was the first to do so, claiming in 1941 that "in Brazil we have one of the purest racial democracies in the Western Hemisphere" (Ramos 1941a, 522; Campos 2004). Ramos had been traveling and lecturing in the United States for most of the preceding year and probably began using the English phrase "racial democracy" in an effort to translate for an English-speaking audience the arguments Freyre had popularized in Brazil. Yet it is important to note the particular audience Ramos was addressing in 1941. His use of the term appeared in a special issue of the *Journal of Negro Education* on the theme of "the Crisis of Democracy in the Western Hemisphere," edited by a group of African American scholars at Howard University and including articles by W. E. B. DuBois, Ralph Bunche, Eric Williams, Rayford Logan, Gilberto Freyre, and quite a few white North American liberals. This setting is important because the term "racial democracy" was already in use among African American scholars, activists, and some white liberals to describe an ideal of egalitarian race relations that, while consistent with the expressed democratic values of the United States, was pointedly yet to be fulfilled (e.g., Stannard Baker 1914; Du Bois 1915; *Daily Boston Globe* 1933; Douglass 1940).

That he first used the term in a special issue dedicated to the "crisis of democracy" also highlights the fact that Ramos introduced US audiences to the idea that Brazil was a racial democracy in the context of a major shift in US policy toward Latin America (see also Ramos 1941b). The Roosevelt administration sought to organize the hemisphere into a new set of alliances on the principle of Pan-Americanism and in the name of democracy. Officials in the State Department hoped to distance their new efforts at regional leadership from the longstanding racist attitudes that had until then served to justify imperialism in the region. They worked with liberal academics in the United States and with intellectuals in Latin America to create positive accounts of Latin America for English speakers, hoping to replace what Bilden had called "intellectual atrocities" (Hanke 1940). They also sought to promote a vision of a hemisphere united in its rejection of "fallacious claims of class or racial superiority" (*Atlanta Constitution* 1938). Mexican intellectuals and diplomats contributed extensively to these conversations and were especially vocal in denouncing racism directed against Mexican migrants and Mexican Americans. Yet Brazil ultimately took center stage in this form of Pan-Americanism, perhaps because most discussions of race in the United States continued to be dominated by the so-called Negro question (echoed in Brazil by what was increasingly called the *problema do negro*) while Mexican intellectuals tended to represent mestizaje as mixture primarily between whites and indigenous people (Rosemblatt 2009).

Brazilian race experts and representatives of the Vargas government offered Brazil as a shining example of a shared hemispheric project to build racial democracy – a project to which (they emphasized) the United States was a latecomer. As Freyre wrote in his contribution to the 1941 special issue of the *Journal of Negro Education*, "The name of the second Roosevelt begins to mean something new in the life of a people which for such a long time has heard only rumors of an imperialistic furor, of a democracy corrupted by plutocracy, and of the hate Anglo-Saxons bear to races they consider inferior" (Freyre 1941, 511). Under pressure from African American activists, the State Department also began a project to include black artists and academics, including several scholars at Howard University, in cultural diplomacy efforts directed at populations of African descent in Latin America (J. L. Graham 2010).

Yet the various participants in conversations about race, democracy, and Pan-Americanism in the early 1940s had competing agendas. Latin American representatives to Pan-American organizations and participants in bilateral negotiations frequently sought to pressure or embarrass the United States on its record of racial discrimination (Henderson 2011; Preece 1945). In the United States, racial liberals and African American journalists picked up on such critiques to argue that the success of US foreign policy in the region urgently required reform at home. A writer for the African American *Chicago Defender*, for instance, noted that the 1942 Pan-American declaration failed because of "America's unpalatable racial superiority as manifested in the outrageous treatment of her black minority – a treatment scarcely distinguishable from that of Jewish minorities in the Hitler dominated countries" (Bolden 1942a, 1942b; *Chicago Defender* 1942). Proponents of reform in the United States, scholars of Latin America, and most notably writers in the African American press also continued to use positive accounts of Latin American race relations in calls for racial democracy in the United States or criticism of US imperialism. Ramos's and Freyre's pronouncements, in particular, were useful for the argument that "Democracy really works in

Brazil" (*New York Amsterdam News* 1943) or reports that the impos-ition of an "American brand of color prejudice" in Puerto Rico risked destroying what "can be one of the finest examples of democracy-in-practice in the whole world" (Little 1942; for similar pronouncements on Cuba and Panama respectively, see Biesanz 1949, 773; E. Williams [1942] 1969, 67).

These debates did not significantly improve the record of the Roosevelt administration on matters of race and civil rights. Indeed, the major New Deal programs would grant the benefits of social democracy principally to white citizens (Katznelson 2005). Yet the conversations about race, democracy, and Pan-Americanism that emerged during the war did have a profound impact on emerging liberal ideologies, which framed the question of race as a fundamentally moral one, a matter of adjusting the "American conscience" to align with the intrinsic values of Americanism. This view was promoted by sociologist Gunnar Myrdal in his 1944 trea-tise *An American Dilemma*, which discussed "the split morality of the nation on the issue of racial democracy" (Myrdal 1944, 645).

This was also the principal message of the most influential English-language interpretation of the arguments put forth by Freyre and Ramos: Frank Tannenbaum's broad comparative theory of race relations in the Americas. In *Slave and Citizen* (1946), Tannenbaum argued that the legal and religious norms governing slavery in Latin America granted "juridical and moral personality" (Tannenbaum [1946] 1992, 98) to slaves, in contrast to the religious and legal institutions in the English colonies, which treated slaves as non-persons. For Tannenbaum, this distinction, though originating in the law, had evolved in the modern era into a question of "values and prejudice" (127). Like other US-based observers before him, Tannenbaum was less concerned with analyzing the actual workings of Latin American racial hierarchies than with using them comparatively to highlight the exceptional "political and ethical biases that have manifestly separated the United States from the rest of the New World in this respect" (42), and to offer hope that these biases might someday fade. This concern, framed around interactions between blacks and whites, helps explain why Tannenbaum drew so heavily on the Brazilian case and shaped his comparison only along dynamics of African slavery, omitting the experiences of indigenous populations with settler colonialism.

During the war, then, North Americans tended to adopt – in the service of a wide range of arguments – Brazilian claims to have perfected "racial democracy." Yet in the United States, the term had emerged first as a way of identifying a fundamental failure of democratic values rather than their triumphant success. Even in the heyday of enthusiasm for Brazilian racial democracy, this logic could easily be applied to Latin America as well – and it was.

This differently accented use of "racial democracy" seems to have emerged earliest in studies of Puerto Rico. A colony administered by the United States and a source of massive migration to the United States, Puerto Rico was one of the first parts of the region where social scientists began to conduct research on racial prejudice and civil rights and to puzzle out the incompatibility between Puerto Rican racial self-concepts and US forms of racial classification. Already by the 1940s, this research had begun to reveal dissonance between claims that race prejudice did not exist and observations of extensive prejudice. Indeed, a year before Arthur Ramos first applied the term "racial democracy" to Brazil, two professors at the University of Puerto Rico published a compendium of testimonies about racial prejudice collected among their students as well as a collection of writings by Puerto Ricans of color. They concluded that racial prejudice existed in Puerto Rico "for all persons who do not close their eyes to reality." They called the silence of Puerto Rican sociologists cowardly, arguing that scholars were responsible for keeping the race question in a state of "damp and unhygienic darkness" (Rosario and Carrión 1940, 2: 88). That same year, Charles Rogler, a University of Kansas anthropologist who generally accepted the view that race prejudice was milder in Puerto Rico, noted that the significance of color differed according to social class and that elite Puerto Ricans were the most likely to "pay lip service to racial democracy" (Rogler 1940, 37; for the contention that Haiti was also not a "racial democracy," see Blanshard 1947, 314).

Some African American scholars also adopted a skeptical approach to claims about racial democracy in Latin America. In the 1941 special issue of the *Journal of Negro Education*, historian Rayford Logan accepted the premise that "[w]hatever the reasons, race prejudice was stronger in the English colonies than in those of the Latin nations." But he noted that "in all the Western Hemisphere, as later in Africa and Asia, membership in the white race ... meant the possession of most of the wealth, power, and the social prerogatives" (R. Logan 1941, 346–47). This led him to the conclusion – quite distinct from the arguments presented by Freyre and Ramos in the same publication – that the "real and unmistakable crisis of democracy ... lies in the failure to recognize the fact that there never has been a democracy [anywhere in the Americas], there is none now, and in the ascertainable future there will be none" (R. Logan 1941, 351). Logan's colleague at Howard University, the African American philosopher and literary critic Alain Locke, made a similar argument in 1943. He thought North Americans did have something to learn from Latin Americans in terms of race relations. But he concluded that the whole of the Western Hemisphere, "one way or the other and to one degree or another, suffers yet from the unhappy consequences of slavery, which in one situation has left us an undemocratic problem of class and in another, an even less democratic situation of color caste." Both Latin America and the United States, Locke argued, still had work to do to achieve "racial democracy" (Locke 1944, 10).

These varied approaches to "racial democracy" had thus been circulating for several years when the phrase reached Brazil toward the end of World War II, where it elicited similarly diverse responses. Roger Bastide, a French sociologist residing in São Paulo, introduced a broad reading public to the Portuguese translation of the term in an article in the *Diário de São Paulo* in 1944. Bastide argued that Brazilian democracy (at the time, Brazil was still a dictatorship) emanated from Brazilian support for the Allies and from a uniquely fluid form of social relations. He suggested that Brazil's "*democracia racial* " could be a lesson for Europeans in how to construct a racially egalitarian post-war social order (Guimarães 2002, 141–44). Arthur Ramos and a growing number of international researchers also supported this view (Maio 1999, 142).

Yet in Brazil as elsewhere, the term caught on because it meant different things to different people. Conservative writers, including Gilberto Freyre himself, continued to make the case that the absence of racial prejudice and conflict was already an essential feature of Brazilian society, rendering further discussion of racial inequalities or injustice unnecessary. But at the same time, as the country returned to political democracy in 1945, many self-defined *negro* thinkers and activists in Rio de Janeiro and São Paulo adopted the banner of "democracia racial" to assert their own symbolic inclusion in a *mestiço* nation and to contest biological theories of race, as well as to demand expanded civil and political rights. Like their counterparts in the United States – and in frequent conversation with them – activists and writers in Brazil's black press promoted the idea that racial democracy was an essential part of the national character, and they mobilized in the hope of achieving what the editors of one Afro-Brazilian newspaper called "the true racial democracy in which we wish to live and which we wish to build" (cited in Alberto 2011, 179).

Alongside these optimistic uses of the term, black thinkers also echoed the skepticism of African American and (some) Puerto Rican scholars, presenting evidence of ongoing racism to argue that this national ideal remained largely unfulfilled. In the black press, in mainstream Brazilian newspapers, and in conversations with African American visitors, black Brazilians often found it necessary to point out that racial democracy was a failure. In 1947, José Correia Leite, a longtime activist and a veteran of São Paulo's early twentieth-century black press, denounced the idea of Brazil's lack of prejudice as "a sentimental lie" that blinded *negros* to the fact that their country was (in an inversion of Freyre's classic formulation) "no more than a vast slave quarters, with only a few blacks in the big house" (cited in Alberto 2011, 202). In 1948, Abdias do Nascimento, the writer, playwright, actor, and activist who became one of the leading voices of black politics in twentieth-century Brazil, made a similar point in an interview to the African American journalist George Schuyler of the *Pittsburgh Courier*: "[a]n effort is made to scatter far and wide before the winds of propaganda the idea that here in Brazil the Negro had found his paradise where he may enjoy equal rights with other men. Don't believe this ... If the race drama here does not take the form of bellicosity and physical clashes, that does not mean that it does not exist. It is something that exists psychologically for a great part of the population, this veiled racial discrimination, mystified among the propositions of a constitution which defines all men equal before the law" (Schuyler 1948). The following year, researcher Maxine Gordon cited this same interview to make a comparison with the race problem in Puerto Rico: "Those who believe prejudice does not exist ... have seen Puerto Rico, we feel, with a casual and uncritical eye" (Gordon 1949, 296–97).

The circulation of these skeptical accounts, however, did little to dampen the enthusiasm over Brazilian racial democracy in international academic and policy circles. This enthusiasm reached its peak in the early 1950s, when the Social Sciences division of the United Nations Educational, Scientific, and Cultural Organization (UNESCO), in collaboration with a series of Brazil experts, decided to fund a major research initiative on Brazilian race relations. Organizers hoped to produce evidence about Brazil's famously mixed-race society that would further discredit myths of biological race and help inspire policies to eradicate racism worldwide.

In 1950, as UNESCO worked to outline the proposed research project, black thinkers in Rio de Janeiro held their own conference on race relations. The Afro-Brazilian sociologist Alberto Guerreiro Ramos urged UNESCO to move beyond "academic or merely descriptive studies that lead to a false consciousness" about racial discrimination and to focus instead on identifying and resolving racial discrimination in Brazil (Maio 1999, 146–47). He lobbied for UNESCO to hold an international conference on race relations that would include black thinkers as producers of knowledge (A. do Nascimento 1968, 153–59). In the end, although UNESCO researchers failed to include black intellectuals as full collaborators, they did find that Brazilians of African ancestry were broadly disadvantaged in access to power and resources. Yet this evidence did not overturn the racial democracy thesis. Scholars working on Brazil's Northeast concluded that class, and not race, was the major reason for discrimination (e.g., T. de Azevedo 1953; Wagley 1963). Those studying the more racially stratified cities of Brazil's industrial Southeast affirmed that racism existed and posed a serious obstacle to the advancement of black and brown Brazilians, but they concluded that it would eventually disappear as Brazil completed the transition to a competitive class society (e.g., Costa Pinto 1953; Bastide and Fernandes 1955). Both of these arguments, in different ways, proved compatible with the idea of Brazil's racial democracy; indeed, the idea that class and not race explained Brazil's patent inequalities became one of racial democracy's most lasting variants (Sheriff 2001, 6). As late as 1963, Charles Wagley, one of the original UNESCO researchers, proclaimed that despite the more complicated picture that had begun to emerge, "Brazilians can still call their society a racial democracy," a "lesson … for the rest of the world" (Wagley 1963, 2).

Nor did Brazilian politicians and intellectuals give up the nationalist narrative of racial exceptionalism in light of the UNESCO findings. At their most extreme, conservative uses of racial democracy portrayed any form of racial consciousness or grievance as "reverse racism" and a violation of the national essence (see examples in Alberto 2011, 196–223). Gilberto Freyre's own arguments in these years shifted even farther to the right as he marshaled his trademark idea of "Lusotropical" harmony in the service of Antonio de Oliveira Salazar's dictatorship and Portugal's overseas empire (Freyre 1953, 1959). By the late 1950s, the retrenchment by defenders of rosy visions of Brazilian racial democracy, together with the inconvenient UNESCO findings, began to provoke open skepticism among Brazilian and foreign academics. Historian Stanley Stein captured this disenchantment in his 1961 review of Freyre's *New World in the Tropics*: "One can condone the fervor of the propagandist of ethnic equality [in an earlier moment of scientific racism]. It is another matter, once the good fight was won, for a social scientist to propagate as fact what are hypotheses about the culture in which random miscegenation occurred, namely slavery, patriarchalism, monarchy, and Portuguese colonialism. The perfervid regionalist who once exhumed the colonial past seems now enamored of a corpse" (Stein 1961, 113).

The issue for the many scholars and activists who expressed such skepticism about racial democracy in Brazil and other parts of Latin America was not just that claims of a more benign form of slavery or harmonious race relations were profoundly mistaken. It was that these "old myths" and "mystifications" actively prevented black people from speaking up on their own behalf. In 1963, sociologist Gordon Lewis concluded his discussion of a report by the Committee on Civil Rights in Puerto Rico by asking, "[H]ow far does all this amount to a genuine racial democracy? Very little, perhaps, in any complete way" (G. K. Lewis 1963, 283). He suggested that racism in Puerto Rico worked precisely through the "vehicle of racial indeterminacy," making it rare for a black Puerto Rican to "adopt an open attitude of racial pride" (286). Finally, he noted, "[t]here is very little, in the Puerto Rican Negro, of the belligerent militancy of his counterpart in the United States" (282). The following year, in 1964, Brazilian sociologist Florestan Fernandes argued still more pointedly that racial democracy was not simply a falsehood but a "technique of domination," a powerful form of "false consciousness about Brazilian racial realities" formulated by elites (Fernandes [1964] 2008, 311). He admitted that in the "hands of blacks and mulattos," the ideology of racial democracy might have become something to be "exploit[ed] in the opposite direction: for their own ends ... a factor in the democratization of wealth, culture, and power" (320). Yet the myth, Fernandes lamented, had been "constructed and used to reduce to a minimum such mobilization," making it instead "a formidable barrier to the progress and autonomy of the 'man of color'" (326).

To be sure, some contemporary readers would likely still have seen this purported absence of "belligerence" and "mobilization" as evidence of the superiority of the Puerto Rican and Brazilian systems of race relations. But during the late 1950s and early 1960s, that view had begun to shift as African Americans created a breathtaking protest movement that gradually forced the nation to contend with racism in housing, schools, and employment, and to curb the use of racist language in public and political speech. In the short run, this movement produced exactly the kind of televised backlash that supported a view of the United States as a society with an exceptionally violent racial system, and of Latin America as a haven of racial harmony. But by the end of the decade, the absence of racial discrimination in the law no longer distinguished Latin American societies from the United States. In the ongoing conversations about race between Anglo- and Latin Americans (Skidmore 1983; Hellwig 1992; Andrews 1996), the question became not why did the United States not have racial democracy, but why did Latin America not have black movements? Why, in particular, did Latin Americans not have the racial "pride" that could spur such movements?

Political events in Brazil further buttressed the emerging myth-of-racial-democracy thesis. The military dictatorship that took power in 1964 made ample use of the image of racial democracy to downplay its own authoritarianism and to prohibit discussion or organizing around racial inequality. This left black Brazilian thinkers and activists little room to persist in their earlier optimism that a shared consensus around racial democracy could be the basis for anti-racist political action. Looking toward African decolonization and black liberation struggles in the United States, they perceived a relative quiescence among Brazilians of African descent and increasingly called for cultural, psychological, and political "decolonization."

It was in this period, then, that the emerging Black Movement (*Movimento Negro*) joined Florestan Fernandes in the shift from endorsing a shared but as-yet-unfulfilled ideal of racial democracy, to mounting a frontal assault on the "myth of racial democracy" (Guimarães 2002; Alberto 2011). This technique would prove powerful, even as it tended to occlude a longer history of black activism. In his research, Fernandes had relied heavily on leading mid-century black activists and thinkers as informants. Many of the insights in his work – including the argument that racial democracy was a false consciousness that could be juxtaposed to Brazilian reality – were possible precisely because black Brazilians were not as blinded or disempowered as he (and now they themselves) suggested.

Puerto Rican activists and scholars who had grown up as migrants inside the United States developed a similar critique of Latin American race relations (including the claim that there was no racism in Latin America) as "brainwashing," "colonized mentality," and "non-conscious ideology." They drew on their personal experiences as well as on Marxist theory, the work of African American psychologists, the writings of Franz Fanon, and their admiration of the Black Power movement (Enck-Wanzer 2010, 22–23). The similarities between these critiques and those leveled at Brazilian racial democracy provide another example of intersecting, rather than parallel, trajectories among African Americans, Brazilians, and Afro-Caribbeans. When Abdias do Nascimento went into exile to escape Brazil's military dictatorship, he worked as a visiting professor at the Puerto Rican Studies Center at SUNY Buffalo from 1970 to 1976. Then, in 1977, Nascimento presented his influential manifesto "'Racial Democracy': Myth or Reality?" at the Second World Black and African Festival of Arts and Cultures in Lagos, Nigeria. In this piece, he described Brazil as a colonized nation and portrayed racial democracy as an ideology expressly aimed at "denying blacks the possibility of self-definition by removing any means of racial identification." As when Arthur Ramos first used the term in the *Journal of Negro Education*, this second, defining Brazilian text about "racial democracy" (later published as A. do Nascimento 1978, 79) appeared first in English, targeting an international, largely Afro-diasporic, audience.

Already by the early 1970s, the results of Fernandes' research and the myth-of-racial-democracy thesis had a major impact on both Brazilian scholars and "Brazilianists" in the United States, as did the vigorous rebuttal of Tannenbaum in the emerging field of comparative slavery. In 1971, anthropologist Sidney Mintz diagnosed what he saw as a division between "those who may have been somewhat deceived by the seemingly harmonious tenor of Brazilian interracial contacts" and those who were not. This division, he suggested, was crucial to understanding scholarly arguments about race in other parts of the region. He also noted a distinction between those who sought to make broad comparisons between racial systems based on "ancient, basic, and murky" differences between the Iberian and English Americas, and those who relied on detailed research into the workings of race in specific local contexts of slavery and free labor (Mintz 1971). The "revisionist" camp (Toplin 1971, 136) grew dramatically during the 1980s and into the 1990s, creating a more complete picture of the workings of racism and racial inequality in Brazil (Dzidzienyo 1971; Skidmore 1974; T. de Azevedo 1975; Silva 1978; Hasenbalg 1979; Hasenbalg and Silva 1988; Moura 1988; Andrews 1991; Lovell 1994; Burdick 1998; Reichmann 1999). In this context, many scholars elaborated the thesis that "myths of racial democracy" hampered the development of racial consciousness and mobilization (Fontaine 1985; Burdick 1992; Hanchard 1994; Marx 1998; Twine 1998; Guimarães 1999; Winant 1999).

The revisionist approach also worked its way deeply into the scholarship on race for the rest of Latin America, informing a wide range of works in this period that sought to document racism and to analyze how ideologies of race across the region had served to perpetuate the subordination of people of color while making them invisible, appropriating their cultures, downplaying their numerical and historical significance, or rendering illegitimate their identities as distinct groups (Rout 1973, 1976; Andrews 1980; Knight 1990; Wright 1990; Montañez 1993; Wade 1993; Kinsbruner 1996; Moore 1997; Frigerio 2000; Rahier 2003; Barragán 2005). Though the term "racial democracy" had previously been applied in specific instances to conversations (both celebratory and skeptical) about Puerto Rico and other parts of the region most closely in contact with the United States, in no other context had the phrase come to dominate local conversations or scholarship about race as it had in Brazil. The proliferation of revisionist scholarship thus led, paradoxically, to an increase in the use of "racial democracy," "myth of racial democracy," or close variants ("myths of mestizaje," "myths of equality") to describe and indict a wide range of ideologies across the region understood to work more or less like Brazil's (Purcell 1985 [on Costa Rica]; Wade 1986; Wright 1988, 1990; Kutzinski 1993; Wade 1993 [on Colombia]; Helg 1995 [on Cuba]; Hasenbalg 1996 [on Latin America]; "Special Issue on Race and Identity" 1996 [on Puerto Rico]; Gould 1998 [on Nicaragua]; Martínez-Echazábal 1998; Safa 1998; Chambers 1999 [on Peru]; Sidanius, Peña, and Sawyer 2001 [on the D. R.]; Herrera Salas 2005 [on Venezuela]; Nobles 2005; Guerrón-Montero 2006 [on Panama]). On one hand, this elevation of "racial democracy" to generic category applicable throughout the region allowed for valuable comparison, permitting authors working in other parts of Latin America to draw on the richness of Brazil-based evidence and theorization even when national literatures on race were less robust. On the other hand, this shorthand use of "racial democracy," especially to mean a mostly one-dimensional "myth," had a homogenizing effect on conversations about race. The term's dominance and its evident Brazilian associations may also have preempted conversations with scholars in Spanish America who did not recognize their national experiences in that particular term. "Racial democracy," after all, explicitly invoked the existence of "races," something at odds with many Spanish American ideologies of mestizaje, whiteness, or racelessness.

### AFTER THE FALL: RECENT SCHOLARLY TRENDS

Several aspects of the myth-of-racial-democracy thesis came under scrutiny at the end of the twentieth century, particularly as some scholars began to move from comparing "race relations" (a set of interactions between identifiable racial groups) to comparing "racial formation" or "racialization" (the social production of racial meanings and their evolution over time). This shift troubled the idea that racial ideas and identities in Latin America were comparatively more "false" or "mystified" than those in the United States. Literary scholar Silvio Torres-Saillant summed up the point eloquently for the case of the Dominican Republic (like Puerto Rico, a society closely connected to the United States as a result of both empire and migration). The challenge for scholars, he noted, was to make sense of the seeming gap between the evident racism in Dominican society and the "lesser place African-descended Dominicans accord to racial traits in articulating their social identity," without "[d]enormalizing Dominicans" or concluding that they "suffer from collective dementia." According to Torres-Saillant, "since the Dominican people's racial language defies the paradigms prevalent in countries like the United States, well-intentioned observers from such countries would wish this community adopted the racial vocabulary generated by the historical experiences of *their* societies. But, apart from safeguarding us all from such ethnocentric compulsions, paying heed to the specificity of the Dominican case can incite reflection on the elusiveness of race as an analytical category both in the Dominican Republic and elsewhere" (Torres-Saillant 2000, 1090; for similar perspectives on race in the US, see Fields 1982; Omi and Winant [1986] 2014; on Brazil, see Fry 1995, 1996; Bairros 1996; Da Matta 1997; Da Silva 1998; cf. Hanchard 1996).

Differences of interpretation between scholars who emphasized the need to debunk nationalist myths of harmony and scholars who emphasized the need to understand racial meaning in local terms reached a crescendo when two French scholars, Pierre Bourdieu and Loïc Wacquant, entered the fray. In a high-profile article on the much-debated Brazilian case, they accused revisionists (especially the African American political scientist Michael Hanchard) of cultural imperialism and ethnocentrism for imposing US ideas of race where they did not belong (Bourdieu and Wacquant 1999). Hanchard and others countered that these scholars' defense of Brazilian "difference" dangerously downplayed Brazilian racism, caricatured US racial politics, misrepresented the positions of the scholars they criticized, and buttressed discourses of racial democracy. The intensity of these exchanges shows how much was at stake for participants. The difficulty of extricating definitions of race, racism, and antiracism from the uneven hemispheric geopolitics in which conversations about "racial democracy" had long been enmeshed was now especially complicated by attacks on the supposed particularism of African

American researchers, in the name of anti-imperialism, universalism, and objectivity (J. D. French 2000; Hanchard 2003; for an overview of these debates see Wade 2004).

Yet in many ways, the scholarship on race in Latin America was already moving past the ostensible impasse. The burgeoning field of comparative slavery had firmly established that it made little sense to compare Spanish, Portuguese, French, and Anglo-Saxon systems of exploitation, or their legacies, as to which was gentler or morally superior (Mintz 1959; Genovese 1968). In the 1970s and 1980s, the field was further energized by work that sought to integrate questions of ideology more thoroughly into the history of capitalism and slavery and to understand how ideas about slavery and freedom emerged from processes of contention among social groups (Davis 1975). By the end of the 1980s, scholars began producing new studies examining the participation of African-descended people in legal and social contests over the "meanings of freedom" (Scott 1988, 1994; Chalhoub 1990; Holt 1992; Mattos 1995; Cooper, Holt, and Scott 2000). Alongside these developments, scholars of Latin America began to historicize the ideological underpinnings and effects of the very categories on which statistical analyses of inequality were based. They examined the social construction of race – the ways that race was recorded in documents and censuses and the ways that it intersected with other elements of social identity like gender, legitimacy, religiosity, public reputation, or class (Martínez Alier 1974; Andrews 1980; Cope 1994; Otero 1997). Decades later, this continues to be an extremely productive area of research (Caulfield 2000; Nobles 2000; Beattie 2001; Cunha 2002; Putnam 2002; Appelbaum, Macpherson, and Rosemblatt 2003b; Martínez 2008; Guzmán 2010; O'Toole 2012; Baerga 2014; Loveman 2014; Rappaport 2014; Twinam 2015).

All of these shifts had a major impact on the way scholars would rethink the myth-of-racial-democracy thesis. As early as 1985, historian Emilia Viotti da Costa, partly inspired by work on ideology and myth in US history and American Studies (see, e.g., R. Williams 1976, 153–57, 210–12; Slotkin 1986; Eagleton 1991, 12–16), presented a new analysis of the production, functioning, and meanings of the Brazilian myth of racial democracy. Da Costa agreed with Fernandes and others that the idea of racial democracy concealed racism and that it "made the development of black consciousness more difficult and racial confrontation less likely" (da Costa 1985, 240). But she was unconvinced by the idea that "ideologies are actually nothing but inverted images of the real world ... artifacts that dominant groups manufacture to disguise forms of oppression or to create political hegemony" (237). "Social myths," she wrote, "are an integral part of social reality and should not be seen merely as epiphenomena. In daily life, myth and reality are inextricably interrelated" (235). Da Costa situated the rise and fall of racial democracy as a competition between the ideologies of two powerful social groups: the intellectuals (like Freyre) who helped create the idea and who were tied to an older, patriarchal social order they saw as imperiled, and a generation of post-war social scientists (like Fernandes) who set about unmasking that same idea as part of their "political struggle against the traditional oligarchies" (245). The social importance of the myth lay in what it revealed about broader contests, mainly among elites, over the nature of Brazilian society and politics.

Perhaps because in her account these struggles over racial democracy were not even primarily about race (238), da Costa did not extend her analysis to contestation between elites and nonelites over the myth's social meanings, or to black thinkers' roles in these debates. These insights would be put forward most compellingly by two scholars working on Cuba, both of whom had been deeply embedded in conversations over the comparative history of "meanings" of freedom and citizenship. Historian Ada Ferrer, drawing on the work of historical anthropologist William Roseberry (1994), argued that the ideology of racelessness that emerged within the Cuban independence movement, and that continued to shape Cuban politics thereafter, was a "language of contention" (Ferrer 1999, 10). This Cuban variant of racial harmony was more than either a mechanism for imposing the interests of a dominant class or the outcome of disputes among different factions of the elite. It was the terrain on which various actors, including people of African descent, positioned themselves in struggles over the shape of their movement and the society it would produce.

Likewise, historian Alejandro de la Fuente argued that the idea of a Cuban nation created "with all and for all" certainly placed constraints on some kinds of independent black politics. But it also worked to "restrain considerably the political options" of white politicians, helping to bring about the right to suffrage for all Cuban men and their inclusion in early republican politics despite considerable opposition (de la Fuente 1999, 42; see also de la Fuente 1998). In extensive dialogue with the Brazil debates, de la Fuente demonstrated that "social myths" of racelessness, far from being mere frauds, were the outcome of intense if uneven political negotiation from above and below. They constituted a kind of "restraining wall" that could, at certain moments, delimit what was acceptable in national discourse about race and citizenship (65).

Historian Nancy Appelbaum has termed this approach to myths of racial harmony "post-revisionist," noting that it combines the revisionist interest in how race has shaped citizenship in modern Latin America with a concern for "how race is 'made'" and "how elite intellectuals and popular forces have interacted in the making of race" (Appelbaum 2005, 207–08; see also Appelbaum, Macpherson, and Rosemblatt 2003a). The post-revisionist moment has produced a wide range of case studies and syntheses rethinking the relationship between racial and national ideologies across disciplines, geographical areas, and historical periods. In the paragraphs that follow, we highlight some key works, themes, and directions in this literature.

Perhaps the most important trend in the last fifteen years is the growth of research on the ideas and activities of Afro-Latin American intellectuals and political activists (see Chapter 6). The myth-of-racial-democracy thesis had focused on white elites' successful construction and manipulation of dominant racial ideologies, perceiving black consciousness and mobilization only, or primarily, in clearly articulated rejections of these "myths." Over the past decade and a half, scholars have not only continued to uncover moments and movements in which Afro-Latin American thinkers or activists contested claims about the absence of racism; they have also noticed when and how Afro-Latin Americans purposefully found or made spaces within national ideologies of mixture or racial inclusiveness, pushed the limits of those ideologies, or even helped to create them. Most of this production has focused on Brazil and Cuba, which in comparison to the United States often appear to lack independent black political activism but which, in regional context, emerge as areas with unusually active black social and political spheres (on Brazil, see Butler 1998; Grinberg 2002; Guimarães 2002; A. do Nascimento and Nascimento 2003; T. de M. Gomes 2004; C. M. M. de Azevedo 2005; Cunha and Gomes 2007; Seigel 2009; Alberto 2011; Pereira 2013; F. Gomes and Domingues 2014; on Cuba, see de la Fuente 2001; Bronfman 2005; Guerra 2005; Scott 2005; Pappademos 2011).

These developments are not confined to scholarship on these "core" regions of Afro-Latin America; indeed, the gradual expansion of such work beyond these areas has helped significantly to historicize the term "racial democracy" as only one instance of a much broader range of ideologies of racial inclusion across time and space. In early nineteenth-century Spanish America, for example, republican "myths of harmony" were shaped by liberal political ideas that conceived of citizenship as necessarily uniform and homogeneous. In the city of Cartagena, where people of African descent made up an important part of the population and wielded significant political power, expressions of this homogeneous ideal included endorsements of racial fusion or coexistence that recognized racial differences (Lasso 2007). In post-independence Buenos Aires, early metaphors of national inclusion also embraced universalist ideas of raceless citizenship but pointedly avoided references to biological mestizaje, consanguinity, or coexistence as means to those ends. Instead, dominant metaphors held that the national soil would create, almost alchemically, a shared sense of belonging among the people of different ancestries who shed their blood for the new nation, giving rise to a single, raceless (and later explicitly white) family tree, with little to no room for a separate Afro-Argentine identity (Quijada 2000; Edwards 2014; Geler 2014). In Puerto Rico, participants in the late-nineteenth-century colonial reform movement upheld an ideal of "cordiality" as an essential feature of Puerto Rican identity, built around the figure of a black schoolteacher who taught white and black children in his classroom (Hoffnung-Garskof 2011). Moving beyond the US-Latin America contrast, this body of work suggests a portrait of many different myths, stories, or metaphors of racial inclusion, set against different kinds of economic and political structures, within different regional and urban geographies, each functioning to limit and facilitate anti-racist politics in different ways (for similar arguments on these and other parts of Latin America, see Dubois 2006; Acree and Borucki 2008; Smith 2009; Vinson 2009; Andrews 2010b; Geler 2010; McGraw 2014; Andrews 2016a, 45–66).

Most of these works focus on individuals or groups who took part in identifiable racial politics or engaged with national ideologies of race as "blacks," "Afrodescendants," or people "of color." However, a second tendency of recent scholarship has been to question whether race-based organizations are, *a priori*, the only or the best way to engage in anti-racist struggles. In light of the broader shifts in comparative studies of race outlined earlier in the chapter, the question of why Latin American societies lacked mass civil rights or black liberation movements – which had helped support the conclusion that myths of racial democracy were demobilizing – increasingly emerged as a question wrongly posed or too hastily answered. In her comparison of post-emancipation Cuba and Louisiana, historian Rebecca Scott, reflecting on the "cross-racial loyalties" that kept many Cubans from adhering to explicitly race-based organizations, cautions against arriving at the conclusion that those who invoked the ideal of racelessness were necessarily cynically racist, opportunistic, or dupes. "It was – and is – an open question whether the concept of caste is best combated through the invocation of solidarity along a color line or across it" (Scott 2005, 247).

George Reid Andrews makes this point more broadly, noting that Afro-Latin Americans most frequently pursued anti-racist policies through cross-class, multiracial popular movements, unions, or political parties that promised to redistribute power and resources to the largely overlapping constituencies of the poor and racially discriminated. This makes sense in a region in which racial distinctions and strictures were formally abolished after independence, where messages of national integration and harmony became hegemonic over the course of the twentieth century, and where populations that were disadvantaged by class and by political marginalization were often significantly or overwhelmingly of African descent (Andrews 2004; for specific country cases, see de la Fuente 2001; Sanders 2004; Velasco e Cruz 2006; Fischer 2008; Á. Nascimento 2008; Adamovsky 2012b; J. L. Graham 2014; Elena 2016). Across Latin America, moreover, movements or uprisings in the name of the "people" or the urban poor often had racial discrimination as a subtext, even if these mobilizations were multiracial in composition and did not always make racial grievances explicit. Finally, as another way of questioning the idea that mass race-based movements are the necessary condition for social change, scholars have examined how several small but vocal and internationally-connected movements (especially in Brazil and Colombia) have incited political changes disproportionate to their size, such as the creation of state policies to combat racial disparities (Hernández 2013; Paschel 2016; on the effects of such policies in Brazil, see Andrews 2014).

A third notable trend in recent academic production on racial ideologies is the evolution of the method of national or region-wide comparisons into something that scholars have termed "transnational," "simultaneous," or "connective" approaches. When comparison takes into account contested and contingent social meanings, as well as the historical importance of the circulation of ideas and people, the reality that those meanings are constructed in relation to one another becomes particularly clear (Scott 2005; Seigel 2009; Cowling 2013; Ferrer 2014). It is notable, for instance, that some of the most important African-descended political thinkers in late nineteenth- and early twentieth-century Cuba, such as Rafael Serra and Martín Morúa Delgado, lived for extended periods as migrants in the United States. They first engaged with Martí's ideal of a raceless nation while living in direct contact with the color line in the United States, and as participants in African American civil rights organizing and in electoral politics within the Republican Party. Transnational circulations and conversations were, in this case, crucial to the origins of the distinct nationalist perspectives on race that, as we have shown, later became the subject of inter-American comparison (Hoffnung-Garskof 2009; Guridy 2010; Hoffnung-Garskof 2019). For societies like Cuba, Puerto Rico, Jamaica, and the Dominican Republic, with long histories of mass migration to the United States, it may not be possible to imagine clear boundaries between Latin American and US systems of racial meaning. It may be better to analyze race-making as something that has occurred both within national frames and also within an uneven transnational social field (Duany 2002; Hoffnung-Garskof 2008; Flores 2010; Putnam 2013; see also Nunes 2008; Alberto 2009; T. Joseph 2015). These transnational frames extend beyond the United States; scholars have highlighted the importance of connections among Afrodescendants in different Latin American nations and between Latin America and Africa (Matory 2005; Alberto 2008; Andrews 2010a; Dávila 2010; Pinho 2010). Collectively, these works suggest that while Afro-Latin Americans often looked abroad for inspiration or models, they also used international contacts and comparisons strategically: to engage in highly public meta-conversations about race and national identity. And they show that far from being frozen in a relationship of normative versus derivative or insufficient blackness, members of African American and Afro-Latin American populations have shifted their politics and their understanding of themselves in relation to one another.

Complementing this transnational approach to racial ideologies is a "sub-national" or regional approach. Recently, scholars have devoted attention not only to the variety of regional histories of race within national contexts, or to the different kinds of politics adopted by Afro-descendants in those regions, but to the ways in which regional ideas about race, racial politics, and racial inclusion compete with one another in defining ostensibly national racial systems (Wade 2000; Appelbaum 2003; Romo 2010; Alberto 2011; L. A. Lewis 2012; Sue 2013; Telles and PERLA 2014). As Barbara Weinstein demonstrates in her work on the Brazilian state of São Paulo, the effort to code modernity as white, and to restrict modernity to certain regions, allowed for deeply racist ideas about the unfitness for citizenship of non-white people to remain powerful but unspoken in a "racial democracy." Weinstein argues that twentieth-century São Paulo, though configured as white rather than *mestiço*, was not an outlier from national discourses of racial harmony and mixture, but one of its variants (Weinstein 2015). A similar point has been made by scholars of Argentina, who demonstrate that whiteness in Argentina is a version of mestizaje rather than its antipode. There, as in other nations and regions with strong whitening ideologies (Telles and Flores 2013), the outcome of mixture and inclusion were conceived as a broadly-defined, phenotypically diverse "white" (Frigerio 2006, 2009; Edwards 2014; Geler 2016; Adamovsky 2016; Alberto and Elena 2016; Andrews 2016b; Elena 2017). Like other ideologies of mixture, whiteness in Argentina was marked by many of the same internal hierarchies and contradictions as ideologies of "racial democracy" elsewhere (Alberto and Elena 2016).

So far, we have discussed works that focus mostly on the relationships between ideologies of racial inclusion and the kinds of political mobilization they enabled or constrained, whether in national politics, in transnational and diasporic conversations, or in sub-national contexts. But much of the recent scholarship has moved beyond the realm of formal politics to ask about the meanings of racial democracy in everyday life. Perhaps the best example of this is Robin Sheriff's ethnography of popular views of race in a Rio de Janeiro favela. Sheriff concludes that racial democracy is best understood as a series of "heteroglot narratives" which, when enunciated by the state or privileged white citizens, quite frequently have a repressive "smoke-screen" quality (Sheriff 2001, 221). But when invoked by those who suffer discrimination, they constitute "a passionately embraced dream" (11), "a story, really, about how people of different colors do, or ought to, relate to one another" (7). Her findings resonate with other work on Brazil by sociologists and anthropologists who argue, to borrow anthropologist Peter Fry's formulation, that racial democracy is "not so much as an 'impediment' to racial consciousness . . . as the foundation of what 'race' still actually means to most Brazilians" (Fry 2000, 97). In Brazil, as sociologist Edward Telles demonstrates, "horizontal" social relations like intermarriage or residential proximity are characterized by fluidity and integration (especially among working-class and poor Brazilians), while vertical social relations like hiring or promotions continue to be markedly stratified by race or color. In other words, the "myth" of racial democracy is neither simply true nor wholly inconsistent with everyday "reality" (Telles 2004). In such a context, national discourses of inclusion can become the basis of a fervent defense of antiracialism among racially mixed lower classes – one that coexists with, rather than precludes, a sense of racial solidarity, commitment, or injustice (Sansone 2003; Bailey 2004, 2009; Collins 2015).

The expansion of research on ideologies of racial inclusion beyond the realm of formal politics and high culture is especially important in a region where nonelites have typically expressed their ideas of national belonging in vocabularies that circulate outside or at the margins of formal politics and citizenship (Owensby 2005). Historians, too, have begun to trace these more diffuse popular understandings through sources produced when the state interacts with everyday life, such as in courtroom transcripts, police records, classrooms, or notarial copybooks (Mattos 1995; Caulfield 2000; Dávila 2003; Fischer 2004; Caulfield, Chambers, and Putnam 2005; Shumway 2005; J. French 2009; Arvey 2010; E. Logan 2010; Morrison 2010; Baerga 2014; Beattie 2015; Chira 2016). Popular culture – music, religion, literature, and even popular ideas of science – has also proved an exceptionally fertile site for grasping how racially mixed popular sectors worked out their own definitions of inclusive ideals of national belonging "from below," often in dialogue with cultural mediators who moved between popular and elite sectors (Wade 2000, 2005; P. Johnson 2002; Chasteen 2004; McCann 2004; Lane 2005; Matory 2005; Feldman 2006; Moore 2006; González 2010; Burdick 2011; Adamovsky 2012a; Karush 2012; Hertzman 2013; Wade et al. 2014; C. Abreu 2015; Pite 2016; Alberto 2016).

## WHITHER RACIAL DEMOCRACY?

The career of the term "racial democracy" as it evolved in the middle of the twentieth century – first to describe something that was absent in the United States and then to describe something that was, by contrast, uniquely present in Brazil – is over. In the United States, by the late 1950s the term was eclipsed by "civil rights," followed in the 1960s and 1970s by "black liberation" and "Black Power" and, more recently, by "multiculturalism" and "racial justice." In Brazil, few in public life invoke the phrase *democracia racial* except in the negative, as when activists and allies of the Black Movement use it to note that Brazil is not a racial democracy and never was. Even conservatives know better than to use the term, which has become mostly radioactive – although related terms with a longer and somewhat less controversial history in Brazil, like *mestiçagem*, *mistura*, or *miscigenação*, remain (e.g., Kamel 2006; Movimento Pardo-Mestiço Brasileiro 2006). New terms and concepts have emerged in Brazil and elsewhere in the region to do the work black thinkers, activists, and allied academics once hoped "racial democracy" might do: terms like "multiculturalism," "human rights," "antiracism," "social inclusion," and, perhaps most salient in recent official discourses, "racial equality," as in Brazil's "Statute of Racial Equality" of 2010.

These changes reflect the success of the Brazilian Black Movement and other black organizations in the region in attacking the myth of racial democracy, as well as the influence of shifting international vocabularies of antiracism. But they also have to do with local politics. Thirty years of democracy in Brazil has not, by itself, yielded racial equality, just as fifty years of legal equality has not produced racial justice in the United States. Many Brazilians now understand the production of racial and other kinds of equality to require active and corrective state interventions. It seems that the "democracy" in racial democracy is at once too lofty a goal and too low a bar – that is, on the one hand, Brazil is not and is not likely to soon become a "true" democracy in the sense of full racial equality; but "democracy" is also too vague, not sufficiently focused on equal outcomes, or too deeply tainted by association with earlier and ongoing celebrations of *mestiçagem*.

We might reasonably argue that "racial democracy" should begin a similar decline in academic work, and in many ways it already has. It would be exceedingly difficult for a manuscript to survive peer review these days while making an unqualified argument that Latin America, or any part thereof, is an example of a successful racial democracy. By the same token, it is no longer particularly useful to frame a research project around evidence that will test or disprove claims to racial democracy – a theory proposed more than sixty years ago and no longer seriously defended by scholars. In fact, it is our hope that the arguments presented in this chapter will encourage scholars to think carefully about continuing to use the term "racial democracy" to stand in for the spectrum of longstanding and deeply contested ideals of racial inclusion we have explored. Demoting "racial democracy" from generic category to specific instance will, we hope, encourage scholars to continue to uncover, analyze, and compare the many terms employed in Latin American ideologies of racial inclusion (not just "democracy" but also "mestizaje," "fraternity," "harmony," "cordiality," "fusion," or the "cosmic race" as well as nationalisms color-coded as "café con leche," "trigueño," "indio," "moreno," "morocho," and even "blanco/branco"), the specific social relations out of which they emerge, their particular political overtones and undertones, and their positions within a wider range of allegorical stories about national belonging.

Key to this demotion is the recognition that, while Brazilian scholars, journalists, and activists no longer use the term "racial democracy" without qualifying it with the word "myth," in many parts of Latin America the wide variety of claims of racial inclusion are not so moribund. Indeed, various claims around mestizo or raceless nationalism continue to inflect politics in many parts of the region even as state action and public opinion mobilize new and evolving kinds of racial exclusion, as in the case of criminal justice and housing policy in early twenty-first century Puerto Rico (Dinzey-Flores 2013; Godreau 2015). Even in Brazil, the aspirational dimensions of racial democracy as an ideal of antiracism continue to do important work even as the term itself is discredited, shaping both formal politics and everyday understandings of race. As historian Marc Hertzman puts it, myths of racial democracy could not continue to hold sway "if large sectors of the population ... did not believe in them," or if nonelites did not themselves "figh[t] tooth and nail to shape them and, above all, to make them their own" (Hertzman 2013, 252). These persistent as well as newly emerging ideas of racial inclusion need continued critical analysis – not least because, as in the past, they will surely continue simultaneously to inscribe or excuse forms of racial exclusion.

Such analysis will not be served by forcing these ideas back into the scaffold of myths or realities of "racial democracy." But that does not mean that those historical debates no longer have an important place in academic work, especially in teaching. In our conversations with students, which we see as an important arena in the project of racial justice, we find ourselves returning to the story of racial democracy's rise, fall, and afterlives as a means of engaging students in the challenging tasks of making comparisons among objects that are unstable and interconnected, and of holding multiple, seemingly contradictory ideas in their minds. We sometimes intentionally emphasize the difference between various Latin American systems of racial meaning and those now operating in the United States to push students to think about the presumptions they make about racial categories and political movements. We also find it useful to involve students in critical analysis of the limits of national ideologies of racial inclusion, both by examining how they can constrain the symbolic meanings of citizenship and by contrasting ideals of inclusion with available social indicators that demonstrate ongoing inequality. In the process, we are delighted if some of our students find their way to the conclusion that racial democracy ideologies were "myths" in the sense argued by Abdias do Nascimento, Florestan Fernandes, and others, and if they are able to articulate a skeptical view of Latin American claims about racial inclusion in classroom debate.

This provides an opportunity for us to encourage them to apply similar critical thinking to their own categories and experiences.

Our tendency to shift our emphasis among different approaches to ideas of racial inclusion in different contexts, to experience the current moment of scholarly production as a challenging counterpoint rather than an easy synthesis, carries beyond teaching. For us, as for our students, it is important not to get too settled in any one perspective, to accept the idea that the topic of race is deeply confusing, and to welcome the confusion. Where conversations, academic or political, take a strongly revisionist tone, we find ourselves emphasizing the limits of the myth-of-racial-democracy thesis – especially when the work of denouncing racism or state repression has the unintended effect of portraying Afrodescendants as passive victims, making it harder to see their historical presence and efforts. Yet in contexts where official and popular discourses of racial inclusiveness remain relatively immune to revisionist critiques, we find ourselves emphasizing the gap between claims of racial inclusion and contrasting "realities." When engaging with scholarship on areas of the Americas, including the United States, where Afro-Latin Americans and Afro-Latinos continue to go unacknowledged, or in places where scholarship on race has been less densely developed than in Brazil and Cuba, we recognize the important work that scholars and activists are doing, often in partnership, to highlight the problems of invisibility and persistent anti-black racism in the face of national ideologies of harmony, mestizaje, or whiteness.

Finally, this same principle helps us to grapple with an apparent disjuncture between the emerging perspective in academia over the last decade and a half and the surge of Afro-Latin American activism in the same period. At first glance, it seems puzzling for scholars to recuperate the social constructedness of race and the affordances of Latin American ideas of racial inclusion, or to seek to reimagine as more than false consciousness the manifold ways that Afro-Latin Americans responded to these ideas, precisely when black activists' assertions of black identities and longstanding denunciations of "myths" of racial harmony begin to get traction with local, national, and supranational organizations. It might seem counterproductive to reconsider class-based and populist politics as meaningful forms of antiracism just at the moment when Latin American governments begin to institute compensatory policies specifically in favor of racial equality. Indeed, some scholars have expressed misgivings about the ease with which these policies have been enacted, seeing them as strategies employed by neoliberal states to gain legitimacy while moving away from commitments to ameliorate class-based inequalities (for a summary of such critiques, see Guimarães 2006). In Brazil, the defense of the distinctiveness of Brazilian ideals (if not realities) of racial inclusion has placed some scholars directly at odds with the Black Movement and allied academics who push for race-based affirmative action (Fry et al. 2007). Likewise, a historical or sociological project designed to understand the emergence of racial categories in Puerto Rico and the Dominican Republic on their own terms, and to understand their complex interactions with US racial categories, might appear to work at cross-purposes with the recent movement to encourage Afro-Latinos in the United States to enumerate themselves as black on the census (Jiménez Roman 2010). These differences in emphasis emerge even though scholars and activists share a commitment to combating racism toward and within Afro-Latino communities.

While the tangled knot of racial democracy can be easier to hold on to if we imagine it as a single debate between myth and reality that has been resolved in favor of "both," in thinking through the relationship between academic work and activism, it may be useful to take the longer view that discussions of racial democracy, and of racial inclusion more broadly, always consisted of multiple conversations taking place in different contexts and registers. Which of the many elements of "racial democracy" writers or speakers emphasized had to do with their particular vantage points and the arguments they hoped to make. The same is true today. Academics do not have a unique ability to see race objectively from outside of our own experience, and scholars' understanding is enriched by the perspectives of activists (indeed, some scholars are activists and vice-versa). By the same token, we think that there is an important role in public discussions of race for academics and teachers who grapple with the outer limits of the idea of race as a social construction as well as a lived reality, even if such work is not immediately useful to political movements. We are optimistic that scholarship that moves beyond the dyad "myth or reality" and that highlights Afro-Latin Americans' agency and political nimbleness, including in the making and unmaking of myths, will prove as energizing to contemporary social movements as an earlier generation of works highlighting the existence of racism. And we hope that literature that emphasizes Afro-Latin Americans' alternative forms of racial consciousness and organizing – rather than their comparative failures or absence – might continue to inform conversations and comparisons with allies in the United States.

## BIBLIOGRAPHY

Abreu, Christina. 2015. *Rhythms of Race: Cuban Musicians and the Making of Latino New York City and Miami, 1940–1960*. Chapel Hill, NC: University of North Carolina Press.

Abreu, Martha. 2000. *O império do divino. Festas religiosas e cultura popular no Rio de Janeiro (1830–1900)*. Rio de Janeiro: Nova Fronteira.

Acree, William, and Alex Borucki. 2008. *Jacinto Ventura de Molina y los caminos de la escritura negra en el Río de la Plata*. Montevideo: Linardi y Risso.

Adamovsky, Ezequiel. 2012a. "El color de la nación argentina. Conflictos y negociaciones por la definición de un ethnos nacional, de la crisis al Bicentenario." *Jahrbuch für Geschichte Lateinamerikas* 49: 343–64.

2012b. *Historia de las clases populares en la Argentina: desde 1880 hasta 2003*. Buenos Aires: Sudamericana.

2016. "A Strange Emblem for a (Not So) White Nation: 'La Morocha Argentina' in the Latin American Racial Context, c. 1900–2015." *Journal of Social History* 49, 4: 1–25.

Adelman, Jeremy. 1999. "Introduction." In *Colonial Legacies: The Problem of Persistence in Latin American History*, edited by Jeremy Adelman, 1–14. New York, NY and London: Routledge.

Alberto, Paulina L. 2008. "'Para africano ver': African-Bahian Exchanges in the Reinvention of Brazil's Racial Democracy, 1961–63." *Luso-Brazilian Review* 45, 1: 78–117.

2009. "When Rio Was Black: Soul Music, National Culture, and the Politics of Racial Comparison in 1970s Brazil." *Hispanic American Historical Review* 89, 1: 3–39.

2011. *Terms of Inclusion: Black Intellectuals in Twentieth-Century Brazil*. Chapel Hill, NC: University of North Carolina Press.

2016. "Indias blancas, negros febriles: Racial Stories and History-Making in Contemporary Argentine Fiction." In *Rethinking Race in Modern Argentina*, edited by Paulina L. Alberto and Eduardo Elena, 289–317. Cambridge and New York, NY: Cambridge University Press.

Alberto, Paulina L., and Eduardo Elena. 2016. "Introduction: The Shades of the Nation." In *Rethinking Race in Modern Argentina*, edited by Paulina L. Alberto and Eduardo Elena, 1–24. Cambridge and New York, NY: Cambridge University Press.

Andrews, George Reid. 1980. *The Afro-Argentines of Buenos Aires, 1800–1900*. Madison, WI: University of Wisconsin Press.

1991. *Blacks and Whites in São Paulo, Brazil, 1888–1988*. Madison, WI: University of Wisconsin Press.

1996. "Brazilian Racial Democracy, 1900–90: An American Counterpoint." *Journal of Contemporary History* 31, 3: 483–507.

2004. *Afro-Latin America, 1800–2000*. Oxford and New York, NY: Oxford University Press.

2010a. "Afro-World: African-Diaspora Thought and Practice in Montevideo, Uruguay, 1830–2000." *The Americas* 67, 1: 83–107.

2010b. *Blackness in the White Nation: A History of Afro-Uruguay.* Chapel Hill, NC: University of North Carolina Press.

2014. "Racial Inequality in Brazil and the United States, 1990–2010." *Journal of Social History* 47, 4: 829–54.

2016a. *Afro-Latin America: Black Lives, 1600–2000.* Cambridge, MA: Harvard University Press.

2016b. "Whiteness and Its Discontents." In *Rethinking Race in Modern Argentina*, edited by Paulina L. Alberto and Eduardo Elena, 318–26. Cambridge and New York, NY: Cambridge University Press.

Appelbaum, Nancy. 2003. *Muddied Waters: Race, Region, and Local History in Colombia, 1846–1948.* Durham, NC: Duke University Press.

2005. "Post-Revisionist Scholarship on Race." *Latin American Research Review* 40, 3: 206–17.

Appelbaum, Nancy, Anne Macpherson, and Karin Rosemblatt. 2003a. "Introduction: Racial Nations." In *Race and Nation in Modern Latin America*, 1–31. Chapel Hill, NC: University of North Carolina Press.

Appelbaum, Nancy, Anne Macpherson, and Karin Rosemblatt, eds. 2003b. *Race and Nation in Modern Latin America.* Chapel Hill, NC: University of North Carolina Press.

Arvey, Sarah R. 2010. "Making the Immoral Moral: Consensual Unions and Birth Status in Cuban Law and Everyday Practice, 1940–1958." *Hispanic American Historical Review* 90, 4: 627–59.

Azevedo, Celia Maria Marinho de. 1987. *Onda negra, medo branco: O negro no imaginário das elites–século XIX.* São Paulo: Annablume.

2005. "A recusa da 'raça': Anti-racismo e cidadania no Brasil dos anos 1830." *Horizontes Antropológicos* 11, 24: 297–320.

Azevedo, Thales de. 1953. *Les élites de couleur dans une ville brésilienne.* Paris: UNESCO.

1975. *Democracia racial: Ideologia e realidade.* Petrópolis: Vozes.

Baerga, María del Carmen. 2014. *Negociaciones de sangre: dinámicas racializantes en el Puerto Rico decimonónico.* Madrid and Frankfurt: Vervuert Iberoamericana.

Bailey, Stanley R. 2004. "Group Dominance and the Myth of Racial Democracy: Antiracism Attitudes in Brazil." *American Sociological Review* 69, 5: 728–47.

2009. *Legacies of Race: Identities, Attitudes, and Politics in Brazil.* Stanford, CA: Stanford University Press.

Bairros, Luíza. 1996. "'Orfeu e Poder': Uma perspectiva afro-americana sobre a política racial no Brasil." *Afro-Ásia* 17: 173–86.

Barbosa, José Celso. 1937. *La obra de José Celso Barbosa: problema de razas.* Edited by Pilar Barbosa de Rosario. San Juan: Imprenta Venezuela.

Barragán, Rossanna. 2005. "The 'Spirit' of Bolivian Law: Citizenship, Patriarchy, and Infamy." In *Honor, Status, and Law in Modern Latin America*, edited by Sueann Caulfield, Sarah C. Chambers, and Lara Putnam, 66–86. Durham, NC: Duke University Press.

Bastide, Roger, and Florestan Fernandes. 1955. *Relações raciais entre negros e brancos em São Paulo.* São Paulo: Anhembi.

Beattie, Peter. 2001. *The Tribute of Blood: Army, Honor, Race, and Nation in Brazil, 1864–1945*. Durham, NC: Duke University Press.

2015. *Punishment in Paradise: Race, Slavery, Human Rights, and a Nineteenth-Century Brazilian Penal Colony*. Durham, NC: Duke University Press.

Berlin, Ira. 2003. *Generations of Captivity: A History of African-American Slaves*. Cambridge, MA: Harvard University Press.

Biesanz, John. 1949. "Cultural and Economic Factors in Panamanian Race Relations." *American Sociological Review* 14, 6: 772.

Bilden, Rüdiger. 1929. "Brazil, Laboratory of Civilization." *The Nation*, January 16.

Blanchard, Peter. 2008. *Under the Flags of Freedom: Slave Soldiers and the Wars of Independence in Spanish South America*. Pittsburgh, PA: University of Pittsburgh Press.

Blanco, Tomás. 1942. *El prejuicio racial en Puerto Rico*. San Juan: Biblioteca de Autores Puertorriqueños.

Blanshard, Paul. 1947. *Democracy and Empire in the Caribbean: An Overview*. New York, NY: Macmillan.

Bolden, Frank E. 1942a. "Pan-America Should Be Considered a Colored Ally." *Pittsburgh Courier*, March 21.

1942b. "Recognition of Color Problem Will Save United States Future Embarrassment." *Pittsburgh Courier*, April 4.

Bomfim, Manoel do. 1929. *O Brasil na América: Caracterização da formação brasileira*. Rio de Janeiro: F. Alves.

Bourdieu, Pierre, and Loïc Wacquant. 1999. "On the Cunning of Imperialist Reason." *Theory, Culture & Society* 16, 1: 41–58.

Bronfman, Alejandra. 2005. *Measures of Equality: Social Science, Citizenship, and Race in Cuba, 1902–1940*. Chapel Hill, NC: University of North Carolina Press.

Burdick, John. 1992. "The Myth of Racial Democracy." *NACLA Report on the Americas* 25, 4: 40–49.

1998. *Blessed Anastácia: Women, Race, and Popular Christianity in Brazil*. New York, NY: Routledge.

2011. *The Color of Sound: Race, Religion, and Music in Brazil*. New York, NY: New York University Press.

Butler, Kim. 1998. *Freedoms Given, Freedoms Won: Afro-Brazilians in Post-Abolition São Paulo and Salvador*. New Brunswick, NJ: Rutgers University Press.

Campos, Maria José. 2004. *Arthur Ramos, luz e sombra na antropologia brasileira*. São Paulo: Biblioteca Nacional.

Caulfield, Sueann. 2000. *In Defense of Honor: Sexual Morality, Modernity, and Nation in Early-Twentieth Century Brazil*. Durham, NC: Duke University Press.

Caulfield, Sueann, Sarah C. Chambers, and Lara Putnam, eds. 2005. *Honor, Status, and Law in Modern Latin America*. Durham, NC: Duke University Press.

Chalhoub, Sidney. 1990. *Visões da liberdade: Uma história das últimas décadas de escravidão na Corte*. São Paulo: Companhia das Letras.

1993. "The Politics of Disease Control: Yellow Fever and Race in Nineteenth-Century Rio de Janeiro." *Journal of Latin American Studies* 25, 3: 441–63.

2006. "The Politics of Silence: Race and Citizenship in Nineteenth-Century Brazil." *Slavery & Abolition* 27, 1: 73–87.

Chambers, Sarah C. 1999. *From Subjects to Citizens: Honor, Gender, and Politics in Arequipa, Peru, 1780–1854.* University Park: Pennsylvania State University Press.

Chasteen, John. 2004. *National Rhythms, African Roots: The Deep History of Latin American Popular Dance.* Albuquerque, NM: University of New Mexico Press.

Chira, Adriana. 2016. "Uneasy Intimacies: Race, Family, and Property in Santiago de Cuba, 1803–1868." PhD diss., University of Michigan.

Collins, John. 2015. *Revolt of the Saints: Memory and Redemption in the Twilight of Brazilian Racial Democracy.* Durham, NC: Duke University Press.

Colombán Rosario, José, and Justina Carrión. 1940. *Problemas sociales: El negro–Haiti, Estados Unidos, Puerto Rico.* Boletín de la Universidad de Puerto Rico, X. Vol. 2. San Juan: Negociado de materiales, imprenta, y transporte.

Cooper, Frederick, Thomas C. Holt, and Rebecca J. Scott. 2000. *Beyond Slavery: Explorations of Race, Labor, and Citizenship in Postemancipation Societies.* Chapel Hill, NC: University of North Carolina Press.

Cope, R. Douglas. 1994. *The Limits of Racial Domination: Plebeian Society in Colonial Mexico City, 1660–1720.* Madison, WI: University of Wisconsin Press.

Costa Pinto, Luiz de Aguiar. 1953. *O negro no Rio de Janeiro: Relações de raças numa sociedade em mudança.* São Paulo: Companhia Editora Nacional.

Cottrol, Robert J. 2013. *The Long, Lingering Shadow: Slavery, Race, and Law in the American Hemisphere.* Athens: University of Georgia Press.

Cowling, Camillia. 2013. *Conceiving Freedom: Women of Color, Gender, and the Abolition of Slavery in Havana and Rio de Janeiro.* Chapel Hill, NC: University of North Carolina Press.

Cunha, Olivia Maria Gomes da. 2002. *Intenção e gesto: Pessoa, cor e a produção cotidiana da (in)diferença no Rio de Janeiro, 1927–1942.* Rio de Janeiro: Presidência da República/Arquivo Nacional.

Cunha, Olivia Maria Gomes da, and Flávio Gomes. 2007. *Quase-cidadão: Histórias e antropologias da pós-emancipação no Brasil.* Rio de Janeiro: Editora FGV.

Da Costa, Emilia Viotti. 1985. *The Brazilian Empire: Myths and Histories.* Chicago, IL: University of Chicago Press.

Daily Boston Globe. 1933. "Call N.R.A.: Reply to Reds, Hitler, Fascism," September 4.

Da Matta, Roberto. 1997. "Notas sobre o racismo à brasileira." In *Multiculturalismo e racismo. Uma comparação Brasil-Estados Unidos*, edited by Jessé Souza, 69–74. Brasília: Paralelo.

Da Silva, Denise Ferreira. 1998. "Facts of Blackness: Brazil Is Not Quite the United States … and Racial Politics in Brazil?" *Social Identities* 4, 2: 201–34.

Dávila, Jerry. 2003. *Diploma of Whiteness: Race and Social Policy in Brazil, 1917–1945.* Durham, NC: Duke University Press.

2010. *Hotel Trópico: Brazil and the Challenge of African Decolonization, 1950–1980.* Durham, NC: Duke University Press.

Davis, David Brion. 1975. *The Problem of Slavery in the Age of Revolution, 1770–1823.* Ithaca, NY: Cornell University Press.

De la Fuente, Alejandro. 1998. "Race, National Discourse, and Politics in Cuba: An Overview." *Latin American Perspectives* 25, 3: 43–69.

1999. "Myths of Racial Democracy: Cuba, 1900–1912." *Latin American Research Review* 34, 3: 39–73.

2001. *A Nation for All: Race, Inequality, and Politics in Twentieth-Century Cuba.* Chapel Hill, NC: University of North Carolina Press.

2004. "Slave Law and Claims-Making in Cuba: The Tannenbaum Debate Revisited." *Law and History Review* 22, 2: 339–69.

2010. "From Slaves to Citizens? Tannenbaum and the Debates on Slavery, Emancipation, and Race Relations in Latin America." *International Labor and Working Class History* 77, 1: 154–73.

De la Fuente, Alejandro, and Ariela J. Gross. 2015. "Manumission and Freedom in the Americas. Cuba, Virginia, and Louisiana, 1500s–1700s." *Quaderni Storici* 148, 1: 15–48.

Di Meglio, Gabriel. 2006. *¡Viva el bajo pueblo!: la plebe urbana de Buenos Aires y la política entre la revolución de mayo y el rosismo (1810–1829).* Buenos Aires: Prometeo.

Dinzey-Flores, Zaire Zenit. 2013. *Locked In, Locked Out: Gated Communities in a Puerto Rican City.* Philadelphia, PA: University of Pennsylvania Press.

Douglass, Harl R. 1940. "The Education of Negro Youth for Modern America: A Critical Summary." *The Journal of Negro Education* 9, 3: 534–46.

Duany, Jorge. 2002. *The Puerto Rican Nation on the Move: Identities on the Island and in the United States.* Chapel Hill, NC: University of North Carolina Press.

Dubois, Laurent. 2006. "An Enslaved Enlightenment: Rethinking the Intellectual History of the French Atlantic." *Social History* 31, 1: 1–14.

Du Bois, William Edward Burghardt. 1915. "Purity of Blood." *Crisis: A Record of the Darker Races*, April, 276–83.

Dzidzienyo, Anani. 1971. *The Position of Blacks in Brazilian Society.* London: Minority Rights Group.

Eagleton, Terry. 1991. *Ideology: An Introduction.* London and New York, NY: Verso.

Edwards, Erika. 2014. "Mestizaje, Córdoba's Patria Chica: Beyond the Myth of Black Disappearance in Argentina." *African and Black Diaspora* 7, 2: 89–104.

Elena, Eduardo. 2017. "Nation, Race, and Latin Americanism in Argentina: The Life and Times of Manuel Ugarte, 1900s–1960s." In *Making Citizens in Argentina*, edited by Benjamin Bryce and David M. K. Sheinin, 62–82. Pittsburgh, PA: University of Pittsburgh Press.

2016. "Argentina in Black and White: Race, Peronism, and the Color of Politics, 1940s to the Present." In *Rethinking Race in Modern Argentina*, edited by Paulina L. Alberto and Eduardo Elena, 184–212. Cambridge and New York, NY: Cambridge University Press.

Enck-Wanzer, Darrel, ed. 2010. *The Young Lords: A Reader*. New York, NY: New York University Press.

Erman, Sam. 2008. "Meanings of Citizenship in the U.S. Empire: Puerto Rico, Isabel González, and the Supreme Court, 1898 to 1905." *Journal of American Ethnic History* 27, 4: 5–33.

Feldman, Heidi. 2006. *Black Rhythms of Peru: Reviving African Musical Heritage in the Black Pacific*. Middletown: Wesleyan University Press.

Fernandes, Florestan. 2008. *A integração do negro na sociedade de classes*. São Paulo: Globo. First published in 1964.

Ferrer, Ada. 1999. *Insurgent Cuba: Race, Nation, and Revolution, 1868–1898*. Chapel Hill, NC: University of North Carolina Press.

2014. *Freedom's Mirror: Cuba and Haiti in the Age of Revolution*. Cambridge and New York, NY: Cambridge University Press.

Fields, Barbara J. 1982. "Race and Ideology in American History." In *Region, Race, and Reconstruction: Essays in Honor of C. Vann Woodward*, edited by J. Morgan Kousser and James Macpherson, 143–77. Oxford and New York, NY: Oxford University Press.

Figueroa, Luis A. 2005. *Sugar, Slavery, and Freedom in Nineteenth-Century Puerto Rico*. Chapel Hill, NC: University of North Carolina Press.

Fischer, Brodwyn. 2004. "Quase pretos de tão pobres? Race and Social Discrimination in Rio de Janeiro's Twentieth-Century Criminal Courts." *Latin American Research Review* 39, 1: 31–59.

2008. *A Poverty of Rights: Citizenship and Inequality in Twentieth-Century Rio de Janeiro*. Stanford, CA: Stanford University Press.

Flores, Juan. 2010. *The Diaspora Strikes Back: Caribeño Tales of Learning and Turning*. New York, NY: Routledge.

Fontaine, Pierre-Michel, ed. 1985. *Race, Class, and Power in Brazil*. Los Angeles, CA: Center for Afro-American Studies, University of California.

French, Jan. 2009. *Legalizing Identities: Becoming Black or Indian in Brazil's Northeast*. Chapel Hill, NC: University of North Carolina Press.

French, John D. 2000. "The Missteps of Anti-Imperialist Reason: Bourdieu, Wacquant and Hanchard's Orpheus and Power." *Theory, Culture & Society* 17, 1: 107–28.

Freyre, Gilberto. 1941. "Brazil and the International Crisis." *The Journal of Negro Education* 10, 3: 510–14.

1943. *Casa-grande & senzala: Formação da família brasileira sob o regime de economia patriarcal*. Rio de Janeiro: J. Olympio. First published in 1933.

Frigerio, Alejandro. 2000. *Cultura negra en el Cono Sur: representaciones en conflicto*. Buenos Aires: Facultad de Ciencias Sociales y Económicas de la Universidad Católica Argentina.

2006. "'Negros' y 'blancos' en Buenos Aires: repensando nuestras categorías raciales." In *Buenos Aires negra: identidad y cultura*, edited by Leticia Maronese, 77–98. Buenos Aires: CPPHC.

2009. "Luis D'Elía y los negros: identificaciones raciales y de clase en sectores populares." *Claroscuro (Revista del Centro de Estudios Sobre Diversidad Cultural)* 8: 13–43.

Fry, Peter. 1995. "O que a cinderela negra tem a dizer sobre a 'política racial' no Brasil." *Revista USP* 28: 122–35.

1996. "Por quê o Brasil é diferente?" *Revista Brasileira de Ciências Sociais* 11, 31: 178–82.

2000. "Politics, Nationality, and the Meanings of 'Race' in Brazil." *Daedalus* 129, 2: 83–118.

Fry, Peter, Yvonne Maggie, Ricardo Ventura Santos, Marcos Chor Maio, and Simone Monteiro. 2007. *Divisões perigosas: Políticas raciais no Brasil contemporâneo.* Rio de Janeiro: Civilização Brasileira.

Gamio, Manuel. 1929. "Observations on Mexican Immigration into the United States." *Pacific Affairs* 2, 8: 463–69.

Geler, Lea. 2010. *Andares negros, caminos blancos: afroporteños, estado y nación. Argentina a fines del siglo XIX.* Rosario: Prohistoria/TEIAA.

2014. "Afro-Porteños at the End of the Nineteenth Century: Discussing the Nation." *African and Black Diaspora: An International Journal* 7, 2: 105–18.

2016. "African Descent and Whiteness in Buenos Aires: Impossible Mestizajes in the White Capital City." In *Rethinking Race in Modern Argentina*, edited by Paulina L. Alberto and Eduardo Elena, 213–40. Cambridge and New York, NY: Cambridge University Press.

Genovese, Eugene D. 1968. "Materialism and Idealism in the History of Negro Slavery in the Americas." *Journal of Social History* 1, 4: 371–94.

Godreau, Isar P. 2015. *Scripts of Blackness: Race, Cultural Nationalism, and US Colonialism in Puerto Rico.* Champaign, IL: University of Illinois Press.

Gomes, Flávio, and Petrônio Domingues, eds. 2014. *Políticas da raça: Experiências e legados da abolição e da pós-emancipação no Brasil.* São Paulo: Selo Negro.

Gomes, Tiago de Melo. 2004. *Um espelho no palco: Identidades sociais e massificação da cultura no teatro de revista dos anos 1920.* Campinas: UNICAMP.

González, Anita. 2010. *Afro-Mexico: Dancing between Myth and Reality.* Austin, TX: University of Texas Press.

Gordon, Maxine W. 1949. "Race Patterns and Prejudice in Puerto Rico." *American Sociological Review* 14, 2: 294–301.

Gould, Jeffrey L. 1998. *To Die in This Way: Nicaraguan Indians and the Myth of Mestizaje, 1880–1965.* Durham, NC: Duke University Press.

Graden, Dale. 1996. "An Act 'Even of Public Security': Slave Resistance, Social Tensions, and the End of the International Slave Trade to Brazil, 1835–1846." *Hispanic American Historical Review* 76, 2: 249–82.

Graham, Jessica L. 2010. "Representations of Racial Democracy: Race, National Identity, and State Cultural Policy in the United States and Brazil, 1930–1945." PhD diss., University of Chicago.

2014. "A virada antirracista do Partido Comunista do Brasil, a Frente Negra Brasileira e a Ação Integralista Brasileira na década de 1930." In *Políticas da raça: Experiências e legados da abolição e da pós-emancipação no Brasil*, edited by Flávio Gomes and Petrônio Domingues, 353–76. São Paulo: Selo Negro.

Graham, Richard. 1999. "Free African Brazilians and the State in Slavery Times." In *Racial Politics in Contemporary Brazil*, edited by Michael Hanchard, 30–58. Durham, NC: Duke University Press.

Graham, Richard, ed. 1990. *The Idea of Race in Latin America, 1870–1940*. Austin, TX: University of Texas Press.

Grinberg, Keila. 2002. *O fiador dos brasileiros: Cidadania, escravidão e direito civil no tempo de Antonio Pereira Rebouças*. Rio de Janeiro: Civilização Brasileira.

Gross, Ariela J. 2008. *What Blood Won't Tell: A History of Race on Trial in America*. Cambridge, MA: Harvard University Press.

Gross, Ariela J., and Alejandro de la Fuente. 2013. "Slaves, Free Blacks, and Race in the Legal Regimes of Cuba, Louisiana, and Virginia: A Comparison." *North Carolina Law Review* 91: 1699–756.

Guerra, Lillian. 2005. *The Myth of José Martí: Conflicting Nationalisms in Early Twentieth-Century Cuba*. Chapel Hill, NC: University of North Carolina Press.

Guerrón-Montero, Carla. 2006. "Racial Democracy and Nationalism in Panama." *Ethnology* 45, 3: 209.

Guimarães, Antonio Sérgio Alfredo. 1999. *Racismo e anti-racismo no Brasil*. São Paulo: Editora 34.

2002. *Classes, raças e democracia*. São Paulo: Editora 34.

2006. "Depois da democracia racial." *Tempo Social* 18, 2: 269–87.

2007. "Racial Democracy." In *Imagining Brazil*, edited by Jessé Souza and Valter Sinder, 119–37. Lanham, MD: Lexington Books.

Guridy, Frank. 2010. *Forging Diaspora: Afro-Cubans and African Americans in a World of Empire and Jim Crow*. Chapel Hill, NC: University of North Carolina Press.

Guzmán, Florencia. 2010. *Los claroscuros del mestizaje: negros, indios y castas en la Catamarca colonial*. Córdoba: Encuentro.

2016. "Manuel M. Barbarín: esclavizado, libre, político y militar (1781–1834). Un análisis sobre las categorías y sus significaciones en tiempos de Revolución e Independencia." Paper presented at the Latin American Studies Association International Congress, New York, NY, May 30.

Hanchard, Michael. 1994. *Orpheus and Power: The Movimento Negro of Rio de Janeiro and São Paulo, Brazil, 1945–1988*. Princeton, NJ: Princeton University Press.

1996. "Resposta a Luíza Bairros." *Afro-Ásia* 18: 227–34.

2003. "Acts of Misrecognition: Transnational Black Politics, Anti-Imperialism and the Ethnocentrisms of Pierre Bourdieu and Loïc Wacquant." *Theory, Culture & Society* 20, 4: 5–29.

Hanke, Lewis. 1940. "Plain Speaking About Latin America." *Harper's Magazine*, June 1.

Hasenbalg, Carlos. 1979. *Discriminação e desigualdades raciais no Brasil*. Rio de Janeiro: Graal.

1996. "Entre o mito e os fatos: Racismo e relações raciais no Brasil." In *Raça, ciência e sociedade*, edited by Marcos Chor Maio and Ricardo Ventura Santos. Rio de Janeiro: Fiocruz/Centro Cultural Banco do Brasil.

Hasenbalg, Carlos, and Nelson do Valle Silva. 1988. *Estrutura social, mobilidade e raça*. São Paulo: Vértice.

Helg, Aline. 1995. *Our Rightful Share: The Afro-Cuban Struggle for Equality, 1886–1912*. Chapel Hill, NC: University of North Carolina Press.

2004. *Liberty and Equality in Caribbean Colombia, 1770–1835*. Chapel Hill, NC: University of North Carolina Press.

Hellwig, David J. 1992. *African-American Reflections on Brazil's Racial Paradise*. Philadelphia, PA: Temple University Press.

Henderson, Timothy J. 2011. "Bracero Blacklists: Mexican Migration and the Unraveling of the Good Neighbor Policy." *The Latin Americanist* 55, 4: 199–217.

Hernández, Tanya Katerí. 2013. *Racial Subordination in Latin America: The Role of the State, Customary Law, and the New Civil Rights Response*. Cambridge and New York, NY: Cambridge University Press.

Herrera Salas, Jesús María. 2005. "Ethnicity and Revolution: The Political Economy of Racism in Venezuela." *Latin American Perspectives* 32, 2: 72–91.

Hertzman, Marc. 2013. *Making Samba: A New History of Race and Music in Brazil*. Durham, NC: Duke University Press.

Hoffnung-Garskof, Jesse. 2008. *A Tale of Two Cities: Santo Domingo and New York after 1950*. Princeton, NJ: Princeton University Press.

2009. "The World of Arturo Schomburg: Afro-Latinos, African Americans, and the Antillean Independence Movement, 1879–1914." In *Afro-Latin@s in the United States: A Reader*, edited by Miriam Jiménez Román and Juan Flores. Durham, NC: Duke University Press.

2011. "To Abolish the Law of Castes: Merit, Manhood, and the Problem of Colour in the Puerto Rican Liberal Movement, 1873–92." *Social History* 36, 3: 312–42.

2012. "Latin American Studies and United States Foreign Policy." *International Institute Journal, University of Michigan* 2, 1: 8–12.

2019. *Racial Migrations: New York City and the Revolutionary Politics of the Spanish Caribbean, 1850–1910*. Princeton, NJ: Princeton University Press.

Holt, Thomas C. 1992. *The Problem of Freedom: Race, Labor, and Politics in Jamaica and Britain, 1832–1938*. Baltimore, MD: Johns Hopkins University Press.

"Hull's Call for Maintenance of a Free Hemisphere: Secretary Warns of Insidious Peril, Says There Is No Place in Americas for Class and Racial Theories." *Atlanta Constitution*. December 11, 1938.

Jiménez-Román, Miriam. 2010. "Check Both! Afro-Latin@s and the Census." *NACLA Report on the Americas* 43, 6: 38–39.

Johnson, Lyman. 2011. *Workshop of Revolution: Plebeian Buenos Aires and the Atlantic World, 1776–1810*. Durham, NC: Duke University Press.

Johnson, Paul. 2002. *Secrets, Gossip, and Gods: The Transformation of Brazilian Candomblé*. Oxford and New York, NY: Oxford University Press.

Joseph, Tiffany. 2015. *Race on the Move: Brazilian Migrants and the Global Reconstruction of Race*. Stanford, CA: Stanford University Press.

Kamel, Ali. 2006. *Não somos racistas: Uma reação aos que nos querem transformar em uma nação bicolor*. São Paulo: Nova Fronteira.

Karush, Matthew B. 2012. "Blackness in Argentina: Jazz, Tango and Race Before Perón." *Past & Present* 216, 1: 215–45.

Katznelson, Ira. 2005. *When Affirmative Action Was White: An Untold History of Racial Inequality in Twentieth-Century America*. New York, NY: Norton.

Kennedy, Philip W. 1971. "Race and American Expansion in Cuba and Puerto Rico, 1895–1905." *Journal of Black Studies* 1, 3: 306–16.

Kinsbruner, Jay. 1996. *Not of Pure Blood: The Free People of Color and Racial Prejudice in Nineteenth-Century Puerto Rico*. Durham, NC: Duke University Press.

Klein, Herbert S., and Ben Vinson. 2007. *African Slavery in Latin America and the Caribbean*. Oxford and New York, NY: Oxford University Press.

Knight, Alan. 1990. "Racism, Revolution, and Indigenismo: Mexico, 1910–1940." In *The Idea of Race in Latin America, 1870–1940*, edited by Richard Graham, 71–113. Austin, TX: University of Texas Press.

Kutzinski, Vera M. 1993. *Sugar's Secrets: Race and the Erotics of Cuban Nationalism*. Charlottesville: University Press of Virginia.

Lane, Jill. 2005. *Blackface Cuba, 1840–1895*. Philadelphia, PA: University of Pennsylvania Press.

Lara, Silvia Hunold. 1988. *Campos da violência: Escravos e senhores na Capitania do Rio de Janeiro 1750–1808*. Rio de Janeiro: Paz e Terra.

Lasso, Marixa. 2007. *Myths of Harmony: Race and Republicanism during the Age of Revolution, Colombia 1795–1831*. Pittsburgh, PA: University of Pittsburgh Press.

Lewis, Gordon K. 1963. *Puerto Rico: Freedom and Power in the Caribbean*. New York, NY: New York University Press.

Lewis, Laura A. 2012. *Chocolate and Corn Flour: History, Race, and Place in the Making of "Black" Mexico*. Durham, NC: Duke University Press.

Lima, Manoel de Oliveira. 1914. *The Evolution of Brazil Compared with that of Spanish and Anglo-Saxon America*. Translated by Percy Alvin Martin. Stanford, CA: Stanford University Press.

Little, George. 1942. "Puerto Rican National Pride and Democracy Are Real World Models!" *Pittsburgh Courier*, March 7.

Locke, Alain L. 1944. "The Negro in the Three Americas." *The Journal of Negro Education* 13, 1: 7–18.

Logan, Enid. 2010. "Each Sheep with Its Mate: Marking Race and Legitimacy in Cuban Ecclesiastical Archives, 1890–1940." *The New West Indian Guide/ Nieuwe West-Indische Gids* 84, 1: 5–39.

Logan, Rayford. 1933. "No Color Line Down in Cuba, Logan Finds." *The Baltimore Afro-American*, September 9.

    1941. "The Crisis of Democracy in the Western Hemisphere." *The Journal of Negro Education* 10, 3: 344–52.

Lovell, Peggy A. 1994. "Race, Gender, and Development in Brazil." *Latin American Research Review* 29, 3: 7–35.

Loveman, Mara. 2014. *National Colors: Racial Classification and the State in Latin America*. New York, NY: Oxford University Press.

Maio, Marcos Chor. 1999. "O projeto Unesco e a agenda das ciências sociais no Brasil dos anos 40 e 50." *Revista Brasileira de Ciências Sociais* 14, 41: 141–58.

Martí, José. 1893. "Mi raza." *Patria*, April 16.

2012. "Nuestra América." In *Nuestra América*, 51–59. Barcelona: Linkgua Digital. First published in 1891.

Martínez Alier, Verena. 1974. *Marriage, Class and Colour in Nineteenth Century Cuba*. Cambridge and New York, NY: Cambridge University Press.

Martínez-Echazábal, Lourdes. 1998. "Mestizaje and the Discourse of National/ Cultural Identity in Latin America, 1845–1959." *Latin American Perspectives* 25, 3: 21–42.

Martínez, María Elena. 2008. *Genealogical Fictions: Limpieza de Sangre, Religion, and Gender in Colonial Mexico*. Stanford, CA: Stanford University Press.

Marx, Anthony W. 1998. *Making Race and Nation: A Comparison of South Africa, the United States, and Brazil*. Cambridge and New York, NY: Cambridge University Press.

Matory, James Lorand. 2005. *Black Atlantic Religion: Tradition, Transnationalism, and Matriarchy in the Afro-Brazilian Candomblé*. Princeton, NJ: Princeton University Press.

Mattos, Hebe. 1995. *Das cores do silêncio: Os significados da liberdade no sudeste escravista, Brasil século XIX*. Rio de Janeiro: Arquivo Nacional.

McCann, Bryan. 2004. *Hello, Hello Brazil: Popular Music in the Making of Modern Brazil*. Durham, NC: Duke University Press.

McGraw, Jason. 2014. *The Work of Recognition: Caribbean Colombia and the Postemancipation Struggle for Citizenship*. Chapel Hill, NC: University of North Carolina Press.

Mintz, Sidney. 1959. "Labor and Sugar in Puerto Rico and in Jamaica, 1800–1850." *Comparative Studies in Society and History* 1, 3: 273–81.

1971. "Groups, Group Boundaries and the Perception of 'Race.'" *Comparative Studies in Society and History* 13, 4: 437–50.

Montañez, Ligia. 1993. *El racismo oculto de una sociedad no racista*. Caracas: Fondo Editorial Tropykos.

Moore, Robin D. 1997. *Nationalizing Blackness: Afrocubanismo and Artistic Revolution in Havana, 1920–1940*. Pittsburgh, PA: University of Pittsburgh Press.

2006. *Music and Revolution: Cultural Change in Socialist Cuba*. Berkeley, CA: University of California Press.

Morais, Evaristo de. 1922. *Brancos e negros: Nos Estados Unidos e no Brasil*. Rio de Janeiro: Typ. Miccolis.

Moreno Fraginals, Manuel. 1978. *El ingenio, complejo económico social cubano del azúcar*. 3 vols. La Habana: Editorial de Ciencias Sociales.

Morrison, Karen Y. 2010. "Slave Mothers and White Fathers: Defining Family and Status in Late Colonial Cuba." *Slavery and Abolition* 31, 1: 29–55.

Moura, Clóvis. 1988. *Sociologia do negro brasileiro*. São Paulo: Ática.

Myrdal, Gunnar. 1944. *An American Dilemma: The Negro Problem and Modern Democracy*. New York, NY: Harper.

Movimento Pardo-Mestiço Brasileiro – Nação Mestiça. 2006. "Nota de Repúdio do Nação Mestiça ao racismo contido no 'Estatuto da Igualdade Racial.'" April 23. www.nacaomestica.org/noticia_060421_repudio_estatuto.htm.

Nascimento, Álvaro. 2008. *Cidadania, cor e disciplina na revolta dos marinheiros de 1910*. Rio de Janeiro: FAPERJ/Mauad X.

Nascimento, Abdias do. 1978. *O genocídio do negro brasileiro*. Rio de Janeiro: Paz e Terra.

Nascimento, Abdias do, ed. 1968. *O Negro revoltado*. Rio de Janeiro: Edições GRD.

Nascimento, Abdias do, and Elisa Larkin Nascimento. 2003. "Apresentação." In *Quilombo: vida, problemas e aspirações do negro*, 7–10. São Paulo: Editora 34.

*New York Amsterdam News*. 1943. "'Democracy Really Works in Brazil': Scholar Makes Timely Study of Racial Harmony in Brazilian Life," October 2.

Nobles, Melissa. 2000. *Shades of Citizenship: Race and the Census in Modern Politics*. Stanford, CA: Stanford University Press.

———. 2005. "The Myth of Latin American Multiracialism." *Daedalus* 134, 1: 82–87.

Nunes, Zita. 2008. *Cannibal Democracy: Race and Representation in the Literature of the Americas*. Minneapolis, MN: University of Minnesota Press.

Omi, Michael, and Howard Winant. 2014. *Racial Formation in the United States*. New York and London: Routledge. First published in 1986.

Ortiz, Fernando. 1978. *Contrapunteo del tabaco y el azúcar*. Caracas: Biblioteca Ayacucho. First published in 1940.

Otero, Hernán. 1997. "Estadística censal y construcción de la nación. El caso argentino, 1869–1914." *Boletín del Instituto de Historia Argentina y Americana "Dr. Emilio Ravignani"* 3, 16–17: 123–49.

O'Toole, Rachel. 2012. *Bound Lives: Africans, Indians, and the Making of Race in Colonial Peru*. Pittsburgh, PA: University of Pittsburgh Press.

Owensby, Brian. 2005. "Toward a History of Brazil's 'Cordial Racism': Race beyond Liberalism." *Comparative Studies in Society and History* 47, 2: 318–47.

Pappademos, Melina. 2011. *Black Political Activism and the Cuban Republic*. Chapel Hill, NC: University of North Carolina Press.

Paschel, Tianna. 2016. *Becoming Black Political Subjects: Movements and Ethno-Racial Rights in Colombia and Brazil*. Princeton, NJ: Princeton University Press.

Pereira, Amilcar. 2013. *O mundo negro: Relações raciais e a constituição do movimento negro contemporâneo no Brasil*. Rio de Janeiro: Universidade Federal Fluminense.

Pérez, Louis A. 2008. *Cuba in the American Imagination: Metaphor and the Imperial Ethos*. Chapel Hill, NC: University of North Carolina Press.

Pinho, Patricia. 2010. *Mama Africa: Reinventing Blackness in Bahia*. Durham, NC: Duke University Press.

Pite, Rebekah. 2016. "La cocina criolla: A History of Food and Race in Twentieth-Century Argentina." In *Rethinking Race in Modern Argentina*, edited by Paulina L. Alberto and Eduardo Elena, 99–125. Cambridge and New York, NY: Cambridge University Press.

Preece, Harold. 1945. "Unity, Equality Without Racial Discrimination: The Negro in Latin America." *Cleveland Call and Post*, April 28.

Purcell, Trevor W. 1985. "Dependency and Responsibility: A View from West Indians in Costa Rica." *Caribbean Quarterly* 31, 3–4: 1–15.

Putnam, Lara. 2002. *The Company They Kept: Migrants and the Politics of Gender in Caribbean Costa Rica, 1870–1960*. Chapel Hill, NC: University of North Carolina Press.

2013. *Radical Moves: Caribbean Migrants and the Politics of Race in the Jazz Age*. Chapel Hill, NC: University of North Carolina Press.

Quijada, Mónica. 2000. "Imaginando la homogeneidad: la alquimia de la tierra." In *Homogeneidad y nación, con un estudio de caso: Argentina, siglos XIX y XX*, by Mónica Quijada, Carmen Bernand, and Arnd Schneider, 179–218. Madrid: CSIC.

Rahier, Jean Muteba. 2003. "Mestizaje, Mulataje, Mestiçagem in Latin American Ideologies of National Identities." *Journal of Latin American Anthropology* 8, 1: 40–51.

Ramos, Arthur. 1941a. "The Negro in Brazil." *The Journal of Negro Education* 10, 3: 515–23.

1941b. "The Scientific Basis of Pan-Americanism." *The Inter-American Quarterly* 3: 28–35.

Rappaport, Joanne. 2014. *The Disappearing Mestizo: Configuring Difference in the Colonial New Kingdom of Granada*. Durham, NC: Duke University Press.

Reichmann, Rebecca Lynn, ed. 1999. *Race in Contemporary Brazil: From Indifference to Inequality*. University Park, PA: Pennsylvania State University Press.

René, Jean Alix. 2014. "Le Culte de l'égalité: Une exploration du processus de formation de l'État et de la politique populaire en Haïti au cours de la première moitié du dix-neuvième siècle." PhD diss., Montreal: Concordia University.

"The Rio Conference." *Chicago Defender*. February 7, 1942.

Rodríguez-Silva, Ileana M. 2012. *Silencing Race: Disentangling Blackness, Colonialism, and National Identities in Puerto Rico*. New York, NY: Palgrave Macmillan.

Rogler, Charles. 1940. *Comerío, a Study of a Puerto Rican Town*. Lawrence: University of Kansas Press.

Rojas, Ricardo. 1951. *Eurindia: ensayo de estética sobre las culturas americanas*. Buenos Aires: Losada. First published in 1924.

Romo, Anadelia. 2010. *Brazil's Living Museum: Race, Reform, and Tradition in Bahia*. Chapel Hill, NC: University of North Carolina Press.

Roseberry, William. 1994. "Hegemony and the Language of Contention." In *Everyday Forms of State Formation: Revolution and the Negotiation of Rule in Modern Mexico*, edited by Gilbert M. Joseph and Daniel Nugent, 355–66. Durham, NC: Duke University Press.

Rosemblatt, Karin Alejandra. 2009. "Other Americas: Transnationalism, Scholarship, and the Culture of Poverty in Mexico and the United States." *Hispanic American Historical Review* 89, 4: 603–41.

Rout, Leslie B. 1973. *Sleight of Hand: Brazilian and American Authors Manipulate the Brazilian Racial Situation, 1910–1951.* Washington, DC.: Academy of American Franciscan History.

    1976. *The African Experience in Spanish America: 1502 to the Present Day.* Cambridge and London: Cambridge University Press.

Safa, Helen I. 1998. "Introduction." *Latin American Perspectives* 25, 3: 3–20.

Sanders, James. 2004. *Contentious Republicans: Popular Politics, Race, and Class in Nineteenth-Century Colombia.* Durham, NC: Duke University Press.

    2014. *The Vanguard of the Atlantic World: Creating Modernity, Nation, and Democracy in Nineteenth-Century Latin America.* Durham, NC: Duke University Press.

Sansone, Livio. 2003. *Blackness without Ethnicity: Constructing Race in Brazil.* New York, NY: Palgrave Macmillan.

Santiago-Valles, Kelvin A. 1994. *Subject People and Colonial Discourses: Economic Transformation and Social Disorder in Puerto Rico, 1898–1947.* Albany, NY: State University of New York Press.

Scarano, Francisco Antonio. 1984. *Sugar and Slavery in Puerto Rico: The Plantation Economy of Ponce, 1800–1850.* Madison, WI: University of Wisconsin Press.

Schmidt-Nowara, Christopher. 1999. *Empire and Antislavery: Spain, Cuba, and Puerto Rico, 1833–1874.* Pittsburgh, PA: University of Pittsburgh Press.

Schuyler, George S. 1948. "Brazilian Color Bias Growing More Rampant." *Pittsburgh Courier*, September 4.

Scott, Rebecca J. 1988. "Exploring the Meaning of Freedom: Postemancipation Societies in Comparative Perspective." *The Hispanic American Historical Review* 68, 3: 407–28.

    1994. "Defining the Boundaries of Freedom in the World of Cane: Cuba, Brazil, and Louisiana after Emancipation." *American Historical Review* 99, 1: 70–102.

    2005. *Degrees of Freedom: Louisiana and Cuba after Slavery.* Cambridge, MA: Harvard University Press.

Seigel, Micol. 2009. *Uneven Encounters: Making Race and Nation in Brazil and the United States.* Durham, NC: Duke University Press.

Serra y Montalvo, Rafael. 1907. *Para blancos y negros. Ensayos políticos, sociales y económicos.* La Habana: El Score.

Sheriff, Robin. 2001. *Dreaming Equality: Color, Race, and Racism in Urban Brazil.* New Brunswick, NJ: Rutgers University Press.

Shumway, Jeffrey. 2005. *The Case of the Ugly Suitor and Other Histories of Love, Gender, and Nation in Buenos Aires, 1776–1870.* Lincoln, NE: University of Nebraska Press.

Sidanius, Jim, Yesilernis Peña, and Mark Sawyer. 2001. "Inclusionary Discrimination: Pigmentocracy and Patriotism in the Dominican Republic." *Political Psychology* 22, 4: 827–51.

Silva, Nelson do Valle. 1978. "Black-White Income Differentials: Brazil, 1960." PhD diss., University of Michigan.

Simpson, Eyler N. 1927. Review of *Aspects of Mexican Civilization; Some Mexican Problems*, by José Vasconcelos et al. *International Journal of Ethics* 38, 1: 106–7.

Skidmore, Thomas E. 1974. *Black into White: Race and Nationality in Brazilian Thought*. Oxford and New York, NY: Oxford University Press.

1983. "Race and Class in Brazil: Historical Perspectives." *Luso-Brazilian Review* 20, 1: 104–18.

Slotkin, Richard. 1986. "Myth and the Production of History." In *Ideology and Classic American Literature*, edited by Sacvan Bercovitch and Myra Jehlen, 70–90. Cambridge and New York, NY: Cambridge University Press.

Smith, Matthew. 2009. *Red and Black in Haiti: Radicalism, Conflict, and Political Change, 1934–1957*. Chapel Hill, NC: University of North Carolina Press.

Soares, Marisa de Carvalho. 2000. *Devotos da cor: Identidade étnica, religiosidade e escravidão no Rio de Janeiro, século XVIII*. Rio de Janeiro: Civilização Brasileira.

"Special Issue on Race and Identity." 1996. *Centro Journal* 8, 1–2: 1–240.

Stannard Baker, Ray. 1914. "The Burden of Being White." *American Magazine*.

Stein, Stanley J. 1961. "Freyre's Brazil Revisited: A Review of New World in the Tropics." *Hispanic American Historical Review* 41, 1: 111.

Stepan, Nancy. 1991. *The Hour of Eugenics: Race, Gender, and Nation in Latin America*. Ithaca, NY: Cornell University Press.

Sue, Christina. 2013. *Land of the Cosmic Race: Race Mixture, Racism, and Blackness in Mexico*. Oxford and New York, NY: Oxford University Press.

Tannenbaum, Frank. 1992. *Slave and Citizen: The Negro in the Americas*. Boston: Beacon Press. First published in 1946.

Telles, Edward. 2004. *Race in Another America: The Significance of Skin Color in Brazil*. Princeton, NJ: Princeton University Press.

Telles, Edward, and René Flores. 2013. "Not Just Color: Whiteness, Nation, and Status in Latin America." *Hispanic American Historical Review* 93, 3: 411–49.

Telles, Edward, and PERLA. 2014. *Pigmentocracies: Ethnicity, Race, and Color in Latin America*. Chapel Hill, NC: University of North Carolina Press.

Toplin, Robert Brent. 1971. "Reinterpreting Comparative Race Relations: The United States and Brazil." *Journal of Black Studies* 2, 2: 135–55.

Torres-Saillant, Silvio. 2000. "The Tribulations of Blackness: Stages in Dominican Racial Identity." *Callaloo* 23, 3: 1086–111.

Turits, Richard Lee. 2002. "A World Destroyed, a Nation Imposed: The 1937 Haitian Massacre in the Dominican Republic." *Hispanic American Historical Review* 82, 3: 589–635.

Twinam, Ann. 2015. *Purchasing Whiteness: Pardos, Mulattos, and the Quest for Social Mobility in the Spanish Indies*. Stanford, CA: Stanford University Press.

Twine, France Winddance. 1998. *Racism in a Racial Democracy: The Maintenance of White Supremacy in Brazil*. New Brunswick, NJ: Rutgers University Press.

Ugarte, Manuel. 1920. *El porvenir de la América española. La raza, la integridad territorial y moral, la organización interior.* Valencia: Prometeo.

Vasconcelos, José. 1976. "Going to School in Texas." *Review: Literature and Arts of the Americas* 10, 17: 14–20. First published in 1935.

— 1979. *La raza cósmica.* Los Angeles, CA: Centro de Publicaciones, Department of Chicano Studies, California State University-Los Angeles. First published in 1925.

Velasco e Cruz, Maria Cecília. 2006. "Puzzling Out Slave Origins in Rio de Janeiro Port Unionism: The 1906 Strike and the Sociedade de Resistência dos Trabalhadores em Trapiche e Café." *Hispanic American Historical Review* 86, 2: 205–45.

Vinson, Ben, ed. 2009. *Black Mexico: Race and Society from Colonial to Modern Times.* Albuquerque: University of New Mexico Press.

Wade, Peter. 1986. "Patterns of Race in Colombia." *Bulletin of Latin American Research* 5, 2: 1.

— 1993. *Blackness and Race Mixture: The Dynamics of Racial Identity in Colombia.* Baltimore, MD: Johns Hopkins University Press.

— 2000. *Music, Race and Nation: Música Tropical in Colombia.* Chicago, IL: University of Chicago Press.

— 2004. "Images of Latin American Mestizaje and the Politics of Comparison." *Bulletin of Latin American Research* 23, 3: 355–66.

— 2005. "Rethinking Mestizaje: Ideology and Lived Experience." *Journal of Latin American Studies* 37, 2: 239–57.

Wade, Peter, Carlos López Beltrán, Eduardo Restrepo, and Ricardo Ventura Santos, eds. 2014. *Mestizo Genomics: Race Mixture, Nation, and Science in Latin America.* Durham, NC: Duke University Press.

Wagley, Charles. 1963. *Race and Class in Rural Brazil.* 2nd ed. New York, NY: UNESCO. First published in 1952.

Walker, Andrew. 2016. "Myths of Harmony and the Unification of Hispaniola." Unpublished manuscript. University of Michigan, Ann Arbor.

Weinstein, Barbara. 2015. *The Color of Modernity: São Paulo and the Making of Race and Nation in Brazil.* Durham, NC: Duke University Press.

Williams, Eric. 1969. *The Negro in the Caribbean.* New York, NY: Negro Universities Press. First published in 1942.

Williams, Raymond. 1976. *Keywords: A Vocabulary of Culture and Society.* Oxford and New York, NY: Oxford University Press.

Winant, Howard. 1999. "Racial Democracy and Racial Identity." In *Racial Politics in Contemporary Brazil*, edited by Michael Hanchard, 98–115. Durham, NC: Duke University Press.

Wright, Winthrop. 1988. "The Todd Duncan Affair: Acción Democrática and the Myth of Racial Democracy in Venezuela." *The Americas* 44, 4: 441.

— 1990. *Café con leche: Race, Class, and National Image in Venezuela.* Austin, TX: University of Texas Press.

# PART III

# CULTURE

# 9

# Literary Liberties

## *The Authority of Afrodescendant Authors*

## Doris Sommer

Black writers in Latin America have been and continue to be inspirations to dream, to think, to reflect, and to remember because by definition creative literature outstrips reality and it can therefore presage change. The literature written by Afrodescendant writers in Latin America is so varied that no single essay can hope to offer a survey or to summarize work already available in the field. I will therefore limit my observations to some shared formal or strategic features of the primary literature, even when particular works stay close to national traditions and may hardly acknowledge connections in other countries. Readers will perhaps share my fascination in exploring at least one thread of different weaves in order to highlight a kind of freedom achieved by Black writers. It is the autonomy inherent in creative writing, a sense of authority in authorship. The redundancy is meant to underline the liberties taken by writers of fiction, poetry, and drama because Afrodescendant authors are sometimes cast as informants who represent groups, or historical periods and experiences, rather than as autonomous artists. In fact, writers are often vanguards of collective consciousness. They capture what Raymond Williams called "structures of feeling"; these are still nameless experiences and intuitions that are too new to amount to ideologies or shared world views, but newly available for shared reflection thanks to the writing (Williams 1977). Imaginative literature communicates self-determination and self-fashioning, despite the burden of slavery and the legacy of bondage.

On my reading, Afrodescendant writing in Latin America displays a strategic attention to formal literary decisions as opportunities for exercising authority, no matter how inevitable the content or the theme of the writing may be. This appreciation for artistic decision-making as a vehicle for freedom makes the study of literature significant beyond the historical or sociological information that creative writing offers. Even before they start writing, creative authors consider questions about how to strategize representations of themes they might not have freely chosen. The freedom is in the *how* not the what. Will a piece be written as fiction, theater, poetry, etc.? If poetry, blank verse, sonnet, *coplas*, *décimas*, etc.? Will it be tragic or ironic? A novel, a short story, a poem, or a play? Will it trap readers and viewers in their own unspoken assumptions about values and desires? Before artful choices are made, the options remain available, still unscripted, like a horizon of freedom.

Among the strategies whose effects have gripped readers of Afrodescendant writers, I will identify only a few and invite you, dear reader, to continue the exploration of literary contributions that run parallel to contributions in music and other arts. The moves that arrest me – and that surely connect with other strategies still to be named – share a general feature which becomes the leitmotiv and even the theory of my reading: It is an unrelenting and structural doubling of codes, of systems, beliefs, meanings, languages, and personae. Afrodescendant literature moves in restless toggling or counterpoint between two (sometimes more) antagonistic systems, without necessarily wanting to settle accounts or to claim that one side wins and the other loses. W. E. B. Du Bois acknowledged this enriching restlessness as "the gift of second sight," even as he protested its humiliating origin as the unfairness of white-dominated Anglo-America (Du Bois 1999). Du Bois admitted that the deficit in power generates a surfeit of perspective, though he lamented the high costs of the philosophical benefit. Whatever the calculation we make of this energizing movement between points of view, Afrodescendant writers remind us that creativity is more about endless and unresolved processes than about final pleasing products.

What distinguishes the liberties taken in Afrodescendant writing from the sometimes-comparable moves made by white Creoles to deal with racialized hierarchies is, I think, the level of complicity with their readers. It's probably fair to say that black writers assume that black readers will recognize the conflicting systems that structure the literature, while white readers may miss the signs. Whites can be surprised, unsettled, or outraged to discover asymmetries of rights and expectations. They can even be the target of texts designed to trap them in complicity, not with the white author who exposes them, but with the murderous white power exposed. (*Cecilia Valdés* [1882] by Cirilo Villaverde is my favorite example, and *Sab* [1842] by Gertrudis Gomez de Avellaneda runs a close second.)

But being black obliges both authors and audiences to navigate unavoidable crosscurrents of culture. Even a commissioned text like enslaved Juan Francisco Manzano's *Autobiography*, meant to fuel abolitionism, sends winks to insiders about privileged information that he keeps unavailable for charitable outsiders. Henry Louis Gates, Jr. offers a brilliant lesson in reading the difference in *The Signifying Monkey* (1988), a study of African American verbal arts as a tradition that catches white readers off guard and that enjoys the inside jokes among black players.

Following a brief comment about the serious sport of positioning readers along lines of privilege and also projecting moves beyond those lines, I offer some background notes on the academic study of Afrodescendant literature in Latin America and a loosely chronological sampling of some strategies found in that literature.

### DANGEROUS SUPPLEMENT

In general, writing in Latin America negotiates a cultural duality inscribed in the name of the region, an oxymoron of a European adjective for a New World noun. A European heritage in the word Latin identifies the languages that helped to shape the area's collective imaginaries and communication. And the word America – despite being the baptismal name used by European conquerors – is the world where Creoles would develop autonomy through a hybrid identity that was both Iberian and indigenous. For this cultural novelty that hoped to be a light brown coherent unity, Africa is an additional element that troubles any apparent truce between Latin Europe and to the New World. The value here includes *difference* itself, in the sense that African American poet and essayist Audre Lorde (1984) understood the right to defer from oppressive structures and the fulcrum for breaking free from "the master's house." Difference enables movement, explains Brent Hayes Edwards (2001, 66): "it is exactly such a haunting gap or discrepancy that allows the African diaspora to 'step' and 'move' in various articulations. Articulation is always a strange and ambivalent gesture, because finally, in the body, it is only difference – the separation between bones or members – that allows movement."

Africa is, in Jacques Derrida's terms, a "dangerous supplement," an internal difference that makes stable constructions tremble. Afrodescendant identity is at least triple, compared to the duality of Creole rhetoricians. Adding Africa complicates the already dizzying toggle between Iberian and American. It inserts an unaccounted piece of architecture into the "Lettered City" that scholars of literature had imagined to be complete but that now needs to be redesigned. Adding the extra piece shows that the entire structure is vulnerable to other possible and unbidden elements for a blueprint of the hemisphere. The standard design has not made much room for names of particular African nations and languages and spirits, for example, or for destabilizing movements among multiple elements of identity. If the term Latin America describes a toggle and a tension, Afro-Latin America expands the range of improvised identities exponentially because one extra piece portents another, and another. Afrodescendant writing takes advantage of these polyrhythmic and syncopated opportunities to compose complex works that improvise play between recognizable but now porous patterns.

Official state-sponsored cultures from one country to the next had no taste for contradiction throughout national histories. Countries had long dreamed of stabilizing the movement back and forth from old world to new, fixing racial complexity into a manageable, coherent, and monochromatic ideal. A people should be one national family, with one language, one religion, and one color. It should be homogeneous, so that racial difference demanded *mestizaje* as a patriotic project. *Raza cósmica* was the term coined by José Vasconcelos in a 1925 book that colored the campaigns of racial neutralization throughout the hemisphere. Leaders were sure that their countries were in conflict (underdeveloped and unstable) because their untutored masses suffered from antagonism among races. The remedy was to erase race. Admittedly, there have been historically more murderous measures for the removal of racial difference. But the state supported cultures of miscegenation turned out rather predictably to do very little to reduce inequality. Instead, they simply claimed that national citizens were already hybrid, which officially unhinged any complaint of racial discrimination and thereby reinforced racism.

Afrodescendant writers and readers were the black sheep of national hybrid families, and many were understandably skeptical about ending racism with mere rhetoric. Too many cultural values on one side and social abuses on the other interfered with the official programs of racial erasure. In any case, giving up one's particular culture was no sure path toward racial equality. And Afro-Latin Americans would have had to sacrifice more cultural elements than anyone else so they kept the pieces in play and the tensions alive to develop agility among multiple tags and codes.

My own supplement to the already dynamic reconstruction site for Afrodescendant literary studies, expanded by the disruptive supplement of Africa in the Americas, runs an underappreciated line of aesthetic analysis through the work in progress. My purpose is to add an underappreciated value to Latin American literary studies in ways that feature black writing as foundational. The focus on literary form as reinforcement for a newly capacious architecture for literary studies recovers attention to artistic strategies as a connecting mortar. Formal analysis has sometimes fallen out of fashion for literary studies, especially in considering ethnically marked literature, because formalism has been allegedly complicit with a conservative ideology of art for art's sake. This helps to explain why Cultural Studies often sidesteps the elite confines of what Angel Rama would famously call the "Lettered City." The contestatory and interdisciplinary field of Cultural Studies prefers to attend to popular arts and to ask questions borrowed from history, ethnography, and sociology rather than from aesthetics. This shift of focus from aesthetics to popular practices demonstrates how slippery the word "culture" can be. Raymond Williams (1976) worried about the term after returning to Oxford from the battlefront of WWII when he realized that the most common key words were no longer clear to him. By then, "culture" had come to mean both a shared system of beliefs and practices – in the language of social scientists – *and* the field of creative trial and error – for artists and humanists. In other words, the concept of culture was used as much to honor existing social patterns as to interrupt those patterns with irreverent provocations. Given the political and ethical impulses of Cultural Studies, on my reading, irreverence was appreciated as a function of popular culture in the sociological sense, without necessarily pushing the boundaries of existing artistic form. This has generated thematic readings (to identify social hierarchies, continuities of belief, and a lingering legacy of inequality, racial and gender discrimination, economic exploitation) more than attention to literary liberties.

All of these approaches are urgent and welcome for a field under construction, but literary analysis has a particular added value to offer, which is to showcase the extraordinarily complex and subtle maneuvers by Afrodescendant artists who turn daunting material and political conditions into the stuff of creative triumphs. Those victories should count toward claiming cultural territory, even when the artists themselves became exiles or martyrs. Although fundamental themes (of African heritage, slavery, and its sequels in color-coding and in identities that weave between national and transnational ties) provide a shared bedrock for literary constructions and historical experiences (along with the shared narratives and interpretations that they have generated) prepare the conditions for creative writing, I choose to underline art. Because art is always new and irreverent; these are its signature effects. It is through the act of writing literature that the burden of experience turns into the ignition for creativity. The work of writers depends on wresting a measure of freedom in order to mold existing material into something else. Creative writers do not simply acknowledge the world as it is and has been; they intervene in the world with a fresh note that opens new structures of feeling and thought. Artists, in this sense, are not victims, but subjects in the full sense of contributors to the world as a work in progress.

## THE FIELD OF AFRO-LATIN AMERICAN LITERATURE

It makes sense that the general field was first surveyed and described at a distance, from the United States, because inside Latin America, country by country, black writers had been read in the context of national literary traditions rather than in transnational relations. During the development of African American studies in North America in the 1960s and 1970s, a fraternal embrace of Spanish and Portuguese writing by Afrodescendant writers was a sequel and a confirmation of family resemblances. Distance in space and in language did not discount a shared American history on the same receiving end of the Atlantic slave trade. And several black intellectuals from Latin America would choose to emigrate to the North, where their work was welcomed more warmly than it had been at home.

Among the North American scholars who broke ground for a companion field in Latin America was Alabama-born Miriam DeCosta. Her *Blacks in Hispanic Literature* (1977; see also DeCosta-Willis 2003) is a collection of essays that showed an already collective effort to develop cross-cultural scholarship about literary family resemblances. Richard Jackson (1979; see also Jackson 1997) would soon publish *Black Writers in Latin America*, in the same year that Martha Cobb brought out *Harlem, Haiti, and Havana: A Comparative Critical Study of Langston Hughes, Jacques Roumain, Nicolás Guillén* (Cobb 1979). Then Marvin Lewis could survey the new routes toward ancient roots (borrowing from the title of a Dorothy Mosby essay on Costa Rica [Mosby 2012]) to develop sustained readings of black writers in particular countries, including Venezuela, Argentina, and Equatorial Africa (Lewis 1983, 1992, 1996, 2007). Surveys and centered essays continued to convene scholars to investigate and general readers to engage with admirable works of literary art written by blacks in Latin America. A recent volume edited by

Jerome Branche (2015) takes good advantage of earlier and contemporary contributions by pioneers in the field. Richard Jackson, for example, added to his broad surveys (Jackson 1979, 1988, 1997) and carefully annotated bibliographies (Jackson 1980, 1989) a study on the bidirectional influences of black writers in the United States and Latin America (Jackson 1998); Marvin Lewis established The Afro-Romance Institute for Languages and Literatures of the African Diaspora at the University of Missouri (www.afroromance.missouri.edu).

If a degree of geographic separation from Latin America enabled a first generation of North American scholars to cast a broad view of the literary landscape to the South, it was to complement the work of local literati who tended to focus on literature often defined by national boundaries. A lasting effect of this expansive move for reading Afrodescendant literature has been that even when the subject of a particular study is a single author or a work, the general area of Latin America remains a context for connections and comparisons. This toggle between local lessons and regional patterns – national formations and transnational dynamics – describes the rhythm of Latin American Studies in general. A nervous movement in and among countries that share some features and differ in others was born of Cold War anxieties among United States business and government leaders regarding countries too close to go unattended by institutional interests and free-market ideology. Area studies in general began as academic vigilantism. But, by a typical and chronic boomerang effect of regional studies and surveillance, Latin America often conquered the hearts and minds of its interrogators. The sentimental reversal from calculated interest to admiration and desire had already undone some of the controlling impulses for area studies by the 1970s, while Black Studies programs were developing in the North. Prescient scholars in the United States understood the urgency to develop parallel projects in Latin America, where far more enslaved Africans had landed and where nationalist rhetoric typically proclaimed that racism had already ended, as one tactic to dismiss the sequels to slavery. In fact, a few racially snubbed and politically disaffected Latin Americans helped to found Black and Puerto Rican Studies in the United States, including Abdias do Nascimento and Carlos Guillermo Wilson (see Chapter 15).

Disciples of these pioneering scholars now come to a field of Afro-Latin American Literature that is, thanks to them, established and available for continuing research and commentary. Current and future researchers can now cultivate some still sparsely developed areas of literary criticism in more countries than most outsiders – and many insiders – associate with significant Afrodescendant experiences and arts. My own necessarily spotty references to only a few authors and works cannot follow the convention of geographical and historical mapping in an essay too brief and too broad to be comprehensive. That work has largely been done by the researchers previously mentioned, and I gratefully acknowledge it as grounding for current investigations, including my own. The reflection I offer does not presume to summarize the extensive work of many writers and literary historians, nor, as I have mentioned, will it approach the field with a lens focused on the themes of Afrodescendant literature. Instead my focus is on form, to add what I can with the tools of my training while I point readers to the major contributions of experts in the field.

The themes are given, indelibly, rather than freely chosen. They are the tragic and dramatic burdens of history. No one who writes seriously in an Afrodescendant framework can ignore the experiences of the Middle Passage, the centuries of slavery, residual and hydra-headed discrimination, heroic movements of resistance, and hybrid identity formation. Attention to themes would offer continuity along the dimensions of space and time; it would confirm the shared heritage that fuels the literary traditions of black writers in English and in Iberian languages in terms shared with the social sciences. But humanistic attention to literary form offers a different order of continuity with a paradoxically political advantage: a line of literary experimentation can upset the hierarchy of history with new unauthorized authority. Writers do not ask for permission to use available materials and methods; they take it. And reading for strategic decisions leads to an appreciation of how writers can use the themes of affliction as the raw matter with which to make something new, something that bears the mark of freedom to create a personal style and signature. A kind of autonomy is already realized in the very act of writing. Burdens identify the victims of history as objects of activity by others, but literary framing shows that victims become the subjects of history by telling it in their own voices. This is an act of taking liberties. Writers are therefore agents and ambassadors of freedom, not so much because of what they write but because of how they do it. Since the effects of bondage often ripple from physical abuse to psychological shackles, the bold agency of self-authorizing black literary arts is a powerful model and motor of activism.

In some ways, the focus on form follows a path like that of subaltern history, which reads momentous events backwards, to identify the often-anonymous people who had evidently made conscious decisions and planned strategies. Otherwise, there would be no world-changing events of formerly disenfranchised people to document. Literary effects are comparable evidence of commanding agents; they are products of artful strategy rather than the themes that we know in advance. How do black writers manage to resist physical and then psychological bondage, and thereby become models of free subjects? What strategies constitute their verbal arts, inherited from Africa, and then combined with unbidden but by now intimate Ibero-American environments? These are my questions.

## EARLY MASTERS

Consider the enslaved Cuban poet and autobiographer Juan Francisco Manzano (1797–1854). After winning the sympathy of Creoles who could pay for his manumission, Manzano got a deal he could not refuse: to write an autobiography as his ticket to freedom. Manzano obliged; how could he not? But in the process, he doubled himself as the predictable object of liberal pity and also the surprisingly authoritative subject of his own narrative. As he wrote the story of his life, for example, Manzano paused at a particularly painful moment that he would not describe. Still enslaved, the writer performs a refusal, a self-authorizing discretion even under his benefactor's pressure to reveal everything. In control now as he narrates, Manzano records an unguarded moment when he attacked the slave drivers who made him watch as his own mother was beaten. He writes of his brutal handling, "I was about to lose my life ... But let us pass over the rest of this painful scene in silence" (Manzano 1996, 73).

Not giving up those desired details is a way of owning his own life. Demure and discrete, Manzano's strategy recalled passages written by former slave Frederick Douglass and by the escapee Harriet Jacobs. They performed similar gestures of resistance under the prurient gaze of white readers. Douglass and Jacobs doubled and divided the public of readers between those who knew slavery and those who only knew about it. "It would afford me great pleasure indeed, as well as materially add to the interest of my narrative, were I at liberty to gratify a curiosity, which I know exists in the minds of many, by an accurate statement of all the facts pertaining to my most fortunate escape," Douglass teases during an intense moment remembered. "But I must deprive myself of this pleasure, and the curious of the gratification which such a statement would afford" (Douglass 1845, chap. 11, para. 1). Jacobs also made sure that readers heard her self-authorizing refusal: "but no, I will not tell you of my own suffering – no, it would harrow up my soul, and defeat the object that

I wish to pursue" (Jacobs 1853). Later, the white novelist Cirilo Villaverde adopted this move and turned it inside out, perversely, to expose a white narrator who pleads ignorance rather than discretion. Instead of a black author who tells readers that they know more than they choose to tell, Villaverde created a clueless white narrator for Cuba's national novel, *Cecilia Valdés* (1882). Any reader of the illicit erotic affair in a slave society would obviously know that the light-skinned heroine is an unacknowledged sister of her spoiled white lover. But the narrator refuses to connect the dots about the perversions of family ties under the abuses of slavery, abuses that require secrecy and then lead to incest. Readers surely enjoy outsmarting the benighted narrator, and the author traps them in their own bad faith and denial because they know that the familiar story depends on the lies that corrupt everyone (Sommer 1999).

Knowing more than white narrators, and knowing when to say so, is a hallmark of black writing in the Americas; it is a feature of layering or doubling. Marvin Lewis makes the point melancholically. "As creative artists, though, [Afro-Hispanic writers] bear the heavier burden of knowing themselves as well as the dominant others" (Lewis 2005, 613). But the burden enables strategic decisions and so doubles as an added value (Du Bois's "second sight"). Jerome Branche credits an early and unconventional production of poetry with formulating a particular Afro-Latin American "episteme," a way of knowing (Branche 2015, 4). Knowing who is who, especially who is "black behind the ears," was cultural capital that circulated freely in the Caribbean, even among Dominicans who have long lived in denial of their blackness, until mass migrations from the 1980s onward brought them into regular contact with Afrodescendant peoples who looked just like family (Torres-Saillant 2014). Dominican Juan Antonio Alix (1833–1918) had taunted his countrymen in rhymes about "El negro tras de la oreja" (Ryan 2001).

Sometimes the added cultural value of being black in Latin America translates into the sheer virtuosity of mastering many codes, as in the case of Candelario Obeso (1849–84). He knew enough elite Spanish and English to translate Shakespeare (before succumbing to the racism and poverty that drove him to suicide at the age of thirty-five). He also outmaneuvered fussy grammarians by mastering their rules and then adding local registers to the Colombian language (Branche 2015, 4). In his collected *Popular Songs from Home*, Obeso outed the patriotism that followed national independence. It was simply a new maneuver to force blacks into brutal labor because civil wars were nothing more than contests for power between elite Creole political parties. Here was a curse on both houses performed in the down-home language of black boatmen along the River Magdalena.

| | |
|---|---|
| Ricen que hai guerra | They say there's a war |
| Con lo cachacos, | With the Capital's band, |
| I a mi me chocan | And I get caught |
| Los zamba-palo... | in the ruckus |
| Cuando los goros | With the right wing |
| Sí fui sordao | Cause then I was a soldier |
| Pocque efendía | Just to defend |
| Mi humirde rancho ... | My humble home ... |

Performing in a range of styles with technical virtuosity is, no doubt, a strategy to outshine white writers the way that Sor Juana Inés de la Cruz outshone men in baroque New Spain. Confronted by male skepticism about female intelligence, she purposefully saturated the possibilities for writing, brilliantly, in everything from sonnets to seguidillas, from psalms to scientific speculation. Black writers in the independence and republican periods shared the challenge to occupy discursive spaces that whites had imagined to be preferential. Like Obeso, Manzano spanned the range of available genres, "from Afro-Creole orality to the Petrarchan sonnet" (Branche 2015, 4). Even more admirable is Gabriel de la Concepción Valdés, known as Plácido (1809–45). Cuba's most famous nineteenth-century poet, of any color, Plácido's inspired improvisations and occasional poems were collected as early as 1838, alongside his sonnets, heroic narratives, and devotional poetry. Critical at times of his society, the way any sensible Cuban would have been, Plácido was to the end of his life "the life of the party," in José Lezama Lima's words (*Damisela* 2006). That brilliant life ended early, after Spanish authorities responded viciously to rumors of a slave revolt, targeting Plácido as part of the suspected conspiracy. "¡A la mar, a la mar!" ordered Plácido's pirate hero of a narrative poem, so that the high seas may cleanse the allegedly illegal crew of the real stench from corruption on land.

Plácido's popularly recited verses inspired generations of poets, including the boom of black poetry and periodicals in Cuba during the 1880s. After two armed rehearsals for Cuba's independence – in which blacks took the lead, as they would again in the third war of independence from 1895 to 1898 – black voices made themselves audible to whites as well as to one another through a range of publications. Though most of the new writing underlined a commitment to the decent values of propriety and patriotism that fueled a shared national project, the very popularity of new black voices created a stir. Literary innovation was found not in the themes but in the prolific participation of black writers; they occupied a good part of the public sphere (Ryan 2015). This was a performance of presence impossible to deny, out on the battlefield and inside the lettered city. Again, the key to appreciate liberties taken is formal rather than thematic.

Along with admiring the virtuosity of a Plácido who challenged white literary masters but remained sanguine, notice too how taciturn an effect mulatto Machado de Assis had on his readers. Machado troubled the hierarchy of literary tastes and values and unsettled everyone with the dangerous supplement of irony during Brazil's late nineteenth century. This was a period when weepy romantic nation-founding novels were being phased out by gritty naturalist narratives that were written in dead earnest. In this context of overstated passions and then scientific, sometimes voyeuristic, attention to daily detail, Machado's sparseness read like a refusal of prurience. He refused to dwell on pain to excite liberal feelings of condescension. Matter-of-factness was a stylistic slap for readers accustomed to the ingratiating embrace of informants. The effect of his zero-degree style of neutrality and equanimity was to double the points of view, underlining the horror of slavery with the dispassionate observations of business as usual.

Slavery brought with it its own trades and tools, as happens no doubt with any social institution. If I mention certain tools, it is only because they are linked to a certain trade. One of them was the iron collar, another the leg iron. There was also the mask of tin plate

(Machado de Assis 1963, 101).

This reversal of style, along with other Caliban-like moves to master the masters with their own rational language, and then to add some value from Africa, describes a range of great Afrodescendant writers in Latin America.

## MAGIC AND REAL

Alejo Carpentier, whose French surname traced his European roots, showed up the shallow European attempts to create a new culture after the moral and physical exhaustion of World War I. He held Europe up to an unflattering mirror of a truly alternative worldview. Old world surrealists and vanguardists of all stripes were trying too hard to plumb below the unnatural facade of civilization. They explored the unconscious, imagined absurd juxtapositions, and exploded recognizable words into constituent sounds that had lost their meaning. The great effort eked out in a disenchanted world produced astonishingly impoverished results, according to Carpentier. The surest way for Europeans to confirm their failure was to compare their tepid fantasies to the cultural hotbed of Afro-Caribbean culture where everyday words and things normally doubled or multiplied their meanings.

In Latin America, more than in the North, white writers would appropriate some of the dynamism in necessarily multicultural Afrodescendant writing, especially from the Vanguard of the 1920s and 1930s on. Formal experiments flourished throughout Latin America after World War I – when European conventions lost their luster of Enlightenment – and again in the heady years following the Cuban Revolution. Experiments took some leads from First World iconoclasts, but Latin American poets also strove to add a local value. Otherwise Latin American literature would continue to play catch-up with an imploding Old World. During the Vanguard, interwar years, Latin American literature strove to refresh and to reframe its project as both universal and particular. Before then, it had been enough for most white authors to claim universality in brotherhood with Europe, even if American versions of European genres dared to improve on the masters. But black writers had always been claiming both more and less from the Old World: more conceptual consistency about freedom and democracy, and less universality regarding cultural practices.

By contrast with North America's Vachel Lindsey, whose horrific but canonical caricature of "The Congo" (1919) turned Africans into primitive foils for venting unprocessed rage, Latin American poets took literary leads from local African artists practiced in processing contradictions (Hyland 2013). The condition of marginality to modernity put the entire region of Latin America into culturally contentious relationships with international literary trends, so that white writers experienced the doubling of identities that blacks knew how to negotiate: Latin Americans were both up-to-date and "developing." Since white Latin Americans were already "others" for metropolitan centers, black writing helped to turn otherness into aesthetic advantage by adding African elements and exploring contradictions, especially after the moral and military disasters of World War I.

The time had come to out-play Europe, and the new moves were often Afrodescendant inspirations. This is to say that alongside the lively literary life of Afro-Latin Americans themselves, elements of Afro-local cultures spiked the experiments of stylistically ambitious Creole writers throughout the region. But one characteristic signature that whites would leave out of their newly blackened writing was the strategic distance that blacks tended to establish between readers who know discrimination and others who only know about it. Creole writers are likely to appropriate black literary arts as if all the elements were equally familiar and available.

Probably Puerto Rico's greatest vanguard poet was as white and privileged as Carpentier. Luis Palés Matos wrote "Ñáñigo al cielo" among other lasting poems in *Tuntún de pasa y grifería* (1937), which helped to found a literary movement called Negrismo. Alongside Alejo Carpentier and other Cuban *negristas* including Nicolás Guillén, Palés turned elite taste toward an Afrocentric aesthetic in seductively syncretic work that was popular and experimental at the same time.

But watch what happens when those elements are reappropriated for a double dose of critical distance that creates havoc for old forms. Mulatto Mário de Andrade combined street-smart *modernista* maneuvers with the energy of resentment against the racism of left-leaning comrades who were "enlightened," meaning white or whitened. Andrade's result was a new inferno, *Paulicéia desvairada* (1922). The book broke all of the rules and set an unbeatably high bar of creativity. Published in English translation, this book of irregular poems was titled *Hallucinated City*, but I prefer to translate the title as "Polly-Town Out of Control." It is world-class poetry that can rival Whitman's paean to the urban "loafer" in a working-class city (as opposed to a Parisian *flaneur*), and it is also an update to Dante's tour of hell.

| | |
|---|---|
| *Profundo. Imundo meu coração . . .* | Deep down. Filthy my heart . . . |
| *Olha o edifício: Matadouros da Continental.* | Look at the building: Continental Slaughterhouses. |
| *Os vícios viciaram-me na bajulação sem sacrifícios* | Vices have corrupted me in false adulation without sacrifices |
| *. . . Minha alma corcunda como a avenida São João.* | , , , My soul hunchbacked like the Avenue St. John. |
| (Andrade 1922, 71) | (Andrade 1968, 41) |

There is a special energy here, a creative fuel that comes from long simmering resentment. I am convinced that we have yet to acknowledge how much art comes from anger. Our contemporary rhetoric of universal caring tends to exhort us to cultivate empathy with the underprivileged (as if difference necessarily marks a lack of privilege, as if identifying with someone else's feelings weren't also an abuse of the other's propriety

[Bloom 2016]). We are even encouraged to respond with forgiveness to unspeakable crimes. So, it may sound unlikely to offer some praise for rage. But rage is a normal and healthy response to abuse (Flaherty 2004). And literature can safely voice revenge through one ventriloquist or another, sometimes to the sound of the kora to invoke the gods: "¡Los esclavos rebeldes/ esclavos fugitivos,/ hijos de Orichas vengadores/ en América nacidos/ lavarán la terrible/ la ciega/ maldición de Changó!" (Zapata Olivella 2010, 70)

Perhaps we are too used to the irony to comment on it, but Nicolás Guillén (1902–89), who was a long-time member of the Partido Socialista Popular, became Cuba's national poet after the 1959 revolution by just such a double-dealing inversion: He enlisted traditional Afro-Cuban rhythms and incantations to the gods to give contemporary (communist) culture its marching orders. Despite the unfriendly atmosphere for religious practices under Fidel Castro's watch, especially vigilant against African-based religions, unstoppable Afro-Cuban culture that included cults to the gods surely signaled an alternative modernity throughout the hemisphere. In other countries of Latin America, ancient traditions were also offering parallel codes for cultural and political activism among Afrodescendant populations. In Peru, for example, musician and popular poet Nicomedes Santa Cruz (1925–1992) had been reviving from 1955 on the Afro-Latino improvisational art of *décimas* and cultivating the taste for traditional instrumental music. The Peruvian *cajón* is by now the preferred percussion instrument for Spanish flamenco as well as for much Latin American music, and many Peruvians are finally proud to call their country the most culturally diverse on the continent (Degregori 2000). But by the end of the decade when Cuba turned a new and autonomous page of history in 1959, Peru's Afrocentric myths, pre-Christian gods, orality, and performance paradoxically gained ground as legitimate companion vehicles toward emancipation and full participation in national life. Freedom for Afrodescendants does not flow in one master register but in counterpoint. Peruvian readers probably remembered the abolitionist novel *Matalaché* (1928) by mulatto Enrique López Albújar. (It competes for the tag of foundational fiction with Clorinda Matto de Turner's Indianist tragedy *Aves sin nido* [1889].) But a recent writer, Lucía Charún Illescas, has refreshed the genre with references to Afrocentric beliefs that López Albújar had left out. In her novel *Malambo* (2001), Charún Illescas takes up ancient African themes to mend gaps in official memory and to make sense for all Peruvians of the broad-based cult to The Lord of Miracles, a black Christ who stands in for the orishas.

Grassroots religion reframed the dream of national unity in Peru without leaving the dream to elite interpretations. Unity throughout the region had appealed to a homogeneous and stifling patina of Catholic *mestizaje* – or worse, to the pretense of collective whiteness – but black aesthetic interventions managed to create a capacious multiculturalism even in Colombia. There, for example, the Caribbean Coast had long been called "Atlantic" to avoid associations with blackness and to claim Europe as its other shore. At the turn of the twentieth century, the Colombian government had preferred to sacrifice the Isthmus of Panama to US interests rather than to profit from plans to build the ambitious canal. Most people cannot explain the evidently irrational decision. But Afrodescendant historian Alfonso Múnera has explained that the territory was identified with "unruly" blacks to whom the Bogota government basically bid good riddance (Múnera 2005). By 1991 the presumably colorless country wrote and ratified a new Constitution that recognized racial diversity for the first time (see Chapter 7). Cultural richness was to be respected and protected. Other countries would follow this lead.

Meanwhile, inside Colombia operating as a harbinger or an agent of change, Manuel Zapata Olivella was writing provocations between justified rancor and seasoned black humor. The counterpoint between outrage and irreverence sustains his epic novel *Changó, el gran putas* (1983). The monumental work is now featured in the Ministry of Culture's officially national "Biblioteca de literatura afrocolombiana." Zapata Olivella tuned readers into an expanded American history made audible through the ritual narration that invoked African orishas. "Mythic realism" is what Zapata called his two-tiered operation in *Changó*; it rescues facts through the offices of fantasy (Henao Restrepo 2010, 23). The choice of Changó for the novel's title, along with the scandalous epithet, is telling because the pantheon of Yoruba deities is populous and other orishas might have served as the spirit of migrations and settlements. Why not the god of the crossroad, or the goddess of ocean waters, or of war, etc.? Zapata Olivella chose Changó to lead – I am convinced – because this god is a double figure. He is a male who passes for female. He is a warrior who is also a seductress. And he wields a double-headed axe that is a sign of his bidirectional agency. The complex figure is practically a model of history itself in Zapata Olivella's strategy to move between myth and realism.

Those moves between fact and material history by a stylist as masterful as Zapata Olivella include another kind of doubling too. I mean the ambivalence of words that explode in puns to haunt the history. Zapata Olivella makes even apparently innocent uses of Spanish pinch the reading painfully. For example, an old word in slave-dealing days for ship, "nao," regularly replaces the more modern "nave" with echoes of "no" and nothingness in the Portuguese-laced language of the traders. The entire first part of *Changó* is a versified invocation to the gods, sung to the sound of the kora with words that elude simple meanings. Do not worry if you cannot understand some; Elegba, god of the crossroads, will show the way. Like Colombia's national novel *María* (1868), written by Sephardic Jew Jorge Isaacs, this updating and upstaging of the country's collective tragedy starts with an intimate note to the reader. But now there are no instructions for weeping at romantic frustration or at the final tragic loss of a beloved by her bereft lover. Instead you are invited to board the slave ships, no matter what race colors your skin. Everyone in the Americas has a history in slavery. Let yourself go, like a curious child, because America is young too, seeking its way with confidence despite the confusion: "Forget school, verb tenses, the border between life and death, because this saga has no traces but the ones you leave: you are the prisoner, the discoverer, founder and liberator." [Olvídate de la academia, de los tiempos verbales, de las fronteras que separan la vida de la muerte, porque en esta saga no hay más huella que la que tú dejes: eres el prisionero, el descubridor, el fundador, el libertador."] (Zapata Olivella 2010, 35).

Quince Duncan (2004) names this layering of mythic and material worlds Afrorealism; his manifesto updates and honors Zapata Olivella's juxtaposition of "myth" and "realism" but also identifies the mythic African elements as formal structures of Afrodescendant literature. The manifesto reappears as a "Prologue" to *A Message from Rosa* (a bilingual book, first published in 2004): "Afrorealism, A Declaration in honor of Richard Jackson, our modern Orisha of Visibility, and Manuel Zapata Olivella, Orisha of Convocation." Duncan's invitation/invocation begins like this: "Multiple voices. Stories stemming from a common original African ethnicity rooted in spirituality and reverence for the Ancestral Lore, a common experience with abduction, enslavement, colonialism, displacement and racism" (Duncan 2007). Meanwhile, in novels such as *Rosa*, and *Hombres curtidos* (1971, Cured Skin of Man), and in many masterful stories, Duncan dares to develop the themes of love and remembrance amid a disabling intolerance of the English language in Costa Rica, where English betrays the Anglo-Caribbean roots of writers, meaning black and often Jamaican. He even managed to spin a web of spirituality thanks to shared ancestral beliefs and traditions – while his Catholic and Protestant characters push their children toward competing churches.

With *Rosa*, Duncan reframed feelings beyond alliances to competing national states and competing Western religions, through the multivoiced dynamism that novels allow. The book draws connections among apparently competing narrative lines and languages. Its title turns out to be a reference to Rosa Parks, who dared to sit at the front of a segregated southern bus, and the informative footnotes explain African terms and prepare readers for a more pointed proposal in his next book. Duncan's *El pueblo afrodescendiente* (2012) is an extended essay on the diasporic process of forming a transnational counter-public (Valero 2015).

Art, academics, and activism go together in Duncan's work, as they do for Zapata Olivella, too. The multiple roles speak to the dangerous supplements they smuggle from one field to another. Luis Camnitzer (2007) argued convincingly that the interface among poetry, politics, and pedagogy is structural for Latin American leadership in general because one activity depends on and fuels the others. Conceptualism for Camnitzer is therefore a constant feature of creativity in the region rather than a limited historical movement or option. The observation finds strong cases among black artists since they cannot avoid making one liberty count for another (see Chapter 6.) In Brazil, it was Abdias Nascimento (1914–2011) who brought together this tripling of approaches to constructing racial justice, and justice in general, in spectacularly public ways. From the time that he was dismissed from the army for acting up, which probably inspired him to found his famous acting company (Black Experimental Theatre) in 1944, until serving as Federal Senator starting in 1994 after years of exile, Nascimento called out racism on stage, in universities, and in government. A jarring voice in his own country – where the official culture of "cordiality" and color-blindness remained resistant to protest – Nascimento joined a new academic movement in his host country, the United States. There he founded departments of Black and of Puerto Rican Studies (Weber 2011). Among the works he wrote in exile during the Brazilian dictatorship (1964–85) was a play titled *Sortilege* (1978). The pretty French name referred to the Latin term for "sorcery." It opens on three female devotees as they sacrifice a rooster and offer incantations to Exu, the orisha who moves in a doubled universe, between two worlds staged as upper and lower platforms with contrasting scenery. These *filhas de santo* celebrate the rite as they recall the trials of a black lawyer, now approaching their site of worship. Escaped from prison after accidentally murdering his white wife, Emmanuel is cast both as a Macbeth and as an Othello. (*Othello* is predictably a leitmotif for Afro-Latin American literature; Plácido impersonates the lovesick Moor in a light-hearted rhyme about misplaced desire [Valdés 1856, 17]. And Candelario Obeso published a translation of Shakespeare's play in 1878.) He is as much the ambition to be an en-lightened Christian as he is the denial of ancestral gods and of the dark-skinned girl who loves him. Here is the double disaster of being black in Brazil. The hero is caught both by his desire for greatness and by his racial self-loathing.

Nascimento's strategy of doubling the levels of staging goes bilingual in Zapata Olivella, who uses enough Yoruba words to send clueless but grateful readers to the last pages of his novel, where he provides a lexicon. In Quince Duncan's works, bilingualism also appears as a strategy of doubling: He outdoes Costa Rican Creoles by lacing local registers of Spanish with English language contraband. "Whoever work, let him be the best. Whoever study, let him devote hisself entirely to it. And, above all, my son. love, love a lot" (Duncan 1993, 44). By now, he and other canonized Spanish-language writers with Anglo surnames highlight the fault line of national be-longing to countries like Costa Rica and Panama. Both nations had passed laws during the 1940s whitening campaigns that explicitly excluded the children of Afrodescendant (often Jamaican) immi-grants from full citizenship. While the short-lived Costa Rican law of 1942 was technically a ban on new immigration (of blacks and non-Christians), it added a restriction on the movement of resident West Indians (Pereira Rocha and Rosa Bezerra 2015, 38). These politically disenfranchised but culturally enriched children of Anglophone families became admirably agile adults who alternately disdained local patriotism and passionately claimed it. They feel simultaneously ironic and bereft, in the toggle that Afrodescendant literature acknowledges and tolerates. No one needs to explain to Duncan or to Shirley Campbell in Costa Rica how utterly "imagined" national communities are. When Campbell calls out to the Afro-coast of many American countries, a young Nicaraguan from Puerto Cabezas responds: "Soy como vos Shirley / Rotundamente negra / Vivo en Managua y desayuno / rice and beans / green banana/ bread fruit / ginger tea / black tea" (Roof 2016, 69).

From the US mainland, Latino writers intrigue monolingual Anglo readers with the added value of Spanish words that interrupt the intimacy of communication. Rather than identify with characters and contexts in Junot Diaz's work, for example, readers experience a measure of exclu-sion and get the equalizing point. This invitation to controlled conversa-tion has marked minority writing from the times of El Inca Garcilaso de la Vega (Sommer 1999).The strategic use of Spanish in Latino literature continues to adjust the terms of interchange between hegemonic readers and subaltern writers. Nevertheless, belonging to a national imaginary can tug at the heart, as it does, for example, in a Dominican very different from Diaz, the novelist Avelino Stanley. His *Tiempo muerto* (Dead Time, 1998) is a tragedy of be-longing to the Dominican Republic, where Stanley's English surname targets him as an undesirable *cocolo*, and where Creole-speaking Haitians sound equally foreign on plantations that employ black workers, sometimes, when there is enough sugar to harvest.

Panamanian Carlos "Cubena" Guillermo Wilson expects nothing good from his home country. Wilson is a self-proclaimed Afro-diasporic writer, repaying Panama's exclusion of black immigrants with a mutual rejection and an extended stay in the United States. This is a typical trajectory for Afro-Caribbeans. And the challenges that migration creates for diasporic families translate into an almost funny airport setting that opens his novel, *The Grandchildren of Felicidad Dolores* (1991). The grandmother of the title and her ancestral stories are foundations that hold together the grandchildren and the narrative. Commuting and criss-crossing national borders is constant among Afro-Panamanian musicians as well. A common complaint among jazz masters (including Luis Russell and Eric Dolphy) is that their national identity is overlooked by both promoters and critics (Zárate n.d.). Ironically, Panama's probably best-known contribution to jazz was to develop a "passing tone" that resists notation and makes mischief with predictable or patriotic sounds. "Passing tone" (like Changó's volatility?) is a leitmotif or an objective correlative for restless diasporic creativity.

### *CONTRAPUNTEO* IN BLACK AND WHITE

Afrodescendant and Afro-inflected arts are complex and multicultural by definition, as can be appreciated in the few cases we have mentioned. They negotiate the distance between Africa and an enslaved new world. On the move in style because they're often unwelcome to stay, black arts develop in *contrapunteos* of competition among contradictions; they hover among perspectives that refuse to blend. Forging responses that develop real or feigned desires to pass under the racial radar, alongside other responses that show-up master codes with a showy virtuosity that outdoes those codes, Afro-Latin American writing makes visible and lays bare the social distances that color creates in the Americas. It scoffs at inherited privilege and even at one's own pursuit of the cultural narrowness that comes with whitening. Only a careless reader can mistake the multiple registers of lasting literature by Afro-Latino writers as simple statements of a single identity. Particularity is not in the theme of identity (which is important and predictable) but in the restless style and rhetorical innovations that creative writing requires in inhospitable hegemonic languages. "You gotta have your tips on fire," is the advice that brown Víctor Hernández Cruz (1985) gives to color-coded, Spanish-inflected, poets in New York City. Meanwhile, black Tato Laviera (1985) played on his identity as *AmeRícan*, making himself doubly authentic as a Puerto Rican and a US mainlander, twice the national that any Anglo could presume to be. Or, and simultaneously, this title poem of his memorable book makes a tragic joke of the always frustrated desire for a national identity when one is black and Latin American (Noel 2014). For Laviera, Puerto Rico had been no more hospitable to his black presence than was the United States. The move, then, is to stay on the move. Mayra Santos Febres does this masterfully too, and adds the difference of gender to her "trans" Afro-Puerto Rican literary liberties. Some readers may prefer the self-affirming effects of more strident tones, as in Shirley Campbell's popular "Rotundamente negra," but literary scholarship is fueled even farther by the moving pieces of a fraught identity that can't afford to congeal into probable performances.

When Nancy Morejón (2003, 196), for example, writes, hauntingly, "Amo a mi amo" (I love my master), how many specters does she raise with this simple, declarative, practically redundant and grammatically tidy transparency? Does the Spanish language itself trap the slave in a double bondage by preparing the perverse interchangeability of "amo" between passion and servitude? Or is the perversity hard-wired into the human condition, so that chains of love can become both a metaphor for slavish submission and the real thing of iron links too? Morejón raises questions, maybe more for women readers than for men, about serving one's master, in all the poem's minutiae of daily drudgery. Does the poem blind us with a wash of courtly love, inherited from Spanish speakers about very different circumstances, when knights pledged obedience to ladies so powerful that they were addressed as Master rather than Mistress?

This double duty of metaphors, when a gesture of speech later shows up as a material reality (e.g., Morejón's inescapable passion is bound by real metal chains), is one of the signature stylistic devices in what has long been called Magic Realism in Latin American writing. Even before Zapata Olivella performed the mythic realism that Quince Duncan much later named Afrorealism, Cuban Alejo Carpentier described the magic realism that would be so popular from the 1960s on, during and after the

Boom in Latin American narrative. He offered a prescient formulation as "lo real maravilloso" in the prologue to *El reino de este mundo* (1994). But it was Gabriel García Márquez, from the culturally Africanized Caribbean coast of Colombia, who brought almost instant international attention to this technique for doubling the uses of fantastic language. "Gabo went to Angola and declared that, suddenly, he realized how black he really was" (Zapata Olivella, quoted in Henao Restrepo 2010, 27). Think of the baby born of incest with the tail of a pig in *One Hundred Years of Solitude*. It sounds like a mere expression of degeneration but later the figurative aberration is described in detail, as a little cartilage corkscrew at the base of the newborn's spine. Or remember the silk rope that binds husband to wife, identified on the following page by its exact color and heft.

The tortuous history of Africa in the Americas affects us all, as Zapata Olivella said in the previous quote, while ushering us into the hull of a slave ship to listen during the endless voyage that will oblige us all to avenge the events of history. Nevertheless, he staged the difference between readers in the know and others who want to know. There is an unavoidable cultural gap here between literature that is authentically black and the *negrista* appropriations, so that strategic location of target readers is part of the literary choreography among notable Afrodescendant writers. If all the inhabitants of the Americas are implicated, where is the distinction between black and white? The faulty line and inevitable slippage between literature that is *negra* and a symbiotic line of *negrista* literature raises a corollary distinction and a concern about the participation of white writers and scholars in the field of Afro-Latin American literature. Does the field mark off Afrodescendant writers and critics from white interlocutors? Or does it include us all along the cautionary lines that good writers can trace? Certainly there are reasons to distinguish subjects who write through one experience of racial difference from those who write through another, as Michael Handelsman (2015) makes clear in a comparative essay.

The case Handelsman considers is about two competing literary treatments of the jazz genius Charlie "Bird" Parker. Who does "Bird" belong to? A simple answer is that he belongs to everybody, but a fuller response considers different styles and tones of the connection. Otherwise readers miss the differential effects of their own levels of musical readiness and they also miss some artful improvisations of the writers. In 1959, Argentine Julio Cortázar wrote a now classic story about Parker titled "El perseguidor" (The Pursuer), and half a century later Ecuadorian Juan

Montaño recuperated that jazz heritage in "Be Bop" (2008). The white aficionado in Cortázar's story is bewitched by Parker's exploration of nonlinear timing, which remains out of reach and unmanageable in the Frenchman's grammar of consecutive verbal tenses that fails to capture his life. But the Afrodescendant jazz columnist in Montaño's narrative hears familiar moves in Parker's experimental music; he hears the cross-cutting histories of collective dream sequences that connect with waking life. Handelsman stages the contrast between the two authors through their references to Miles Davis. Both had read and interpreted in culturally specific ways the reflection that Davis offers on the beginning of bebop: "White people back then liked music they could understand, that they could *hear* without training. Bebop didn't come out of them and so it was hard for many of them to hear what was going on in the music. It was an all-black thing" (Handelsman 2015, 111).

It would be wrong to defend an imagined, and putatively ethical, desire to cross the color line in liberal or empathic ways that understate the indelible differences that color has stained into Latin American cultures. The (familiar, nationalistic) efforts to erase color are themselves disrespectful of the structurally unequal experiences of racism. In fact, a now quite popular validation of empathy – the presumption that one can feel another's feelings – undermines a necessary acknowledgment of distinct experiences and associations (Bloom 2013). But recognizing difference does not absolve either side from engagement. Difference depends precisely on relationality, so that white interlocutors like myself are, by default, collaborators in the construction of Afro-Latin American literary studies. The point is made boldly by Toni Morrison with regard to literature in the United States: No serious writer during the formative nineteenth century, for example, was free from the burden of slavery.

All the classic texts in the United States are haunted by the African American experience. Even when the themes of slavery do not seem evident, the tone is. Mutual fear and the guilt fuel the white writers' imagination. Morrison's *Playing in the Dark: Whiteness and the Literary Imagination* (1993) reframes the hegemonic canon of a triumphalist nation as a series of tormented wrestles with racism. Her review of the African American experience in US literature is too subtle to miss even the writers who seem to demur. Poe, Melville, Cather, and Hemingway are among the respondents to American anxieties raised for everyone in the company of enslaved people. What can it mean to be free, or to be innocent, or original, when freedom and innocence and originality can founder because of institutional injustice? Melville's Bartleby the

Scrivener stands in for a long history of reluctance to know and to say. And Morrison's writers stand in for American readers whom they hope to seduce into thinking and feeling differently, including those who would feign ignorance or indifference to racially coded cultures.

A strong case for Morrison's thesis about race at the core of American cultures is the literature written in Latin America, starting with the Spanish Caribbean and Brazil where the vast majority of enslaved Africans landed in the Americas. Here, feigning indifference to blackness is not an option any more, not since even Colombia has started to call its coastline "Caribbean" instead of "Atlantic." Engagement does not have to risk the ethical trap of impersonating the other; it does not need to sacrifice the difference between positions on the inside or the outside of a color line. But it does take on the task of acknowledging racial difference and the cultural constructions of racism. Fernando Ortiz (1881–1969) famously formulated his country's polyrhythmic productions in agriculture, society, and the arts as a ceaseless contest of one [each?] race trying by all means to outdo and to confound the other. Cuba is a *Contrapunteo del tabaco y el azúcar* (Ortiz, 1940). The contest was sometimes colored as black versus white, or free labor versus slavery, or pungent masculine clouds of dark tobacco smoke versus the sweet meats of frothy feminine sugar. (Ortiz's obviously untroubled patriarchal handling of the gendered terms call attention now and did even then. See the alternative offered by Lydia Cabrera, who responded to Afro-Cuban forms with unconventional writing that doubled as both creative and scientific [Rodríguez-Mangual 2004.])

The very trope of *contrapunteo* is an Afrodescendant reference. It refers to a verbal competition between improvisational poets. Here "counterpoint" does not refer to a European musical genre in which scripted melodies collide and continue to play. Instead it names a versified joust in which opponents repeat the same melody but change the words in order to upstage one another in clever rhymes. Neither side really wants a final victory over the other. Simply winning would eliminate the counterpart and cut short the sport. Playing and shining require a surviving competitor to raise the ante turn after turn. Calling his book a Caribbean counterpoint signals the side Ortiz would take on the question of Cuba's cultural identity. He was categorical, knowing that his Africanist position would keep the country's racial differences in a dynamic *contrapunteo*, compared to the murderous monotone imaginations that preferred whitening or a mixed homogeneous race: "Cuba will be Black or it will not be." Underscoring his conclusion, with glaring clarity, is the fact that

Ortiz himself was white, not to mention also that he was schooled in the elitist culture of white privilege. In fact, Fernando Ortiz was a recovered racist, if you trace his publications back to his first books on criminology and blackness (Ortiz 1906, 1986).

## RETELLING IT LIKE IT IS

Years later, Manuel Zapata Olivella (1997, 143) would extend Ortiz's embrace of Afrodescendant Cuban counterpoint to hear African verbal sparring throughout the American hemisphere: "La presencia africana no puede reducirse a un fenómeno marginal de nuestra historia. Su fecundidad inunda todas las arterias y nervios del nuevo hombre americano." [African presence cannot be reduced to a marginal phenomenon of our history. Its generative power floods all the arteries and nerves of the new American man.] Every schoolchild in Colombia knows how the narrator of *María* (1868) learned from the bondswoman Nay to tell stories of love and war, displacement and slavery. The white storyteller hero learns African orality and is therefore able to narrate his own tragedy to countless readers. But Zapata Olivella raises Nay from supporting role to the rank of heroic narrator, and then multiplies her through thousands of griots whose African voices retell the genuine and tortuous history of Africa in the Americas. Thanks to this kind of rewriting of a foundational novel – replacing it without eliminating other versions – Afrodescendant literature in Latin America continues to open dynamic routes for research and for reading pleasure. The *contrapunteo* with national canons of literature will ensure the survival of traditional classics that now respond to new and newly appreciated challengers among black artists. The double and multiple registers of Afro-Latin American style allow the contests and combinations to flourish on all sides.

Attention to literary form promotes these transnational readings of Afrodescendant writers and readers throughout the hemisphere. The resemblances pull away from country-coded traditions while a counterpull continues toward particular patriotisms. Afrodescendant literature deals in these doublings. And a conundrum about how to be-long follows like a thread from one writer to another, interrogating the value of patriotism for fatherlands that remain reluctant to acknowledge multicolored mothers and their families. Attention to style and literary effects, as I have been suggesting, appreciates the agility of writers who carve out spaces for maneuver between the countervailing currents of identity, spirituality, language, and homeland. Authors wield authority. Even in apparently impossible predicaments, the act of writing is an exercise of agency. Despite frustrations when formal decisions miss their mark, as standard literary criticism is quick to note, an author's choice of genre, tone, and words shows the spark of literary liberties that can ignite readers to rehearse future freedoms.

## BIBLIOGRAPHY

Andrade, Mário de. 1922. *Paulicéia Desvairada*. São Paulo: Casa Mayença.
  1968. *Hallucinated City: Paulicéia Desvairada*, translated by Jack E. Tomlins. Nashville, TN: Vanderbilt University Press.
Ballagas, Emilio. 1946. *Mapa de la poesía negra americana*. Buenos Aires: Editorial Pleamar.
  ed. 1935. *Antología de poesía negra hispanoamericana*. Madrid: M. Aguilar.
Bloom, Paul. 2013. "The Baby in the Well: The Case Against Empathy." *The New Yorker*, May 20. www.newyorker.com/magazine/2013/05/20/the-baby-in-the-well.
  2016. *Against Empathy: The Case for Rational Compassion*. New York, NY: HarperCollins.
Branche, Jerome C. 2015. *Black Writing, Culture, and the State in Latin America*. Nashville, TN: Vanderbilt University Press.
Camnitzer, Luis. 2007. *Conceptualism in Latin American Art: Didactics of Liberation*. Austin, TX: University of Texas Press.
Carpentier, Alejo. 1994. "Prólogo." In *El reino de este mundo*. San Juan, Puerto Rico: Editorial de la Universidad de Puerto Rico. First published in 1945.
Charún-Illescas, Lucía. 2001. *Malambo*. Lima: Universidad Nacional Federico Villarreal, Editorial Universitaria.
Cobb, Martha. 1979. *Harlem, Haiti, and Havana: A Comparative Critical Study of Langston Hughes, Jacques Roumain, Nicolas Guillén*. Washington DC: Three Continents Press.
*Damisela*. 2006. "Gabriel de la Concepción Valdés 'Plácido.'" www.damisela.com/literatura/pais/cuba/autores/placido/index.htm.
Davis, Miles and Quincy Troupe. 1989. *Miles, The Autobiography*. New York, NY: Simon and Schuster.
DeCosta, Miriam. 1977. *Blacks in Hispanic Literature*. Port Washington, NY: Kennikat Press.
DeCosta-Willis, Miriam, ed. 2003. *Daughters of the Diaspora: Afra-Hispanic Writers*. Kingston: I. Randle.
Degregori, Carlos Iván, ed. 2000. *No hay país más diverso: Compendio de antropología peruana*. Lima, Peru: Instituto de Estudios Peruanos.
Douglass, Frederick. 1845. *Narrative of the Life of Frederick Douglass: An American Slave*. Boston: Anti-Slavery Office. www.gutenberg.org/files/23/23-h/23-h.htm.
Du Bois, W. E. B. 1999. *The Souls of Black Folk*, edited by H. L. Oliver. New York, NY: W. W. Norton.

Duncan, Quince. 1993. *Una canción en la madrugada*. San Jose: Editorial Costa Rica.

——— 2004. "El Afrorealismo, una dimensión nueva de la literatura latinoamericana." *Revista Virtual Istmo*. http://istmo.denison.edu/n10/articulos/afrorealismo.html.

——— 2007. *Un mensaje de Rosa*. San José, Costa Rica: Editorial Universidad Estatal a Distancia.

——— 2014. *A Message from Rosa*. Bloomington, IN: Palibrio.

Edwards, Brent Hayes. 2001. "The Uses of Diaspora." *Social Text* 19, 1–66: 45–73.

Flaherty, Alice. 2004. *The Midnight Disease: The Drive to Write, Writer's Block, and the Creative Brain*. Boston: Houghton Mifflin.

Gates, Henry Louis, Jr. 1988. *The Signifying Monkey: A Theory of Afro-American Literary Criticism*. New York, NY: Oxford University Press.

Handelsman, Michael. 2015. "Situando a Charlie 'Bird' Parker entre Julio Cortazar y Juan Montano. Una lectura de pertenencias." *Revista de Crítica Literaria Latinoamericana* 41, 81: 109–28.

Henao Restrepo, Dario. 2010. "Prólogo: Los hijos de Changó. La epopeya de la negritud en América." In *Changó, el Gran Putas*, edited by Manuel Zapata Olivella, 11–29. Bogotá: Ministerio de Cultura.

Hernández Cruz, Víctor. 1985. "You Gotta Have Your Tips on Fire." *Mainland: Poems*. New York, NY: Random House.

Hyland, Richard. 2013. "Richard Hyland on Vachel Lindsay's 'The Congo.'" https://jacket2.org/commentary/richard-hyland-vachel-lindsays-congo.

Isaacs, Jorge. 1867. *María*. Bogotá.

Jackson, Richard. 1979. *Black Writers in Latin America*. Albuquerque, NM: University of New Mexico Press.

——— 1980. *The Afro-Spanish American Author: An Annotated Bibliography of Criticism*. New York, NY: Garland.

——— 1988. *Black Literature and Humanism in Latin America*. Athens, GA: University of Georgia Press.

——— 1989. *The Afro-Spanish American Author II. The 1980s: An Annotated Bibliography of Recent Criticism*. West Cornwall, CT: Locust Hill Press.

——— 1997. *Black Writers and the Hispanic Canon*. New York, NY: Twayne's World Authors Series.

——— 1998. *Black Writers and Latin America: Cross-Cultural Affinities*. Washington DC: Howard University Press.

Jacobs, Harriet A. 1853. "LETTER FROM A FUGITIVE SLAVE. Slaves Sold under Peculiar Circumstances." *New York Daily Tribune*, June 2. docsouth.unc.edu/fpn/jacobs/support16.html.

Laviera, Tato. 1985. *AmeRícan*. Houston, TX: Arte Público Press.

Lewis, Marvin A. 1983. *Afro-Hispanic Poetry, 1940–1980: From Slavery to Negritud in South American Verse*. Columbia, MO: University of Missouri Press.

——— 1992. *Ethnicity and Identity in Contemporary Afro-Venezuelan Literature: A Culturalist Approach*. Columbia, MO: University of Missouri Press.

——— 1996. *Afro-Argentine Discourse: Another Dimension of the Black Diaspora*. Columbia, MO: University of Missouri Press.

2005. "Literature, Black, in Spanish America." In *Africana: The Encyclopedia of the African and African American Experience*, 2nd ed., edited by Anthony Appiah and Henry Lewis Gates Jr., 612–13. New York, NY: Oxford University Press.

2007. *An Introduction to the Literature of Equatorial Guinea: Between Colonialism & Dictatorship*. Columbia, MO: University of Missouri Press.

López Albújar, Enrique. 1928. *Matalaché: Novela retaguardista*. Piura, Perú: Talleres de "El Tiempo."

Lorde, Audre. 1984. "The Master's Tools Will Never Dismantle the Master's House." In *Sister Outsider: Essays and Speeches*, 110–13. Trumansburg, NY: Crossing Press.

Machado de Assis, Joaquim Maria. 1963. "Father Versus Mother." In *The Psychiatrist and Other Stories, translated by David Grossman and Helen Caldwell*, 101–12. Berkeley, CA: University of California Press.

Manzano, Juan Francisco. 1996. *Autobiography of a Slave*, edited by Ivan Schulman. Detroit, MI: Wayne State University Press.

Matto de Turner, Clorinda. 1889. *Aves sin nido (Novela peruana)*. Lima: Imprenta del Universo.

Morejón, Nancy. 2003. *Looking Within: Selected Poems, 1954–2000/Mirar adentro: Poemas escogidos, 1954–2000*. Detroit, MI: Wayne State University Press.

Morrison, Toni. 1993. *Playing in the Dark: Whiteness and the Literary Imagination*. New York, NY: Vintage Books.

Mosby, Dorothy E. 2007. *An Introduction to the Literature of Equatorial Guinea: Between Colonialism & Dictatorship*. Columbia, MO: University of Missouri Press.

2012. "Roots and Routes: Transnational Blackness in Afro-Costa Rican Literature." In *Critical Perspectives on Afro-Latin American Literature*, edited by Antonio D. Tillis, 5–29. New York, NY: Routledge.

Múnera, Alfonso. 2005. "Panamá, la última frontera." In *Fronteras imaginadas: La construcción de las razas y de la geografía en el siglo XIX colombiano*, 88–128. Bogotá: Editorial Planeta.

Nascimento, Abdias do. 1995. "Sortilege (Black Mystery)." *Callaloo*, 18, 4: 821–62.

Noel, Urayoán. 2014. *In Visible Movement: Nuyorican Poetry from the Sixties to Slam*. Iowa City, IA: University of Iowa Press.

Obeso, Candelario. 1877. *Cantos populares de mi tierra*. Bogotá: Imprenta de Borda.

Ortiz, Fernando. 1906. *Los negros brujos*. Madrid: Librería de F. Fé.

1940. *Contrapunteo* cubano del *tabaco* y el azúcar. Havana: J. Montero.

1986. *Los negros curros*. Havana: Editorial de Ciencias Sociales.

Palés Matos, Luis. 1937. *Tuntún de pasa y grifería: Poemas afroantillanos*. San Juan: Biblioteca de Autores Puertorriqueños.

Pereira Rocha, Elaine, and Nielson Rosa Bezerra, eds. 2015. *Another Black Like Me: The Construction of Identities and Solidarity in the African Diaspora*. Newcastle upon Tyne: Cambridge Scholars Publishing.

Pereda Valdés, Ildefonso, ed. 1936. *Antología de la poesía negra americana*. Santiago de Chile: Ediciones Ercilla.

Rodríguez-Mangual, Edna M. 2004. *Lydia Cabrera and the Construction of an Afro-Cuban Cultural Identity*. Chapel Hill, NC: University of North Carolina Press.

Roof, Maria. 2016. "The Nicaribbeans: African-Descended Writers in Nicaragua." *Cincinnati Romance Review* 40: 45–86.

Ryan, Marveta. 2001. "Border-Line Anxiety: Dominican National Identity in the 'Diálogo Cantado.'" *Afro-Hispanic Review* 20, 2: 23–33.

"Seeking Acceptance from Society and the State: Poems from Cuba's Black Press, 1882–1889." In *Black Writing, Culture, and the State in Latin America*, edited by Jerome C. Branche, 33–60. Nashville, TN: Vanderbuilt University Press.

Sommer, Doris. 1999. "Who Can Tell? Villaverde's Blanks." In *Proceed with Caution When Engaged by Minority Writing in the Americas*, 187–201. Cambridge, MA: Harvard University Press.

Stanley, Avelino. 1998. *Tiempo muerto*. Santo Domingo: Cocolo Editorial.

Torres-Saillant, Silvio. 2014. "Tribulations of Dominican Racial Identity." In Roorda, Eric, Lauren Hutchinson Derby, and Raymundo González, eds. *The Dominican Republic Reader: History, Culture, Politics.* 423–26. Durham, NC: Duke University Press.

Valdés, Gabriel de la Concepción. 1856. *Poesias completas de Plácido (Gabriel de la Concepción Valdés)*. Paris: Librería Española. archive.org/stream/poesias completaooplgoog/poesiascompletaooplgoog_djvu.txt.

Valero, Silvia. 2015. "La construcción del 'sujeto afrodiaspórico' como sujeto político en *Un mensaje de Rosa* (2004) y *El pueblo afrodescendiente* (2012), de Quince Duncan." *Revista de Crítica Literaria Latinoamericana*, 41, 81: 83–107.

Vasconcelos, José. 1925. *La raza cósmica. Misión de la raza iberoamericana. Notas de viajes a la América del Sur*. Paris: Agencia Mundial de Librería.

Villaverde, Cirilo. 1882. *Cecilia Valdés*. New York, NY: Impr. de El Espejo.

Weber, Bruce. 2011. "Abdias do Nascimento, Rights Voice, Dies at 97." *New York Times*, May 20. www.nytimes.com/2011/05/31/world/americas/31nascimento.html.

Williams, Raymond. 1976. *Keywords: A Vocabulary of Culture and Society*. New York, NY: Oxford University Press.

1977. "Structures of Feeling." In *Marxism and Literature*, 128–35. New York, NY: Oxford University Press.

Wilson, Carlos Guillermo. 1991. *Los nietos de Felicidad Dolores*. Miami, FL: Ediciones Universal.

Zapata Olivella, Manuel. 1983. *Changó, el gran putas*. Bogotá: Oveja Negra.

1997. *La rebelión de los genes: El mestizaje americano en la sociedad futura*. Bogotá: Altamir Ediciones.

2010. *Changó, el gran putas*. Bogotá: Ministerio de Cultura.

Zárate, Patricia. "Afro-Panamanians in Jazz History." Unpublished paper.

# Afro-Latin American Art

## Alejandro de la Fuente[1]

It is a remarkable moment, barely perceptible, tucked at the edge of the image. Titled "Mercado de Escravos," the 1835 Johann Moritz Rugendas (1802–58) lithograph depicts a group of African slaves who wait to be purchased, while some potential buyers walk around and a notary or scribe appears ready to make use of the only visible desk (see Figure 10.1). In the background, a Catholic Church coexists harmoniously with the market and overlooks a bay and a vessel, perhaps the same ship that brought those Africans from across the Atlantic. While they wait, most of the slaves socialize, sitting around a fire. Others stand up, awaiting their fate, between resignation and defiance. One slave, however, is doing something different: he is drawing on a wall, an action that elicits the attention of several of his fellow slaves (see Figure 10.1A).

What was this person drawing on the wall? What materials was he using? Who was his intended audience? Did these drawing partake of the graphic communication systems developed by some population groups in the African continent? Was he drawing one of the cosmograms used by the Bantu people from Central Africa to communicate with the ancestors and the divine? (Thompson 1981; Martínez-Ruiz 2012). Was he leaving a message for other Africans who might find themselves in the same place at

[1] I gratefully acknowledge the comments, suggestions, and bibliographic references that I received from Paulina Alberto, George Reid Andrews, David Bindman, Raúl Cristancho Álvarez, Thomas Cummins, Lea Geler, María de Lourdes Ghidoli, Bárbaro Martínez-Ruiz, and Doris Sommer. Special thanks to Emanoel Araujo and his team for sharing materials about their work. My students and collaborators Laura Correa Ochoa, Cary García Yero, Angélica Sánchez Barona, and Miari Stephens read the manuscript, asked poignant questions, and made numerous suggestions.

FIGURE 10.1 Johann Moritz Rugendas, *Mercado de Escravos*, 1835, lithograph. Courtesy of Fine Arts Library, Harvard University.

some point in the future? The slave seems to be drawing a ship, perhaps a slave ship, but this representation may well be a function of Rugenda's own expectations.

We may never be able to answer these questions, or to rescue the visual representations that the Africans arriving in the New World used to cope with the uprootedness, isolation, and despair produced by enslavement and the middle passage. What the Rugendas lithograph does capture, regardless of its romantic undertones, is how even the most dehumanized circumstances, the moment in which slaves were traded as commodities, were "punctuated by . . . episodes of resistance" (Johnson 1999, 9) and by the slaves' attempts to counteract how they were being represented by others.

As slaves confronted the unknown and sought to shape their circumstances, re-create lost worlds, and construct new imaginaries, they engaged in art. Mackandal's brave new world, a world without masters, was, at least according to Alejo Carpentier (2006, 24), contained in "an account book stolen from the plantation's bookkeeper, its pages showing heavy signs drawn in charcoal." Afro-Cuban carpenter José Antonio Aponte, the leader of a famous anti-colonial, abolitionist revolt, was also

FIGURE 10.1A Rugendas, *Mercado de Escravos*, detail.

an artist. Aponte's views about history, justice, race, and freedom were articulated in a "book of paintings" populated by black kings, soldiers, and mythical creatures. The book has not been found, but colonial officials in early nineteenth-century Cuba used it to ascertain Aponte's intentions and were terrified by his images and collages (Palmié 2002; Childs 2006). And in his famous slave autobiography, Juan Francisco Manzano (1996, 67–68) remembered with sadness the day that his father "took away [his] box of colors," "prohibited [him] from taking up [his] paint brushes," and destroyed an image that Manzano had painted, in which a joyful witch was helping a sad-looking demon. Manzano does not elaborate on the reasons behind his father's actions, but it is possible that he perceived rebelliousness and anticipated danger in his son's pictorial musings. What did Manzano's witch and demon look like?

Conflicts over representation and authorship lie at the heart of what we may term Afro-Latin American art. Most of the art produced by the

Afrodescendants themselves, particularly prior to the twentieth century, has been lost. This would include the vast body of ritual artifacts produced by the Africans to support themselves and to cope with enslavement. As with the Rugendas lithograph, we are frequently unable to ascertain the identity, personal histories, aspirations, and training of the producers of such artifacts, which hold a foundational place in Afro-Latin American art. We know that Africans were able to reconstruct kinship networks and cultural practices in the colonies. Religious practices, customs, spirituality, beliefs, and musical forms survived the middle passage and were reconstituted under enslavement (Thornton 1998; Sweet 2003). Music, rituals, and the transmission of knowledge implied the production of instruments, representations, and ritual objects – that is, they sustained artistic creativity, often in hidden spaces. As art historian Leslie King-Hammond states, "artistic innovation" was key to the constitution of "safe and sacred 'spaces of blackness'" where a new sense of identity could be nourished in the New World (2008, 58). The widespread belief that colonial blacks or people of color were talented craftsmen and artists (Arrate 1949; Araujo 2010, 1:16; Alacalá 2014, 32) is probably anchored not only on Iberian associations between manual labor and dishonor, but on the skills and sensibilities of the Africans who arrived in the Americas. Slave owners contributed to the development of these skills, as they placed young slaves as apprentices with master artists, many of whom were themselves of African origin or descent. Traditional African techniques and visual cues found their way into colonial societies, contributing to the functionality and aesthetics of a variety of sumptuary and common-use objects. Even if these traces are not always easily identifiable, they must be taken into account as we seek to conceptualize Afro-Latin American art. The important work done by scholars of Afro-diasporic visual cultures represents a fundamental contribution to these studies (Thompson 1981, 1983; Blier 1995; Lawal 2004; Martínez-Ruiz 2010, 2012, 2013).

One possible approach to this question identifies the art of the various Afro-Latin American populations of the region with the personal and racial background of the creators. In this view, Afro-Latin American art is the art produced by people of African descent, regardless of theme, inspiration, or purpose. Emanoel Araujo's pathbreaking exhibit, *A Mão Afro-Brasileira*, organized to reflect on the centennial of abolition in Brazil (1988), is perhaps one of the best articulations of this view (see Figures 10.2 and 10.3). The exhibit did not link "Afro-Brazilian" art to any particular expression, theme, epistemology, or school, but to the artists' ancestry.

FIGURE 10.2 *A Mão Afro-Brasileira I*, exhibition poster, 1988. Courtesy of Emanoel Araujo.

FIGURE 10.3 *A Mão Afro-Brasileira III*, exhibition poster, 1988. Courtesy of Emanoel Araujo.

All the participants, including the curator, were widely perceived to be black. As Araujo (2010, 1:15) explains, his goal was to search for concrete illustrations of the "cultural contributions of blacks and their descendants to our arts since the arrival of the first groups of slaves in Portuguese America."

Araujo's *The Afro-Brazilian Touch* sought to conceptualize the Afro-diasporic art of Brazil away from the racially tinged *arte negra* of the past, a label that was infused with primitivist and derogatory meanings associated with the European gaze on African and other world cultures (Cleveland 2013, 12). Furthermore, his vision of what constituted Afro-Brazilian culture was capacious enough to include not only historical references to the links between African cultures and Brazil, but also contemporary art forms that did not explicitly comment on traditional African cultural forms, such as religion.

By 1988, however, the term *Afro* was widely used to denote a wide variety of cultural expressions, processes, and practices. Although linked to populations of African descent, these practices made reference to processes of creolization, hybridization, syncretism, and cultural nationalization that could not be reduced to the creativity of a racially defined group, a move that some critics and scholars criticized as essentialist (Angola and Cristancho Álvarez 2006; Conduru 2012, 9). Indeed, a definition of Afro-Latin American art tied to the ancestry of its creators would not only imply an endorsement of the primacy of racial genealogies, but would likewise negate the Africans' own abilities to borrow, appropriate, and re-create elements of European cultures. Afro-Latin American art cannot be conceived outside the (asymmetrical, to be sure) processes of exchange, recognition, and borrowing that took place in colonial societies, not only between the Africans and the Europeans, but among Africans of different origins as well. Recognition means, precisely, knowing again – a fundamentally creative process. Even in areas inhabited by large contingents of Africans from the same region or linguistic family, borrowings and learning were unavoidable, as the Africans were forced to experiment with new materials and tools and to produce in the context of new communities, environments, and constraints.

That is why some scholars favor definitions of *Afro* art centered on thematic elements and influences. Some, like anthropologist Mariano Carneiro da Cunha, highlight the connections between Afro-Brazilian religions and art. Cunha (1983, 994) defines "Arte afro-brasileira" as a "conventional artistic expression that plays a role in the cult of the Orixas or deals with a subject related to the cult." Curator and anthropologist Kabengele Munanga (2000, 104) concurs with this position, noting that "the first form of real Afro-Brazilian art is a ritual, religious art." Others, however, include secular expressions as well. Brazilian anthropologist Marta Heloísa Leuba Salum (2000, 113), for instance, conceptualizes Afro-Brazilian art as a contemporary phenomenon "encompassing any expression in the visual arts that recaptures, on one hand, traditional African aesthetics and religiosity, and, on the other, the socio-cultural context of blacks in Brazil."

A definition of Afro–Latin American art would then combine thematic and authorial elements. First, following Araujo's lead, the label would include artworks produced by Africans and by people of African descent in the region, regardless of theme, style, or influence. The known corpus of this production is considerably richer for the twentieth and twenty-first centuries than for previous periods, but we do have information about some artists of African descent in the colonial period and the nineteenth century. The artistic production of maroon communities would be included in this group (Price and Price 1999). African background was fundamental in the constitution and organization of runaway communities, which provided a safe haven for the proliferation of African artistic practices (Thornton 1998). Yet these communities could not survive in total isolation and incorporated materials, references, and techniques from their surrounding world, including those linked to indigenous groups. As Sally and Richard Price argue, "the arts of the Maroon represent a unique balance of continuity and change that makes them, in the fullest sense, Afro-American" (1999, 277).

Second, Afro-Latin American art would encompass works that either claim or display African influences, particularly but not exclusively in the areas of religion, music, and dance, regardless of the ancestry and personal circumstances of the author. Finally, a significant body of Afro-Latin American art encompasses works that comment on blackness and on issues of race, difference, and nation in the region. With deep roots in the colonial period, this production has processed anxieties concerning purity and miscegenation; channeled ethno-racial conflicts over questions of inclusion and access to resources; and contributed to the development of racial imaginaries that portray Latin American nations as racially homogenous, usually through the metaphor of *mestizaje* or *mestiçagem*.

This capacious definition of Afro-Latin American art includes representations that could be characterized as openly racist, as well as those that celebrate blackness as "a reference point against which whiteness and a future of whitened modernity could be defined" (Wade 2001, 855). It conceives Afro-Latin American art as a distinctive discursive space where multiple, contradictory visions of race, origin, difference, and nation are articulated and debated through a variety of visual media. Afrodescendant artistic producers represent a distinct and fundamental voice in these debates, but their creative work cannot be placed outside broader processes of colonialism, slavery, and imperial expansion.

This conceptualization of Afro-Latin American art has important disciplinary implications as well. Anchored in Parisian fascinations with primitivism, the study of black art or *l'art nègre* was frequently the domain of anthropologists preoccupied with questions of cultural survival and ethnic origins. As physician and ethnologist Raimundo Nina Rodrigues (1904) asserted in his pioneer study of "black sculptures" in Brazil, such pieces had "real ethnographic value" and represented "a phase in the development of [the country's] artistic culture." Some of the best-known scholars of the African presence in Latin America (Fernando Ortiz 1906, 1952–1955; Arthur Ramos 1946; Pierre Verger 2000) worked in this tradition. By contrast, the study of Afro-Latin American art, in any of its national variants, is preoccupied primarily with the artistic production of Afrodescendants and with the thematic approaches previously discussed. As sources, images can be used to raise different, perhaps new, questions. Their study is undertaken by scholars working on a variety of disciplines besides anthropology, including growing numbers of art historians, historians, and art critics.

This body of scholarship has increased significantly in the last few decades, in tandem with the rise of the Afrodescedendant movement in the region and the deployment of art as a weapon in the struggle against racism. Exhibits such as *A Mão Afro-Brasileira* in Brazil, *Queloides* (1997, 1999, and 2010–12) in Cuba, and the creation of Afro-Brazil Museum in São Paulo in 2004 are all important moments in this itinerary. Some of the questions addressed by scholars working on visual art, which I will discuss later in the chapter, connect with larger questions in Afro-Latin American studies. For instance, research on the influence of African aesthetics in the production of colonial art and objects, made in many cases by African slaves, speaks to wider debates about the ability of Africans to reproduce cultural systems in the Americas (Gomez 1998; Thornton 1998; Sweet 2003; see Chapter 12) and can benefit from recent scholarship that analyzes creolization processes within Africa (Ferreira 2012; Candido 2013). The study of visual representations of blacks during colonial times can add new perspectives to the analysis of the Iberians' perceptions of Africans and their descendants (Sweet 1997; Brewer-García 2015). A similar argument can be made about the development of nationalist iconographies after independence. Were images of black deployed for nationalistic purposes in ways similar to those of indigenous people, studied by Earle (2007)? In the twentieth century, the visual arts are central to debates concerning the content and meaning of processes of cultural nationalization (Martínez 1994; Moore 1997; Chasteen 2004; Andrews 2007; Hertzman 2013). Ideologies of mestizaje and racial fraternity found frequent and powerful articulation in visual arts, with social effects that are still open to debate. Also debatable, to end, is whether efforts to denounce racism through art can be dismissed as culturalist efforts (Hanchard 1994) or constitute effective means of social action.

This chapter offers a historical overview of Afro-Latin American art, as previously defined, since colonial times to the present. The chapter seeks to identify how this production changed over time, in tandem with broader shifts in the history of Afro–Latin America (Andrews 2004), to highlight some of the main contributions to this area of artistic creation, especially among Afrodescendant artists, and to suggest questions for future research. It seeks to delineate the contours of the known corpus of Afro-Latin American art and its serious limitations, which are grounded on utterly inadequate research into this production. The chapter does not use specific media (painting, photography, sculpture, installation) as a basis for analysis, although many of the artists discussed below worked on a variety of art forms.

## COLONIAL ART

Afrodescendants left important traces in colonial art, both as authors and as subjects of representation, in secular as well as religious art. As producers, they were particularly active in the religious sphere, as it was frequently through the labor of enslaved Africans that churches were built and chapels, altars, retables, and liturgical objects and images were made. The "making of altarpieces involved coordinating specialized artists, including sculptors, joiners, gilders, and painters" (Katzew 2014, 152) and it was not unusual for master artisans to own and to employ slaves as assistants and apprentices in their shops (de la Fuente 2008a). This allowed African workers to make use of a variety of skills and to insert their own interpretations and aesthetic sensibilities into such products, however difficult it may be to single out and to identify such contributions with any degree of precision. Indeed, the development of specific methodologies and the identification of sources that would allow us to study how

African visual idioms and techniques shaped the production of colonial religious art and other objects constitutes a fruitful area for future research (Conduru 2012). Archaeologists have made important contributions to the study of these aesthetic interventions. In Brazil, for instance, scholars have studied how body scarification signs and patterns used by some African populations were reproduced in pottery and pipes (Torres de Souza and Agostini 2012). In his study of two Jesuit wine-producing estates in seventeenth- and eighteenth-century Nasca, Peru, archaeologist Brendan Weaver (2015, 335) has found remains that allow him to argue that slaves chose to embellish some of their tools, including notably those for personal use, with "African stylistic elements." These archaeological studies open up new and exciting opportunities for further research into the aesthetic sensibilities and interventions of African slaves; scholars of Afro-Latin American art would benefit from studying their methods and results.

The famous mural of the Señor de los Milagros in Lima, dated around 1650 and attributed to an anonymous slave from Angola, is one of the earliest known art images produced by African slaves in the New World (Costilla 2015). The image was probably linked to the Andean god Pachacámac and became the subject of a broad popular cult (Rostworowski. 1998). In Brazil, the Rio de Janeiro–born Manuel da Cunha (1737–1809) represents one of the earliest known examples of a painter in the Americas who was born to an enslaved mother and also one of the first identifiable Afrodescendant artists to produce religious works. Thanks to the protection of a powerful patron, da Cunha obtained his freedom, studied in Lisbon, and returned to Rio, where he established a school and devoted himself to the production of religious paintings, portraits, and sculptures (Teixeira Leite 2010a). Also in eighteenth-century Brazil, but better known, are the examples of Antônio Francisco Lisboa (Aleijadinho) (1738–1814) and Valentim da Fonseca e Silva (Mestre Valentim) (c. 1745–1813), two mulatto artists that modernists would elevate in the 1920s to the status of foundational figures of Brazilian national culture (Andrade 1965).

A gifted architect and sculptor born to a female slave, Aleijadinho designed the church of São Francisco de Assis in Ouro Prêto and carved ornamentations in this and several other religious buildings, including pulpits, retables, choirs, chancels, and statues. Almost all of the artist's known works are of religious nature (Ribeiro de Oliveira 2010). He probably learned his trade from his Portuguese father, architect Manoel Francisco Lisboa, who immigrated to the Minas Gerais region around

1720 and who was responsible for the planning and execution of several important buildings in the region (Ribeiro de Oliveira 2000). Aleijadinho drew inspiration from, or, in the language of Brazilian modernists (Andrade 1928), cannibalized European engravings and architectural treatises to produce an original and highly personal synthesis that occupies a singular place in the history of Luso-Brazilian rococo. Aleijadinho is said to have made extensive use of African formal conventions (Cunha 1983) but other authors emphasize his stylistic debts to European influences, particularly to German rococo (Ribeiro de Oliveira 2010).

Unlike his contemporary Aleijadinho, sculptor, woodcarver, and architect Mestre Valentim received a formal education in Portugal and is mostly remembered today for his contributions to civil architecture and the urbanization of Rio de Janeiro. His earlier works (1770s), however, are mostly religious, including ornaments in the church Nossa Senhora do Carmo, and he continued to produce religious works until the end of his life, as exemplified by the carving of the altar of the church of São Francisco de Paula in Rio, which he executed between 1800 and 1813 (Pontual 2000). But it was as the planner and executor of major public works, particularly of Rio de Janeiro's Public Promenade or *Passeio Público*, that Mestre Valentim is remembered today. Guarded by an iron gate, this majestic park was inspired by European urbanization developments and filled with fountains, pavilions, terraces, waterfalls, and stone benches. Perhaps its most interesting innovation was Valentim's inclusion of local elements, particularly in the form of locally produced bronze statues celebrating tropical fauna and vegetation, which replaced the more traditional dolphins and tritons found in European parks (Ribeiro de Oliveira 2010).

Outside Brazil, Afrodescendant artists also made important contributions to the development of colonial art. Like Aleijadinho and Valentim, some of these artists are today remembered as key, even foundational figures of their respective national pictorial traditions. In the case of Puerto Rico, this perspective is illustrated by the figure of José Campeche (1751–1809) (Quero Chiesa 1945). The son of a freedman and a Spanish woman from the Canary Islands, Campeche was a gifted painter, woodcarver, architect, and musician who probably learned some of the basics of his various trades from his father, a gilder and church decorator who also played music in the cathedral of San Juan (Libin 2006; Temin 2006). As was usual at the time, ecclesiastical institutions and elite patrons commissioned most of Campeche's works, which were devoted to religious themes and portrayals of the island's colonial elite (Traba 1972;

Sullivan 2014). Despite his close personal connection to slavery, black subjects rarely appear in his paintings. When they do, as in his 1792 portrait of Governor Don Miguel Antonio de Ustáriz, they are placed in the background, as anonymous workers paving the way to Bourbon progress (Temin 2006, 164).

Contemporary to Campeche was painter Vicente Escobar (1762–1834), the son of pardo parents who were members of the upper echelons of the free colored community of Havana. Escobar's father and maternal grandfather were both officers in the Colored Militias in Havana and belonged to families with long and distinguished military pedigrees (Barcia 2009). Thanks to his family's networks and resources, Escobar managed to study at the San Fernando Royal Academy of Arts in Madrid and to establish his own atelier in Havana, devoted mostly to the production of portraits and religious paintings (López Núñez 1997). It is significant that Escobar obtained an appointment as a painter of the Royal Chamber in 1827, but only after getting a dispensation under the cédula of *Gracias al Sacar*, by which people of mixed parentage could obtain a certificate of legal whiteness (Twinam 2014). Although critics have described his work as formulaic and unimaginative (Méndez Martínez 2013), Escobar's claim to fame was guaranteed by Cuban novelist Cirilo Villaverde, who referred to him as "the famous Vicente Escobar" (Villaverde 2005, 55) in *Cecilia Valdés*.

Blacks also entered colonial art as objects of representation, both in religious and secular art. In addition to a handful of black saints such as St. Benedict of Palermo, Santa Iphigenia and Saint Martin de Porres, Africans were frequently included in representations of the adoration of the magi, which "acquired the status of a pictorial paradigm for an entire art industry" around the time of the European expansion into Africa and the Americas (Koerner 2010, 17). The dissemination of these images increased in the late sixteenth century across the Spanish empire and some representations did not cast blackness in a negative light (Brewer-García 2015). Blacks were occasionally represented as devout Christians, as illustrated by Guamán Poma de Ayala's *Cristianos Negros* (1615) and by José Campeche's *Exvoto de la Sagrada Familia* (ca. 1778), in which three fully dressed black women kneel piously before the Holy Family (Taylor 1988, 13; Brewer-García 2015, 117).

Representations of black Christians raise questions of belonging, creolization, and civility, but it was in profane art that those questions found a privileged space. As visual artists represented Africans and their descendants, they spoke to the tensions and anxieties that surrounded the creation of creolized, multiracial societies in the Americas. *Negros* did not fit comfortably with the metaphor of the two republics, Spanish and indigenous, which functioned as the organizing principle of colonial society. On the one hand the Africans and their descendants were deemed to be *gente de razón* and as such they were subject to the jurisdiction of the Inquisition. In at least some social relations, they were vassals of the Crown and given access to benefits such as *vecindad* (Bennett 2003). On the other hand, however, blackness was a debased and dishonorable social condition. Colonial authorities made significant efforts to equate blackness and African origin with enslaved status, which leads some authors to categorically state that blacks did not have access to vassalage (O'Toole 2012).

Painters and engravers processed these tensions concerning difference, inclusion, and notions of purity and lineage in a variety of ways. An early and remarkable example is that of *Los Mulatos de Esmeraldas*, a 1599 portrait of Francisco de la Robe, the leader of an African community in the Ecuadorian coast, and his two sons. Executed by an indigenous painter trained in the arts school of Quito, Andrés Sánchez Galque, the painting offers an extraordinary combination of visual cues to illustrate the lack of civilization of these barbarous subjects (indigenous facial gold ornaments, arrows) as well as their acceptance of Spanish rule, illustrated by their poise and clothing (Cummins 2013). The portrait is also an early illustration of processes of mixture and creolization, as the subjects combine European, indigenous, and African attributes. Francisco de la Robe was himself a *criollo* born to an African slave and an indigenous woman from Central America.

Although Sánchez Galque portrayed these individuals in ways that were legible to the King – the painting was commissioned as a gift for Philip III – it conveyed the exoticism of its distant colonial subjects. A similar sense of exoticism can be appreciated in the ethnic paintings executed by an otherwise very different artist, Albert Eckhout, who differentiated individuals according to origin, ethnicity, skin color, and levels of civility. Part of an effort by the Dutch West India Company to study and document the land and inhabitants of its newly acquired Brazilian colony in the mid-seventeenth century, the paintings of Eckhout portrayed several indigenous groups, blacks, and people of mixed Afro- and Indo-European ancestry. Missing, however, are portraits of Dutch and Portuguese subjects, which reinforces "the strangeness of the country" and the "natural history perspective" chosen by the author (Boogart 2012, 229–30).

These paintings also highlight a central feature of colonial societies and a key preoccupation of colonial art: heterogeneity. On the one hand these representations – of which the casta paintings of the eighteenth century are the most elaborate example – sought to capture the multiplicity of factors that produced a bewildering number of ranks, qualities, and social stations among colonial populations. Eckhout's rendering of a mulatto, for instance, differs from his indigenous and black subjects not only in skin color, but also in terms of clothing – a primary marker of difference in the early modern world (Wheeler 1999) – in his access to what Arnold Bauer (2001) called "civilizing goods" (musket, sword), and even in the surrounding background. Whereas commercial tropical plants (sugarcane) escort the mulatto, the semi-naked indigenous people are surrounded by the wilderness of the rainforest (Boogart 2012).

On the other hand, these visual representations marked the dividing line between Europeans and a creolized, diverse, multiracial, and increasingly mixed underclass. The casta paintings of the eighteenth century sought to convey precise information about different types and degrees of mixture, but they did so by reinforcing the association between "castas" and "mixture" in general. Perhaps because of their sheer complexity, these taxonomies conveyed the notion that a large portion of the colonial population was of mixed parentage and that the socially relevant line was not between different forms of mixture, but between a racially mixed Creole population and a small and allegedly pure elite of European ancestry. By the late eighteenth century the label "castas" was applied in Mexico to people of mixed descent regardless of origin (Cope 1994) and similar capacious and inclusive terms had emerged in other areas of the colonial world. In the Nuevo Reino de Granada, for instance, the multiracial lower classes were included in the category of *libres de todos los colores* (free people of all colors) (Rappaport 2014). The early casta paintings contributed to the rise and consolidation of new criollo feelings and identities in New Spain during the seventeenth century and conveyed a certain pride about the land and its peoples (Katzew 2004; Katzew 2014). In this sense they represented an early and precocious response to Europeans' disparaging views about the New World, an early articulation of an American vision in which mixture was not a mark of inferiority and impurity (Martínez 2008), but a point of pride.

The existence of a multiracial and racially mixed plebeian world was occasionally captured in other forms of colonial art as well. A folding screen produced in Mexico City circa 1660, for instance, represents the main square of the city as a space inhabited by laborers of various backgrounds and colors, including some Africans or Afrodescendants, "without any tension between the ethnic groups" (Fracchia 2012, 202). Likewise, the workers depicted in the background of Campeche's portrait of Governor Ustáriz (1792) appear to be a multiracial crowd in which blacks labor alongside workers from other backgrounds (Taylor 1988, 20).

Criollo elites would be able later to construct narratives of American mixture and harmony that built on these colonial precedents. Indeed, it may well be that discourses of harmony and mestizaje were first articulated in the visual arts, a point that requires further research and that would alter established chronologies of Afro-Latin American history. When issues of representation came to be discussed at the Cortes de Cádiz, the criollos countered Spanish concerns about mixture and disorder with discourses of interracial intimacy and harmony that decried casta classifications as the barbarous policies of a decrepit, crumbling empire (Lasso 2007). Colonial tensions surrounding difference, inclusion, social worth, and community were not solved by independence, but the elimination of casta distinctions and the dissemination of republican egalitarian ideals and practices created opportunities for the development of new imaginaries of race and nation. At the same time, notions of equality were promptly contested and circumscribed by a powerful new body of knowledge that anchored older notions of human difference in the new language of biology and, later in the nineteenth century, evolution (Fredrickson 2002). Scientific racism would generate a new and powerful language, including visual language, for discrimination and exclusion.

## INDEPENDENCE AND NATION MAKING

Although the wars for independence forced questions of race, origin, and belonging to the forefront of the political arena, historians of Latin American art have devoted minimal attention to the important question of how such tensions and debates may have been echoed by the visual arts. The dearth of research is particularly acute when it comes to representations of blacks, despite the well-known fact that Afrodescedendants made up a significant portion of both patriot and royalist armies. Their prominent participation in the wars allowed slaves and blacks to inject their own visions and aspirations into the political and legal agendas of the nations in the making (Ferrer 1999; Andrews 2004; Reales 2007; Blanchard 2008; Sartorius 2014; Echeverri 2016). Indigenous themes and allegories have received more scholarly attention, among other reasons because America was sometimes represented as an indigenous woman since colonial times (Ades 1989) and also because after independence indigenous civilizations were invoked as historical precedents to construct new genealogies for the emerging nations (Gisbert 1980; Earle 2007). Even in places with large populations of African descent that lacked indigenous people, such as Cuba, Amerindian images were deployed for nationalistic purposes (Niell 2016).

Afrodescendants entered the iconography of the new nations either as part of the vast patriotic iconography that sought to celebrate the heroes of independence, through abolitionist art or, most frequently, through the romantic and ethnographic gaze of foreign traveling artists and scientists who visited the region during the nineteenth century. The postindependence years were not only years of self-exploration and nationalist myth-making, but also of intense exploration by outsiders bent on depicting and translating the new, exotic republics to the world (Catlin 1989). With roots in colonial representations, the views of scientific and traveling artists frequently adopted the language of "types," by which different human groups were classified using a variety of physical, phenotypical, cultural, and environmental attributes. Such classification efforts were anchored in bodies of biological and racial knowledge that allocated different civilizational worth and mental abilities to different groups. Similar concerns and ideas informed the production of *costumbristas*, local artists interested in capturing local colors, customs, and costumes.

Since a relatively large number of people of African descent rose to positions of prominence within the patriot armies, it is not surprising that at least some of them were subsequently memorialized among the heroes and martyrs of independence. This process, however, was not free from conflict, as some of the most prominent black patriots were conveniently whitened in order to insert them among the founders of the new nations. Among these was patriot and statesman Vicente Guerrero, who was president of Mexico in 1829. Representations of Guerrero vary, depending on the purpose of the artist. Those who sought to portray him as a member of the nation's military and political elite tended to lighten his complexion, offering a whitened version of Guerrero. Those who sought to portray the individual, however, tended to represent him as a person of mixed race, with a darker complexion similar to that of many Mexicans of African descent (Ballesteros Páez 2011).

Like Guerrero, other Afrodescendant patriots were visually inserted in the pantheon of the martyrs of independence during the nineteenth century even though (or perhaps because) they fell victim to the racial conflicts and tensions that frequently surrounded processes of nation making. Many of these figures were represented posthumously as part of broader efforts to construct a historical genealogy for the new republics. Examples of this iconography would include the portraits of Admiral José Prudencio Padilla and Colonel Leonardo Infante, created in the 1870s–1880s by nationalist painter and historian Constancio Franco Vargas (1842–1917), or the portrait of the Venezuelan General Manuel Carlos Piar, authored by Pablo Hernández (1890–1928), probably in the early twentieth century. Neither Padilla nor Piar nor Infante died in combat. Rather, they were subsequently executed by their former comrades in arms, who frequently opposed the social ascent of individuals of mixed and Afrodescendant ancestry (Helg 2004; Lasso 2007; Reales 2007).

The creation of a visual register of the heroes of independence in South America owes much to the work of José Gil de Castro (1785–1841), an Afro-Peruvian painter who has been rightly termed "the painter of liberators" (Majluf et al. 2012). The legitimate son of a free pardo and a black freedwoman, Gil de Castro painted some of the best-known images of the heroes of independence, from Simón Bolívar or José de San Martín to Bernardo O'Higgins. He also authored the best-known portrait of José Olaya, an Afro-Peruvian courier who served the republican forces and was executed by the Spaniards in 1823. Gil de Castro's representation of Olaya is fully dignified and lauds his courage and service to the homeland.

Born in Lima, Gil de Castro produced some of his work in Chile, where he joined the famous regiment of Infantes de la Patria, a military formation composed by free pardos (Blanchard 2008). Despite achieving prominence as a republican painter and despite his own efforts to distance himself from a family background that was painfully close to slavery, Gil de Castro died in obscurity and was later dismissed as a minor painter, graphically described as "el negro Jil" (Majluf 2015, 49).

Another Afro-Peruvian artist, Francisco "Pancho" Fierro (ca. 1807–79) made a fundamental contribution to documenting black patriotism after independence (see portrait in Figure 10.4). The son of a slave mother and a white criollo who grew up as a free mulatto in Lima (León y León 2004), Fierro's watercolors depict black participation in processions and other public displays of support for independence and the republic. In 1821, the same year that José de San Martín proclaimed the independence of Peru, Fierro produced several images that captured Afro-Peruvian support for independence. Particularly interesting is a trilogy devoted to the "civic processions of blacks" on occasion of the declaration of

FIGURE 10.4 Estudio Courret Hermanos, Lima, Peru, *Portrait of Francisco "Pancho" Fierro*, ca. 1870–80. Courtesy of Fine Arts Library, Harvard University.

independence, analyzed by Melling (2015). The trilogy depicts black subjects of a variety of socioeconomic backgrounds – as inferred by their clothing and poise – as well as of various gender and age categories. Some are barefoot, others are clothed in middle-class garb, wearing hats and walking canes. What unites all these characters is their celebratory tone, as indicated by the festive nature of the procession and the display of flags and other symbols of republican allegiance.

The characters in the trilogy appear to be all Afro-Peruvian, but other Fierro watercolors that speak to issues of patriotism and citizenship depict cross-racial crowds. In another watercolor probably produced around the same date as the trilogy (1821), Fierro displays a patriot soldier holding the effigy of Saint Rosa, a symbol of independence, surrounded by a crowd of men and women of various ethnic and racial backgrounds (see Figure 10.5). The crowd is clearly celebrating, as indicated by the dancing and by the accompanying fireworks.

It is difficult to determine whether some of the Afrodescendant subjects portrayed in these and other images were enslaved. As Melling (2015, 192)

FIGURE 10.5 Pancho Fierro, *Effigy of Saint Rosa of Lima*, ca. 1821, watercolor on paper. Courtesy of Fine Arts Library, Harvard University.

notes, "the range of black types portrayed indicates that they would potentially be representative of a variety of occupations ... they may also be free, slaves, *libertos* or any combination of these." The wars of independence dealt a significant blow to slavery across much of Latin

America, but the road to emancipation proved to be much longer and tortuous than many of the slaves who participated in the wars probably anticipated. In areas where conflict was minimal, such as Brazil or in the Spanish colonies of the Caribbean – Cuba and Puerto Rico – slavery actually expanded, fueling the development of plantation agriculture. This expansion took place in an adverse international context, however, as abolitionist forces gained steady ground throughout the century.

Abolitionists used print culture to disseminate their message and believed that "images were very effective tools to proselytize their cause" (Patton 1998, 75). Such images sought to humanize blacks and appealed to the public's sentiments and to their sympathy for fellow humans. Examples of this genre exist in Latin America, as illustrated by the work of Francisco Oller (1833–1917) in Puerto Rico (Sullivan 2014; Temin 2006) and by Juan Jorge Peoli's (1825–93) sympathetic representation of an aging slave to illustrate Anselmo Suárez y Romero's abolitionist story "El Guardiero" in Cuba (Ramos-Alfred 2011). In Brazil, abolitionist Joaquim Nabuco described the massive graphic work of Angelo Agostini (1843–1910) in Rio de Janeiro's *Revista Illustrada* in the 1870s as "an abolitionist bible for those who do not know how to read" (Wood 2013, 136). By then abolitionist discourse and mobilization were in full swing in Brazil, but sympathetic representations of Afro-Brazilians circulated at least since the 1850s, when a leading newspaper in Rio, *Marmota Fluminense*, edited and owned by abolitionist Francisco de Paula Brito, published a sympathetic portrait of the enslaved sailor Simão, who became famous for saving the lives of thirteen white individuals during a shipwreck. The lithograph disseminated in Brito's newspaper was based on an oil portrait authored by José Correia de Lima (1814–57). Exhibited at the Imperial Academy's 1859 salon, Correia de Lima's portrait offered a positive and dignified representation of the slave (Cardoso 2015).

Antislavery sentiments in Europe help explain why traveling artists and scientists produced a significant visual corpus of Africans and their descendants in Latin America. Representations of slaves and of blacks appear in the works of traveling artists such as Claudio Linati (Mexico), Johann Moritz Rugendas (Brazil, Mexico, Chile, Argentina, Uruguay, Peru and Bolivia), Jean-Baptiste Debret (Brazil), Thomas Ender (Brazil), Armand Reclus (Panama), Camille Pissarro (Venzuela), and Frédéric Mialhe and Eduardo Laplante (Cuba). Some of these representations were highly stereotyped and critical, but others were sympathetic and denounced slavery's violence. Linati's clearly pejorative representation of an Afro-Mexican couple from Alvarado, Veracruz, is an excellent example of the former. His *Nègre d'Alvarado etendu dans son Hamac, faisant travailler sa femme* (1828) depicts a black man who rests on his hammock while whipping his working wife. Of a different sort, but equally unsympathetic, are Laplante's representations of sugar slaves in Cuba. A celebration of the technologically advanced mills that made Cuba a world leader of sugarcane production, Laplante's lithographs present "anonymous slaves dressed in monochromatic uniforms [who] are either pegs in a mechanical system, visually indistinguishable from the actual machinery around them, or black dots scattered in a natural landscape" (Ramos-Alfred 2011, 104; García Mora and Santamaría García 2006). On the other end of the spectrum, however, are Debret's sympathetic depictions of slave life in Brazil. Debret not only captured how slaves performed every imaginable form of labor in the country, but he also denounced, in graphic and striking ways, the various forms of punishment and torture that slaves were forced to endure (Wood 2013).

Travelers and artists from within the region also engaged in efforts of recognition, representation and dissemination that frequently included people of African descent. In Colombia, Ramon Torres Méndez (1809–85), often labeled as the country's first national visual artist, produced a large number of watercolors that captured popular customs and "types," some of whom were of African descent (González 1986). The illustrators that accompanied the Comisión Corográfica, a nationalist scientific project that sought to map the territory of Colombia and to document the country's varied geography and riches, also produced visual representations of the Afrodescendant population of Colombia, particularly numerous along the Pacific coast (Villega Vélez 2011; Appelbaum 2016). In Ecuador, Afrodescendants are registered in the watercolors of musician, painter, and educator Juan Agustín Guerrero (1818–80), founder of a "democratic school" of art that privileged local landscapes, customs, and topics (Hallo 1981).

Many of these representations refer to generic and abstract "types," a discourse that early photography helped to consolidate (Catlin 1989). Even some individual portraits, like the *Retrato de Mulata* (1875) painted by Mexican artist and educator Felipe Santiago Gutiérrez (1824–1904), who traveled to Colombia in the 1870s, seek to capture a socio-racial type rather than an individual. Gutiérrez's *Retrato* portrays a dignified, well-dressed, middle-class Afro-Colombian woman, but her individual identity remains buried under and subsumed by the "mulata" label

(Morton 2014; Vásquez 2014). By contrast, his portraits of white women frequently referred to individuals (Garrido et al. 1993). Only exceptionally did prominent individuals of African descent get individualized in nineteenth century paintings. Examples include Pancho Fierro's watercolor portrait of doctor José Manuel Valdéz, who was appointed Protomedicato General de la Republica, the top medical post of Peru, in 1830; Francisco Oller's portrait of Afro–Puerto Rican schoolteacher Rafael Cordero; and Rodolpho Bernadelli's (1852–1931) portrait of abolitionist and engineer André Rebouças (Temin 2006; Melling 2015; Cardoso 2015).

These artists created a body of work of significant historical value and left powerful and graphic testimonies about popular customs, celebrations, dress, labor activities, class distinctions, and gender and racial norms in the new republics. Latin American costumbristas are frequently credited with being the first exponents of a new, criollo nationalist art. Fierro, for instance, has been characterized as the first Peruvian artist who interpreted "the figure and soul of its people" (Sabogal 1945, 31). Torres Méndez is described as the artist who achieved "the pictorial emancipation" of Colombia (Sánchez 1991, 17). In Cuba, Victor Patricio Landaluze (1828–89) has been described as "the most clearly Cuban artist of the nineteenth century" despite his Spanish origin (Ramos-Alfred 2011, 162). Criollo art conveyed the image of plural, multiracial, and harmonious social settings that superseded the caste distinctions of colonial societies, thus contributing to the creation of new nationalist imaginaries that sought to reconcile republican notions of political equality with socioracial distinctions (Majluf 2008).

At the same time, costumbrista criollo artists displayed a fascination for the exotic and the popular that was frequently indistinguishable from the ethnographic gaze of traveling and scientific artists. Costumbrista images illustrated travel books and albums and shaped the perceptions and representations of traveling artists. Although frequently characterized as local, the costumbrista genre produced commercial images for the international market, trespassing "the national frontiers that the genre helped to construct" (Majluf 2008, 45). The images of the new nations were produced in dialogue with international markets, preferences, and ideas and in response to tourists' needs (Villegas 2011).

This dialogue took place in a context in which notions of racial difference acquired new scientific credence. Race explained not only individual differences, but the alleged backwardness of entire nations as well. "What we term national character," the Count of Gobineau

(1856, 31) wrote, "is the aggregate of the qualities preponderating in a community.... The same is the case with the races ... the black race is intellectually inferior to the white." On top of that, race mixture, so prevalent in Latin America, led to debasement of the superior white race and ultimately to degeneration. "If there is a decided disparity in the capacity of the two races, their mixture, while it ennobles the baser, deteriorates the nobler," explained Gobineau (1856, 159–60). By the late nineteenth century, American and European scientists had produced a significant body of research demonstrating that miscegenation resulted in "mongrelization" and decadence (Tucker 1994). Visiting Brazil in the 1860s, Swiss-American naturalist Louis Agassiz commented on the deleterious effects of racial mixture: "Let any one who doubts the evil of this mixture of races, and is inclined, from a mistaken philanthropy, to break down all barriers between them, come to Brazil. He cannot deny the deterioration consequent upon an amalgamation of races, more widespread here than in any other country in the world, and which is rapidly effacing the best qualities of the white man, the negro, and the Indian, leaving a mongrel nondescript type, deficient in physical and mental energy" (Agassiz 1868, 293).

Agassiz (1868, 124) noted the absence of "a pure *type*" among Brazilians, a loaded scientific concept that permeated the language and representations of local costumbrista and traveler painters (see Figure 10.6). This notion implied that humans could be divided and classified into discrete groups or categories and that group boundaries could be determined through a variety of phenotypical, cultural, and intellectual features. Artistic depictions of popular "types" echoed the racialized, scientific misgivings that were associated with the trope of human types and conveyed ambivalence about the Latin American nations' capacity for civilization and progress.

For instance, a comment published in a Bogotá magazine in 1852 apropos of Torres Méndez's aquatint *Champán en el Río Magdalena* (1851), which depicts black rowers or *bogas* transporting a white family (Torres Méndez 1860), noted that this was not the main form of transportation on the river and that steamboats, "that powerful agent of civilization," were "slowly replacing the barbarous and primitive system of the champanes and canoes" operated by the bogas (Sánchez 1991, 39). The representations commissioned by the Comisión Corográfica shared these civilizing concerns, which were tied to ideas of race. The Commission sought to highlight Colombia's potential and to attract white, European migrants that would develop the country's vast natural

Head of Alexandrina.

FIGURE 10.6 "Head of Alexandrina." "The adjoining sketch is a portrait of my little house-maid, Alexandrina, who, from her mixture of Negro and Indian blood, is rather a curious illustration of the amalgamation of races here." From Louis and Elizabeth Agassiz, *A Journey in Brazil*. Boston: Ticknor and Fields, 1868, 245–46. Courtesy of Widener Library, Harvard University.

resources (Villega Vélez 2011). Many of the "types" of Quibdó in the Chocó province, represented by the Commission's artists, are individuals of visible African descent who appear poorly clothed and barefooted (Hernández de Alba 1986). These individuals were placed beyond the Commission's racial improvement hopes, which were centered on the "absorption of the indigenous race by the European" and the formation of a "homogeneous, vigorous and well conformed population" (Villega Vélez 2011, 107). In Cuba, costumbrista painter Victor Patricio Landaluze constructed highly stereotyped images of Afro-Cubans and captured elite fears concerning the possible Africanization of the island after the mid-nineteenth century (Ramos-Alfred 2011). In Argentina, caricatures of grotesque black subjects were deployed to illustrate their barbarism and that of the Juan Manuel de Rosas regime, with which blacks were supposedly allied (Ghidoli 2016c).

Even Pancho Fierro's depictions of black patriotism and citizenship are burdened by stereotypical representations linking blackness with music,

dance, and entertainment. The characters participating in patriotic processions carry flags and other republican symbols, but they invariably
carry musical instruments as well, as if no other form of black political
demonstration was conceivable. The same images that celebrate black
citizenship, then, also introduce "the prevalent association of blackness
with leisure, entertainment and festive pursuits of a public nature in the
post-independence visual tradition" (Melling 2015, 190).

These anxieties concerning race, civilization, and progress had a deep
impact on cultural production and public policy in Latin America toward
the late nineteenth century, as many members of the elite felt that the
region's future depended on its ability to embrace European civilization
and whiten its population. To achieve these goals, they promoted two sets
of interrelated policies. On the one hand, many countries promoted
whitening through state-sponsored immigration programs that sought
to attract European settlers to the region. On the other hand, African
cultural forms were conceptualized as obstacles to progress, incompatible
with the creation of modern nations. Latin American white elites
launched what George Reid Andrews (2004, 118) has aptly called a
"war on blackness." In the 1880s, Afro-Cuban cabildos were prohibited
from forming comparsas – street carnival musical and dance formations –
and taking them to the streets. Brazilian authorities banned capoeira in
1890. The Peruvian church prohibited the "Son de los Diablos," an
Afro-Peruvian dance form captured masterfully by Pancho Fierro in
several watercolors, from being performed in religious celebrations as
early as 1817. Brazilian authorities launched "a kind of war" against
Candomblé, even if repression was neither consistent nor effective (Reis
2015, 145). Everywhere African-based religious practices were seen as
primitive, retrograde, and potentially criminal (Moore 1997; Andrews
2004; Feldman 2006).

In this context, the production of Afro-Latin American art other than
ritual art probably hit a low point. During the nineteenth century painting
was transformed, from a mechanical trade performed by low-class individuals, to a refined form of academic creation. Majluf (2015) notes that
not a single artist of African or indigenous descent can be identified in
Chile and Peru after Gil Castro. Pancho Fierro would be an exception, but
Fierro was a self-taught aquarellist, a minor genre compared to painting.
In the Rio de la Plata region, where a large population of African descent
lived by the time of independence, it is possible to identify only a handful
of Afrodescendant artists during the nineteenth century. In addition to
Fermín Gayoso (1782–1832), a late colonial portrait painter who was

born a slave but obtained his freedom, there is reference to three other figures: Juan Blanco de Aguirre (1855–92), Rosendo Mendizábal (1810–79), and Bernardino Posadas (1861–?). Little is known about their lives and work. Blanco de Aguirre studied in Florence with a government fellowship, opened a school of painting in Buenos Aires, and taught at the prestigious Colegio Nacional of Buenos Aires. Unlike the others, he also left an important body of written work, including several texts devoted to issues of race. The son of two free pardos, Mendizábal specialized in the production of hair art, a genre that was popular during the Victorian era, and devoted much of his time to politics. Posadas was a student of Blanco Aguirre who also taught drawing at the Colegio Nacional (Andrews 1980; Picotti 1998; Cirio 2009; Ghidoli 2016a, 2016b).

In Brazil, a few black and mulatto artists managed to graduate from the Imperial Academy of Fine Arts, transformed into the National School of Fine Arts in 1890, but their work conveys little sense of their ancestry and little concern for some of the social themes that had preoccupied the costumbrista painters. Indeed, some scholars and critics contend that the only way for these artists to survive was by embracing the dominant whitening cultural project under which they lived (Teixeira Leite, 2010b). In this predicament painters were not alone. All over Latin America, black middle-class individuals distanced themselves from Africa and from African-based cultural practices, seeking standing and respectability in openly racist societies (Andrews 2004; de la Fuente 2001).

These trends are perhaps best exemplified by the careers and works of two of the most successful and accomplished Afrodescendant artists of the period, the Rio de Janeiro–born Arthur Timótheo da Costa (1882–1922) and the Havana-born Pastor Argudín Pedroso (1880–1968). Both artists received academic training. Argudín attended the San Alejandro Fine Arts Academy, while Costa entered the National School of Fine Arts in 1894. Both gained some notoriety and obtained support to continue their education in Europe. Costa won a prize at a national art exhibit in 1907 and traveled to Paris to continue his studies there. In 1911 he returned to Europe, this time to work on the Brazilian pavilion at the Turin International Exhibit. Argudín traveled to Spain in 1912, with a fellowship from the city council of Havana, to study at the Royal Academy San Fernando in Madrid. Upon graduation in 1914, he moved to Paris, where he seems to have lived until 1931, when he returned to Havana (Marques 2010; Teixeira Leite 2010b; Comesañas Sardiñas 2008). In 1935, the "Cuban Negro artist" (*New York Times,*

Feb. 15, 1935) exhibited his work at the Harmon Foundation in New York City, thanks to the support of Arthur Schomburg, in whose house Argudín lived and whose portrait he painted.

Although it has been argued that impressionism had a limited impact on Latin American art (Ades 1989), both Costa and Argudín appear to have incorporated some of the language and the palette of French impressionists during their European travels. Neither artist appears to have seriously explored issues of African ancestry or social themes concerning race in their oeuvre, although Costa did devote several portraits to Afrodescendant subjects.[2] Costa also produced a *Self-Portrait* (1908) that "puts the viewer face to face with a serious-looking, twenty-six-year-old artist who brandishes his brushes fiercely, almost as a shield to defend himself against the envious slings and arrows sure to be launched in his direction after winning the travel prize to Europe in 1907" (Cardoso 2015, 502). The artist is properly clothed in middle-class fashion, but there is no visible whitening effort in the canvas. A later *Self-Portrait* (1919), however, shows a significantly less-defiant Costa who appears to be considerably lighter, if not white. It is a remarkable transformation, one that coincides with wider efforts by middle-class blacks in the region to escape from blackness (Cardoso 2015).

Whitening found one of its most coherent pictorial expressions in Modesto Brocos's (1852–1936) graphically titled *The Redemption of Ham* (1895). Brocos was himself an immigrant and his canvas depicts the successful whitening of a Brazilian family that in three generations of miscegenation has transited from black to mulatto to white. The image captures the centrality of sex and reproduction to national dreams of racial improvement, a process that constructed women's bodies as the sites where progress and modernity were literally gestated (Stepan 1991). The white father looks approvingly at his light-skinned baby, while the black grandmother looks up to heaven to say thanks for the redemption of her progeny. Whitening was also promoted through visual representations that clearly depicted black subjects as cultural and national outsiders, as exemplified by the Buenos Aires cartoons studied by Frigerio (2011) and Ghidoli (2016b, 2016c).

This fascination of Latin American elites with Europe had contradictory and unexpected consequences. On the one hand, the immigrants who did arrive in Latin America were Europe's working poor, not the cultured

---

[2] It should be noted, however, that Argudín's career and work are vastly understudied. A serious look at his work may change the assessment advanced here.

and allegedly superior "stock" imagined by elites. As these immigrants sought to make opportunities for themselves and their families in their new homes, they moved into the poor and working-class areas of Latin American cities such as São Paulo, Rio de Janeiro, Havana, or Montevideo. They joined multiracial working-class communities where African-based cultural forms such as music, dance, and religion were common. They moved into the Brazilian *cortiços*, the *conventillos* of Montevideo, and the *solares* of Havana. In those spaces they contributed to the processes of mixture that elites envisioned as the path to progress, but they also adopted local cultural forms, frequently of perceived African origin, to claim national belonging (Andrews 2007). Instead of cultural and demographic whitening, the integration of immigrants into Latin America resulted in cultural browning. Aluisio Azevedo captured this process masterfully in *O cortiço* (1890), where several of the novel's main characters are European immigrants who mingle with Afro-Brazilians, adopt local ways, and succumb to the "lascivious virus" of Brazilian culture (Azevedo 2000, 155).

Ironically, Europe also contributed to the reassessment of African-based cultural forms and practices in Latin America. Artists from the region frequently traveled to Paris to continue their studies and to absorb European culture, but in the process they encountered Paris's fascination with *l'art nègre*. To the white avant-garde that embraced "negrophilia," black-ness was a marker of their own modernity, even if their voyeuristic gaze helped to reaffirm Africans and their cultures as primitive and exotic. Afrodescendant artists made use of these spaces to advance their careers and to express their own visions of worth and modernity, but they frequently had to "fit primitivist projections that better suited the vanguard's taste for vitality, sexual potency, and things African" (Archer 2014, 136).

Paris made yet another important contribution: it provided a shared space where artists from all over Latin America came together and recognized each other. Paris was the place where it became possible to articulate "transnational connections stitching together racial and national schemas throughout the Americas" (Seigel 2009, 238). In the 1920s and 1930s over 300 artists from Latin America traveled to Paris and it was there that the first exhibit of "Latin American art" was ever held. This exhibit, the *Exposition d'Art Américain-Latin* (see Figure 10.7) at the Galliéra Museum (1924) brought together over 260 works by forty-two artists from Latin America, many of whom were Paris-based or had exhibited there before (Greet 2014). It was in Paris, and only in Paris, where artists such as Afro-Cuban painter Pastor Argudín could meet and

**VILLE DE PARIS**

- 15 Mars -
15 Avril 1924

*Paris –*

# MUSÉE GALLIÉRA

10, Avenue Pierre-1ᵉʳ-de-Serbie

# Exposition

# d'Art Américain-Latin

ORGANISÉE PAR

## La Maison de l'Amérique Latine

ET

## L'Académie Internationale

## des Beaux-Arts

# CATALOGUE

FIGURE 10.7  Musée Galliéra, *Exposition d'Art Américain-Latin. Catalogue* (Paris, 1924).

exhibit with Latin American luminaries such as Tarsila do Amaral (1886–1973), who completed her famous *A Negra* in Paris in 1923, and with Uruguayan Pedro Figari (1861–1938), who exhibited two of his candombe paintings at the Galliéra Museum exhibit, where Argudín also displayed his works. The organizers of *Exposition d'Art Américain-Latin* described the exhibit as a moment of self-recognition for the "nearly one hundred million men" of the region, whose "similar ethnicity, religion, historical tradition, customs, and democratic ideals" informed the collective will to shape "humanity's future" (Greet 2014, 216–17).

In this search for commonalities and in the urge to shape their future, Latin American intellectuals and artists turned to indigenous and African roots, reassessing their importance and value. What Paris admired as exotic is what Latin America was precisely made of. The alternative modernity that Negrophile Paris intellectuals searched for had been achieved already. Brazilian poet Oswald de Andrade, at the time married to Tarsila do Amaral, summarized the new vision beautifully in "Manifesto Antropófago" (1928): "Without us, Europe would not even have its wretched declaration of the rights of man. The golden age proclaimed by America. . . . We already had communism. We already had the surrealist language." Latin America was the future and this future was imagined, at least in part, through the exaltation, incorporation, and nationalization of black culture.

### MESTIZO DREAMS

As previously noted, the Creole art of the late colonial period and some of the patriotic art after independence anticipated visions of Latin American plebeian societies as multiracial and mixed. More elaborate ideas of racial mixture and blending as something quintessentially Latin American began to circulate in the late nineteenth century in various forms, and they were systematized into dominant nationalist visions in the 1920s–1940s. The two world wars raised serious doubts about the alleged superiority of European culture, including the racial science that linked mixture to degeneration and backwardness, a link much emphasized by American scholars. After World War II, racial science in general, including the very concept of race, came under serious scrutiny and was generally rejected (Barkan 1992; Tucker 1994). Indeed, by the time international agencies sought to understand how, in a world beset with racial conflicts and Nazi genocide, some nations had managed to create racially harmonious societies, they turned to Latin America, particularly to Brazil, which was seen as "one of the rare countries which have achieved a 'racial democracy'" (Métraux 1952, 6; Maio 2001).

The articulation of nationalist myths of mestizaje or mestiçagem and racial democracy is usually tied to the writings of a few prominent intellectuals such as Manuel Gamio, José Vasconcelos, Gilberto Freyre, Andrés Eloy Blanco, Jose Martí, and Fernando Ortiz. However, the origin of these ideologies is invariably linked to episodes of popular mobilization and to the intellectual contributions of Afrodescendant thinkers (Andrews 2004; Alberto 2011; see also Chapters 6 and 8). Although these were national ideologies, they were created in conversation with, and as creative reactions to, ideas of social Darwinism and scientific racism that condemned all Latin American nations to perpetual subordination and backwardness. At least in part, it was in response to allegations that "mongrel-ruled" Latin America was hopeless, as Lothrop Stoddard put it in *The Rising Tide of Color against White World-Supremacy* (1920), that intellectuals in Latin America began to speak of cosmic races and mixed, tropical civilizations.

National cultures were central to these debates. Whitening was always a demographic and cultural project and black inferiority was frequently explained in cultural terms. Because Latin American constitutions embraced notions of equality and legal impediments to citizenship and voting rights were not articulated in the language of race (Engerman and Sokoloff 2005), racism was experienced "not in legal form, but as a set of 'dogmas' about racial and cultural inferiority" (Alberto 2011, 36). Debates about race, equality, and nation were consequently waged in cultural spaces linked to music, dance, carnival, and literature (Moore 1997; Andrews 2004; Chasteen 2004; Hertzman 2013).

Such debates also found expression in the visual arts. Ideologies of mestizaje articulated myths of history and origins, but they were essentially utopian visions about Latin America's future. When Afro-Cuban poet Nicolás Guillén referred to "Cuba's soul" as "mestizo" in *Sóngoro Cosongo* (1931), he was referring to a historical process of national formation, but one that served as the foundation for a future nation: "it is from the soul, not the skin, that we derive our definite color. Someday it will be called 'Cuban color'" (Guillén 1974, 1:114).

The visual arts were a privileged space to weave these historical narratives about the future, a place where new identities could be visually represented and where tensions between the local and the modern, as well as inclusion and exclusion, could be negotiated. Although systematic comparative scholarship on this artistic production is lacking, the avant-garde movements that swept the region after the 1920s articulated discourses of race and nation that rescued the cultural contributions of African and indigenous groups and celebrated mestizaje and fusion as the very essence of the region. Even in countries where the whitening project was most successful, as in Argentina, representations of the "people" and "criollismo" implicitly acknowledged processes of mestizaje and racial mixing (Adamovsky 2016a).

In Brazil, the artists linked to the modernist movement in the 1920s and 1930s epitomize this new vision (Ades 2014; Conduru 2012). Even if these artists were not the first to represent black subjects (Cardoso 2015), they articulated a new national discourse grounded on racial mixture, racial pluralism, and the importance of black and indigenous contributions. Cândido Portinari's (1903–62) famous O Mestiço (1934), painted after his inevitable pilgrimage to Paris, is perhaps the best-known representation of Brazilian mestiçagem and racial democracy. Portinari's Brazil is linked to the dignity and strength of a racially mixed rural labor force that proudly displays its African heritage (Ades 2014). In Cuba, the Vanguardia of the 1920s and 1930s also sought to articulate a new national identity based on the recovery of black cultural forms and the celebration of mestizaje. Along with musicians and writers, visual artists embraced afrocubanismo, a cultural movement that identified cubanidad with its African roots (Kutzinski 1993; Martínez 1994; Moore 1997; Anderson 2011). Cuba's mestizaje was visually articulated by Víctor Manuel (1897–1969) in his *Gitana Tropical*, a 1929 canvas painted during a trip to Paris. Widely recognized as "the first classic of Cuban artistic modernity," the painting portrays a racially mixed woman who, in Victor Manuel's own words, is "a mestiza, a mulata, but I gave her the almond shape eyes of an Indian from Peru, Mexico" (Vázquez Díaz 2010, 92, 97).

Afrodescendant subjects were also represented in visions of mestizaje that were constructed primarily around indigenous contributions. The Mexican muralists, for instance, included black subjects in representations of the working class or to highlight the slave-like condition of the peon (Ades 2014). In Colombia, the artists of the *Bachué* group (1920s–1940s), named after a deity of the Muisca people, celebrated indigenous elements as a fundamental contribution to Colombian culture (Pineda García 2013). However, some of their paintings made reference to blacks, as in Ignacio Gómez Jaramillo's (1910–70) fresco *La Liberación de los Esclavos* (1938), part of his murals in Bogota's National Capitol.

Art historian Raúl Cristancho Álvarez describes this mural as "the first important work in Colombian visual arts that thematically is fully devoted to Afro-Colombians" (Maya Restrepo and Cristancho Álvarez 2015, 28). Like many artists of his generation Gómez Jaramillo studied in Europe, but he also traveled to Mexico in the mid-1930s to study the work of the muralists (Solano Roa 2013). The movement appears to have had a limited impact on the Colombian Caribbean coast, although the artistic production of this crucial area of Afro–Latin America is seriously understudied (Lizcano Angarita and González Cueto 2007). The early work of Cartagenero painter Enrique Grau (1920–2004) can be included in these artistic movements, especially his *Mulata Cartagenera* (1940) (Márceles Daconte 2010), although Grau himself did not recognize such influences on his work (Goodall 1991).

Rightly described as "sensual" (Rodríguez 2003, 16) Grau's *Mulata* illustrates some of the racial, gender, and discursive tensions that animated these avant-garde pictorial movements. Representations of black subjects varied widely. Despite their claims to originality, some artists echoed ingrained stereotypes and reproduced visual cues from the traditional costumbrista genre, presenting Afrodescendants as sensual, dancing, and musically-oriented subjects. Some titles – "The Negress," "A Mestizo," "Tropical Gipsy" – suggest that nineteenth-century idioms concerning *types* carried over into the 1920s and 1930s. Figari's renderings of candombe in Uruguay, Emiliano di Cavalcanti's (1897–1976) representations of Afro-Brazilian samba, Jaime Colson's (1901–75) *Merengue* (1938) in the Dominican Republic, and works by Eduardo Abela (1899–1965) and Mario Carreño (1913–99) in Cuba illustrate this approach (Cunha 1983; Martínez 1994; Ades 2014).

Interested in downplaying the histories of conflict and violence through which actual mestizaje took place, some of these artists celebrated mestiza women as symbols of national beauty, the site where racial conflicts were solved and national harmony achieved (Kutzinski 1993). In the process, they contributed to the "sexual objectification" (Conduru 2012, 58) of the black female and reproduced stereotypes about black sexuality and eroticism. Brazilian scholar Mariano Carneiro da Cunha (1983) even questions whether these representations should be included in studies of Afro-Latin American art at all.

At the same time, these artists, who have variously been described as modernist, avant-garde, populist, and nationalist, did what artists do best: they created opportunities for new imaginaries and social practices. On the one hand, several artists emphasized not only processes of racial fusion, but used their work to highlight class stratification and conflict (Ades 2014). A few artists of African descent, such as Alberto Peña (a.k.a. Peñita) (1897–1938) in Cuba, offered a radical reading of social realities. They painted strikes and unemployment, denounced the shortcomings of nationalist ideals, and highlighted the specificity of the plight of black workers (Martínez 1994; de la Fuente 2001). Most importantly, after the 1940s a new group of artists, building on the cultural spaces opened up by their predecessors in the 1920s and 1930s, began to study African-based religions seriously and to explore new ways to incorporate ritual knowledge, idioms, and objects into national art. As the pioneer and most accomplished of these artists, Afro-Cuban Wifredo Lam (1902–82), put it, they wanted to go further and create a new language that was authentically African, not a "pseudo" national art for tourists. "I refused to paint cha-cha-cha. I wanted with all my heart to paint the drama of my country, but by *thoroughly expressing the negro spirit* ... I could act as a Trojan horse that would spew forth hallucinating figures with the power to surprise, to disturb the dreams of the exploiters ... a true picture has the power to set the imagination to work, even if it takes time" (Fouchet 1976, 188–89, emphasis added). New figures, new pictures, new imaginations, all based on an authentic "negro spirit," that lived – could only live – in the popular sectors. Artists such as Lam took some of the avant-garde anticipations and dreams to their logical consequences. And such consequences, even when expressed in non-realist (surrealist) languages, were almost inevitably African.

The search for African authentic idioms was animated by three additional interrelated factors. First, African decolonization processes in the 1960s and 1970s created new hopes, new paradigms, and new spaces for Afro-diasporic cultural forms. International events such as the World Black and African Festivals of Arts and Cultures (FESTAC) in Senegal (1966) and Nigeria (1977), and the First Congress of Black Culture of the Americas (Cali, 1977), provided opportunities for artists from across the diaspora to come together and share their work. International organizations such as OSPAAL gave Third World decolonization and anti-imperialist movements a platform and a singular motif for artistic creation (Frick 2003). Second, the civil rights movement in the United States and the struggle against apartheid in South Africa provided powerful examples for international antiracist movements worldwide – movements that found in Africa a common link.

Last, but certainly not least, many black artists and intellectuals became frustrated with the shortcomings of populism, racial democracy, and mestizaje, and with the lack of real social change in their countries. As the ideologies of mestizaje transited from utopian dreams to state-sanctioned dogmas, they were deployed as tools to stifle popular mobilization and to delegitimize demands for racial justice. In countries such as Brazil and Cuba this transit produced contradictory consequences. On the one hand, it created some opportunities for artistic creation and facilitated the development of cultural and diplomatic relations with African nations. Artists from Brazil attended the World Conferences of 1966 and 1977 (Conduru 2009; Alberto 2011; Cleveland 2013). Cuba was apparently not invited to Dakar in 1966 (Kula 1976), but artists from the island did participate in FESTAC 1977 (Bettelheim 2013). On the other hand, attempts by black intellectuals to transform these international gestures into opportunities to debate racism and discrimination at home met with hostility and outright repression (Moore 1988; Alberto 2011; Guerra 2012).

The work of Afro-Brazilian activist, writer, cultural promoter, and self-taught artist Abdias do Nascimento (1914–2011) exemplifies some of these trends (photograph in Figure 10.8). Nascimento was a member of the Frente Negra Brasileira in his youth and the creator of the Teatro Experimental do Negro in 1944, an organization that combined cultural promotion with antiracist activism. By the 1960s, under the military dictatorship, Nascimento became a fierce critic of Brazilian racial democracy and went into exile (Alberto 2011; Hanchard 1994). It was then that he began to paint, developing a body of work that celebrated the vitality and currency of Afro-Brazilian Candomblé. He defined the central problem of his art as "the restoration of the values of African culture in Brazil" and, using language similar to that of Lam's, noted that his main concerns were not aesthetic, but "the spiritual vitality of the black race in my country" (Cleveland 2013, 48).

Other artists, in Brazil and beyond, have expressed similar concerns about spirituality, "the values of African culture," and artistic expression. In Brazil, following Cunha's (1983) lead, one would have to include artists usually grouped under the "primitive" and "popular" labels, whose work reflects African influences not only thematically, but also in terms of formal expressions. Also in this group would be artists whose production is squarely placed within ritual art, such as sculptor Mestre Didi (Deoscóredes Maximiliano dos Santos, 1917–2013) and those who articulate their Afro-Brazilian religious grounding through new formal solutions and visual languages. Among these would be Rubem Valentim (1922–91), São Paulo female artist Niobe Xandó (1915–2010), and Ronaldo Rego (b. 1935) (Salum 2000; Conduru 2009; Cleveland 2013).

FIGURE 10.8  Abdias do Nascimento (ca. 1950) Coleção Fotos Correio da Manhã, PH/FOT 35917. Acervo do Arquivo Nacional, Rio de Janeiro, Brasil. Courtesy of Paulina Alberto.

There are important parallels between the proposals and concerns of these Brazilians artists and the work of their peers in Cuba. In the 1960s and 1970s sculptors such as Agustín Cárdenas (1927–2001), Rogelio Rodríguez Cobas (1925–2013), and Ramón Haití Eduardo (1932–2008); sculptor and engraver Rafael Queneditt Morales (1942–2016); and painter Manuel Mendive Hoyo (b. 1944) created a body of work that was openly celebratory of Afro-Cuban Santería and its orishas. Like Nascimento in Brazil, these artists did not see African-based cultural practices as a root or a heritage, but as vital expressions of Cuban popular culture. Many of them appear to have shared the vision, articulated by Afro-Cuban intellectual and activist Walterio Carbonell (1961), that Santería represented a progressive intellectual and cultural force in the construction of Cuban socialist society. This vision, however, was not shared by Cuban authorities, who in the late 1960s actively discouraged all religious practices, and any artistic production related to them (Ramos Cruz 2009; de la Fuente 2013; Martínez-Ruiz 2013).

The search for African connections and black spirituality was not confined to Brazil and Cuba, although it found its most visible and numerous exponents in those countries. Afro-Uruguayan painters Ramón Pereyra (1919–54) and especially Rubén Galloza (1923–2002) devoted a good portion of their work to reconstruct and disseminate the religious practices and popular culture of Afro-Uruguayans. Pereyra was, along with Figari, the artist best represented in an exhibit commemorating the one-hundred-year anniversary of slave emancipation in Uruguay, organized by the National Commission of Tourism in 1942. Some of the titles of his works – *Barrio Negro*, *La Comparsa*, *Spiritual* – reflect his involvement with Afro-Uruguayan popular culture (Diggs 1952). He shared this trait with Galloza, the son of a black domestic servant who grew up in the working-class neighborhood of Barrio Sur in Montevideo. Galloza became a tireless promoter of candombe and other forms of popular culture, subjects that dominated his vast body of work (Olivera Chirimini 2001; Sztainbok 2008). Pereyra and Galloza were also activists involved in civil rights struggles for racial equality and cultural recognition in mid-twentieth-century Montevideo (Andrews 2010). The work of Carlos Páez Vilaró (1923–2014) was animated by similar concerns. In the 1950s, he opened his studio in one of the popular conventillos of Montevideo, which facilitated his immersion in Afro-Uruguayan culture and the production of a later body of works with explicit denunciations of racism and colonialism. For instance, one section of his famous *Roots of Peace* 1960 mural at the tunnel connecting the buildings of the Organization of American States in Washington, D.C., is devoted, precisely, to the "struggle against racial discrimination" (Kiernan 2002; Sztainbok 2008).[3]

In Colombia, the work of Afro-Colombian painter Cogollo (Herberto Cuadrado Cogollo, b. 1945) illustrates superbly how international anti-racist movements such as Black Power, and artistic influences such as Wifredo Lam's surrealism, shaped the work of individual artists elsewhere. Cogollo settled in Paris in the late 1960s and began a process of research and discovery of African cultural influences without Western filters that was very much akin to that of Lam (Fabre 1980; Rosemont and Kelley 2009; Medina 2000). This search resulted in the creation of a

---

[3] I thank Roberto Rojas, from the Department of Social Inclusion of the OAS, for showing me the mural, which is not easily accessible to the public.

personal catalog of "Afro-Caribbean symbols" (Márceles Daconte 2010, 225). In 1973, on the occasion of a personal exhibit at Galerie Suzanne Visat in Paris, Cogollo even defined himself as an African sorcerer, a "nohor" who had the ability to see and represent the entrails of others (Cogollo 1973).

It is probably not a coincidence that many of these artists were or are themselves of African descent and that many of them grew up in families and communities where African-based cultural practices were common. Lam was born in a sugarcane community and was exposed to Afro-Cuban religiosity since his childhood. Nascimento was the grandson of slaves. Mestre Didi, himself a Candomblé priest, grew up in a religious family in Bahia and was initiated at an early age. Mendive grew up in a Havana slum in a Santería-practicing family, Cogollo in the multiracial port city of Cartagena. Galloza grew up close to some of the conventillos of Montevideo, where Afro-Uruguayan culture thrived. Rego is white but is a priest in the Afro-Brazilian religion of Umbanda. Páez Vilaró was also white, but he worked from a conventillo and traveled extensively in Africa. For these artists, connections to Africa were personal, intense, and intimate, part of living, contemporary cultures that functioned as reservoirs against racism and prejudice. By the time black mobilization exploded in Latin America in the 1970s, 1980s, and 1990s, visual artists were already well positioned to play leading roles in the formulation of new demands for inclusion and justice.

## THE ART OF BLACK MOBILIZATION

The Primer Congreso de la Cultura Negra de las Americas that Afro-Colombian writer and activist Manuel Zapata Olivella organized in 1977 was not an isolated event. It was in fact one of the initial salvos in what would soon become a continental, transnational wave of black mobilization demanding equal access to material resources and to power. One of the central goals of the Congress was to affirm black culture in the Americas, but this agenda was linked to a more general discussion concerning racism and discrimination in the region. Intellectuals and artists such as Nascimento attended, while one of the sections was devoted to artistic creativity and headed by artist and folklorist Delia Zapata Olivella. Clearly, the organizers saw art and culture as platforms for demands and activism. Subsequent congresses were organized in Panama (1980) and Brazil (1982). By 1978 a national black political movement, the Movimento Negro Unificado, had been created in Brazil (see Chapter 7).

In part because many of the activists were themselves artists or intellectuals, or due to the fact that many civil rights organizations began as study groups and cultural initiatives, art and culture were always conceived as part of the movement. In some countries, such as Peru, Costa Rica, and Paraguay, activists demanded the designation of specific days for Afro-Peruvian, Afro–Costa Rican, and Afro-Paraguayan Culture. In countries with larger populations of African descent, such as Brazil and Cuba, artists-activists used cultural projects to denounce the persistence of racism, to revisit the memories of slavery and emancipation, and to highlight the shortcomings of mestizaje and racial democracy.

An early example of visual artists' involvement in debates about race and justice is that of Grupo Antillano (1978–83) in Cuba (see Figure 10.9). Founded by sculptor and engraver Rafael Queneditt, the Group came into existence after the so-called *Quinquenio Gris*, a "grey" period of neo-Stalinist censorship during the 1970s characterized by a dogmatic approach to culture in general and to Afro-Cuban religiosity in particular. The Group's foundational manifesto stated clearly that their raison d'être was to search for the Caribbean and African roots of an authentic Cuban culture. In this search, they claimed to build on a generation of previous artists, among them Wifredo Lam (who became honorary president of the Group and exhibited with them) and Afro-Cuban artist Roberto Diago (1920–55).

Grupo Antillano placed Santeria and other African religious and cultural practices at the very center of Cuba's national formation, a position that openly contested official characterizations of such practices as primitive obstacles in the construction of a modern socialist society. Furthermore, the Group engaged the sympathy and support of a large group of collaborators. Among these were not only key figures in Cuban visual arts, but also writers, musicians, historians, and art critics who shared their views and concerns about the African and Caribbean roots of Cuban culture. Prominent among these collaborators were some of the best-known Afro-Cuban intellectuals of the period: historians José Luciano Franco and Pedro Deschamps Chapeaux; ethnographers and ethnomusicologists Rogelio Martínez Furé and Odilio Urfé; musicians such as Martha Jean Claude, Mercedita Valdés, and pianist Rosario Franco; playwright Eugenio Hernández Espinosa; and Afrocubanista poetry performer Luis Carbonell. The Group built a true Afro-Cuban cultural movement and their exhibits became cultural and social events that transcended the visual arts. Their exhibits were also a searing critique of Cuban art academies,

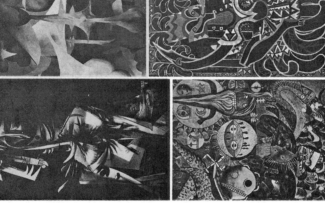

**Grupo**

Kubánský Dům Kultury / Praha
Kubánský Fond Kulturnich Statků
Ministersvo Kultury / Kuba
"Antiliska Skupina"
**1980**

FONDO CUBANO DE BIENES CULTURALES  MINISTERIO DE CULTURA

**Antillano**

**CASA
DE LA CULTURA
CUBANA/PRAGA**

**FONDO CUBANO
DE BIENES
CULTURALES**

**Exposición
Grupo Antillano**
Enero 1980

FIGURE 10.9  Exhibition poster, Grupo Antillano (Havana, 1980). From Alejandro de la Fuente, ed. *Grupo Antillano: The Art of Afro-Cuba*. Pittsburgh: University of Pittsburgh Press, 2013.

where new trends in Western art found a privileged space, and of a cultural bureaucracy that insisted on relegating black culture to the spaces of folklore (de la Fuente 2013; Ramos Cruz 2013; Bettelheim 2013).

Grupo Antillano took advantage of a propitious moment, as in the late 1970s the Cuban government became embroiled in the African civil wars and built new alliances in the Caribbean, especially with the New Jewel Movement in Grenada. Brazilian artists followed a similar strategy when, in 1988, they used the centennial of the abolition of slavery to highlight the persistence of racism and discrimination in their country. It was in this context that Araujo organized the exhibit *A Mão Afro-Brasileira*, mentioned at the outset of this chapter, which was accompanied by a profusely illustrated volume that highlighted the key contributions of Afrodescendants to Brazilian culture. The exhibit and the volume openly called for a new, Afrocentric and revolutionary art history of Brazil (Araujo 2014). Presented at the Museum of Modern Art in São Paulo, *A Mão Afro-Brasileira* offered the first comprehensive assessment of the artistic production of people of African descent in the country, from colonial times to contemporary art. Araujo would go on to organize other important exhibits of Afro-Brazilian art in the 1990s and 2000s (Cleveland 2013), and he would organize a new version of his own pathbreaking exhibit, *A Nova Mão Afro-Brasileira*, in 2014. In contrast to the original exhibit, *A Nova Mão Afro-Brasileira* highlights the work of a selected group of contemporary artists, including highly acclaimed artists such as Rosana Paulino (b. 1967) and photographer Eustáquio Neves (b. 1955) (Araujo 2014). Paulino's work was also featured, along with the work of Ronaldo Rêgo, Rubem Valentim, Niobe Xandó, Mestre Didi, Araujo, and others, in the "Arte Afro-Brasileira" section of the important *Mostra do Redescobrimento* exhibited at the São Paulo Biennale in 2000 (Salum 2000; Aguilar 2000).

Two additional curatorial projects are also connected to broader patterns of black mobilization: *Viaje sin Mapa* (2006) in Colombia and *Queloides* (1997–2012) in Cuba. Curated by Mercedes Angola and Raúl Cristancho Álvarez, two faculty members at the Universidad Nacional de Colombia, *Viaje sin Mapa* sought to offer the first comprehensive survey of "afro representations in Colombian contemporary art." Probably not coincidentally, the exhibit took place at a time when debates concerning how to count people of African descent in the Colombian national census were raging (Angola and Cristancho Álvarez 2006; Paschel 2013). *Viaje sin Mapa* was presented at the Luis Angel Arango Library in Bogotá and its main goal was to neutralize the invisibility that has traditionally affected black artists in Colombia. Cristancho went on to organize, along with Luz Adriana Maya Restrepo, *¡Mandinga Sea! África en Antioquia* (2013–14), an ambitious exhibition that sought to trace the impact of West African cultures in Antioquia and that looked at representations of blackness from the colonial period to the present (Maya Restrepo and Cristancho Álvarez 2015).

In Cuba, *Queloides* represented the angst of a group of young, mostly black artists as they experienced the collapse of the Cuban socialist welfare state in the 1990s (de la Fuente 2008a). "Queloides" are raised, pathological scars, a title that makes reference both to the traumatic effects of racism and to the widespread belief that the black skin is especially susceptible to developing these scars. The first exhibit, *Queloides I Parte*, was presented alongside an anthropology conference in 1997, organized by artist Alexis Esquivel and by art critic Omar Pascual Castillo (see Figure 10.10). A second, larger edition took place at the Centro de Desarrollo de Artes Visuales in Havana in 1999, thanks to the curatorial intervention of Afro-Cuban writer and art critic Ariel Ribeaux Diago (1969–2005). These exhibits received very limited state support and were ignored by the Cuban media, despite being unprecedented events in Cuban art. Because of this, in 2010 Afro-Cuban artist Elio Rodríguez (b. 1966) and the author of this chapter organized a new edition of the exhibit under the title *Queloides: Raza y Racismo en el Arte Cubano Contemporáneo*. It was the first and only time that the terms "race" and "racism" appeared in an art exhibit in Cuba (de la Fuente 2010; Casamayor 2011; Martín-Sevillano 2011). The artists participating in each of these exhibits have varied, but five of them – Manuel Arenas (b. 1964), Alexis Esquivel (b. 1968), Douglas Pérez (b. 1972), René Peña (b. 1957), and Elio Rodríguez – have participated in all of them.

Collectively, these curatorial projects have achieved at least two important goals. First, they have created opportunities for artists interested in issues of race and identity, including a growing group of Afrodescendant artists, to share and disseminate their work, in Latin America and beyond. Notably, this includes the work of a small but growing number of female Afrodescendant artists, who have traditionally been grossly underrepresented in the region's art scene. Second, the artists participating in these exhibits have articulated potent critiques of Latin American societies and contributed to make racism and discrimination socially visible. Their work can be located in, and be understood as, contributions to current debates concerning race, gender, and justice in the region.

# QUELOIDES
## I PARTE

Alvaro Almaguer

Manuel Arenas

Roberto Diago

Aléxis Esquivel

Omar-Pascual C.

René Peña

Douglas Pérez

Gertrudis Rivalta

Elio Rodríguez

José Angel Vincench

**CASA DE AFRICA**

Enero 1997

---

### PROLEGOMENO No. 1

El proceso de inter-acción cultural Africa-Europa en el contexto latinoamericano, y más específicamente, en el caribeño, o sea, el nuestro, como es sabido, estuvo condicionado por relaciones socio-económicas violentas (esclavistas), las cuales dotaron al propio proceso de integración cultural de una compleja especificidad de carácter traumático, que aun en nuestros días no deja de problematizarnos constantemente, pues dicho proceso es en la actualidad la imagen de un cuerpo con borrosas cicatrices y notables *QUELOIDES*, que precisan de una fina y sofisticada cirugía, que junto a los métodos más contemporáneos de lectura de los fenómenos culturales sea capaz de "esbozar" (finalmente) una "nueva" re-lectura de esta FRANKESTEIN (sincrética) que es nuestra cultura.

El MODELO multicultural es una tendencia que parece rimar con el desarrollo de los medios de homogenización macro-cultural, a la vez, que parece ser contrarrestada por ellos mismos esta ambigüedad le da una complejidad inusitada al fenómeno en sí, de ahí que sea tan importante desarrollar una comprensión actualizada de los MODELOS de HETERODOXIA cultural en sus sentidos más específicos, para luego contar con herramientas eficaces para el desarrollo ulterior de cualquier programa de emancipación o democratización cultural a escala global.

Es ya tradicional en el campo de las Artes Visuales en Cuba una preocupación de los artistas por acercarse a los procesos de integración (hibridación, o sincretismo) cultural desde un punto de vista etnológico, etnográfico y en el peor de los casos folklóricos (y/o folklorizantes); dar una visión "otra" desde un punto de vista sociológico es la preocupación fundamental de los artistas jóvenes aquí reunidos, para intentar manifestar una arista poco reflejada (explícitamente) por el Arte, pero que no por ello resulta menos sintomática a la hora de penetrar en el análisis de estos tópicos, y que por demás permite una postura de distancia crítica que posibilitan figurarse el problema como proceso continuo y presente. No como pretérito investigable.

Alexis Esquivel. Enero/1997

---

**PROYECTO Y CURADURIA**
Alexis Esquivel Bermúdez
Omar Pascual Cas'illo

**DISEÑO DE CATALOGO**
Orlando Silvio Silvera Hdez

---

**QUELOIDES I PARTE**, es una muestra que se integra de manera modesta al ENCUENTRO DE ANTROPOLOGIA DE LA TRANSCULTURACION, efectuado en el mes de Enero de 1997, en La Habana, CUBA.

---

FIGURE 10.10 Exhibition brochure, Queloides I Parte (Havana, 1997). From Alejandro de la Fuente, ed. *Queloides: Race and Racism in Cuban Contemporary Art*. Pittsburgh: Mattress Factory Museum, 2010.

## FUTURE AGENDA

Art has frequently been a force for social change, a space where new futures and agendas for racial justice become possible. That is why, in their *Éloge de la Creolité*, Bernabé, Chamoiseau, Confiant and Khyar (1990) argue that art is the key to "the indeterminacy of the new" and "the richness of the unknown." Afro-Latin American art has played a major role in the construction of new imaginaries of race and nation and made key contributions to Latin American culture.

This field is still in its infancy, however, and truly basic research questions and areas of study remain unexplored (Munanga 2000). First and foremost, a better knowledge of the artistic production of Afrodescendants in the region since colonial times is badly needed. Such knowledge would radically alter – Araujo (2010) is correct – how we study art history in Latin America. Neglected by scholars, museums, art collectors, curators, and art critics, the very existence and production of numerous artists of African descent are barely known, or simply unknown. With the partial (and admittedly crucial) exception of Brazil, this is still virgin territory. Yet both in terms of locus of production and subject formation, Afrodescendant artists represent a distinct voice in continental debates on race, difference, nation, and representation. Many of these artists have not only experienced and have been forced to contend with racial barriers of various sorts, but have lived in communities constituted around African-based cultural practices. Writing in 1943 about his piece *Negra Vieja*, which had been acquired by the Museum of Modern Art in New York City, MoMA, Afro-Cuban sculptor Teodoro Ramos Blanco reflected about the importance of this distinction:

Black form has been interpreted, or to be precise has been dealt with by great artists, but they have only achieved the exterior part, without content. They have given us the vessel, but visibly empty; they have lacked emotion and when they have tried to feel it, it has looked fake to us, as something neither felt nor experienced. Let us say that it was a matter of fashion or 'snobbism'... How different is the effect when the form is interpreted – and now the expression is valid – by a sincere artist who is proud of his inspiration ... The touch is not about making a white or yellow form painted of black; you must feel it, model its expression, its rhythm, its beauty, its interior. And even if it is made of white marble, the form will be black because its essence is black.[4]

---

[4] Teodoro Ramos Blanco, "Comentario a propósito de mi 'Negra Vieja'," Havana, March 1943, reel 2169, Giulio V. Blanc Papers, Archives of American Art. I am grateful to Cary García Yero for sharing this document with me.

In addition to research centered on issues of authorship, many concrete questions remain. The important subject of how African aesthetic sensibilities may have shaped the production of religious and secular artifacts during the colonial period needs serious and detailed attention. Archaeologists have done valuable research on how slaves reproduced African aesthetic traditions in the production of work tools and in pottery and pipe decorations. That these aesthetic interventions fall outside the canon of art is, of course, a matter of definitions. A dialogue between archaeologists, historians, and art historians around these interventions would open new and exciting opportunities for further research into slaves' contributions to Afro-Latin American art.

Further research is also needed on the question of black representations in the patriotic art of the nineteenth century, a theme that has not been properly and systematically surveyed, despite its obvious importance. A related question concerns the transformation of art from a colonial mechanical trade to a cultured form of knowledge and its impact on black artistic communities in the region. Several authors note the relative absence of Afrodescendant artists, indeed of black subjects in general, in the art of the late nineteenth century and the turn of the twentieth century. Recent research in Brazil suggests, however, that this may be a function of our own lack of knowledge rather than a reflection of reality (Marques 2010; Teixeira Leite 2010b; Cardoso 2015).

Given how much remains to be done at the national level, where the work of many Afrodescendant artists is still barely known, the dearth of comparative studies is perhaps understandable. Even the well-known modernist and avant-garde movements, which share so much in common concerning their views of race and nation, as well as their cross-fertilization in transnational nodes such as Paris or New York, have not been seriously studied from a regional point of view. How did these artists contribute to the consolidation of racial democracy and populist regimes in the region? Did they open up spaces for new ideas and formulations? The contributions that visual artists have made to the contemporary Afrodescendant movement – another promising area of comparative research – have deep roots that we need to understand better.

As we reflect on the contributions of Afro-Latin American art, it is worth considering how visual representations articulate ideas about race, class, gender, nation, and belonging that are otherwise difficult to convey in the public sphere. Through the creative recombination and synthesis of a variety of discourses, the visual arts are able to produce and disseminate new contents even in environments in which the explicit discussion of such contents is not welcome. The important work done by several Argentine historians about stereotypical representations of blacks illustrates how the popular media articulates racist meanings without an explicit or "verbal" discussion of blackness (Frigerio 2011; Adamovsky 2016b; Alberto 2016; Ghidoli 2016b, 2016c; Lamborghini and Geler 2016). Similar research could be fruitfully done across the region, particularly, but not exclusively, in countries were the black population supposedly disappeared and where Afrodescendants are poorly represented in more-conventional sources (for postrevolutionary Cuba, see Benson 2016).

Art, however, can also operate in the opposite direction. As Adamovsky (2016b, 158) has argued, "visual culture is one of the fundamental resources for hegemony-building, but it is also a fertile ground for counter hegemonic exercises." For instance, art played a prominent role in rupturing the thick nationalist silence frequently associated with state ideologies of racial democracy. To mention one example, when the celebrations of the fourth centennial of the foundation of the city of São Paulo failed to make any reference to slavery, to Africa, or to blacks, what the members of a local Afro-Brazilian club demanded was, of all things, an artistic intervention: a sculpture of Mãe Preta, a project that was implemented despite the objections of the city's white major (Alberto 2011). When open debates about race, racism, and the vitality of African religious practices were officially proscribed in Cuba during the 1970s, the visual arts became a privileged space to raise issues and to insinuate views that were otherwise unspeakable, as exemplified by the work of Grupo Antillano (de la Fuente 2013). A somewhat different but related example is that of Peronist Argentina. While the Peronista leadership rejected any open discussion of race, the regime's visual imagery celebrated a racially mixed population, an unstated but potent recognition of the political importance and might of the lower-class "cabecitas negras," migrant workers from the interior (Lamborghini and Geler 2016; Adamovsky 2016b). As I have argued elsewhere, "things that are not speakable in other realms become possible in the realm of art" (Gates, Rodríguez Valdés, and de la Fuente 2012, 35).

In the articulation of this research agenda, it is important to note the creation of the Afro-Brazil Museum in São Paulo in 2004 (see Figures 10.11 and 10.12), an institution that not only provides a much-needed sense of historical tradition to the Afrodescendant population in

FIGURE 10.11 Museu Afro Brasil (1). Photo, Nelson Kon. Courtesy of Museu Afro Brasil.

FIGURE 10.12 Museu Afro Brasil (2). Photo, Nelson Kon. Courtesy of Museu Afro Brasil.

Brazil (Cleveland 2015), but also provides a specialized space for the study of Afro-Latin American art. The field now has an institutional home, one that is properly located in the region. One museum is certainly not enough to capture the rich history of this artistic production, but it is a start.

## BIBLIOGRAPHY

Adamovsky, Ezequiel. 2016a. "La cultura visual del criollismo: Etnicidad, 'color' y nación en las representaciones visuales del criollo en Argentina, c. 1910–1955." *Corpus: Archivos virtuales de la alteridad americana* 6, 2, http://corpusarchivos.revues.org/1738.

  2016b. "Race and Class through the Visual Culture of Peronism." In *Rethinking Race in Modern Argentina*, edited by Paulina Alberto and Eduardo Elena, 155–83. New York, NY: Cambridge University Press.

Ades, Dawn. 1989. *Art in Latin America: The Modern Era, 1820–1980.* New Haven, CT: Yale University Press.

  2014. "The Image of the Black in Latin America." In *The Image of the Black in Western Art*, edited by David Bindman and Henry Louis Gates Jr., vol. 5, 1, 227–56. Cambridge, MA: Belknap Press of Harvard University Press.

Agassiz, Louis, and Elizabeth Agassiz. 1868. *A Journey in Brazil.* Boston, MA: Ticknor and Fields.

Aguilar, Nelson, ed. 2000. *Mostra do redescobrimento: Arte afro-brasileira.* São Paulo: Associação Brasil 500 Anos Artes Visuais.

Alberto, Paulina. 2011. *Terms of Inclusion: Black Intellectuals in Twentieth-Century Brazil.* Chapel Hill, NC: University of North Carolina Press.

  2016. "El Negro Raúl: Lives and Afterlives of an Afro-Argentine Celebrity, 1886 to the Present." *Hispanic American Historical Review* 96, 4: 669–710.

Alcalá, Luisa Elena. 2014. "Painting in Latin America, 1550–1820: A Historical and Theoretical Framework." In *Painting in Latin America: 1550–1820*, edited by Luisa Elena Alcalá and Jonathan Brown, 15–68. New Haven, CT: Yale University Press.

Anderson, Thomas F. 2011. *Carnival and National Identity in the Poetry of Afrocubanismo.* Gainesville, FL: University Press of Florida.

Andrade, Mário de. 1965. *Aspectos das artes plásticas no Brasil.* São Paulo, Livraria Martins.

Andrade, Oswald de. 1928. "Manifiesto antropofago." *Revista de Antropofagia* 3: 7.

Andrews, George Reid. 1980. *The Afro-Argentines of Buenos Aires, 1800–1900.* Madison, WI: University of Wisconsin Press.

  2004. *Afro-Latin America, 1800–2000.* New York, NY: Oxford University Press.

  2007. "Remembering Africa, Inventing Uruguay: Sociedades de Negros in the Montevideo Carnival, 1865–1930." *Hispanic American Historical Review* 87, 4: 693–726.

  2010. *Blacks in the White Nation: A History of Afro-Uruguay.* Chapel Hill, NC: University of North Carolina Press.

Angola, Mercedes, and Raúl Cristancho. 2006. *Viaje sin mapa: Representaciones afro en el arte contemporáneo colombiano.* Bogotá: Banco de la República.

Appelbaum, Nancy P. 2016. *Chorographic Commission of 19th Century Colombia.* Chapel Hill, NC: University of North Carolina Press.

Araujo, Emanoel, ed. 2010. *A mão afro-brasileira: Significado da contribuição artística e histórica*. São Paulo: Imprensa Oficial do Estado de São Paulo/ Museu Afro Brasil. 2 vols.

  ed. 2014. *A nova mão afro-brasileira*. São Paulo: Museu Afro Brasil.

Archer, Petrine. 2014. "Negrophilia, Josephine Baker, and 1920s Paris." In *The Image of the Black in Western Art*, edited by David Bindman and Henry Louis Gates Jr., vol. 5, 1, 135–52. Cambridge, MA: Belknap Press of Harvard University Press.

Arrate, José Martín Félix. 1949. *Llave del Nuevo Mundo*. Mexico City: Fondo de Cultura Económica.

Azevedo, Aluísio. 2000. *The Slum*. Translated by David H. Rosenthal. New York, NY: Oxford University Press.

Ballesteros Páez, María Dolores. 2011. "Vicente Guerrero: Insurgente, militar y presidente afromexicano" *Cuicuilco* 51: 23–41.

Barcia, María del Carmen. 2009. *Los ilustres apellidos: Negros en La Habana colonial*. Havana: Ediciones Boloña.

Barkan, Elazar. 1992. *The Retreat of Scientific Racism: Changing Concepts of Race in Britain and the United States between the World Wars*. New York, NY: Cambridge University Press.

Bauer, Arnold. 2001. *Goods, Power, History: Latin America's Material Culture*. New York, NY: Cambridge University Press.

Benson, Devyn. 2016. *Antiracism in Cuba: The Unfinished Revolution*. Chapel Hill, NC: University of North Carolina Press.

Bennett, Herman L. 2003. *Africans in Colonial Mexico: Absolutism, Christianity, and Afro-Creole Consciousness, 1570-1640*. Bloomington, IN: Indiana University Press.

Bernabé, Jean, Patrick Chamoiseau, Raphaël Confiant, and Mohamed B. Taleb Khyar. 1990. "In Praise of Creoleness" *Callaloo*, 13, 4: 886–909.

Bettelheim, Judith. 2005. *AFROCUBA: Works on Paper, 1968–2003*. San Francisco, CA: International Center for the Arts, San Francisco State University.

  2013. "Grupo Antillano, Revisited." In *Grupo Antillano: The Art of Afro-Cuba*, edited by Alejandro de la Fuente, 37–50. Pittsburgh, PA: Fundacion Caguayo and University of Pittsburgh Press.

Blanchard, Peter. 2008. *Under the Flags of Freedom: Slave Soldiers and the Wars of Independence in Spanish South America*. Pittsburgh, PA: University of Pittsburgh Press.

Blier, Suzanne P. 1995. *African Vodun: Art, Psychology, and Power*. Chicago, IL: University of Chicago Press.

Boogart, Ernst van den. 2012. "Black Slavery and the 'Mulatto Escape Hatch' in the Brazilian Ensembles of Frans Post and Albert Eckhout." In *The Slave in European Art: From Renaissance Trophy to Abolitionist Emblem*, edited by Elizabeth McGrath and Jean Michel Massing, 217–52. London: The Warburg Institute.

Brewer-García, Larissa. 2015. "Imagined Transformations: Color, Beauty, and Black Christian Conversion in Seventeenth-Century Spanish America." In

*Envisioning Others: Race, Color and the Visual in Iberia and Latin America,* edited by Pamela A. Patton, 111–41. Leiden: Brill.

Carbonell, Walterio. 1961. *Crítica, cómo surgió la cultura nacional.* Havana: Editorial Yaka.

Cardoso, Rafael. 2015. "The Problem of Race in Brazilian Painting, c. 1850–1920," *Art History* 38, 3: 488–511.

Carpentier, Alejo. 2006. *The Kingdom of This World.* New York, NY: Farrar, Straus, and Giroux.

Casamayor Cisneros, Odette. 2011. "Queloides: inevitables, lacerantes. En torno a la exposición Queloides. Raza y racismo en el arte Cubano contemporáneo." *Artecubano. Revista de Artes Visuales* 2: 22–29.

Catlin, Stanton Loomis. 1989. "Traveller-Reporter Artists and the Empirical Tradition in Post-Independence Latin America." In *Art in Latin America: The Modern Era, 1820–1980,* edited by Dawn Ades, 41–100. New Haven, CT: Yale University Press.

Chasteen, John Charles. 2004. *National Rhythms, African Roots: The Deep History of Latin American Popular Dance.* Albuquerque, NM: University of New Mexico Press.

Childs, Matt. 2006. *The 1812 Aponte Rebellion in Cuba and the Struggle against Atlantic Slavery.* Chapel Hill, NC: University of North Carolina Press.

Cirio, Norberto P. 2009. *Tinta negra en el gris del ayer: Los afroporteños a través de sus periódicos entre 1873 y 1882.* Buenos Aires: Teseo.

Cleveland, Kimberly. 2013. *Black Art in Brazil: Expressions of Identity.* Gainesville, FL: University Press of Florida.

2015. "Preserving African Art, History, and Memory: The AfroBrazil Museum." In *African Heritage and Memories of Slavery in Brazil and the South Atlantic World,* edited by Ana Lucia Araujo, 285–311. Amherst, NY: Cambria Press.

Cogollo, Herberto Cuadrado. 1973. *Cogollo: Le monde d'un nohor.* Paris: Galerie Suzanne Visat.

Comesañas Sardiñas, Zeida. 2008. *Great Masters of Cuban Art: Ramos Collection.* Daytona Beach, FL: Museum of Arts and Sciences.

Conduru, Roberto. 2009. "Negrume Multicor: Arte, África e Brasil para além de raça e etnia." *Acervo* 22, 2: 29–44.

2012. *Arte afro-brasileira.* Belo Horizonte: Editora C/Arte.

Costilla, Julia. 2015. "'Guarda y custodia' en la Ciudad de los Reyes: La construcción colectiva del culto al Señor de los Milagros (Lima, siglos XVII y XVIII)." *Fronteras de la Historia* 20, 2: 152–79.

Cummins, Thomas. 2013. "Three Gentlemen from Esmeraldas: A Portrait for a King." In *Portraits of Slaves,* edited by Agnes Lugo-Ortiz and Angela Rosenthal, 118–45. New York, NY: Cambridge University Press.

Cunha, Mariano Carneiro da. 1983. "Arte afro-brasileira," in *História geral da arte no Brasil,* edited by W. Zanini, C. T. Costa, and M. S. Albequerque, vol. 2, 973–1033. São Paulo: Instituto Walther Moreira Salles and Fundação Djalma Guimarães.

De la Fuente, Alejandro. 2001. *A Nation for All: Race, Inequality, and Politics in Twentieth-Century Cuba.* Chapel Hill, NC: University of North Carolina Press.

2008a. *Havana and the Atlantic in the Sixteenth Century*. Chapel Hill, NC: University of North Carolina Press.

2008b. "The New Afro-Cuban Cultural Movement and the Debate on Race in Contemporary Cuba." *Journal of Latin American Studies* 40, 4: 697–720.

ed. 2010. *Queloides: Race and Racism in Cuban Contemporary Art*. Pittsburgh, PA: Mattress Factory and University of Pittsburgh Press.

2013. *Grupo Antillano: The Art of Afro-Cuba*. Pittsburgh, PA: Fundacion Caguayo and University of Pittsburgh Press.

Diggs, Irene. 1952. "Negro Painters in Uruguay," *The Crisis* (May), 299–301.

Earle, Rebecca. 2007. *The Return of the Native: Indians and Myth-Making in Spanish America, 1810–1930*. Durham, NC: Duke University Press.

Echeverri, Marcela. 2016. *Indian and Slave Royalists in the Age of Revolution: Reform, Revolution, and Royalism in the Northern Andes, 1780-1825*. New York, NY: Cambridge University Press.

Engerman, Stanley L. and Kenneth L. Sokoloff. 2005. "The Evolution of Suffrage Institutions in the New World." *Journal of Economic History* 65, 4: 891–921.

Fabre, Michel. 1980. "Herberto Cuadrado Cogollo." *Callaloo*, 8/10: 19–26.

Feldman, Heidi Carolyn. 2006. *Black Rhythms of Peru: Reviving African Musical Heritage in the Black Pacific*. Middletown, CT: Wesleyan University Press.

Ferrer, Ada. 1999. *Insurgent Cuba: Race, Nation, and Revolution, 1868-1898*. Chapel Hill, NC: University of North Carolina Press.

Fouchet, Max-Pol. 1976. *Wifredo Lam*. New York, NY: Rizzoli International Publications.

Fracchia, Carmen. 2012. "The Urban Slave in Spain and New Spain." In *The Slave in European Art: From Renaissance Trophy to Abolitionist Emblem*, edited by Elizabeth McGrath and Jean Michel Massing, 195–216. London: The Warburg Institute.

Fredrickson, George M. 2002. *Racism: A Short History*. Princeton, NJ: Princeton University Press.

Frick, Richard. 2003. *Cartel tricontinental de solidaridad*. Bern, Switzerland: Commedia-Verlag.

Frigerio, Alejandro. 2011. "'Sin otro delito que el color de su piel.' Imágenes del "negro" en la revista Caras y Caretas (1900–1910)." In *Cartografías afrolatinoamericanas: Perspectivas situadas para análisis transfronterizos*, edited by Florencia Guzmán and Lea Geler, 151–72. Buenos Aires: Biblos.

García Mora, Luis Miguel, and Antonio Santamaría García, eds. 2006. *Los ingenious: Colección de vistas de los principales ingenios de azúcar de la isla de Cuba*. Madrid: Ediciones Doce Calles.

Garrido, Esperanza et al. 1993. *Felipe Santiago Gutiérrez: Pasión y destino*. Toluca: Instituto Mexiquense de Cultura.

Gates Jr., Henry Louis, Elio Rodríguez Valdés, and Alejandro de la Fuente. 2012. "Race and Racism in Cuban Art." *Transition* 108: 33–51.

Ghidoli, María de Lourdes. 2016a. "En pelo y al lápiz: La trayectoria de dos pintores afrodescendientes en la Buenos Aires del siglo XIX." In *Afrolatinoamérica: Estudos comparados*, edited by Viviana Gelado and María Verónica Secreto, 69–94. Rio de Janeiro: Editora Mauad.

2016b. *Estereotipos en negro: Representaciones y autorrepresentaciones visuales de afroporteños en el siglo XIX*. Rosario: Prohistoria Ediciones.

2016c. "La trama racializada de lo visual. Una aproximación a las representaciones grotescas de los afroargentinos." *Corpus: Archivos virtuales de la alteridad americana* 6, 2, http://corpusarchivos.revues.org/1744.

2016d. "Posadas, Bernardino." In *Dictionary of Caribbean and Afro Latin American Biography*, edited by Franklin Knight and Henry Louis Gates Jr. New York, NY: Oxford University Press.

Gisbert, Teresa. 1980. *Iconografía y mitos indígenas en el arte*. La Paz: Apartado 195.

Gobineau, Arthur, Comte de. 1856. *The Moral and Intellectual Diversity of Races*. Philadelphia, PA: J. B. Lippincott & Co.

Gomez, Michael A. 1998. *Exchanging Our Country Marks: The Transformation of African Identities in the Colonial and Antebellum South*. Chapel Hill, NC: University of North Carolina Press.

González, Beatriz. 1986. *Ramón Torres Méndez: Entre lo pintoresco y la picaresca*. Bogotá: C. Valencia Editores.

Goodall, Donald. 1991. "Interview: Enrique Grau." *Latin American Art*: 37–38.

Greet, Michele. 2014. "Occupying Paris: The First Survey Exhibition of Latin American Art." *Journal of Curatorial Studies* 3, 2–3: 212–36.

Guerra, Lillian. 2012. *Visions of Power in Cuba: Revolution, Redemption, and Resistance, 1959–1971*. Chapel Hill, NC: University of North Carolina Press.

Guillén, Nicolás. 1974. *Obra poética*. 2 vols. Havana: Unión de Escritores y Artistas de Cuba.

Hallo, Wilson. 1981. *Imágenes del Ecuador del siglo XIX: Juan Agustín Guerrero*. Madrid: Espasa-Calpe.

Hanchard, Michael. 1994. *Orpheus and Power: The Movimento Negro of Rio de Janeiro and São Paulo, Brazil, 1945–1988*. Princeton, NJ: Princeton University Press.

Hernández de Alba, Guillermo. 1986. *Acuarelas de la Comisión Corográfica, Colombia, 1850–1859*. Bogotá: Litografía Arco.

Hertzman, Marc A. 2013. *Making Samba: A New History of Race and Music in Brazil*. Durham, NC: Duke University Press.

Johnson, Walter. 1999. *Soul by Soul: Life Inside the Antebellum Slave Market*. Cambridge, MA: Harvard University Press.

Katzew, Ilona. 2004. *Casta Painting*. New Haven, CT: Yale University Press.

2014. "Valiant Styles: New Spanish Painting, 1700–1785." In *Painting in Latin America: 1550–1820*, edited by Luisa Elena Alcalá and Jonathan Brown, 149–203. New Haven, CT: Yale University Press.

Kiernan, James Patrick. 2002. "The Bright Side of the Tunnel," *Americas* (March–April), 54–55.

King-Hammond, Leslie. 2008. "Identifying Spaces of Blackness: The Aesthetics of Resistance and Identity in American Plantation Art." In *Landscape of Slavery: The Plantation in American Art*, edited by Angela D. Mack and Stephen G. Hoffius, 58–85. Columbia, SC: University of South Carolina Press.

Koerner, Joseph Leo. 2010. "The Epiphany of the Black Magus circa 1500." In *The Image of the Black in Western Art*, edited by David Bindman and Henry

Louis Gates Jr., vol. 3, 1: 7–92. Cambridge, MA: Belknap Press of Harvard University Press.

Kula, Morgan. 1976. "The Politics of Culture: The Case of Festac." *Ufahamu: A Journal of African Studies* 7, 1: 166–92.

Kutzinski, Vera M. 1993. *Sugar's Secrets. Race and the Erotics of Cuban Nationalism.* Charlottesville, VA: University Press of Virginia.

Lamborghini, Eva, and Lea Geler. 2016. "Presentación del Debate: Imágenes racializadas: políticas de representación y economía visual en torno a lo 'negro' en Argentina, siglos XX y XXI." *Corpus: Archivos virtuales de la alteridad americana* 6, 2, http://corpusarchivos.revues.org/1735.

Lawal, Babatunde. 2004. "Reclaiming the Past: Yoruba Elements in African American Arts." In *The Yoruba Diaspora in the Atlantic World,* edited by Toyin Falola and Matt D. Childs, 291–324. Bloomington, IN: Indiana University Press.

León y León, Gustavo. 2004. *Apuntes histórico genealógicos de Francisco Fierro: Pancho Fierro.* Lima: Biblioteca Nacional del Perú.

Libin, Laurence. 2006. "Musical Instruments in Two Portraits by José Campeche." *Music in Art,* 31, 1/2: 127–31.

Linati, Claudio. 1828. *Costumes civils, militaires et réligieux du Mexique.* Brussels: Lithographie Royale de Gobard.

Lizcano Angarita, Martha, and González Cueto, Danny. 2007. "El negro en las letras, la historiografía y el arte del Caribe colombiano: Notas para su studio." *Huellas* 78–79: 23–31.

López Núñez, Olga. 1997. "Notas sobre la pintura colonial en Cuba." In *Pintura europea y cubana en las colecciones del Museo Nacional de La Habana,* 49–73. Madrid: Fundación Cultural Mapfre.

Maio, Marcos Chor. 2001. "UNESCO and the Study of Race Relations in Brazil: Regional or National Issue?" *Latin American Research Review* 36, 2: 118–36.

Majluf, Natalia. 2008. *Tipos del Perú. La Lima criolla de Pancho Fierro.* Madrid: Ediciones El Viso.

2015. *José Gil de Castro: Pintor de libertadores.* Santiago de Chile: Museo Nacional de Bellas Artes.

Majluf, Natalia et al. 2012. *Más allá de la imagen: Los estudios técnicos en el proyecto José Gil de Castro.* Lima: MALI.

Manzano, Juan Francisco. 1996. *Autobiography of a Slave.* Detroit, MI: Wayne State University Press.

Márceles Daconte, Eduardo. 2010. *Los recursos de la imaginación: Artes visuales del Caribe colombiano.* Barranquilla: Artes Gráficas Industriales.

Marques, Luiz. 2010. "O século XIX e o advent da Academia das Belas Artes e o novo estatuto do artista negro." In *A mão afro-brasileira: Significado da contribuição artística e histórica,* edited by Emanoel Araujo, vol. 1, 225–30. São Paulo: Imprensa Oficial do Estado de São Paulo: Museu Afro Brasil.

Martín-Sevillano, Ana Belén. 2011. "Crisscrossing Gender, Ethnicity, and Race: African Religious Legacy in Cuban Contemporary Women's Art." *Cuban Studies* 42: 136–54.

Martínez, Juan A. 1994. *Cuban Art and National Identity: The Vanguardia Painters, 1927–1950.* Gainesville, FL: University Press of Florida.

Martínez, María Elena. 2008. *Genealogical Fictions: Limpieza De Sangre, Religion, and Gender in Colonial Mexico.* Stanford, CA: Stanford University Press.

Martínez-Ruiz, Bárbaro. 2010. "Ma kisi Nsi: L'art des habitants de région de Mbanza Kongo." In *Angola figures de pouvoir,* edited by Christiane Falgayrettes-Leveau, 2–39. Paris: Musée Dapper.

    2012. *Escritura gráfica Kongo y otras narrativas del signo.* Mexico City: El Colegio de México.

    2013. *Things That Cannot Be Seen Any Other Way: The Art of Manuel Mendive.* Miami, FL: Frost Museum of Art.

Maya Restrepo, Luz Adriana and Raúl Cristancho Álvarez, eds. 2015. *¡Mandinga Sea! África en Antioquia!* Bogota: Ediciones Uniandes.

Medina, Álvaro. 2000. *El arte del Caribe colombiano.* Cartagena: Gobernación del Departamento de Bolívar.

Melling, Helen. 2015. "'Colourful Customs and Invisible Traditions': Visual Representations of Black Subjects in Late Colonial and 19th-Century Post-Independence Peru (1750s–1890s)." PhD diss., King's College, London.

Méndez Martínez, Roberto. 2013. "Vicente Escobar, talento y mascara." *Palabra Nueva* (Nov.), http://palabranueva.net/pn-old/index.php?option=com_content&view=article&id=596:vicente-escobar-talento-y-mascara&catid=210:cultura&Itemid=255.

Métraux, Alfred. 1952. "An Inquiry into Race Relations in Brazil," *UNESCO Courier 6.*

Moore, Carlos. 1988. *Castro, the Blacks, and Africa.* Los Angeles, CA: UCLA Center for Afro-American Studies.

Moore, Robin. 1997. *Nationalizing Blackness: Afrocubanismo and Artistic Revolution in Havana, 1920–1940.* Pittsburgh, PA: University of Pittsburgh Press.

Morton, Javier López. 2014. "Del mundo de las subastas: La Mulata" (June 24). Accessed June 15, 2016, at https://javierlmorton.wordpress.com/tag/felipe-santiago-gutierrez.

Munanga, Kabengele. 2000. "Arte afro-brasileira: o que é, a final?" In *Mostra do redescobrimento: Arte afro-brasileira,* edited by Nelson Aguilar, 98–111. São Paulo: Associação Brasil 500 Anos Artes Visuais.

Niell, Paul. 2016. "Bolivarian Imagery and Racial Ideology in Early Nineteenth-Century Cuba." In *Simón Bolivar: Travels and Transformations of a Cultural Icon,* edited by Maureen G. Shanahan and Ana Maria Reye, 62–77. Gainesville, FL: University Press of Florida.

Olivera Chirimini, Tomás. 2001. "Candombe, African Nations and the Africanity of Uruguay." In *African Roots/American Cultures: Africa in the Creation of the Americas,* edited by Sheila S. Walker, 259–74. Lanham, MD: Rowman & Littlefield.

Ortiz, Fernando. 1906. *Los negros brujos (apuntes para un estudio de etnología criminal).* Madrid: Librería de Fernando Fe.

    1952–1955. *Los instrumentos de la música afrocubana.* 5 vols. Havana: Ministerio de Educación. Dirección de Cultura.

O'Toole, Rachel Sarah. 2012. *Bound Lives: Africans, Indians, and the Making of Race in Colonial Peru*. Pittsburgh, PA: University of Pittsburgh Press.

Palmié, Stephan. 2002. *Wizards and Scientists: Explorations in Afro-Cuban Modernity and Tradition*. Durham, NC: Duke University Press.

Paschel, Tianna. 2013. "'The Beautiful Faces of My Black People': Race, Ethnicity and the Politics of Colombia's 2005 Census." *Ethnic and Racial Studies* 36, 10: 1544–63.

Patton, Sharon F. 1998. *African-American Art*. New York, NY: Oxford University Press.

Picotti, Dina V. 1998. *La presencia africana en nuestra identidad*. Buenos Aires: Ediciones del Sol.

Pineda García, Melba. 2013. "Rómulo Rozo, la diosa Bachué y el indigenismo en Colombia (1920–1950)," *Baukara* 3: 41–56.

Pontual, Roberto. 2000. "Fonseca e Silva, Valentim da." In *Encyclopedia of Latin American Art*, edited by Jane Turner. New York, NY: Macmillan.

Price, Sally and Richard Price. 1999. *Maroon Arts: Cultural Vitality in the African Diaspora*. Boston, MA: Beacon Press.

Quero Chiesa, Luis. 1945. "Arte nacional puertorriqueño." *Alma Latina, Semanario de Cultura* 524 (Dec. 15): 13, 40.

Ramos, Arthur. 1946. *As culturas negras no Novo Mundo: O negro brasileiro*. São Paulo: Companhia Editora Nacional.

Ramos-Alfred, Evelyn Carmen. 2011. "A Painter of Cuban Life: Victor Patricio de Landaluze and Nineteenth-Century Cuban Politics (1850–1889)." PhD diss., University of Chicago.

Ramos Cruz, Guillermina. 2009. *Lam y Mendive, arte afrocubano*. Barcelona: Ediciones Linkgua.

2013. "Tribute to the Grupo Antillano." In *Grupo Antillano: The Art of Afro-Cuba*, edited by Alejandro de la Fuente, 19–36. Pittsburgh, PA: Fundacion Caguayo and University of Pittsburgh Press.

Rappaport, Joanne. 2014. *Disappearing Mestizo: Configuring Difference in the Colonial New Kingdom of Granada*. Durham: Duke University Press.

Reales, Leonardo. 2007. "The Contribution of the Afro-Descendant Soldiers to the Independence of the Bolivarian Countries (1810–1826)." *Revista de Relaciones Internacionales, Estrategia y Seguridad* 2:2: 11–31.

Reis, João José. 2015. *Divining Slavery and Freedom: The Story of Domingos Sodré, an African Priest in Nineteenth-Century Brazil*. New York, NY: Cambridge University Press.

Ribeiro de Oliveira, Myriam A. 2010. "O Aleijadinho e Mestre Valentim." In *A mão afro-brasileira: Significado da contribuição artística e histórica*, edited by Emanoel Araujo, vol. 1, 75–102. São Paulo: Imprensa Oficial do Estado de São Paulo / Museu Afro Brasil.

Rodrigues, Raimundo Nina. 1904. "As bellas artes nos colonos pretos do Brasil: A esculptura." *Kósmos: Revista Artistica, Scientifica e Literaria* 1, 1.

Rodríguez, Bélgica. 2003. *Enrique Grau: Homenaje*. Bogotá: Villega Editores.

Rosemont, Franklin, and Robin Kelley, eds. 2009. *Black, Brown, & Beige: Surrealist Writings from Africa and the Diaspora*. Austin, TX: University of Texas Press.

Rostworowski, Maria. 1998. "Pachacamac and Señor de los Milagros." In *Native Traditions in the Postconquest World*, edited by Elizabeth Boone and Tom Cummins, 345–59. Washington, DC: Dumbarton Oaks.

Sabogal Diéguez, José. 1945. *Pancho Fierro, estampas del pintor peruano*. Buenos Aires: Editorial Nova.

Salum, Maria Helena Leuba. 2000. "Cem anos de arte afro-brasileira." In *Mostra do redescobrimento: Arte afro-brasileira*, edited by Nelson Aguilar, 112–21. São Paulo: Associação Brasil 500 Anos Artes Visuais.

Sánchez, Efraín. 1991. "Ramón Torres Méndez y la pintura de tipos y costumbres." *Boletín Cultural y Bibliográfico* 28, 28: 16–39.

Sartorius, David. 2014. *Ever Faithful: Race, Loyalty, and the Ends of Empire in Spanish Cuba*. Durham, NC: Duke University Press.

Seigel, Micol. 2009. *Uneven Encounters: Making Race and Nation in Brazil and the United States*. Durham, NC: Duke University Press.

Solano Roa, Juanita. 2013. "The Mexican Assimilation: Colombia in the 1930s: The Case of Ignacio Gómez Jaramillo." *Historia y Memoria* 7: 79–111.

Stepan, Nancy Leys. 1991. *"The Hour of Eugenics": Race, Gender, and Nation in Latin America*. Ithaca, NY: Cornell University Press.

Stoddard, Lothrop. 1920. *The Rising Tide of Color Against White World-Supremacy*. New York, NY: Scribner.

Sullivan, Edward. 2014. *From San Juan to Paris and Back: Francisco Oller and Caribbean Art in the Era of Impressionism*. New Haven, CT: Yale University Press.

Sweet, James H. 1997. "The Iberian Roots of American Racist Thought." *William and Mary Quarterly* 54, 1: 143–46.

———. 2003. *Recreating Africa: Culture, Kinship, and Religion in the African-Portuguese World, 1441–1770*. Chapel Hill, NC: University of North Carolina Press.

Sztainbok, Vannina. 2008. "National Pleasures: The Fetishization of Blackness and Uruguayan Autobiographical Narratives." *Latin American and Caribbean Ethnic Studies* 3, 1; 61–84.

Taylor, René. 1988. *José Campeche y su tiempo*. Ponce: Museo de Arte de Ponce.

Teixeira Leite, José Roberto. 2010a. "Negros, pardos e mulatos na pintura e na escultura brasileira do século XVIII." In *A mão afro-brasileira: significado da contribuição artística e histórica*, edited by Emanoel Araujo, vol. 1, 25–74. São Paulo: Imprensa Oficial do Estado de São Paulo / Museu Afro Brasil.

———. 2010b. "Valorosos pintores negros do oitocentos." In *A mão afro-brasileira: significado da contribuição artística e histórica*, edited by Emanoel Araujo, vol. 1, 187–224. São Paulo: Imprensa Oficial do Estado de São Paulo / Museu Afro Brasil.

Temin, Christine. 2006. "José Campeche and Francisco Oller." *Antiques* (Nov.): 162–69.

Thompson, Robert F. 1981. *The Four Moments of the Sun*. Washington, DC: National Gallery of Art.

1983. *Flash of the Spirit: African and Afro-American Art and Philosophy*. New York, NY: Random House.

Thornton, John. 1998. *Africa and Africans in the Making of the Atlantic World, 1400–1800*. New York, NY: Cambridge University Press.

Torres de Souza, Marcos, and Camilla Agostini. 2012. "Body Marks, Pots, and Pipes: Some Correlations between African Scarifications and Pottery Decoration in Eighteenth- and Nineteenth-Century Brazil." *Historical Archaeology* 46, 3: 102–23.

Torres Méndez, Ramón. 1860. *Album de cuadros de costumbres*. París: A. De la Rue.

Traba, Marta. 1972. "El ojo alerta de Campeche." *La Torre, Revista General de la Universidad de Puerto Rico*, 77: 43–51.

Tucker, William H. 1994. *The Science and Politics of Racial Research*. Urbana, IL: University of Illinois Press.

Twinam, Ann. 2014. *Purchasing Whiteness: Pardos, Mulattos, and the Quest for Social Mobility in the Spanish Indies*. Stanford, CA: Stanford University Press.

Vásquez, William. 2014. "Antecedentes de la Escuela Nacional de Bellas Artes de Colombia 1826–1886: De las artes y oficios a las bellas artes." *Cuadernos de Música, Artes Visuales y Artes Escénicas* 9, 1: 35–67.

Vázquez Díaz, Ramón. 2010. *Víctor Manuel*. Madrid: Ediciones Vanguardia Cubana.

Verger, Pierre. 2000. *Notas sobre o culto aos orixás e voduns na Bahia de Todos os Santos, no Brasil, e na antiga costa dos escravos, na África*. São Paulo: EDUSP. First published in 1957.

Villaverde, Cecilio. 2005. *Cecilia Valdes or El Angel Hill*. New York, NY: Oxford University Press.

Villegas, Fernando. 2011. "El costumbrismo americano ilustrado: El caso peruano. Imágenes originales en la era de la reproducción técnica." *Anales del Museo de América* 19: 7–67.

Villegas Vélez, Álvaro. 2011. "Paisajes, experiencias e historias en las dos primeras expediciones de la Comisión Corográfica. Nueva Granada, 1850–1851." *Historia y Sociedad* 20: 91–112.

Wade, Peter. 2001. "Racial Identity and Nationalism: A Theoretical View from Latin America." *Ethnic and Racial Studies* 24, 5: 845–65.

Weaver, Brendan. 2015. "Fruit of the Vine, Work of Human Hands: An Archaeology and Ethnohistory of Slavery on the Jesuit Wine Haciendas of Nasca, Peru." PhD diss., Vanderbilt University.

Wheeler, Roxann. 1999. *The Complexion of Race: Categories of Difference in Eighteenth-Century British Culture*. Philadelphia: University of Pennsylvania Press

2000. *The Complexion of Race: Categories of Difference in Eighteenth-Century British Culture*. Philadelphia, PA: University of Pennsylvania Press.

Wood, Marcus. 2013. *Black Milk: Imagining Slavery in the Visual Cultures of Brazil and America*. New York, NY: Oxford University Press.

# A Century and a Half of Scholarship on Afro-Latin American Music

## Robin D. Moore

This chapter provides an overview of research on Afro-Latin American music, both historically and in the present. It begins by discussing the development of Afro-Latin American musical research in the late nineteenth and early twentieth centuries, often written by authors implicated in racist ideologies and projects. It continues with commentary on early studies of Afro-Latin American music by researchers such as Fernando Ortiz and Mário de Andrade, who came to understand Afro-Latin American heritage as valuable and studied it as part of projects of nation-building. Next, the chapter discusses authors from the mid-twentieth century such as Melville Herskovits, Roger Bastide, and others. These "retentionist" scholars have come under criticism in recent decades because of their rather essentialist notions of culture and their at times obsessive focus on the African origins of particular forms of expression; yet their work contributed in important ways to the documentation of Afro-Latin American heritage and the expansion of an entire field of study. Finally, the chapter provides an overview of changes in scholarship on Afro-Latin American music since the 1970s. Many publications from this period studied the grassroots cultural initiatives of Afro-Latin American artists or critically examined ideologies surrounding Afro-Latin American music, including commercial repertoire. The chapter concludes with discussion of publications from the last two or three decades on topics such as nationalism, globalization, hybridity, whiteness, cultural citizenship, and activist scholarship. It underscores the interventions and contributions of music scholars in broader academic dialogues related to blackness in Latin America and the Caribbean.

## THE COLONIAL ERA THROUGH THE TURN OF THE TWENTIETH CENTURY

As George Marcus (1999) and countless others in recent decades have pointed out, the discipline of anthropology (as well as ethnomusicology and Latin American studies) emerged in the wake of colonialist expansion.[1] After centuries of warfare, genocide, the conquest and subjugation of native peoples, the mass importation of slaves to the Americas, and extremely disdainful views of practices such as Afro-Latin American music making, local residents slowly gained a greater appreciation for such expression. This was a painfully slow process, one that is far from complete even today. Colonialist expansion in Latin America led to highly stratified societies, largely along lines of race and ethnicity (see Chapters 3 and 4). For many years, African-influenced culture served as a marker of marginal status; elite society used belief in the superiority of European cultural practices as an important means of differentiating itself from the masses, and as a justification for slavery. Conventional wisdom throughout the Americas and Europe through at least the 1930s perpetuated belief in evolutionism, a hierarchy of more and less "advanced" races and cultures. Elite authors for many years characterized Afro-Latin American music as part of an extremely rudimentary culture and as representative of a people who had not progressed far beyond the senseless howling of animals.[2] Only in the mid-twentieth century did such views begin to shift substantially.

In such a context, it is not surprising that rigorous scholarship on Afro-Latin American music is a relatively recent phenomenon. Prior to the mid-twentieth century, specialists in the study of such music did not exist, as it was not considered deserving of attention. This view was particularly widespread among Latin American elites; many early written descriptions of African-influenced music come not from them but from travelers who visited the region and wrote memoirs of their experiences. Travelers often viewed such expression as exotic or quaint and worthy of mention for

---

[1] Note that Gilbert Chase (1906–1992), one of the first scholars of Latin American music based in the United States, became interested in the topic after having been born in Cuba following the United States' first military occupation of that country (1898–1902). His father was a military officer.

[2] See, for instance, the references to colonial-era condemnation of African dances in Andrews (1980), 156–64, or (2004), 28–31. Additional citations are available in Chasteen (2004), 91–113. Such racist characterizations of black music from the Americas persisted well into the twentieth century (e.g., Merriam 1964, 241–43).

that reason. Examples of their writings include those of French Calvinist Jean de Léry (1536–1613), who lived in Rio de Janeiro in the 1550s and published *History of a Voyage to the Land of Brazil* (1578; see de Léry 1990), and Jean-Baptiste Labat (1663–1738), who published similar material on the Caribbean about a century later (Labat 1970). Foreign visitors of note who wrote about music and dance in the late eighteenth and early nineteenth centuries include Moreau de Saint-Méry (1798) in the Caribbean and Johann Baptist von Spix (1976) on Brazil. Later in the nineteenth century, Swedish author Fredrika Bremer (1995) wrote similar accounts while in Cuba.[3] Local descriptions of slave festivities appeared in the press, in municipal legislation and police regulation,[4] and in popular literature during the colonial era as well, of course,[5] but in general the views of the authors tended to be strongly biased against local black expression.

Many of the first writers who examined Afro-diasporic culture in detail were trained in medicine or law rather than the humanities and began to pursue such work after having been exposed to the writings of Cesare Lombroso (1835–1909) and other authors in the field of criminology. This new form of pseudo-science added gravitas and legitimacy to long-held dominant views about blacks' biological and cultural inferiority. Lombroso, an Italian physician of Jewish ancestry who studied populations in asylums and prisons, is largely credited with the creation of criminology as a discipline. Drawing on concepts from physiognomy, degeneration theory, phrenology, and social Darwinism, Lombroso suggested that human criminal tendencies were inherited or physically innate and largely associated with non-Caucasian races. Thus, he presumed some individuals to be born with criminal predispositions that could be determined through an examination of their bodies. Particular features identified them as less evolved members of the human species who had not acquired an adequate moral sense. Lombroso's 1876 publication *Criminal Man* (*L'Uomo Delinquente*) presents many of these ideas (Gould 1981). His professional career and its intellectual legacy suggest how academic work on Afro-Latin American expressive culture for decades contributed directly to the subjugation of Afro-Latin peoples.

---

[3] See Wade 1999 for discussion of similar travel writings discussing black music in New Granada.

[4] Andrews (1980, 28–31) and de la Fuente (2008, 169–70), for instance, provide examples of police regulations banning gatherings and musical events by Africans and their descendants, which were commonplace for centuries.

[5] In the case of Cuba, for instance, see comments by authors such as Ramón Meza and Aurelio Pérez Zamora, reprinted in Ortiz 1984a.

Raymundo Nina Rodrigues (1862–1906), another physician, was one of the first authors to study Afro-diasporic cultures in the Americas; his work manifests strong influences from criminology. Nina Rodrigues began practicing medicine in Salvador, Brazil in the 1880s, eventually growing interested in Afro-Brazilian religion and attending *Candomblé* events. As a doctor, he participated in professional organizations related to internal medicine, surgery, and infectious disease. This seems to have contributed to his view of black cultures as a pathology and his adoption of the Portuguese phrase *"antropologia patológica"* in his discussion of them. He began collecting black religious fetishes and totems, resulting in 1900 in the publication of *O animismo fetichista dos negros da Bahia* (Rodrigues 1935). Nina Rodrigues was an early instigator of criminal anthropology and phrenology in Brazil. His 1899 book *Mestiçagem, degenerescência e crime* continued to influence publications on Afro-Latin American culture through the 1930s. Two decades later, the career of Brazilian Arthur Ramos (1903–49) paralleled that of Nina Rodrigues in that he studied medicine and psychology, began work that pathologized black populations by publishing on topics such as insanity and hygiene, and slowly became interested in black culture and religion as a result (Ramos 1937). While much more progressive than Nina Rodrigues, Ramos's work continued to manifest misguided views that suggested blacks were culturally stunted and inferior to whites.

Fernando Ortiz Fernández (1881–1969) is a key figure in the gradual transition of Afro-Latin American studies from works based on racist presuppositions to scholarship of the mid-twentieth century that began to accept and valorize such expression (Moore 2018). He helped "break the taboo" (Le Riverend 1961, 38; Price-Mars 1965, 12) surrounding black cultures of the Americas and to study them comprehensively. Born in Havana, Ortiz completed a doctorate in Madrid at the newly founded Instituto Sociológico. There he was first exposed to writings on the "penitentiary sciences" and criminology, a strong influence on his first book, *Los negros brujos* (Ortiz 1906). Hired as a public prosecutor for the city of Havana, Ortiz supported campaigns against African-derived religions by incarcerating devotees believed to be involved in "witchcraft" and advocating the suppression of what he considered deviant and dangerous behavior. Many of the instruments and other ritual objects originally belonging to incarcerated individuals eventually became part of Ortiz's personal collection and supported his research; others he destroyed or donated to the newly established Museum of Ethnography in Havana (Helg 1995, 114).

Through the 1910s and into the 1920s, Ortiz largely maintained his biases against African-derived heritage. By 1921, however, he began to suggest that "purified" versions of such music and dance might be worthy of preservation. He noted that "even in *comparsas* [black carnival bands] of evident primitiveness we find something artistic ... why should we eliminate them when we can transform, improve, and incorporate them, thus purifying our national folklore? Don't we maintain other traditions just as savage, impure and impossible to purify, of corrupting and anti-social transcendence, such as the lottery and cock fighting?" (Ortiz 1984b, 34). In 1923 Ortiz advocated for the "descriptive study, with a goal of true social therapy, of certain antisocial practices such as acts of witchcraft and *ñañiguismo* " (1923, 48–49).[6] By the early 1930s, his attitudes toward Afro-Latin American cultural study had definitively shifted away from such views, influenced in part by strong nationalist and anti-imperialist sentiment in Cuba and by the international vogue of jazz and other Afro-diasporic musics. An essay from 1934 provides an example of this transformation in the tone of his scholarship.

In these times of national suffering and profound tragedy, in which Cubans must begin a reconquest of their own country, economically and politically, so that they survive in the face of the destructive force of foreign imperialism, it is absolutely necessary that all affirmations of the Cuban spirit of its own creation be supported. Ideological imperialism, if not as insidious as the economic imperialism that sucks the blood of our nation, is also deleterious...Let us try to better understand ourselves ... And let us not forget that vernacular music represents one of a nation's most vital forms, and that Cuban music resonates throughout the world, among all people.

(Ortiz 1934, 113)

Ortiz now argued that Cubans of all racial backgrounds had the same inherent potential in an intellectual sense and that racism had no place in modern Cuba. It was from this period on that he wrote his best and most widely influential works on black music and dance including *La africanía de la música folklórica de Cuba* (1950), *Los bailes y los teatros de los negros en el folklore de Cuba* (1951), and the five-volume *Los instrumentos de la música folklórica de Cuba* (1952–55). These works contain important scholarly information, yet are not free of anti-black sentiment. Until the end of his life, Ortiz tended to view culture through an evolutionist lens and suggested that it developed in a fairly unilinear fashion

---

[6] *Ñañiguismo* refers to Afro-Latin American religious and musical practices derived from the Cross River Delta region between present-day Cameroon and Nigeria.

from savage to complex. His disavowal of racism per se, combined with an ongoing belief in cultural hierarchy, led to recurrent tensions in his writing. His work attests both to the significant progress made by scholars of Afro-Latin American arts in the early twentieth century and to the extent to which much of their thinking remained confined to white supremacist presuppositions of the colonial period.

Early scholars of Afro-Latin American heritage tended to characterize Afrodescendant populations as simply African, a savage and exotic other. They concentrated their efforts on describing black cultural phenomena in detail and discussing their possible points of origin in Africa. Authors tended to view the *maracatu* phenomenon in Recife or the *terreiros* of Candomblé worship, for instance, as "African islands in Brazil," thus labeling the practices foreign and implicitly denying their members full citizenship (Lima 2012, 72). The period of the 1920s and 1930s, however, marked a transition to new ideological paradigms in which African-derived heritage throughout the region began to achieve greater acceptance.

## SCHOLARSHIP OF THE MID-TWENTIETH CENTURY

Many authors have discussed the rise of modern nation-states and the importance of nationalist political movements to the widespread acceptance of local forms of culture (e.g., Hall 1984; Hobsbawm 1990). Beginning at least with the writings of Johann Gottfried Herder (1744–1803), Western authors have suggested that individuals in emergent nation-states shared certain customs, including language and religion but also folklore, dance, and music. Many elites used shared identification with folklore as a way of generating patriotism and allegiance to new and more centralized forms of government, an important corollary to populist politics. Latin American elites adopted such discourses surrounding local musical traditions later than those in Europe, owing in part to the fact that political independence came later to the region and in part to the heavily stratified societies created in the wake of colonial rule. Additionally, the evolutionist mindset of the nineteenth and early twentieth centuries made the adoption of Afro-Latin American culture difficult, as mentioned; it tended to be viewed as a "*cosa de negros,*" a lesser form of expression rather than heritage shared by everyone. For many years nationalist movements in Latin America promoted what might be described as "white nationalism" (León 1991), an invitation for minorities to take part in projects of liberation or self-rule that presumed an acceptance of European cultural norms. Only gradually did various forms of

Afrodescendant, mestizo, or indigenous heritage (initially of a decidedly stylized nature) begin to achieve recognition as bona-fide national expression in the region.

The first half of the twentieth century in Latin America, therefore, might be described as one of an incipient cultural nationalism in which authors undertook studies of Afro-diasporic heritage fraught with bias. Yet the pioneers in this area represented the decidedly progressive thinkers of their day. Despite the limitations of their work, they undertook it in the face of tremendous resistance as mainstream society still had little or no interest in such topics. Some, such as Fernando Ortiz, hoped to find ways to "improve" and "elevate" the Afrodescendant musics of their respective countries. Others, perhaps influenced by a desire to understand the ultimate origins of all music and especially "primitive" musics, demonstrated an obsessive concern for the specific African origins of certain cultural practices. A focus on origins characterized the work of Francisco Augusto Pereira de Costa (1851–1923) in northeastern Brazil, for instance, as well as subsequent generations of scholars influenced by his work.[7] Others believed non-European traditional music to be in decline owing to contact with "superior" Western forms of music and collected them primarily for purposes of historical documentation (Miñana Blasco 2016, 94). Still others, embracing the positivistic ethos of the day, simply sought to catalogue and classify all cultural forms they encountered. Through the 1940s, even the most rigorous and least biased early publications tended to be heavily descriptive rather than analytical (Béhague 1982, 17).

Contextualizing the greater concern for Afrodescendant music among academics at this time was of course the rise of the popular music industry, phonograph sales, the growth of radio, and the prominent place that new forms of black, urban, working-class music held within the repertoires being marketed and disseminated internationally through the mass media. Eric Hobsbawm has characterized the development of the mass culture industry at this time as a revolutionary process in which musics from the margins of postcolonial society effectively displaced previous bourgeois arts institutions in the space of only a few decades, taking the world by storm. He considers this process the most important cultural development of the twentieth century (Hobsbawm 1987, 236). Jazz in its many forms as well as blues, Cuban *son,* tango, calypso, mento, samba,

---

[7] These individuals included Katarina Real, Roberto Benjamin, and Leonardo Dantas da Silva (see LaFevers 2016).

and a host of other Afrodescendant musical styles that had developed in the Americas gained widespread audiences during the 1910s and 1920s and established a dominance in the commercial sphere that they have retained ever since. As a consequence, black music became less a rural, peripheral phenomenon in the mid-twentieth century and more a part of the mainstream. Academics tended to ignore this new reality for some time, denouncing commercial music making as crass, tainted with foreign influence, or otherwise undeserving of study. Yet the avoidance of such trends made their publications increasingly less relevant, and they eventually revised their opinion as will be discussed.

Mário de Andrade (1893–1945) is a good example of the sorts of self-trained scholars who began to write on Afro-Latin American traditions in the early twentieth century in this context. His work illustrates how the slow collapse of oligarchic regimes in early twentieth-century Latin America led over time to a tentative embrace of non-European cultures and eventually to widespread social movements espousing multiculturalism of a sort beginning in the 1930s. A classically trained Brazilian pianist, poet, and novelist, Andrade demonstrated strong interest in traditional music and undertook extensive fieldwork in the 1930s, recording countless rural genres, Afro-Brazilian and otherwise (Simonett and Marcuzzi 2016, 4). Many of his recordings and accompanying notes have been reissued on CD recently (Camarga Toni 2010). Andrade called for conservatory-trained composers to take inspiration in the nation's folk music, advocating for a synthesis of academic and traditional repertoire in concert halls as an overt manifestation of Brazilianness. The case for such an approach is made in his influential "Ensaio sobre a música brasileira" (1928) and in later publications (Andrade 1937, 1941). Andrade preferred nationalistic composition strongly inflected by modernist and experimentalist trends; in this sense, his aesthetic sense closely parallels that of Alejo Carpentier in Cuba, Carlos Chávez in Mexico, José Enrique Rodó in Uruguay, Heitor Villa-Lobos in his own country, and others of the same generation. In much the same vein as Andrade's writings, Carpentier's publication *La música en Cuba* (1946) deserves mention. It provides an insightful overview of Cuban music from the earliest days of the colony through the mid-twentieth century, yet focuses primarily on nationalist concert music and academic compositions at the expense of popular (or even traditional) genres.

In these and other authors of the mid-twentieth century such as Gilberto Freyre (1900–87) and José Vasconcelos (1882–1959), one finds the origins of Latin American discourses of *mestizaje* and creolization that continue to have a strong influence on regional ideologies. Their rhetorical celebration of indigenous, Afrodescendant, and other cultures within the nation, and (grudgingly) of popular culture with similar influences, represents an important step forward in the struggle for cultural diversity. And yet to the extent that such authors accepted local traditional music as national heritage, they deemed it acceptable only if infused with or subordinated to European influences. The specific manifestations of this emergent ideology took various forms but invariably tended to gloss over longstanding practices of domination and oppression. In Mexico, Afrodescendant contributions effectively disappeared in Vasconcelos' writings and conception of a "cosmic race." In Brazil, the Vargas regime touted Afrodescendant forms such as *choro*, *maxixe*, and samba as quintessentially Brazilian even as it suppressed discussion of racial conflict. In Colombia, Cuba, and elsewhere intellectuals similarly embraced notions of racial mixture, yet studied such heritage in decidedly apolitical ways that disenfranchised Afrodescendant communities themselves. Frequently their scholarship portrayed Afro-Latin American music as timeless and unchanging forms of pre-modern expression (Miñana Blasco 2016, 94–95). To the extent that such music became a central focus of their research, it tended to be presented in regional or national festivals or studied without regard to its social meanings or uses in the present.

Additional examples of the sorts of publications described previously include Gallet's *Estudos do folklore* (1934), discussing the instrumentation and stylistic features of many forms of Afro-Brazilian traditional music and dance; Grenet's *Popular Cuban Music* (1939) with its overview of "African," "Spanish," and other influences; Coopersmith's work in the Dominican Republic (Coopersmith 1949); Alvarenga's *Música popular brasileira* (1950); Ortiz's later publications from the 1940s and 1950s; Ramón y Rivera's *El joropo* (1953); Pardo Tovar's publications on Afro-Colombian music (Pardo Tovar and Pinzón Urrea, 1961; Pardo Tovar 1966); and Howard's survey of drums in the Americas (Howard 1967), among others. All of these works were important and groundbreaking studies, helping to establish a literature where none had existed before. Most of the individuals writing such material worked without consistent institutional support and were trained in areas other than musicology or anthropology (Romero 2016, 85). Organological studies (focusing on systems of instrument classification, performance techniques, and instrument construction) featured prominently in their writings, as well as analyses of musical scales employed in particular repertoires, pitches, and melodies, and musical form or other stylistic elements. Many publications consisted of panoramic overviews describing the musics of a particular country or region in broad strokes and were not based on extended firsthand observation. Recent authors have critiqued this scholarship as devoid of critical analysis (Miñana Blasco 2016, 96).

Greater possibilities for commercial travel, international communication, film documentation, and sound recording facilitated extended ethnographic research in the mid-twentieth century. In conjunction with the further development of sociocultural anthropology as a discipline and recognition of the importance of extended fieldwork, these changes led to much more rigorous studies of Afro-diasporic heritage. The trend was particularly evident among academics based in the United States and Europe, many of whom were members of the newly established Society for Ethnomusicology, the International Folk Music Council, or similar organizations. New approaches to scholarship were also evident among academics in Latin America, many of whom studied abroad and/or incorporated influences from foreign research into their publications. The establishment of commercial air travel facilitated work by Harold Courlander in the Caribbean, Africa, and Southeast Asia, for instance. Born into a family of Jewish immigrants, Courlander developed an interest in black culture as he listened to the folk tales of black migrants from the US South in his hometown of Detroit, Michigan. Later based in New York, he made some of the first ethnographic recordings of Afrodescendant music of the Americas for the newly founded Folkways record label and published *The Drum and the Hoe* (1960) based on ethnographic work in Haiti in the 1930s and 40s. In Cuba, Lydia Cabrera's (1899–1991) career was similarly shaped by close contact with her local black community as a young girl, and later by studies in Paris. In addition to seminal publications on Afro-Cuban religion and mythology, she and her collaborator Josefina Tarafa made some of the earliest recordings of *batá* and *Palo* drumming in Havana and Matanzas in the 1950s, many of which have been recently re-released (Cabrera and Tarafa 2001a, 2001b, 2003; see also Simonett and Marcuzzi 2016, 15).

One of the most influential figures of the mid-twentieth century on Afro-diasporic cultural studies was Melville Herskovits (1895–1963). Also a son of Jewish immigrants, he studied anthropology with Franz Boas at Columbia University, graduating in the 1920s after conducting fieldwork in East Africa. Herskovits later conducted additional research in Haiti, Suriname, and elsewhere in the Americas, helping to establish African American studies and African diaspora studies as distinct fields of study. His monumental work *The Myth of the Negro Past* appeared in 1941, a pivotal period in which Nazi propaganda and racial atrocities led the international community to seriously challenge evolutionist notions of race. The book was the first to focus on African American culture and society throughout the hemisphere and to consider their influence on contemporary society. It documented the widespread ignorance and bias in previous academic publications on African American history and culture and discussed the influences of African-derived religion, music, and folklore on US society. Herskovits also focused on issues of cultural change (acculturation), at that time still a relatively new topic to anthropologists and scholars of traditional music. He trained several prominent students who focused on Afro-diasporic music later in their careers, including Alan Merriam, Richard Waterman, Robert Thompson, and Katherine Dunham, and at times collaborated directly with them (Herskovits and Waterman 1949). More recent authors have criticized many aspects of Herskovits' writings – their decidedly apolitical nature, the fact that they document but do not consider the reasons for the perpetuation of Afro-diasporic cultural forms, that they fail to provide an overarching theory with which to understand either cultural retentions or processes of acculturation – but for its day his work represented an unprecedented achievement. Though a focus on the African origins of particular styles of music and dance is no longer common, some scholars continue to embrace it, for instance Ivor Miller who has initiated transatlantic dialogues between performers in Cuba and the Niger Delta as part of his research (Miller 2009).

After World War II, it became increasingly common to find publications on Afro-diasporic culture written by authors with formal training in the social sciences who brought a more critical lens to their focus of study. The work of such individuals drew on anthropology, history, sociology, and other disciplines, and their interest in Afro-Latin American music touched on topics including religion, linguistics, the history of slavery, broad demographic trends, and interactions between Euro- and Afrodescendant populations. Such publications often framed their research in terms of trends in Latin America as a whole and drew data from multiple sites. Afro-diasporic religion became an especially intense focus of study, with data on music similarly contributing to interdisciplinary academic initiatives (see Chapter 12).

In the United States, some of the first individuals conducting research along these lines included students of Herskovits. Richard Waterman (1914–71), for instance, wrote a dissertation in the late 1940s on perceived Africanisms in the music of Trinidad and Tobago and shortly thereafter conducted fieldwork in Brazil, Cuba, and Puerto Rico. His publications attempted to assess the nature of African-derived musical practices of the Americas in terms of musical style (Waterman 1952). Waterman also made important early recordings of traditional music for the Library of Congress. Alan Merriam (1923–80), a co-founder of the Society for Ethnomusicology, wrote a dissertation on musical performance in the context of Brazilian Candomblé ritual (1951) before turning his attention to African and Native American musics, and to broader questions of theory. Folklorist and cultural anthropologist William Bascom (1912–81) published extensively on Yoruba and Yoruba-derived religions in Africa and the Americas in the 1940s through 1980 (Bascom 1972, 1980). To this group might also be added Norman Whitten, who conducted groundbreaking work in the 1960s on Afro-Ecuadorian and Afro-Colombian musical practices such as the *currulao* (Whitten 1967, 1974) and made numerous recordings for the Smithsonian Institute. All these authors continued to pursue research in small, tightly knit communities, frequently in rural areas. While their work made significant contributions, their choice of focus and modes of analysis continued to exclude almost all urban and mass-mediated repertoire.

Various French ethnographers and researchers conducted important studies of Afro-diasporic religions and expressive culture of a similar nature at approximately the same time. Photographer, self-taught ethnographer, and *babalawo* (an individual trained in the art of ritual divination in Yoruba-derived religions) Pierre Verger (1902–96) explored many parts of the world before settling in Salvador, Bahia in the 1940s. Thereafter he devoted his life to studying traditions of the African diaspora in that city, amassing substantial amounts of material and publishing some of it (e.g., Verger 1954). The non-profit Pierre Verger Foundation in Salvador holds tens of thousands of his photographs as well as many of his written documents, recordings, and other materials. Roger Bastide (1898–1974), a specialist in sociology and Brazilian literature, is also known for his contributions to the study of Afro-diasporic religions (Bastide 1971, 1978). Swiss anthropologist and human rights activist Alfred Métraux (1902–63) published extensively on indigenous communities of the Americas, largely through his affiliations with the Smithsonian Institute and UNESCO, before turning his attention to Afrodescendant populations. His book on Haitian *Vodoun* (Métraux 1959 contains important information about the role of music and dance in religious ceremonies).

Within Latin America as well, the period from 1950 to 1970 witnessed a gradual trend away from descriptive studies or facile discussion of tripartite racial heritage and toward more focused concern with particular minority groups and their music, as well as with other topics such as the migration of populations within or beyond Latin America and the effects of such movement on cultural forms. These trends coincided with the rapid urbanization of many regions in Latin America and the formation of expanded Latin American communities abroad. The efforts of individual scholars to document local cultures were bolstered by the establishment of many new research centers and cultural institutes: the Instituto Musical de Investigaciones Folklóricas in Cuba (1949); the Instituto Nacional de Folklore in Venezuela (1953); the Instituto de Cultura Puertorriqueña (1955); the Instituto Colombiano de Etnomusicología y Folklore (1964); as well as the creation of new journals: the *Revista Musical Chilena* in 1945, the *Inter-American Music Bulletin* in 1957, and *Actas del Folklore* in 1961, to name only a few.

Despite the migratory trends previously mentioned, most of the anthropologists and ethnomusicologists who conducted research on Afro-diasporic musical traditions in the 1950s and 1960s still worked in only one or two locations and focused their research on relatively isolated traditional communities. British-derived models of structural-functionalist analysis were central to their analysis, especially in the case of researchers from the United States. They viewed culture as a relatively static and homogeneous set of shared practices and behaviors. They perceived the ritual music they studied as reinforcing existing structures of social power by underscoring gender divisions, serving to mark transitions from adolescence into adulthood, and so on (e.g., Merriam 1964; , Nettl 1964; Turner 1967, 1969). While increasingly interested in issues such as acculturation, their analytical models often did not allow for a view of culture as emergent or contested, or in ascribing individual agency to performers or community members. Similarly, their focus on present-time studies of isolated societies made it difficult for them to recognize interactions or influences among multiple locations and resultant changes in cultural practices over time. Finally, this period was also one of firm belief in the objectivity of the researcher, faith in etic or external analysis as opposed to local views, and general lack of recognition of the political implications of foreign research by those from developed countries in the developing world, something that would change in the decades to come.

## TRENDS SINCE THE 1970S

The significant changes to the focus and tenor of scholarship on Afro-Latin American music since 1970, and to a majority of scholarship in the humanities and social sciences, derive in large part from broader processes. The critiques of colonialism and neocolonialism that began to emerge following World War II increased in intensity, leading to armed uprisings for independence in much of the developing world. In that context, scholars began to reexamine the frequent disconnect between their research and the concerns of the communities they studied, and the ways in which academic endeavors might be complicit in perpetuating structures of dominance. Postcolonial authors (Franz Fanon, Aimé Césaire, etc.) began disseminating their perspectives on the negative influences of the developed world on others, contributing to further self-scrutiny and making Latin America a less comfortable research site for those from the United States and Europe. New social movements (the feminist movement, gay rights, black power, liberation theology, etc.) and the anti-war movement in the United States and internationally led to a reevaluation of conventional views more broadly. The work of Michel Foucault reverberated through academic disciplines, demonstrating the positioned and political nature of all discourse, including academic writing, and again forcing researchers to consider the relationship of their work to structures of power. The Birmingham School in England, based on the work of Marxist-influenced scholars (Raymond Williams, Stuart Hall, Dick Hebdige), began to study culture as politically charged rather than autonomous and neutral, with renewed attention to class struggle, the repression of minorities, and other subcultures. Birmingham School scholars increasingly analyzed culture as a form of ideology with direct impact on the social order. All these influences led to greater focus among music scholars on the cultural projects of black communities themselves, on cultural agency, and on politics, resulting in essays such as Paulo de Carvalho Neto's "Folklore of the Black Struggle in Latin America" (1978).

The politicized turn in musical study in the United States and Europe, initiated in the 1970s by scholars such as John Blacking, Charles Keil, and Kenneth Gourlay, gained momentum and made scholars aware of the importance of discussing the relationships between themselves and the communities they worked with, as well as their own positioned perspectives. Certainly many individuals continued to write apolitically on themes of longstanding interest in the 1970s and 1980s based on ethnographic observation in small communities. But music publications increasingly demonstrated a greater sensitivity to the views of local communities, including discussion of "ethno-aesthetics." Gerard Béhague, for instance, and many of his colleagues in anthropology at the University of Texas continued to champion a model of performance ethnography well into the 1980s that used close observation of ritualistic events as the basis of research (Béhague 1975, 1984) yet foregrounded emic perspectives in the discussion of songs, dance movements, ritual objects, and actions. Afro-diasporic religious music and related activity inspired many new studies into the 1980s, 1990s, and beyond, both by foreign researchers (Barnes 1989; Brandon 1993; Hagedorn 2001; Brown 2003), by those living in Latin America (Lizardo 1975, 1979; Carvalho 1984), and increasingly by analysts who were initiates themselves. This period in which researchers first began to recognize the political resonance of musical expression represented an important step toward the more fully engaged forms of engaged or activist scholarship that emerged later.

In Latin America, the same tendencies involving gradual movement away from descriptive musical studies or concern for the origins of particular instruments or performance practices and toward socially informed scholarship and studies in urban areas are evident. Yet perhaps because of a lack of sustained institutional support for such research, or the lack of exposure to international publications, the process took longer (Simonett and Marcuzzi, 2016, 20). Certainly Marxist-influenced scholarship circulated widely in post-revolutionary Cuba and resonated throughout the region, including the work of José Luciano Franco (1959, 1968), Argeliers León (1964, 1974), and Leonardo Acosta (1982, 1983), among others. These individuals viewed black music, as well as that of other communities, within a framework of class struggle, colonialism, and postcolonialism. Studies of Afro-Latin American performers linked to notions of national patrimony (e.g., Castillo Faílde 1964; Rodríguez Domínguez 1978) were typical of the period as well, at least in part a reaction to perceived cultural imperialism and the imposition of foreign genres and artists. The 1980s gave rise to an expansion of musicological studies in Cuba generally, owing in part to the economic support of the Soviet Union and the use of culture in promoting an anti-imperialist agenda (Pérez Rodríguez; 1982, 1988; Pérez Fernández 1988; see also Moore 2006, 267–69). In various countries, detailed studies of particular Afro-Latin American music communities began to appear and researchers more consistently based their publications on sustained fieldwork (Vázquez Rodríguez 1982; Vinueza 1988).

A final significant trend of musical scholarship of the 1980s was greater interest in popular music repertoire, as researchers began to overcome their disciplinary biases and to study such forms in earnest. In the United States, one of the first individuals to publish on popular Afro-Latin American musical topics was John Storm Roberts (1972, 1979), followed by Gerard Béhague (1973, 1980), and Peter Manuel (1988). The new focus on popular music greatly enhanced the scope and relevance of musical study generally and has come to dominate subsequent publications. At the same time, the focus on commercial recordings and their dissemination through radio, television, and film created methodological problems in terms of how to study musical circulation and meaning. It also tended to blur the categories of "black" or "Afro-Latin American" music, since established popular genres (ska, roots reggae, salsa, hip-hop, reggaeton, cumbia) increasingly circulated among and were performed by non-black performers, and black stylistic influences increasingly fused with others (Afro-diasporic or not) derived from Europe, the United States, and elsewhere.

The 1990s and 2000s gave rise to a significant expansion in the study of Latin American music generally, and to the publication of many new scholarly resources. As one example, the Latin American branch of the International Association for the Study of Popular Music (IASPM), founded in 1997, has become a vibrant forum for the discussion and dissemination of musical research and has expanded dialogue among researchers throughout the region, facilitated greatly by the rise of the internet. The Brazilian Association for Ethnomusicology (Associação Brasileira de Etnomusicologia or ABET), founded in 2001, represents another locus of Afro-Latin American musical study, corresponding to the rise of Brazil as a global economic power. Graduate programs for the study of Latin American music were established in São Paulo, Rio de Janeiro, and other Brazilian cities and in Spanish-speaking America in Bogotá, Mexico City, Santiago de Chile, and elsewhere. Encyclopedias such as that edited by Malena Kuss (2007) provided additional sources of information on music of the African diaspora, and specialized textbooks appeared to support the classroom instruction of such repertoire (Dudley 2003; Murphy 2006; Moore 2010).

The turn of the twentieth century is also associated with the publication of case studies focusing on Afro-Latin American traditions that surpassed previous work in terms of their detail and the incorporation of extended musical analysis (e.g., Schechter 1999). Biographical studies of Afro-Latin American performers appeared for the first time (Vélez 2000;

Garcia 2006) and publications focusing on unique and forgotten histories of local musical styles (Dufrasne-González 1994; Moreno 1994; Pedroso 1995; McAlester 2002; Lima 2005, 2008; Guillen 2007). The tendency to focus on musical forms associated with black political struggle has intensified (Carvalho 1984, 1994; Carvalho and Segato 1992; Crook and Johnson 1999; Cunha 1998; Sheriff 1999; Fryer 2000; Sansone 2003; Pereira de Tugny and Caixeta de Queiroz 2006; Guilbault 2007; Pardue 2008; Sneed 2008), and studies that emphasize hidden Africanisms within mainstream musical practices have appeared (Quintero Rivera 1999).

Discussion of mestizaje and creolization have long been part of the analysis of cultural forms in Latin America and the Caribbean, as mentioned. But as notions of race, ethnicity, and the frequently self-conscious construction of identity became more central to musical study in the 1980s and beyond, the fragmented or hybrid nature of culture rose to prominence again as a focus. Kenneth Bilby (1985) considered such issues in relation to the British Caribbean, noting among other tendencies striking forms of inter-Afro-diasporic fusion in Jamaica and a tendency toward "polymusicality," the movement of musicians through distinct musical worlds or idioms. Paul Gilroy's work recognized that "black music" can frequently be an overly essentialized category, given that the process of colonial and postcolonial encounter accentuates "the inescapable fragmentation and differentiation of the black subject" (Gilroy 1993, 35). Similar issues are raised in García Canclini's *Hybrid Cultures* (1990, translated 1995), centered on processes of globalization and the interpenetration of the foreign and local in Latin American culture.

A focus on international cultural flows is evident in many publications from the first years of the twentieth century (e.g., Guilbault 1993; Flores 2000; Galinsky 2002; Rivera 2003; Perna 2005; Rivera et al., 2007). They are linked to the rise of globalization studies more generally, in turn inspired by neoliberal economic trends, free trade agreements such as NAFTA, the rise of new political and economic world powers such as China, India, and Brazil, and the ever more pervasive influence of internet music communities. Music scholars have responded to critiques of globalist/hybridity scholarship – that it often represents an apolitical discourse, that it may over-fetishize established cultural categories such as "traditional music," that it fails to recognize the hybrid nature of virtually all expression, or that it can be viewed as an extension of outmoded notions of mestizaje (Nederveen Pieterse 2001) – by framing their analysis either vis-à-vis the broader objectives of local communities or in terms of increasing international cultural influences within overarching structures of dominance (Stokes 2004). Studies considering the intersections of race, gender, and music appeared during this time as well, such those as examining the prohibitions surrounding women's performance of Afro-Cuban *batá* drums (Prior 1999; Sayre 2000).

Critiques of historical cultural processes of various kinds characterize publications of the 1990s and 2000s. Part of this tendency undoubtedly derives from the influence of work in the 1980s on "invented traditions," which called into question longstanding national or regional practices by considering how they had developed and whose interests they ultimately served (Hobsbawm and Ranger 1983). Rowe and Schelling (1991) explored related themes such as how local cultures in Latin America have been altered or manipulated in negotiation with foreign influences. García Canclini's (1995) interest in "stagings of the popular" intersects with such research as well, examining processes of folklorization in Latin America and manipulations of heritage in the service of political interests. Musical studies with a related focus include Hagedorn's (2001) study of the secularizing of black sacred repertoire in Cuba, Lane's work on blackface theater (2005), Rivero's study of racialized performance on early Puerto Rican television (2005), Thomas's work on race in *zarzuela* performance (2009), and Abreu's study of black and white Latino artists in the US media (2015).

Publications on cultural nationalism over the last twenty years present a similarly critical interrogation of local histories, with recent work exploring the conscious manipulation of cultural forms toward political ends. Such analysis coincides with the rise of multiculturalist politics in Latin America, renewed attempts on the part of racialized minorities to claim rights to land and full citizenship, and ongoing critiques of dominant discourses about national character and heritage (Hale 2005; Engle 2010). As noted, elite sectors of Latin American society have manifested decidedly ambivalent attitudes toward working-class cultural forms that develop through processes of fusion. Yet these are precisely the sorts of expression best suited to serve as national symbols. Thus, representing the nation through music can be highly problematic, and recent studies of Latin American musical nationalism have been useful in unearthing lines of social division as well as the strategies employed to hide or mitigate them. Many such publications have focused on case studies from the Caribbean (Glasser 1995; Pacini Hernandez 1995; Austerlitz 1997; Moore 1997; Largey 2006). Colombia (Wade 1993, 2000) and Brazil (Vianna 1999; Raphael 1990; Shaw 1999; Quintero-Rivera 2000; Sandroni 2001; McCann 2004; Magaldi 2008) have been the site of similar studies.

Another trend associated with the 1990s and beyond is the study of the racialized music of Latin America as a hemispheric or even global phenomenon. This sort of work recognizes the increasingly interconnected ideological worlds of the late twentieth century and beyond, facilitated by global transportation and media networks. Gilroy's *The Black Atlantic* (1993) represents one such study. Building on the work of Stuart Hall and others, the author emphasizes the permeability and emergent nature of blackness and also the many interrelationships and systems of exchange among distinct Afro-diasporic communities. While Gilroy's book has been critiqued for downplaying Third-World experience in favor of a focus on music making in the United Kingdom and United States, failing to recognize nation-states as ongoing axes of power (Puri 2004, 28), and over-essentializing the nature of Afro-diasporic music more generally (Radano 2003, 40–41), it remains influential. Recent studies adopting a similar hemispheric or transnational frame of reference in the analysis of music and race include Seigel's work on musical and racial interactions among residents in Brazil and the United States (2010), Putnam's study of jazz and calypso among Caribbean migrants throughout the hemisphere (2013), and others (Chasteen 2004; Feldman 2006; Rommen 2011).

## CONCLUSION

A concluding overview of publications since 2010 suggests possible trends in future research. John Gray's exhaustive bibliographic compilations on Afro-Latin American music (2010, 2011, 2012, 2013, 2014, 2015, 2016) have laid much of the groundwork for additional study of Afro-diasporic populations throughout Latin America and beyond. New books dedicated to Afro-Latin American musical performance (Ochoa, Santamaría and Sevilla 2010; Schweitzer 2013; Miller 2014) have added substantially to previous literature (Chao Carbonero 1980; Amira 1992; García and Minichino 2001). These works pose a substantive challenge to conservative musical institutions in ways that studies by historians and social scientists can not. Their analysis of sound, aesthetics, and improvisation documents the virtuosity and complexity of Afro-diasporic traditions and presents them in a way that composers, performers, music theorists, and others oriented toward Western notation can understand and dialogue with. Publications of this nature are slowly impacting the canonical, Eurocentric orientation of conservatories and schools of music throughout the hemisphere and should allow Afrodescendant repertoire to become more central to music pedagogy in the future.

In terms of collaborative academic work, institutions such as the Lauro Ayestarán National Center for Musical Sudy (or Centro Nacional de Documentación Musical Lauro Ayestarán, founded 2009, Montevideo) bring regional and international scholars together into dialogues over the music of the African diaspora (Aharonián 2013). With contributions by authors from Africa, Europe, the United States, and various parts of Latin America, the Center's publications represent a continuation of efforts initiated by Béhague, Crook, and Johnson in the 1990s (Béhague 1994; Crook and Johnson 1999).

Themes of racial politics and division continue to be evident in recent publications through the lens of nationalism (Hertzman 2013), regionalism (Bodenheimer 2015), commercial dance music performance (Vaughn 2012), racial memory and performance (Wirtz 2014), the self-conscious staging of local heritage (Sharp 2014), the spread of Latin American hip-hop scenes (Baker 2011; Pardue 2012; Burdick 2013; Saunders 2015; LaFevers and Santiago da Silva 2014; Perry 2016), music for tourists (Rommen and Neely 2014), and other topics. Following in the wake of George Yúdice's influential book on cultural expediency (Yúdice 2003) and examinations of the self-conscious and strategic uses of culture toward particular ends, topics related to black music and cultural rights/ activism remain prominent, as in Avelar and Dunn's edited collection (2011). This corresponds to a broader trend toward applied or activist scholarship within music studies generally (Harrison 2012), and to broader issues of cultural rights (Weintraub and Yung 2009).

Other relatively new areas of inquiry include a focus on whiteness and the racialized boundaries of black expression; on black music and nostalgia/memory; and critiques of black expression as represented in academic publications. Whiteness studies in music emerged some years after the topic gained currency in the humanities and social sciences (Rasmussen 2001), though one can find antecedent publications that address related topics.[8] Early examples of studies explicitly focused on whiteness focused on US expression (Kajikawa 2009, but the topic has only recently been

---

[8] Studies of musical nationalism in the 1990s, for instance, often emphasized the ways that white performers and composers altered black music stylistically as it came to be accepted as "everyone's music," thus making it conform more closely to white middle-class aesthetic norms. In terms of both its sound and its forms of social circulation, such music could therefore be described as whitened. Publications on blackface minstrelsy in the United States and elsewhere also anticipated recent whiteness studies in emphasizing the anxieties of groups who identify as white and their reactions to the mass popularization of non-white culture.

applied to Latin American music. Certainly various Afro-diasporic traditions such as marimba music or the bolero that developed in black communities and have now lost all direct association with blackness merit investigation from that perspective. Gidal's (2016) study of Umbanda religion in southern Brazil as practiced primarily by Brazilians who do not identify as black represents another interesting case in point. The *danzón*, yet another Afro-diasporic form no longer associated with blackness, has been studied by Madrid and Moore (2013). They focus both on its radically shifting racial associations through the years, the nostalgia that currently surrounds the music for its many fans, the ways it has been adopted by new, primarily non-black communities, and how it is reimagined based on particular views of the past.

While it is difficult to predict with certainty the future of Afro-Latin American music scholarship, the broad contours of such work are evident. Music will continue to be studied as an active part of broader social processes and as contributing to particular racial projects. Increasing emphasis will be placed on the emergent, shifting nature of blackness, its strategic deployment at particular moments, and the many forces that can influence perceptions of it on the part of black and non-black communities alike. Racialized music will increasingly be understood as part of hemisphere-wide or even global phenomena, and notions of blackness, Latin-ness, and mestizo-ness put into sustained dialogue with one another. Musical scholarship will maintain its links to other topics of interest in the humanities and social sciences such as individual and collective memory, national consciousness, regional character, Afro-diasporic allegiances, gender studies, activist scholarship, collaborations with local communities, and so on. Scholars will examine how in-group perspectives of black music are formed through dialogue with external groups and even broader transnational processes. The exploration of such interconnected histories, and of the fundamental interpenetration of Afro-descendant and Eurodescendant aesthetics in much present-day black music, will undoubtedly reveal important new insights.

## BIBLIOGRAPHY

Abreu, Christina D. 2015. *Rhythms of Race: Cuban Musicians and the Making of Latino New York City and Miami, 1940–1960.* Chapel Hill, NC: University of North Carolina Press.

Acosta, Leonardo. 1982. *Música y descolonización.* Mexico City: Presencia Latinoamericana.

1983. *Del tambor al sintetizador.* Havana: Editorial Letras Cubanas.

Aharonián, Coriun, ed. 2013. *La música entre África y América*. Montevideo: Centro Nacional de Documentación Musical Lauro Ayestarán.

Altmann, Thomas. 1998. *Cantos lucumí a los orichas*. Hamburg: Oché.

Alvarenga, Oneyda. 1950. *Música popular brasileira*. Rio de Janeiro: Editora Globo.

Amira, John, and Steven Cornelius. 1992. *The Music of Santería: Traditional Rhythms of the Batá Drums*. Crown Point, IN: White Cliffs Media.

Andrade, Mário de. 1928. "*Ensaio sobre a música brasileira*." São Paulo: I. Chiarato.

    1937. "O samba rural paulista." *Revista do Arquivo Municipal* 4, 41: 37–116.

    1941. *Música do Brasil*. Curitiba: Editora Guaira.

Andrews, George Reid. 1980. *The Afro-Argentines of Buenos Aires, 1800–1900*. Madison, WI: University of Wisconsin Press.

    2004. *Afro-Latin America. 1800–2000*. New York, NY: Oxford University Press.

Austerlitz, Paul. 1997. *Merengue: Dominican Music and Dominican Identity*. Philadelphia, PA: Temple University Press.

Avelar, Idelber, and Christopher Dunn, eds. 2011. *Brazilian Popular Music and Citizenship*. Durham, NC: Duke University Press.

Baker, Geoffrey. 2011. *Buena Vista in the Club: Rap, Reggaetón, and Revolution in Havana*. Durham, NC: Duke University Press.

Barnes, Sandra T., ed. 1989. *Africa's Ogun: Old World and New*. Bloomington, IN: Indiana University Press.

Bascom, William. 1950. "The Focus of Cuban *Santería*." *Southwestern Journal of Anthropology* 6, 1: 64–68.

    1972. *Shango in the New World*. Austin, TX: African and Afro-American Research Institute, University of Texas.

    1980. *Sixteen Cowries: Yoruba Divination from Africa to the New World*. Bloomington, IN: Indiana University Press.

Bastide, Roger. 1971. *African Civilizations in the New World*. New York, NY: Harper & Row. First published in 1967.

    1978. *The African Religions of Brazil: Toward a Sociology of the Interpenetration of Civilizations*. Baltimore, MD: Johns Hopkins University Press. First published in 1960.

Béhague, Gerard. 1973. "Bossa and Bossas: Recent Changes in Brazilian Urban Popular Music." *Ethnomusicology* 17, 2: 209–33.

    1975. "Notes on Regional and National Trends in Afro-Brazilian Cult Music." In *Tradition and Renewal*, edited by Merlin H. Forster, 68–80. Urbana, IL: University of Illinois Press.

    1980. "Brazilian Musical Values of the 1960s and 70s: Popular Urban Music from Bossa Nova to Tropicalia." *Journal of Popular Culture* 14, 3: 437–52.

    1982. "Ecuadorian, Peruvian, and Brazilian Ethnomusicology: A General View." *Latin American Music Review* 3, 1: 17–35.

    1984. "Patterns of Candomblé Music Performance: An Afro-Brazilian Religious Setting." In *Performance Practice: Ethnomusicological Perspectives*, edited by Gerard Béhague, 222–54. Westport, CT: Greenwood Press.

    1991. "Reflections on the Ideological History of Ethnomusicology." In *Comparative Musicology and Anthropology of Music*, edited by Bruno Nettl and Philip Bohlman, 56–68. Chicago, IL: University of Chicago Press.

2002a. "Recent Studies of Brazilian Music: Review-Essay." *Latin American Music Review* 23, 2: 235–51.

2002b. "Bridging South America and the United States in Black Music Research." *Black Music Research Journal* 22, 1: 1–11.

ed. 1994. *Music and Black Ethnicity: The Caribbean and South America.* Miami: University of Miami Press.

Bilby, Kenneth. 1985 "The Caribbean as a Musical Region." In *Caribbean Contours*, edited by Sidney Mintz and Sally Price, 181–218. Baltimore, MD: Johns Hopkins University Press.

Bodenheimer, Rebecca. 2015. *Geographies of Cubanidad: Place, Race, and Musical Performance in Contemporary Cuba.* Jackson, MI: University of Mississippi Press.

Brandon, George. 1993. *Santeria from Africa to the New World: The Dead Sell Memories.* Bloomington, IN: Indiana University Press.

Bremer, Fredrika. 1995. *Cartas desde Cuba.* Havana: Editorial Arte y Literatura.

Brown, David. 2003. *Santería Enthroned.* Chicago, IL: University of Chicago Press.

Burdick, John. 2013. *The Color of Sound: Race, Religion, and Music in Brazil.* New York, NY: New York University Press.

Cabrera, Lydia, and Josefina Tarafa. 2001a. *Havana, Cuba ca. 1957: Rhythms and Songs for the Orishas.* Washington DC: Smithsonian Folkways. CD 40489.

2001b. *Matanzas, Cuba, ca. 1957: Afro-Cuban Sacred Music from the Countryside.* Washington DC: Smithsonian Folkways. CD 40490.

2003. *Havana and Matanzas, Cuba ca. 1957: Batá, Bembé, and Palo Songs from the Historic Recordings of Lydia Cabrera and Josefina Tarafa.* Washington DC: Smithsonian Folkways. CD 40434.

Camarga Toni, Flávia, et al. 2010. *Missão de pesquisas folclóricas.* São Paulo: Associação Amigos do Centro Cultural São Paulo.

Carpentier, Alejo. 1946. *La música en Cuba.* Mexico City: Fondo de Cultura Económica.

Carvalho, José Jorge de. 1984. "Music of African Origin in Brazil." In *Africa in Latin America: Essays on History, Culture, and Socialization,* edited by Manuel Moreno Fraginals, 227–50. New York, NY: Holmes and Meier.

1994. *The Multiplicity of Black Identities in Brazilian Popular Music.* Brasilia: Universidade de Brasilia.

Carvalho, José Jorge de, and Rita L. Segato. 1992. *Shango Cult in Recife, Brazil.* Caracas: FFUNDEF, CONAC.

Carvalho Neto, Paulo de. 1978. "Folklore of the Black Struggle in Latin America." *Latin American Perspectives* 5, 2: 53–88.

Castillo Faílde, Osvaldo. 1964. *Miguel Faílde, creador musical del danzón.* Havana: Editora del Consejo Nacional de Cultura.

Chao Carbonero, Graciela. 1980. *Bailes yorubas de Cuba.* Havana: Editorial Pueblo y Educación.

Chasteen, John Charles. 2004. *National Rhythms, African Roots: The Deep History of Latin American Popular Dance.* Albuquerque, NM: University of New Mexico Press.

Coopersmith, Jacob. 1949. *Music and Musicians of the Dominican Republic.* Washington, DC: Pan American Union.

Coronil, Fernando. 1995. "Introduction. Transculturation and the Politics of Theory: Centering the Center, Cuban Counterpoint." In *Cuban Counterpoint: Tobacco and Sugar*, edited by Fernando Ortiz, ix–lvi. Durham, NC: Duke University Press.

Courlander, Harold. 1960. *The Drum and the Hoe: Drum and Lore of the Haitian People.* Berkeley, CA: University of California Press.

Crook, Larry, and Randal Johnson, eds. 1999. *Black Brazil: Culture, Identity, and Social Mobilization.* Los Angeles, CA: UCLA Latin American Center Publications.

Cunha, Olivia Maria Gomes da. 1998. "Black Movements and the 'Politics of Identity' in Brazil." In *The Cultures of Politics and the Politics of Culture: Re-Visioning Social Movements in Latin America*, edited by Sonia E. Alvarez, et al. Boulder, CO: Westview.

De la Fuente, Alejandro. 2008. *Havana and the Atlantic in the Sixteenth Century.* Chapel Hill, NC: University of North Carolina Press.

De Léry, Jean. 1990. *History of a Voyage to the Land of Brazil, Otherwise Called America.* Translated by Janet Whatley. Berkeley, CA: University of California Press.

Dudley, Shannon. 2003. *Carnival Music in Trinidad: Experiencing Music, Expressing Culture.* New York, NY: Oxford University Press.

Dufrasne-González, J. Emmanuel. 1994. *Puerto Rico tambien tiene – tambó! Recopilación de artículos sobre la plena y la bomba.* Rio Grande: Paracumbé.

Dunn, Christopher, and Charles A. Perrone, eds. 2001. *Brazilian Popular Music and Globalization.* Gainsville, FL: University Press of Florida.

Engle, Karen. 2010. *The Elusive Promise of Indigenous Development: Rights, Culture, Strategy.* Durham, NC: Duke University Press.

Feldman, Heidi. 2006. *Black Rhythms of Peru: Reviving African Musical Heritage in the Black Pacific.* Middletown, CT: Wesleyan University Press.

Flores, Juan. 2000. *From Bomba to Hip-Hop: Puerto Rican Culture and Latino Identity.* New York, NY: Columbia University Press.

Franco, José Luciano. 1959. *Folklore criollo y africano.* La Habana: Junta Nacional de Arqueología y Etnología.

     1968. *La presencia negra en el Nuevo Mundo.* Havana: Casa de las Américas.

Fryer, Peter. 2000. *Rhythms of Resistance: African Musical Heritage in Brazil.* Hanover, NH: Wesleyan University Press.

Galinsky, Philip. 2002. *"Maracatu Atômico": Tradition, Modernity, and Post-modernity in the Mangue Movement of Recife, Brazil.* New York, NY: Psychology Press.

     2015. *Maracatu Atômico: Tradition, Modernity, and Postmodernity in the Mangue Movement and the "New Music Scene" of Recife, Pernambuco, Brazil.* New York, NY: Routledge.

Garcia, David. 2006. *Arsenio Rodríguez and the Transnational Flows of Latin Popular Music.* Philadelphia PA: Temple University Press.

García, Nanette, and Maurice Minichino. 2001. *The Sacred Music of Cuba: Batá Drumming Matanzas Style.* New York, NY: Melantone Productions.

García Canclini, Néstor. 1990. *Culturas híbridas: estrategias para entrar y salir de la modernidad.* México, D. F.: Random House Mondadori.

1995. *Hybrid Cultures. Strategies for Entering and Leaving Modernity.* Minneapolis, MN: University of Minnesota Press.

Gallet, Luciano. 1934. *Estudos do folklore.* Rio de Janeiro: C. Wehrs.

Gidal, Marc. 2016. *Spirit Song: Afro-Brazilian Religious Music and Boundaries.* New York, NY: Oxford University Press.

Gilroy, Paul. 1993. *The Black Atlantic: Modernity and Double Consciousness.* Cambridge, MA: Harvard University Press.

Glasser, Ruth. 1995. *My Music Is My Flag. Puerto Rican Musicians and Their New York Communities, 1917–1940.* Berkeley, CA: University of California Press.

Gould, Stephen Jay. 1981. *The Mismeasure of Man.* New York, NY: W. W. Norton.

Gray, John. 2010. *From Vodou to Zouk: A Bibliographic Guide to Music of the French-Speaking Caribbean and Its Diaspora.* Nyack, NY: African Diaspora Press.

2011. *Jamaican Popular Music, From Mento to Dancehall Reggae: A Bibliographic Guide.* Nyack, NY: African Diaspora Press.

2012. *Afro-Cuban Music: A Bibliographic Guide.* Nyack, NY: African Diaspora Press.

2013. *Baila!: A Bibliographic Guide to Afro-Latin Dance Musics from Mambo to Salsa.* Nyack, NY: African Diaspora Press.

2014. *Afro-Brazilian Music: A Bibliographic Guide.* Nyack, NY: African Diaspora Press.

2015. *Carnival, Calypso and Steel Pan: A Bibliographic Guide to Popular Music of the English-Speaking Caribbean and Its Diaspora.* Nyack, NY: African Diaspora Press.

2016. *Hip-Hop Studies: An International Bibliography and Resource Guide.* Nyack, NY: African Diaspora Press.

Grenet, Emilio. 1939. *Popular Cuban Music: 80 Revised and Corrected Compositions Together with an Essay on the Evolution of Music in Cuba.* Havana: Carasa y Cía.

Guilbault, Jocelyne. 1993. *Zouk: World Music in the West Indies.* Chicago, IL: University of Chicago Press.

2007. *Governing Sound: The Cultural Politics of Trinidad's Carnival Musics.* Chicago, IL: University of Chicago Press.

Guillen, Isabel Cristina Martins. 2007. "Rainhas coroadas: Historia e ritual nos maracatus-nação do Recife." In: *Cultura afro-descendente no Recife: maracatus, valentes e catimbós*, edited by Ivaldo Marciano de França Lima and Isabel Cristina Martins Guillen, 179–202. Recife: Edições Bagaço.

ed. 2014. *Inventário Cultural dos Maracatus Nação.* Recife: Editora UFPE.

Hagedorn, Katherine. 2001. *Divine Utterances: The Performance of Afro-Cuban Santería.* Washington, DC: Smithsonian Institution Press.

Hale, Charles. 2005. "Neoliberal Multiculturalism: The Remaking of Cultural Rights and Cultural Dominance in Central America." *PoLAR* 28, 1: 10–28.

Hall, Stuart. 1984. *The Idea of the Modern State*. Philadelphia, PA: Open University Press.

Harrison, Klisala. 2012. "Epistemologies of Applied Ethnomusicology." *Ethnomusicology 56*, 3: 505–29.

Helg, Aline. 1995. *Our Rightful Share: The Afro-Cuban Struggle for Equality, 1886–1912*. Chapel Hill, NC: University of North Carolina Press.

Henry, Clarence Bernard. *Let's Make Some Noise: Axé and the African Roots of Brazilian Popular Music*. Jackson, MS: University Press of Mississippi, 2008.

Herskovits, Melville. 1941. *The Myth of the Negro Past*. Boston: Beacon Press.

  1944. "Drums and Drummers in Afro-Brazilian Cult Life." *Musical Quarterly* 30: 477–92.

Herskovits, Melville, and Richard Waterman. 1949. "Música de culto afrobahiana." *Revista de Estudios Musicales 1*, 2: 65–127.

Hertzman, Marc A. 2013. *Making Samba: A New History of Race and Music in Brazil*. Durham, NC: Duke University Press.

Hobsbawm, Eric. 1987. *The Age of Empire, 1875–1914*. New York, NY: Vintage Books.

  1990. *Nations and Nationalism since 1780: Programme, Myth, Reality*. New York, NY: Cambridge University Press.

Hobsbawm, Eric, and Terrence Ranger, eds. 1983. *The Invention of Tradition*. New York, NY: Cambridge University Press.

Howard, Joseph H. 1967. *Drums in the Americas*. New York, NY: Oak Publications.

Issa, Daniela. 2008. "Praxis of Empowerment: Mística and Mobilization in Brazil's Landless Rural Workers' Movement." In *Latin American Social Movements in the Twenty-First Century: Resistance, Power, and Democracy*, edited by Harry D. Vanden, et al. Plymouth, UK: Rowman & Littlefield.

Kajikawa, Loren. 2009. "Eminem's 'My Name Is': Signifying Whiteness, Rearticulating Race." *Journal of the Society for American Music 3*, 3: 341–63.

Kuss, Malena, ed. 2007. *Music in Latin America and the Caribbean*. Vol. 2. *Performing the Caribbean Experience*. Austin, TX: University of Texas Press.

Labat, Jean-Baptiste. 1970. *The Memoirs of Père Labat, 1693–1705*. Translated and abridged by John Eaden. London: F. Cass.

LaFevers, Cory. 2010. "The Sounds of Blackness in Brazil: Musical Affordance, Regional Identity, and Activism in Recife's Black Movements." Master's thesis, Syracuse University.

  2016. "Past, Present, and Future Trends in Brazilian Ethnomusicology. A General Overview." Unpublished paper.

LaFevers, Cory, and Viviane Santiago da Silva. 2014. "Projeto Yabas: Reflections on Hip-Hop and Black Women's Self-making in Brazil." *Alter/nativas Latin American Cultural Studies Journal 2*. http://alternativas.osu.edu/en/issues/spring-2014.html#essays1.

Lane, Jill. 2005. *Blackface Cuba, 1840-1895*. Philadelphia, PA: University of Pennsylvania Press.

Largey, Michael. 2006. *Voodoo Nation. Haitian Art Music and Cultural Nationalism*. Chicago, IL: University of Chicago Press.

León, Argeliers. 1964. *Música folklore: Yoruba, Bantú, Abakuá*. Havana: Ediciones del C.N.C.

1974. *Del canto y el tiempo*. Havana: Editorial Letras Cubanas.

1991. "Of the Axle and the Hinge: Nationalism, Afro-Cubanism, and Music in Pre-Revolutionary Cuba." In *Essays on Cuban Music: North American and Cuban Perspectives*, edited by Peter Manuel, 267–82. Lanham, MD: University Press of America.

León, Javier, and Helena Simonett, eds. 2016. *A Latin American Music Reader: Views from the South*. Urbana, IL: University of Illinois Press.

Le Riverend, Julio. 1961. "Fernando Ortiz cumple 80 años." *INRA* 2, 8: 38–43.

Lima, Ivaldo Marciano de França. 2005. *Maracatus-nação*. Ressignificando velhas histórias. Recife: Edições Bagaço.

2008. *Maracatus e maracatuzeiros: Desconstruindo certezas, batendo afayas e fazendo histórias. Recife, 1930–1945*. Recife: Edições Bagaço.

2009. "Afoxés: Manifestação cultural baiana ou pernambucana? Narrativas para uma história social dos afoxés." *Revista Esboços* 16, 2: 89–110.

2012. *Maracatus do Recife: Novas considerações sob o olhar dos tempos*. Recife: Edições Bagaço.

Lizard, Fradique. 1975. *Danzas y bailes folklóricos dominicanos*. Santo Domingo: Fundación García-Arevalo.

1979. *Cultura africana en Santo Domingo*. Santo Domingo: Taller.

Lombroso, Cesare. 2006. *Criminal Man*. Translated by Mary Gibson and Nicole Hahn Rafter, with translation assistance from Mark Seymour. Durham, NC: Duke University Press. First published in 1876.

Madrid, Alejandro, and Robin Moore. 2013. *Danzón: Circum-Caribbean Dialogues in Music and Dance*. New York, NY: Oxford University Press.

Magaldi, Cristina. 2008. "Before and after Samba: Modernity, Cosmopolitanism, and Popular Music in Rio de Janeiro at the Beginning and End of the Twentieth Century." In *Postnational Musical Identities: Cultural Production, Distribution, and Consumption in a Globalized Scenario*, edited by Ignacio Corona and Alejandro L. Madrid, 173–184. Lanham, MD: Lexington.

McAlester, Elizabeth. 2002. *Rara*. Berkeley, CA: University of California Press.

McCann, Brian. 2004. *Hello, Hello Brazil: Popular Music in the Making of Modern Brazil*. Durham, NC: Duke University Press.

Manuel, Peter. 1988. *Popular Musics of the Non-Western World: An Introductory Survey*. New York, NY: Oxford University Press.

Marcus, George. 1999. *Anthropology as Cultural Critique*. Chicago, IL: University of Chicago Press.

Merriam, Alan. 1951. "Songs of the Afro-Bahian Cults: An Ethnomusicological Analysis." PhD dissertation, Northwestern University.

1964. *The Anthropology of Music*. Evanston, IL: Northwestern University Press.

Métraux, Alfred. 1959. *Voodoo in Haiti*. New York, NY: Oxford University Press.

Miller, Ivor. 2009. *Voice of the Leopard: African Secret Societies and Cuba*. Jackson, MS: University of Mississippi Press.

Miller, Sue. 2014. *Cuban Flute Style: Interpretation and Improvisation*. Lanham, MD: Scarecrow Press.

Miñana Blasco, Carlos. 2016. "Between Folklore and Ethnomusicology. Sixty Years of Folk and Vernacular Music Studies in Colombia." In *A Latin American Music Reader. Views from the South*, edited by Javier León and Helena Simonett, 94–119. Urbana, IL: University of Illinois Press.

Moore, Robin D. 1997. *Nationalizing Blackness: Afrocubanismo and Artistic Revolution in Havana, 1920–1940*. Pittsburgh, PA: University of Pittsburgh Press.

    2006. *Music and Revolution: Cultural Change in Socialist Cuba*. Berkeley, CA: University of California Press.

    2010. *Music in the Hispanic Caribbean: Experiencing Music, Expressing Culture*. New York, NY: Oxford University Press.

    ed. 2018. *Fernando Ortiz on Music. Selected Writings on Afro-Cuban Culture*. Philadelphia, PA: Temple University Press.

Moreau de Saint-Méry, Médéric Louis Elie. 1798. *Description Topographique, Physique, Civile, Politique et Historique de la Partie Française de l'isle Saint-Domingue*. Paris: Dupont.

Moreno, Dennis. 1994. *Un tambor arará*. Havana: Editorial de Ciencias Sociales.

Murphy, John P. 2006. *Music in Brazil: Experiencing Music, Expressing Culture*. New York, NY: Oxford University Press.

Nederveen Pieterse, Jan. 2001. "Hybridity, So What? The Anti-Hybridity Backlash and the Riddles of Recognition." *Theory, Culture & Society* 18, 2–3: 219–45.

Nettl, Bruno. 1964. *Theory and Method in Ethnomusicology*. New York, NY: Free Press of Glencoe.

Nina Rodrigues, Raymundo. 1935. *O animismo fetichista dos negros da Bahia*. Rio de Janeiro, Civilização Brasileira.

Ochoa, Juan Sebastián, Carolina Santamaría, and Manuel Sevilla, eds. 2010. *Músicas y prácticas sonoras en el Pacífico afrocolombiano*. Bogotá: Editorial Pontficia Universidad Javeriana.

Oliveira, Jailma Maria. 2014. "Mulheres nos maracatus-nação pernambucanos." In *Inventário cultural dos Maracatus-Nação*, edited by Isabel Cristina Martins Guillen, 139–63. Recife: Editora UFPE.

Oliveira, Jailma Maria, and Lady Selma Ferreira Albernaz. 2011. "Homens travestidos no maracatu-nação pernambucano: Trânsito entre masculinidade e feminilidade." Paper delivered at *XI Congresso Luso Afro Brasileiro de Ciências Socias*. Salvador, August 7–10, 2011. Universidade Federal da Bahía.

Ortiz, Fernando. 1906. *Los negros brujos. Apuntes para un estudio de etnología criminal*. Madrid: Librería de Fernando Fé.

    [pseudonymn Juan del Morro]. 1923. "La Sociedad del Folkore Cubano." *Revista Bimestre Cubana*, 18, 1: 47–52.

    1934. "De la música afrocubana: Un estímulo para su estudio." *Universidad de la Habana* 1, 3: 111–25.

    1950. *La africanía de la música folklórica de Cuba*. Havana: Ministerio de Educación.

    1951. *Los bailes y el teatro de los negros en el folklore de Cuba*. Havana: Ministerio de Educación.

1952–55. *Los instrumentos de la música afrocubana.* 5 vols. Havana: Cárdenas y Cía.

1984a. "La antigua fiesta afrocubana del Día de Reyes." In Fernando Ortiz, *Ensayos etnográficos*, 41–78. Havana: Editorial de Ciencias Sociales. First published in 1920.

1984b. "Los cabildos afro-cubanos." In Fernando Ortiz, *Ensayos etnográficos*, 11–40. Havana: Editorial de Ciencias Sociales. First published in 1921.

Quintero Rivera, Angel G. 1999. *Salsa, sabor y control: Sociología de la música tropical.* San Juan: Siglo Veintiuno Editores.

Quintero-Rivera, Mareia. 2000. *A cor e o som da nação: A idea de mestiçagem na crítica musical do caribe hispánico e do brasil (1928–1948).* São Paulo: FFLCH-USP.

Pacini Hernandez, Deborah. 1995. *Bachata: A Social History of a Dominican Popular Music.* Philadelphia, PA: Temple University Press.

Packman, Jeff. 2011. "Musicians' Performances and Performances of 'Musician' in Salvador da Bahia, Brazil." *Ethnomusicology* 55, 3: 414–44.

Pardo Tovar, Andrés 1966. *La cultura musical en Colombia.* Bogotá: Ediciones Lerner.

Pardo Tovar, Andrés, and Jesús Pinzón Urrea. 1961. *Rítmica y melódica del folclor chocoano.* Bogotá: Universidad Nacional de Colombia.

Pardue, Derek. 2008. *Ideologies of Marginality in Brazilian Hip Hop.* New York, NY: Palgrave Macmillan.

2012. "Taking Stock of the State: Hip-Hoppers' Evaluation of the Cultural Points Program in Brazil." *Latin American Perspectives* 39, 2: 93–112.

Pedroso, Lázaro (Ogún Tolá). 1995. *Obbedi, cantos a los orishas: Traducción e historia.* Havana: Artex.

Pereira de Costa, Francisco Augusto. 1908. *Folk-lore pernambucano.* Rio de Janeiro: O Verl.

Pérez Fernández, Rolando Antonio. 1988. *La binarización de los ritmos ternarios africanos en América Latina.* Havana: Casa de las Américas.

Pérez Rodríguez, Nancy. 1988. *El carnaval santiaguero.* 2 vols. Santiago de Cuba: Editorial Oriente.

et. al. 1982. *El cabildo carabalí Isuama.* Santiago de Cuba: Editorial Oriente.

Periera de Tugny, Rosângela, and Ruben Caixeta de Queiroz, eds. 2006. *Músicas africanas e indígenas no Brasil.* Belo Horizonte: Editora UFMG.

Perna, Vincenzo. 2005. *Timba: The Sound of the Cuban Crisis.* London: Ashgate.

Perry, Marc. 2016. *Negro soy yo: Hip Hop and Raced Citizenship in Neoliberal Cuba.* Durham, NC: Duke University Press.

Price-Mars, Jean. 1965. "Homenaje a Fernando Ortiz." *La Gaceta de Cuba* 4, 42: 12–13. First published in 1956.

Prior, Andrea. 1999. "The House of Añá: Women and Batá." *CBMR Digest* 12, 2: 6–8.

Puri, Shalini. 2004. *The Caribbean Postcolonial: Social Equality, Post-nationalism, and Cultural Hybridity.* New York, NY: Palgrave Macmillan.

Putnam, Lara. 2013. *Radical Moves: Caribbean Migrants and the Politics of Race in the Jazz Age.* Chapel Hill, NC: University of North Carolina Press.

Radano, Ronald. 2003. *Lying Up a Nation: Race and Black Music*. Chicago, IL: University of Chicago Press.

Ramón y Rivera, Felipe. 1953. *El joropo, baile nacional de Venezuela*. Caracas: E. Armitano.

Ramos, Arthur. 1937. *As culturas negras no Novo Mundo*. Rio de Janeiro: Civilização Brasileira.

Raphael, Alison. 1990. "From Popular Culture to Microenterprise: The History of Brazilian Samba Schools." *Latin American Music Review* 11, 1: 73–83.

Rasmussen, Brander, et al., eds. 2001. *The Making and Unmaking of Whiteness*. Durham, NC: Duke University Press.

Rivera, Raquel. 2003. *New York Ricans From the Hip Hop Zone*. New York, NY: Palgrave Macmillan.

Rivera, Raquel, Wayne Marshall, and Deborah Pacini Hernandez, eds. 2007. *Reggaeton*. Durham, NC: Duke University Press.

Rivero, Yeidy. 2005. *Tuning Out Blackness: Race and Nation in the History of Puerto Rican Television*. Durham, NC: Duke University Press.

Roberts, John Storm. 1972. *Black Music of Two Worlds*. New York, NY: Original Music.

1979. *The Latin Tinge: The Impact of Latin American Music on the United States*. New York, NY: Oxford University Press.

Rodríguez Domínguez, Ezequiel. 1978. *Trío Matamoros: Treinta y cinco años de música popular*. Havana: Editorial Arte y Literatura.

Romero, Raúl. 2016. "Music Research in South America." In *A Latin American Music Reader: Views from the South*, edited by Javier León and Helena Simonett, 75–93. Urbana, IL: University of Illinois Press.

Rommen, Timothy. 2007. *"Mek some noise": Gospel Music and the Ethics of Style in Trinidad*. Berkeley, CA: University of California Press.

2011. *Funky Nassau: Roots, Routes, and Representation in Bahamian Popular Music*. Berkeley, CA: University of California Press.

Rommen, Timothy, and Daniel T. Neely, eds. 2014. *Sun, Sea, and Sound: Music and Tourism in the Circum-Caribbean*. New York, NY: Oxford University Press.

Rowe, William, and Vivian Schelling. 1991. *Memory and Modernity: Popular Culture in Latin America*. London: Verso.

Sandroni, Carlos. 2001. *Feitiço decente: Transformações do samba no Rio de Janeiro (1917–1933)*. Rio de Janeiro: Jorge Zahar Editor/Editora UFRJ.

Sansone, Livio. 2003. *Blackness without Ethnicity: Constructing Race in Brazil*. New York, NY: Palgrave MacMillan.

Saunders, Tanya. 2015. *Cuban Underground Hip Hop: Black Thoughts, Black Revolution, Black Modernity*. Austin, TX: University of Texas Press.

Sayre, Elizabeth. 2000. "Cuban Batá Drumming and Women Musicians: An Open Question." *Kalinda*, 13, 1: 12–15.

Schechter, John, ed. 1999. *Music in Latin American Culture: Regional Traditions*. New York, NY: Schirmer.

Schweitzer, Kenneth. 2013. *The Artistry of Afro-Cuban Batá Drumming: Aesthetics, Transmission, Bonding, and Creativity*. Jackson, MS: University Press of Mississippi.

Seigel, Micol. 2005. "The Disappearing Dance: Maxixe's Imperial Erasure." *Black Music Research Journal* 25, 1–2: 93–117.

2010. *Uneven Encounters: Making Race and Nation in Brazil and the United States*. Durham, NC: Duke University Press.

Sharp, Daniel B. 2014. *Between Nostalgia and Apocalypse: Popular Music and the Staging of Brazil*. Middletown, CT: Wesleyan University Press.

Shaw, Lisa. 1999. *The Social History of the Brazilian Samba*. Aldershot, UK: Ashgate.

Sheriff, Robin E. 1999. "The Theft of Carnaval: National Spectacle and Racial Politics in Rio de Janeiro." *Cultural Antrhopology* 14, 1: 3–28.

Simonett, Helena, and Michael Marcuzzi. 2016. "One Hundred Years of Latin American Music Scholarship: An Overview." In *A Latin American Music Reader: Views from the South*, edited by Javier León and Helena Simonett, 1–67. Urbana, IL: University of Illinois Press.

Sneed, Paul. 2008. "Favela Utopias: The *Bailes Funk* in Rio's Crisis of Social Exclusion and Violence." *Latin American Research Review* 43, 2: 57–79.

Stokes, Martin. 2004. "Music and the Global Order." *Annual Review of Anthropology* 33: 47–72.

Thomas, Susan. 2009. *Cuban Zarzuela: Performing Race and Gender on Havana's Lyric Stage*. Urbana, IL: University of Illinois Press.

Spix, Johann Baptist von. 1976. *Viagem pelo Brasil, 1817-1820*. São Paulo: Edições Melhoramentos.

Turner, Victor. 1967. *The Forest of Symbols: Aspects of Ndemu Ritual*. Ithaca, NY: Cornell University Press.

1969. *The Ritual Process: Structure and Anti-Structure*. Chicago, IL: Aldine.

Vaughn, Umi. 2012. *Rebel Dance Renegade Stance: Timba Music and Black Identity in Cuba*. Ann Arbor, MI: University of Michigan Press.

Vázquez Rodríguez, Rosa Elena "Chalena." 1982. *La práctica musical de la población negra en el Perú: La danza de negritos de El Carmen*. Havana: Casa de las Américas.

Vélez, María Teresa. 2000. *Drumming for the Gods: The Life and Times of Felipe García Villamil, Santero, Palero and Abakuá*. Philadelphia, PA: Temple University Press.

Verger, Pierre. 1954. *Dieux d'Afrique: culte des Orishas et Vodouns à l'ancienne Côte des esclaves en Afrique et à Bahia, la baie de tous les saints au Brésil*. Paris: P. Hartmann.

Vianna, Hermano. 1999. *The Mystery of Samba*. Translated by John Charles Chasteen. Chapel Hill, NC: University of North Carolina Press.

Vinueza, María Elena. 1988. *Presencia arará en la música folklórica de Matanzas*. Havana: Casa de las Américas.

Wade, Peter. 1993. *Blackness and Race Mixture: The Dynamics of Racial Identity in Colombia*. Baltimore, MD: Johns Hopkins University Press.

1999. "Representations of Blackness in Colombian Popular Music." In *Representations of Blackness and the Performance of Identities*, edited by Jean M. Rahier, 173–91. Westport, CT: Greenwood Press.

2000. *Music, Race, and Nation: Música tropical in Colombia*. Chicago, IL: University of Chicago Press.

Waterman, Richard. 1952. "African Influence on the Music of the Americas." In *Acculturation in the Americas: Proceedings and Selected Papers of the 29th International Congress of Americanists*, edited by Sol Tax, vol. 2, 207–18. Chicago, IL: University of Chicago Press.

Weintraub, Andrew, and Bell Yung, eds. 2009. *Music and Cultural Rights.* Urbana, IL: University of Illinois Press.

Whitten Jr., Norman. 1967. "Música y relaciones sociales en las tierras bajas colombianas y ecuatorianas del Pacífico." *América Indígena* 27, 4: 635–66.

1974. *Black Frontiersmen: A South American Case.* Cambridge, MA: Schenkman Publishing.

Wirtz, Kristina. 2014. *Performing Afro-Cuba: Image, Voice, Spectacle in the Making of Race and History.* Chicago, IL: University of Chicago Press.

Yúdice, George. 2003. *The Expediency of Culture: Uses of Culture in the Global Era.* Durham, NC: Duke University Press.

# 12

# Afro-Latin American Religions

## Paul Christopher Johnson and Stephan Palmié

This chapter presents a concise overview of scholarship on religious formations in Latin America that are historically or currently associated with notions of African origin. It covers a broad spectrum of traditions and regions, yet we place considerable emphasis on two areas that were the recipient of the most intensive slave traffic, and were thus often thought to harbor the "most African" ritual traditions: Cuba and Brazil. This is a deliberate decision, and it has implications for both the structure and content of this chapter, which oscillates regularly between Cuba and Brazil, while periodically ranging to other regions in order to spur wider comparative reflection. We begin with a consideration of the empirical and theoretical questions informing a realistic conception of the historical transmission of forms of religious culture from Africa to the Ibero-American colonies. We then turn to matters of inter-religious encounter. In the third section, we consider post-abolition and twentieth-century constraints and affordances posed by law, the social sciences, and the nation-state. Here we explain why neither the qualifier "Afro" nor the concept of "religion" ought to be taken at face value when considering traditions of varying depth that locate their sources of legitimacy, authenticity, and ritual efficacy in notions of African origin. In the last section, we describe the features of contemporary praxis in some traditions, and the kinds of transversal effects generated by various forms of mediation between formerly distinct Afro-Latin American ritual traditions now gathered, at least in certain venues, as a unified superform.

## TRANSMISSION

The existence of ritual traditions that can be subsumed under the label "Afro-Latin American religions" is the result of the violent displacement of upwards of six million enslaved Africans (almost two-thirds of all slaves shipped to the Americas) to the New World colonies of Spain and Portugal. Africans who survived the horrors of the Middle Passage carried with them complex conceptions of the world including ideas about the relation between humans and forces or entities that we might be inclined to categorize, rightly or wrongly, as belonging to the realm of the religious. Just as the Spanish and Portuguese engaged the New World through the lens of Christian hierophanies and by means of rituals directed toward Christ, the Virgin, and various saints, so did their African slaves populate the Americas with deities and forces originating in their former social environments.

There is much to commend this view. As the young Cuban lawyer Fernando Ortiz (1973, 24) wrote in 1906, "African fetishism entered Cuba with the first black." His disparaging formulation notwithstanding, Ortiz was echoed some forty years later by an informant of the ethnographer Lydia Cabrera (1983,147). "Ever since the first slave ship landed," the man whom she chose to call José del Rosario told her, "the first Congo who stepped on Cuban soil cut branches [of vegetation], disinterred the dead, and began to work with his [spirit of the dead], and taught his children [to do so, too]." Archival evidence supports such a view. Practices among African slaves and freedmen perceived as "superstitious" or "idolatrous" by ecclesiastical and secular authorities appear in the colonial record even before the formal institution of the Holy Inquisition in Mexico in 1571, and in Lima and Cartagena de las Indias thereafter. According to documents scrutinized by María Teresa de Rojas (1956, 1285), as early as 1568, Havana's city commander, Bartolomé Ceperos, deplored the "scandalous" antics of Congolese blacks who called themselves "kings and queens" and engaged in ritual gatherings of profoundly African nature. African practices likewise appear in the early records of Brazil, and the terms of inquisitorial condemnation – most often as *feitiçaria* (fetishism) or *curandeirismo* – were early established by the Portuguese, not only on the Central West African coast but also among Jesuit descriptions of Tupi-speaking indigenes of the Brazilian coast (Souza 1986; Vainfas 1989; Mott 2010). By the 1600s we find clear evidence of African ritual complexes. The seventeenth-century Bahian-born poet, Gregório de Matos, famously described in one poem,

All these quilombos,
With peerless masters,
Teaching by night
Calundus and fetishism
Thousands of women
Attend them faithfully.
So does many a bearded man [a Portuguese]
Who thinks himself a new Narcissus.

(Sweet 2003, 146–47).

De Matos must have presumed that the word "calundu" – the earliest term used in Brazil to name African possession rituals – was recognizable to at least some readers, suggesting that such events were a known part of the city's social life. By the early 1700s, Bahian clergy established a catechism to properly evangelize to slaves, suggesting a perceived threat posed by slaves' own practices. Shortly thereafter appeared the first detailed description of said calundu in print, in Nuno Marques Pereira's 1728 *Compêndio narrativo do peregrino da América*. So-called *bolsas de mandinga* – fetish-objects or small sacks worn on the body as amulets of protection – also frequently appeared in early reports (Reis 1993; Harding 2000; Parés 2013).

Slaveholding planters, priests, and secular authorities alike recognized that the enslaved engaged in practices that could not simply be explained by their conditions of captivity, but related to their past lives in Africa, and the worldviews that had given structure and coherence to such lives. Nevertheless, the perspective of an unbroken continuity of African ritual practice in the New World implied by such sources is by no means unproblematic. This so because any *historical* consideration of African-derived (or "African inspired" as authors like Ochoa [2010] have recently put it) ritual formations in the Americas has to take account of a bewildering range of variables. These include New World variations in regional patterns of slave importation from Africa over time, but also variations in the local conditions under which the enslaved may have been able to transform African cosmologies and the ritual practices associated with them into viable social institutions (Morgan 1997).

African Americanist scholarship long tended toward direct equations between demographic input from specific African regions and cultural "output" in specific New World localities (as pioneered by Melville J. Herskovits [1941]). This chapter, in contrast, attends to the gaps, fissures, interstices and, at times, sheer inventiveness of African religions in the Americas. In both Cuba and Brazil, we now know too much about the concrete histories of ritual formations that claim African origins for themselves, to entertain a view that would argue for specific African input alone. We know, for example, that even though Yoruba-speaking slaves arrived in Cuba no later than the late eighteenth century, it took at least three generations after that until the Cuban version of the Ifá oracle finally was put on a reproducible institutional footing there, at the very end of the nineteenth century, when a small group of elderly Africans innovated a genuinely New World basis for its initiatory reproduction (Brown 2003a). In Brazil, the prominence of Ifá and then its decline (before its recent recuperation via Cubans in Rio de Janeiro [Capone 2016]) likewise seems to have hinged on the careers of relatively few key figures like Domingos Sodré (Reis 2008), Agenor Miranda Rocha, and Martiniano Eliseu de Bonfim and the travels between Brazil and then-British Nigeria of the likes of Martiniano (Matory 2005). Different temples (*terreiros*) emerged and gained notoriety in part through their idiosyncratic African "recoveries" – most famously the abrupt institution of a committee of twelve "Ministers of Xangô" at the terreiro called Axé Opô Afonjá, born in 1910. Or, among many other transformations of "the tradition," the move from a mostly male priesthood in the early 1800s to a priesthood more evenly divided by gender at the close of the century (Parés 2013) – while still prominently advertising the orthodoxy of female leadership in at least one nation (Ketu) of Candomblé (Landes 1947).

We will have to give up the view of unmediated continuities between Africa and the Americas. As Roger Bastide (1978:47) perceptively wrote in the case of Brazil, incipient traditions of African ritual practice were subject to multiple contingencies.

Time, in the long run, would erode all traditions, however firmly anchored in the new habitat. But the slave trade continuously renewed the sources of life by establishing continuous contact between old slaves, or their sons, and the new arrivals, who sometimes included priests and medicine men. In this way, throughout the whole period of slavery, religious values were continuously rejuvenated at the same time that they were being eroded. We know little about the Afro-Brazilian religions in those distant times, but we should certainly give up the notion of cult centers surviving though the centuries to the present day (something that slavery precluded), and think rather of a chaotic proliferation of cults or cult fragments arising only to die out and give way to others with each new wave of arrivals.

Bastide's caveats are relevant both in a temporal and a spatial sense. Particularly in the case of Spain, which was excluded from direct trade with Africa, regions of African origin fluctuated widely in response to the *asiento* contracts that Spain had to conclude with Portuguese and later northern European purveyors of enslaved Africans to its New World colonies (see Chapter 2). But the developmental stages and corresponding labor needs of specific locations within Spain's imperial purview also dictated not only numbers of newly imported slaves but often their African provenance as well. Thus, while the mining and incipient hacienda industry in Mexico (and to a lesser extent, Peru) absorbed the bulk of slaves imported into the Spanish American empire in the sixteenth and seventeenth centuries, the rapid decline of the economic utility of slave labor in New Spain, New Granada, and Peru after the beginning of the eighteenth century also made for the radical decline of any recognizably "African" forms of ritual praxis there. In contrast, it was the late development (or redevelopment) of slave-labor-based sugar economies in Cuba and Brazil that led to massive surges in legal and illegal slave importations to these regions in the nineteenth century. The conjuncture of these late sugar booms in Cuba and Brazil with the political developments that plunged into prolonged warfare the Yoruba-speaking city-states of what today is southwestern Nigeria may explain the eventual emergence of the Yoruba-inspired traditions of Regla de Ocha and Candomblé as well as the Gbe-inspired traditions of Jeje Candomblé. Indeed, some research now points to the rivalry between Oyo and Dahomey, the two dominant city-states around the Bight of Benin, as extending into the Americas and driving the emergence of marked nations of Candomblé, as well as the development of nations of spirits in Haitian Vodou (Silveira 2006; Hébrard 2012; Parés 2013).

CONFLUENCES

## Afro-Catholicisms

Enslaved Africans entered institutional frameworks that generated locally specific opportunities and constraints when it came to reasserting notions of their relation to entities – spirits, deities, ancestors, forces of nature – that formed part and parcel of their world. African religious traditions did not find their best chance of reassertion in the New World in the plantation zones where, during the heyday of the Atlantic slave trade, grueling labor conditions, excessive mortality rates, and highly unbalanced sex ratios made for a constant turn-over of the labor force, and so inhibited the social reproduction of whatever traditions temporarily took hold (Moreno Fraginals 1983, 24–49). Instead, chances for such incipient traditions to perdure were greater in urban contexts, especially when colonial power structures unwittingly provided them with institutional sites of germination. In the Latin American case, institutions such as the Spanish American *cabildos de nación* and Catholic lay brotherhoods (*cofradías*, or *irmandades* in Brazil, as will be discussed) were some of the most efficient incubators of Afro-Latin American ritual traditions. Modeled on voluntary associations of resident foreigners in Seville (Pike 1967), such corporations were designed as an instrument of control over African slaves and freedpeople who were expected to congregate along what were presumed to be "ethnic" or "ethnolinguistic" lines (hence the qualifier "de nación").

Such *cabildos* and *cofradías* organized along the lines of emergent New World African ethnicities existed in the slaveholding urban Spanish Americas as early as the second half of the sixteenth century (Aimes 1905, Ortiz 1921, Acosta Saignes 1955, Friedemann 1988; de la Fuente 2008), and their ritual practices diverged from clerical and secular colonial expectations (for recent analyses, see Farias, Soares, and Gomes 2005; Soares 2011; Cañizares-Ezguerra, Childs, and Sidbury 2013). The extent to which such practices were informed by direct continuities between ethnically specific African cultures and their colonial American equivalents is subject to debate. But it is clear that such institutional frameworks provided Africans with cultural and linguistic commonalities, and the opportunity to adapt prior ritual practices and cosmological notions not just to New World contexts of enslavement, but to the formal dictates and practical routines of Iberian versions of the Catholic faith. In 1755, the newly installed Bishop of Havana, Pedro Agustín Morell de Santa Cruz, thus made a concerted effort to register the city's then existing twenty-one *cabildos de nación* in order to target them for missionization, suggesting that priests in whose parishes these cabildos were located acquaint themselves with the African languages spoken by their members (Marrero 1971–1978, VIII: 160). Little came of Morell's enlightened project. But it indicates that, by this time, incipient African-derived ritual traditions were evolving within a complex ecology of religious practices. These included not just official versions of Catholicism, but Iberian folk practices such as heterodox forms of saintly devotions, healing and divination practices, and curses and spells with deep histories on the Iberian peninsula.

In Brazil likewise, Catholicism provided the encompassing colonial religious framework. At least some arriving Africans were already nominally Catholic, given the missionization of the Kongo by Capuchins and

Dominicans since the late 1400s and in the late sixteenth century by the Jesuits. Catholicism was the state religion of the Kingdom of Kongo from 1509 to 1542, and early Afro-Catholic institutions were established, including confraternities devoted to specific saints (Thornton 1998; Fromont 2014). Afro-Catholicism also became integral to the currency of metropolitan Portuguese society, in part via the popularity of saints like Ephigenia, Benedict, Antônio, and Gonçalo and the material practices applied to their cultivation. Gilberto Freyre went so far as to attribute Loyola's *Spiritual Exercises* and the birth of the Jesuits to "African sources," via the mysticism of Moors (Freyre 1956, 78). We need not fully endorse Freyre's notorious hyperbole to concede the broad point of an African influence on Iberian versions of Portuguese Catholicism.

In some parts of Brazil, like São Paulo, the first African slaves arriving from Portugal (Heywood 1999) brought with them versions of Luso-African Catholicism. There were multiple sources for what Bastide (1978, 109–25) called Brazil's "two Catholicisms": the version carried to Brazil by enslaved Central Africans, already at least nominally Catholic; the version of Portuguese popular Catholicism that was already, in part, "Africanized"; and of course to these we must add the new versions of Afro-Catholic practice that came into being in Brazil, Cuba, Saint Domingue, New Spain, and elsewhere through the mandated Christianization of slaves. The result of that transculturation, to take Fernando Ortiz's term, was a baroque Catholicism that placed a heavy emphasis on the exchange with saints (Souza 1986), on festivals and processions (Reis 2003a), and on *diabolismo,* possession, and physical vulnerability to magical attacks, or *feitiço* (Mott 1993, 59–65; Parés 2013, 78). Still, we should be cautious in the simplistic attribution of Catholic religious identifications since what Cécile Fromont called "Kongo Christianity," like Afro-Brazilian Catholicism a century later, or indeed all popular Catholicism, was selective, pragmatic, aesthetically developed, and variable (Sweet 2003, 197–98; Fromont 2014). Certain saints attracted interest while others were ignored. Medallions, amulets, and talismans protecting the body enhanced luck or life chances. They were valued in Brazil as in Africa, such that rosaries were popular power objects, sometimes even regarded as *nkisi* (Karasch 1979). Such unevenness applied equally to the making of "African religion" in the Americas, with African rituals related to healing gaining ascendancy over, say, sociopolitical rites or ones related to warfare, since political sovereignty and the possibilities for armed resistance were mostly foreclosed.

As elsewhere, Africans in Brazil formed confraternities (Mulvey 1980, Kiddy 2005; Soares 2011). With the support of both the Pope and the Portuguese king, Jesuits in Pernambuco initiated a confraternity specifically for slaves by 1552 (Mulvey 1980, 254), since Africans and Afro-Brazilians were barred from "white" brotherhoods. The inverse was not inevitably the case, such that by the nineteenth century whites sometimes made up a third or more of "black" brotherhoods. Women were also able to join and did so in substantial numbers. By founding their own lay confraternities Africans and their descendants created their own expressions of Afro-Catholic devotion, even as they became "Brazilian" through taking part in the brotherhoods' events. Most famous among the Afro-Brazilian brotherhoods was Nossa Senhora do Rosário, both in Bahia and in Rio. In Bahia the order initially accepted only Angolans before later also accepting Brazilian-born slaves and freemen and then, in the nineteenth century, coming to be dominated by Gbe-speaking Jejes, or Dahomeans (Reis 1993, 151). Other orders and churches were associated with Yoruba-speaking Nagôs – such as Nossa Senhora da Boa Morte, exclusive to slaves and freemen who identified with the city-state of Ketu – while still other orders were open only to *pardo*, or mixed-race members.

While some organizations had as few as twenty participants, others grew to over 500 in densely populated cities of Minas Gerais, Pernambuco, Bahia, and Rio de Janeiro (Mulvey 1980, 268). Some 80 percent of Africans and Afro-Brazilians in the colony joined confraternities, often dividing their time between several at the same time (Reis 2003a, 45). The confraternities generated consequential social affinities and distinctions. White brotherhoods were divided by class, trade or craft guilds, and property-ownership; black brotherhoods likewise segmented the population in multiple ways, dividing slaves and freemen at times by language and ethnicity (initially forming the Afro-Brazilian complex of "nation"), and at times by "race," distinguishing African-born from Creole blacks, and mulattos from both of these (Bastide 1978, 115; Reis 2003a, 44). Despite their diverse fields of stratification, the Catholic brotherhoods served as rare sites of shared humanization in an otherwise often brutal slavocratic society. In the brotherhoods, Africans and Afro-Brazilians earned positions of merit and respect, found the guarantee of a respectable burial for their family members upon death, and, most importantly, collected funds for mutual aid and manumission. Still, the birth of Afro-Brazilian religions cannot be understood solely as a form of resistance to slavery. The leaders of Afro-Brazilian institutions in the nineteenth century were overwhelmingly free Africans, an elite class that sometimes owned slaves themselves. To take two examples, Marcelina da Silva, priestess of one of the earliest and most prestigious terreiros of Brazil, the Casa Branca, continued buying slaves until 1875, even after antislavery laws like the Law of the Free Womb had come into effect and the end of the slave system was clearly in sight (Parés and Castillo 2010, 20). The well-known diviner Domingos Sodré likewise owned slaves (Reis 2008).

That said, it is clear that the Portuguese master-class mostly feared the emerging Afro-Brazilian traditions as a threat of rebellion. To counter that threat, ethnic divisions were instituted through Catholic brotherhoods as colonial policy. It was hoped that this would prevent any prospect of total solidarity among Africans and Afro-Brazilians. Even after an uprising in 1816, the governor of Bahia continued to grant slaves the liberty of assembly on Sundays and saints' days in specific locales, arguing that the freedom for ethnic groups to follow their own customs would prevent dangerous inter-ethnic alliances (Reis 1986, 115). Such limited "official" spaces allowed slaves' religious practices to be performed, conserved and created.

Comparable scenarios unfolded in Cuba, Mexico, and elsewhere. As Herman Bennett (2005, 2009) has shown in considerable detail for seventeenth-century Mexico City, Catholic *cofradías* provided a primary space of socialization and civil life for Afro-Mexicans. Afro-Mexicans also contributed to the development of an aesthetically rich Catholicism replete with images, processions, and saints (Germeten 2006). Afro-Mexican piety was in many regards comparable to Cuba's or Brazil's Catholic baroque (Ortiz 1975; Reis 2003a, 39). Bastide noted that, "wherever black brotherhoods existed, African religion survived – in Uruguay, Argentina, Peru, and Venezuela – and that these African religions disappeared in those countries where the church refused to allow the brotherhoods to meet for dancing outside the church after mass" (1978, 54). George Reid Andrews (1980, 139–70) confirmed Bastide's hypothesis for Argentina. In one of the Latin American nations that most aggressively effaced Africanness from its national mythology, Afro-Argentine Catholic confraternities – which mostly predated Euro-Argentine *cofradías* in the nineteenth century – allowed for the emergence of particular dance styles, most famously the tango via the candombe – a precursor to the *congada* dances accompanied by two-drum (in Argentina) or three-drum (in Uruguay and in Minas Gerais, Brazil) ensembles, systems of mutual aid, and even ethnic "nations."

A key part of the social lives of confraternities was the cultivation and celebration of the group's specific patron saint, and thus, through the overall complex of confraternities, the production of a collective *pantheon* of saints – their icons, sites, processions, proclivities, colors, and dates. Not coincidentally, the generation of "Afro-Brazilian religion" also depended on the creation of institutions that would support an intersecting network of "saints," or gods (*orixás, voduns, inquices*), and cues us to bridges between Catholic and later Afro-Brazilian ritual assemblages. In some instances, Afro-Brazilians not only reinforced the importance of select saints already canonized by the Church, they generated their own. Such was the story of Rosa Maria Egipcíaca da Vera Cruz, discovered by Luiz Mott (1993). Rosa was enslaved and shipped from Ouidah at age six, landing in Rio de Janeiro in 1725. After twenty-five years of slave labor, abuse, and forced prostitution (as a so-called "profit slave," *escrava de ganho*), by the mid-eighteenth century she began to have mystical visions and to recount them in vivid detail. She came to be revered as a popular saint, and everyday people sought contact with her to produce miraculous results. As perhaps the earliest African-born author in Brazil, she wrote at length about her visions in terms that eventually attracted authorities' attention. In 1765 she was accused by the Office of the Inquisition and sent to Lisbon for trial.

There are many examples of slaves acquiring a sublime, saintly status in Brazil, even in the twentieth century, as in the case of Escrava Anastácia (Slave Anastácia) (Hayes and Handler 2009; Burdick 1998; Sheriff 1996; Karasch 1986; Wood 2011; Johnson, forthcoming). Popular Catholic saints – such as Rosa Egipcíaca and Escrava Anastácia, like others indexing mixed-race fusions such as María Lionza in Venezuela (Ferrándiz 2003, Canals 2017), or, today, the Mayan rogue "saint" Maximón in Guatemala who eventually migrated to some Garifuna altars in Honduras – demonstrate the creative vitality of Afro-Catholicism, despite the severe restrictions placed on it. Official agents of the Church were overwhelmingly hostile toward African and Afro-American practices through at least the middle of the twentieth century. Only since Vatican II, and under threat by burgeoning Neo-Pentecostal sects in Brazil that since 1970 have come to command about a quarter of Brazilians' expressed religious affiliations, has the Catholic Church made a concerted effort to incorporate "Africanisms" into its liturgies, such as using putatively African drum and dance styles in the "inculturated mass" (Burdick 1998). Yet in spite of the centuries-long battle against African and indigenous practices, and certainly without intent, the Church supplied spatio-temporal frames, and material niches of attachment, where African religious ideas and practices were developed and performed.

Much like Regla de Ocha in Cuba, Afro-Brazilian Candomblé emerged out of, or at least in near proximity to, Catholicism. The core members of one of the earliest and most famous houses (terreiros) of Candomblé, Casa Branca (also called Engenho Velho, the "old sugar mill"; and Ilê Iyá Nassô Oká), assembled in the shadow of the Barroquinha church in first decades of the 1800s, and the terreiro was born of two confraternities associated with that church, Bom Jesus dos Martírios and Nossa Senhora da Boa Morte (Silveira 2006; Harding 2000, 100). The Sunday Sabbath provided a "day of rest" for slaves to be at church, though many slave-masters disregarded the injunction to allow slaves to attend mass (Sweet 2003, 200–201). Though multi-deity cults also emerged in West Africa (Apter 1995; Parés 2013, 208-9), the model of joining all of the disparate orixás into one space and paradigm may have derived in part from observations of how the Catholic saints were cultivated in one space. Similarly, Candomblé's methods of creating fictive kin for the initiatory "family of the saint" seem to parallel the Catholic institution of god-parenthood, crucial in the brotherhoods.

Such issues draw us toward a reluctant invocation of "syncretism." In the twentieth century, this concept became dear to foundational writers on "Afro-Latin American religions" from Melville J. Herskovits and Arthur Ramos to Pierre Verger and Roger Bastide, and through these canonical figures to many still writing today. The term was central to the study and practice of Afro-Latin religions for nearly a century, but we invoke it here not for its analytical utility – which is questionable – but rather to indicate its frequent use both by key scholars past and present, and by Afro-Latin American religious leaders themselves, in various "anti-syncretism" campaigns. In our view it will be more productive to speak of layered affiliations: of multi-religious practices, "shifting arenas" (Sweet 2003, 114, 203), and strategic cultivating of "parallelisms" and "double participation" (Parés 2013, 76–77) within larger, heterogeneous religious ecologies. Africans and Afro-Brazilians appropriated the saints and rites selectively and humanized them. They founded their own brotherhoods, built their own churches, and sometimes pressed their own saints into service. Some Africans and Afro-Brazilians began to carry out their own masses, like Pedro Congo in Itaubira, Mina Gerais (Sweet 2003, 208). Postrevolutionary Haiti saw the emergence of the *prêt savane*, an officiant who recreated parts of Catholic liturgy in the context of Vodou (Herskovits 1937), and early twentieth century Cuba seemed overrun by *hombres dioses* who liberally borrowed from local folk Cath-olicism, nineteenth-century Spiritism, and elements of indigenized African traditions (Román 2007). Afro-Latin Americans elsewhere also selectively appropriated the memories and repertoires carried by Africans to the Americas, according to salience, viability, and sociological capacity to sustain a practice.

## Emergence

From this complex set of practices and powers, what would be sanctified as authentically African? The question is resonant, since the capacity to transform idiosyncratic or domestic rituals into social institutions was crucial to the emergence of something like "Afro-Brazilian religion" (or Afro-Cuban, or Afro-Mexican religion, not to mention the meta-cluster of "Afro-Latin American religions"). The key period of transposition from the presence of African religious practices extant in Brazil or Cuba, to Afro-Brazilian and Afro-Cuban religious *institutions*, seems to fall in the first three decades of the nineteenth century in Brazil, and the last two decades of that century in Cuba (Harding 2000; Parés 2013, 92; Brown 2003a).

We can point to several reasons for this crucial transformation: First, because the conflict and then fall of major West African powers like Oyo or Dahomey, and the jihad led by the northern Yoruba warlord Afonjá, produced enormous numbers of new African slaves at the precise period when Brazil and especially Cuba were expanding sugar production in the wake of the Haitian Revolution. The arrival of large numbers of ethnically related slaves with shared ritual repertoires put pressure on other Afro-American groups to define their own practices and boundaries. Second, by the early decades of the nineteenth century a sufficient number of African-born and Creole freemen were present in urban environs to give birth to and sustain networks of fictive kin adjacent to and even outside of Catholic Church sponsorship. In Brazil, the intersections between brotherhoods' social networks, the domestic and clientelistic practices of various famous *curandeiros* and *feitiçeiros*, and the ritual dance and drum societies called *calundus* or *batuques* until the early 1800s first gave rise to the word "candomblé" in 1807, when it was invoked in association with a "president" and thus by inference an established institution (Parés 2013, 88; Harding 2000). Third and related, was the gradual detachment from the model of ethnic associations in the brotherhoods to a model of fictive kin produced in and through initiatic procedures. By 1829 there were police invasions of established buildings and communities devoted to "candomblé," and reports of multiethnic and multiracial congregations (Reis 1986). Only at this point can we start to speak of institutions of "Afro-Brazilian religion," organized around the cultivation of multiple African deities in a single space, via a shared extra-domestic "altar-offering complex" (Parés 2013, 84, 87).

The emergence of a bona fide institutional form of Afro-Brazilian religion coincided with increasing multiracial and multiethnic ritual constituencies; such that even the very early police invasion of a candomblé in 1829 reported the fact that a white attorney was a participant. In Cuba, too, such transformations from ethnolinguistic or descent-based forms of association to initiatory ones are documentable by the second half of the nineteenth century. In 1863, Andrés Facundo de los Dolores Petit, the famous holder of the *Isué*-title in the *potencia* (chapter) of the male esoteric sodality Abakuá known as Aguana Bakokó Efó, swore in a new Abakuá chapter composed entirely of white men (Ortiz 1952–55, IV: 68–71, Sosa Rodríguez 1982, 142), and in 1900, i.e., only about a decade after five elderly Africans had established an initiatory protocol for the cult of the Ifá oracle, we get documentary evidence for the initiation of a white Creole of Spanish descent named Bonifácio Valdés as a *babalawo* (Brown 2003a, 68–73). What is more, both the white *potencia* known as Ocóbio Efó Mucarará and Bonifácio Valdés, in turn, initiated Cuban Creoles of both European and African descent, thereby effectively becoming racially "white" vectors of the transmission of "African" ritual knowledge, and so generating the contemporary pattern where Africanity does not, and indeed need not, correspond to social blackness. As the Cuban ethnographer Teodoro Díaz Fabelo (1960, 16) wrote on the eve of the Cuban Revolution, "Havana's best oriaté [ritual specialist in Regla de Ocha] and the Abakuá titleholder who possesses the most exalted knowledge and reputation are white."

As the earlier version of "nations" defined by ethnicity, language, and a predominant social blackness thus blurred toward the later nineteenth century, what came into being was a more or less theological idea of "nation," defined by initiation and the ritual family (*família de santo* in Brazil, *casa de santo* or *ilé ocha* in Cuba) into which one was integrated by ritual kinship rather than biological descent or socio-racial criteria (Costa Lima 1977). In this sense the discursive assertion of a strong, stable, and proximate Africanness in terms of ritual diacritics was closely correlated with the increasing uncertainty of ethno-racial Africanness among the participating populations. That is to say, discourses of authenticity and purity gained in force because it was mainly in a competitive economy of reputation that such matters were adjudicated (Johnson

2002; Brown 2003a). This disjuncture between ritually generated experiences of Africanness and ethno-racial codings of black identity has only expanded in the late twentieth and early twenty-first centuries, such that, according to some scholars, at least half of all practitioners of African religions in Brazil do not – at least outside of venues explicitly calling for such identifications – consider themselves black (Prandi 1991; Silva 1995; Pierucci and Prandi 2000). Rather, they imagine and present themselves as *religiously* African. This process yielded famous cases of European priestesses of Candomblé like the Frenchwoman Giselle Cossard Binon (1923–2016), who became known across Brazil and beyond as Mãe Giselle of Iemanjá.

### African Amerindian Religions

The religions that eventually became part of an "Afro-Latin American" complex, however, emerged from more than only African European or inter-African transculturations. African Amerindian encounters were also religiously prolific. Much of this is now beyond documentary reconstruction. But in some instances, we have good indications of how such processes unfolded. For example, enslaved Africans destined for Caribbean labor in the mid-seventeenth century were several times cast onto the shores and mercy of the Island Caribs of St. Vincent, as well as elsewhere. In the case of St. Vincent, some Africans survived and, together with the Caribs, founded the new ethnicity and religious culture of the "Black Caribs." Surviving Africans were tolerated and partly assimilated by the Island Caribs for reasons that remain opaque. Caribs also sometimes captured Africans, like the five hundred they captured from a shipwreck near Grenada (Thornton 1998, 284). As early as 1546, a letter to the city council of San Juan, Puerto Rico, advised the council to watch for Carib Indians and "blacks who go with them" (Thornton 1998, 288). Another report from Dominica, 1574, noted the Island Caribs integrating into their society both Spanish and African captives acquired in periodic raiding expeditions (Gonzalez 1988, 26); in 1576 an Afro-Puerto Rican woman named Luiza de Navarette was returned to her home isle after four years as a slave to the Caribs (Thornton 1998, 290). Garifuna religious practice today, anchored by the large-scale ritual complex called the *dügü*, in which the ancestors return, shows evidence of this history of encounter (Kerns 1983; Johnson 2007).

In Brazil, too, new practices emerged from Afro-Amerindian confluences. Robert Slenes (1991, 2006, 2008; see also Hébrard 2012) showed how Kongo nkisi priests working as slaves in Brazil sometimes availed themselves of indigenous territorial powers. These encounters generated new sects like *cabula,* a forerunner of so-called *macumba,* in which Amerindian and other Brazilian spirits are manifested alongside African ones. Such confluences also planted the seeds of the *jurema* cult, entailing the use of psychoactive plants as a technique of ongoing revelation from spirits. *Jurema* appeared around quilombos of Pernambuco as a meeting of slaves' and indigenous people's ritual techniques (Santos 1995; Motta 1997; Carvalho 2012). In practically every slaveholding Iberian colony such convergences took place between originally African and Native American practices concerning the harnessing of numinous forces to everyday goals. The particularly well-mined archives of the Mexican Inquisition (Palmer 1976; Behar 1987; Alberro 1993; Lewis 2003) yield a picture of a highly complex occult economy in which Africans, Indians, Europeans, and their Creole offspring eclectically drew on locally coexisting forms of knowledge and ritual skills deriving from all three continents in order to heal various maladies, cast spells on each other, or seek avenues to better fortune. Though the records of the tribunals of the Holy Office in Lima (Ballesteros Gaibrois 1955; Silverblatt 2004) and Cartagena de las Indias (Maya Restrepo 2005; Gómes, 2013, 2014; Germeten 2013) have so far not received sufficient attention, recent and ongoing work is beginning to reveal just how complex, protean, and in many ways cosmopolitan early local ritual worlds in the Iberian Atlantic really were.

### Afro-Latin American Islam

Another factor on which we lack adequate documentation is the impact of Islam on the religious syntheses and transformations underway in Afro-Latin America. Some portraits of Islamic leaders in the Americas are now being brought into focus, like the leader called Rufino who served a community of Muslims in Porto Alegre in the 1830s before moving north to work in the slave trade in Rio de Janeiro (Reis, Gómes, and Carvalho 2010), and the Damascus-raised teacher Al-Bagdali, who arrived in Brazil in 1866 and taught in Rio, Bahia, and Pernambuco (Farah 2007). Elsewhere we catch only brief glimpses of Islam in the ethnonyms under which Mande-speaking captives were registered in the Americas (e.g., "Mandingas"). There is the intriguing possibility that the Jamaican-born Boukman Dutty, a leader of the initial 1791 insurrection that was to evolve into the Haitian Revolution was a "man of the book," i.e., a Muslim (Khan 2012).

It is not until the so-called Malé Rebellion in Salvador de Bahia in 1835 that we get a sharper view of the spread of Islam (Reis and Morães Farías 1989) in the Americas. The Malé Rebellion – named after the Yoruba term for Muslim, *imalé* – was one of the largest slave insurrections in Brazil, following at least eight smaller revolts. The massive inquest that it generated (Reis 2003b) proved beyond doubt that, like some of the earlier uprisings, it was "somehow" Islamically inspired. Yet just *how* this was so has remained opaque.

The Malés of Bahia were comprised mostly of Hausa and Islamicized Yoruba slaves captured and shipped in the early nineteenth-century wars around the Bight of Benin, and there are clear indications that some of them were actively proselytizing non-Islamicized slaves and free blacks. The inquest revealed copious writings in Arabic among the possessions of some conspirators, and it seems that a shed lent to some of the supposed ring-leaders may have served as a madrasa in which aspiring converts acquired some degree of Arabic literacy. The Jesuit missionary Ignace Etienne reported that four major Sunni schools of thought (*madhahib*) may have been taught (Farah 2007, 12). For these reasons, both Brazilian authorities then, and scholars since, have tended to assume a jihadic inspiration to the revolt (Reis 1993). Yet as the most astute scrutiny of the documentary record (Reis and Morães Farias 1989) concludes, the Arabic writings reveal no jihadic intent, and had the rebellion met with success, it is not at all clear that its political result would have been a Yoruba-style city-state like Ibadan (itself a conglomerate of Muslim and pagan refugees from the nineteenth-century Yoruba wars), or a Sokoto-style caliphate. The Malés' material practices of manufacturing talismans made of quranic scripts and wrapped in a sack to be worn on the body as protection, mirrored Afro-Catholic practices and aims. Moreover, their use of white garments, especially on Fridays, matched the practices of Nagô devotees of Oxalá, whose color was also white and whose sacred day was Friday (Reis 1993). It is possible, then, that Afro-Catholic and Afro-Muslim slaves and freemen found sufficiently common codes of ritual comportment and religious power to begin to act together in the largest urban slave rebellion of Brazil's history.

Despite severe reprisals against Muslims in Brazil thereafter, Islam continued to survive, albeit perhaps in attenuated forms secretly maintained in homes. When the Iraqi imam Al-Bagdali taught on the outskirts of Brazil's coastal cities in the late 1860s, he found ready if uninformed audiences for his words. He expressed disappointment at constantly having to address lapses in the basics, such as the need to constantly revisit the Five Pillars and the requirement of visiting Mecca (*hajj*), or the injunction against drinking alcohol; to emphasize that women too, and not only men, were responsible for fasting during Ramadan; or to demonstrate how to conduct a proper Muslim burial (Farah 2007, 9–15). Al-Bagdali's travel narrative offers a window on the late nineteenth-century decline of Islam among Afrodescendants in Brazil, as least as a self-sustaining tradition, notwithstanding periodic twentieth-century revivals spurred by new immigrant groups.

## Espiritismo

Additional social and intellectual currents arrived in the Americas to interact with emergent Afro-Latin American traditions, such as French Spiritism. Copies of Allan Kardec's *Le livre des esprits* (1857) were in the Brazilian capital by 1860. Kardec's early works were translated into Portuguese by 1866, and Spiritist groups were meeting by 1873 (Aubrée and Laplantine 1990, 10). The monthly review *Revista Espirita* began publication in 1875, and the Federação Espírita Brasileira convened in 1884 (Aubrée and Laplantine 1990, 112–14; Hess 1991, 86; Giumbelli 1997, 56, 61). By the 1880s, Spiritism was an everyday topic of newspaper pages. Espiritismo perhaps found fertile ground in Brazil in relation to an older folk spiritism descended from Portuguese Sebastianism, with its nostalgia for a golden past and mystic expectations of a glorious, if as yet unseen, future (Warren 1968).

Though Kardecian Spiritism spread rapidly in Spain during the same decade (Abend 2004) and undoubtedly diffused from there to Cuba and Puerto Rico, it is also possible that American Spiritualism reached Cuba as well. During the first Cuban War of Independence (1868–78), Cuban exiles in New York regularly held séances to consult with the spirits of deceased *independentistas* (Bermúdez 1967). By 1880, the Sociedad Antropológica de la Isla de Cuba held a special session on the phenomenon. The 1880s and 1890s saw a rapid proliferation of Spiritist publications and societies, and the merging of (implicitly "white") European Spiritism with popular healing and divinatory practices among racially indeterminate populations that often coalesced around charismatic individuals described in the press as "hombres dioses" or "man-gods" (Román 2007). By the beginning of the twentieth century we thus see an increasing split between elite "scientific" Spiritism and a proliferation of more or less "Africanized" varieties of "espiritismo cruzado" – a division that persists to this day, even though "orthodox" "espiritistas científicos" are a dwindling minority in present-day Cuba (Espírito Santo 2015). In turn, virtually all more obviously African-derived Cuban ritual traditions have absorbed elements of spiritist doctrine concerning the role of the dead in the lives of the living, a trend that has aided the integration of historically heterogeneous ritual systems into a complex religious ecology.

Brazil experienced an analogous transfusion. In the 1920s, a city across the bay from Rio called Niterói spawned a new Afro-Latin American religion called Umbanda, a hybrid of Espiritismo and Candomblé (Montero 1985; Brown 1986; Hale 2009). In Umbanda, Afro-Brazilian deities were transmuted into systematic military ranks and phalanxes of spirits, and indeed Umbanda seems to have benefited from the support of the military class in Brazil. Umbanda practices drew from and mimicked those of Candomblé, like spirit possession, but scaled back the sacrificial exchanges with the gods and the complexity and duration of initiatic processes. This rendered Umbanda accessible to members of all ethnic groups and classes, especially in southern cities like Rio, São Paulo, and Porto Alegre. Spiritism and its offspring Umbanda relied upon representations of primitive "Africanness," yet offered the promise of Afro-Brazilian spirit-possession practices with few of the social liabilities. To the contrary, even if it was not quite respectable, it was thoroughly "French," cosmopolitan, and à la mode. And yet, as Stefania Capone described (1999), precisely by virtue of Umbanda's ready accessibility and convenience, it eventually came to appear "not as strong" as the putatively more authentic, more African Candomblé, leading to a wave of conversions from Umbanda to Candomblé in southern Brazilian cities from the 1980s to the present.

## TOWARD THE TWENTIETH CENTURY: LAW, STATE, SCHOLARS, AND THE VEXATIONS OF RELIGION

Having sketched some of the key historiographical problems confronting the study of Afro-Latin religious formations, we now turn to daunting questions of how to conceptualize such phenomena. The domain of religion long served as a touchstone for the study of the cultural interrelations between Africa and the Americas. Since the pioneering research of Raimundo Nina Rodrigues (1862–1906) in Brazil, Fernando Ortiz (1881–1969) in Cuba, Jean Price-Mars (1876–1969) in Haiti, and the North American anthropologist Melville J. Herskovits (1895–1963) in Suriname, Haiti, Trinidad, and Brazil, practices understood as "survivals" of African religious traditions in New World societies were assigned crucial status for investigations of African cultural continuities in the Americas (Johnson 2011, 2014). These founders of African Americanist scholarship perceived the field of the religious to be particularly resistant to change, and therefore of heightened importance for determining what became known as the African cultural heritage in the Americas. Such a legacy is nowadays beyond dispute. Yet not only has the methodological basis for its assessment by morphological comparison of ill-contextualized ethnographic data from both sides of the Atlantic become subject to sustained critique; the conceptual apparatus that once allowed for the seemingly unproblematic recognition of "African" forms of "religion" in the Americas has also been called into question.

Partly, this is so because the term "religion" does not represent a self-evident, universally valid designator of delimitable segments of human experience, thought, and behavior. Instead, conceptions of religion, as they consolidated in modern secularist liberal thought, carry a heavy ideological burden (Harrison 1990; Asad 1993; McCutcheon 1997; Smith 2004; Masuzawa 2005). This is because the modern use of "religion" to demarcate an institutional realm based on faith and separate from the domain of "rational" action is informed by both post-Reformation Christian notions of faith and transcendence, and normative Western secularist presuppositions concerning the role that "religious belief" ought to play in civic life. To characterize forms of thought and action in pre-modern or non-Western contexts as religious thus opens the door to anachronistic or ethnocentric distortions of social worlds in which "religion," as a realm of experience presumably separable from the sphere of mundane rationalities, simply did not exist.

Obviously, enslaved Africans carried into the diaspora views of the world that included propositions about deities, ancestral spirits, and forces with which humans had to reckon and interact in ritually regulated ways. The enslaved unquestionably drew upon such notions in shaping the institutions that came to integrate the slave societies of the New World. Yet the majority of Africans who reached the Americas during the more than 350 years of the slave trade can hardly be said to have been practicing a "religion" in the modern sense. It was in the course of the operation of local slave regimes that certain of their practices were objectified as magic, witchcraft, or insubordination based on harmful superstition – either in accordance with laws regulating slave behavior, or in the context of forced Christianization. Whatever traditions of ritual praxis emerged and consolidated among enslaved Africans and their descendants in the New World must therefore be viewed as products of a context in which alien and oppressive legal and ecclesiastical regimes sought to repress what they construed, on the basis of Christian notions of "religious" propriety, as dangerous signs of African alterity.

Yet for precisely that reason, right from the start, notions of what constitutes "religion" informed colonial Latin American discourses on and engagements with ritual practices among the enslaved. At least formally, the authority of the Roman Catholic Church underwrote all aspects of the colonial ventures in the Iberian Americas, including the obligatory baptism and nominal catechization of the enslaved, and so set the terms under which African cultural forms could take root in the New World. Only very slowly was the term "religion" adopted by Africans and Afro-Americans, and then primarily in the post-independence period, to gain legal and socio-cultural standing vis-à-vis established institutions of the postcolonial state.

We see this moment with particular clarity in the immediate aftermath of the first American occupation of Cuba (1899–1902), in the course of which Catholicism was disestablished and (under American pressure) a clause guaranteeing freedom of religion was appended to the constitution of the newly independent Cuban republic. In the midst of massive persecutory campaigns against alleged practitioners of "African witchcraft" (brujería) that had been instigated by social reformers keen on modernizing Cuba, Afro-Cuban cult groups such as the Sociedad Lucumí Santa Rita de Casio y San Lázaro and the Sociedad de Socorros Mutuos bajo la Advocación de Santa Barbara began to shrewdly inscribe themselves into postcolonial law (Palmié 2002, 2013, Bronfman 2004). They did so by claiming legal protection for practices in accordance with what they called a "Christian Lucumí morality," mirroring the language of the constitution; but they also engaged their detractors in print, and actively courted public intellectuals, such as Fernando Ortiz, to come to their defense. (Ortiz's 1906 book, *Los negros brujos*, had played a major role in driving the anti-witchcraft campaigns that shook Cuba between 1904 and 1920).

Such self-conscious attempts to rationalize Afro-Cuban ritual practices in light of the legitimacy afforded by the label "religion" endured, with various degrees of success, throughout the twentieth century, both on the island and in its diaspora. This process reached a culmination in the 1993 US Supreme Court victory of the Cuban-American *obá oriaté* (ritual specialist in Regla de Ocha) Ernesto Pichardo that legalized animal sacrifice for his officially incorporated Church of the Lukumí Babalu Ayé

(Palmié 1996; Johnson 2005). But similar processes also underlay the revolutionary Cuban state's 1991 official accreditation of the Asociación Cultural Yoruba de Cuba (note the switch from "religion" to "culture"!) as an institution led by babalawos that supposedly mediates between the state and practitioners of Afro-Cuban religions (though it remains controversial among the latter – cf. Routon 2009).

Similar maneuvers are well documented in the Brazilian case. Following abolition (1888) and the founding of the First Republic (1889), Decree 119A, handed down on January 7, 1890, followed the French and US constitutional models as well as the tenets of Positivism by declaring a clear separation of church and state. While religious tolerance had been in law since 1824, the new constitution mandated the complete liberty of religious groups and terminated the patronage of the Catholic Church. Notwithstanding the newfound constitutional freedom of religion, Afro-Brazilian practices gained no protection. They were not deemed bona fide "religions," and continued to be regulated and policed under laws of "public health" instituted in the Penal Code of 1890, which prohibited illegal medicine, curing and the practice of "magic" and "spiritism" (Maggie 1992; Borges 1993, 1995; Johnson 2002, 85–96). Since Afro-Brazilian religions were considered a dangerous detriment to national progress, they were repressed under an alternative category to "religion."

Scholars working on Afro-Brazilian religions were part and parcel of the uneven processes of repression, tolerance and legalization, often splitting practices "of the left hand" like Macumba, Quimbanda, or Candomblé de Caboclo, from practices of the "right hand" associated with Nagô terreiros (in particular, specific prestigious houses tracing a lineage to the Yoruba city-state of Ketu). Beatriz Góis Dantas (1988) showed how scholars misrecognized categories of religious practice–in which temples emphasizing Yoruba origins were regarded as the most authentically African compared to others emphasizing Angolan, indigenous or plural origins–for analytical categories. Scholars mostly validated the Yoruba-centric pretensions claimed by certain Candomblé priests, serving as authorizers and amplifiers of a religious hierarchy. And by repeatedly reproducing studies of the same allegedly "authentic" temples of Candomblé, anthropologists and historians fortified and sedimented those distinctions, lending their authority to legal and financial distinctions according to which some Afro-Brazilian practitioners came to be valorized while others were left on the margins, or even subjected to state harassment (Hayes 2007). Dantas acknowledged that religious practitioners have their own uses for such distinctions – prestige, financial gain, power – yet her work was squarely focused on intellectuals' duplicity, as they played the part of hustling busybodies producing the "really African" religions they then go out and "find." Even more insidiously, the cultural appreciation of Yoruba (nagô) terreiros arguably served to mask the denial of social equality (Fry 1982; Hanchard 1994; Dantas 2009, 133). Full rights of freedom of religion were not accorded practitioners of Candomblé until 1976, coinciding with the beginnings of its promotion as a cultural attraction and, later, as national patrimony, especially in Bahia (Matory 2005; Sansi 2007; Selka 2007; Pinho 2010).

This process was roughly mirrored in Cuba, where Fernando Ortiz was clearly the key figure. Having once advocated the annihilation of what, in 1906, he had branded as socially noxious African superstitions, by the 1930s Ortiz had turned himself into a prolific ethnographer of Afro-Cuban culture and an effective exponent of a Cuban national project in which the country's African heritage ought to play a prominent role. Beginning in the late 1920s, he was joined in such efforts (informed in part by opposition to European and North American visions of "racial purity") by a host of artists and intellectuals (like the poet Nicolás Guillén, the novelist Alejo Carpentier, or the painter Wilfredo Lam) who, partly inspired by European modernist primitivism, similarly extolled the virtues of Cuba's African cultural heritage. The epitome of this tendency can perhaps be seen in the work of Lydia Cabrera (1899–1991), whose prolific ethnographically-based writings deliberately and consistently blur the distinctions between literature and the social sciences.

Raimundo Nina Rodrigues played a similar role in Brazil, moving from the posture of criminal psychiatrist seeking to diagnose Afro-Brazilian religions as more or less a medical malady to becoming a sympathetic and keen-eyed ethnographer of Candomblé (Nina Rodrigues 2006 [1896–7]). He died in 1906 and so did not live long enough to become a broker in the nationalizing of the Afro-Brazilian cults, in the mode of Ortiz for the Afro-Cubans. Instead those roles fell to his students, admirers and rivals like Arthur Ramos, Edison Carneiro and Manuel Querino. The period after 1930 presented new risks and opportunities in the public sphere for Afro-Brazilian religions, under the dictatorship of Getúlio Vargas. Under the leadership of scholars like Ramos, Carneiro and Gilberto Freyre, "Afro-Brazilian culture" gained purchase in Brazil's national identity with the state granting its approval to the first black political organization, the Black Brazilian Front (1931), the first Afro-Brazilian Congresses (in Recife, 1934, and Bahia, 1937), and the Black Brazilian National

Convention (1945) (Hanchard 1994; Alberto 2011). The creation of Umbanda occurred at roughly the same moment, expressing and fomenting a nascent "racial democracy" mythology (see Alberto and Hoffnung-Garskoff in this volume). Umbanda was presented as the true Brazilian religion, a genuinely autochthonous creation combining the three large cultural strands of Brazil: the Amerindian, the African and the Iberian, expressing and mediating a unique non-European character (Montero 1985; Brown 1986; Ortiz 1986, 1989). By 1942 certain practices of spirit mediumship had gained enough organizational structure and military and middle-class support to be rewarded by the state and removed from the list of criminal acts against public health (Maggie 1992, 47; Giumbelli 1997). Many such openings were sharply constrained after 1937's stronger dictatorial turn. The state held the power to officially determine which terreiros qualified as the "traditional" sites of Candomblé. Legal rights protecting certain terreiros were passed, or so it is told in oral tradition, due to the persistent initiative of the famous priestess of the terreiro Axé Opô Afonjá, Mother Aninha, and her initiated "son," the diplomat and statesman Oswaldo Aranha (Serra 1995, 53). Yet if the state indirectly affirmed that select forms of "traditional" Candomblé could constitute a genuine religion and ought to be protected by law, it simultaneously implied that most terreiros were not traditional or legitimate. Vargas' acts of widespread repression punctuated by piecemeal toleration left the issue of "religion" versus "magic" – authentic Candomblé versus malevolent Macumba or sorcery– open as a valid distinction. The high stakes of the relatively arbitrary distinctions between terreiros said to preserve the "real" tradition in contradistinction to the "low spiritism" and "sorcery" of the rest, initiated rifts within Afro-Brazilian communities themselves, spurred by the privileged position accorded the Nagô (Ketu) houses at the expense of Angolan, Jeje, and Caboclo houses of Candomblé.

If these were hierarchies produced mostly by agents S of the state and the academy, they were also maximally exploited by savvy Afro-Brazilian priests and leaders. "Afro-Brazilian tradition" was not only decreed from the top down, as Stefania Capone's (1999, 2010) and J. Lorand Matory's (1999, 2005) research demonstrated. Rather it was woven of a transatlantic web of religious actors, scholars, objects, and practices. Candomblé's particular form of legitimate authority emerged not only out of debates and conflicts internal to the religion but also in relation to repressive state regimes adjudicating the legal situation of Afro-Brazilian religions, and in relation to scholars' publications on them over the course of the twentieth century. Scholarly depictions of traditional African religion came to inform the orthopraxic quest itself, as Candomblé practitioners eagerly devoured academic books. The state, the academy and the terreiros collaborated in authorizing hierarchies of putative African purity and authenticity, with the terreiros rooted in the Yoruba (Nagô), and more specifically the Ketu nation gaining most. Despite recent research belatedly recuperating the histories of the Angolan and Jeje "nations," these hierarchies persist in the form not only of prestige or numbers of initiates but in monetary and legal forms like patrimonialization and thus financial sponsorship by the state.

The process of nationalization can be traced not only at a macro-institutional level, but also in micro-histories of ritual practice. For example, Capone's work (1999a, trans. 2010) showed how the orixá named Exú moved from being identified as a diabolical imp in early twentieth-century studies of Candomblé, a period in which the religion was regarded as a social danger, to being reworked as a beneficial mediator and messenger after the 1930s, as certain versions of Afro-Brazilian practice began to acquire national legitimacy. Jocélio Teles dos Santos (1995) showed how, as the discourse of African authenticity became ascendant in the twentieth century, terreiros devoted to the Amerindian figure of the *caboclo* transformed themselves, and the caboclo entities, into Angola-nation houses and beings, respectively. Not only the modes of ritual practice but also the very nature of deities themselves acquired new contours and qualities.

In Cuba, similar visions of a thoroughly "transculturated" (Ortiz's term) national project eventually came to guide the revolutionary government's conflicted post-1959 policies toward what it variously regarded as genuine expressions of popular resistance against racist and classist oppression but nonetheless could not tolerate as "religion." Thus while the 1960s saw concerted efforts at documenting Cuba's African traditions, these were undertaken with a view toward salvaging their "cultural value" before they would inevitably melt away under the glaring light of socialist rationality (Guanche 1983; Argüelles Medeiros and Hodge Limonta 1991; Hagedorn 2001; Ayorinde 2004). By the time the revolutionary state declared a policy of scientific atheism in the 1970s, such efforts had already stopped, and it was only after the end of Soviet support and the formal 1991 declaration of the Congress of the Cuban Communist Party to no longer consider religious practice an impediment to Party membership (and the social benefits it carries) that efforts to study Afro-Cuban religions resumed.

By then, however, Cuban and international researchers were looking at a world that had changed significantly since the time that Fernando Ortiz had mounted the stage at an event organized, in 1937, by the prestigious Instituto Hispanocubano de Cultura, and pronounced the Yoruba-derived tradition of chanting to the sound of *batá* drums (in order to induce divine possession) as the "classical music" of Cuba. By that time, Ortiz had already begun to make his extensive library of Africanist ethnographies available to his local interlocutors. What he set in motion, thereby, was the assimilation (or reassimilation) into Afro-Cuban religious repertoires of data on what, by then, had begun to congeal, in southwestern Nigeria (and largely under British missionary influence), as "the Yoruba." As in the Brazilian case, what resulted was not only a process of the "Yorubanization" of cultic practice in some quarters, but a general evaluation of putatively Yoruba-derived cultural forms as normatively more valuable in terms of the folkloricization (and eventual heritagization) of practices that were once persecuted as inimical to visions of rational (and implicitly "white," or European-oriented) visions of Latin American national viability. This is a moment that, if anything, has attained even more influence in contexts that the Argentine sociologist Alejandro Frigerio (2004) has usefully described as "secondary diasporas." But before we go into that we will now turn to a descriptive synthesis of the current ethnographic literature on Afro-Latin American religions in Cuba and Brazil.

## Cuba

Generalizing about contemporary Afro-Cuban religious formations is a daunting task. Partly, this is because their history already indicates a complex situation of partial accommodation and mutual calibration among originally heterogeneous but now multiply articulated traditions. Practitioners themselves distinguish at least five distinct but practically overlapping component traditions: the Yoruba-inspired Santería or, more properly, Regla de Ocha and Ifá (also known as Lucumí or Regla de Ocha-Ifá); the so-called Reglas de Congo, which draw on western Central African sources and comprise four sub-traditions (Palo Monte, Mayombe, Brillumba and Kimbisa); the Fon/Gbe- inspired Regla de Arará; the male esoteric sodality of Abakuá, which historically relates to similar institutions in the Cross River region of contemporary Nigeria and Cameroon; and various forms of Spiritist praxis ranging from the most austere, European-style "espiritismo científico" to diverse and highly idiosyncratic modalities of "espiritismo cruzado" and, arguably, a new ritual genre, the "cajón pa' los muertos," that emerged in Havana in the 1990s.

There also exists a spectrum of regional differences on the island (mainly between eastern and western Cuba), as well as between urban and rural areas. Regla de Ocha and Ifá originated in urban Havana and Matanzas (López Valdés 1985; Brown 2003a; Palmié 2002, 2013) and only reached the eastern parts of the island in the 1930s when the Havana-initiated Matancero Reyniero Pérez relocated to Santiago de Cuba (Lachatañeré 1992; Wirtz 2007; Larduet Luaces 2014). The Regla de Arará is largely restricted to rural Matanzas (Sogbossi 1998), and Abakuá only exists in five port towns in western Cuba (Regla, Guanabacoa, Habana, Matanzas and Cárdenas) (Cabrera 1959; Sosa Rodríguez 1982; Brown 2003b, Palmié 2008). Eastern Cuba is known for varieties of "espiritismo cruzado" such as "espiritismo de cordón" and "muertería" not found elsewhere (Wirtz 2007; Román 2007; Espírito Santo 2015). And while the Reglas de Congo, particularly Palo Monte, are spread fairly evenly across the island, the practices of individual cult groups are so idiosyncratic that sometimes little seems to be comparable beyond their focus on power objects known as *ngangas*, "prendas" or *enquices* and the spirits of the dead (*nfumbis*) that animate them (Cabrera 1983; Ochoa 2010; Kerestetzi 2011).

Further undermining efforts to generalize about Afro-Cuban religious practice is the highly individualized, pragmatic way in which practitioners and cult groups in all Afro-Cuban religious formations compose their own varieties of praxis from a variety of options present in a highly complex ritual ecology. As in other instances of non-centralized "folk religions," key features of modern conceptions of "religion" – such as the mutual exclusivity of membership in different religions – simply do not apply. Even though most Afro-Cuban religious formations are characterized by initiatory pathways to full ritual competence, few practitioners of any Afro-Cuban ritual tradition only practice *one* tradition. Most are initiated into more than one, and even people who merely consult ritual experts for reasons of personal health and wellbeing do so eclectically, treating each tradition (including Spiritism and Catholic masses) as distinct but ultimately complementary or even continuous sets of sacred resources (Argyriadis 1999; Espírito Santo 2015). It is thus not at all uncommon to find individuals who have undergone initiations in more than one Afro-Cuban religion, and who advise their clients to seek recourse not only in rituals pertaining to those, but in ones they do not practice themselves. This is so because the entities ruling one's fate – deities known as *orichas* (or orishas) in Regla de Ocha and Ifá, and differently conceived as spirits of the dead ("muertos") in the case of the Reglas de Congo and Espiritismo – form part and parcel of one and the same numinous universe to which all forms of "religion" seek to respond.

The emphasis here falls on the term "response." In all instances, it is the orichas or muertos with whom the initiative for interchanges with humans rests. Deities and the dead communicate with the living through various divinatory systems (*ifá*, *diloggún* and *obí* in Regla de Ocha, *chamalongo* in the Reglas de Congo), they speak directly to them during possession trance, make themselves known in dreams, or visit otherwise inexplicable afflictions on humans. The orichas and the dead do so in order to compel humans (whether they already are their devotees or not) to engage with them through public ceremonies ("tambores"), sacrifices (*ebó*), the fashioning of protective amulets ("resguardos"), or by embarking on a course of increasingly binding initiatory commitments that can, but need not, culminate in their full-scale consecration to an oricha (*kari ocha* or "hacer santo") in the case of Regla de Ocha, or the rituals ("rayamiento") that establish a lifelong interdependence between a practitioner of a Regla de Congo and the spirit (*nfumbi*) housed in an animate power object known as *nganga*.

Crucial to the theology of recruitment underlying such graded pathways to initiation is the notion that even though all of our fates are decided at birth, we can fall short of living up to the best potential outcome – e.g., if someone who is destined to become a devotee of an oricha fails to heed the deity's call. As a result, human volition plays no role in "joining" an Afro-Cuban religion (particularly Regla de Ocha and Ifá). One does not become a Santero because one wishes to; rather the initiative lies with the divine. A corollary to this (which probably relates to innovations in initiatory praxis dating back to the early twentieth century) is that because all human heads are potentially "owned" by an *oricha*, social race is an entirely irrelevant criterion. Since initiation places a person in an initiatory genealogy ("rama") which is expected to begin with a late-nineteenth- or early-twentieth-century African founding figure ("fundamento"), socially white persons hailed by the oricha thus inevitably acquire African ancestors as part and parcel of the "rama" within which their new status as *omo oricha* or *olocha* places them.

While characterized by similarly graded pathways to full ritual competence, in Palo Monte (and the other Reglas de Congo) human agency plays a somewhat greater role in establishing a relation to the spirit of a dead person ("muerto") who will become the animating force of a nganga object. Such "muertos" may manifest themselves in dreams or through afflictions, but in the majority of cases a *palero* aspiring to become a *tata nganga* will search out the grave of a deceased person and propose to give the "muerto" a new form of embodiment in a *nganga* object if the dead enters into a pact to perform "works" ("trabajos") for its future owner and master in return for sacrifices and other forms of ritual attention. Once such a pact ("trata") is concluded, the palero will extract bone fragments (ideally the skull) from the grave, and ritually mount ("montar") them in an iron cauldron together with an array of mineral, plant and animal substances and artifacts (coins, chains, knives, etc.). Perhaps not surprisingly, relations between tata ngangas and their nfumbis are surrounded by an agonistic (even antagonistic) imagery drawing on slavery and wage labor. But as Palmié (2002) has argued, the reputation of Palo as the fast-acting and morally ambiguous, even sorcerous, counterpoint to the reciprocal relationship between *oricha* devotees and their gods (who, after all cannot be coerced into action) may be a product of the mutual calibration toward each other, within the context of Cuban slavery and post-emancipation labor regimes, of Yoruba- and western Bantu-inspired ritual formations. As recent ethnographies (Ochoa 2010, Kerestetzi 2011) have shown, despite the bravado many paleros display in presenting their practices as a more effective counterpoint to those of santeros, much of their activities similarly revolve around healing and solving their client's problems.

The last Cuban tradition to be discussed here, that of Abakuá, is anomalous in several respects. Perhaps the most puzzling fact about it is that even though slaves from its putative region of African origin were exported in large number to both the British and Spanish Caribbean, nowhere but in Cuba have sodalities of this type ever been documented in the Americas (see the discussion in Palmié 2008). Anomalous, too, is that Abakuá never effectively spread beyond five Cuban port towns and nowadays explicitly refuses to found chapters outside these areas (let alone abroad). It features no individually personalized relations to divine entities, has no divination system, no healing functions, and has integrated elements of Christianity to only a highly superficial degree. Even more unusually, oral tradition and documentary evidence both indicate a precise moment of origin in 1836, when African members of a Regla-based "cabildo de la nación carabalí brikamó ápapa efí" swore in the first Cuban chapter, composed of Cuban Creoles and known as Efique Butón (Sosa Rodríguez 1982). Indeed, given its historical function – Abakuá soon came to control the labor market at Havana's dockside (López Valdés 1985) and still plays an important economic role – interpretations of it as an institution akin to proto-syndicalist movements are tempting. But they miss the mark insofar as such interpretations cannot do justice to the sheer symbolic excess of the 12- to 14-hour-long ceremonies known as *barocos* or "plantes" during which members and title-holders of Abakuá potencias relive a complex mythology that recounts the first encounter between human actors and the mystical, law-giving "voice of écue" in a primordial time-space that contemporary *obonecues* (literally: brothers in écue) call *Enllenisón* (Cabrera 1959; Routon 2005; Palmié 2006).

Although members of Abakuá nowadays use the label "religion" to characterize their practices, the rituals around which this male esoteric sodality organizes itself may be compared to Greek mystery cults (Ortiz 1981) or medieval European morality plays. Abakuá has also repeatedly been traced to similar sodalities among the Efik and Ekoi of southeastern Nigeria and the Cameroons known as "ekpe" or "ngbe" (Miller 2009), though any straightforward narrative of linear transmission ought to be tempered not only by the likely simultaneity of the emergence of these associations on both sides of the Atlantic (Palmié 2008) but also by contemporary Abakuá members' notions of the fundamental irrelevance of such "origin stories" to their contemporary pursuits (Routon 2005).

## Brazil

Candomblé shares affinities with other traditions in Brazil's religious field. Rival religions that offer a similarly intimate incorporation of spirit in flesh include Kardecist Spiritism (Cavalcanti 1983; Aubrée and Laplantine 1990; Hess 1991, 1994), Umbanda (Bastide 1978 Brown 1986; Cavalcanti 1986; Ortiz 1986, 1991; Brumana and Martinez 1991; Burdick 1993; Birman 1995), and, albeit more distantly, Pentecostalism or "third-wave" Protestantism (Ireland 1991; Burdick 1998; Kramer 2001), this last on the rise in extraordinary fashion since the 1950s. What are the teguments of relation and distinction among entities in this religious field?

A spiritist "session" often opens with a brief inspirational message from the teachings of Kardec. The inspirational messages convey his metaphysics composed of magnetisms, fluids, and vibrations in full scientistic splendor. Healing or "therapy," read as the cleansing of the body from negative forces and the restoration of corporeal order, represents the main objective of the session (Montero 1985). Mediums transmit the skill of more ancient, enlightened souls to this end, offering "passes" (*passos*) over subjects' bodies, moving their fingertips over the skin to attract negative vibrations or energies to their grip, and then cast them into the air, at the same time transmitting positive spirits and energies to the "client." The healing spirits invoked are from so-called evolved civilizations – doctors or healers from Europe, ancient Egypt, or the Aztec empire – and mediums' garb and solemn decorum reflect this elevated status. Africanness is strikingly marginalized from the spirit pantheon typically activated in Kardecist sessions.

Unlike most spiritists, Umbandists work with at least some of the *orixás*. Umbanda houses vary widely, some hewing closer to Kardecist Spiritism (so-called Umbanda "of the white line"), while others hew more toward Candomblé. There are also "crossed" houses of "Umbandomblé" that practice both Umbanda and Candomblé out of the same space and within the same group, alternating formats weekly or monthly. If Kardecist centers often disallow African spirits as "primitive," Umbanda reverses this valuation, summoning the orixás (as in Candomblé, also called *santos,* "saints") as leaders of families of spirits. Still, Umbanda centers are often highly rationalized, in Weber's sense of bureaucratic efficiency. The spirits arrive with relatively little ritual preparation (compared to Candomblé) to possess their mediums, and they "manifest" in several standard genres. *Pretos-velhos* ("old blacks") are the spirits of former slaves. *Caboclos* are spirits of Amerindians who can be stern and dignified, in accord with popular myths of the noble savage. *Erês*, also called *crianças*, are spirits of children, playful and whimsically infantile. The *exus* are mischievous troublemakers and tricksters, but also messengers or go-betweens, and *ciganas* are stereotyped gypsies with mystical insight. There are often subgroups within each family like the "women of the street" exus called *pomba-giras* (Hayes 2011). Some Umbanda centers have elaborated new categories of spirits attired like gang-members (*exu mirim*), and drawn on the repertory of spirits from Candomblé de caboclo for cowboys (*boiadeiros*). All of these spirit "guides" (*guias*) seek to help humans in order to themselves gain merit and advance in the spirit world. Song lyrics to call the spirits are sung in Portuguese, and initiation procedures are relatively simple compared with Candomblé.

By now we must acknowledge Neo-Pentecostal Protestantism as an Afro-Latin American religion, given its enormous growth among Afro-descendants not only in Brazil but also in Guatemala, Honduras, and

Haiti. Early Pentecostal sects like Assembly of God arrived in Brazil in 1910, while "native" Brazilian Pentecostal groups began to proliferate from 1952, followed by so-called third-wave groups in the 1970s (Corton and Marshall-Fratani 2001; Silva 2005). Pentecostals or *crentes* (believers) see themselves as avowed enemies of Afro-Brazilian religions like Umbanda and Candomblé, though in practice there are important commonalities. Neo-Pentecostals attribute automatic, magical force to the invocation of certain words, use special oils and color-coded flowers as transformers, and give heavy emphasis to the exorcism of bad spirits – typically performed as Afro-Brazilian *exu* spirits – in order to properly incorporate the Holy Spirit (Oro and Semán 2001, 183–88; Silva 2005, 153).

In an Assembly of God community studied by John Burdick, conversion includes involuntary possession by the Holy Spirit, not unlike a beginning novice in Candomblé or Umbanda and, as in Candomblé, much attention is given to material objects as containers of power and to procedures of contagion and mimesis (Burdick 1993, 64). The idiom of spirit warfare and the ritual concern for the "closed body" strongly resemble analogous preoccupations of members of Afro-Brazilian terreiros, though the techniques of procuring such protections are more directly commoditized in relation to a money economy (Kramer 2001) than in Candomblé where such exchanges – protection for purchase, say – are often masked, though ever-present (Brazeal 2014).

If the similarities are striking, at least in practice, the Holy Spirit and the orixás or voduns present quite divergent conceptions and performances of extraordinary power. Most obviously, the orixás of Candomblé are seen as "African"; they carry the names of West African rivers (Oyá, Obá) and ancient kings (Xangô, Odudua). The god of Pentecostals, by contrast, is depicted as the absolute, universal, and super-cultural figurehead of a world religion. The *orixá* system resists totalization by dividing human experience into separate types of action and power that must be classified, negotiated and balanced. Taken together as a pantheon the *orixás* (and in Jeje terreiros, the voduns, and in Angola Candomblé, the *inquices*) construct a total worldview and classificatory system, yet in practice they are fragmentary and partial as each initiate is first and foremost a "son" or "daughter" of a particular deity. Problems and features of human life are parsed into categories and embedded within cross-cutting classificatory schemas: "hot" and "cool," "male" and "female" (Birman 1995), "domestic" and "wild," as well as colors, days of the week, natural sites, recipes and kinds of food, rhythms, and psychological tendencies. A total ritual system is only achieved through the collective calibration of myriad specializations and roles. The kinds of forces gathered under a brazilianized Yoruba word like *axé*, are each first distilled in order to then be "worked" through specific ritual attention to their accentuation, diminution, and ultimate balance. Finally, the techniques of working such forces are, at least traditionally, kept secret from general public view, and learned only through long initiations and apprenticeship in the terreiro. The Pentecostal model, contrariwise, is a totalizing one of a single, shared narrative, revealed to all in a single sacred text which is carried in public whenever possible, as conspicuously as possible.

If tropes like obedience and revelation are central in Pentecostal practice, "making" is key to Candomblé. Initiation is the simultaneous "making of the head," and the "making of the saint" (*fazer cabeça, fazer santo*) (Capone 1999a; Sansi 2007; Latour 2010). Work figures in all of the daily activities that keep a terreiro going. Indeed, ritual efforts to alter the course of life though ritual techniques are frequently called "jobs" (*trabalhos*). Changes in life chances and the balance of powers can be altered through such ritual labor.

In summary, the Afro-Brazilian groups – Candomblé, Umbanda, Xangô (in Pernambuco) – and hybrid Afro-Brazilian/Amerindian assemblages like Jurema – all live in a context of relentless border-work. Who are we as a community vis-à-vis neighboring traditions, nations, spirits, techniques? Brazil is statistically as densely "religious" as the United States yet more open-ended in terms of what that means. Many people avail themselves of multiple spirit-repertoires, following the logic that "more is better than one." Within such multi-religious possibilities, Afro-Brazilian practices are probably underreported on census responses, registering little over 1 percent in terms of formal affiliation (IBGE 2012, table 1.4.1). At the same time, virtually all Brazilians know about, sometimes think in terms of, or have not infrequently consulted the entities of Candomblé, Umbanda, Batuque, Jurema, Xangô, and more. The Afro-Brazilian religious network – its gods, ancestors, music, recipes, and aesthetics – feature in films, music, journalism, and public space and are assumed as part of the everyday grammar of life across Brazil. This suggests the need to distinguish analytically between formal participants in a terreiro of Candomblé and the tastes, practices, and semiotic codes we might call "public Candomblé" (Johnson 2002), which may or may not involve initiation or other long-lasting commitments.

## SUPERFORM: TRANSREGIONAL DIFFUSION, GLOBALIZATION, VIRTUALIZATION

The twentieth century history of several Afro-Latin American religions is one of rapid expansion from their local centers of consolidation (such as Havana and Matanzas in the case of Regla de Ocha and Salvador da Bahia and Rio de Janeiro in the case of Candomblé) toward ever more expansive peripheries. Yoruba-derived ritual forms arrived in eastern Cuba in the early 1930s (Lachatañeré 1942, 1992; Larduet Luaces 2014) and in New York by the end of that decade. In fact, the first babalawo, Pancho Mora, became active in New York in 1946, more than a decade before Ifá reached Santiago de Cuba at the beginning of the 1960s (Larduet Luaces 2014, 142). In a similar fashion, Candomblé, Umbanda, and the Batuque of Porto Alegre began to gradually spread not just outside their original regional centers of inception, but beyond Brazil's national borders into Uruguay and Argentina (Prandi 1990; Frigerio and Carozzi 1993; Hugarte 1998; Oro 1999).

Ironically, what accelerated these developments were Cold War political constellations and events. Had it not been for the massive emigrant waves from post-1959 revolutionary Cuba and from Brazil under military rule (post-1964), the growth and ritual viability of "secondary diasporas" (Frigerio 2004) would likely have been far more protracted. In the Afro-Cuban case, migrant streams toward the United States carried thousands of initiated practitioners of Regla de Ocha, Ifá, and Palo Monte to emerging exile communities in New York, New Jersey, and Miami, where they built up ritual infrastructures that allowed for the first initiations in exile by 1961 in the case of New York (Brandon 1993, 105–06), and by 1971 in Miami (Palmié 1991, 194–95). The advent of 125,000 Cuban exiles in South Florida during the Mariel exodus of 1980 led to further massive expansion of the number of practitioners and increasing public controversy about what many Anglo-Americans perceived as a morally subversive foreign cult. These controversies came to a head when, in 1987, the *oriaté* (ritual specialist) Ernesto Pichardo opened his legally incorporated Church of the Lukumí Babalu Ayé in the city of Hialeah. This event sparked a protracted series of legal battles that, in 1993, led to a US Supreme Court decision that not only recognized Pichardo's church (and so implicitly Santería) as a religion under American law, but also legalized animal sacrifice for its members (Palmié 1996).

Another event of lasting significance occurred in late 1958, when the US black nationalist and cultural entrepreneur Walter Serge King traveled to Matanzas to be initiated into Regla de Ocha. After returning to New York City, King initially collaborated with Cuban and Puerto Rican initiates but soon embarked on a course of purging what came to be called the American Yoruba Movement or Yoruba Reversionist Movement of what he perceived as spurious Cuban admixtures. In the late 1960s, he broke with the Cubans who rejected his re-Africanization practices as untraditional. In 1970 King and his African American followers moved to South Carolina where they founded the theocratic community of Oyoyunji, which he ruled under the name Oba Efuntola Adelabu Adefunmi I until his death in 2005 (Hunt 1979; Brandon 1993,114–20; Hucks 2012; Palmié 2013, 113–48).

In 1981, Oba Efuntola traveled to Nigeria, where the Ooni of Ifé ratified his status as the ruler of an extraterritorial Yoruba kingdom. In part, this constituted an outgrowth of a conjuncture of transatlantic scope that had taken shape during the decade of the 1970s. By then, traditional Yoruba rulers and the Nigeria state had begun to send academically trained figures such as the literary scholar and babalawo Wande Abimbola and the linguist Olabiyi Babalola Yai on a mission of drawing proponents of Yoruba-derived religious traditions in the Americas into the orbit of an emerging pan-Yoruba cultural project. Both spent ample time in Brazil, where in 1968 Abimbola bestowed the Yoruba title of *bálè* (town chief) of Salvador da Bahia on the Candomblé priest and ethnographer Deoscoredes Maximiliano dos Santos, and where Ambimbola, Yai, and other traveling Nigerians actively promoted a "return" to linguistic and ritual "Yoruba orthodoxy." Probably through the mediation of Abimbola, in 1981 dos Santos traveled to New York, where he met with Oba Efuntola and the Puerto Rican santera Marta Moreno Vega. Together they hatched the idea of an International Congress of Òrìṣà Tradition and Culture that has since been held at several-year intervals in locations such as Ilé Ifé, Salvador, Port of Spain, Havana, Rio de Janeiro, and San Francisco.

Paralleling these developments, we find a trend where cult leaders aspiring to rid themselves of their relations of dependence upon the ritual authority of their initiators in "primary diasporas" (such as Havana or Salvador) turned toward Nigerian priestly figures such as Abimbola or the Oshogbo-based Babalawo Ifá Yemi Elebuibon. As Brown (2003a) and Palmié (2013) documented, such returns to the putative source authority in contemporary Yorubaland likely commenced with the travels of the Miami-based Babalawo José Miguel Gómez Barberas to Oshogbo in 1978. This set a pattern that has become a major source of friction between practitioners who cling to the traditions that originated in their own New World contexts and those who seek African ratification in Nigeria. More recent are attempts by priests of various Afro-Latin American traditions to enhance, restore, or complete their own ritual repertoires by transversally "recuperating," from other diasporic traditions in the Americas, elements felt to have been lost in their own religion. Cases in point are the Miami-based oriaté Miguel "Willie" Ramos's travels to Bahia in 1988, from where he (re)introduced the cults of Oxumarê and Logunedê into Regla de Ocha (Capone 2007), or the (re)introduction of Ifá into the Brazilian Candomblé by traveling Cuban babalawos (Capone 2016).

Two final conjunctures need mentioning here. The first pertains to the onset in Cuba of the so-called Special Period, after the end of Soviet support plunged the island into a massive economic crisis. This led not only to the island's opening to international tourism as a major generator of revenues, but (at least arguably) to the Cuban Communist Party's declaration in 1991 that the practice of religion was no longer an impediment to party membership. While the latter move led to a near-instantaneous explosion of Afro-Cuban religious expressions into Cuban daily life, the former led to the intensification of ritual ties between members of primary and secondary diasporas such as had grown in Puerto Rico and on the US mainland, and even "tertiary" off-shoots in Venezuela, Colombia, and Mexico. It also led to the increasing exposure – and attraction – of foreign (mainly European, but also Latin American) visitors to traditions of Afro-Cuban ritual practice (Argyriadis 2008). As a result, Afro-Cuban ritual diasporas now exist not just in the Americas but also in Europe, where Santería cult groups have been documented in France, Germany, and Spain (Argyriadis 2001–2002; Rossbach de Olmos 2009; Amores 2011).

The second moment that is likely to inform the future history of Afro-Latin American religion is the emergence of a web-borne "virtual diaspora." Even before the dawn of the millennium, Capone (1999b) took note of a growing trend in which debates concerning matters of theology and ritual among literate and media-savvy elites "went viral" on the internet. She also noted a trend of proliferating orisha websites, and a growing use of those websites as a means to bypass more traditional lines of authority and deference in both primary and secondary diasporas. This moment has accelerated since then to a degree where the internet and other forms of digital mediation (Brandon 2008; Murphy 2008; Guanche 2010; Canals 2014, Beliso-De Jesús 2015) have become fora for launching and cultivating priestly careers, or for theological debates about the relative merits of Cuban or Brazilian traditions versus re-Africanized ones (Palmié 2013, 173–221). Such media constitute a – perhaps *the* – prime vehicle for what Frigerio (2004) foresaw, and scholars from Sandra Barnes (1989) to Olupona and Rey (2008) have proclaimed as a "world religion" in the making.

As already mentioned, Afro-Brazilian religions have also circulated well beyond the terreiros. They are by now public, on radio shows since 1962 (Capone 2010, 103), and, increasingly, on film and online (Van de Port 2011). This has created a profile of public Candomblé (Johnson 2002; Matory 2005) that exists with partial autonomy from the actual practice of the tradition. Running parallel to the paradigm of initiation into a specific house and lineage, a whole class of "samplers" has emerged who range among houses, traditions, even "nations" and, via their knowledge of published sources on Afro-Brazilian religions, feel unbeholden to the authority of any particular priestess or priest. Much like the growing number of people in the United States and Europe who identify as "spiritual" but not "religious," these practitioners show how "Afro-Latin American religion" and other diasporic markers can be adopted to various degrees on a voluntary basis. One can join a diaspora, become diasporic, or engage a given "diasporic horizon" (Johnson 2007, 7), with varying degrees of commitment or investment.

This expansion of authentic "African" religiosity has pushed the orixás, voduns, *eguns* and *nkisi* far beyond the specific spaces of their local ritual cultivation, as well as beyond a specific ethno-racial provenance. This raises new and as yet mostly unresearched questions. Given that Afro-Brazilians have long found meanings, value, and situations of status in the figurations, and ritually produced experiences, of traditional Africa – situations that were unavailable to them in mainstream society – what do Brazilian "whites," Asians, and others get from "Africa's" ritual cultivation? It remains unclear why those with other options available to them voluntarily cast themselves into this economy of scarcity – in terms of the prestige of origins – striving to produce the effect of authentic African tradition to distinguish their temple or their knowledge from those of rivals. After all, there is nothing inevitable about the value of authentic African origins and nothing perennial about its parameters; until the 1970s Umbanda's virtues of innovation and mixture held greater prestige than the claims of authenticity borne by Candomblé (Capone 1999a). We need to learn more about the construction and specific attraction of "African authenticity" for groups not of African descent, in comparison with other construals.

## THE NEW DIASPORIC SUPERFORM

The phenomenon of public Candomblé and its digital circulations opens Afro-Brazilian and indeed all Afro-Latin American religions to even wider calibrations with meta-categories like "African diaspora religions" on the global stage. In mega-cities like New York or London, Montreal or São Paulo, diasporic situations allow and even require that previously distinct and separate groups begin to engage each other, forge cross-referential identifications, and collectively build an African diaspora meta-religion. These "religions" – for they all go by the rubric of "religion" in the competitive context where being or becoming a "religion" has important material yields – can begin to be read against and recombined with each other. Spiritual Baptists emigrated from St. Vincent are influenced by Trinidadian religious style in Brooklyn, and may even adopt the Yoruba orishas in their practice (Zane 1999, 167–69, 175). In Spanish Harlem, Santería takes on a Puerto Rican style as *santerismo*, combined with Espiritismo to reduce the range of orichas to "Seven African Powers" (Murphy 1988, 48; Brandon 1993, 107–8). At a Garifuna ceremony in the Bronx, a woman in possession trance behaves in a manner learned in an event in a Vodou in Brooklyn (Johnson 2007, 58). In Mexico City, the saint called Santa Muerte is now revered together with certain Afro-Cuban orichas (Argyriadis and Juárez Huet 2008). And in Barcelona, Venezuelan immigrants and native Catalans are busily integrating elements of both Palo Monte and Regla de Ocha into (often highly digitally mediated) Euro-diasporic versions of María Lionza (Canals 2014, 2017).

This relatively new global superform, *African diasporic religion*, within which *Afro-Latin American religion* takes its place, raises new horizons of self-understanding and shared history, and offers new possibilities of solidarity and legitimacy. Scholars of particular traditions should ask, however, what the consequences are for "local" practice, and for specific religious traditions, when they adopt and engage this religious superform and try to adapt to its norms.

## BIBLIOGRAPHY

Abend, Lisa. 2004. "Specters of the Secular: Spiritism in Nineteenth-Century Spain." *European History Quarterly* 34, 4: 507–34.

Acosta Saignes, Miguel.1955. "Las cofradías coloniales y el folklore." *Cultura Universitaria* 27: 79–102.

Aimes, Hubert S. 1905. "African Institutions in America." *Journal of American Folklore* 18, 68:15–32.

Alberro, Solange.1993. *Inquisición y sociedad en México*. México: Fondo de Cultura Económica.

Alberto, Paulina. 2011. *Terms of Inclusion: Black Intellectuals in Twentieth-Century Brazil*. Chapel Hill, NC: University of North Carolina Press.

Amores, Grecy Pérez. 2011. "Un Elegguá en mi bolso (Sobre las relaciones de poder en el tránsito de objetos y símbolos de las religiones afrocubanas en el siglo XXI. De Cuba a Canarias)." *Revista Atlántida: Revista Canaria de Ciencias Sociales* 3: 129–44.

Andrews, George Reid. 1980. *The Afro-Argentines of Buenos Aires, 1800–1900*. Madison, WI: University of Wisconsin Press.

Apter, Andrew. 1995. "Notes on Orisha Cults in the Ekiti Yoruba Highlands." *Cahiers d'Études Africaines* 138–39: 369–401.

Argüelles Mederos, Aníbal, and Ileana Hodge Limonta.1991. *Los llamados cultos sincreticos y el espiritismo*. La Habana: Editorial Academía.

Argyriadis, Kali. 1999. *La religion à La Havane*. Amsterdam: Archives Contemporaines.

2001–2002. "Les Parisiens et la santería: de l'attaction esthétique à la implication religieuse," *Psychopathologie Africaine* 31: 17–44.

2008. "Speculators and Santuristas: The Development of Afro-Cuban Cultural Tourism and the Accusation of Religious Commercialism." *Tourist Studies* 8, 2: 249–65.

Argyriadis, Kali, and Nahayeilli Juárez Huet. 2008. "Acerca de algunas estrategias de legitimación de los practicantes de la santería en el context mexicano." In *Raíces en movimiento: prácticas religiosas tradicionales en contextos translocales*, edited by Kali Argyriadis et al., 281–308. Mexico City: Centro de Estudios Mexicanos y Centroamericanos.

Asad, Talal. 1993. *Genealogies of Religion*. Baltimore, MD: Johns Hopkins University Press.

Aubrée, Marion and François Laplantine. 1990. *La table, le livre et les esprits: Naissance, evolution et actualité du mouvement social spirite entre France et Brésil*. Paris: J. C. Lattès.

Ayorinde, Christine. 2004. *Afro-Cuban Religiosity, Revolution and National Identity*. Gainesville, FL: University Press of Florida.

Azevedo, Maria Stella de, and Cleo Martins. 1988. *E daí aconteceu o encanto*. Salvador: Axé Opô Afonjá.

Azevedo, Maria Stella de. 1991. "A Call to the People of Orisha," In *African Creative Expressions of the Divine*, edited by Kortright Davis and Elias Farajaje-Jones. Washington DC: Howard University School of Divinity.

Ballesteros Gaibrois, Manuel. 1955. "Negros en la Nueva Granada" in *Miscelanea de estudios dedicados a Fernando Ortiz*, vol. 1, 108–23. Havana: Úcar García.

Barnes, Sandra, ed. 1989. *Africa's Ogun: Old World and New*. Bloomington, IN: Indiana University Press.

Bastide, Roger. 1958. *Le Candomblé de Bahia*. Paris: La Haye, Mouton.

1960. *Les religions africaines au Brésil. Vers une sociologie des interpénétrations de civilisations*. Paris: PUF.

1978. *The African Religions of Brazil: Toward a Sociology of the Interpenetration of Civilizations*. Translated by Helen Sebba. Baltimore, MD: Johns Hopkins University Press.

Behar, Ruth. 1987. "Sex and Sin, Witchcraft and the Devil in Late-Colonial Mexico." *American Ethnologist* 14: 34–54.

Beliso-De Jesús, Aisha M. 2015. *Electric Santería: Racial and Sexual Assemblages of Transnational Religion*. New York, NY: Columbia University Press.

Bennett, Herman. 2005. *Africans in Colonial Mexico: Absolutism, Christianity, and Afro-Creole Consciousness, 1570–1640*. Bloomington, IN: Indiana University Press.

2009. *Colonial Blackness: A History of Afro-Mexico*. Bloomington, IN: Indiana University Press.

Bermúdez, Andrés Armando. 1967. "Notas para la historia del espiritismo en Cuba." *Etnología y Folklore* 5: 5–22.

Birman, Patrícia. 1995. *Fazer estilo criando gêneros: Possessão e diferenças de gênero em terreiros de umbanda e candomblé no Rio de Janeiro*. Rio de Janeiro: EdUERJ.

Borges, Dain. 1993. "'Puffy, Ugly, Slothful and Inert': Degeneration in Brazilian Social Thought, 1880–1940." *Journal of Latin American Studies* 25, 2: 235–56.

1995. "The Recognition of Afro-Brazilian Symbols and Ideas, 1890–1940." *Luso-Brazilian Review* 32, 2: 59–78.

Brandon, George. 1993. *Santería from Africa to the New World: The Dead Sell Memories*. Bloomington, IN: Indiana University Press.

2008. "From Oral to Digital: Rethinking the Transmission of Tradition in Yorùbá Religion." In *Òrìṣà Devotion as World Religion: The Globalization of Yorùbá Religion*, edited by Jacob K. Olupona and Terry Rey, 448–69. Madison, WI: University of Wisconsin Press.

Brazeal, Brian. 2014. "The Fetish and the Stone: A Moral Economy of Charlatans and Thieves." In *Spirited Things: The Work of "Possession" in Afro-Atlantic Religions*. Edited by Paul Christopher Johnson. Chicago, IL: University of Chicago Press, 131–54.

Bronfman, Alejandra. 2004. *Measures of Equality: Social Science, Citizenship, and Race in Cuba, 1902–1940*. Chapel Hill, NC: University of North Carolina Press.

Brown, David H. 2003a. *Santería Enthroned: Art, Ritual, and Innovation in an Afro-Cuban Religion*. Chicago, IL: University of Chicago Press.

2003b. *The Light Inside: Abakuá Society Arts and Cuban Cultural History*. Washington, DC: Smithsonian Institution.

Brown, Diane D. 1986. *Umbanda: Religion and Politics in Urban Brazil*. Ann Arbor, MI: UMI Research.

Brumana, Fernando G., and Elba G. Martinez. 1991. *Marginália sagrada*. Campinas: Editora Unicamp.

Burdick, John. 1993. *Looking for God in Brazil: The Progressive Catholic Church in Urban Brazil's Religious Arena*. Berkeley, CA: University of California Press.

1998. *Blessed Anastácia: Women, Race, and Popular Christianity in Brazil*. New York, NY: Routledge.

Cabrera, Lydia. 1983. *El Monte*. Miami: Colección del Chicherekú. First published in 1954.

Canals, Roger. 2014. "Dioses de tarifa plana: El culto de María Lionza y las nuevas tecnologías." In *Mitos religiosos afroamericanos*, edited by Nicolás Cortes Rojano, 227–258. Barcelona: Centre d'Estudis i Recerques Socials i Metropolitanes.

2017. *A Goddess in Motion: Visual Creativity in the Cult of María Lionza*. Oxford: Berghahn Books.

Cabrera, Lydia. 1959. *La sociedad secreta Abakuá, narrada por viejos adeptos*. Havana: Ediciones C.R.

Cañizares-Esguerra, Jorge, Matt D. Childs, and James Sidbury, eds. 2013 *The Black Urban Atlantic in the Age of the Slave Trade*. Philadelphia, PA: University of Pennsylvania Press.

Capone, Stefania. 1999a. *La quête de l'Afrique: pouvoir et tradition au Brésil*. Paris: Karthala.

1999b. "Les Dieux sur le Net: L'essor des religions d'origine africaine aux Etats-Unis." *L'Homme* 151: 47–74.

2005. *Les Yoruba du Nouveau Monde: Religion, ethnicité et nationalism noir aux États-Unis*. Paris: Karthala.

2007. "The 'Orisha Religion' between Syncretism and Re-Africanization." In *Cultures of the Lusophone Black Atlantic*, edited by Nancy Priscilla Naro, Roger Sansi-Roca, and Dave Treece, 219–32. New York, NY: Palgrave Macmillan.

2010. *Search for Africa in Brazil*. Durham, NC: Duke University Press.

2016. "The Pai-de-Santo and the Babalawo: Religious Interaction and Ritual Rearrangements within Orisha Religion." In *Ifá Divination, Knowledge, Power, and Performance*, edited by Jacob K. Olopuna and Rowland O. Abiodun, 223–45. Bloomington, IN: Indiana University Press.

Carvalho, Marcus. 2012. "João Pataca et sa 'tranquille' bande du *quilombo* de Catucá." In *Brésil: quatre siècles d'esclavage*, edited by Jean Hébrard, 215–42. Paris: Karthala.

Castillo, Lisa Earl and Luis Nicolau Pares. 2010. "Marcelina da Silva: A Nineteenth- Century Candomblé Priestess in Bahia." *Slavery and Abolition* 31: 1–27.

Cavalcanti, Maria Laura Viveiros de Castro. 1983. *O mundo invisível: cosmologia, sistema ritual e noção de pessoa no espiritismo*. Rio de Janeiro: Zahar Editora.

1986. "Origins, para que as quero? Questões para uma investigação sobre a Umbanda." *Religião e sociedade* 13: 84–102.

Chidester, David. 2014. *Empire of Religion: Imperialism and Comparative Religion*. Chicago, IL: University of Chicago Press.

Clarke, Kamari M. 2004. *Mapping Yoruba Networks: Power and Agency in the Making of Transnational Communities*. Durham, NC: Duke University Press.

Coelho, Ruy. 1955. "The Black Carib of Honduras: A Study in Acculturation." PhD diss., Northwestern University.

Corten, André and Ruth Marshall-Fratani, editors. 2001. *Between Babel and Pentecost: Transnational Pentecostalism in Africa and Latin America*. Bloomington, IN: Indiana University Press.

Costa Lima, Vivaldo da. 1976. "O conçeito de 'nação' nos candomblés da Bahia." *Afro-Asia* 12: 65–90.

1977. "A família-de-santo nos candomblés da Bahia: Um estudo de relações intra-grupais." Master's thesis, Universidade Federal da Bahia, Salvador.

Dantas Gois, Beatriz.1988. *Vovó Nagô e Papai Branco*. Rio de Janeiro: Graal.

2009. *Nagô Grandma and White Papa: Candomblé and the Creation of Afro-Brazilian Identity*. Translated by Stephen Berg. Chapel Hill, NC: University of North Carolina Press.

De la Fuente, Alejandro. 2008. *Havana and the Atlantic in the Sixteenth Century*. Chapel Hill, NC: University of North Carolina Press.

De Rojas, María Teresa. 1956. "Algunos datos sobre los negros esclavos y horros en la Habana del siglo XVI," in *Miscelanea de estudios dedicados a Fernando Ortiz*, vol. 2, 1276–87. Havana: Úcar García.

Díaz Fabelo, Teodoro. 1960. *Olorun*. La Habana: Úcar García.

Espírito Santo, Diana. 2015. *Developing the Dead: Mediumship and Selfhood in Cuban Espiritismo*. Gainesville, FL: University Press of Florida.

Farah, Paulo Daniel Elias, translator and editor. 2007. *O deleite do estrangeiro em tudo o que é espantoso e maravilhoso: Estudo de um ralato de viagem bagdali*. Rio de Janeiro: Biblioteca Nacional.

Farias, Juliana Barreto, Carlos Eugênio Líbano Soares, and Flávio dos Santos Gomes. 2005. *No labirinto das nações: Africanos e identidades no Rio de Janeiro, século XIX*. Rio de Janeiro: Arquivo Nacional.

Ferrándiz, Francisco. 2003. "Malandros, María Lionza and Masculinity in a Venezuelan Shantytown." In *Changing Men and Masculinities in Latin America*, edited by Matthew C. Gutmann, 115–33. Durham, NC: Duke University Press.

Freyre, Gilberto. 1956. *The Masters and the Slaves: A Study in the Development of Brazilian Civilization*. Translated by Samuel Putnam. New York, NY: Alfred A. Knopf.

Friedemann, Nina S de. 1988. *Cabildos negros: Refugios de Africanía en Colombia*. Caracas: Universidad Catolica Andres Bello.

Frigerio, Alejandro. 2004. "Re-Africanization in Secondary Religious Diasporas: Constructing a World Religion." *Civilisations* 51: 39–60.

Frigerio, Alejandro, and María Julia Carozzi. 1993. "As religiões afrobrasileiras na Argentina." *Cadernos de Antropologia* 10: 39–68.

Fromont, Cécile. 2014. *The Art of Conversion: Christian Visual Culture in the Kingdom of Kongo*. Chapel Hill, NC: University of North Carolina Press.

Fry, Peter. 1982. *Para inglês ver: Identidade e política na cultura brasileira*. Rio de Janeiro: Zahar.

Germeten, Nicole von. 2006. *Black Blood Brothers: Confraternities and Social Mobility for Afro-Mexicans*. Gainesville, FL: University Press of Florida.

2013. *Violent Delights, Violent Ends: Sex, Race, and Honor in Colonial Cartagena de Indias*. Albuquerque, NM: University of New Mexico Press.

Giumbelli, Emerson. 1997. *O cuidado dos mortos*. Rio de Janeiro: Arquivo Nacional.

Gleason, Judith. 2000. "Oya in the Company of Saints." *Journal of the American Academy of Religion* 68, 2: 265–92.

Gómez, Pablo F. 2013. "The Circulation of Bodily Knowledge in the Seventeenth-Century Black Spanish Caribbean." *Social History of Medicine* 26, 3: 383–402.

2014. "Transatlantic Meanings: African Rituals and Material Culture in the Early Modern Spanish Caribbean." In *Materialities of Ritual in the Black Atlantic*, edited by Akinwumi Ogundiran and Paula Saunders, 125–41. Bloomington, IN: Indiana University Press.

Gonzalez, Nancie L. 1988. *Sojourners of the Caribbean: Ethnogenesis and Ethnohistory of the Garifuna*. Urbana, IL: University of Illinois Press.

Gordon, Edmund T. 1998. *Disparate Diasporas: Identity and Politics in an African Nicaraguan Community*. Austin, TX: University of Texas Press.

Guanche, Jesús. 1983. *Procesos etnoculturales de Cuba*. Havana: Editorial Letras Cubanas.

2010. "Cuba en Venezuela: orichas en la red." *Temas* 61:117–25.

Hagedorn, Katherine. 2001. *Divine Utterances: The Performance of Afro-Cuban Santería*. Washington, DC: Smithsonian Institution.

Hale, Lindsay L. 2009. *Hearing the Mermaid's Song: The Umbanda Religion in Rio de Janeiro*. Albuquerque, NM: University of New Mexico Press.

Hanchard, Michael George. 1994. *Orpheus and Power: The Movimento Negro of Rio de Janeiro and São Paulo, Brazil, 1945–1988*. Princeton, NJ: Princeton University Press.

Handler, Jerome S., and Kelly E. Hayes. 2009. "Escrava Anastácia: The Iconographic History of a Brazilian Popular Saint." *African Diaspora* 2: 25–51.

Harding, Rachel E. 2000. *A Refuge in Thunder: Candomblé and Alternative Spaces of Blackness*. Bloomington, IN: Indiana University Press.

Harrison, Peter. 1990. *"Religion" and the Religions in the English Enlightenment*. New York, NY: Cambridge University Press.

Hayes, Kelly E. 2007. "Black Magic and the Academy: Macumba and Afro-Brazilian 'Orthodoxies.'" *History of Religions* 46, 4: 283–315.

2011. *Holy Harlots: Femininity, Sexuality and Black Magic in Brazil*. Berkeley, CA: University of California Press.

Hébrard, Jean. 2012. "L'esclavage au Brésil: le débat historiographique et ses racines." In *Brésil: quatre siècles d'esclavage*, edited by Jean Hébrard, 7–61. Paris: Karthala & CIRESC.

Herskovits, Melville J. 1937. "African Gods and Catholic Saints in New World Negro Belief." *American Anthropologist* 39: 635–43

1941. *The Myth of the Negro Past*. New York, NY: Harper.

Hess, David J. 1991. *Spirits and Scientists: Ideology, Spiritism, and Brazilian Culture*. University Park, PA: Pennsylvania State University Press.

1994. *Samba in the Night: Spiritism in Brazil*. New York, NY: Columbia University Press.

Heywood, Linda M. 1999. "The Angolan-Afro-Brazilian Cultural Connections." *Slavery and Abolition* 20: 9–23.

Hucks, Tracey. 2012. *Yoruba Traditions and African American Religious Nationalism*. Albuquerque, NM: University of New Mexico Press.

Hugarte, Renzo Pi, and Mariel Cisneros López, eds. 1998. *Cultos de posesión en Uruguay: Antropología e historia*. Montevideo: Ediciones de La Banda Oriental.

Hulme, Peter, and Neil Whitehead, editors. 1992. *Wild Majesty: Encounters with Caribs from Columbus to the Present, an Anthology*. New York, NY: Oxford University Press.

Hunt, Carl M. 1979. *Oyotunji Village: The Yoruba Movement in America*. Washington, DC: University Press of America.

Ireland, Rowan. 1991. *Kingdoms Come: Religion and Politics in Brazil*. Pittsburgh, PA: University of Pittsburgh Press.

IBGE (Instituto Brasileiro de Geografia e Estatística). 2012. *Censo demográfico 2010: Características da população, religião e pessoas com deficiência*. Rio de Janeiro: IBGE.

Johnson, Paul Christopher. 2002. *Secrets, Gossip and Gods: The Transformation of Brazilian Candomblé*. New York, NY: Oxford University Press.

2005. "Three Paths to Legitimacy: African Diaspora Religions and the State." *Culture and Religion* 6, 1: 79–105.

2007. *Diaspora Conversions: Black Carib Religion and the Recovery of Africa*. Berkeley, CA: University of California Press.

2011. "An Atlantic Genealogy of 'Spirit Possession.'" *Comparative Studies in Society and History* 53, 2: 393–425.

2014. "Introduction: Spirits and Things in the Making of the Afro-Atlantic World." In *Spirited Things: The Work of "Possession" in Afro-Atlantic Religions*, edited by Paul Christopher Johnson. Chicago, IL: University of Chicago Press.

Forthcoming. "Material Modes and Moods of 'Slave Anastácia,' Afro-Brazilian Saint." *Journal de la société des américanistes*.

Karasch, Mary C. 1979. "Central African Religious Tradition in Rio de Janeiro." *Journal of Latin American Lore* 5: 233–53.

1986. "Anastácia and the Slave Women of Rio de Janeiro," In *Africans in Bondage*, edited by Paul Lovejoy, 29–105. Madison, WI: University of Wisconsin Press.

Kerestetzi, Katerina. 2011. "Vivre avec les morts. Réinvention, transmission et legitimation des pratiques du palo monte (Cuba)." PhD diss., Paris-Nanterre.

Kerns, Virginia. 1983. *Women and the Ancestors: Black Carib Kinship and Ritual*. Urbana, IL: University of Illinois Press.

Khan, Aisha. 2012. "Islam, Vodou, and the Making of the Afro-Atlantic." *New West Indian Guide* 86: 29–54.

Kiddy, Elizabeth W. 2005. *Blacks of the Rosary: Memory and History in Minas Gerais, Brazil*. University Park, PA: Pennsylvania State University Press.

Kramer, Eric W. 2001. "Possessing Faith: Commodification, Religious Subjectivity and Collectivity in a Neo-Pentecostal Church." PhD diss., University of Chicago.

Lachatañeré, Romulo. 1942. *Manual de santería*. Havana: Editorial Caribe.

1992. *El sistema religioso de los afrocubanos*. Havana: Editorial Ciencias Sociales.

Landes, Ruth. 1947. *The City of Women*. New York, NY: Macmillan.

Larduet Luaces, Abelardo. 2014. *Hacia una historia de la santería santiaguera y otras consideraciones*. Santiago: Casa del Caribe.

Latour, Bruno. 2010. *On the Modern Cult of the Factish Gods*. Translated by Heather MacLean and Cathy Porter. Durham, NC: Duke University Press.

Lewis, Laura A. 2003. *Hall of Mirrors: Power, Witchcraft, and Caste in Colonial Mexico*. Durham, NC: Duke University Press.

Lincoln, Bruce, 2003. *Holy Terrors: Thinking about Religion after September 11*. Chicago, IL: University of Chicago Press.

López Valdés, Rafael. 1965. "La sociedad secreta 'Abakuá' en un grupo de obreros portuarios." *Etnología y Folklore* 2: 5–26.

Maggie, Yvonne. 1992. *Medo do feitiço: Relações entre magia e poder no Brasil*. Rio de Janeiro: Arquivo Nacional.

Marrero, Lévi. 1971–78. *Cuba, economía y sociedad*. Madrid: Playor.

Masuzawa, Tomoko. 2005. *The Invention of World Religions*. Chicago, IL: University of Chicago Press.

Matory, J. Lorand. 1999. "The English Professors of Brazil: On the Diasporic Roots of the Yoruba Nation." *Comparative Studies in History and Society* 41, 1: 72–103.

2005. *Black Atlantic Religion*. Princeton, NJ: Princeton University Press.

Maya Restrepo, Adriana. 2005. *Brujería y reconstrucción de identidades entre los africanos y sus descendientes en la Nueva Granada, siglo XVII*. Bogotá: Ministerio de Cultura.

McCutcheon, Russell T. 1997. *Manufacturing Religion*. New York, NY: Oxford University Press.

Miller, Ivor. 2009. *Voice of the Leopard: African Secret Societies and Cuba*. Jackson: University Press of Mississippi.

Montero, Paula. 1985. *Da doença à desordem: A magia na umbanda*. Rio de Janeiro: Edições Graal.

Moreno Fraginals, Manuel. 1983. *La historia como arma*. Barcelona: Editorial Crítica.

Morgan, Philip D. 1997. "The Cultural Implications of the Atlantic Slave Trade: African Regional Origins, American Destinations, and New World Developments." *Slavery and Abolition* 18: 122–45.

Mott, Luiz. 1993. *Rosa Egipcíaca: Uma santa africana no Brasil*. Rio de Janeiro: Editora Bertrand Brasil.

2010. *Bahia: Inquisição e sociedade*. Salvador: EdUFBA.

Motta, Roberto. 1997. "Religiões afro-recifenses: Ensaio de classificação." *Revista Antropológicas* 2: 11–34.

Mulvey, Patricia A. 1980. "Black Brothers and Sisters: Membership in the Black Lay Brotherhoods of Colonial Brazil." *Luso-Brazilian Review* 17, 2: 253–79.

Murphy, Joseph M. 1988. *Santería: An African Religion in America*. Boston: Beacon Press.

2008. "Òrìṣà Traditions and the Internet Diaspora." In *Òrìṣà Devotion as World Religion: The Globalization of Yorùbá Religion*, edited by Jacob K. Olupona and Terry Rey, 470–84. Madison, WI: University of Wisconsin Press.

Nina Rodrigues, Raimundo. 2006. *O animismo fetichista dos negros baianos*. Rio de Janeiro: Biblioteca Nacional. First published in 1896–1897.

Nongbri, Brent. 2013. *Before Religion: A History of a Modern Concept*. New Haven: Yale University Press.

Ochoa, Todd Ramón. 2010. *Society of the Dead: Quita Mananquita and Palo Praise in Cuba*. Berkeley, CA: University of California Press.

Olupona, Jacob K., and Terry Rey. 2008. "Introduction." In *Òrìṣà Devotion as World Religion: The Globalization of Yorùbá Religious Culture*, edited by Jacob K. Olupona and Terry Rey, 3–28. Madison, WI: University of Wisconsin Press.

Oro, Ari Pedro. 1999. *Axé Mercosul: As religiões afro-brasileiras nos países do Prata*. Rio de Janeiro: Editora Vozes.

Oro, Ari Pedro, and Pablo Semán. 2001. "Brazilian Pentecostalism Crosses National Borders." In *Between Babel and Pentecost: Transnational Pentecostalism in Africa and Latin America*, edited by André Corten and Ruth Marshall-Fratani, 181–215 Bloomington, IN: Indiana University Press.

Ortiz, Fernando. 1921. "Los cabildos afrocubanos." *Revista Bimestre Cubana* 16, 1: 5–39.

———. 1952–55. *Los instrumentos de la música afrocubana*. Havana: Ministerio de Educación.

———. 1973. *Los negros brujos*. Miami: Ediciones Universal. First published in 1906.

———. 1975. *Historia de una pelea cubana contra los demonios*. Havana: Editorial de Ciencias Sociales. First published in 1959.

———. 1981. *Los bailes y el teatro de os negros en el folklore de Cuba*. Havana: Editorial Letras Cubanas. First published in 1951.

Ortiz, Renato. 1986. "Breve nota sobre a umbanda e suas origens." *Religião e Sociedade* 13: 133–37.

———. 1989. "Ogum and the Umbandista Religion." In *Africa's Ogun: Old World and New*, edited by Sandra T. Barnes. 90–103. Bloomington, IN: Indiana University Press.

———. 1991. *A norte branca do feiticeiro negro: Umbanda e sociedade brasileira*. São Paulo: Editora Brasiliense. First published in 1978.

Palmer, Colin A. 1976. *Slaves of the White God: Blacks in Mexico, 1570–1650*. Cambridge, MA: Harvard University Press.

Palmié, Stephan. 1991. *Das Exil der Götter: Geschichte und Vorstellungswelt einer afrokubanischen Religion*. Frankfurt: Peter Lang.

———. 1996. "Which Center, Whose Margin? Notes Towards an Archaeology of U.S. Supreme Court Case 91–948, 1993." In *Inside and Outside the Law*, edited by Olivia Harris, 184–209. New York, NY: Routledge.

———. 2002. *Wizards and Scientists: Explorations in Afro-Cuban Modernity and Tradition*. Durham, NC: Duke University Press.

———. 2005. "The Cultural Work of Yoruba-Globalization." In *Christianity and Social Change in Africa*, edited by Toyin Falola, 43–83. Chapel Hill, NC: Carolina Academic Press.

———. 2006. "A View from Itía Ororó Kande." *Social Anthropology* 14: 99–118.

———. 2008. "Ecué's Atlantic: An Essay in Method." In *Africas of the Americas: Beyond the Search for Origins in the Study of Afro-Atlantic Religions*, edited by Stephan Palmié, 179–222. Leiden: Brill.

2013. *The Cooking of History: How Not to Study Afro-Cuban Religion.* Chicago, IL: University of Chicago Press.

Parés, Luis Nicolau. 2013. *The Formation of Candomblé: Vodun History and Ritual in Brazil.* Translated by Richard Vernon. Chapel Hill, NC: University of North Carolina Press.

Paton, Diana. 2009. "Obeah Acts: Producing and Policing the Boundaries of Religion in the Caribbean." *Small Axe* 28: 1–18.

Pereira, Nuno Marques. 1988. *Compêndio narrativo do peregrino da América.* Rio de Janeiro: Academia Brasileira de Letras.

Pérez y Mena, Andrés I. 1995. "Puerto Rican Spiritism as a Transfeature of Afro-Latin Religion." In *Enigmatic Powers: Syncretism with African and Indigenous Peoples' Religions Among Latinos,* edited by Anthony M. Stevens-Arroyo and Andrés I. Pérez y Mena, 137–58. New York, NY: Bildner Center.

Pike, Ruth.1967. "Sevillan Society in the 16th Century: Slaves and Freedmen." *Hispanic American Historical Review* 47, 3: 344–59.

Pierucci, Antônio Flávio, and Reginaldo Prandi. 2000. "Religious Diversity in Brazil: Numbers and Perspectives in a Sociological Evaluation." *International Journal of Sociology* 15, 4: 629–40.

Pinho, Patricia de Santana. 2010. *Mama Africa: Reinventing Blackness in Bahia.* Durham, NC: Duke University Press.

Prandi, Reginaldo. 1990. "Linhagem e legitimidade no candomblé paulista." *Revista Brasileira de Ciencias Sociais* 14: 18–31.

1991. *Os candomblés de São Paulo: A velha magia na metrópole nova.* São Paulo: Hucitec and Edusp.

Raboteau, Albert. 1978. *Slave Religion in Antebellum America: The "Invisible Institution" in the Antebellum South.* New York, NY: Oxford University Press.

Rauhut, Claudia. 2012. *Santería und ihre Globalisierung in Kuba: Tradition und Innovation in einer afrokubanischen Religion.* Würzburg: Ergon Verlag.

Reis, João José. 1986. "Nas malhas do poder escravista: A invasão do candomblé do Accú na Bahia, 1829." *Religião e Sociedade* 13, 3: 108–27.

1993. *Slave Rebellion in Brazil: The Muslim Uprising of 1835 in Bahia.* Translated by Arthur Brakel. Baltimore, MD: Johns Hopkins University Press.

2003a. *Death Is a Festival: Funeral Rites and Rebellion in 19th-Century Brazil.* Chapel Hill, NC: University of North Carolina Press.

2003b. *Rebelião escrava no Brasil.* 2nd edition. São Paulo: Companhia das Letras.

2008. *Domingos Sodré um sacerdote Africano: Escravidão, liberdade e candomblé na Bahia do século XIX.* São Paulo: Companhia das Letras.

Reis, João José, Flávio dos Santos Gomes, and Marcus Joaquim de Carvalho. 2010. *O alufá Rufino: Tráfico, escravidão e liberdade no Atlântico negro (1822–1853).* São Paulo: Companhia das Letras.

Reis, João José, and Paulo F. Morães de Farías. 1989. "Islam and Slave Resistance in Bahia, Brazil." *Islam et Sociétés au Sud du Sahara* 3: 41–66.

Richman, Karen. 2008. "Peasants, Migrants, and the Discovery of African Traditions: Ritual and Social Change in Lowland Haiti." In *Africas of the*

*Americas: Beyond the Search for Origins in the Study of Afro-Atlantic Religions*, edited by Stephan Palmié, 293–321. Leiden: Brill.

Román, Reinaldo. 2007. *Governing Spirits: Religion, Miracles, and Spectacles in Cuba and Puerto Rico, 1898–1956*. Chapel Hill, NC: University of North Carolina Press.

Rossbach de Olmos, Lioba. 2009. "Santería: The Short History of an Afro-Cuban Religion in Germany by Means of Biographies of Some of Its Priests." *Anthropos* 104:1–15.

Routon, Kenneth. 2005. "Unimaginable Homelands? 'Africa' and the Abakuá Historical Imagination." *Journal of Latin American Anthropology* 10: 370–400.

———. 2011. *Hidden Powers of the State in the Cuban Imagination*. Gainesville, FL: University Press of Florida.

Sansi Roca, Roger. 2007. *Fetishes and Monuments: Afro-Brazilian Art and Culture in the 20th Century*. Oxford and New York, NY: Berghahn.

Santos, Jocélio Teles dos. 1995. *O dono da terra: O caboclo nos candomblés da Bahia*. Salvador: Sarah Letras.

Scott, David. 1999. *Refashioning Futures: Criticism after Postcoloniality*. Princeton, NJ: Princeton University Press.

Selka, Stephen. 2007. *Religion and the Politics of Ethnic Identity in Bahia, Brazil*. Gainesville, FL: University Press of Florida.

Serra, Ordep. 1995. *Aguas do rei*. Petrópolis: Vozes.

Sheriff, Robin E. 1996. "The Muzzled Saint: Racism, Cultural Censorship and Religion in Urban Brazil." In *Silence: The Currency of Power*, edited by Maria-Luisa Achino-Loeb, 113–40. New York and Oxford: Berghahn.

Silva, Vagner Gonçalves da. 1995. *Orixás da metrópole*. Petrópolis: Vozes.

———. 2005. "Concepções religiosas afro-brasileiras e neopentecostais: Uma análise simbólica." *Revista USP* 67: 150–175.

Silveira, Renato da. 2006. *O candomblé da Barroquinha: Processo de constituição do primeiro terreiro baiano de keto*. Salvador: Edições Maianga.

Silverblatt, Irene. 2004. *Modern Inquisitions: Peru and the Colonial Origins of the Civilized World*. Durham, NC: Duke University Press.

Slenes, Robert W. 1991. "'*Malungu, Ngoma Vem!*': África coberta e descoberta no Brasil." *Revista USP* 12: 48–67.

———. 2006. "A árvore de *Nsanda* trans-plantada: Cultos Kongo de aflição e identidade escrava no Sudeste brasileiro (século XIX)." In *Trabalho livre, trabalho escravo: Brasil e Europa, séculos XVIII e XIX*, edited by Douglas Cole Libby and Júnia Ferreira Furtado, 273–314. São Paulo: Annablume.

———. 2008. "Saint Anthony at the Crossroads in Kongo and Brazil: 'Creolization' and Identity Politics in the Black South Atlantic, ca. 1700/1850." In *Africa, Brazil, and the Construction of Trans-Atlantic Black Identities*, edited by Boubacar Barry, Élisée Soumonni, and Lívio Sansone, 209–254. Trenton, NJ: Africa World Press.

Smith, Jonathan Z. 1998. "Religion, Religions, Religious." In *Critical Terms for Religious Studies*, edited by Mark C. Taylor, 269–84. Chicago, IL: University of Chicago Press.

Smith, Wilfred Cantwell. 1963. *The Meaning and End of Religion*. Minneapolis: Fortress Press.

Soares, Mariza de Carvalho. 2011. *People of Faith: Slavery and African Catholics in Eighteenth-Century Rio de Janeiro*. Translated by Jerry D. Metz. Durham, NC: Duke University Press.

Sogbossi, Hippolyte Brice. 1998. *La tradición ewé-fon en Cuba*. Havana: Fundación Fernando Ortiz.

Sosa Rodriguez, Ernesto. 1982. *Los ñáñigos*. Havana: Ediciones Casa de las Américas.

Souza, Laura de Mello e. 1986. *O diabo e a Terra de Santa Cruz*. São Paulo: Companhia de Letras.

Stewart, Charles, and Rosalind Shaw, editors. 1994. *Syncretism/ Anti-Syncretism: The Politics of Religious Synthesis*. London and New York, NY: Routledge.

Sweet, James Hoke. 2003. *Recreating Africa: Culture, Kinship, and Religion in the African-Portuguese World, 1441–1770*. Chapel Hill, NC: University of North Carolina Press.

Thornton, John K. 1998. *The Kongolese Saint Anthony: Dona Beatriz Kimpa Vita and the Antonian Movement, 1684–1706*. New York, NY: Cambridge University Press.

Vainfas, Ronaldo. 1989. *Trópico dos pecados: Moral, sexualidade e Inquisição no Brasil*. Rio de Janeiro: Nova Fronteira.

Van de Port, Mattjis. 2011. *Ecstatic Encounters: Bahian Candomblé and the Quest for the Really Real*. Amsterdam: Amsterdam University Press.

Van der Leeuw, Gerardus. 1963 [1933]. *Religion in Essence and Manifestation: A Study in Phenomenology*. Translated by J. E. Turner. New York, NY: Harper and Row.

Warren, Donald Jr. 1968. "The Portuguese Roots of Brazilian Spiritism." *Luso-Brazilian Review* 5, 2: 3–33.

Wirtz, Kristina. 2007. *Ritual, Discourse, and Community in Cuban Santería*. Gainesville, FL: University Press of Florida.

2014. *Performing Afro-Cuba: Image, Voice, Spectacle in the Making of Race and History*. Chicago, IL: University of Chicago Press.

Wood, Marcus. 2011. "The Museu do Negro in Rio and the Cult of Anastácia as a New Model for the Memory of Slavery." *Representations* 113, 1: 111–49.

Zane, Wallace. 1999. *Journeys to the Spiritual Lands: The Natural History of a West Indian Religion*. New York, NY: Oxford University Press.

# 13

# Environment, Space, and Place: Cultural Geographies of Colonial Afro-Latin America

## Karl Offen[1]

A section of railroad track protrudes from the ground a block from my office on the campus of Oberlin College in Northeast Ohio. Erected in 1977, the sculpture commemorates Oberlin's participation in the Underground Railroad, a network of safe houses and passages that helped fugitive slaves find freedom across Lake Erie in Canada. I must have walked by the site a dozen times before I noticed the patch of waist-high shrubs on the exhibit's south side. Concealed by growth are small red signs providing each plant's common names – Evening Primrose, Butterfly Weed, Worm Wood – their Latin names, and their medical uses. A larger but no less obscure placard announced the shrubbery as the Underground Railroad Healing Garden, a celebration of African American herbal healing arts. The easy-to-overlook patch contains several plants – all native to the Americas – used by African Americans for healing and solace during their journey north.

On the one hand, the sculpture and garden exemplify a typical display found on many college campuses across North America. On the other hand, the site conveys the essential relationship that Afrodescendant peoples established with New World nature, as well as the importance of geography more generally in their lives. As a cultural landscape, the place reminds us that African Americans were both constrained and

[1] Oberlin College student Britni Wallace contributed to the research for this paper. Judith Carney and Jane Landers encouraged me to pursue this project and provided vital suggestions and material support at the beginning. Amanda Minks and the editors, Reid Andrews and Alejandro de la Fuente, provided substantial feedback on an earlier version of the chapter. I alone am responsible for continued shortcomings.

enabled by the biophysical environments they came to know and interact with. My experience with this particular site also demonstrates that we can easily overlook evidence of African American cultural and historical geographies, even when they are woven into the spaces of our everyday lives. In this chapter, I take up these subjects – all of them concerns of cultural geography – to review how African and Afrodescendant peoples established meaningful relationships with the Neotropical environments of Latin America and the Caribbean – that swath of the Americas that straddles the equator approximately 23 degrees north and south, or from northern Cuba and Mexico to southern Brazil.

At a basic level, cultural geography seeks to understand the relationship between collective human life and the natural environment, including social relations, the spatiality of life, and the role of culture in shaping and reflecting these interactions (Tuan 1977; Foote, Hugill, Mathewson, and Smith 1994). As a subdiscipline of geography in North America, cultural geography has been profoundly shaped by Latin America because some of its most illustrious practitioners worked in the region (e.g., West 1952, 1957; Parsons 1956; Sauer 1966; Watts 1987; Butzer 1992). Since the 1990s, many cultural-historical geographers have focused on the African legacy in Latin America, and specifically African and Afrodescendant environmental knowledges, African agency in the co-creation of Neotropical landscapes, and the African plants and animals participating in the so-called Columbian Exchange – the two-way transfer of biological resources and the associated social-environmental changes initiated with the Columbian voyages (Voeks 1997; Carney 2001, 2003, 2004, 2005, 2010; Carney and Voeks 2003; Carney and Rosomoff 2009; Sluyter 2012a; Voeks and Rashford 2012a; Watkins 2015). My focus in this chapter, however, is not to underscore geographic scholarship of Afro-Latin America but rather to highlight the many cultural geographies evident in colonial Afro-Latin American scholarship more generally. Specifically, I seek to bring the range of studies examining colonial Afro-Latin American religious practices and medical plant use into dialogue with those on Afro-Latin American house gardens, agriculture, and the broader creation of cultural landscapes, or landscapes that shape and reflect the peoples that created them. Scholars of Afro-Latin America often take up the concerns of cultural geography, but they rarely set out to explore how the cultural dimensions of environment, landscape, space, and place constitute broader lived experiences of Afrodescendants, or the importance of these experiences to the historical development of Latin America more generally. The argument presented here is that Afro-Latin

Americans established meaningful cultural relationships with their environments, which profoundly influenced other dimensions of their lives. As
I discuss briefly in the final section, some of the shared cultural geographies of colonial Afro-Latin America influence the social and political discourses surrounding Afro-Latin American land and environmental issues
to this day.

The essay is divided into four sections. The first contextualizes colonial
Afro-Latin American cultural geographies within recent and revisionist
scholarship that underscores not only the diversity of African and Afrodescendant activities and experiences in America but the distinct disciplinary approaches used to examine them in a new light. The section
highlights scholarship addressing African and Afrodescendant agency –
or self-directed, intentional, and mindful practices – primarily within the
institution of slavery. A second section considers how African perceptions
of Neotropical nature were anchored within the beliefs and practices that
people brought with them and adapted to American environments and
social conditions. A third section distinguishes between place and space
within cultural geography to examine the importance of subsistence
agricultural opportunities within the context of the disruptures tied to
forced migration and the Columbian Exchange. A final section briefly
illustrates some of the ways that colonial Afro-Latin American cultural
geographies remain relevant for Afro-Latin Americans today.

### DIVERSITY OF EXPERIENCE AND AGENCY IN THE DIASPORA

A great deal of recent historical scholarship on Latin America highlights
the ubiquity of the African presence in the region, the diversity of African
experiences, and the need to better understand the African role in the
overall development of Iberian America (Restall and Landers 2000;
Cáceres 2001; Vinson 2006; de la Fuente 2008; Carney and Rosomoff
2009; Gudmundson and Wolfe 2010; Jefferson and Lokken 2011;
Bryant, O'Toole, and Vinson III 2012; Wheat 2016). Such research departs
from the important but often constraining lenses of plantation slavery,
*mestizaje*, and colonial systems of racial domination to instead focus on
the cultural and diasporic dimensions of African and Afrodescendant
lives, and to view Africans and Afrodescendants as creative subjects
contributing to their own experiences. Foundational to this recent scholarship is an examination of black and slave life beyond the sugar plantation and, specifically, the wider range of activities in which Africans and
their descendants participated. David Wheat (2016), for example, has

recently shown that Africans in the Spanish Caribbean to 1640 served as "surrogate settlers," or colonists who replaced the broad range of work that Spanish peasants would have done in Spain. In so doing, Africans and their descendants strengthened and expanded Spanish dominion in the New World. African majorities, including a significant number of free Afrodescendants, arose quickly on farms around Havana, Santo Domingo, Cartagena, and Panama City. These people were overwhelmingly involved in raising food crops, tending livestock, and doing the bulk of work that established Spain's foothold in the Caribbean basin. While many of the more recent Afro-Latin American studies, including Wheat's, are not concerned with cultural geography, or even human-environmental relations per se, they reflect insights from earlier studies that demonstrate how biophysical conditions influenced economic and social life in America, whether under conditions of slavery or not (West 1957; Watts 1987; Carney 2010, 2012).

The seminal work by Ira Berlin and Philip Morgan (1993) explicitly showed historians how the environment influenced the opportunities for Afro-Latin Americans to create independent economies, to bequeath property, and to shape black family and community life more generally (see also Bennett 2003). This work focused greater attention on the role of free and enslaved Afrodescendants in economies other than sugar and paved the way for research on colonial-era coffee, tobacco, cotton, cacao, rice, ginger, indigo, viticulture, ranching, stock raising, hides, timber, resins, dyewoods, mining, marine harvesting (pearls, fishing, turtling, whaling), wild resource extraction, navigation and piloting (Sharp 1976; Bolland 1977; Shepherd 2002; Dawson 2006, 2013; Brockington 2008; Rupert 2009; Zabala 2010; Offen 2000, 2010, 2011b, 2013b; Van Norman 2012; Sluyter 2012a; Lohse 2014; Cromwell 2014; Stark 2015; Wheat 2016; Warsh 2018). Other scholarship discusses free and enslaved African and Afrodescendant roles in defense, transportation, urban ports, and artisanal activities (Lane 2002; Restall 2000, 2009; de la Fuente 2008; Cáceres 2010; Cañizares-Esguerra, Childs, and Sidbury 2013; Wheat 2016). The diversity of these works, both implicitly and explicitly, testifies to the role of environmental conditions in shaping not only the lives of Afrodescendants but also the ways that Afrodescendants contributed to colonial Latin America more generally.

Extractive resource economies on the margins of plantation systems and within imperial borderlands demonstrate how a regional political ecology influenced the conditions of slavery (Offen 2010, 2013b). The extraction of mahogany in Belize and the Mosquitia region of what is today Honduras, for example, illustrates some of the relations between slavery, ecology, and the agency of Afrodescendants. In the British enclaves of Mosquitia and Belize, mahogany grew inland on the frontier with Spanish Central America, and the nature of political boundaries was continually negotiated by all parties including Afrodescendants and Amerindians. Starting in the second half of the eighteenth century, British merchants employed African slaves to locate, cut, and transport mahogany to the coast. Most Afrodescendant slaves in Mosquitia arrived from Jamaica, where they had been sold-off the island for "crimes" (i.e., slave revolts). An enslaved population with a reputation for rebellion, combined with the relative defenseless position of the settlement and the lack of soldiers or an effective militia, helped ensure that slave owners granted their slaves greater independence and social autonomy (Offen 2010; 2013b).

Starting in January, slave-majority groups would spend up to eight months in the forest at a stretch. From remote base camps, teams of slaves would locate, cut, and roll logs with oxen to where flood waters could float them downstream in July. The labor involved in this work was difficult and required a great deal of skill. Because mahogany grew dispersed, only about one tree per hectare, the most valued skill was locating trees by soil preference, hard-to-see tree crowns, and by other environmental indicators; the slave possessing this skill could shape the conditions for all. Hunting was also central to the success of any venture; as one Englishman put it without irony in 1742, slaves "need[ed] to have maximum freedom to acquire game and provisions or people would starve" (Offen 2013b). It is also probable that groups of slaves organized themselves by ethnic or kinship considerations (Finamore 2008, 79). Given the frontier setting and the possibility of freedom should slaves reach Spanish settlements, the mahogany economy – and by extension other economies that relied on the distant extraction of wild resources such as sarsaparilla, marine turtles, vanilla, and medicinal plants – "necessitated a relatively flexible form of bondage" (Anderson 2012, 157; see also Bolland 1977; Offen 2010, 2013b, 2015; Lentz 2014; Restall 2014). In short, the ecology and the biophysical and political setting of desired resource economies shaped and reflected the social relations of production and influenced the ability of the enslaved to negotiate the terms of their servitude.

Recognition of African and Afrodescendant agency and diversity of experience in America has been matched in Afro-Latin American studies by a more nuanced and quantitative picture of where Africans came from, when they left, and how they traveled. Part and parcel of this trend has been the development and widespread use of the Trans-Atlantic Slave Trade Database (Eltis, Behrendt, Richardson, and Klein 1999; Eltis and Richardson 2010; Eltis, Behrendt, Florentino, and Richardson 2013). By documenting some 36,000 slave voyages, from port of departure to embarkation point, from ship captain to a demographic description of the enslaved passengers, the database demonstrates flows and patterns of African arrivals over time throughout the Americas. The database records just part of the Old to New World migration patterns, of course, but it helps verify that almost three-fourths of all westward migrants to cross the Atlantic between 1500 and 1820 came from Africa, and forces us to take the implications of this seriously. The data shows with greater certainty that the slave trade was not "as randomizing a process as posited by those who argue that Africans had to start from scratch culturally" in the New World (Thornton 1998, 204; see also Sweet 2003, 116). As Walter Hawthorne (2010, 7) puts it, Africans in the Americas "were not any more randomly distributed than were Europeans." So, for example, when the Portuguese held the *asiento*, or contract, for bringing slaves to Spanish America, we know that the West Central Africans crossing the Atlantic between 1590 and 1640 gave a recognizable Angolan character to many ports throughout the Americas (Miller 2002; Heywood 2002; Heywood and Thornton 2007; Lokken 2010, 2013; Wheat 2016) – just as Upper Guineans made up similarly large majorities through the 1580s (Newson and Minchin 2007; Wheat 2016). But timing also mattered to the shaping of what came afterwards. The Haitian Revolution – and the disruption of the world's largest producer of sugar – inspired Cuban planters to import as many as 300,000 slaves between 1790 and 1820, three times the number of Africans brought to the island in the preceding 280 years (Eltis 2000; Andrews 2004, 69; Childs 2006; Klein and Vinson III 2007; Wheat 2016; see also Chapter 2).

Nowhere is agency and environment more evident in the cultural geographies of Afro-Latin Americans than among communities established by fugitive slaves. Such places are called many things across Latin America, from *mocambos* and *quilombos* in Brazil (from Kimbundu terms, referred to as the "language of Angola" in many colonial sources), to *palenques* (palisades) from Mexico to Colombia, to *manieles* in the Dominican Republic (from the Taino term for both African and Amerindian fugitive communities), and maroon communities throughout the British Caribbean and in English (see Chapter 7). In the preface to the third edition of the formative volume *Maroon Societies* (1996, xv), Richard Price suggests that maroon communities "were even more frequent and geographically widespread than anyone was aware just a few years ago." He wrote that more than twenty years ago, but it remains true even today. An updated statement might also include reference to how such communities formed earlier and, literally, everywhere Africans went, contained some free African but also non-African peoples, and were more connected to and, therefore, more significant for, colonial society than previously thought. They also remain very much a part of the historical imagination and the volatile land politics of Afrodescendants throughout Latin America to this day (e.g., dos Anjos and Sanzio 2005; Price 2010; Farfán-Santos 2016).

Among the biggest recent development in maroon studies is the correction to the idea that maroons sought to create isolated societies in remote forest redoubts – an image that Price's early work contributed to (Price 1983, 1990; Stedman, Price and Price 1992; see also Diouf 2014). The most famous quilombo of all – Palmares (1605–1694) of colonial Brazil – comprised several communities, included people of all races, collectively held some 11,000–20,000 people at its peak, and remained well-connected to colonial society (Schwartz 1992; Reis and Gomes 1996; Anderson 1996; Weik 2004; Funari 2007). Funari (2007, 367) suggests that Palmeres sheltered one in three African slaves in colonial Brazil in the late seventeenth century, and that the towns together were comparable to the largest city in the colony at the time. Moreover, it is possible that the majority of maroons that lived in Latin America resided close to urban areas, moved between them when possible, relied significantly on trade with colonial society, and associated with Catholic institutions and practices on a regular basis (Schwartz 1992; Anderson 1996; Landers 1999, 2000, 2002, 2005b, 2006, 2013; Romero and Lane 2002; Corzo 2003; Lokken 2004; Beatty-Medina 2006; Pike 2007; McKnight 2009; Amaral 2016).

By the late eighteenth century, the proximity among rural, urban, and quilombo spaces shrank around Salvador, Bahia, Cartagena, and several provincial cities across Afro-Latin America (Schwartz 1992; Reis and Gomes 1996; Andrews 2004, 74; Landers 2013; Reis 2013). Salvador – a city surrounded by up to 100 quilombos – had a population ca. 1830 that was 80 percent black or mulatto, with 60 percent of its enslaved population born in Africa (Reis 2013, 64). João José Reis describes the outskirts of Salvador as a place where freed Africans, Creoles, and *quilombolas* established themselves as small farmers who raised fowl and cultivated a range of crops that they sold in Salvador markets. Bahia's colonial governor, the Count of Ponte (1805–1810), described these black suburbs as being mixed with quilombos containing vagabonds, the sick, imposters, criminals, and medicine men, and religious temples – not just fugitive slaves. The count described these transgressive communities as places where "[blacks] lived in absolute liberty, dancing, wearing extravagant dress, [practicing] false medicine, uttering fanatical prayers and blessings; they used to rejoice, to eat and indulge themselves, violating all rights, laws, orders, and the public peace" (Reis 2013, 74–75). Schwartz (2006), moreover, finds quilombos around Salvador deeply entangled with the planning and execution of slave rebellions in that city. Likewise, the many palenques outside of Cartagena maintained vital relations with urban slaves, suburban haciendas, and representatives of the Church, including convent sisters (Borrego Plá 1973; Vidal Ortega 2002; McKnight 2009; Landers 2013; Soulodre-La France 2015).

Shipwrecks also brought many Africans upon coastal areas before they experienced New World slavery. One of the more well-known events occurred off what is today northwest Ecuador in the mid-sixteenth century (Lane 2002; Beatty-Medina 2006), while another important wreck took place off Cape Gracias a Dios in eastern Central America in the early seventeenth century – the latter likely due to a slave mutiny combined with piracy (Offen 2011b; Thornton 2017). In both these cases, complex Afro-Amerindian, or so-called *zambo*, dynasties emerged. In Ecuador, African and zambo leaders united mulatto "chieftains" (Beatty-Medina 2006, 127), and, in eastern Nicaragua and Honduras, an Afro-Amerindian Miskitu Kingdom combined both Miskitu zambos and Miskitu Amerindians (Offen 2002, 2007, 2010; Thornton 2017). These were not Neo-African kingdoms but rather New World polities of compulsion profoundly entangled with colonial designs. Both groups adapted well to diverse ecosystems – subsisting on New World crops, game, and trade. They also subordinated neighboring indigenous peoples and established treaties with Spaniards and, in the case of the Miskitu, with the British, too. Through spatial practices from tribute and tax collection and the monitoring of borders, to discourses of territorial autonomy and defiance communicated via colonial symbols of dominion and authority, these mixed Afrodescendant peoples carved out independent polities on the margins of and in between colonial empires (Lane 2002; Offen 2007; Beatty-Medina 2006, 2009, Williams 2014). Unlike the majority of maroon communities throughout Latin America, however, colonial regimes never vanquished these polities, and only in the national period did they become integrated into state-building projects. Their accomplishments – reflecting

African, Amerindian, and European cultural and political forms and traditions – continue to influence the cultural geographies of Afro-Latin America by bridging the ideological, historical, and political divides between Amerindians and Afrodescendants throughout Latin America and the Caribbean (see Chapter 4).

Disputes about the relative role of Africa in colonial Afro-Latin American studies continues to influence scholarship. Heated debates pitting African cultural continuities and "survivals" against various models of creolization following the deracination of the Middle Passage endure. But, most scholars probably accept a need to focus on both creative cultural change and "African" persistence, and recognize that continuity and change both require a degree of agency.[2] For most geographers this debate is distracting. An important geographic concept is diffusion, the movement of something from its place of origin to a new destination where it must adapt anew. The concept refers to people, of course, but also ideas, technologies, and biological organisms such as cattle (Sauer 1966; Sluyter 2012a), rice (Carney 2001), or mosquitos (McNeill 2010). For geographers, the biophysical environment and the transformations humans enact upon it influence social life and, thus, unquestionably affected Afro-Latin American experiences in America and vice versa. This is why the groundbreaking research on the role of Africa – its crops, animals, and peoples – in the Columbian Exchange by geographer Judith Carney forces us to reconsider the material and emotive relationships African and Afrodescendants established with the American landscapes that they co-created (2001, 2003, 2004, 2005, 2010, 2012; Carney and Rosomoff 2009). What makes Carney's work so important is her insistence that African peoples brought with them sophisticated knowledge, skills, and techniques that were pre-adapted to tropical climates. Why would we assume, she posits rhetorically, that "slaves" possessed a limited understanding of New World environments and agro-ecosystems, especially when contemporaneous Europeans made no such assumptions? As Carney and Voeks (2003, 145) put it, to classify African men and women simply as slaves is to dispossess them "of their pre-existing ethnic

---

[2] In contrast, Philip Morgan argues that any emphasis on "Africanity" makes "excessive claims for the autonomy of slaves and the primacy of their African background ... belittles the slaves' achievements by minimizing the staggering obstacles they faced in forging a culture" (Morgan 1998, 657). This view builds off Sidney Mintz and Richard Price's seminal articulation of creolization in their short book – originally published in 1976 – *The Birth of African-American Culture* (Mintz and Price 1992; see also Price 2006).

and gendered forms of knowledge, robbing them of their real contributions to the Americas," and, in effect, robs them twice.

Many historians of the African legacy in America explicitly connect their studies to Africa, and, indeed, this is arguably the hallmark of recent Diaspora studies. By reminding us that African peoples and cultures were never static, and by historicizing change in Africa – whether via traders and Islam in West Africa, via the Portuguese and Catholicism in West Central Africa, or through internal dynamics and warfare – many historians emphasize that "creolization" started in Africa (Thornton 1998; Sweet 2003; Lovejoy 2005; Ferreira 2014; Candido 2015). Sweet argues that "the cultural flexibility and adaptability that have so often been associated with slave communities in the Americas were already institutionalized in various Central African social and cultural forms, forms that were also essential to cultural survival and transformation in the diaspora." He finds this to be especially evident in seventeenth-century Brazil where Central Africans made up 90 percent of the enslaved population (Sweet 2007, 244). Sweet (2011) also demonstrates that an understanding of African ontologies and epistemologies is necessary for scholars to interpret African and Afrodescendant beliefs and practices in the Americas, and to overcome a documentary record that systematically obscures African categories of knowledge. As I will discuss, one of the things Sweet's work shows is that etiological understandings of sickness and healing reveal a great deal about African peoples' understanding of nature and thus form a key point from which to parse out meanings associated with new Afro-Latin American cultural geographies.

The either-or approach to African continuities or American creolization is also misleading. Many scholars have shown that Africans would have been quite familiar with Atlantic ideas, crops, and goods long before leaving Africa. Thornton has shown that on the eve of the Columbian voyages, thousands of West Central Africans were already practicing a local form of Christianity (Thornton 1998, 2002, 2006). We know that "most Africans who entered slavery were already aware of some of the commodities that were circulating in the Atlantic world or were inspired by the Atlantic encounters before their capture" (Ogundiran and Falola 2007, 22). Studies by Robert Voeks (1997, 2012), Carney and Voeks (2003), and Carney and Rosomoff (2009) – building off the work of others – have shown that many American crops such as maize, capsicum peppers, manioc (cassava), peanuts, tobacco, papayas, and pineapples were cultivated in West Africa by the end of the seventeenth century. Moreover, colonizing or stowaway weeds – often providing the basis for

leaves and herbs used in many New World African-based religious ceremonies and healing practices – moved between Africa and America. For
Voeks (2012, 395), this two-way flow led to a transatlantic "botanical
homogenization" that familiarized Africans with many American plants
before they left home, greatly enhancing their abilities and those of their
descendants in the Americas to reassemble their ethnobotanical traditions
in what would otherwise have been an alien floristic environment. Indeed,
many New World plants in Suriname are known by their African names –
suggesting people recognized what they had already known in Africa (van
Andel et al. 2014; van Andel 2015).

Fundamental to any understanding of Afro-Latin American cultural
geographies is the origin and development of environmental knowledge.
There are at least two separate issues here and both are related to method.
The first issue concerns the need to include the landscape and the memory
of landscape as sources of information. To do this we need to step outside
written texts and archives and look for evidence within a variety of
disciplines, from biogeography and botany to linguistics and archaeology
(Carney and Rangan 2015). By knowing, for example, that the Saramaka
maroons of Suriname attribute the arrival of rice to their forest homes to a
woman named Paánza fleeing a plantation with grains woven into her
hair, and that, although the maroons plant and harvest multiple varieties
of rice today, only an African variety is milled by hand, offered to
ancestors, and even exported at a premium to descendants residing in
the Netherlands, tells us a great deal about the long-standing relationship
between this ancient rice variety, religious integration with food and
nature, and the broader cultural geographies of these Afrodescendant
people (Price 1983; Carney 2004, 2005; van Andel 2010).

In related fashion, for geographer Andrew Sluyter, reading the colonial
landscapes of the Americas with an understanding of who had knowledge
of open range cattle ranching, and who did not, shows that Africans and
their descendants are largely responsible for the herding ecologies found
throughout Latin America and the Caribbean. Landscape patterns and
material vestiges are all key to reconstructing the role of African peoples
in the creation of herding ecologies that emerged in the Americas, and that
it was Africans' prior knowledge and adaptive capacities that were most
important in this process, not their labor. For Sluyter, then, landscapes
contain a record of past human activities and agency, and can be reconstructed and interpreted in conjunction with documents, drawings,
and maps to reveal African and Afrodescendant agency in landscape
co-creation. The range of evidence marshaled to support the argument

sets this sort of cultural and historical geography apart from studies that focus exclusively on written documents (Sluyter 2009, 2012a, 2012b, 2015; see also Sluyter and Duvall 2016).

The second issue related to environmental knowledge and method concerns peeling back more recent and virulent forms of racism to see that Europeans themselves valued (and later feared) African and Afrodescendant environment knowledges, but that this changed at various points in the eighteenth century. Research investigating the cultures of natural history by Susan Scott Parrish (2008, 283), shows that whites "believed that Africans possessed zones of knowledge that they themselves did not" (see also Voeks 1997, 46). When Africans and Afrodescendants became majorities in Anglo-American colonies, for example, Afrodescendant knowledge of plants and the environment fueled colonial anxieties and contributed to more systemically racist policies. In pre-1720 North America, "when slave familiarity with marshes, swamps, rivers, woods was still regarded as a manageable asset, slaves were called on frequently to collect natural specimens for colonials, travelers, and metropolitan correspondents" (Parrish 2008, 289; see also Schiebinger 2004; Knight 2010; Offen 2011b; Voeks and Rashford 2012b). It was through this type of exploited knowledge that a vaccination for smallpox was learned from a slave. Parrish (2008, 305) concludes that, "The ambivalent Anglo attitude toward this knowledge – wherein slaves could be executed for the use of poisons but manumitted for the disclosure of antidotes – both reflected a self-interested set of rewards and punishments and indicated the Enlightenment's lingering belief that what was invisible or hidden in nature could be potentially manipulated for dangerous or curative ends by adepts closer to nature than themselves."

That African Americans contributed knowledge to Enlightenment science should not be doubted. The celebrated Afrodescendant, Graman Kwasi, an enslaved healer and botanist who acquired his freedom through his talents, traveled from Suriname to the Netherlands and corresponded with the father of modern taxonomy, the Swede Carl Linnaeus. The latter named a species of Bitter-wood (*Quassia amara*) in his honor because Kwasi shared with Linnaeus how a tea made from the plant could be used to treat intestinal parasites (Stedman, Price and Price 1992, 246, 300–03; Carney and Rosomoff 2009, 90). But Kwasi was just one well-known individual. When others have looked they have found similar evidence for Afro-Latin American empirical study of nature and sophisticated understanding of the environment, healing, and etiology (Maya Restrepo 2000; Garofalo 2006; Carney and Rosomoff 2009;

Knight 2010; Voeks and Rashford 2012a; Jouve Martin 2014). These findings suggest there are important and meaningful Afro-Latin American relationships with the natural world that contributed not only to Afro-Latin American experiences with nature in the hemisphere but also to broader intellectual currents in the Atlantic world.

An exploration of the cultural geographies of Afro-Latin America necessarily involves multiple ways of conceptualizing and understanding space from the point of view of Africans and their descendants. My colleagues and I have argued elsewhere that maps can help us do this, even if they remain an underutilized resource to examine Latin American history overall. Although Europeans and *criollos* – American-born people of European ancestry – drew most extant colonial-era maps, those documents can still be read to reveal the cultural geographies of Afro-Latin Americans (Offen 2003, 2007, 2011a; Dym and Offen 2011, 2012). A map of the *mocambo* Buraco do Tatu in Bahia, Brazil, from the mid-eighteenth-century, for example, illustrates limited agricultural activity, suggesting the community relied primarily on raids and trade (Schwartz 1970; 1992, 113; Reis 1996; Anderson 1996). In contrast, maps of the fugitive communities of Ambrósio and São Gonçalo in Minas Gerais reveal a distinctive cultural geography by illustrating a particular spatial relationship between land-use, defensive structures and inner residential zones (Reis and Gomes 1996; Carney and Rosomoff 2009, 84–87; Rarey 2014). In general, extant maps of maroon communities combine with written accounts detailing, for example, the central location of churches, to suggest that many maroon spaces in Latin America represent a hybridization of Iberian rectilinear and grid-like ordering, with circular and defensive layouts and techniques more common to Central and West Africa. Historical maps have also been used in the Caribbean to verify slave gardens and small farm and orchard plots (Pulsipher 1994, 205; Higman 2001).

Ethnographic maps drawn in the present can also reveal a great deal about Afro-Latin American cultural geographies in the past (Offen 2011a), just as oral histories have done for maroon studies (Price 1983, 1990, 2007; Bilby 2005). Ethnographic maps drawn under the auspices of collective land titling in Pacific Colombia over the last twenty years illustrate the cultural-ecological history of Afrodescendant *tronco* rights in the region. As first described by Nina de Friedmann in the 1980s, troncos represent kinship networks of Afrodescendants along a specific river and its tributaries who trace their ancestry to an initial settler (Friedmann 1998; Offen 2003, 2011a). Troncos also reflect the efforts

of fugitive and manumitted slaves to establish communities while maintaining social ties with mining communities along the Pacific slope before
and after the abolition of slavery in 1851 (Romero and Lane 2002; Offen
2003, 2011a). As I discuss again later, the ethnographic maps combine
notions of race with place to reveal historical cultural geographies in ways
that influenced collective land titling in Colombia today.

More common than the study of historical maps to elicit Afro-Latin
American spatial imaginations is the turn toward digital humanities to
spatialize the content of written sources. Many of these studies reinsert
the biophysical environment into an understanding of past human activities and help us think anew about how the world looked from the point
of view of historical subjects (Higman 2001; Frank and Berry 2010;
Hopkins, Morgan and Roberts 2011; Offen 2013b). Vincent Brown's
spatial history of the 1760–61 slave revolt in Jamaica is an excellent
example (Brown 2015; see also http://revolt.axismaps.com/). Brown's
work shows how plotting the movements of combatants in space reveals
pathways, routes, and strategic objectives of the rebels, and how different
groups traversed landscapes in distinct ways. This sort of work could be
broadened to show how human-environmental knowledge and relationships informed the spatial strategies that rebels and their supporters took
up in the first place.

## COSMOLOGY AND THE PERCEPTION OF NATURE

African ideas of nature must be a starting point to understand how
African and Afrodescendant peoples perceived and established meaningful relations with New World environments. And, just as with other
peoples of the fifteenth and sixteenth centuries, including Europeans,
African and Afro-Latin American ideas of Neotropical nature were
guided by religious beliefs and cosmologies. This means a conviction that
events on earth were intimately linked to the divine and, for Africans
specifically, a hierarchy of otherworldly deities, ancestors, territorial and
lesser spirits who shaped life on earth (see Chapter 12). In James Sweet's
words, many Africans in the fifteenth and sixteenth centuries viewed their
religions "as a way of explaining, predicting, and controlling events in the
world around them. African rituals and beliefs were designed to deal
directly with the fortunes and the dangers of the temporal realm – disease,
drought, hunger, sterility, and so on" (Sweet 2003, 108). Afro-Latin
American religions share a common purpose and practice, "the resolution
of earthly problems, the everyday dilemmas of the now, the health and

prosperity of the adherents, and of the African American community at large" (Voeks 1997, 4; see also Voeks 2012).

Afro-Latin American peoples sought to balance or manipulate their relationships with the supernatural world through divination and healing practices, all of which involved important relationships with the natural world. It was through these related activities that the principal Afro-Latin American religions of today emerged, specifically the various Yoruba- and Angolan-influenced Candomblé traditions in Brazil, the Yoruba and Catholic influenced Santería (or Regla Ocha) and the Angola-derived Reglas de Congo (Palo Monte) in Cuba, Vodou in Haiti, Obeah in Jamaica, and many other integrative and regional practices such as Winti in Suriname and María Lionza in Venezuela (Falola and Childs 2005; van Andel et al. 2012; Parés 2013; Chapter 12). It is not my purpose to survey the breadth or characteristics of these Afro-Latin American religions – most of which only became institutionalized in the nineteenth century – but rather to focus on understanding how African religious beliefs and cosmologies contributed to Afrodescendants' relations with Neotropical environments, well before the consolidation of the previously named and much better studied Afro-Latin American religions.

The challenges of understanding how African religions affected early African perceptions of New World nature are immense. Few scholars have tackled this question head on, even as they reconsider African "religions" in general or African agency within environmental history specifically. Ras Michael Brown (2012) has commented on this lacuna and finds existing scholarship on the relationship between religious beliefs and environmental perception incomplete because it fails "to recover older fundamental meanings attached to the relationship between people and the natural world within the African-Atlantic cultures." For Brown, the rich cultural background essential to understand religious beliefs is an indispensable starting point to explore this relationship, "an insight that only a small number of prescient scholars of early African America have developed to any appreciable degree" (Brown 2012, 24). His point is that only through consideration of key African religious concepts can early African and Afrodescendant ideas of American environments and spaces be fully formulated.

Colonial Afro-Latin American relations with and understandings of New World nature were constrained, but not determined, by slavery. Although African peoples were forcibly settled in alien environments devoid, initially, of ancestors, local shrines or hallowed places, preexisting cosmologies formed the basis to understand that which was new and unfamiliar. Displacement did not dislodge expectations about the natural world. Moreover, exile from African homes, kinship networks, and ancestors – a trauma that Sweet considers "unimaginable for most Westerners" (Sweet 2003, 32) – would have created a strong desire to culturally domesticate unfamiliar environments and spaces. As Brown (2012, 35) puts it, the agonizing experience of transatlantic captivity meant that Africans sought some solace by "aligning their understandings of the physical dimensions of their surroundings with the spiritual dimensions of their environment." Likewise, making a new home in America involved "the transformation of a strange new land into a place where people could belong and establish communities." It was through this process that "African-descended people took a landscape of enslavement ... and recreated it as a land of the living, where they nurtured their bonds with African nature spirits and each other" (Brown 2012, 89; see also Sweet 2011, 226). In this way, New World environments were not solely a place of captivity, but also an "African conceptual space that connected the visible, physical domain with the invisible, spiritual realm" (Brown 2012, 143). Not surprisingly, this was particularly the case in maroon communities, where many aspects of life involved ritual communication with nature spirits (Price 1983, 1990, 136, 345–46, 1991).

The cultural diversity of thought and practice in Africa was vast, yet the degree of this diversity "can easily be exaggerated" (Thornton 1998, 191; see also Hanserd 2015). Many Africans, for example, shared core understandings about how the world worked, about another world known only through revelation and divination (Thornton 1998, 236; Sweet 2003, 2004, 2011), about death and ancestral spirits (Brown 2010, 65), about the nature of corporal and social illness and healing (Sweet 2003, 157; Janzen 2015), and about a supernatural hierarchy from a higher god and lesser territorial spirits to ancestor and nature spirits (Thornton 2002, 75; Brown 2010, 65; Offen 2014, 29–30) – understandings that were often interconnected. Although different peoples held different notions about the characteristics of nature spirits specific to their homes, "they also held in common key ideas about the centrality of nature spirits to daily existence" (Brown 2012, 22). Divination, or the communication between the world of the living and of the spirits, was also a shared practice and included acts performed to invoke ancestral spirits and learn their intentions for those on earth (Sweet 2004, 139; see also Hanserd 2015).

Many African peoples held worldviews that were "flexible, integrative, and imminently responsive to the vagaries of historical change"

(Sweet 2011, 48). Afro-Latin American followers of one faith could also practice the teachings of other distinct faiths (Voeks 1997, 61). Catholicism, because of its focus on revelation, the spiritual world, miracles and rituals, figures prominently in this discussion (Andrews 2004, 70–74; Chapter 12). Thornton argues that the idea of revelation was easily understood by Africans and was central to the formation of African Christianity. This is also why, perhaps, many maroon leaders embraced certain dimensions of Catholicism, erected churches in their fortified settlements, and often hosted long-term visits by priests (Anderson 1996; Thornton 1998, 268–70; Lane 2002; Romero and Lane 2002; Landers 2005b, 2006, 2013, 153–55; Beatty-Medina 2006. 2009). While the Catholic Church considered revelations to be rare, for Central Africans revelation "was ordinary, continuous, and included a variety of local deities and ancestral spirits" (Sweet 2003, 110; see also Thornton 1998, 255–70).

Likewise, the work of Catholic priests casting out evil spirits is not that far removed from African "priests," specifically Angolan *calundeiros,* or *vodunons* among Gbe-speaking peoples. As Sweet argues, Catholic priests in Brazil needed to Africanize their doctrine to remain viable and salient, and Afrodescendant adherents understood this doctrine very much through their own cosmologies (Sweet 2011, 62). When Gbe-speaking West Africans – called Mina by the Portuguese – began replacing West Central Africans as the source of Portuguese slaves in Brazil by the beginning of the eighteenth century, they brought with them a strong belief in voduns, forces or powers, deities or spirits – what Europeans called fetishes. The deeply rooted nature of this belief was so significant that Sweet suggests that Brazilian Catholicism "was largely grafted onto the structures and meanings of vodun" (Sweet 2011, 60). In 1741, a Portuguese-Mina dictionary translated Christian concepts into the lexicon of Vodun, thus God was the "white man's vodun," and *padre* was translated as *Avóduno,* or *vodunon* (Sweet 2011, 58–59). The larger argument here is that Catholicism did not displace African cosmologies in colonial Brazil and this had significant implications for Afro-Latin American cultural geographies in that colony and, by extension, any place continually connected to Africa via the slave trade.

African-based religious beliefs often involved healing, and Afrodescendant peoples in America eagerly valued and appropriated useful medicinal knowledge, ethnobotanical information, and healing strategies from Native Americans and Europeans. This led to shared networks of information interpreted through a related set of filters (Voeks 1997; Maya Restrepo 2000; Moret 2012; Hanserd 2015; Gómez 2015). The historical record shows remarkable similarity among Afrodescendant medical practices in distant American places, such as cupping, cutting, sucking, and the use of ritual objects such as *bolsas de mandinga* – protective amulets of Islamic origin (Gómez 2015, 233; see also Sweet 2003, 179–85, 2009; Newson and Minchin 2007, 249). Such integrative practices and networks thrived particularly well in Catholic places where black majorities "provided spaces for the consumption of Afro-Atlantic healing procedures" that could not be sustained so easily in Anglo- and Dutch colonies, where blacks were more isolated (Gómez 2015, 233–34). These centripetal practices began early on during the slave trade and, as Sweet argues, "facilitated a process of 'Africanization' [in America, normalizing an] essential 'African' religious core that emerged from these shared beliefs" (Sweet 2003, 132).

Many Africans also "held some common assumptions about death" and relations between the living and the dead (Brown 2010, 65). Vincent Brown considers these relations through what he calls "mortuary politics," political acts associated with death, burial, and ancestral places that "mediated group cohesion, property relations, struggles to give public influence a sacred dimension, contests over the colonial moral order, and efforts to politicize local geography and history" (Brown 2010, 11). In this way, Afrodescendant plots or houses that contained the remains of ancestors came to hold particular importance and meaning for the living (Mintz 1974, 237, 246; Armstrong 1999, 179–81; Heath and Bennett 2000, 41; Singleton 2010, 714). As Brown explains, "Africans and their descendants valued [land] and sought to possess it, in order to manifest a preexisting respect for their ancestors" (Brown 2010, 120). Africans in Jamaica, for example, "revered ancestral lands partly because they were burial sites and places of social attachment and incorporation, where forebears afforded spiritual protection from evil and chaos" (Brown 2010, 121). Thus, the cultural geographies of Afro-Latin Americans often combined ancestors and the meanings associated with the landscapes that contained their legacies.

Europeans and *criollos* often considered Afro-Latin American practices associated with ancestor divination, communication with spirits, medical plant uses, and other activities associated with African religious beliefs to be a form of witchcraft (*brujería*) and sorcery (*hechicería* in Spanish and *feitiçaria* in Portuguese) (Parés and Sansi 2011). As Ana Díaz Burgos (2013, 250) points out, many contemporaneous European writers distinguished between witchcraft and sorcery. The latter used spells, incantations, and superstitious practices, whereas the former was much graver because it implied a pact with the devil and the use of psychic powers to cause physical injury, emotional impairment, or murder. Of course, the distinctions among witchcraft, sorcery, magic, superstition, spells, pagan prayers, incantations, hexes, and religious activities reflect European cosmologies more than those of Africans or Afro-Latin Americans. It follows that much of our knowledge of these practices within colonial Latin America come from Europeans, and specifically from the voluminous records of the Inquisition, inquisitorial courts that operated in select places in Spanish America to combat heresy and to maintain Catholic orthodoxy.[3] Where members of the inquisition courts saw *brujería*, Maya Restrepo (2005, 501) sees "a particular form of resistance to slavery: *el cimarronaje simbólico*" (symbolic flight). For his part, Sweet sees African healing practices as a form of "revelatory politics," an African-commentary on social and political ills of colonial America that challenged colonial, racist, and violent systems of inequality (Sweet 2011, 121–22).

Two recent monographs convey the significance of these topics for colonial Afro-Latin American studies in general and colonial cultural geographies of Afro-Latin America in particular. The first is James Sweet's *Domingos Álvares, African Healing, and the Intellectual History of the Atlantic World* (Sweet 2011) and the second is Ras Michael Brown's *African-Atlantic Cultures and the South Carolina Lowcountry* (Brown 2012). Although situated outside Latin America, Brown's work details the role of the *simbi*, a type of nature spirit that originated in Kongo (*basimbi* or *bisimbi*) and took on related meanings across the African Diaspora. Brown (2012, 5) situates his study within a "Bantu-Atlantic spiritual landscape rooted in West-Central Africa with branches that extended throughout the diaspora," including Brazil, Cuba, Dutch Guiana, and Saint-Domingue. Although simbi manifest themselves differently in each place, "the simbi as a kind of spirit existed everywhere" West Central Africans went.

In the South Carolina Lowcountry the simbi occupied features of the environment, particularly pools or springs, waterfalls, rivers, rocks, stones, forests, and mountains and this is where people encountered

---

[3] The Spaniards established inquisitorial courts first in Lima and Mexico City in 1571 and, then, in Cartagena in 1610. Portugal established the Holy Office in 1536 and tried its American subjects in Lisbon. Studies of the Inquisition in Iberia and Latin America are numerous, but a sample of those that deal with Africans and Afro-Latin Americans include McKnight 2003; Bristol 2007; Guengerich 2009; Sweet 2011; Santos 2012.

them intentionally or by accident. As with shrine-based spirits of West Central Africa, the simbi also affected the weather and condition of the flora and fauna, thus controlling to a certain extent the natural environment (Brown 2012, 29). Although West Central Africans represented a minority of the early captives in the South Carolina colony, their conceptual landscapes took root and influenced others. Brown's study is not a case of crude cultural survival but one of creative transformation, in part because in West Central Africa the simbi was tied to ancestors and beings who once lived: but American landscapes initially had no ancestors (Brown 2012, 101–05). Through an exploration of how a greater Niger-Congo cosmology took root in the South Carolina Lowcountry, Brown shows that simbi served as "guardians of the landscape" into the nineteenth century through the "conscious and repeated choices by African-descended people" to retain particular ways of conceptualizing plants, animals, and subsistence activities (Brown 2012, 145). By so doing, Afrodescendant peoples created evocative and consequential cultural geographies that significantly textured their lives and experiences.

Through an exploration of the life and times of Domingos Álvares, Sweet (2011) takes his readers on a journey that follows Álvares from his home in Naogon, Dahomey, where both his parents were likely Vodun priests, to his wartime capture, along his Middle Passage, to his enslavement in 1733 on a sugar plantation in Recife, Pernambuco, Brazil, where he developed a reputation as a *feiticeiro*. The story then moves to Rio de Janeiro where Álvares joins a slave population that was almost 75 percent African-born and becomes a respected healer (Sweet 2011, 77–82). In his new role, Álvares buys his freedom in 1739 and sets up a "ritual space," or *terreiro*, in the rural suburbs of southern Rio de Janeiro near the new parish church Nossa Senhora da Glória. There, he built new webs of kinship through the reconstitution of a spiritual community. He is eventually arrested and tried by inquisitorial courts in Lisbon and exiled to rural Portugal where he continued to practice. Throughout his study, Sweet shows how Álvares tapped into a shared religious system centered on Vodun that equated healing and revelation with political power, resistance, and community-building. Álvares's cosmology remained closely tied to a belief in voduns, but he also adopted rituals and therapeutic methods from Central Africa, Native Americans, and Portuguese Catholicism in ways that resonated with his fellow colonial residents. Álvares's knowledge and practice were dynamic and responsive to change, but were grounded in a West African intellectual history that survived the Middle Passage, adapted to New World conditions, and filled needs waiting to be met.

The history of the life of Domingos Álvares can also be read as an Afro-Latin American cultural geography. From his home in Dahomey where the power of voduns had a lineage that was place-specific (Sweet 2011, 17), to his methods for gathering medicinal plants in New World forests and his application of them in ceremonies that sought to resolve the myriad social ills of plantation slavery (Sweet 2011, 66–71), to his movements and celebrated practices among a like-minded spiritual community throughout Rio's urban spaces (Sweet 2011, 82–85), to his creation of a terreiro, or temple, in suburban Rio – throughout it all Álvares inscribed the core of his cosmological beliefs upon a new environment, contributing to the creation of an Afro-Latin American cultural landscape in colonial Brazil. But it is Sweet's description of the terreiro that is most evocative of a cultural geography that must have been replicated hundreds if not thousands of times across Afro-Latin America with little notice. Sweet illustrates how Álvares's selection of a property near the foot of Igreja de Nossa Senhora da Glória do Outeiro, a spectacular baroque church that sat atop a hill above the sea, was very deliberate. "The spiritual significance of the environment was not lost on Rio's African population. For Domingos, this majestic setting very likely represented the confluence of earth, sea, and sky voduns" (Sweet 2011, 109). The site represented "a potent passageway to the world of the sea and sky voduns, as well as a temporal symbol of the human life cycle. All that was required to tap this power and "render account" was the consecration of the space to the earth voduns" (Sweet 2011, 110). Again, this exact practice must have been commonplace throughout Afro-Latin America, yet went unnoticed by Europeans and criollos as a meaningful act. Sweet notes that even today the church remains spiritually important to Rio's Afrodescendant population, that the Candomblé goddess of the sea, Yemanjá, is directly associated with the saint, Nossa Senhora da Glória, and that both deities are celebrated yearly on August 15th (Sweet 2011, 257).

At his terreiro, Álvares established an altar under a large orange tree where he healed and made offerings to voduns every Saturday. "The construction of the altar would have been unthinkable without previous knowledge, extensive training, and a bloodline tied to the priesthood of the vodun." The choice of a tree was important as a site for the altar because with deep roots in the soil occupied by the earth vodun and other ancestors, from which the altar's power emanates, the tree is a powerful representation of the spirit world (Sweet 2011, 110; on the importance of trees in African and Afrodescendant religious practices, and especially trees of the genus *Ceiba* see also Rashford 1985; Thompson 1993, 114–26; Voeks and Rashford 2012a; Niell 2015; Hanserd 2015). Here Álvares worked with a group of initiates and treated visitors with medicinal plants and their ritual application. What separated Álvares's terreiro from other African healing sites around Rio, according to Sweet, was that it was a sustainable, collective endeavor, "a space where refugees and strangers could reconstitute kinship ties under the banner of public healing" (Sweet 2011, 140). In his testimony at the inquisition, Álvares said he made infusions from plants, and attributed their ability to cure to their "natural" power, not by his own virtue. If his treatment failed it meant he did not appease the vodun properly (Sweet 2011, 171). Even after two decades removed from Dahomey, Álvares continued to order his ideas about nature, healing, and religion within what Western science considered to be "the supernatural." Sweet's careful reconstruction shows that the spatialities of many Africans and Afrodescendants reflected a form of geomancy tied to beliefs in the innate powers of certain landscapes and natures, vividly illustrating the importance of cultural geography in the lives of many Afro-Latin Americans.

## SPACE AND PLACE

Space and place are key concepts in cultural geography. They share common assumptions about the importance of "the spatial" in people's lives but the two notions are distinct. Place brings together a cultural appraisal of the environment with lived experiences in a specific location in ways that anchor and shape social relationships, as was illustrated with the terreiro established by Domingos Álvares. As a concept, place combines biophysical nature, social relations, and the cultural meanings their interactions generate. Space is more abstract, less experiential. It reflects the relative location of things, as well as the social (economic and political) networks that connect them. For Yi-Fu Tuan (1977) space is formless and profane, whereas place is meaningful and sacred. In this section, I use these concepts to organize the experiences of Afrodescendants working with the environment, not primarily as slaves for masters, but for themselves, for their own subsistence, economic gain, and personal solace. This is not to say that all peoples had these opportunities, but many did. This section starts off, then, by looking at the biogeographical setting of the tropics, the transfer of important cultigens, African and Amerindian exchanges, and slave gardens – places that relied on a direct, emotional, and visceral interaction with the environment but also the spiritual dimension just described.

European and American slave traders brought the vast majority of enslaved Africans to the American or Neotropics and subtropics. Most of this region is distinguished from lands at higher latitudes by a relative lack of seasonal variation in the length of the day over the course of the year, a more limited range of climatic conditions (rainfall and temperature), weathering processes and leaching associated with soil formation, the resultant patterns of vegetation in general, and the relatively high plant and animal biodiversity in particular. Unlike European and most Euro-American enslavers, the overwhelming majority of Africans arriving in the New World also came from similar tropical spaces, essentially sub-Saharan Africa south through the Kongo. The two tropical regions were not biogeographically the same, of course, but Africans were encountering New World environments – tidal estuaries, mangrove and palm forests, swamps, moist and dry savannas, and tropical dry and moist forests – that were relatively familiar. Although Latin America and Africa share only a few hundred plant species, nineteen genera from fifteen botanical families occur in both regions, and they share almost 70 percent of their total plant families (Carney and Rosomoff 2009, 89; van Andel et al. 2014, E5350). This means that many plants were taxonomically related and that they may have shared appearances, biogeographical associations, and properties that African peoples came to understand and make use of (Moret 2012, 221).

Whatever the floristic divide was initially between the tropics of Africa and America, Voeks (2012, 396–97) argues that "the anthropogenic landscapes of tropical America were [already] floristically similar to their sub-Saharan counterparts by the time the largest contingent of slaves" came to America (1780–1830s). The two-way transfer of plants – both purposeful and accidental as stowaways – produced a "wholesale reorganization and dramatic enrichment of the humanized landscapes of the tropical latitudes" (Voeks 2012, 407). As mentioned previously, this view is supported by the recent analysis of some 2,350 Afro-Surinamese plant names by van Andel et al. (2014; see also van Andel 2015; van Andel, van der Velden, and Reijers 2016). Their works demonstrate that enslaved Africans named and, hence, recognized substantial parts of the New World flora based on their knowledge of plants and their properties in Africa. The other argument embedded in this research, however, is that African peoples drew upon, and passed along to their descendants, adaptive capacities and environmental knowledge that allowed them to culturally respond to alien spaces, soil types, plant properties, and animal behaviors – in short, to adapt to New World environments (Knight 2010, 64; Carney and Rosomoff 2009). Given that Africans were brought from one "tropical or subtropical landscape to another and were obviously well versed in the exigencies of tropical cultivation and floristic foraging," Voeks and Rashford find it "paradoxical that they should have been considered such ineffective transporters of agricultural and ethnobotanical skills as compared to Europeans" (2012b, 4). This revisionist scholarship gives us a better biogeographical basis to understand how Afrodescendants established corporeal and emotive relations with Neotropical environments – even in the absence of extensive written documentation.

The underappreciated tenacity with which African cultigens crossed the Atlantic and found their way into American farming systems, and especially "the botanical gardens of the dispossessed," has been the focus of research by Judith Carney over the last three decades (see also van Andel, van der Velden, and Reijers 2016). Carney's work suggests that virtually every slave ship coming to the Americas carried African plants for food, flavorings, bedding, medicines, and fuels. In this way, "slave ships became the unwitting vessels of Africa's botanical heritage by carrying seeds, tubers, and the people who valued them to the Americas" (Carney and Rosomoff 2009, 66; Carney 2012). This dimension of the Columbian Exchange occurred relatively rapidly throughout the circum-Caribbean and northeastern Brazil (Price 1991; Voeks 1997, 22; Carney and Rosomoff 2009, 91–96).

Although some introductions might have been instigated by Europeans and Euro-Americans, Carney and Rosomoff argue that African knowledge informed their ideas about tropical plants. Carney and Rosomoff's work summarizes what is known about how African cultigens such as sorghum, millet, yams, watermelon, okra, African rice (*Oryza glaberrima*), black-eyed and pigeon peas, and other useful plants such as the castor oil bean, African oil palm, and melegueta pepper, found early homes in Neotropical gardens of Afrodescendants (see also van Andel, van der Velden, and Reijers 2016). They do the same for tropical crops originally domesticated in South, East, or Southeast Asia thousands of years ago but that generally reached the Americas first by way of Africa and with African knowledge – including sesame, plantains and bananas (*Musa spp.*), Asian rice (*Oryza sativa*), eggplant, tamarind, taro (*Colocasia esculenta*), and Asian yams (*Dioscorea spp.*) (Carney and Rosomoff

2009; see also Newson and Minchin 2007). As Carney and Rosomoff put it, plantation owners often first encountered African crops in the fields of their slaves, where "a shadow world of cultivation ... evolved in the struggle of the first generations of enslaved Africans to ensure food availability" (Carney and Rosomoff 2009, 125).

The establishment of Afrodescendant tropical agroecosystems was not a simple transfer from one place to another, nor was it done in isolation from other peoples. Some of the first Africans in America learned about New World environments and crops from Amerindians. Many Africans crossing the Atlantic as slaves before 1680 worked in close contact with Amerindians in gold mining (West 1952; Sharp 1976; Newson 1982; Friedmann 1993, 1998; Lane 2002, 2005), cattle ranching (Guitar 2006, 47; Brockington 2008; Sluyter 2012a, 2015), agriculture (Schwartz 1985; Guitar 2006; Lokken 2008; Brockington 2008; Hawthorne 2010; Knight 2010; Wheat 2016), and in other ways, including as adversaries (Schwartz and Langfur 2005; Restall 2009; Zabala 2010). It should also be remembered that about half of all Africans brought to the Americas before 1640 went to what is today Mexico and Central America, where indigenous populations remained large (Carroll 2001; Cáceres 2001; Restall 2005, 2009). Meanwhile, many of the earliest fugitive slave settlements across the Americas comprised both Africans and Amerindians – not always by mutual consent (Hulme and Whitehead 1992; Price 1996; Landers 1999, 2000, 2005a, 2006; Lane 2002; Weik 2004; Lokken 2004, 2008, 2010; Guitar 2006; Beatty Medina 2006; Sweet 2007; Funari 2007; Offen 2011b, 2015; Thornton 2017). Early contact would have affected later forms of adaptation, even across parts of the Caribbean such as Cuba and Hispaniola where indigenous peoples no longer resided (Corzo 2003; Andrews 2004, 74; Weik 2004; Singleton 2010). The "cumulative significance of this fusion of African and Amerindian knowledge systems [can be seen] in the longstanding homeopathic medicinal tradition of the circum-Caribbean region" (Carney and Rosomoff 2009, 89). The circumstances and locations of African and Amerindian interactions were as diverse as they were ubiquitous, but as Africans replaced Amerindians in the Caribbean they became, according to Carney (2010, 108), "custodians of [Amerindian] botanical knowledge systems, including [their] subsistence achievements."

As we saw in the previous section, many African peoples set about creating and domesticating American places by populating them with familiar spirits. Part and parcel of creating meaningful cultural landscapes was subsistence, the raising of and preparing one's own foods. Among maroons, for example, Price finds that subsistence activities were "deeply infused with social and cultural meaning," especially for women (Price 1991, 123), and there is no reason to think this was not the case for all Afrodescendants. For Carney, "subsistence reveals the centrality of the African Atlantic as a historical geographical unit of identity, memory, and resistance" (2010, 108). Subsistence implies a measure of autonomy and provides the opportunity to pass along foods and dishes steeped in other places and other times. The importance of food among all diaspora peoples is well-known, as migrants always bring their dietary preferences and cooking practices with them:

These traditions are rarely forsaken, even when food preferences cannot be reconstituted in full. Food gives material expression to the ways exiles commemorate the past and shape new identities amid alien cultures, diets, and languages. Food is vested with symbolic ties to the homelands left or lost. The emphasis on meaningful foods and familiar forms of preparation enriches the memory dishes with which migrants connect past and present.

(Carney and Rosomoff 2009, 185)

Slave preference for their own foods, and the provision grounds to raise them on, merged with slave owners' self-interest by limiting their own responsibilities for feeding slaves and by tempering resentment. As planters in Rio de Janeiro province put it, "Slaves who have [provision grounds] neither flee nor make trouble"; the garden plots "distract them a bit from slavery and delude them into believing that they have a small right to property" (Andrews 2004, 26). For slaves, "the advantages of a more secure and plentiful food supply, cash from the sale of surpluses, and periods of unsupervised activity were apparent" (Marshall 1993, 205).

Conventional wisdom posits that enslaved Africans first seized the right to grow their own crops in northeastern Brazil. This is based on the understanding that when the Dutch fled northeastern Brazil in 1654 they brought the tradition of slave-self-provisioning to the Guianas and the Caribbean where the practice was called the Pernambuco system (Barickman 1994, 657; Thornton 1998, 174; Carney and Rosomoff 2009, 108, 127). At the turn of the eighteenth century, however, the Portuguese were still debating whether planters had to offer slaves a day off to cultivate their own gardens (Schwartz 1985, 137; Conrad 1994, 58; Sweet 2011, 46–47). Recent research by Wheat (2016) suggests that African peoples – both free and enslaved – throughout the circum-Caribbean circa 1570 and 1640 farmed and marketed the majority of food crops there, suggesting that the diffusion of the so-called Pernambuco system only applies to non-Spanish colonies of the Caribbean, but even this caveat does not address early African subsistence farming in Anglo colonies such as that on Providence Island (e.g., Offen 2011b). Other areas of Iberia America, particularly in lucrative mining areas such as in Venezuela or Minas Gerais, often ignored these provisioning conventions (Berlin and Morgan 1993, 26; Thornton 1998, 168; Carney and Rosom-off 2009, 82). In contrast, more remote mining areas, such the Chocó in Pacific Colombia, often needed slaves to grow their own food (Sharpe 1976, 133–35), but the evidence that they allowed for this is contradict-ory (Jiménez Meneses 1998, 223–26). Many Caribbean locales such as Jamaica, French Guiana, and the Windward Islands became "home fed" colonies whereas slave societies in the British colonies of Barbados and North America relied on provisions produced elsewhere (Marshall 1993, 204; Barickman 1994, 658). In contrast, many rural Afrodescendants throughout Spanish America farmed non-export food crops, and some had access to their own garden plots. This was especially common on Jesuit estates – and the Jesuits were the largest slaveholders in Latin America before their removal in the 1760s. But this was also true on *estancias* or ranches, cacao plantations, suburban farms, and on the frontier (Barickman 1994; Díaz 2000; Cáceres 2000, 2001; Soulodre-La France 2006; Brockington 2008; Carney and Rosomoff 2009; Lohse 2014; Wheat 2016). Personal gardens helped generate a sense of belonging, an attachment to place, improved diets and, and the customary right to bequeath and inherit personal property.

Much of our knowledge of slave gardens comes from the Caribbean, where scholars have identified three main garden types: common grounds, distant ravine or mountain grounds, and houseyard gardens (Mintz 1974; Marshall 1993; Pulsipher 1994; Heath and Bennett 2000; Carney and Rosomoff 2009).[4] Common grounds were flat lands set aside by planta-tion owners to increase the supply of caloric foods such as yams, sweet potatoes, plantains, and manioc. In many cases these grounds were not controlled by Afrodescendants and so it is the other two types that are more important to discuss here. Planters apparently cared little about the location of distant provision grounds unless their surplus production and sales competed with crops raised by former white smallholders

---

[4] My hope is that one day this field and archaeological-based research will combine better with archival materials used by Wheat (2016, 180–215) to show the profound significance of food production by free and enslaved Afrodescendants throughout the circum-Caribbean by the mid-sixteenth century.

(Marshall 1993, 207; Pulsipher 1994, 207).[5] But, for slaves these places "formed a nodal point within the social relations of slavery that allowed slave practices, values, and interests to emerge and develop and to assume autonomous forms of organization and expression" (Tomich 1993, 234). Pulsipher found ravine plots on Monserrat to represent a completely different concept of agriculture from that practiced in common grounds. Ravine plots illustrated "complex systems of environmental management that took into consideration angle of slope ... moisture availability, cycles of soil fertility, wind patterns, propitious lunar phases for planting, tending and harvesting, and the specific ecological requirements of dozens of species grown" (Pulsipher 1994, 210). Perhaps imparting the sentiments of her field collaborators, Pulsipher claimed slave cultivation "on high remote slopes early in the morning calls up feelings of freedom and independence, of affinity with nature, of solidarity of black people in landscapes where whites rarely tread. The cultivators feel close to ancestors who worked the same spots and their labors give them the sense of prosperity that abundant food symbolizes" (Pulsipher 1994, 217).

The houseyard gardens of Afrodescendants contain a myriad of cultural geographies in miniature. Heath and Bennett (2000, 38) define a houseyard "as the area of land, bounded and usually enclosed, which immediately surrounds a domestic structure and is considered an extension of that dwelling." The houseyard has "particular personal or group uses, including, but not limited to, food production and preparation, care and maintenance of animals, domestic chores, storage, recreation, and aesthetic enjoyment. It is at once a part of the domestic compound and a mediating space between the natural, public world and the constructed, private world of the dwelling." And, just as today, "shaping one's yard is an action laden with meaning" (Heath and Bennett 2000, 38; see also Mintz 1974, 247). We know that the houseyard gardens of Afrodescendants contained ground and tree crops; vegetables and greens; plants sown for medicinals, teas, flavorings, coloring, cosmetics, soaps, shampoos, fibers, and containers; and plants grown for household tasks such as making rope, sweeping, scrubbing pots, carrying things with head pads, and wrapping foods. Shade trees such as coconuts, bananas, and

---

[5] It may seem paradoxical that planters would concern themselves with the welfare of their former indentured servants upon completion of their contracts, but we know planters across the Caribbean shared deep-rooted anxieties about black majorities and, thus, often did address financial concerns of white smallholders and craft workers.

plantains were particularly popular (Pulsipher 1994, 214; Heath and Bennett 2000, 40; Carney and Rosomoff 2009).[6] Archaeologists have shown that houseyards preserve "evidence of communal activities and of time spent gardening, performing chores, and building and maintaining friendships" (Heath and Bennett 2000, 51; see also Armstrong 1999, 179; Chan 2007, 28).

Colonial residents and travelers frequently commented on the house-yard gardens of the slave quarters and how they provided their owners with a sense of pride. Writing about Jamaica in the second half of the eighteen century, longtime resident Bryan Edwards reported that "the cottages of the Negroes usually compose a small village.... They seldom placed much regard to order, but being always intermingled with fruit-trees, particularly the banana, the avocado pear and the orange (the Negroes own planting and property) they sometimes exhibit a pleasing and picturesque appearance" (Heath and Bennett 2000, 40; see also Pulsipher 1994, 214; Brown 2010, 115–21). Writing about houseyards encountered in the Caribbean of the 1950s, Mintz likely conjures up the way these *places* constituted communal life in the past: "decisions are made, food is prepared and eaten, the household group – whatever its composition – sleeps and socializes, children are conceived and born, death is ceremonialized ... Together, house and yard form a nucleus within which the culture expresses itself, is perpetuated, changed and reintegrated" (Mintz 1974, 231–32).

The gardens of free and enslaved Afrodescendants also produced surpluses that helped provision colonial society, increased Afrodescendant economic opportunities, and generated increased autonomy. Women have rightly received special attention in this regard (Berlin and Morgan 1993; Gaspar and Hine 1996, 2004; Carney and Rosomoff 2009; Wheat 2016). In Saint-Domingue "free women of color who owned small pieces of rural property earned their livelihoods by cultivating garden plots ... Proprietors produced enough fruits and vegetables to feed themselves and to supply the markets of the city" (Socolow 1996, 282). Throughout the Recôncavo – the fertile sugar cane lands around the Bay of All Saints in the Captaincy of Bahia – slave provision grounds called *roças* contributed significantly to slave diets and helped feed urban populations in Salvador and elsewhere (Barickman 1994, 1998; Graham 2010). As we saw previously, free Afrodescendants and quilombolas also

---

[6] The many varieties of bananas and plantains (*Musa spp.*) are the world's largest herbs, and not trees at all.

raised abundant crops in this area, especially in the far southern Recôn-cavo. Richard Graham suggests that free people of African descent had few economic opportunities other than agriculture, and many thrived by growing cassava or manioc on poorer soils and marketing the flour (*farinha*) (Carney and Rosomoff 2009, 128; Graham 2010, 86; see also Schwartz 1985). Case Watkins (2015) examines this story at length. He shows how the diffusion and cultural significance of the African oil palm, the extraction of resources in coastal mangrove forests by Afrodescendant peoples, and their use of fire in manioc cultivation, all combined to create favorable conditions for the spread of African oil palms or *dendé* – from the Kimbundu word *ndende* – and, thus, how Afrodescendants' choices, preferences, and subsistence and marketing practices quite literally, created the distinctive Dendé landscape running south of Jaguaripe toward Ilhéus along the Brazilian coast (Watkins 2015, 32–34).

Afrodescendant women throughout Latin America and the Caribbean also prepared and sold foods – what Carney and Rosomoff (2009, 177) call "memory dishes of the African Diaspora." Work by Alejandro de la Fuente suggests such activities began very early in colonial society when slave owners allowed their slaves to find their own work in exchange for a portion of their earnings; these individuals were called *ganadoras*. As early as 1528 the Audiencia complained that many slaves were working under this practice in Santo Domingo (de la Fuente 2008, 159). Writing about Havana at the turn of the seventeenth century, de la Fuente finds "slaves and free (or freed) blacks nearly monopolized street sales of foods, an activity that allowed them to gain a knowledge of the urban space, build potentially valuable social networks, and establish control over some portion of their labor." Women were particularly active in this role. A petition to the town council in 1601 claimed that more than 300 women made a living as ganadoras (de la Fuente 2008, 154). For the most part, free and enslaved Afrodescendants outside Havana cultivated what the ganadoras sold (Wheat 2016, 191–97). This Afro-Latin American urban practice of preparing and selling food was common throughout the circum-Caribbean and Brazil (Reis 2005; Wheat 2016, 142–80).

Though beyond the scope of this chapter, there were many different types of Afro-Latin American urban and colonial organizations related to cultural geographies that merit more attention, such as *cantos* (work groups), *cabildos de nación* (councils organized by "nation" or ethnicity), Catholic brotherhoods, *calundu* temples, black barrios, and convents. Recent scholarship has suggested that these cultural geographies were created by both free and enslaved Africans and Afrodescendants before

1820 in cities like Havana, Cap Français, Santo Domingo, Cartagena, Vera Cruz, Lima, and throughout Brazilian cities (e.g., Reis 1993, 2005; Gaspar and Hine 1996; Vidal Ortega 2002; Andrews 2004; van Deusen 2004; Schwartz 2006; Childs 2006; Von Germeten 2006; de la Fuente 2008; Zabala 2010; Cañizares-Esguerra, Childs, and Sidbury 2013; Díaz Burgos 2013; Soulodre-La France 2015; Wheat 2016; Symanski 2016).

## CONTEMPORARY IMPLICATIONS OF AFRO-LATIN AMERICAN CULTURAL GEOGRAPHIES

Since the late 1980s, seventeen Latin American countries have enacted constitutional reforms to redefine themselves as multiethnic and pluricultural. This has opened political spaces in which many Afro-Latin Americans have advanced agendas seeking collective cultural rights, specifically to land. One of the issues involved when pursuing collective cultural rights in Latin America is the ongoing distinction made between "race" and "ethnicity" (Wade 1997; Hooker 2005; Mollett 2013; Farfán-Santos 2016; Goett 2017). To simplify, today in many parts of Latin America, Afrodescendants are considered "outsiders" associated with a black racial phenotype while Amerindians are considered "insiders" associated with an original ethnic authenticity. This is, of course, ironic because in the colonial period Spaniards and Portuguese considered Africans to be *"gente de razón,"* or "rational people," and therefore closer to themselves. In contrast, Spaniards classified Amerindians separately, often allowing them to govern themselves at the village level within a *República de Indios*, a Republic of Indians – a political concept not related to the current meaning of republic. Afrodescendants – with few exceptions (see Landers 2006) – lived as members of the *República de Españoles*. Thus, the insider-outsider duality of today is the reverse of what it was in the colonial period and this affects the strategies, discourses, and legal apparatus within which contemporary Afro-Latin Americans pursue collective rights to land, just as many Amerindians rely on their former and distinct political status to claim ancestral rights to their traditional lands and territories.

The important language of the new constitutions and international conventions further reifies perceived distinctions between race and ethnicity that divides Afrodescendants and Amerindians and encourages a politics steeped in past cultural geographies, some of which are imagined and at odds with the narrative provided here. To make inroads within this differential classification scheme many Afrodescendant groups seeking collective land rights have hewed close to an idealization of maroon isolation and independence. Because national mythologies and many elites have upheld maroons as symbols of resistance to colonial rule, certain kinds of maroon communities have received a sort of privileged status within the African-Amerindian conceptual divide. In some cases, these Afrodescendant communities have received collective cultural rights to land in ways that other Afrodescendants have not. Part of this relates to their perceived spatial and cultural proximity to Amerindian peoples, their history of self-governance, and their embrace of an environmentalist identity. This latter positionality adds an important international dimension of support to territorial struggles of Afro-Latin Americans in many Neotropical countries. By residing in and claiming title to ostensibly "natural" areas, many maroon and rural Afrodescendants fit into the mythology of defiant rebels living in harmony with nature. Such conceptual constructs have greatly influenced which Afrodescendants have had their collective land rights recognized and upheld by the state and which groups of Afrodescendants have not.

In Brazil, for example, transitory Article 68 of the 1988 constitution granted property rights to the descendants of quilombo communities who are still occupying their lands. As Elizabeth Farfán-Santos (2016) describes, subsequent laws set out to define "quilombo descendant" and, now, nearly 2,000 quilombo descendant communities have been recognized, though less than ten percent have received their collective land titles (Futemana, Munari, and Adams 2015). The arduous and costly legal tasks of proving quilombola descent and confronting continual occupation, and of fighting resistance from wealthy landowners have limited the success of an otherwise progressive policy, and has also ensured that most Afrodescendants in Brazil remain unaffected.

In her study examining the process of proving quilombo descent among of the quilombolas of Grande Paraguaçu in Bahia, Farfán-Santos (2016, 7) finds that the "quilombolas want the state and society to see quilombola rights as exactly what they are, reparations for hundreds of years of exclusion from the right of black Brazilians to own land as well as a recovered cultural ancestry and past – a legitimate claim to space and a cultural and racial identity." That this has not happened suggests that progressive laws benefiting Afro-Latin American land rights that affect a majority of citizens can be passed and implemented only to the extent that they do not challenge the status quo system of white privilege and power. In this dominant ideology, the recognition of Afro-Latin American rights and land devolutions are allowed when they are imagined to occur "out there," in distant forests that do not challenge the status quo. This geohistorical imagination, as this chapter has shown, relies on a distorted interpretation of how African and Afrodescendant peoples – even maroon peoples – created and recreated their own cultural geographies as active members of colonial society across the hemisphere.

The limited scope of recent legal changes applies to other Latin American countries with important histories involving Afrodescendant peoples. In Colombia, for example, only Afrodescendants residing in the Pacific watershed initially received collective land rights under the celebrated Law 70 of 1993 (following the constitutional reform of 1991), yet the majority of Afro-Colombians live outside this region. The complexity of this development, and specifically the creation of Law 70, circumvented the race/ethnicity divide by implicitly intellectualizing the Afrodescendants of Pacific Colombia as "natives of the place" (Offen 2003, 57), in effect viewing them as "Indian-like." Many environmental activists and scholars in the lead up to Law 70 supported this position by upholding the tronco form of riverine settlement described earlier in this chapter as an ideal ecological adaptation. This historical development – which is one appropriate adaptation to a challenging environment – helped justify the right to collective tronco territories claimed by Afro-Colombians in the Pacific watershed because doing so would contribute to environmental conservation in one of the most biodiverse regions on the planet (Offen 2003, 2011a). Indeed, following the 1989 approval of the International Labor Organization's Convention on Indigenous and Tribal Peoples (ILO 169), many Afrodescendants living in rural and biodiverse parts of Latin America explicitly sought to emulate indigenous discourses of nature stewardship, cultural difference, and ethnic authenticity to advance their own territorial rights. On the one hand, this was politically astute and in some cases genuinely validated sustainable environmental practices, but on the other hand it established a difficult legacy to uphold for Afro-Colombians who live outside the Pacific watershed.

In Nicaragua, neither the Miskitu nor the Afrodescendant Creoles are considered by themselves or others to be maroons and instead are considered by many to be outsiders who have historically aided foreign interests in the eastern half of the country. Thus, to blunt a complex national mythology that I cannot do justice to here, the Miskitu work hard to distinguish themselves from the Afrodescendant Creoles of the region despite many historical commonalities. In effect, the Miskitu consider themselves to be simply "Indian," an English loan word used in the Miskitu language for Amerindians, despite a long history of mixing with different peoples. Likewise, to help establish their own legitimacy in the eyes of the state – who often views them as recent arrivals from the West Indies – many Creoles take pains to point out their own indigenous ancestors. In both cases, the important cultural geographies created by Afrodescendants – whether Miskitu or Creole – in Nicaragua are downplayed, undervalued, or obscured by national myths of mestizaje, a legacy of foreign intervention, and state efforts promoting territorial integration (Gordon 1998; Offen 2004; Hooker 2005; Gudmundson and Wolfe 2010; Chapter 4). In short, unlike the neighboring Garifuna of Honduras, who in Mark Anderson's words consider themselves proudly to be both "black and indigenous" (Anderson 2009; see also Mollet 2013), the Miskitu generally reject their African ancestry for multifaceted historical reasons that are augmented by more recent forms of racism. Hopefully the research outlined here has the potential to contribute to a more inclusive and integrative picture of Afrodescendants in Latin America, particularly with respect to land, and to shrink the insider/outsider divide that pits Afro-Latin Americans against Amerindians to the benefit of dominant society.

Future work connecting the cultural geographies of colonial Afro-Latin America discussed here with those of the present would need to fulfill at least six different tasks: 1) to document how different places remained connected to Africa in the nineteenth century through the continued forced migration of African peoples, as well as the diasporic relations that were maintained following the end of the slave trade – the cases of Cuba and Brazil are particularly relevant here; 2) to distinguish between societies where the slave trade became less important than the internal dynamics of late colonial societies in shaping the lives of Afrodescendants – Mexico and Peru come to mind here; 3) to confront the Afro-Latin American struggles to retain lands and resources acquired after independence and abolition in the face of Liberal economic reforms in the second half of the nineteenth century; 4) to examine black proletarianization and the differentially higher rates of black urbanization by the late nineteenth century – in part a direct outcome of Liberal economic reforms in the countryside – as well as the new social and political organizations and movements that emerged in urban spaces, including the consolidation of African-based religious institutions; 5) to chart the impacts of more ideological, "scientific," and systemic forms of racism and the denial of full rights as citizens of emerging nations; and 6) to detail more methodically how ideas about the Afro-Latin American cultural geographies of the past inspire political action today, both by Afrodescendants themselves and by the institutions reproducing dominant society.

## BIBLIOGRAPHY

Amaral, Adela L. 2016. "The Archaeology of a Maroon Reducción: Colonial Beginnings to Present Day Ruination." PhD diss., University of Chicago.

Anderson, Jennifer L. 2012. *Mahogany: The Costs of Luxury in Early America.* Cambridge, MA: Harvard University Press.

Anderson, Mark. 2009. *Black and Indigenous: Garifuna Activism and Consumer Culture in Honduras.* Minneapolis, MN: University of Minnesota Press.

Anderson, Robert Nelson. 1996. "The *Quilombo* of Palmares: A New Overview of Maroon Society in Seventeenth-Century Brazil." *Journal of Latin American Studies* 28, 3: 545–66.

Andrews, George Reid. 2004. *Afro-Latin America.* Oxford: Oxford University Press.

Armstrong, Douglas V. 1999. "Archaeology and Ethnohistory of the Caribbean Plantation." In *"I, Too, Am America": Archaeological Studies of African-American Life*, edited by Theresa A. Singleton, 173–92. Charlottesville, VA: University of Virginia Press.

Barickman, B. J. 1994. "'A Bit of Land, Which They Call Roça': Slave Provision Grounds in the Bahian Recôncavo, 1760–1840." *Hispanic American Historical Review* 74, 4: 649–87.

 1998. *A Bahian Counterpoint: Sugar, Tobacco, Cassava, and Slavery in the Recôncavo, 1780–1860.* Stanford, CA: Stanford University Press.

Beatty-Medina, Charles. 2006. "Caught between Rivals: The Spanish-African Maroon Competition for Captive Indian Labor in the Region of Esmeraldas during the Late Sixteenth and Early Seventeenth Centuries." *The Americas* 63, 1: 113–36.

 2009. "Maroon Chief Alonso de Illescas' Letter to the Crown, 1586." In *Afro-Latino Voices: Narratives from the Early Modern Ibero-Atlantic World, 1550–1812*, edited by Kathryn Joy McKnight and Leo J. Garofalo, 30–37. Indianapolis, IN: Hackett Publishing Company, Inc.

Bennett, Herman L. 2003. *Africans in Colonial Mexico: Absolutism, Christianity, and Afro-Creole Consciousness, 1570–1640.* Bloomington, IN: University of Indiana Press.

Berlin, Ira, and Philip D. Morgan. 1993. "Labor and the Shaping of Slave Life in the Americas." In *Cultivation and Culture: Labor and the Shaping of Slave Life in the Americas*, edited by Ira Berlin and Philip D. Morgan, 1–45. Charlottesville, VA: University of Virginia Press.

Bilby, Kenneth M. 2005. *True-Born Maroons.* Foreword by Kevin Yelvington. Gainesville, FL: University Press of Florida.

Bolland, O. Nigel. 1977. *The Formation of a Colonial Society: Belize, from Conquest to Crown Colony.* Baltimore, MD: The Johns Hopkins University Press.

Borrega Plá, María del Carmen. 1973. *Palenques de negros en Cartagena de Indias a fines del siglo XVII.* Seville: Escuela de Estudios Hispano-Americanos de Sevilla.

Bristol, Joan. 2007. *Christians, Blasphemers, and Witches: Afro-Mexican Ritual Practice in the Seventeenth Century.* Albuquerque, NM: University of New Mexico Press.

Brockington, Lolita Gutiérrez. 2008. *Blacks, Indians, and Spaniards in the Eastern Andes: Reclaiming the Forgotten in Colonial Mizque, 1550–1782*. Lincoln, NE: University of Nebraska Press.

Brown, Ras Michael. 2012. *African-Atlantic Cultures and the South Carolina Lowcountry*. New York, NY: Cambridge University Press.

Brown, Vincent. 2010. *The Reaper's Garden: Death and Power in the World of Atlantic Slavery*. Cambridge, MA: Harvard University Press.

2015. "Mapping a Slave Revolt: Visualizing Spatial History through the Archives of Slavery." *Social Text* 33, 4: 134–41.

Bryant, Sherwin K., Rachel Sarah O'Toole, and Ben Vinson III, eds. 2012. *Africans to Spanish America: Expanding the Diaspora*. Bloomington, IN: University of Illinois Press.

Butzer, Karl W., ed. 1992. *The Americas before and after 1492: Current Geographical Research*. Special Issue. *Annals of the Association of American Geographers* 82, 3: 345–568.

Cáceres Gómez, Rina. 2000. *Negros, mulatos, esclavos y libertos en la Costa Rica del siglo XVII*. Mexico City: Instituto Panamericano de Geografía e Historia.

2010. "Slavery and Social Differentiation: Slave Wages in Omoa." In *Blacks and Blackness in Central America: Between Race and Place*, edited by Lowell Gudmundson and Justin Wolfe, 130–49. Durham, NC: Duke University Press.

ed. 2001. *Rutas de la esclavitud en Africa y América Latina*. San José: Editorial de la Universidad de Costa Rica.

Candido, Mariana P. 2015. *An African Slaving Port and the Atlantic World: Benguela and Its Hinterland*. New York, NY: Cambridge University Press.

Cañizares-Esguerra, Jorge, Matt D. Childs, and James Sidbury, eds. 2013. *The Black Urban Atlantic in the Age of the Slave Trade*. Philadelphia, PA: University of Pennsylvania Press.

Carney, Judith A. 2001. *Black Rice: The African Origins of Rice Cultivation in the Americas*. Cambridge, MA: Harvard University Press.

2003. "African Traditional Plant Knowledge in the Circum-Caribbean Region." *Journal of Ethnobiology* 23, 2: 167–85.

2004. "'With Grains in Her Hair': Rice in Colonial Brazil." *Slavery and Abolition* 25, 1: 1–27.

2005. "Rice and Memory in the Age of Enslavement: Atlantic Passages to Suriname." *Slavery and Abolition* 26, 3: 325–48.

2010. "Landscapes and Places of Memory: African Diaspora Research and Geography." In *African Diaspora and the Disciplines*, edited by Tejumola Olaniyan and James H. Sweet, 101–18. Bloomington, IN: Indiana University Press.

2012. "Seeds of Memory: Botanical Legacies of the African Diaspora." In *African Ethnobotany in the Americas*, edited by Robert Voeks and John Rashford, 13–33. New York, NY: Springer.

Carney, Judith A., and Haripriya Rangan. 2015. "Situating African Agency in Environmental History." *Environment and History* 21, 1: 1–11.

Carney, Judith A., and Richard Nicholas Rosomoff. 2009. *In the Shadow of Slavery: Africa's Botanical Legacy in the Atlantic World*. Berkeley, CA: University of California Press.

Carney, Judith A., and Robert A. Voeks. 2003. "Landscape Legacies of the African Diaspora in Brazil." *Progress in Human Geography* 27, 2: 139–52.

Carroll, Patrick J. 2001. *Blacks in Colonial Veracruz: Race, Ethnicity, and Regional Development, 1570–1830*. 2nd ed. Austin, TX: University of Texas Press.

Chan, Alexandra A. 2007. "Bringing the Out Kitchen In? The Experiential Landscapes of Black and White New England." In *Archaeology of Atlantic Africa and the African Diaspora*, edited by Akinwumi Ogundiran and Toyin Falola, 249–76. Bloomington, IN: Indiana University Press.

Childs, Matt D. 2006. "'The Defects of Being a Black Creole': The Degrees of African Identity in the Cuban *Cabildos De Nación*, 1790–1820." In *Slaves, Subjects, and Subversives: Blacks in Colonial Latin America*, edited by Jane G. Landers and Barry M. Robinson, 209–45. Albuquerque, NM: University of New Mexico Press.

Conrad, Robert Edgar, ed. 1994. *Children of God's Fire: A Documentary History of Black Slavery in Brazil*. 2nd edition. University Park, PA: Pennsylvania State University Press.

Corzo, Gabina la Rosa. 2003 [1988]. *Runaway Slave Settlements in Cuba: Resistance and Repression*. Chapel Hill, NC: University of North Carolina Press.

Cromwell, Jesse. 2014. "More than Slaves and Sugar: Recent Historiography of the Trans-Imperial Caribbean and Its Sinew Populations." *History Compass* 12, 10: 770–83.

Dawson, Kevin. 2006. "Enslaved Swimmers and Divers in the Atlantic World." *Journal of American History* 92, 4: 1327–55.

——— 2013. "The Cultural Geography of Enslaved Ship Pilots." In *The Black Urban Atlantic in the Age of the Slave Trade*, edited by Jorge Cañizares-Esguerra, Matt D. Childs, and James Sidbury, 163–84. Philadelphia, PA: University of Pennsylvania Press.

De la Fuente, Alejandro. 2008. *Havana and the Atlantic in the Sixteenth Century*. Chapel Hill, NC: University of North Carolina Press.

Díaz, María Elena. 2000. *The Virgin, the King, and the Royal Slaves of El Cobre: Negotiating Freedom in Colonial Cuba, 1670–1780*. Stanford, CA: Stanford University Press.

Díaz Burgos, Ana. 2013. "A Cartography of Sorcery: Mapping the First *Auto de Fe* in Cartagena de Indias, 1614." *Colonial Latin American Historical Review* 1, 3: 243–72.

Diouf, Sylviane A. 2014. *Slavery's Exiles: The Story of the American Maroon*. New York, NY: New York University Press.

Dos Anjos, Araújo and Rafael Sanzio. 2005. *Territórios das Comunidades Quilombolas do Brasil: Segunda Configuração Espacial*. Brasilia: Mapas Editora and Consultoria.

Dym, Jordana and Karl Offen. 2012. "Maps and the Teaching of Latin American History." *Hispanic American Historical Review* 92, 2: 213–44.

Dym, Jordana, and Karl Offen, eds. 2011. *Mapping Latin America: A Cartographic Reader*. Chicago, IL: University of Chicago Press.

Eltis, David. 2000. *The Rise of African Slavery in the Americas*. New York, NY: Cambridge University Press.

Eltis, David, Stephen D. Behrendt, David Richardson, and Herbert S. Klein, eds. 1999. *The Trans-Atlantic Slave Trade: A Database on CD-ROM Set and Guidebook*. New York, NY: Cambridge University Press.

Eltis, David, and David Richardson. 2010. *Atlas of the Transatlantic Slave Trade*. New Haven, CT: Yale University Press.

Eltis, David, Stephen D. Behrendt, Manolo Florentino, and David Richardson. 2013. *Voyages: The Trans-Atlantic Slave Trade Database*. Emory University. www.slavevoyages.org.

Falola, Toyin, and Matt D. Childs, eds. 2005. *The Yoruba Diaspora in The Atlantic World*. Bloomington, IN: Indiana University Press.

Farfán-Santos, Elizabeth. 2016. *Black Bodies, Black Rights: The Politics of Quilombolismo in Contemporary Brazil*. Austin, TX: University of Texas Press.

Ferreira, Roquinaldo. 2014. *Cross-Cultural Exchange in the Atlantic World: Angola and Brazil during the Era of the Slave Trade*. New York, NY: Cambridge University Press.

Finamore, Daniel. 2008. "Furnishing the Craftsmen: Slaves and Sailors in the Mahogany Trade." *In American Furniture*, 61–87.

Foote, Kenneth E., Peter J. Hugill, Kent Mathewson, and Jonathan M. Smtih, eds. 1994. *Re-Reading Cultural Geography*. Austin, TX: University of Texas Press.

Frank, Zephyr, and Whitney Berry. 2010. "The Slave Market in Rio De Janeiro circa 1869: Context, Movement and Social Experience." *Journal of Latin American Geography* 9, 3: 85–110.

Friedemann, Nina S. de. 1998. "Gold Mining and Descent: Güelmambí, Nariño [Colombia]." In *Blackness in Latin America and the Caribbean: Social Dynamics and Cultural Transformations. Central America and Northern and Western South America*, edited by Norman E. Whitten and Arlene Torres, vol. 1, 183–99. Bloomington, IN: Indiana University Press.

Funari, Pedro P. 2007. "The Archaeological Study of the African Diaspora in Brazil." In *Archaeology of Atlantic Africa and the African Diaspora*, edited by Akinwumi Ogundiran and Toyin Falola, 355–71. Indianapolis, IN: Indiana University Press.

Futemana, Célia, Lúcia Chamlian Munari, and Cristina Adams. 2015. "The Afro-Brazilian Collective Land: Analyzing Institutional Changes in the Past Two Hundred Years." *Latin American Research Review* 54, 4: 26–48.

Garofalo, Leo J. 2006. "Conjuring with Coca and the Inca: The Andeanization of Lima's Afro-Peruvian Ritual Specialists, 1580–1690." *The Americas* 63, 1: 53–80.

Gaspar, David Barry, and Darlene Clark Hine, eds. 1996. *More than Chattel: Black Women and Slavery in the Americas*. Bloomington, IN: Indiana University Press.

Gaspar, David Barry, and Darlene Clark Hine, eds. 2004. *Beyond Bondage: Free Women of Color in the Americas*. Urbana, IL: University of Illinois Press.

Geggus, David. 2013. "The Slaves and Free People of Color of Cap Français." In *The Black Urban Atlantic in the Age of the Slave Trade*, edited by Jorge Cañizares-Esguerra, Matt D. Childs, and James Sidbury, 101–21. Philadelphia, PA: University of Pennsylvania Press.

Goett, Jennifer. 2017. *Black Autonomy: Race, Gender, and Afro-Nicaraguan Activism.* Stanford, CA: Stanford University Press.

Gómez, Pablo F. 2015. "Healing, African American." In *The Princeton Companion to Atlantic History*, edited by Joseph C. Miller, 233–34. Princeton, NJ: Princeton University Press.

Gordon, Edmund T. 1998. *Disparate Diasporas: Identity and Politics in an African-Nicaraguan Community.* Austin, TX: University of Texas Press.

Graham, Richard. 2010. *Feeding the City: From Street Market to Liberal Reform in Salvador, Brazil, 1780–1860.* Austin, TX: University of Texas Press.

Gudmundson, Lowell and Justin Wolfe, eds. 2010. *Blacks and Blackness in Central America: Between Race and Place.* Durham, NC: Duke University Press.

Guengerich, Sara Vicuña. 2009. "The Witchcraft Trials of Paula de Eguiluz, a Black Woman, in Cartagena de Indias, 1620–1636." In *Afro-Latino Voices: Narratives from the Early Modern Ibero-Atlantic World, 1550–1812*, edited by Kathryn Joy McKnight and Leo J. Garofalo, 175–93. Indianapolis, IN: Hackett Publishing Company, Inc.

Guitar, Lynne. 2006. "Boiling it Down: Slavery on the First Commercial Sugarcane Ingenios in the Americas (Hispaniola, 1530-45)." In *Slaves, Subjects, and Subversives: Blacks in Colonial Latin America*, edited by Jane G. Landers and Barry M. Robinson, 39–82. Albuquerque, NM: University of New Mexico Press.

Hanserd, Robert. 2015. "Okomfo Anokye formed a tree to hide from the Akwamu: Priestly power, freedom, and enslavement in the Afro-Atlantic." *Atlantic Studies* 12, 4: 522–44.

Hawthorne, Walter. 2010. *From Africa to Brazil: Culture, Identity, and an Atlantic Slave Trade, 1600–1830.* New York, NY: Cambridge University Press.

Heath, Barbara J., and Amber Bennett. 2000. "'The Little Spots Allow'd Them': The Archaeological Study of African American Yards." *Historical Archaeology* 34, 2: 38–55.

Heywood, Linda M., ed. 2002. *Central Africans and Cultural Transformations in the American Diaspora.* New York, NY: Cambridge University Press.

Heywood, Linda M., and John K. Thornton. 2007. *Central Africans, Atlantic Creoles, and the Foundation of the Americas, 1585–1660.* New York, NY: Cambridge University Press.

Higman, Barry. 2001. *Jamaica Surveyed: Plantation Maps and Plans of the Eighteenth and Nineteenth Centuries.* Kingston: University of the West Indies Press.

Hooker, Juliet. 2005. "Indigenous Inclusion/Black Exclusion: Race Ethnicity and Multicultural Citizenship in Latin America." *Journal of Latin American Studies* 37, 2: 285–310.

Hopkins, Daniel, Philip Morgan, and Justin Roberts. 2011. "The Application of GIS to the Reconstruction of the Slave-Plantation Economy of St. Croix, Danish West Indies." *Historical Geography* 39: 85–104.

Hulme, Peter and Neil L. Whitehead, eds. 1992. *Wild Majesty: Encounters with Caribs from Columbus to the Present Day.* Oxford: Clarendon Press.

Janzen, John M. 2015. "Healing, African." In *The Princeton Companion to Atlantic History*, edited by Joseph C. Miller, 230–32. Princeton, NJ: Princeton University Press.

Jefferson, Ann, and Paul Lokken. 2011. *Daily Life in Colonial Latin America*. Santa Barbara: Greenwood.

Jiménez Meneses, Orián. 1998. "La conquista del estómago: Viandas, vituallas y ración negra, siglos XVII-XVIII." In *La Geografía Humana de Colombia: Los Afrocolombianos*, edited by Luz Adriana Maya Restrepo, vol. 6, 221–40. Bogotá: Instituto Colombiano de Cultura Hispánica.

Jouve Martín, José R. 2014. *The Black Doctors of Colonial Lima: Science, Race, and Writing in Colonial and Early Republican Peru*. Montreal: McGill-Queens University Press.

Klein, Herbert S., and Ben Vinson III. 2007. *African Slavery in Latin America and the Caribbean*. 2nd edition. New York, NY: Oxford University Press, 2007.

Knight, Franklin C. 2010. *Working the Diaspora: The Impact of African Labor on the Anglo-American World, 1650–1850*. New York, NY: New York University Press.

Landers, Jane G. 1999. *Black Society in Spanish Florida*. Champaign, IL: University of Illinois Press.

2000. "Cimarrón Ethnicity and Cultural Adaptation in the Spanish Domains of the Circum-Caribbean, 1503–1763." In *Identity in the Shadow of Slavery*, edited by Paul E. Lovejoy. New York, NY: Continuum.

2002. "The Central African Presence in Spanish Maroon Communities." In *Central Africans and Cultural Transformations in the American Diaspora*, edited by Linda M. Heywood, 227–41. New York, NY: Cambridge University Press.

2005a. "Africans and Native Americans on the Spanish Florida Frontier." In *Beyond Black and Red: African-Native Relations in Colonial Latin America*, edited by Mathew Restall, 53–80. Albuquerque, NM: University of New Mexico Press.

2005b. "Leadership and Authority in Maroon Settlements in Spanish America and Brazil." In *Africa and the Americas: Interconnections during the Slave Trade*, edited by José C. Curto and Renée Soulodre-La France, 173–84. Trenton, NJ: Africa World Press.

2006. "Cimarrón and Citizen: African Ethnicity, Corporate Identity, and the Evolution of Free Black Towns in the Spanish Circum-Caribbean." In *Slaves, Subjects, and Subversives: Blacks in Colonial Latin America*, edited by Jane G. Landers and Barry M. Robinson, 111–45. Albuquerque, NM: University of New Mexico Press.

2013. "The African Landscape of Seventeenth-Century Cartagena and Its Hinterlands." In *The Black Urban Atlantic in the Age of the Slave Trade*, edited by Jorge Cañizares-Esguerra, Matt D. Childs, and James Sidbury, 147–62. Philadelphia, PA: University of Pennsylvania Press.

Lane, Kris. 2002. *Quito 1599: City and Colony in Transition*. Albuquerque, NM: University of New Mexico Press.

2005. "Africans and natives in the mines of Spanish America." In *Beyond Black and Red: African-Native Relations in Colonial Latin America*, edited by Mathew Restall, 159–84. Albuquerque, NM: University of New Mexico Press.

Lentz, Mark W. 2014. "Black Belizeans and Fugitive Mayas: Interracial Encounters on the Edge of Empire, 1750–1803." *The Americas* 70, 4: 645–75.

Lohse, Russell. 2014. *Africans into Creoles: Slavery, Ethnicity, and Identity in Colonial Costa Rica.* Albuquerque, NM: University of New Mexico Press.

Lokken, Paul. 2004. "A Maroon Moment: Rebel Slaves in Early Seventeenth-Century Guatemala." *Slavery and Abolition* 25, 3: 44–58.

———. 2008. "Génesis de una comunidad afro-indígena en Guatemala: La Villa de San Diego de la Gomera en el siglo XVII." *Mesoamérica* 50: 37–65.

———. 2010. "Angolans in Amatitlán: Sugar, African Migrants, and Gente Ladina in Colonial Guatemala." In *Between Race and Place: Blacks and Blackness in Central America and the Mainland Caribbean,* edited by Lowell Gudmundson and Justin Wolfe, 27–56. Durham, NC: Duke University Press.

———. 2013. "From the 'Kingdoms of Angola' to Santiago de Guatemala: The Portuguese Asientos and Spanish Central America, 1595–1640." *Hispanic American Historical Review* 93, 2: 171–203.

Lovejoy, Paul E. 2005. "Trans-Atlantic Transformation: The Origins and Identity of Africans in the Americas." In *The Atlantic World: Essays on Slavery, Migration, and Imagination,* edited by Wim Klooster and Alfred Padula, 126–46. Upper Saddle River, NJ: Pearson/Prentice Hall.

Marshall, Woodville K. 1993. "Provision Ground and Plantation Labor in Four Windward Islands: Competition for Resources during Slavery." In *Cultivation and Culture: Labor and the Shaping of Slave Life in the Americas,* edited by Ira Berlin and Philip D. Morgan, 203–20. Charlottesville, VA: University of Virginia Press.

Maya Restrepo, Luz Adriana. 2000. "Medicina y botánica africanas en la Nueva Granada, siglo XVII." *Historia Crítica* 19, 1: 24–42.

———. 2005. *Brujería y reconstrucción de identidades entre los africanos y sus descendientes en la Nueva Granada Siglo XVII.* Bogotá: Imprenta Nacional.

McClure, Susan. 1982. "Parallel usage of Medicinal Plants by Africans and their Caribbean Descendants." *Economic Botany* 36, 3: 291–301.

McKnight, Kathryn Joy. 2003. "'En su tierra lo aprendió': An African Curandero's Defense before the Cartagena Inquisition." *Colonial Latin American Review* 12, 1: 63–84.

———. 2009. "Elder, Slave, and Soldier: Maroon Voices from the Palenque del Limón, 1634." In *Afro-Latino Voices: Narratives from the Early Modern Ibero-Atlantic World, 1550–1812,* edited by Kathryn Joy McKnight and Leo J. Garofalo, 64–81. Indianapolis, IN: Hackett Publishing Company, Inc.

McNeill, J. R. 2010. *Mosquito Empires: Ecology and War in the Greater Caribbean, 1620–1914.* New York, NY: Cambridge University Press.

Miller, Joseph C. 2002. "Central Africa During the Era of the Slave Trade, c. 1490s–1850s." In *Central Africans and Cultural Transformations in the American Diaspora,* edited by Linda M. Heywood, 21–69. New York, NY: Cambridge University Press.

Mintz, Sidney W. 1974. *Caribbean Transformations.* Baltimore, MD: Johns Hopkins University Press.

Mintz, Sidney W., and Richard Price. 1992. *The Birth of African-American Culture: An Anthropological Perspective*. Boston: Beacon Press.

Mollett, Sharlene. 2013. "Mapping Deception: The Politics of Mapping Miskito and Garifuna Space in Honduras." *Annals of the Association of American Geographers* 103, 5: 1227–41.

Moret, Erica S. 2012. "Trans-Atlantic Diaspora Ethnobotany: Legacies of West African and Iberian Mediterranean Migration in Central Cuba." In *African Ethnobotany in the Americas*, edited by Robert Voeks and John Rashford, 217–45. New York, NY: Springer.

Morgan, Philip D. 1998. *Slave Counterpoint: Black Culture in the Eighteenth-Century Chesapeake and Lowcountry*. Chapel Hill, NC: University of North Carolina Press.

Newson, Linda. 1982. "Labour in the Colonial Mining Industry of Honduras." *The Americas* 39, 2: 185–203.

Newson, Linda A., and Susie Minchin. 2007. *From Capture to Sale: The Portuguese Slave Trade to Spanish South America in the Early Seventeenth Century*. Leiden: Brill.

Niell, Paul. 2015. *Urban Space as Heritage in Late Colonial Cuba: Classicism and Dissonance on the Plaza de Armas of Havana, 1754–1828*. Austin, TX: University of Texas Press.

Offen, Karl H. 2000. "British Logwood Extraction from the Mosquitia: The Origin of a Myth." *Hispanic American Historical Review* 80, 1: 113–35.

2002. "The Sambo and Tawira Miskitu: The Colonial Origins and Geography of Miskitu Differentiatio n in Eastern Nicaragua and Honduras." *Ethnohistory* 49, 2: 319–72.

2003. "The Territorial Turn: Making Black Territories in Pacific Colombia." *Journal of Latin American Geography* 2, 1: 43–73.

2004. "The Geographical Imagination, Resource Economies, and Nicaraguan Incorporation of the Mosquitia, 1838–1909." In *Territories, Commodities and Knowledges: Latin American Environmental Histories in the Nineteenth and Twentieth Centuries*, edited by Christian Brannstrom, 50–89. London: Institute for the Study of the Americas.

2007. "Creating Mosquitia: Mapping Amerindian Spatial Practices in Eastern Central America, 1629–1779." *Journal of Historical Geography* 33, 2: 254–82.

2010. "Race and Place in Colonial Mosquitia, 1600–1787." In *Between Race and Place: Blacks and Blackness in Central America and the Mainland Caribbean*, edited by Lowell Gudmundson and Justin Wolfe, 92–129. Durham, NC: Duke University Press.

2011a. "Making Black Territories." In *Mapping Latin America: A Cartographic Reader*, edited by Jordana Dym and Karl Offen, 288–92. Chicago, IL: University of Chicago Press.

2011b. "Puritan Bioprospecting in the West Indies and Central America." *Itinerario* 35, 1: 15–47.

2013a. "Historical Geography II: Digital Imaginations." *Progress in Human Geography* 37, 4: 562–74.

2013b. "Place between Empires: Africans and Afro-Amerindians in Colonial Mosquitia." Paper presented at the Omohundro Institute for Early American

History and Culture, *Africans in the Americas: Making Lives in a New World, 1675–1825*, Cave Hill, Barbados, March 14–16.

2014. "Introduction: The Awakening Coast." In *The Awakening Coast: An Anthology of Moravian Writings from Mosquitia and Eastern Nicaragua, 1849–1899*, edited by Karl Offen and Terry Rugeley, 1–40. Lincoln, NE: University of Nebraska Press.

2015. "Mapping Amerindian Captivity in Colonial Mosquitia." *Journal of Latin American Geography* 14, 3: 35–65.

Ogundiran, Akinwumi, and Toyin Falola. 2007. "Pathways in the Archaeology of Transatlantic Africa." In *Archaeology of Atlantic Africa and the African Diaspora*, edited by Akinwumi Ogundiran and Toyin Falola, 5–33. Bloomington, IN: Indiana University Press.

Parés, Luis Nicolau. 2013. *The Formation of Candomblé: Vodun History and Ritual in Brazil*. Chapel Hill, NC: University of North Carolina Press.

Parés, Luis Nicolau, and Roger Sansi, eds. 2011. *Sorcery in the Black Atlantic*. Chicago, IL: University of Chicago Press.

Parrish, Susan Scott. 2008. "Diasporic African Sources of Enlightenment Knowledge." In *Science and Empire in the Atlantic World*, edited by James Delbourgo and Nicholas Dew, 281–310. New York, NY: Routledge.

Parsons, James J. 1956. *San Andrés and Providencia: English-Speaking Islands in the Western Caribbean*. Berkeley, CA: University of California Press.

Pike, Ruth. 2007. "Black Rebels: The Cimarrons of Sixteenth-Century Panama." *The Americas* 64, 2: 243–66.

Price, Richard. 1983. *First-Time: The Historical Vision of an Afro-American People*. Baltimore, MD: Johns Hopkins University Press.

1990. *Alabi's World*. Baltimore, MD: The John Hopkins University Press.

1991. "Subsistence on the Plantation Periphery: Crops, Cooking, and Labour among Eighteenth-Century Suriname Maroons." *Slavery and Abolition* 12, 1: 107–27.

2006. "'On the Miracle of Creolization.'" In *Afro-Atlantic Dialogues: Anthropology in the Diaspora*, edited by Kevin A. Yelvington, 113–45. Santa Fe: School of American Research Press.

2007. *Travels with Tooy: History, Memory, and the African American Imagination*. Chicago, IL: University of Chicago Press.

2010. *Rainforest Warriors: Human Rights on Trial*. Philadelphia, PA: University of Pennsylvania Press.

ed. 1996. *Maroon Societies: Rebel Slave Communities in the Americas*. 3rd edition. Baltimore, MD: Johns Hopkins University Press.

Pulsipher, Lydia M. 1994. "The Landscapes and Ideational Roles of Caribbean Slave Gardens." In *The Archaeology of Garden and Field*, edited by Naomi F. Miller and Kathryn L. Gleason, 202–22. Philadelphia, PA: University of Pennsylvania Press.

Rarey, Matthew Francis. 2014. "Aquilombado: Fugitive Landscapes and the Politics of Cartography in Colonial Brazil." Congress of the Latin American Studies Association, Chicago, Illinois, May 22.

Rashford, John. 1984. "Plants, Spirits and the Meaning of 'John' in Jamaica." *Jamaica Journal* 17, 2: 62–70.

1985. "The Cotton Tree and the Spiritual Realm in Jamaica." *Jamaica Journal* 18, 1: 49–57.

Reis, João José. 1993. *Slave Rebellion in Brazil: The Muslim Uprising of 1835 in Bahia*. Baltimore, MD: Johns Hopkins University Press.

1996. "O mapa do buraco do tatu." In *Liberdade por um fio: História dos quilombos no Brasil*, edited by João José Reis and Flávio dos Santos Gomes, 501–05. São Paulo: Campanhia das Letras.

2005. "Street Labor in Bahia on the Eve of the Abolition of Slavery." In *Africa and the Americas: Interconnections during the Slave Trade*, edited by José C. Curto and Renée Soulodre-La France, 141–72. Trenton, NJ: Africa World Press.

2013. "African Nations in Nineteenth-Century Salvador, Bahia." In *The Black Urban Atlantic in the Age of the Slave Trade*, edited by Jorge Cañizares-Esguerra, Matt D. Childs, and James Sidbury, 63–82. Philadelphia, PA: University of Pennsylvania Press.

Reis, João José, and Flávio dos Santos Gomes, eds. 1996. *Liberdade por um fio: História dos quilombos no Brasil*. São Paulo: Campanhia das Letras.

Restall, Matthew. 2000. "Black Conquistadors: Armed Africans in Early Spanish America." *The Americas* 57, 2: 171–205.

2009. *The Black Middle: Africans, Mayas, and Spaniards in Colonial Yucatan*. Stanford, CA: Stanford University Press.

2014. "Crossing to Safety? Frontier Flight in Eighteenth-Century Belize and Yucatan." *Hispanic American Historical Review* 94, 3: 381–419.

ed. 2005. *Beyond Black and Red: African-Native Relations in Colonial Latin America*. Albuquerque, NM: University of New Mexico Press.

Restall, Matthew, and Jane Landers, eds. 2000. *The African Experience in Early Spanish America*. Special Issue. *The Americas* 57, 2: 167–308.

Romero, Mario Diego, and Kris Lane. 2002. "Miners & Maroons: Freedom on the Pacific Coast of Colombia and Ecuador." *Cultural Survival Quarterly* 25, 4: 32–37.

Rupert, Linda M. 2009. "Marronage, Manumission and Maritime Trade in the Early Modern Caribbean." *Slavery and Abolition* 30, 3: 361–82.

Santos, Vanicléia Silva. 2012. "Africans, Afro-Brazilians and Afro-Portuguese in the Iberian Inquisition in the Seventeenth and Eighteenth Centuries." *African and Black Diaspora: An International Journal* 5, 1: 49–63.

Sauer, Carl O. 1966. *The Early Spanish Main*. Berkeley, CA: University of California Press.

Schiebinger, Londa. 2004. *Plants and Empire: Colonial Bioprospecting in the Atlantic World*. Cambridge, MA: Harvard University Press.

Schwartz, Stuart B. 1970. "The 'Mocambo': Slave Resistance in Colonial Bahia." *Journal of Social History* 3, 4: 313–33

1985. *Sugar Plantations in the Formation of Brazilian Society: Bahia, 1550–1835*. New York, NY: Cambridge University Press.

1992. *Slaves, Peasants, and Rebels: Reconsidering Brazilian Slavery*. Urbana, IL: University of Illinois Press.

2006. "Cantos and Quilombos: A Hausa Rebellion in Bahia, 1814." In *Slaves, Subjects, and Subversives: Blacks in Colonial Latin America*, edited by Jane

G. Landers and Barry M. Robinson, 247–69. Albuquerque, NM: University of New Mexico Press.

Schwartz, Stuart B. and Hal Langfur. 2005. "Tapanhuns, Negros da Terra, and Curibocas." In *Beyond Black and Red: African-Native Relations in Colonial Latin America*, edited by Mathew Restall, 81–114. Albuquerque, NM: University of New Mexico Press.

Sharp, William Frederick. 1976. *Slavery on the Spanish Frontier: The Colombian Chocó, 1680–1810*. Norman: University of Oklahoma Press.

Shepherd, Verene A., ed. 2002. *Slavery without Sugar: Diversity in Caribbean Economy and Society since the 17th Century*. Gainesville, FL: University Press of Florida.

Singleton, Theresa. 2010. "Archaeology and Slavery." In *The Oxford Handbook of Slavery in the Americas*, edited by Robert L. Paquette and Mark M. Smith, 702–24. New York, NY: Oxford University Press.

Sluyter, Andrew. 2009. "The Role of Black Barbudans in the Establishment of Open-Range Cattle Herding in the Colonial Caribbean and South Carolina." *Journal of Historical Geography* 35, 2: 330–49.

    2012a. *Black Ranching Frontiers: African Cattle Herders of the Atlantic World, 1500–1900*. New Haven, CT: Yale University Press.

    2012b. "The Role of Blacks in Establishing Cattle Ranching in Louisiana in the Eighteenth Century." *Agricultural History* 86, 2: 41–67.

    2015. "How Africans and Their Descendants Participated in Establishing Open-Range Cattle Ranching in the Americas." *Environment and History* 21, 1: 77–101.

Sluyter, Andrew, and Chris Duvall. 2016. "African Fire Cultures, Cattle Ranching, and Colonial Landscape Transformations in the Neotropics." *Geographical Review* 106, 2: 294–311.

Socolow, Susan M. 1996. "Economic Roles of the Free Women of Color of Cap Français." In *More than Chattel: Black Women and Slavery in the Americas*, edited by David Barry Gaspar and Darlene Clark Hine, 279–97. Bloomington, IN: Indiana University Press.

Souldore-La France, Renée. 2006. "Los esclavos de su Majestad: Slave Protest and Politics in Late Colonial New Granada." In *Slaves, Subjects, and Subversives: Blacks in Colonial Latin America*, edited by Jane G. Landers and Barry M. Robinson, 175–208. Albuquerque, NM: University of New Mexico Press.

    2015. "Sailing Through the Sacraments: Ethnic and Cultural Geographies of a Port and Its Churches – Cartagena de Indias." *Slavery and Abolition* 36, 3: 460–77.

Stark, David M. 2015. *Slave Families and the Hato Economy in Puerto Rico*. Gainesville, FL: University of Florida Press.

Stedman, John Gabriel, Richard Price, and Sally Price, eds. 1992. *Stedman's Surinam: Life in an Eighteenth-Century Slave Society*. Baltimore, MD: Johns Hopkins University Press.

Sweet, James H. 2003. *Recreating Africa: Culture, Kinship, and Religion in the African-Portuguese World, 1441–1770*. Chapel Hill and London: University of North Carolina Press.

    2004. "'Not a Thing for White Men to See': Central African Divination in Seventeen-Century Brazil." In *Enslaving Connections: Changing Cultures of*

Africa and Brazil during the Era of Slavery, edited by José C. Curto and Paul E. Lovejoy, 139–48. Amherst, NY: Humanity Books.

2007. "African Identity and Slave Resistance in the Portuguese Atlantic." In *The Atlantic World and Virginia, 1550–1624*, edited by Peter C. Mancall, 225–47. Chapel Hill, NC: University of North Carolina Press.

2009. "Slaves, Convicts, and Exiles: African Travellers in the Portuguese Atlantic World, 1720-1750." In *Bridging the Early Modern Atlantic World: Peoples, Products, and Practices on the Move*, edited by Caroline A. Williams, 193–202. Farnham, Surrey, UK: Ashgate.

2011. *Domingos Álvares, African Healing, and the Intellectual History of the Atlantic World*. Chapel Hill, NC: University of North Carolina Press.

Symanski, Luís Cláudio P., ed. 2016. *Archaeology of African Diaspora Contexts in Brazil*. Special Issue. *Journal of African Diaspora Archaeology and Heritage* 5, 2: 63–221.

Thompson, Robert Farris. 1993. *Face of the Gods: Art and Altars of Africa and the African Americas*. New York, NY: Museum for African Art.

Thornton, John K. 1998. *Africa and Africans in the Making of the Atlantic World, 1400–1800*. 2nd edition. New York, NY: Cambridge University Press.

2002. "Religious and Ceremonial Life in *Kongo* and *Mbundu* Areas, 1500–1700." In *Central Africans and Cultural Transformations in the American Diaspora*, edited by Linda M. Heywood, 71–90. New York, NY: Cambridge University Press.

2006. "Central Africa in the Era of the Slave Trade." In *Slaves, Subjects, and Subversives: Blacks in Colonial Latin America*, edited by Jane G. Landers and Barry M. Robinson, 83–110. Albuquerque, NM: University of New Mexico Press.

2017. "The Zambos and the Transformation of the Miskitu Kingdom, 1636–1740." *Hispanic American Historical Review* 97, 1: 1–28.

Tomich, Dale. 1993. "Une Petite Guinée: Provision Ground and Plantation in Martinique, 1830–1848." In *Cultivation and Culture: Labor and the Shaping of Slave Life in the Americas*, edited by Ira Berlin and Philip D. Morgan, 221–42. Charlottesville, VA: University of Virginia Press.

Tuan, Yi-Fu. 1977. *Space and Place: The Perspective of Experience*. Minneapolis, MN: University of Minnesota Press.

Van Andel, Tinde R. 2010. "African Rice (*Oryza glaberrima Steud.*): Lost Crop of the Enslaved Africans Discovered in Suriname." *Economic Botany* 64, 1: 1–10.

2015. "African Names for American Plants." *American Scientist* 113: 268–75.

Van Andel, Tinde R., Amber van der Velden, and Minke Reijers. 2016. "The 'Botanical Gardens of the Dispossessed' Revisited: Richness and Significance of Old World Crops Grown by Suriname Maroons." *Genetic Resources and Crop Evolution* 63, 4: 695–710.

Van Andel, Tinde R, Charlotte I. E. A. van't Klooster, Diana Quiroz, Alexandra M. Towns, Sofie Ruysschaert, and Margot van Den Berg. 2014. "Local Plant Names Reveal That Enslaved Africans Recognized Substantial Parts of the New World Flora." *Proceedings of the National Academy of Sciences of the United States of America* 111, 50: E5346–53.

Van Andel, Tinde R., Sofie Ruysschaert, Kobeke Van de Putte, and Sara Groe-
    nendijk. 2012. "What Makes a Plant Magical? Symbolism and Sacred Herbs
    in Afro-Surinamese *Winti* Rituals." In *African Ethnobotany in the Americas*,
    edited by Robert Voeks and John Rashford, 247–84. New York, NY:
    Springer.
Van Deusen, Nancy. 2004. *The Souls of Purgatory: The Spiritual Diary of a
    Seventeenth-Century Afro-Peruvian Mystic, Ursula de Jesús*. Albuquerque,
    NM: University of New Mexico Press.
Van Norman, William C., Jr. 2012. *Shade-Grown Slavery: The Lives of
    Slaves on Coffee Plantations in Cuba*. Nashville, TN: Vanderbilt Univer-
    sity Press.
Vidal Ortega, Antoni. 2002. *Cartagena de Indias y la región histórica del Caribe,
    1580–1640*. Seville: Escuela de Estudios Hispano-Americanos.
Vinson III, Ben, ed. 2006. *The African Diaspora in the Colonial Andes*. Special
    Issue. *The Americas* 63, 1: 1–196.
Voeks, Robert A. 1993. "African Medicine and Magic in Brazil." *The Geograph-
    ical Review* 83: 66–78.
    1997. *Sacred Leaves of Candomblé: African Magic, Medicine, and Religion in
        Brazil*. Austin, TX: University of Texas Press.
    2012. "Ethnobotany of Brazil's African Diaspora: The Role of Floristic Hom-
        ogenization." In *African Ethnobotany in the Americas*, edited by Robert
        Voeks and John Rashford, 395–416. New York, NY: Springer.
Voeks, Robert, and John Rashford, eds. 2012a. *African Ethnobotany in the
    Americas*. New York, NY: Springer.
    2012b. "Introduction." In *African Ethnobotany in the Americas*, edited by
        Robert Voeks and John Rashford, 1–9. New York, NY: Springer.
Von Germeten, Nicole. 2006. *Black Blood Brothers: Confraternities and
    Social Mobility for Afro-Mexicans*. Gainesville, FL: University Press of
    Florida.
Wade, Peter. 1997. *Race and Ethnicity in Latin America*. London: Pluto Press.
Warsh, Molly A. 2018. *American Baroque: Pearls and the Nature of Empire,
    1492–1700*. Chapel Hill, NC: Omohundro Institute of Early American His-
    tory and Culture and the University of North Carolina Press.
Watkins, Case. 2015. "African Oil Palms, Colonial Socioecological Transform-
    ation and the Making of an Afro-Brazilian Landscape in Bahia, Brazil."
    *Environment and History* 21, 1: 13–42.
Watts, David. 1987. *The West Indies: Patterns of Development, Culture and
    Environmental Change since 1492*. New York, NY: Cambridge University
    Press.
Weik, Terrance. 2004. "Archaeology of the African Diaspora in Latin America."
    *Historical Archaeology* 38, 1: 32–49.
West, Robert Cooper. 1952. *Colonial Placer Mining in Colombia*. Baton Rouge:
    Louisiana State University Press.
    1957. *The Pacific Lowlands of Colombia: A Negroid Area of the American
        Tropics*. Baton Rouge: Louisiana State University Press.
Wheat, David. 2016. *Atlantic Africa and the Spanish Caribbean, 1570–1640*.
    Chapel Hill, NC: University of North Carolina Press.

Whitten, Norman. 1986. *Black Frontiersmen: Afro-Hispanic Culture of Ecuador and Colombia*. Prospect Heights, IL: Waveland Press.

Williams, Caroline A. 2014. "'If You Want Slaves Go to Guinea': Civilisation and Savagery in the 'Spanish' Mosquitia, 1787–1800." *Slavery and Abolition* 35, 1: 121–41

Zabala, Pilar. 2010. "The African Presence in Yucatan: Sixteenth and Seventeenth Centuries." In *Natives, Europeans, and Africans in Colonial Campeche: History and Archaeology*, edited by Vera Tiesler, Pilar Zabala, and Andrea Cucina, 152–74. Gainesville, FL: University Press of Florida.

# PART IV

# TRANSNATIONAL SPACES

# 14

# Transnational Frames of Afro-Latin Experience:

## *Evolving Spaces and Means of Connection, 1600–2000*

### Lara Putnam

Which kinds of long-distance connections have shaped Afro-Latin experiences? How have these means of connection and the geographies they weave together changed over time? Which places, within and beyond the Americas, have been so linked by densely overlapping circuits of migration, communication, and exchange as to constitute what anthropologists label "transnational social fields"? How have these evolving geographies of Afro-Latin connection been shaped – or truncated – by the territorial and political claims of empires and nations? And how has awareness of the shifting transnational dimensions of Afro-Latin life shaped scholars' practice: the questions we ask, the sources we seek, the answers we find?

Scholarship on Afro-Latin America has never had the luxury of insularity. From Mahommah Gardo Baquaqua to Fernando Ortiz to Melville Herskovits to Sidney Mintz and Richard Price and beyond, both insiders and outsiders have placed long-distance mobility and its complex consequences at the crux of Afro-Latin experience. For several generations of scholars, attention centered on the long-distance connections built by forced migration from Africa in the age of the slave trade, and debate centered on the ways that cultural knowledge and practices were maintained or transformed in sites of arrival (Morgan 1997; Midlo-Hall 2005; Price 2006). Over the past two decades, scholars have increased their attention to the more recent multi-dimensional flows and impacts that have knit together what Paul Gilroy labeled "the Black Atlantic" from post-emancipation to the present (Gilroy 1993).

Most recently, the accumulation of fine-grained research has begun to make it possible to move beyond blanket assertions of connection and begin to reconstruct specific patterns of supralocal ties as they evolved over time. This is in line with developments in the social sciences more broadly. Sociologists like Peggy Levitt and anthropologists like Nina Glick-Schiller argue that the task of scholars of transnational connection is to determine empirically the spatial contours, components, and impact of the particular transnational (and national, and subnational) social fields – each one a "set of multiple interlocking networks of social relationships through which ideas, practices, and resources are unequally exchanged, organized, and transformed" – that shaped the cases they seek to explain (Levitt and Glick Schiller 2004, 1009).

As scholars advocating transnational approaches have underlined, meaningful arguments for the importance of connection require attention to its necessary counterpoints: places of relative isolation, eras of inward turns, moments when national boundaries or audiences mattered most (Clavin 2005; Osterhammel 2009; Struck, Ferris, and Revel 2011; Saunier 2013). Those advocating this approach use the term "transnational" for research based on the reconstruction of connection across political-territorial boundaries, be those national frontiers or lines of colony or empire.

Such an approach – framing one's research within specific transnational fields empirically mapped over time – can usefully complement overarching interpretive concepts like "African diaspora," "Atlantic History," and "the Black Atlantic" (Palmer 1998; Kelley and Patterson 2000; Dubois and Scott 2010; Miller 2015). All of these macrolevel frames of reference have been and will continue to be useful and generative. This chapter, however, targets a smaller scale of observation, asking about communities and the specific places far and near with which they were systematically engaged. In this sense it responds to Fred Cooper's call for improved "ways of analyzing processes that cross borders but are not universal, that constitute long-distance networks and social fields but not on a planetary scale" (Cooper 2001, 189).

Those border-crossing processes included networks of capital, commodities, and authority, which wove a multitude of partially overlapping geographies only some of which I will choose to foreground here. To be sure, for instance, commodity histories from Sidney Mintz's classic *Sweetness and Power* to recent works on mahogany, cocoa, and pearls have much to show us about the production chains and distant demand that shaped Afro-Latin lives in the Americas (Mintz 1985; Anderson 2012). Critical histories placing metropole and colony in a single frame have been another scholarly focus: for instance in regard to abolition movements, deeply relevant to the history covered here (Schmidt-Nowara 1999).

However, this chapter chooses to focus on those transnational connections visible to Afro-Latin historical subjects themselves: the ties that shaped the scope of the world they knew as relevant to their lives. This is the scale on which the generative interactions J. Lorand Matory has conceptualized as "live dialogue" across the African diaspora has taken place (2006, 2014).

One way to stay close to the actor's perspective is to sleuth out stories of individual transnational lives, as Martha Hodes (2006), James Sweet (2011), Rebecca Scott and Jean Hébrard (2012), and Greg Grandin (2014) among others have done. The present chapter does not dial the microscope down that far. Rather it attempts to scope the hemispheric panorama of patterned connection over time. Awareness of this panorama should allow us to see where and how particular travelers were exceptional, and in which cases or ways they were commonplace. The kinds of insights we should draw will shift accordingly.

Academic studies that are not just multi-sited but multiply grounded – based in intensive, contextualized research both in and about more than one place – remain comparatively rare. Constraints of language, funding, and expertise limit such work. So too, the urgent need to speak to national political debates has favored nationally framed accounts of Afro-Latin trajectories (Pérez 2002). Nevertheless, the few in-depth multi-grounded studies that do exist have been extraordinarily revealing, complementing nation-based historiography in vital ways. This suggests great scope for future projects that can marshal skills and resources to investigate cross-border ties in depth, from multiple locations. Hopefully the pages that follow can signal some of the specific, far-flung, entangled locales that would be fruitful targets for such approaches.

In sum, this chapter makes a preliminary effort to identify the most significant transnational fields that have shaped and been shaped by Afro-Latin lives over time. It seeks to mark the chronology of those fields' emergence, their shifting boundaries, and their contraction or decline: and to give some examples of ways they mattered.

## THE TRANSATLANTIC SLAVE TRADE AND ITS SECONDARY CURRENTS: SEVENTEENTH AND EIGHTEENTH CENTURIES

Such a reconstruction must begin, of course, with the broad swath of connections between West and Central Africa and the plantation societies of the Americas that swelled as the slave trade swelled, carrying in the eighteenth century alone two million captives from Africa to the British Caribbean, one million to the French Caribbean, and over two million to Brazil.

The painstaking digitization of data from nearly 35,000 slave ship voyages in the extraordinary Transatlantic Slave Trade Database project, under the leadership of David Eltis, David Richardson, and Stephen Behrendt and with the help of many other scholars, has made it possible to map the routes that channeled this mass traffic (Eltis and Richardson 2010; Eltis, et al. 2013; see also Chapter 2). Sometimes these routes were diffuse and heterogeneous, when the dictates of profits and local politics demanded broad catchment and dispersed destinations. But at other times they were highly concentrated for decades or generations, giving purchase for the establishment of social, political, and economic ties, especially among elites profiting from the trade. Transatlantic traffic to Cartagena and Veracruz, for instance, came heavily from Angola at the start of the seventeenth century (Wheat 2011; Borucki, Wheat, and Eltis 2015). As the volume soared in the following century, multiple dense pairings between sending region and receiving port emerged, linking Luanda and Benguela to Rio de Janeiro, the Mina Coast to Bahia, and the region north of the Congo River estuary to Saint-Domingue (Eltis and Richardson 2008).

By the eighteenth century, secondary circuits of semi-clandestine commerce, which traded enslaved workers and other contraband across imperial lines, had created even closer connections between particular sets of American ports. One network centered on Kingston, Havana, and Cartagena, with secondary nodes like Veracruz, Omoa, Portobelo (O'Malley 2014; Wheat 2016). Transatlantic crossings by Dutch slave traders powered a second subregional network, based in Curaçao, tied to Riohacha, Coro, La Guaira, and Cumaná along the northern South American coast (Klooster 1998; Cwik 2010; Rupert 2012; Borucki 2012). Another web of enslaved commerce, gaining importance in the second half of the eighteenth century, linked the Danish West Indies to Puerto Rico, Cuba, and Venezuela. Finally, and most importantly in numerical terms, the ports along the Río de la Plata and its tributaries formed a fourth cluster, linked to Brazilian ports and their Angolan networks (Borucki 2009; Borucki 2011; Schultz 2015).

The Transatlantic Slave Trade Database's attainment of a critical mass of voyage coverage by the late 1990s was sped by and in turn furthered a set of highly fruitful collaborations between historians of Africa and historians of the Spanish and Portuguese Americas (Lovejoy 2009; Curto and Soulodre-La France 2004). One result was a series of collective publications, some bringing together scholars to trace the disparate American destinations of a single African sending region (Heywood 2002; Falola and Childs 2005), others tracing the range of dyads between African ports and locales within a single receiving society – Brazil – which by the end of the eighteenth century dwarfed all other destinations combined with the exception of French Saint-Domingue (Curto and Lovejoy 2004). The same scholarly infrastructure undergirded the training of a generation of new PhDs equally grounded in African and Latin American history, whose multi-sited research projects revealed the intense enmeshment of political developments (Lovejoy 2012; Mobley 2015), family networks (Cândido 2013a, 2013b), and cultural exchange (Ferreira 2014; see also Hawthorne 2010) in linked sites that spanned the Atlantic. These overlapping connections formed precisely the kind of dense transnational social fields that Nina Glick Schiller described. In case after case, the new researchers find prior understanding of events within individual plantation societies to be partial at best, and argue that explanations must be widened to include specific historical developments within the African side of each field.

Some scholars argue that the dislocations and existential impact of transatlantic slavery created religions that were inherently transnational, and transnational fields within which spiritual forces and ritual practices were pervasively central (Matory 2009; Ogundiran and Saunders 2014; see also Chapter 12). Certainly, the wealth of scholarship on transnational dimensions of religion and healing in the seventeenth- and eighteenth-century Afro-Atlantic would seem to support this. While classic works by early twentieth-century ethnologists sought to prove cultural origins and collective retentions, more recent scholarship tracks ritual practices shaped by the impact of enslavement on each side of the Atlantic (Vanhee 2002; Sweet 2003; Fromont 2013; Krug 2014) and highlights the importance of specialists who deployed expertise and fused new sources of spiritual knowledge (McKnight 2003; Sweet 2011; Gómez 2013; Gómez 2014).

Meanwhile, even as forced migration and trade routes that sustained it were binding Caribbean, South American, and West and Central African ports into tight subsets, flights from slavery were creating their own geographies within the Americas. More diffuse and small scale, these nevertheless created identifiable Afro-Latin hinterlands laced by patterned routes along coasts and rivers. We see these along the northern Gulf of Mexico (Landers 1990; Usner 1992), western Caribbean rimlands (Offen 1999; Offen 2002; Lokken 2004; Marín Araya 2004; Tompson 2008,

2012; Restall 2009; Thornton 2017), and northern South America's Pacific Coast (Lane 1998; Beatty-Medina 2012). Far from the coasts, similar zones of refuge emerged in cases where the competing territorial claims of European states created imperial fringes with possibilities for evasion, leverage, or even alliance (Price 2002; Gomes 2002; Miki 2011; Yingling 2015; Borucki 2017).

### THE AGE OF REVOLUTION: ROUTES TRAVELED AND REMADE

The tumultuous Age of Revolution and the challenges to slavery within it remade these patterns. The successful revolt in Saint-Domingue resonated across the slave societies of the Americas: in ways that were anything but random. The regional and transatlantic networks in which Spanish American and circum-Caribbean ports were enmeshed channeled the individuals, rumors, and texts that carried news of successive republican revolutions in North America, France, and the French Caribbean (Scott 1986; Landers 2011; Bassi 2012). Free people of color, local white Creoles, and enslaved port-dwellers all engaged with the ideas and possibilities of the moment – in some instances in alliance with each other; at other moments, in stark separation. Both in the Río de la Plata and in northern South America's ports and towns, the networks bringing news from abroad connected to local networks that routinely crossed socioracial lines (Helg 2004; Johnson 2011; Borucki 2015; Echeverri 2016; Soriano 2018). In such places, *pardos* and free blacks followed political news from afar alongside white Creole plebeians and artisans. Nevertheless, in those same places, the news arriving from 1791 onward provoked elite fears of cataclysmic, separatist black rebellion.

The enslaved of Saint-Domingue had taken up arms, and a decade of military, political, and ideological upheaval that would eventually be known as the Haitian Revolution would follow. In France's eastern Caribbean colonies the enslaved likewise armed themselves to claim freedom and citizenship; there, re-enslavement would be brutally reimposed in 1802 (Dubois 2004). Saint-Domingue's leaders, in contrast, would proclaim independence in 1804, and successfully defend it. Reversing generations of scholarly neglect, studies of Haiti's reverberation now abound (Gaspar and Geggus 1997; Geggus 2001; Dubois 2006; Garraway 2008; Munroe and Walcott 2008; Cáceres and Lovejoy 2008; Dillon and Drexler 2016). On their basis we can begin tracing different means through which these events resounded, in different directions and with different consequences.

Gruesome tales and fear of becoming "another Haiti" shook white leaders across the hemisphere, from Philadelphia to Havana to Buenos Aires and beyond, sped by the era's burgeoning periodical press (Johnson 2011; Ferrer 2014; Dun 2016). Simultaneously, and often in dialogue with that print coverage and local white reactions to it, news of revolution in the French Antilles traveled by word of mouth, song, and broadside across the seaborne networks of the Greater Caribbean. Ideas and individuals arriving from the French conflagration along these routes in the 1790s were linked to uprisings by Afrodescendants on the northern coasts of Colombia and Venezuela and in Curaçao: locales that as we have seen were tightly connected by commerce, contraband, and marronage (Geggus 2001; Oostindie 2011; Aizpurúa 2011; Soriano 2018).

The impact of the military upheaval and of the creation of a new state, which banned slavery within its borders, at the heart of the Greater Antilles was not merely symbolic. It opened new possibilities for flight and new terrain of confrontation, as the territorial struggles of military and diplomatic agents continually remade (and were remade by) the geography of freedom struggle on the ground. Although most vivid within the island of Hispaniola (shared by Haiti and Santo Domingo), this dynamic encompassed Jamaica and Cuba, each just a sea channel away, as well (Ferrer 2012; Johnson 2012; Gonzalez 2014; Smith 2014; Yingling 2015; Gaffield 2015; Nessler 2016; Eller 2016). As Cuban slavery expanded, in an Atlantic market remade by Saint-Domingue's exit, personal experiences and knowledge of Haiti would remain explosive touchstones on the island (Childs 2006; Ferrer 2014).

Meanwhile, to the north, Afro-North Americans watched and debated the destiny of Haiti as place of freedom and as sovereign state. Such debate was prominent in the print public sphere but not limited to it: it was shaped by personal contact with refugees, sailors, and others as well (Fanning 2007; White 2010; Yingling 2013; Jones 2013). Once military upheaval settled, mobility would not be a one-way street. As many as 13,000 African Americans emigrated to Haiti in the 1820s (Fanning 2015). Haiti's symbolic importance within Afro-North America would continue to spread via prints and performative culture across subsequent generations (Nwankwo 2005; Calagé, Dalleo, Duno-Gottberg, and Headley 2013; Wirzbicki 2015) and take on new significance in the wake of slavery's end (Polyné 2010; Byrd 2015).

In sum, the revolutionary struggles against slavery in the French Antilles at the dawn of the nineteenth century echoed along channels set by a preexisting geography of supralocal connection. But the struggles themselves also remade that geography. The flight of planters seeking to reestablish slave societies and people of color seeking shelter from violence intensified connections among Haiti, Cuba and New Orleans in the northwest Caribbean (Scott 2005; Dessins 2007; Sublette 2008; Scott and Hébrard 2012; Vidal 2013; Johnson 2016) and among the francophone Windwards, Trinidad, and Venezuela in the south (Brereton 1981; Soriano 2012; Candlin 2012). These ties would in turn shape flows of trade, migration, and information across subsequent generations.

## THE "SECOND SLAVERY": AFRICA, BRAZIL, AND CUBA ENTWINED

The rise of the "second slavery" over the first half of the nineteenth century generated a new transatlantic geography of intense familial and commercial ties between ports in Brazil (Bahia, Rio de Janeiro) and West (Ouidah, Lagos) and Central Africa (Luanda, Benguela, and the northern Angola coast). The range of destinations in the Americas had been radically reduced by British slave trade abolition and the slow successive demise of slavery in the Danish, British, and French colonies and Spanish American republics. Now skirting international law, profitable trafficking required close oversight and ongoing ties of kinship and trust. Merchants succeeded by deploying family, capital, and residence between the port dyads their ships traversed (Law and Mann 1999; Mann and Bay 2001; Curto and Lovejoy 2004; Ferreira 2008). Microlevel inquiry reveals how the consolidation of this bicoastal elite, the ongoing trade in captives, the ancillary trade in consumer products, and small-scale return migration overlapped and fed each other: as when Brazilian-born traders of African parentage, now resident in Ouidah, imported Afro-Brazilian artisans back to the Bight of Benin to build the Brazilian-style houses they missed (Law and Mann 1999, 325; Ferreira 2007; Naro 2007).

As in the previous centuries, the violence of slavery continued to drive mobility across political frontiers. But in the nineteenth century it was not the spread of European domain but the uneven spread of abolition that created new frontiers of enslavement within the Americas. Moreover, by this era, centuries of forced immigration and local survival along imperial frontiers meant that there were often culturally-linked Afrodescendant communities on both sides of the thermoclines of freedom created by uneven abolition. Such frontiers could favor fugitives seeking freedom – or cross-border raiding and illegal enslavement. Both became prominent on the Uruguayan/Rio Grande do Sul frontier from the 1840s to 1860s

(Palermo 2008; Monsma and Dorneles Fernandes 2013; Grinberg 2016, 2017). Similarly on South America's northern fringes, Afrodescendant youths from the Trinidad and the Windward Islands risked loss of freedom in Venezuela (Toussaint 2007).

These were only small eddies, however, in a mid-nineteenth century Atlantic whose main currents were massive and focalized flows of captives from West and Central Africa to Brazil and a rapidly accelerating current from Africa to Cuba. Cuba-based slave traders carried away hundreds of thousands of Africans, from rather more dispersed ports of origin than their Luso-African counterparts. These included Bonny and Old Calabar in the 1820s and 1830s, Ouidah in the 1830s, and Luanda and other West Central African sites in the 1850s (Eltis and Richardson 2008b; Grandío 2008; Zeuske 2015; Pérez Morales 2017). As in previous eras, the transatlantic routes of enslavement also generated ancillary circuits of enslaved as contraband: in this era, for instance, channeling to Puerto Rico both new African arrivals via Havana and free or formerly free laborers from British colonies (Dorsey 2003; Chinea 2005).

The rapid expansion of slave imports to Cuba in the 1820s coincided with years of military upheaval in inland West Africa. Manuel Barcia suggests we should think of West Africa's Atlantic states as undergoing an "Age of Revolution," in which issues of sovereignty and slavery entwined, just as colonies at the other end of the Atlantic had done nearly simultaneously (Barcia 2014; also Dubois 2006). In the West African variant, military campaigns for Islamic reform were central, resulting in transport to the Americas of both Muslims and experienced soldiers, a pattern understood at the time (and by scholars since) as a dangerous driver of rebellions, for instance in Bahia and central Cuba (Reis 1993; Barcia 2012; cf. Lovejoy 2012; Finch 2015).

One route of return to Africa was exile in the wake of failed rebellion, as with the 1835 Malê Rebellion of Bahia, or the 1844 La Escalera in Cuba (Reid-Vazquez 2011). Thousands of others returned voluntarily after having gained freedom in Brazil, whether at mid-century by proving they had been illegally introduced, or at century's end after nation-wide abolition (1888). Individual and collective fortunes varied. In some locales, self-proclaimed "Brazilians" claimed status based on skills acquired or trading access to New World goods, forging and keeping a communal identity (Lindsay 1994; Guran 2007). Other returnees found themselves unable to locate or recreate community (Lawrence 2014).

All told, in the six decades between British slave trade abolition in 1807 and the transatlantic trade's final suppression, 1.6 million enslaved

Africans were transported to Brazil and 685,000 to Cuba. Some 180,000 more were "recaptured" en route by the British navy under treaties barring the trade. Recaptives were settled in Sierra Leone or sent under contract of indenture – often involuntarily – to labor in colonies where the end of slavery had left planters hunger for workers. Some 55,000 recaptives were sent under indenture to the British Caribbean, most to British Guiana, Jamaica, and Trinidad (Adderley 2002, 2006; da Silva et al. 2014). Another 16,000 indentured Africans were contracted by the French directly in East Africa and sent to labor in Guadeloupe and Martinique (Laurence 2011).

Because the formalities of record-keeping were carefully followed by British authorities in this process – even as commitments to voluntary contract and free labor were not – nominal-level information on the great bulk of recaptives has been retained. It is now being processed with public input on name ethnicities and more, via digital outreach initiatives (www .liberatedafricans.org/, www.african-origins.org/). The process has the potential to yield an unprecedentedly precise panorama of points of origin (rather than just ports of embarkation) – and, importantly, not just for those recaptured, but for the 2.3 million enslaved Africans whose Brazil- or Cuba-bound transports avoided intervention (Schwarz 2012; da Silva et al. 2014; Lovejoy 2016). Our ability to map routes of connection and frame multi-sited research around them will expand apace.

Such research will complement work already undertaken in regard to religion in particular. The intensely focalized transatlantic slave trade of the nineteenth century, and the dense transnational fields it created, generated particular kinds of religious innovation. From the start of transatlantic enslavement, spiritual belief and ritual had been forced to grapple with violent rupture, distance, and loss. New nineteenth-century iterations of this dynamic were shaped by transport routes, technologies, and entrepreneurial networks that sped communication and brought people on opposite sides of the Atlantic into a partially shared marketplace of religious ideas and practice. Scholars have used multi-grounded research strategies to reconstruct how religious "traditions" emerged in dialogue between Cuba and Brazil and West/Central Africa in this era (Parés 2001; Brown 2003; Matory 2005; Lovejoy 2012). Rituals, concepts, and collective identities in the New World's last slave-importing societies changed in dialogue with coeval developments in African locales: which were themselves being remade by the rise and fall of human trafficking and the violence, political shifts, and wealth-making it brought (Blier 1995; Palmié 2002; Shaw 2002; Palmié 2008).

By the start of the twentieth century print culture became an added vector of connection in the realm of spiritual practice. Summaries of African "belief" or "witchcraft" published by European travelers – often composed in collaboration with literate, multilingual West Africans, some of them Afro-Brazilian or Afro-Caribbean by birth or ancestry – were read and republished at sites from Bahia to Port of Spain to Havana, where they shaped the understanding of practitioners and opponents alike (Matory 1999; Reis 2001; Paton and Forde 2012; Reis 2015). With the final end of the Cuban and Brazilian slave trades and African indenture to the British colonies, and as the first wave of post-emancipation return dissipated, transnational ties between the Americas and Africa would increasingly look like this: exoticized communication and commerce, spidery remnants of the dense social fields of the preceding generations.

## POST-INDEPENDENCE REPUBLICS: INWARD REGIONS, OUTER BORDERLANDS

Thus, the nineteenth century saw new lines and new kinds of transatlantic and inter-hemispheric connection. Yet for many Afro-Latins, this was an era in which relevant social fields shrank and reoriented inward. Across much of post-Independence Spanish America, the formation of new nation-states made subnational regions more salient than ever before. Subnational regions – often formalized as *provincias* or *estados* – formed economic units, housed elective offices worth fighting for, and shaped militarized patron-client networks. Afro-Latin communities within the new republics sat near the centers of these processes. Indeed, they enthusiastically furthered them (Graham 1990; Andrews 2004; Sanders 2004; Lasso 2007; Mayes 2014).

The early republican era saw black empowerment far outside these consolidating regions as well, at the outer frontiers of the new nations: in black borderlands like the Caribbean lowlands of Central America (Euraque, Gould, and Hale 2004) and Pacific coast enclaves like Mexico's Costa Chica, Colombia's Chocó, and Ecuador's Esmeraldas (Wade 1993; Lewis 2012; see also Chapters 4 and 13). These colonial-era zones of refuge, created by Afro- and indigenous-descended peoples at the interstices of empires, now sustained themselves through small-scale commerce and exchange that routinely cut across political borders. In the western Caribbean, where Miskitu and others sold turtles and other tropical products to European markets, and foreign missions sought new souls, such ties are becoming well studied (Gordon 1998; Everingham and

Taylor 2009; Crawford 2013; Crawford and Márquez 2016). The supra-local ties of the black borderlands of the Pacific have not.

The movement of refugees and workers between Cuba and Miami, Key West, and Tampa and of exiles from the Hispanic Caribbean to New York from the 1860s to 1890s represents yet a third variety of transnational connection in this era: highly focalized and highly responsive to international politics (Mirabal 2001, 2017; Daniel 2010). New research traces the integration of Mexican ports including Veracruz and Mérida to these circuits, which were mobilized and reinforced by Cuban exile activism around the Ten Years' War and independence struggle. The findings suggest the importance of a "transnational Gulf world" scholars have yet to fully assess (Muller 2017).

By the 1860s the final iteration of the transatlantic slave trade, based in Cuba, had ended, and with Brazil's 1888 abolition, chattel slavery in the Americas was no more. From then on, it would be free rather than coerced mobility by Afro-Latins that wove crucial transborder connections. Some long-distance travel by high-impact individuals continued, like that of Candomblé leaders to Lagos seeking goods, knowledge, and prestige to advance the position of their own "houses" (Matory 2005). But, for the bulk of freedpeople, mobility in the first generation after slavery was short in distance, although weighty in consequence. Across plantation societies, these decades saw small-range movement rise in importance. Landowners sought to bind freedpeople in place through new mechanisms of sharecropping and debt; freedpeople sought autonomy by reconstituting peasant communities outside the bounds of planter control, yet still near enough to markets and wages.

### LABOR, MIGRATION, AND RIGHTS IN A POST-EMANCIPATION HEMISPHERE

As Afro-Latin populations cleaved to small-scale movement and interstitial spaces, imperial and new national states helped local employers and distant entrepreneurs create new transoceanic geographies of unfree labor – now in the Pacific. Over 100,000 Chinese workers traveled under contract of indenture to Cuba alone in the second half of the nineteenth century. Similar numbers sailed for Peru, where sugar fields and guano mines offered backbreaking labor. Upon contracts' completion many Chinese migrants returned home, but some stayed, mobilizing kin ties to create dispersed commercial networks with outposts in ports and small towns across the hemisphere (Hu-DeHart and López 2008; López 2013; Young 2014).

Within the British colonies, indentured migration pulled nearly a half million souls from India to the Caribbean in the eighty years after the end of slavery, their subsidized labor a steady prop for sugar planters' profits. Some 240,000 indentured East Indians went to British Guiana, 145,000 to Trinidad, 35,000 to Jamaica, 34,000 to Surinam, and smaller numbers to smaller islands. Across the generations in which formal labor structures separated these immigrants from the Afrodescended "Creoles" around them and continued arrivals renewed the Hindi language and Hindu and Muslim ritual arrays, communities remained largely segregated. Only with the end of empire in the 1960s would these boundaries be challenged, eroding in some places while becoming fodder for politicized violence in others (Williams 1991; Munasinghe 2001; Khan 2004).

By the dawn of the twentieth century, new patterns of investment and growth began to power long-distance migrations among Afro-Latin populations once more, redrawing racialized regions. On the one hand, in South America – Brazil most of all – incipient industrialization drew rural-born Afrodescendants from former plantation zones toward growing cities, creating large-scale long-distance flows within rather than across national borders. (The North American variant of this trend is known as the "Great Migration.") On the other hand, around the Caribbean basin, surging US investment brought new plantation and infrastructure projects to sparsely populated black borderlands. Such investment generated highly focalized cross-border mobility, drawing above all from heavily populated former sugar colonies: the British West Indies and Haiti (Putnam 2002; Giovannetti 2014; Casey 2017). Migratory movements organized by foreign employers with a predilection for segregated workforces created highly visible enclaves, with racial and cultural divides made salient (Bourgois 1989; Putnam 2014a).

Yet even at the height of US canal-building and banana-planting, circum-Caribbean migration included far more own-account mobility than employer-organized contracting: including the entirety of women's labor migration, which made up as much as one-third of total departures from the British Caribbean in the early twentieth century. Female predominance was strongest among the Jamaicans, Barbadians, and Trinidadians who left for Harlem and Brooklyn in accelerating numbers by the early 1920s. Indeed, by 1924 more British Caribbean women and girls lived in New York City than in either Kingston or Port of Spain (Putnam 2016c).

Overall the degree of return or sequential migration varied widely among subcircuits of the Greater Caribbean, as did the numbers of men versus women arriving. So did the degree to which these French or English patois-speaking Afrodescended newcomers created distinct communities of their own, or instead blended among the Spanish- or patois-speaking locals they encountered. The latter pattern could lead to retroactive erasure of the very fact of cross-border movement. Conversely, as national leaders sought to assert control over borders, taxes, and loyalties, these mixed borderlands could face fierce intervention, geared to make black border-crossers hypervisible as aliens rather than invisible as neighbors. This is the story of the Dominican-Haitian frontier, where the Trujillo regime's active efforts to disempower and disenfranchise Haitian migrants and their descendants have been revealed by an extraordinary series of recent research (Derby 1994; Turits 2002; Paulino 2005, 2006; Hintzen 2016).

Even beyond Hispaniola's particularly fraught internal frontier, the tense counterpoint between grassroots transnational ties and state-asserted barriers to them resonated across the interwar Greater Caribbean. On the one hand, as men, women, children, remittances, and news circulated within dense circuits of ongoing connection, wrestling their way toward upward mobility in the face of racisms encountered, the region saw a flowering of black-led transnational civic organizations, of which Marcus Garvey's Universal Negro Improvement Association (UNIA) is the largest and best known (Giovannetti and Roman 2003; Guridy 2010; Hill 2011; Corinealdi 2011; Putnam 2013; Sullivan 2014; Davidson 2015; Morris 2016). On the other hand, these same years saw the heyday of scientific racism, international white supremacism, and ethnically-defined populisms, all of which converged in the imposition of new barriers to cross-border movement and new vulnerabilities for non-citizens of color. Scholars have located in this conjuncture the drivers of the era's manifold black internationalism, as Afro-Caribbean sojourners articulated new visions of peoplehood, destiny, and rights and forged new alliances to give them force (James 1998; Parascandola 2005; Makalani 2011; Putnam 2013).

Entwined with these developments were technological shifts with profound impact on the means and reach of transnational connection. The spread of literacy and linotype meant that local black newspapers sprung up in multiple sites, and the increasing density of shipping meant that the new papers circulated between sites with ease. Articles were reprinted and read far from home. In city after city, the local black press became a window offering a panoramic view of the struggles of Afrodescendants elsewhere (Seigel 2009; Andrews 2010a; Alberto 2011; Andrews 2016, 67–87; Putnam 2016a; Alamo Pastrana 2016; Flórez Bolívar 2016). The circulation of recorded music, in particular Afro-associated genres like tango, *son*, calypso, *cumbia*, and *plena*, created another realm of self-conscious intradiasporic encounter (Waxer 1994; Wade 2000; Allen 2012; Hertzman 2013; Madrid and Moore 2013; Putnam 2013, 2016b; see also Chapter 11).

The new media undergirded new ideas of supranational belonging. They also sped the spread of race-conscious social and political organizations. Some had formal supranational structures, Garvey's UNIA most prominent among them. Many others remained either local or national in their organization and their targets of political pressure, yet drew inspiration and tactics from the movements elsewhere which they could now closely follow. We see this among Afrodescended communities in Uruguay, Brazil, Colombia, and Cuba, as well as among communities of British Caribbean ancestry in Panama, Costa Rica, and beyond (Andrews 2010b; Alberto 2011; Corinealdi 2013; Flórez Bolívar 2016).

By the time the U-Boat scares of World War II followed the economic crises of the Great Depression, unfettered movement for Afrodescendants around the Greater Caribbean was largely a thing of the past. Those British Caribbean sojourners who had settled in the Spanish-speaking republics (a mere fraction of those who passed through, yet still several hundred thousand in all) began a multigenerational process of becoming Afro-Latin. Variegated local paths of cultural and social integration and fraught national politics of formal citizenship would together shape this process, which by the 1970s and 80s had sharply attenuated any ties to grandparents' home islands (Martínez 1999; Charlton 2005; Senior Angulo 2007; Nwankwo 2009; Crawford 2011; Szok 2012; Whitney and Chailloux Laffita 2013; Putnam 2014b; Queeley 2017).

## THE "US CENTURY" FOR AFRO-LATIN AMERICA: 1940S–?

The twentieth century would be marked by the increasing weight of the United States within transnational Afro-Latin circuits: both those driven by human mobility, and those built on the mobility of media. Although further immigration to the United States from Europe's Caribbean colonies was blocked in 1924, migration from US neocolonies in the Caribbean continued and, in the wake of World War II, accelerated and spread. Puerto Rican Harlem, Philadelphia, and Chicago and the Dominican

Bronx joined Cuban Miami and Tampa as Afro-Latin centers in the continental United States (Greenbaum 2002; Haslip-Vieira, Falcón, and Matos Rodríguez 2004; Hoffnung-Garskof 2008; Duany 2011). Shipping routes and naval bases created new instances of the personal ties and transport infrastructure that drive focalized migration, and thus, densely particular Afro-Latin immigrant communities grew: Garifuna Los Angeles, Honduran New Orleans, British West Indian Panamanians in Brooklyn.

Each community was tied to households back home by the circulation of children, remittances, and consumer goods, even as each also built new ties (and found new tensions) with the receiving society around it. Settling in cities with large already-existing populations of immigrants and people of color, Afro-Latinos found themselves navigating a US taxonomy of race, ethnicity, and identity in which immigrant, Latino, and black were presumed to be exclusive rather than overlapping categories (Candelario 2007; Flores 2009; Rivera-Rideau, Jones, and Paschel 2016; see also Chapter 15). In a sense, they too were confronted with a multigenerational process of becoming Afro-Latin.

Distinct, and as yet understudied, were the migratory flows that carried Afrodescendants across "South-South" borders: Haitians to the Dominican Republic and the Bahamas, Dominicans to Puerto Rico, Afro-Colombians to Venezuela, Guyanese to Brazil, Brazilians to Uruguay. Racialization, xenophobia, citizenship struggles, and community formation in each case have been just as fraught, sometimes more so, as in the North American case. Meanwhile, smaller in scale but still visible are the flows of third-generation British Caribbean-descendants departing the Cuban, Dominican, or Panamanian economies of their birth for their grandparents' Jamaica, Barbados, or Trinidad: or reuniting with literal or metaphorical cousins from those islands in London, Toronto, or Brooklyn.

Meanwhile, in the post-World War II era, forms of media that supported transnational resonance of black politics and black popular culture proliferated. The weight of US politics and popular culture intensified. Increasingly, though, the US-based popular culture spilling outward was itself Afro-Latin, from salsa to bachata to reggaeton (Allen and Wilcken 1998; Waxer 2002; Fernandez 2006; Rivera, Marshall, and Pacini-Hernandez 2009; Rivera-Rideau 2015; Abreu 2015). As before, expressive culture – and music in particular – functioned as a rich site for the recognition of commonality across difference. Sometimes that commonality was framed in terms of shared cultural roots, other times in terms of common current oppressions. Increasingly, twentieth and twenty-first-century Afro-Atlantic music has stressed both at once, via lyrics and rhythmic/chromatic references alike.

A wealth of recent research has upended binary frameworks that once saw traditional/authentic/local and modern/commercial/cosmopolitan as opposing poles. Rather, scholars show us how musical practices understood as local gain political valence precisely in the context of consumers' engagement with cosmopolitan musical scenes. In sites across the Afro-Americas, by the last third of the twentieth century musical claim-staking over the diversity of "black" and "African" essences powered dances and politics alike. Consider three case studies.

Heidi Feldman has reconstructed how Lima-based activists began looking to the Afrodescended hinterlands of Pacific Peru as a source of African musical traditions in the late 1950s, their quest shaped by global events (Third World decolonization; US civil rights organizing) that raised the cachet of Afro-linked cultural roots. Feldman posits the "Black Pacific" as a human geography spread across multiple Latin American nations, within which African cultural resonance is linked to ruralness, isolation, and preservation (Feldman 2007). Yet the activists' engagement with these spaces was anything but hermetic. Like black activists in Uruguay in the same years (Andrews 2010a), Afro-Peruvian musical entrepreneurs looked to Afro-Cubans, Afro-Brazilians, and Afro-North Americans as well for exemplars of black cultural radicalism.

Meanwhile, musicologist Kenneth Bilby reports that in those same 1970s, Surinamese Creoles (from coastal areas firmly within the colonial cultural domain) began looking to previously denigrated Maroon communities for traces of African cultural resistance. Here too the context included both national and international events, including Surinam's formal independence and accelerating migration to the Dutch metropole. And here too, musical fusions mapped out an eclectic but meaningful array of Afro-diasporic connection. Genres created by Creole and Maroon musicians and their publics in this era ranged from "Sranan Bubbling," a "fusion of kaseko with Jamaican reggae and dance-hall rhythms" to "Fonki (Funky) Aleke," a "distinctive substyle of aleke with rhythmic structure derived in part from US funk instrumentation" (Bilby 1999, 286).

And meanwhile, in the same 1970s, politically engaged party-goers in Rio de Janeiro were embracing Afro-American funk music alongside a collective self-identification as "black" and the term "Black Power." Their racially defined, loud, and funky street parties took the opening that the waning military dictatorship offered, and leveraged US labels and rhythms to challenge Brazil's own racial inequalities (Alberto 2009).

CONCLUSION

Summarizing her findings on the social meaning of music for Haitians in the diaspora (or aspiring to leave home for diaspora), Elizabeth McAlister observes, "Music making is one way individuals and groups position themselves towards privileged geographies and locate themselves in the spaces they construct . . . [I]magined geographies of diaspora feature multiple horizons . . . and can be focused on Haiti, the Dominican Republic, or all of Hispaniola and simultaneously on a past Kongo Kingdom or on the future Christian Kingdom of God. These cognitive maps, in turn, open up possibilities for multiethnic networks and forms of group belonging" (McAlister 2012, 27).

McAlister's notion of "cognitive maps," "imagined geographies of diaspora" that both reflect past connections and shape future ones, pushes us to recognize that non-material lines of transnational connection can have concrete consequences for individuals and groups alike. Music, religion, news media, and other cultural products circulate and overlap, reflecting past lines of connection and shaping new ones. The circulation of media takes place not in a vacuum, but within transnational social fields built by the daily labors – physical, emotional, intellectual, organizational – of each generation of Afro-Latin Americans in turn. The imagined geographies of diaspora shift and stretch in consequence. The transnational frames of Afro-Latin experience are not new, but they are made anew in each era, by the lives and actions of those who see themselves within them.

BIBLIOGRAPHY

Abreu, Christina D. 2015. *Rhythms of Race Cuban Musicians and the Making of Latino New York City and Miami, 1940–1960.* Chapel Hill, NC: University of North Carolina Press.
Adderley, Rosanne. 2002. "'African Americans' and 'Creole Negroes': Black Migration and Colonial Interpretations of 'Negro' Diversity in Nineteenth-Century Trinidad." In *Marginal Migrations: The Circulation of Cultures within the Caribbean,* edited by Shalini Puri, 17–42. London: Macmillan Education/Warwick University Caribbean Studies Series.
2006. *'New Negroes from Africa:' Slave Trade Abolition and Free African Settlement in the Nineteenth-Century Caribbean.* Bloomington, IN: Indiana University Press.
Aizpurúa, Ramón. 2011. "Revolution and Politics in Venezuela and Curaçao, 1795–1800." In *Curaçao in the Age of Revolutions, 1795–1800,* edited by Wim Klooster and Gert Oostindie, 97–123. Leiden: KITLV Press.

Alamo Pastrana, Carlos. 2016. *Seams of Empire: Race and Radicalism in Puerto Rico and the United States.* Gainesville, FL: University Press of Florida.

Alberto, Paulina. 2009. "When Rio Was *Black*: Soul Music, National Culture, and the Politics of Racial Comparison in 1970s Brazil." *Hispanic American Historical Review* 89, 1: 3–39.

2011. *Terms of Inclusion: Black Intellectuals in Twentieth-Century Brazil.* Chapel Hill, NC: University of North Carolina Press.

Allen, Ray and Lois Wilcken, eds. 1998. *Island Sounds in the Global City: Caribbean Popular Music and Identity in New York.* Urbana, IL: University of Illinois Press.

Allen, Rose Mary. 2012. "Music in Diasporic Context: The Case of Curaçao and Intra-Caribbean Migration." *Black Music Research Journal* 32, 2: 51–65.

Anderson, Jennifer L. 2012. *Mahogany: The Costs of Luxury in Early America.* Cambridge, MA: Harvard University Press.

Andrews, George Reid. 1991. *Blacks and Whites in São Paulo, Brazil, 1888–1988.* Madison: University of Wisconsin Press.

2004. *Afro-Latin America, 1800–2000.* New York, NY: Oxford University Press.

2010a. "Afro-World: African-Diaspora Thought and Practice in Montevideo, Uruguay, 1830–2000," *The Americas* 67, 1: 83–107.

2010b. *Blackness in the White Nation: A History of Afro-Uruguay.* Chapel Hill, NC: University of North Carolina Press.

2016. *Afro-Latin America: Black Lives, 1600–2000.* Cambridge, MA: Harvard University Press.

Barcia, Manuel. 2012. *The Great African Slave Revolt of 1825: Cuba and the Fight for Freedom in Matanzas.* Baton Rouge: Louisiana State University Press.

2014. *West African Warfare in Bahia and Cuba: Soldier Slaves in the Atlantic World, 1807–1844.* New York, NY: Oxford University Press.

Bassi, Ernesto. 2012. "Turning South before Swinging East: Geopolitics and Geopolitical Imagination in the Southwestern Caribbean after the American Revolution." *Itinerario* 36, 3: 107–32.

2017. *An Aqueous Territory: Sailor Geographies and New Granada's Transimperial Greater Caribbean World.* Durham, NC: Duke University Press.

Beatty-Medina, Charles. 2012. "Between the Cross and the Sword: Religious Conquest and Maroon Legitimacy in Colonial Esmeraldas." In *Africans to Spanish America: Expanding the Diaspora*, edited by Sherwin Bryant, Rachel O'Toole, and Ben Vinson, 95–113. Urbana, IL: University of Illinois Press.

Bilby, Kenneth. 1999. "'Roots Explosion': Indigenization and Cosmopolitanism in Contemporary Surinamese Popular Music." *Ethnomusicology* 43, 2: 256–96.

Blier, Suzanne Preston. 1995. *African Vodun: Art, Psychology, and Power.* Chicago, IL: University of Chicago Press.

Borucki, Alex. 2009. "The 'African Colonists' of Montevideo. New Light on the Illegal Slave Trade to Rio de Janeiro and the Río de la Plata (1830–1842)." *Slavery and Abolition* 30, 3: 427–44.

2011. "The Slave Trade to the Río de la Plata. Trans-Imperial Networks and Atlantic Warfare, 1777–1812." *Colonial Latin American Review* 20, 1: 81–107.

2012. "Trans-Imperial History in the Making of the Slave Trade to Venezuela, 1526–1811." *Itinerario* 36, 2: 29–54.

2015. *From Shipmates to Soldiers: Emerging Black Identities in the Río de la Plata*. Albuquerque, NM: University of New Mexico Press.

2017. "Across Imperial Boundaries: Black Social Networks across the Iberian South Atlantic, 1760–1810." *Atlantic Studies* 14, 1: 11–36.

Borucki, Alex, David Wheat, and David Eltis. 2015. "Atlantic History and the Slave Trade to Spanish America." *American Historical Review* 120, 2: 433–61.

Bourgois, Philippe. 1989. *Ethnicity at Work: Divided Labor on a Central American Banana Plantation*. Baltimore, MD: Johns Hopkins University Press.

Brereton, Bridget. 1981. *A History of Modern Trinidad, 1783–1962*. Port of Spain, Trinidad: Heinemann.

Brown, David H. 2003. *Santería Enthroned: Art, Ritual, and Innovation in an Afro-Cuban Religion*. Chicago, IL: University of Chicago Press.

Byrd, Brandon R. 2015. "Black Republicans, Black Republic: African-Americans, Haiti, and the Promise of Reconstruction." *Slavery & Abolition* 36, 4: 545–67.

Cáceres, Rina, and Paul Lovejoy, eds. 2008. *Haití. Revolución y emancipación*. San José, Costa Rica: Editorial UCR.

Calagé, Carla, Raphael Dalleo, Luis Duno-Gottberg, Clevis Headley, eds. 2013. *Haiti and the Americas*. Jackson: University Press of Mississippi.

Candelario, Ginetta E. B. 2007. *Black behind the Ears: Dominican Racial Identity from Museums to Beauty Shops*. Durham, NC: Duke University Press.

Cândido, Mariana. 2013a. *An African Slaving Port and the Atlantic World: Benguela and Its Hinterland*. New York, NY: Cambridge University Press.

2013b. "South Atlantic Exchanges: The Role of Brazilian-Born Agents in Benguela, 1650–1850." *Luso-Brazilian Review* 50, 1: 53–82.

Candlin, Kit. 2012. *The Last Caribbean Frontier, 1795–1815*. New York, NY: Palgrave Macmillan.

Casey, Matthew. 2017. *Empire's Guest Workers: Haitian Migrants in Cuba during the Age of US Occupation*. New York, NY: Cambridge University Press.

Charlton, Audrey K. 2005. "'Cat Born in Oven Is not Bread': Jamaican and Barbadian Immigrants in Cuba between 1900 and 1959." PhD diss., Columbia University.

Childs, Matt. 2006. *The 1812 Aponte Rebellion in Cuba and the Struggle against Atlantic Slavery*. Chapel Hill, NC: University of North Carolina Press.

Chinea, Jorge. 2005. *Race and Labor in the Hispanic Caribbean: The West Indian Immigrant Worker Experience in Puerto Rico, 1800–1850*. Gainesville, FL: University Press of Florida.

Clavin, Patricia. 2005. "Defining Transnationalism." *Contemporary European History* 14, 4: 421–39.

Cooper, Frederick. 2001. "What Is 'Globalization' Good For? An African Historian's Perspective." *African Affairs* 100: 189–213.

Corinealdi, Kaysha. 2011. "Redefining Home: West Indian Panamanians and Transnational Politics of Race, Citizenship, and Diaspora, 1928–1970." PhD diss., Yale University.

———. 2013. "Envisioning Multiple Citizenships: West Indian Panamanians and Creating Community in the Canal Zone Neocolony." *The Global South* 6, 2:87–106.

Crawford, Sharika. 2011. "A Transnational World Fractured but not Forgotten: British West Indian Migration to the Colombian Islands of San Andrés and Providence." *New West Indian Guide/Nieu West-Indische Gids* 85, 1–2: 31–52.

———. 2013. "Politics of Belonging on a Caribbean Borderland: The Colombian Islands of San Andrés and Providencia." In *Crossing Boundaries: Ethnicity, Race, and National Belonging in a Transnational World*, edited by Brian D. Behnken and Simon Wendt, 19–37. Lanham, MD: Lexington Books.

Crawford, Sharika, and Ana Isabel Márquez. 2016. "A Contact Zone: A Turtle Commons in the Western Caribbean." *International Journal of Maritime History* 28, 1: 64–80.

Curto, José C., and Paul E. Lovejoy, eds. 2004. *Enslaving Connections: Changing Cultures of Africa and Brazil during the Era of Slavery.* Amherst, NY: Humanity Books/Prometheus Books.

Curto, José C., and Renée Soulodre-La France, eds. 2004. *Africa and the Americas: Interconnections during the Slave Trade.* Trenton, NJ: Africa World Press.

Cwik, Christian. 2010. "Curazao y Riohacha: Dos puertos caribeños en el marco del contrabando judío, 1650–1750." In *Ciudades portuarias en la Gran Cuenca del Caribe*, edited by Jorge Elías Caro and Antonino Vidal, 298–327. Barranquilla: Universidad del Norte.

Daniel, Evan Matthew. 2010. "Rolling for the Revolution: A Transnational History of Cuban Cigar Makers in Havana, Florida, and New York City, 1853–1895." PhD diss., New School University.

Da Silva, Daniel Domingues et al. 2014. "The Diaspora of Africans Liberated from Slave Ships in the Nineteenth Century." *Journal of African History* 55, 3: 347–69.

Davidson, Christina Cecelia. 2015. "Black Protestants in a Catholic Land: The AME Church in the Dominican Republic 1899–1916." *New West Indian Guide* 89: 258–88.

Derby, Lauren. 1994. "Haitians, Magic, and Money: Raza and Society in the Haitian-Dominican Borderlands, 1900 to 1937." *Comparative Studies in Society and History* 36, 3: 488–526.

Dessins, Nathalie. 2007. *From Saint-Domingue to New Orleans: Migration and Influences.* Gainesville, FL: University Press of Florida.

Dillon, Elizabeth Maddock, and Michael Drexler, eds. 2016. *Haiti and the Early United States: Histories, Geographies, Textualities.* Philadelphia, PA: University of Pennsylvania Press.

Dorsey, Joseph C. 2003. *Slave Traffic in the Age of Abolition: Puerto Rico, West Africa, and the Non-Hispanic Caribbean, 1815–1859.* Gainesville, FL: University Press of Florida, 2003.

Duany, Jorge. 2011. *Blurred Borders: Transnational Migration between the Hispanic Caribbean and the United States*. Chapel Hill, NC: University of North Carolina Press.

Dubois, Laurent. 2004. *A Colony of Citizens: Revolution and Slave Emancipation in the French Caribbean, 1787–1804*. Chapel Hill, NC: University of North Carolina Press

   2006. "An Enslaved Enlightenment: Rethinking the Intellectual History of the French Atlantic." *Social History* 31, 1: 1–14.

Dubois, Laurent, and Julius Scott. 2010. *Origins of the Black Atlantic*. New York, NY: Routledge.

Dun, James Alexander. 2016. *Dangerous Neighbors: Making the Haitian Revolution in Early America*. Philadelphia, PA: University of Pennsylvania Press.

Echeverri, Marcela. 2016. *Indian and Slave Royalists in the Age of Revolutions: Reform, Revolution, and Royalism in the Northern Andes, 1780–1825*. New York, NY: Cambridge University Press.

Eller, Anne. 2016. *We Dream Together: Dominican Independence, Haiti, and the Fight for Caribbean Freedom*. Durham, NC: Duke University Press.

Eltis, David, and David Richardson. 2010. *Atlas of the Transatlantic Slave Trade*. New Haven, CT: Yale University Press.

   eds. 2008. *Extending the Frontiers: Essays on the New Transatlantic Slave Trade Database*. New Haven, CT: Yale University Press.

   2008b. "A New Assessment of the Transatlantic Slave Trade." In *Extending the Frontiers: Essays on the New Transatlantic Slave Trade Database*, edited by David Eltis and David Richardson, 1–62. New Haven, CT: Yale University Press.

Eltis, David, Stephen D. Behrendt, Manolo Florentino, and David Richardson. 2013. *Voyages: The Trans-Atlantic Slave Trade Database*. Emory University. www.slavevoyages.org.

Euraque, Darío A., Jeffrey L. Gould, and Charles R. Hale, eds. 2004. *Memorias del mestizaje: Cultura política en Centroamérica de 1920 al presente*. Antigua, Guatemala: Centro de Investigaciones Regionales de Mesoamérica.

Everingham, Mark, and Edwin Taylor. 2009. "Encounters of Moravian Missionaries with Miskitu Autonomy and Land Claims in Nicaragua, 1894–1936." *Journal of Moravian History* 7: 31–57.

Falola, Toyin, and Matt D. Childs, eds. 2005. *The Yoruba Diaspora in the Atlantic World*. Bloomington, IN: Indiana University Press.

Fanning, Sara. 2007. "The Roots of Early Black Nationalism: Northern African Americans' Invocations of Haiti in the Early Nineteenth Century." *Slavery & Abolition* 28, 1: 61–85.

   2015. *Caribbean Crossing: African Americans and the Haitian Emigration Movement*. New York, NY: New York University Press.

Feldman, Heidi. 2007. *Black Rhythms of Peru: Reviving African Musical Heritage in the Black Pacific*. Middletown, CT: Wesleyan University Press.

Fernández, Raúl A. 2006. *From Afro-Cuban Rhythms to Latin Jazz*. Berkeley, CA: University of California Press.

Ferreira, Roquinaldo. 2007. "Atlantic Microhistories: Mobility, Personal Ties, and Slaving in the Black Atlantic World (Angola and Brazil)." In *Cultures of the Lusophone Black Atlantic*, edited by Nancy Priscilla Naro, Roger Sansi-Roca, and David Treece, 99–128. New York, NY: Palgrave Macmillan.

2008. "The Suppression of the Slave Trade and Slave Departures from Angola, 1830s–1860s." In *Extending the Frontiers: Essays on the New Transatlantic Slave Trade Database*, edited by David Eltis and David Richardson, 313–34. New Haven, CT: Yale University Press.

2014. *Cross-Cultural Exchange in the Atlantic World: Angola and Brazil during the Era of the Slave Trade*. New York, NY: Cambridge University Press.

Ferrer, Ada. 2012. "Haiti, Free Soil, and Antislavery in the Revolutionary Atlantic." *American Historical Review* 117, 1: 40–66.

2014. *Freedom's Mirror: Cuba and Haiti in the Age of Revolution*. New York, NY: Cambridge University Press.

Finch, Aisha K. 2015. *Rethinking Slave Rebellion in Cuba: La Escalera and the Insurgencies of 1841–1844*. Chapel Hill, NC: University of North Carolina Press.

Flores, Juan. 2009. *The Diaspora Strikes Back: Caribeño Tales of Learning and Turning*. New York, NY: Routledge.

Flórez Bolívar, Francisco Javier. 2016. "En sus propios términos: Negros y mulatos y sus luchas por la igualdad en Colombia, 1885–1947." PhD diss., University of Pittsburgh.

Fromont, Cécile. 2013. "Dancing for the King of Congo from Early Modern Central Africa to Slavery-Era Brazil." *Colonial Latin American Review* 22, 2: 184–208.

Gaffield, Julia. 2015. *Haitian Connections in the Atlantic World: Recognition after Revolution*. Chapel Hill, NC: University of North Carolina Press.

Garraway, Doris L., ed. 2008. *Tree of Liberty: The Haitian Revolution in the Atlantic World*. Charlottesville, VA: University of Virginia Press.

Gaspar, David Barry, and David Geggus, eds. 1997. *A Turbulent Time: The French Revolution and the Greater Caribbean*, Bloomington, IN: Indiana University Press.

Geggus, David, ed. 2001. *The Impact of the Haitian Revolution in the Atlantic World*. Columbia: University of South Carolina Press.

Geggus, David, and Norman Fiering, eds. 2008. *The World of the Haitian Revolution*. Bloomington, IN: Indiana University Press.

Gilroy, Paul. 1993. *The Black Atlantic: Modernity and Double Consciousness*. Cambridge, MA: Harvard University Press.

Giovannetti, Jorge. 2014. "Migración en las Antillas: Episodios de transterritorialidad, 1804–1945." In *Historia comparada de las Antillas*, edited by José A. Piqueras, 595–616. Madrid: CSIC.

Giovannetti, Jorge L., and Reinaldo L Roman, eds. 2003. *Caribbean Studies Special Issue: Garveyism in the Hispanic Caribbean* 31, 1: 1–260.

Gomes, Flávio dos Santos. 2002. "A 'Safe Haven': Runaway Slaves, Mocambos, and Borders in Colonial Amazonia, Brazil." *Hispanic American Historical Review* 82, 3: 469–98.

Gómez, Pablo F. 2013. "The Circulation of Bodily Knowledge in the Seventeenth-Century Black Spanish Caribbean." *Social History of Medicine* 26, 3: 383–402.

———. 2014. "Incommensurable Epistemologies? The Atlantic Geography of Healing in the Early Modern Black Spanish Caribbean." *Small Axe: A Caribbean Journal of Criticism* 44: 95–107.

Gonzalez, John Henry. 2014. "Defiant Haiti: Free-Soil Runaways, Ship Seizures and the Politics of Diplomatic Non-Recognition in the Early Nineteenth Century." *Slavery and Abolition* 35, 2: 124–35.

Gordon, Edmund T. 1998. *Disparate Diasporas: Identity and Politics in an African Nicaraguan Community*. Austin, TX: University of Texas Press.

Graham, Richard. 1990. *Patronage and Politics in Nineteenth-Century Brazil*. Stanford, CA: Stanford University Press.

Grandin, Greg. 2014. *The Empire of Necessity: Slavery, Freedom, and Deception in the New World*. New York, NY: Metropolitan Books/Henry Holt.

Grandío Moráguez, Oscar. 2008. "The African Origins of Slaves arriving in Cuba, 1789–1865." In *Extending the Frontiers: Essays on the New Transatlantic Slave Trade Database*, edited by David Eltis and David Richardson, 176–204. New Haven, CT: Yale University Press.

Greenbaum, Susan D. 2002. *More Than Black: Afro-Cubans in Tampa*. Gainesville, FL: University Press of Florida.

Grinberg, Keila. 2016. "The Two Enslavements of Rufina: Slavery and International Relations on the Southern Border of Nineteenth-Century Brazil." *Hispanic American Historical Review* 96, 2: 259–90.

———. 2017. "Illegal Enslavement, International Relations, and International Law on the Southern Border of Brazil." *Law and History Review* 35, 1: 31–52.

Guran, Milton. 2007. "Agudás from Benin: 'Brazilian' Identity as a Bridge to Citizenship." In *Cultures of the Lusophone Black Atlantic*, edited by Nancy Priscilla Naro, Roger Sansi-Roca, and David Treece, 147–58. New York, NY: Palgrave Macmillan.

Guridy, Frank Andre. 2010. *Forging Diaspora: Afro-Cubans and African Americans in a World of Empire and Jim Crow*. Chapel Hill, NC: University of North Carolina Press.

Haslip-Vieira, Gabriel, Angelo Falcón, and Félix Matos Rodríguez, eds. 2004. *Boricuas in Gotham: Puerto Ricans in the Making of Modern New York City*. Princeton, NJ: Markus Wiener.

Hawthorne, Walter. 2010. *From Africa to Brazil: Culture, Identity, and an Atlantic Slave Trade, 1600–1830*. New York, NY: Cambridge University Press.

Helg, Aline. 2004. *Liberty and Equality in Caribbean Colombia, 1770–1835*. Chapel Hill, NC: University of North Carolina Press.

Hertzman, Marc A. 2013. *Making Samba: A New History of Race and Music in Brazil*. Durham, NC: Duke University Press.

Heywood, Linda M., ed. 2002. *Central Africans and Cultural Transformations in the American Diaspora*. New York, NY: Cambridge University Press.

Hill, Robert A., ed. 2011. *The Marcus Garvey and Universal Negro Improvement Association Papers*, vol. 11, *The Caribbean Diaspora, 1910–1920*. Durham, NC: Duke University Press.

Hintzen, Amelia. 2016. "'A Veil of Legality': The Contested History of Anti-Haitian Ideology under the Trujillo Dictatorship." *New West Indian Guide* 90: 28–54.

Hodes Martha. 2006. *The Sea Captain's Wife: A True Story of Love, Race, and War in the Nineteenth Century*. New York, NY: W. W. Norton.

Hoffnung-Garskof, Jesse. 2008. *A Tale of Two Cities: Santo Domingo and New York after 1950*. Princeton, NJ: Princeton University Press.

Hu-DeHart, Evelyn, and Kathleen López, eds. 2008. Special issue, "Afro-Asia." *Afro-Hispanic Review* 27, 1: 1–256.

James, Winston. 1998. *Holding Aloft the Banner of Ethiopia: Caribbean Radicalism in Early Twentieth-Century America*. New York, NY: Verso.

Johnson, Lyman L. 2011. *Workshop of Revolution: Plebeian Buenos Aires and the Atlantic World, 1776–1810*. Durham, NC: Duke University Press.

Johnson, Rashauna. 2016. *Slavery's Metropolis: Unfree Labor in New Orleans during the Age of Revolutions*. New York, NY: Cambridge University Press.

Johnson, Sara E. 2012. *The Fear of French Negroes: Transcolonial Collaboration in the Revolutionary Americas*. Berkeley, CA: University of California Press.

Jones, Martha S. 2013. "The Case of Jean Baptiste, un Créole de Saint-Domingue: Narrating Slavery, Freedom, and the Haitian Revolution in Baltimore City." In *The American South and the Atlantic World*, edited by Brian Ward, Martin Bone, and William A. Link, 104–28. Gainesville, FL: University Press of Florida; University of Michigan Public Law Research Paper No. 376. Available at https://ssrn.com/abstract=2326760

Kelley, Robin D. G., and Tiffany Patterson. 2000. "Unfinished Migrations: Reflections on the African Diaspora and the Making of the Modern World." *African Studies Review* 43, 1: 11–45.

Khan, Aisha. 2004. *Callaloo Nation: Metaphors of Race and Religious Identity among South Asians in Trinidad*. Durham, NC: Duke University Press.

Klooster, Wim. 1998. *Illicit Riches: Dutch Trade in the Caribbean, 1648–1795*. Leiden: KITLV Press.

Krug, Jessica A. 2014. "Social Dismemberment, Social (Re)membering: Obeah Idioms, Kromanti Identities and the Trans-Atlantic Politics of Memory, c. 1675–Present." *Slavery & Abolition* 35, 4: 537–58.

Landers, Jane. 1990. "Gracia Real De Santa Teresa De Mose: A Free Black Town in Spanish Colonial Florida." *American Historical Review* 95, 1: 9–30.

2011. *Atlantic Creoles in the Age of Revolutions*. Cambridge, MA: Harvard University Press.

Lane, Kris. 1998. "Taming the Master: Brujería, Slavery, and the Encomienda in Barbacoas at the Turn of the Eighteenth Century." *Ethnohistory* 45, 3: 477–507.

Lasso, Marixa. 2007. *Myths of Harmony: Race and Republicanism during the Age of Revolution, Colombia, 1795–1831*. Pittsburgh, PA: University of Pittsburgh Press.

Laurence, K. O. 2011. "The Importation of Labour and the Contract Systems." In *General History of the Caribbean*, vol. 4, *The Long Nineteenth Century: Nineteenth-Century Transformations*, edited by K. O. Laurence, 191–222. Paris: UNESCO.

Law, Robin, and Kristin Mann. 1999. "West Africa in the Atlantic Community: The Case of the Slave Coast." *William and Mary Quarterly* 56, 2: 307–34.

Lawrence, Benjamin. 2014. *Amistad's Orphans: An Atlantic Story of Children, Slavery, and Smuggling*. New Haven, CT: Yale University Press.

Levitt, Peggy, and Nina Glick Schiller. 2004. "Conceptualizing Simultaneity: A Transnational Social Field Perspective on Society." *International Migration Review* 38, 145: 1002–1039.

Lewis, Laura A. 2012. *Chocolate and Corn Flour: History, Race and Place in the Making of "Black" Mexico*. Durham, NC: Duke University Press.

Lindsay, Lisa. 1994. "'To Return to the Bosom of Their Fatherland': Brazilian Immi-grants in Nineteenth-Century Lagos." *Slavery and Abolition* 15, 1: 22–50.

Lokken, Paul. 2004. "A Maroon Moment: Rebel Slaves in Early Seventeenth-Century Guatemala." *Slavery & Abolition* 25, 3: 44–58.

López, Kathleen. 2013. *Chinese Cubans: A Transnational History*. Chapel Hill, NC: University of North Carolina Press.

Lovejoy, Henry B. 2012. "Old Oyo Influences on the Transformation of Lucumí Identity in Colonial Cuba." PhD diss., UCLA.

2016. "The Registers of Liberated Africans of the Havana Slave Trade Commission: Implementation and Policy, 1824–1841." *Slavery & Abolition* 37, 1: 23–44.

Lovejoy, Paul, ed. 2009. *Identity in the Shadow of Slavery*. 2nd ed. London: Continuum. First published in 2000.

Madrid, Alejandro L. and Robin D. Moore. 2013. *Danzón: Circum-Caribbean Dialogues in Music and Dance*. New York, NY and London: Oxford University Press.

Makalani, Minkah. 2011. *In the Cause of Freedom: Radical Black Internationalism from Harlem to London, 1917–1939*. Chapel Hill, NC: University of North Carolina Press.

Mann, Kristen, and Edna Bay, eds. 2001. *Rethinking the African Diaspora: The Making of a Black Atlantic World in the Bight of Benin and Brazil*. London: Frank Cass.

Marín Araya, Giselle. 2004. "La población de Bocas del Toro y la Comarca Ngöbe-Buglé hasta inicios del siglo XIX." *Anuario de Estudios Centroamericanos* 30, 1–2: 119–62.

Martínez, Samuel. 1999. "From Hidden Hand to Heavy Hand: Sugar, the State, and Migrant Labor in Haiti and the Dominican Republic," *Latin American Research Review* 34, 1: 57–84.

Matory, J. Lorand. 1999. "The English Professors of Brazil: On the Diasporic Roots of the Yorùbá Nation." *Comparative Studies in Society and History* 41, 1: 72–103.

2005. *Black Atlantic Religion: Tradition, Transnationalism, and Matriarchy in the Afro-Brazilian Candomblé*. Princeton, NJ: Princeton University Press.

2006. "The 'New World' Surrounds an Ocean: Theorizing the Live Dialogue between African and African American Cultures." In *Afro-Atlantic Dialogues: Anthropology in the Diaspora*, edited by Kevin A. Yelvington, 151–92. Santa Fe: School of American Research Press.

2009. "The Many Who Dance in Me: Afro-Atlantic Ontology and the Problem with 'Transnationalism.'" In *Transnational Transcendence: Essays on Religion and Globalization*, edited by T. J. Csordas, 231–62. Berkeley, CA: University of California Press.

2014. "From 'Survival' to 'Dialogue': Analytic Tropes in the Study of African-Diaspora Cultural History." In *Transatlantic Caribbean: Dialogues of People, Practices, Ideas*, edited by Ingrid Kummels, Claudia Rauhut, Stefan Rinke, and Birte Timm, 33–56. Bielefeld, Germany: Transcript Verlag.

Mayes, April. 2014. *The Mulatto Republic: Class, Race, and Dominican National Identity*. Gainesville, FL: University Press of Florida.

McAlister, Elizabeth. 2012. "Listening for Geographies: Music as Sonic Compass Pointing toward African and Christian Diasporic Horizons in the Caribbean." *Black Music Research Journal* 32, 2: 25–50.

McKnight, Kathryn Joy. 2003. "'En su tierra lo aprendió': An African Curandero's Defense before the Cartagena Inquisition." *Colonial Latin American Review* 12, 1: 63–84.

Midlo-Hall, Gwendolyn. 2005. *Slavery and African Ethnicities in the Americas: Restoring the Links*. Chapel Hill, NC: University of North Carolina Press.

Miki, Yuko. 2011. "Diasporic Africans and Postcolonial Brazil: Notes on the Intersection of Diaspora, Transnationalism, and Nation." *História Unisinos* 15, 1: 126–130. doi: 10.4013/htu.2011.151.14

Miller, Joseph C., ed. 2015. *The Princeton Companion to Atlantic History*. Princeton, NJ: Princeton University Press.

Mintz, Sidney. 1985. *Sweetness and Power: The Place of Sugar in Modern History*. New York, NY: Viking Penguin.

Mirabal, Nancy Raquel. 2001. "'No Country but the One We Must Fight for': The Emergence of an Antillean Nation and Community in New York City, 1860–1901." In *Mambo Montage: The Latinization of New York*, edited by Arlene Dávila and Augustín Laó-Montes, 57–72. New York, NY: Columbia University Press.

2017. *Suspect Freedoms: The Racial and Sexual Politics of Cubanidad in New York, 1823–1957*. New York, NY: New York University Press.

Mobley, Christina Frances. 2015. "The Kongolese Atlantic: Central African Slavery & Culture from Mayombe to Haiti." PhD diss., Duke University.

Monsma, Karl, and Valéria Dorneles Fernandes. 2013. "Fragile Liberty: The Enslavement of Free People in the Borderlands of Brazil and Uruguay, 1846–1866." *Luso-Brazilian Review* 50, 1: 7–25.

Morgan, Philip D. 1997. "The Cultural Implications of the Atlantic Slave Trade: African Regional Origins, American Destinations and New World Developments." *Slavery and Abolition* 18, 1: 122–45.

Morris, Courtney Desiree. 2016. "Becoming Creole, Becoming Black: Migration, Diasporic Self-Making, and the Many Lives of Madame Maymie Leona Turpeau de Mena." *Women, Gender, and Families of Color* 4, 2: 171–95.

Muller, Dalia. 2017. *Cuban Emigres and Independence in the Nineteenth Century Gulf World*. Chapel Hill, NC: University of North Carolina Press.

Munasinghe, Viranjini. 2001. *Callaloo or Tossed Salad? East Indians and the Cultural Politics of Identity in Trinidad*. Ithaca: Cornell University Press.

Munroe, Martin, and Elizabeth Walcott, eds. 2008. *Echoes of the Haitian Revolution, 1804–2004.* Mona, Jamaica: University of the West Indies Press.

Naro, Nancy Priscilla. 2007. "Colonial Aspirations: Connecting Three Points of the Portuguese Black Atlantic." In *Cultures of the Lusophone Black Atlantic,* edited by Nancy Priscilla Naro, Roger Sansi-Roca, and David Treece, 129–46. New York, NY: Palgrave Macmillan.

Nessler, Graham. 2016. *An Islandwide Struggle for Freedom: Revolution, Emancipation, and Reenslavement in Hispaniola, 1789–1809.* Chapel Hill, NC: University of North Carolina Press.

Nwankwo, Ifeoma. 2005. *Black Cosmopolitanism: Racial Consciousness, and Transnational Identity in the Nineteenth-Century Americas.* Philadelphia, PA: University of Pennsylvania Press.

   ed. 2009. *African Routes, Caribbean Roots, Latino Lives.* Special issue of *Latin American and Caribbean Ethnic Studies* 4, 3: 221–317.

O'Malley, Gregory. 2014. *Final Passages: The Intercolonial Slave Trade of British America, 1619–1807.* Chapel Hill, NC: Omohundro Institute of Early American History and University of North Carolina Press.

Offen, Karl H. 1999. "The Miskitu Kingdom: Landscape and the Emergence of a Miskitu Ethnic Identity, Northeastern Nicaragua and Honduras, 1600–1800." PhD diss., University of Texas.

   2002. "The Sambo and Tawira Miskitu: The Colonial Origins and Geography of Intra-Miskitu Differentiation in Eastern Nicaragua and Honduras." *Ethnohistory* 49, 2: 319–72.

Ogundiran, Akinwumi, and Paula Saunders, eds. 2014. *Materialities of Ritual in the Black Atlantic.* Bloomington, IN: Indiana University Press.

Oostindie, Gert. 2011. "Slave Resistance, Colour Lines, and the Impact of the French and Haitian Revolutions." In *Curaçao in the Age of Revolutions 1795–1800*, edited by Wim Klooster and Gert Oostindie, 1–23. Leiden: KITLV Press.

Osterhammel, Jürgen. 2009. "A 'Transnational' History of Society: Continuity or New Departure?" In *Comparative and Transnational History: Central European Approaches and New Perspectives*, edited by Heinz-Gerhard Haupt and Jürgen Kocka, 39–51. New York and Oxford: Berghahn Books.

Palermo, Eduardo R. 2008. "Secuestros y tráfico de esclavos en la frontera uruguaya: Estudio de casos posteriores a 1850." *Revista Tema Livre*, 13. http://revistatemalivre.com/palermo13.html.

Palmer, Colin. 1998. "Defining and Studying the Modern African Diaspora." *Perspectives: American Historical Association Newsletter* 36, 6: 1, 22–25.

Palmié, Stephan. 2002. *Wizards and Scientists: Explorations in Afro-Cuban Modernity and Tradition.* Durham, NC: Duke University Press.

   2008, ed. *Africas in the Americas: Beyond the Search for Origins in the Study of Afro-Atlantic Religions.* Leiden: Brill.

Parascandola, Louis J., ed. 2005. *Look for Me All around You: Anglophone Caribbean Immigrants in the Harlem Renaissance.* Detroit: Wayne State University Press.

Parés, Luis Nicolau. 2001. "The Jeje in the Tambor de Mina of Maranhão and in the Candomblé of Bahia." *Slavery and Abolition* 22, 1: 83–90.

Paton, Diana, and Maarit Forde, eds. 2012. *Obeah and Other Powers: The Politics of Caribbean Religion and Healing.* Durham, NC: Duke University Press.

Paulino, Edward. 2005. "Erasing the Kreyol from the Margins of the Dominican Republic: The Pre- and Post-Nationalization Project of the Border, 1930–1945." *Wadabagei* 8, 2: 35–71.

2006. "Anti-Haitianism, Historical Memory, and the Potential for Genocidal Violence in the Dominican Republic." *Genocide Studies and Prevention: An International Journal* 1, 3: 265–88.

Pérez, Jr., Louis A. 2002. "We Are the World: Internationalizing the National, Nationalizing the International." *Journal of American History* 89, 2: 558–66.

Pérez Morales, Edgardo. 2017. "Tricks of the Slave Trade: Cuba and the Small-Scale Dynamics of the Spanish Transatlantic Trade." *New West Indian Guide* 91: 1–29.

Polyné, Millery. 2010. *From Douglass to Duvalier: U.S. African Americans, Haiti, and Pan-Americanism, 1870–1964.* Gainesville, FL: University Press of Florida.

Price, Richard. 2002. *First-Time: The Historical Vision of an African American People.* Chicago, IL: University of Chicago Press.

2006. "On the Miracle of Creolization." In *Afro-Atlantic Dialogues: Anthropology in the Diaspora*, edited by Kevin A. Yelvington, 115–48. Santa Fe: School of American Research Press.

Putnam, Lara. 2002. *The Company They Kept: Migrants and the Politics of Gender in Caribbean Costa Rica, 1870–1960.* Chapel Hill, NC: University of North Carolina Press.

2013. *Radical Moves: Caribbean Migrants and the Politics of Race in the Jazz Age.* Chapel Hill, NC: University of North Carolina Press.

2014a. "Borderlands and Border-Crossers: Migrants and Boundaries in the Greater Caribbean, 1840–1940." *Small Axe* 42: 7–21.

2014b. "The Panama Cannonball's Transnational Ties: Migrants, Sport, and Belonging in the Interwar Greater Caribbean." *Journal of Sport History* 31, 4: 401–24.

2016a. "Circum-Atlantic Print Circuits and Internationalism from the Peripheries in the Interwar Era." In *Print Culture Histories Beyond the Metropolis*, edited by James Connolly, 215–40. Toronto: University of Toronto Press.

2016b. "Jazzing Sheiks at the 25 cent Bram: Panama and Harlem as Caribbean Crossroads, circa 1910–1940." *Journal of Latin American Cultural Studies* 25, 3: 1–21.

2016c. "Cities of Women: Gender Divides in Circum-Caribbean Migration, 1880–1930." 32nd Annual Elsa Goveia Memorial Lecture, University of the West Indies, Mona, Jamaica.

Queeley, Andrea. 2017. "Pensions, Politics, and Soul Train: Anglo-Caribbean Diasporic Encounters with Guantánamo from the War to the Special Period." In *Caribbean Military Encounters: A Multidisciplinary Anthology from the Humanities*, edited by Shalini Puri and Lara Putnam. London and New York, NY: Palgrave Macmillan.

Reid-Vazquez, Michele. 2011. *The Year of the Lash: Free People of Color in Cuba and the Nineteenth-Century Atlantic World*. Athens: University of Georgia Press.

Reis, João José. 1993. *Slave Rebellion in Brazil: The Muslim Uprising of 1835 in Bahia*. Translated by Arthur Brakel. Baltimore, MD: Johns Hopkins University Press.

———. 2001. "Candomblé in Nineteenth-Century Bahia: Priests, Followers, Clients." *Slavery and Abolition* 22, 1: 91–115.

———. 2015. *Divining Slavery and Freedom: The Story of Domingos Sodré, an African Priest in Nineteenth-Century Brazil*. Translated by H. Sabrina Gledhill. New York, NY: Cambridge University Press.

Restall, Matthew. 2009. *The Black Middle: Africans, Mayas, and Spaniards in Colonial Yucatan*. Stanford, CA: Stanford University Press.

Rivera-Rideau, Petra R. 2015. *Remixing Reggaetón: The Cultural Politics of Race in Puerto Rico*. Durham, NC: Duke University Press.

Rivera-Rideau, Petra R., Jennifer A. Jones, and Tianna S. Paschel, eds. 2016. *Afro-Latin@s in Movement: Critical Approaches to Blackness and Transnationalism in the Americas*. New York, NY: Palgrave MacMillan.

Rivera, Raquel, Wayne Marshall, and Deborah Pacini-Hernandez, eds. 2009. *Reggaeton*. Durham, NC: Duke University Press.

Rupert, Linda M. 2012. *Creolization and Contraband: Curaçao in the Early Modern Atlantic World*. Athens: University of Georgia Press.

Sanders, James. 2004. *Contentious Republicans: Popular Politics, Race, and Class in Nineteenth-Century Colombia*: Durham, NC: Duke University Press.

Saunier, Pierre-Yves. 2013. *Transnational History*. Houndmills, Basingstoke: Palgrave Macmillan.

Schmidt-Nowara, Christopher. 1999. *Empire and Antislavery: Spain, Cuba, and Puerto Rico, 1833–74*. Pittsburgh, PA: University of Pittsburgh Press.

Schultz, Kara D. 2015. "'The Kingdom of Angola Is Not Very Far from Here': The South Atlantic Slave Port of Buenos Aires, 1585–1640." *Slavery and Abolition* 36, 3: 424–44.

Schwarz, Suzanne. 2012. "Reconstructing the Life Histories of Liberated Africans: Sierra Leone in the Early Nineteenth Century." *History in Africa* 39, 1: 194–201.

Scott, Julius. 1986. "The Common Winds: Currents of Afro-American Communication in the Era of the Haitian Revolution." PhD diss., Duke University.

Scott, Rebecca, and Jean M Hébrard. 2012. *Freedom Papers: An Atlantic Odyssey in the Age of Emancipation*. Cambridge, MA: Harvard University Press.

Scott, Rebecca J. 2005. *Degrees of Freedom: Louisiana and Cuba after Slavery*. Cambridge MA: Harvard University Press.

Seigel, Micol. 2009. *Uneven Encounters: Making Race and Nation in Brazil and the United States*. Durham, NC: Duke University Press.

Senior Angulo, Diana. 2007. "*La incorporación social en Costa Rica de la población afrocostarricense durante el siglo XX, 1927–1963*." MA thesis, Universidad de Costa Rica.

Shaw, Rosalind. 2002. *Memories of the Slave Trade: Ritual and the Historical Imagination in Sierra Leone*. Chicago, IL: University of Chicago Press.

Smith, Matthew. 2014. *Liberty, Fraternity, Exile: Haiti and Jamaica after Emancipation.* Chapel Hill, NC: University of North Carolina Press.

Soriano, Cristina. 2012. "Revolutionary Voices: The Presence of Visitors, Fugitives and Prisoners from the French Caribbean in Venezuela (1789–1799)." *Storia e Futuro, Rivista di Storia e Storiografia* 30.

2018. *Tides of Revolution: Information and Politics in Late Colonial Venezuela.* Albuquerque, NM: University of New Mexico Press.

Struck, Bernhard, Kate Ferris, and Jacques Revel. 2011. "Introduction. Space and Scale in Transnational History." *International History Review* 33, 4: 573–84.

Sublette, Ned. 2008. *The World That Made New Orleans: From Spanish Silver to Congo Square.* Chicago, IL: Lawrence Hill Books/Chicago Review Press.

Sullivan, Frances Peace. 2014. "'Forging Ahead' in Banes, Cuba: Garveyism in a United Fruit Company Town." *New West Indian Guide* 88: 231–61.

Sweet, James H. 2003. *Recreating Africa: Culture, Kinship, and Religion in the African-Portuguese World, 1441–1770.* Chapel Hill, NC: University of North Carolina Press.

Sweet, James. 2011. *Domingos Álvares, African Healing, and the Intellectual History of the Atlantic World.* Chapel Hill, NC: University of North Carolina Press.

Szok, Peter. 2012. *Wolf Tracks: Popular Art and Re-Africanization in Twentieth-Century Panama.* Jackson: University Press of Mississippi,

Thornton, John K. 2017. "The Zambos and the Transformation of the Miskitu Kingdom, 1636–1740." *Hispanic American Historical Review* 97, 1: 1–28.

Tompson, Doug. 2008. "Refugiados, libertos y esclavos asalariados: Entre la esclavitud y libertad en la costa atlántica de Honduras, ca. 1800." *Mesoamérica* 50: 96–111.

2012. "Between Slavery and Freedom on the Atlantic Coast of Honduras," *Slavery and Abolition* 33, 3: 403–16.

Toussaint, Michael. 2007. "Post-Abolition Trinidad-Venezuela Relations in the Nineteenth Century: The Problem of the Manumisos and Aprendizajes." *The Arts Journal* 3, 1–2: 184–201.

Turits, Richard Lee. 2002. "A World Destroyed, A Nation Imposed: The 1937 Haitian Massacre in the Dominican Republic." *Hispanic American Historical Review* 82, 3: 589–635.

Usner, Daniel H. 1992. *Indians, Settlers, and Slaves in a Frontier Exchange Economy: The Lower Mississippi Valley Before 1783.* Chapel Hill, NC: University of North Carolina Press for the Omohundro Institute of Early American History and Culture, Williamsburg, Virginia.

Vanhee, Hein. 2002. "Central African Popular Christianity and the Making of Haitian Vodou Religion." In *Central Africans and Cultural Transformations in the American Diaspora*, edited by Linda Heywood, 243–64. New York, NY: Cambridge University Press.

Vidal, Cécile, ed. 2013. *Louisiana: Crossroads of the Atlantic World.* Philadelphia, PA: University of Pennsylvania Press.

Wade, Peter. 1993. *Blackness and Race Mixture: The Dynamics of Racial Identity in Colombia*. Baltimore, MD: Johns Hopkins University Press.

2000. *Music, Race, and Nation: Música Tropical in Colombia*. Chicago, IL: University of Chicago Press.

Waxer, Lise. 1994. "Of Mambo Kings and Songs of Love: Dance Music in Havana and New York from the 1930s to the 1950s." *Latin American Music Review / Revista de Música Latinoamericana* 15, 2: 139–76.

2002. *The City of Musical Memory: Records, Salsa Grooves and Local Popular Culture in Cali, Colombia*. Middletown, CT: Wesleyan University Press.

Wheat, David. 2011. "The First Great Waves: African Provenance Zones for the Transatlantic Slave Trade to Cartagena de Indias, 1570–1640." *Journal of African History* 52, 1: 1–22.

2016. *Atlantic Africa and the Spanish Caribbean, 1570–1640*. Chapel Hill, NC: Omohundro Institute of Early American History and Culture/University of North Carolina Press.

White, Ashli. 2010. *Encountering Revolution: Haiti and the Making of the Early Republic*. Baltimore, MD: Johns Hopkins University Press.

Whitney, Robert, and Graciela Chailloux Laffita. 2013. *Subjects or Citizens: British Caribbean Workers in Cuba, 1900–1960*. Gainesville, FL: University Press of Florida.

Williams, Brackette F. 1991. *Stains on My Name, War in My Veins: Guyana and the Politics of Cultural Struggle*. Durham, NC: Duke University Press.

Wirzbicki, Peter. 2015. "'The Light of Knowledge Follows the Impulse of Revolutions': Prince Saunders, Baron de Vastey and the Haitian Influence on Antebellum Black Ideas of Elevation and Education." *Slavery and Abolition*, 36, 2: 275–97.

Yingling, Charlton. 2013. "No One Who Reads the History of Hayti Can Doubt the Capacity of Colored Men: Racial Formation and Atlantic Rehabilitation in New York City's Early Black Press, 1827–1841." *Early American Studies* 11, 2: 314–48.

2015. "The Maroons of Santo Domingo in the Age of Revolutions: Adaptation and Evasion, 1783–1800." *History Workshop Journal* 79: 25–51.

Young, Elliott. 2014. *Alien Nation: Chinese Migration in the Americas from the Coolie Era through World War II*. Chapel Hill, NC: University of North Carolina Press.

Zeuske, Michael. 2015. *Amistad: A Hidden Network of Slavers and Merchants*. Princeton, NJ: Markus Wiener.

# 15

## Afro-Latinos

### *Speaking through Silences and Rethinking the Geographies of Blackness*

### Jennifer A. Jones[1]

INTRODUCTION

In the landmark edited volume, *The Afro-Latin@ Reader*, Pablo "Yoruba" Guzmán recalls the impetus behind the formation of the Young Lords in New York in the 1960s.

> Our original viewpoint in founding the Party was a New York point of view – that's where the world started and ended. As we later found out, New York is different from most other cities that Puerto Ricans live in. But even in New York, we found that on a grass-roots level a high degree of racism existed between Puerto Ricans and Blacks, and between light-skinned and dark-skinned Puerto Ricans. We had to deal with this racism because it blocked any kind of growth for our people, any understanding of the things Black people had gone through. So rather than watching Rap Brown on TV, rather than learning from that and saying, "Well, that should affect me too," Puerto Ricans said, "Well, yeah, those Blacks got a hard time, you know, but we ain't going through the same thing." This was especially true for the light-skinned Puerto Ricans. Puerto Ricans like myself, who look like Afro-Americans, couldn't do that, 'cause to do that would be to escape into a kind of fantasy. Because before people called me a spic, they called me a nigger. So that was, like, one reason as to why we felt the Young Lords Party should exist
>
> (Jiménez Román and Flores 2010, 236).

Guzmán's sense of political efficacy was shaped not only by experiences of discrimination and injustice as a Puerto Rican, but by the role of race and skin color in shaping his experiences as an Afro-Latino: a person

---

[1] Portions of this chapter appear in "Introduction: Theorizing Afro-Latinidades" in *Afro-Latinos in Movement: Critical Approaches to Blackness and Transnationalism in the Americas*, edited by Petra Rivera-Rideau, Jennifer Jones, and Tianna Paschel. New York, NY: Palgrave MacMillan Press.

of both Afrodescendant and Latin American origins, living in the United States. Occupying such a space within the US landscape, in which the racial categories of black and Latino have been largely understood to be mutually exclusive, means that such a duality is often unintelligible and untenable. To be Afro-Latino means possessing a sophisticated, multivalent analysis of race and politics as shaped by personal experience. This complex existence at the intersection of various racialized experiences provides important insights into the construction of US racial categories and spaces, as well as Latin American racial formation.

This chapter examines the emerging field of Afro-Latino Studies and its relationship to Afro-Latin American Studies. It seeks to define and situate the field of Afro-Latino Studies, not necessarily as a coherent theoretical project, but rather as a coalescence of works from various disciplines and regional specialties that contribute to our understanding of blackness and *Latinidad* both in the United States and in Latin America. These works offer three core insights.

First, they are a source of critique. Afro-Latino Studies undermines efforts to marginalize and invisibilize Afrodescendants across the Americas, and their contributions to national identities, cultural production, economic development, social interaction, and geographies of race. It also questions the *mestizaje* paradigm, both hemispherically and within the US context, by examining a population that is fundamentally excluded from *mestizo* racial frameworks, and the work that such exclusion does to both trouble and reproduce racial boundaries.

Second, Afro-Latino Studies portrays and documents a group of people. While Afro-Latinos in the United States have never been a numerically large proportion of the US population, they have made an indelible mark on major metropoles such as New York, Miami, and Chicago. They have also contributed significantly to the social and political history of the hemisphere by projecting ideas and activism back out across the region. Afro-Latino Studies seeks to tell the story of this group of people and the contributions they have made to modern history.

Third, Afro-Latino Studies constitutes a theoretical position. As we see in the case of the Young Lords, Afro-Latinos are central to our understanding of race-making practices in the United States and Afro-Latin America. They serve to undermine *mestizo* nationalism, expand the boundaries of blackness, unpack within and between group conflicts, and open up our narratives of migration, citizenship, and diaspora.

Afro-Latino Studies seeks to illuminate and theorize the presence of black Latinos and *Afro-Latinidad* in the United States. The concept of

*Afro-Latinidad* seeks, in part, to examine how comparable conceptual meanings and experiences of blackness move and take root in various parts of the Americas. It also offers a critical analysis of the forces that sustain anti-blackness throughout the region, despite what many consider dramatically different national discourses about race.

Afro-Latino Studies has progressed in what I consider to be three major articulations: Puerto Rican Studies, the visibility/invisibility paradigm, and the transnational turn. Initiated by the Puerto Rican Studies literature in the 1960s and 1970s (see Flores 2009; Godreau 2015), the emergence of Afro-Latino Studies as a scholarly field corresponded to the demographic and political recognition of Latinos in the United States in the 1970s and 1980s as well as the increasing diversity of migratory streams from across the hemisphere in the same period (Rivera-Rideau, Jones, and Paschel 2016).

As Puerto Rican Studies continued to blossom and develop an analysis of race, coloniality, emplacement, migration, and transnational relations, the expanding diversity of Afro-Latin American migrants prompted a second theoretical perspective, crystallizing in the 1990s and 2000s. This perspective was aligned with work on Afro-Latin Americans more generally, in that it sought to make visible not just Afro-Dominicans, Afro-Cubans, and Afro-Puerto Ricans, but also Afro-Mexicans, Garifuna, and other Latino groups that have been invisible both in the United States and in Latin America more broadly. I call this analytical push the *visibility/ invisibility paradigm*, as it sought to apply insights from research on Puerto Ricans and to a lesser extent, Cubans, to other Afro-Latino populations that have historically been ignored. Scholars in this paradigm argue that Afro-Latin Americans hailed from throughout the hemisphere, each bringing with them distinct cultural, political, and social experiences, not to mention local, national, and diasporic understandings of race (Sarduy and Stubbs 2000; Dzidenyo and Oboler 2005; Burgos 2009).

A third research paradigm has sought to explicitly link the experiences of Afro-Latinos to Latin Americans throughout the hemisphere, highlighting the importance of the flow of people, culture, ideas, and politics across borders, putting the hemisphere in conversation, not just comparison. I call this approach the *transnational turn* (Candelario 2007; Roth 2012; Joseph 2015; Rivera-Rideau 2015; Rivera-Rideau, Jones, and Paschel 2016). This body of scholarship foregrounds the experiences of Afro-Latinos in the United States as a lens through which scholars can better understand the social dynamics of both global and local racial formation. It also situates Afro-Latinos as qualitatively distinct because of their liminality – shaped by the United States, and in conversation with Latin America – brightening and blurring the boundaries of race and nation.

As Miriam Jiménez Román and Juan Flores note in the introduction to *The Afro-Latin@ Reader* (2010), the concept of Afro-Latino is a relatively new one, despite the centuries-long presence of black Latinos in the United States. Indeed, Afro-Latin Americans have been in North America since the 1500s, arriving as soldiers, servants, sailors, slaves, and settlers of the Spanish empire. Yet Afro-Latinos' deep roots in territories now known as Florida, the Carolinas, Louisiana, and Alabama were largely ignored in US scholarship until the initial emergence of Afro-Latino Studies in the 1960s and 1970s (Forbes 1966; Gould 2010; Wood 2010).

This is not to suggest that articulations of *Afro-Latinidad* did not exist prior to that era. Nineteenth-century scholars and major ideological figures in Caribbean nationalist movements such as José Martí and Rafael Serra, who settled in Florida and New York in the 1880s, spearheaded anti-racist, anti-imperialist movements that centered blackness and took inspiration from black Americans as well as West Indian and Caribbean migrants' rise to social and economic power during the Reconstruction Era (Fusté 2016, 222). Martí, Serra, and others were engaged in an Afro-Antillean intellectual project that sought to integrate blackness into the hemispheric project of Latin American identity and independence. Such efforts were diasporic in nature and predated W. E. B. DuBois and Marcus Garvey by decades (Alamo-Pastrano and Candelario 2016).

Ultimately, however, just as the clock was quickly turned back on black advancement in the United States with the advent of Jim Crow, nationalist movements, the rise of US imperialism, and modernist aspirations that relied on the re-centering of whiteness truncated the success of these Afro-Antillean intellectual movements across the hemisphere (Alamo-Pastrana and Candelario 2016). Throughout Latin America, nationalist efforts to appear modern erased slavery, and by extension, black bodies from official versions of national history, engaging in *blanqueamiento* campaigns to whiten the nation through immigration, marginalization, and violence. By the early twentieth century, as Latin American and Caribbean migration to the United States picked up steam, few scholars of Latin America and *Latinidad* were interested in blackness as a social and intellectual project. *Mestizaje*, nationalism, and *criollismo* erased slavery, race, and blackness from the hemispheric conversation, and these were not recuperated until the global anti-colonial and civil rights movements of the 1960s and 1970s. It was these efforts that paved the way for Afro-Latino Studies.

In the United States, as noted, racial politics by the early twentieth century replaced Reconstruction with Jim Crow, emphatically blocking black progress. As in Latin America, modernist eugenicist race-making was strategized through immigration and naturalization law in an attempt to shore up whiteness, while still expanding economically and benefiting from labor migrants and imperial expansion. In the United States, policies regarding the immigration and integration of newcomers ranged from recruitment (in the case of Western Europeans) to outright exclusion (as in the case of Asians), all with the intent of whitening. Because Latin American claims to whiteness or whitening were marginally accepted, at least politically, Latin-American-origin peoples were left to negotiate an official ambiguity in terms of racial status and foreign policy (FitzGerald and Cook-Martín 2014). Throughout the nineteenth and twentieth centuries, constant social and political negotiations over how to racialize people of Latin-American-origin were deeply consequential.

For example, the Johnson-Reed Act of 1924 severely restricted immigration with the intent of preserving the ideal of racial homogeneity, yet no limits were placed on immigrants from Latin America, suggesting a kind of provisional whiteness. However, efforts to suspend immigration during the Great Depression in the 1930s targeted Mexicans for repatriation in massive numbers, including those with citizenship (Ngai 2004; FitzGerald and Cook-Martín 2014). Latin American migrants, especially Mexicans, were discriminated against and uniquely subject to medical inspection and harassment at the border; but as *mestizos*, Latin Americans and Latinos were legally white and were afforded some protections as such (Ngai 2004; Hattam 2007; FitzGerald and Cook-Martín 2014; Stern 2015).[2]

---

[2] In the post-14th amendment, post-slavery era, US-born Latinos were marginally included as racialized minorities, often denied access to institutions and services due to their skin color and national origin (Haney Lopez 2003; Almaguer 2009; Gonzales 2011; Stern 2016). The 14th Amendment was ratified in 1868 as part of a cluster of amendments that guaranteed rights to African Americans following the Civil War. The amendment established birthright citizenship, a privilege previously only granted to whites. While some Latin American origin groups, such as Mexicans, were declared white for the purpose of obtaining citizenship (negotiated under the treaty of Hidalgo Guadalupe to end the Mexican American War in 1848), this Amendment also had the de facto result of expanding citizenship rights to all nonwhite groups and their children.

Afro-Latin Americans did not fit into this framework; they were racialized as black, but located as foreign. These complications did not fit into a modernist world order in which racial lines were bright, fixed, and deeply hierarchical. In Tampa, for example, Afro-Cubans who came to work in the cigar industry in the late 1800s and early 1900s were subject to the rules of Jim Crow at the same time that they were afforded privileges and protections as Cubans and Cuban Americans, accessing resources unavailable to African Americans (Greenbaum 2002). Even during a period where we imagine racial boundaries in the United States to be quite stark, Tampa's Afro-Cubans experienced a kind of situational identity at the intersection of race and ethnicity that is part and parcel of the Afro-Latino experience that has long troubled racial rules, and yet remained largely invisible in our scholarship.

Evelio Grillo writes of his experiences of the "Colored Children's Day" at the South Florida Fair, and the relationship between African Americans and Afro-Cubans. "Social class, different languages, and different cultures divided the two communities. Black Cubans still built dependent relationships with black Americans, especially our black American teachers, with whom we formed deep affectionate bonds. But we lived clearly on the margins of black American society, while we worked out our daily existence in the black Cuban ghetto in Ybor city. Yet our identity as black Americans developed strongly" (Grillo 2000, 16).

Writing on Afro-Cuban textile workers in early twentieth-century New York, Mirabal (2003) finds that even though state-mandated segregation did not apply in that city, Afro-Cubans nevertheless lived in primarily segregated spaces. Like the Cubans in Tampa, however, there was flexibility at the margin, and Afro-Cubans were sometimes able to acquire better housing and employment by highlighting their Latin American ancestry and knowledge of Spanish. Moreover, separations within the Cuban community itself revealed the multiple workings of race" that could not be "solely understood in terms of binary United States racial definitions or ethnic affiliations (Mirabal 2003, 378).

Other scholars have pointed to major figures in Afro-diasporic activism and scholarly thought from that period who had settled in the United States such as Arturo Schomburg, Puerto Rican and Cuban independence activist who moved from Puerto Rico to New York in 1891 (Hoffnung-Garskof 2010). As the coalition for Cuban and Puerto Rican independence dissolved, Schomburg shifted his attentions to scholarly pursuits, pointedly pursuing an Afro-diasporic intellectual agenda through projects like the Negro Society for Historical Research, which would "provide firm historical footing for racial pride and unity" (Hoffnung-Garskof 2010, 71). Contemporary debates over whether Schomburg's strong simultaneous identification as a Puerto Rican, an American Negro, and a member of the broader African diaspora made him a political and social aberration or a window in to a broader constellation of political and social engagements among Afro-Latinos in New York in the early twentieth century, underscore the importance of Afro-Latinos' presence at the intersection of both communities, and their challenge to racial boundaries and meanings in the United States (Hoffnung-Garskof 2010).

### Shifting Populations

Despite the importance of Afro-Latinos who settled in the United States to its development, it was not until the political and demographic change at the end of the nineteenth and early twentieth century that the question of race and nation in the United States, was amplified, and by extension, concerns over the role of Latin-American-origin peoples in it. At a moment in which scientific racism shaped policy and public institutions, this was not without consequences. In turn, the changing empirical context signaled a need for a scholarly shift that examined questions of race and immigration. While the field of Afro-Latino Studies was not initiated until the 1960s, demographic and political changes laid the groundwork for its emergence during this period.

Following the 1848 seizure of large swaths of Mexican territory (and by extension, the people in it),[3] the Latin-American-origin population in the United States rapidly expanded. It is estimated that 75,000–100,000 Mexican nationals became citizens under the Treaty of Guadalupe Hidalgo. Mexicans continued to arrive in the United States in search of expanded labor market opportunities. In 1900, there were just over 100,000 Mexican-born residents in the United States (about 1 percent of all immigrants); by 1950 there were 450,000 Mexican-born residents (Migration Policy Institute 2013). Although some Afrodescendants can be counted among the Mexican-origin population, the largely Mestizo Mexican population played (and continues to play) a significant role in shaping the size and character of the Latino population, including its racialization.

---

[3] This included not only Mexican citizens but significant tracts of sovereign indigenous territories and numerous indigenous nations (Klein 2008).

Large numbers of Cubans who circulated in the United States also contributed significantly to the Latino populations, having an outsized impact on culture and society. That influence increased with major migration waves during the Batista regime, and again following the Castro Revolution. Between 1950 and 1960, the population of Cuban migrants living in the United States doubled, rising from 71,000 to 163,000 (Migration Policy Institute 2015). While Cubans were racialized as white, Afro-Cubans have long settled in the United States, playing an important role in shaping ideas of blackness both at home and throughout the region.

In 1917, the provision of citizenship to Puerto Ricans as residents of the newly acquired US territory was significant, as the island of Puerto Rico numbered approximately 1.3 million residents in 1920. Puerto Rican settlement on the mainland began to accelerate after World War II. Industrial expansion and formal policies like Operation Bootstrap and the establishment of the Bureau of Employment and Migration drew hundreds of thousands of Puerto Ricans to the mainland in the 1940s and 1950s (Perez 2004). Puerto Ricans settled in cities across the Northeast and the Midwest, but overwhelmingly landed in New York City; in the post-war period, 85 percent of Puerto Rican migrants migrated there, building and expanding Puerto Rican neighborhoods alongside African American communities (Gibson 2017). Because Puerto Rico was a former slave colony and home to hundreds of thousands of Afrodescendant Puerto Ricans (in 1950, the Puerto Rican census classified approximately 20 percent of the population as black[4]), Puerto Rican migration helped to create a "field of blackness in the United States" (Flores 2009).

Still, despite significant growth in the Afro-Latino population, Afro-Latin-American-origin people remained invisible, even in the context of racial conflict. For example, the 1935 race riots in Harlem were spurred by an incident involving an Afro-Puerto Rican youth that later spurred the production of a major report: "The Negro in Harlem: A Report on Social and Economic Conditions Responsible for the Outbreak of March 19, 1935," led by noted sociologist E. Franklin Frazier. The report attested to anti-black discrimination and police harassment, but it seemed

---

[4] These numbers are considered to be low and the result of significant "social whitening." In 1899, the census indicated that 61.8 percent of the population was enumerated as white, compared to 79.7 percent in 1950. The discrepancy in proportion cannot be accounted for through migration, births, or deaths and has been attributed to social whitening ideologies popularized throughout Latin America in the early twentieth century (Loveman and Muniz 2007).

to omit the presence of Puerto Ricans and other Afro-Latinos in Harlem altogether, reporting on the boy in question simply as "Negro."

As Latin-American-origin immigrants settled in the United States increasing numbers, the debate over where they fit in the racial hierarchy continued to intensify. Discrimination on the basis of race was legal until the 1960s, so incentives for exposing racial difference were minimal. By the late 1950s however, the growing dissatisfaction among non-whites and their allies with the current racial order drew attention to the various facets of racialized existence, including the spaces of racial liminality. As political movements for equal rights and racial pride emerged, they also sparked new dialogues about shared status, space, and politics that led to new artistic movements, political coalitions, and intellectual engagements that would pave the way for the possibilities of Afro-Latino recognition.

## CIVIL RIGHTS ERA: POLITICAL, SOCIAL AND SCHOLARLY CHANGE

Following the end of WWII and leading up to the passage of civil rights legislation in the 1960s, a sea change in immigration policy and a broader social and cultural shift regarding the identity politics of non-white groups spurred major changes in the presence and meaning of Latinos in the United States. Until the 1960s, the Latin-American-origin population was primarily composed of Mexican-, Puerto Rican-, and Cuban-origin peoples. These national origin groups were regionally distinct, incorporated into the United States under distinct immigration and citizenship regulations, and were not considered, nor did they consider themselves, a unified racial group (Mora 2014).

Beginning in the 1960s, social movement organizations such as the National Association for the Advancement of Colored People (NAACP), The Student Nonviolent Coordinating Committee (SNCC), the Southern Christian Leadership Conference (SCLC) and others, effectively demanded not only a change in law, providing equal accommodation for African Americans in public spaces and in institutional access, but also ushered in an era in which African Americans argued that blackness had value. The success of these movements rapidly expanded to other arenas, such as labor rights and gender rights and became the basis of claims made by other non-white groups, including Cubans, Puerto Ricans, and Mexicans.

For the Latin-American-origin population, which had long benefited from tenuous but historically significant claims to whiteness, this ushered in a new period of racialized consolidation, in which it became important to be able to make claims as a collective. The rise of social movements such as the Brown Power movement and the Chicano movement, alongside growing populations of native-born Latinos and increasing representation in government and the business elite, shifted the landscape for race-making and group membership. By the late 1960s, Cubans, Puerto Ricans, and Mexicans, who had already begun to organize and make legal claims as national origin groups, began to consolidate under the umbrella of "Hispanic" (Mora 2014).

Although racialization and group coherence are always complex social processes, the collectivization process was more difficult and complex for those of Latin-American-origin than for African Americans, who faced overt legal barriers and openly discriminatory treatment. Latin-American-origin populations did face outright racism. But due to the vast differences in social and legal experiences between national origin groups and the local social and demographic configurations they encountered, their inclusion in civil rights legislation was as language minorities, rather than racialized ones, further obscuring their liminal racial status (Montejano 1987; Gutiérrez 1995; López 1996; Ngai 2004; Hattam 2007; López and Olivas 2008).[5] Still, by the late 1970s, the consolidated Hispanic category was born, finally shifting away from claims to whiteness. However, because the content of this category, as I will discuss, was conceived as "brown," Afro-Latinos continued to be marginalized from *Latinidad*.

## Immigration

Civil rights victories and racial claims by African Americans were seen by other non-whites and their allies as tools to fight for institutional inclusion in foreign policy and immigration. Using anti-racism as a tool to press for more equitable international relations, Latin American countries

---

[5] While US policymakers rarely considered Latin-American-origin peoples to be white, often denigrating the continent for its "mongrelized" population, racial status was the subject of significant contention and debate between Latin American policymakers and diplomats and the United States (Cook-Martín and FitzGerald 2014). The degree to which specific nations within the region were considered white or non-white was also the subject of debate and change over time. Within the United States, numerous organizations such as the League of United Latin American Citizens (LULAC) advocated for white status, pushing back against US social conventions of racialization (Mora 2014). As a result, the extent to which Latin-American-origin peoples in the United States were considered white or non-white was not a given, but a deeply contested process.

leveraged internal civil rights efforts to push for the United States to change its largely restrictive and discriminatory immigration laws. In response, the United States instituted the Hart-Celler Immigration Bill in 1965, eliminating national origin quotas and prioritizing immigrants who had families and labor market opportunities in the United States (FitzGerald and Cook-Martín 2014).[6]

Ironically, these efforts to end formal immigration bans by nationality and discrimination within the letter of the law, and which were, in part, the result of negotiations and efforts by postcolonial governments in Asia and Latin America to end racial preferences for Europeans, also created the first numerical restrictions on immigrants from the western hemisphere. Combined with the end of the Bracero program in 1964 and other wartime labor recruitment programs, the net result of these changes was a major increase in unauthorized immigration. Mexicans, and to a lesser extent Central Americans, became permanently linked to the trope of the undocumented or illegal immigrants – a racialized framework that would be extended to all Latinos despite distinct immigration and racialized experiences (Ngai 2004).

This massive change to immigration law was quickly followed by the Cuban Adjustment Act of 1966, which legally positioned all Cubans as political refugees and provided for a special procedure through which Cubans could receive permanent residency. Despite the historical presence of Afro-Cubans in the United States, Cuban Americans at this time were imagined as white by the public, media, and policymakers, with the potential to assimilate into the American mainstream. It was not until the Mariel boatlifts in the 1980s that this perception shifted, linking Afro-Cubans who arrived in that wave with criminality. White Cubans had been and continue to be associated with upward mobility and elite status. Puerto Ricans, for their part, continued to resettle on the mainland as economic stagnation on the island pushed new surges of islanders to migrate in the 1950s and 1960s. This migration further expanded the reach of Puerto Rican enclaves and organizations and deepened the field of blackness they created in these spaces.

Shifts in immigration law had two additional effects. One is that Cubans' and Puerto Ricans' experience of Latino racialization was not

---

[6] While the Hart-Celler act ended racial quotas, the policy change severely restricted immigration for Latin Americans. Under the new law, quotas were imposed for the hemisphere for the first time, even though the law is often portrayed as ending racial restrictions.

only distinct from the growing numbers of Mexican and Central American immigrants because of their large proportion of Afrodescendants, but also because they were not included in the newly racialized ideas of Latino citizenship. Two, these changes greatly diversified and increased the size of the Latino population, further obscuring blackness within the popular construction of *Latinidad*, but also creating political and social leverage for recognition. That is, demographic and policy change transformed race-making for Latinos.

Since the 1960s, the influx of "new" groups of Latinos such as Panamanians and Dominicans has further complicated the relationship between race, blackness, and *Latinidad*.[7] The population of immigrants from the Americas grew from approximately 19 percent of all immigrants currently residing in the United States in 1960 to 46 percent in 1990 (Migration Policy Institute 2016).[8] This new wave of Latin Americans in the United States meant that not only would this population have demographic leverage to make themselves heard and accounted for politically, but also that there was an increasing demand to study and locate this population within our scholarly understanding of social life in the United States.

### Race-Making: Latino Studies and *Latinidad*

A major intellectual and political project that emerged as a result of these political and social changes was the concept of *Latinidad*. As previously noted, *Latinidad* in the United States has long been understood as a puzzle – an ongoing social and political project, rather than an empirical fact. Scholars such as G. Christina Mora (2014), Clara Rodriguez (2000), Laurie K. Sommers (1991), Arlene Dávila (2008, 2012), and others, have decisively argued that *Latinidad* has been constructed and produced, not merely through individual processes of identity formation, but

---

[7] This is not to suggest that Panamanians and Dominicans were not migrating and settling in the United States prior to the 1960s. However, political upheavals such as the end of the Trujillo regime in the Dominican Republic and the destabilization of Central America in the 1980s spurred large-scale migration to the United States, greatly diversifying the Latin-American-origin population in the United States.

[8] Quota restrictions meant that an increasing proportion of the Mexican and Central American population was arriving without documentation during this period, bringing thousands more Latin-American-origin immigrants across the border (Migration Policy Institute 2016).

through institutional engagement, social movements, demographic change, legislative action, and federal policy (Oboler 1995; Flores-Gonzalez 1999; Portes and Rumbaut 2001, 2011; DeGenova and Ramos-Zayas 2003; Jiménez 2010; Menjivar 2013).

Underlying these processes of constructing *Latinidad* historically has been the issue of race. In a context in which black/white boundaries were clearly marked, and Asians and American Indians marked as foreigners or national others, the meaning of Latino identity, and whether it was racial, was uniquely unclear. Latino racialization has long been skirted in US policy, in which Latinos alone have been counted as an ethnic group or language minority. Legislative and judicial action dictated Latino racialization and categorization as early as the judicial exception for Mexicans to be classified as white under the treaty of Guadalupe Hidalgo, in which Mexican-origin people, regardless of indigenous and even African ancestry, were legally declared white, even if they were considered de facto "others" (Montejano 1987; Gutiérrez 1995; López 1996).

By the 1960s, in reaction to their ambiguous legal and racial status, disparate Latin-American-origin groups sought to leverage their new demographic power. As scholars, policymakers, advocates, and media executives worked to create Latinos as a social category, that category, to the extent that it was racialized, was thought of as brown. As *Latinidad* gained conceptual traction, it was linked explicitly by activists and scholars to a politics of *mestizaje* – an ideology lifted from hemispheric nationalist projects that venerated race mixture (see Chapter 8). For many Latinos who had been excluded from the benefits of whiteness, the veneration of the *mestizo* was a positive affirmation of Latino identity where other options were not available. Many argued that Latinos shared important experiences and a structural position worthy not only of shared classification but also of scholarly inquiry, and the turn toward *mestizaje* was an effort to affirm a sense of unity and shared culture in the face of anti-white racism (Padilla 1985; Bean and Tienda 1987). In turn, activists and scholars began to call for Ethnic Studies and Latino Studies programs, developing a theoretical framework for understanding *Latinidad* and concretizing its position in US social history.

As Latinos sought to define their place in US society, many considered themselves to be white, either marking white on the census or choosing identities that suggest a desire to assimilate into whiteness. Others expressed a preference for national origin based identities (Alba 1990;

Oboler 1995; Alba and Nee 2003; Darity, Dietrich and Hamilton 2005; Bonilla-Silva and Embrick 2006; Jiménez- Román and Flores 2010). In response, many Latino Studies scholars embraced fluidity and ambiguity as a defining part of the Latino experience, articulating a kind of *Latinidad* that emphasized mixture, brownness, and the migratory experience (Anzaldúa 1981; Valle and Torres 2000; Pérez-torres 2006).

Much of this work was produced on the heels of social movements such as the Chicano movement, which embraced Aztlán as spiritual homeland and as the crux of Chicano identity. In a similar vein, Gloria Anzaldúa's seminal *Borderlands/La Frontera* (1987) and collaboration with Cherrie Moraga, *This Bridge Called My Back* (1981), both exemplified and cemented the influence of the borderland narrative in the US context, arguing for an identity politics that embraces being both mixed and between – a kind of liminal identity that is defined by the experience of crossing borders.[9] Anzaldúa produced what Juan Flores has called Latino Studies' guiding metaphor of "*la frontera*," which brought to the fore an understanding of *Latinidad* shaped primarily by both movement across borders, both racial and national, just as the concept of Latino or Hispanic was consolidated in the United States by activists, bureaucrats, and a developing Spanish language media (Mora 2014).

Transnationalism therefore, has been central to the construction of *Latinidad*, in part because of the significant movement of people across borders, but largely in a manner that emphasized the US-Mexico border rather than other transnational crossings (DeGenova and Ramos-Zayas 2003). In subsequent decades, this conceptualization of the US Latino as a *mestizo*, transnational subject, became the core of much of the scholarship that seeks to articulate *Latinidad* (Oboler 1995; Almaguer 2003; Beltran 2004). The growth of the Latino population into the largest minority group in the United States, its increasing national, ethnic, and racial diversity since the 1980s, and the rising numbers of Latinos in virtually every state, continue to make immigration central to theorizing *Latinidad*. In the United States, immigration continues to be framed both productively and problematically as a Latino issue, infusing *Latinidad* with a necessarily transnational subject position. Latino Studies scholarship, however, despite its important and productive emphasis on transnationalism and border crossing, often failed to consider the Afro-Latino experience.

---

[9] Piri Thomas' *Down These Mean Streets* (1967) is often referenced as the autobiographical Afro-Latino corollary to Anzaldúa, grappling with the experience of Afro-Latino identity.

## Critique: The Problem with Mestizaje and Latino Studies

While *mestizo* nationalism is being challenged and, in some cases, dismantled in Latin America, it serves as a central political self-assertion in the United States that continues to invisibilize Afro-Latinos or push them outside of *Latinidad* into the African diaspora or Caribbeanness. These racial silences, in turn, created different possibilities for collective organizing through a racialized framework. Thus, perhaps ironically, just as attachments to *mestizaje* began to loosen in Latin America in the 1970s and 1980s, scholars of US Latinos borrowed from *mestizaje* to argue that there is something uniquely mixed about Latinos that both gives them collective meaning and transcends national origins (Anzaldúa 1987; Valle and Torres 1995; Pérez-Torres 2006).

Moreover, because distinctive citizenship policies shape the experiences of Latinos of different national origins in profoundly different ways, many scholars and policymakers wonder whether Latinos' diverse origins and transnational attachments may preclude an internal sense of cohesion. Some argued that *Latinidad*, and by extension, the labels 'Hispanic' and 'Latino' homogenized the diverse experiences of Latin-American-origin peoples in the United States in ways that not only problematized cohesion, but were in and of themselves, problematic (Oboler 1995). The dominance of *mestizo* identity and mestizaje as an anchoring framework means that only certain sending regions and receiving destinations are made visible within *Latinidad*. In addition, while *mestizaje* intends to emphasize hybridity, in practice, it continues to denigrate, if not erase, blackness, while simultaneously relegating indigenous populations to a historical past (Menacha 2001; Hernández 2004; Pérez-Torres 2006).

With few exceptions, *Latinidad* was conceptualized by scholars, bureaucrats, and activists as consistent with hemispheric racial attitudes that venerated race mixture or mestizaje as a kind of hybrid identity that obscured or denied racial difference and, by extension, inequality (but see Menacha 2001). As in the Caribbean and much of Latin America, blackness was extraterritorial, emplaced, invisible, denied, and largely unacknowledged by scholars, policymakers and activists as part of the Latino experience (Hooker 2005; Jones 2013; Godreau 2015; Paschel 2016). That is, rather than conceiving of blackness as a constitutive component of *Latinidad*, blackness was excised, constructed as marginal, historical, or a characteristic of immigrant populations (as in the case of Haitians in the Dominican Republic or Cubans in Mexico) rather than a piece of national racial identity. As a result, Afro-identified people were largely erased from *Latinidad* or even presumed to be antithetical to *Latinidad* (DeGenova and Ramos-Zayas 2003; Milian 2013). This erasure occurred not only in popular discourse and within political and cultural movements (Dávila 2001; Mora 2014) but in scholarly works as well, which in many ways emerged from those movements (but see: Milian 2013 and Pérez-Torres 2006 for a critical analysis of race and *Latinidad*). Thus, Afro-Latinos remained invisible within *mestizaje* and, by extension, Latino Studies.

Still, it should be noted, the marginalization of Afro-Latino Studies in the wider Latino and Latin American scholarship is not merely intellectual or ideological omission. The problematic of the invisibility of Afro-Latinos is also due in part to the demographic reality that shapes Latinidad in the United States. As of the 2014 census, the Mexican-origin population represented 64 percent of US Latinos, while Puerto Ricans accounted for about 9.4 percent, Salvadorans outnumbered Cubans at 3.8 percent and 3.7 percent, respectively, and Dominicans are not far behind at 3.2 percent (Pew Hispanic Center 2016). In part as a result of this demographic composition, the proportion of the population that identifies as black Hispanic was only 2.8 percent of Latinos, or 1.24 million people (Ennis, Rios-Vargas and Albert 2011). Because of these demographic shifts, any understanding of Latinidad is shaped by both widespread diversity on the one hand, and the overwhelming majority of Mexicans on the other.

The tensions within *Latinidad* between diversity and unity are reflected in changes in the census over time, in which Latinos have never consistently abided by census conventions (with as many as 40 percent of Latinos marking some other race), and in new efforts to consolidate *Latinidad* as a coherent category that is distinct from blackness. The difficulty of capturing Latinos in the census reflects the complexity of racialization among Latinos. Moving to a racialized Latino category would almost certainly create a de facto *mestizo* Latino identity that does, in fact, reflect the vast numerical majority of Latinos in the United States. However, it would also obscure the diversity within that category, particularly blackness, which gets erased not only as a racially meaningful experience for many Latinos, but also its role in the larger construction of *Latinidad* throughout the hemisphere (López 2013).

Moreover, it is important to remember that US racial categories, hypodescent rules, and anti-black racism serve as deterrents from identifying as black and Latino, as US racial norms have only recently accommodated identification with two or more races (changed on the census in 2000).[10] As highlighted in this chapter, the categories of Latino and black do not meaningfully make space for Afro-Latino identity formation. Because Latino is largely understood as *mestizo*, and therefore inclusive of various race mixtures, but emphatically not black – and black, is understood as inclusive of any proportion of African ancestry as *only* black, changes to the census would continue to exacerbate the purportedly neat division between black and Latino.[11] The category of Afro-Latino is productive precisely because it unsettles all that is complex about race, forcing engagement with race as puzzle, rather than a given.

### Theorizing Afro-Latinidad

In making a claim for the importance of Afro-Latino scholarship, Miriam Jiménez Román and Juan Flores assert that *Afro-Latinidad* requires a "triple consciousness "(2005). Building on DuBois's conception of double consciousness in the United States, Jiménez Román and Flores posit that *Afro-Latinidad* adds another challenging layer to the racialized experience, undermining dominant conceptions of *Latinidad*, blackness, and Americanness as incompatible identities. Triple consciousness thus makes evident the ways that, as Tanya Katerí Hernández argues, Afro-Latinos, and therefore blackness, remain unintelligible within our understandings of *mestizo Latinidad*, and therefore outside of the Latino imaginary (Hernández 2003).

This is especially important because Cubans and Puerto Ricans have not only long served as significant contributors to the Latino population in the United States, but the deep connections between the United States and these countries have tied together their social, cultural, and racial histories. Politically and demographically, ties have been forged between the Spanish-speaking Caribbean and the United States as early as 1823 as

---

[10] Census convention until the emergence of the Latino category as an ethnic group, rather than a racial group, was to count Afro-Latinos as racially black.

[11] Throughout the slavery period, the United States had race terms similar to those in Latin America, accounting for race mixture through words such as mulatto or octoroon, referring to African Americans of one-half or one-eighth African ancestry. However, under Jim Crow, as race mixing became more common and the rules of citizenship and property ownership became intimately tied to race, social rules were adjusted so that the one-drop rule, or hypodescent, applied. Under these rules, status among African Americans was flattened, and any person with any fraction of African ancestry was considered African American. See Davis, 1991.

a product of the Monroe Doctrine. Later in the century, independence from Spain gave way to US hegemony and increased migration from the islands to the mainland (Flores 2009, 59). Moreover, "*Afroantillianos* constitute by far the largest non-English-speaking black population in US history, and Caribbean Latino history thus overlaps with the history of Afro-Latinos in the United States. To a significant degree, in fact, what marks off caribeños within the Latino pan-ethnicity as a whole is precisely this interface with blackness and an Afro-Atlantic imaginary. As Afro-Latinos, they embody the compatibility of blackness with the notion of Latino identity in the United States" (Flores 2009, 64). Indeed, the invisibility of such overlapping identities, particularly among Afro-Caribbean Americans, underscores an important interstitial racial space that is crucial to our understanding of *Latinidad* (Greenbaum 2002). Despite, or perhaps because of the marginal position of Afro-Latinos, Afro-Latino scholarship has emerged as a way to think not only about the invisible and ignored experience of black Latinos, but also to trouble US frameworks and concepts of *Latinidad* that do engage questions of race but fail to deal adequately with blackness.

## THE EVOLUTION OF AFRO-LATINO SCHOLARSHIP

Afro-Latino Studies, like other bodies of scholarship, has also been shaped by major political and demographic changes in the United States, emerging in direct response to the opening up of discourses and inquiry that sought to theorize and value non-white populations, including through enumeration in the census, social movements, civil rights protections, and integration into the academy in the post-civil rights era, as elaborated previously. Thus, while Afro-Latinos have had a long and distinguished history in the United States from the beginning of North American settlement, Afro-Latino Studies is largely a contemporary area of inquiry, not quite representing a field, but rather a consolidating area of research that aims to empirically examine the experiences of Afrodescendants in place, the migration of Afrodescendant people, and the circulation of ideas that emerge from these experiences. Through these approaches, works from various disciplines and regional specialties contribute to our understanding of blackness and *Latinidad* through critique, visibility, and theoretical intervention. Anchored by key foundational works by Juan Flores (2003), Anani Dzidzienyo and Suzanne Oboler (2005), Miriam Jiménez Román and Juan Flores (2010), Agustín Laó-Montes (2007b) and others, Afro-Latino Studies is emerging as a generative multidisciplinary, mixed-method approach that expands and links Afro-Latin American Studies to Latino Studies and African Diaspora Studies in empirically and theoretically productive ways. Collectively, this scholarship argues that Afro-Latinos are more than a mere group or designation, but carriers of "a legacy of shared and distinctive cultural values and expression that has traversed national particularities and differentiated itself from the group history of both African Americans and other Latin@s" (Jiménez Román and Flores 2010, 4).

### Puerto Rican Studies

Puerto Rico plays an enormously important role in our understanding of Latin America and the Caribbean, hemispheric relations, migration, and racial formation; in so doing, it also initiated Afro-Latino Studies. Its unique place within Latin America as one of Spain's last two colonies meant that it had the longest Hispanic influence. Following the 1898 Spanish-American war, Puerto Rico was transferred to the United States, and through its status as a commonwealth, has experienced the most penetrating American influence, while never enjoying political independence (Duany 2002). Despite these long-standing colonial relationships, and massive migration between island and mainland, Puerto Rico has retained its own identity and culture as a "Spanish-speaking Afro-Hispanic Caribbean Nation" (Duany 2002, 1). While Puerto Rico has a large Afrodescendant population, and at times celebrates its African ancestry as a contributor to its unique history and culture, it has throughout the twentieth century nevertheless constructed a modern racialized identity that excludes and erases racial minorities from its nation-building project (Duany 2002).

While Afro-Puerto Rican identity was not emphasized in scholarship produced on the island, it was nevertheless part of the lived experience of many Nuyoricans of the period. From the perspective of islanders and elites writing in the 1940s and 1950s, the question of race was about proximity to whiteness and adherence to a kind of *blanqueamiento* respectability. This view persisted among many politicians and spokespeople who tried to downplay blackness, even as their communities were being rejected by white New Yorkers on racial grounds. Thus, for Puerto Ricans writing from the US perspective, the question of race was always close at hand. As a result, scholars began to argue that the experience of Puerto Ricanness in the United States was, in part, an experience of blackness.

For example, writing on Puerto Rican identity and settlement in Chicago from the 1940s to the 2000s, Mérida Rua (2012) emphasizess the ways in which Puerto Ricans troubled the city's racial order, suggesting that the whitening perspective of the 1940s and 1950s did not accurately reflect the experience of many Puerto Ricans in those years. In an interview with William Rios, in which he notes that many Puerto Ricans would get jumped when venturing into the neighboring Italian communities, Rios recalled that "because I was black, they thought I was...African American. I walked all over there and never-...was I harassed" (2012, 34). The ambiguity of Afro-Puerto Ricans in the landscape of the cities they resided in afforded them a kind of flexibility and racial unintelligibility that opened up new spaces for political alliances, intimate relationships, and blended cultural expression in a broad context of segregation, racialized conflict, and marginalization.

As early as the 1960s, Nuyorican activists, artists, and everyday residents reckoned with these complicated racialized encounters, in which blackness, largely a liability on the island as well as in the United States, could nevertheless be a locus of empowerment, security, solidarity, and cultural production (Flores 1993; Rivera 2003; Dávila 2004). As scholars took these insights to the academy to develop Puerto Rican Studies, the embryonic field of Afro-Latino Studies began to explore and analyze Puerto Rican spaces, primarily in New York but also in Chicago, Florida, and New Jersey.

Thus Puerto Rican scholars, activists, and artists have, since the late 1960s and 1970s, loudly and forcefully argued for a Latino identity politics in the United States that is inclusive of the Caribeño and Afro-Caribeño roots of the second largest Latino population.[12] Throughout this period, Nuyoricans engaged in political activism through groups such as the Young Lords, mobilized for research and intellectual engagement of their own experiences and communities, and created new cultural forms that spoke to their daily lives. Writers and poets such as Jesus Colón, author of *A Puerto Rican in New York and Other Sketches* (1961), inspired a generation through their work.

Puerto Rican writer Piri Thomas' memoir *Down These Mean Streets* (1967) is widely considered one of the first descriptions of being identified

---

[12] This calculation of course omits Puerto Ricans on the island, a US territory.

as both black and Latino in the United States.[13] Portraying the experience of being Puerto Rican and black, Thomas' work is considered a classic narrative of the Puerto Rican experience in East Harlem – one that is emphatically, though not named as such, Afro-Latino (Higgins 2007). Also considered a classic in Latino Studies more broadly, Thomas' work opened up a space of analysis in the 1970s and 1980s in which race and identity, particularly blackness, could be interrogated as part and parcel of the US Nuyorican experience. Along with memoirists such as Nuyorican Bernardo Vega who wrote of their racialized experiences in New York, these writers were the foundation of the Afro-Latino canon (Flores 2009).

Emerging alongside Latino Studies, Puerto Rican Studies in the United States developed out of the insights of Nuyorican artists and activists (who sometimes were also scholars themselves) as both a counter and complementary discourse to the *mestizo* framework that emphasized indigeneity while eschewing blackness (Flores 1993, 2009). Expanding these insights into a scholarly analysis of the Puerto Rican diaspora, scholars such as Frank Bonilla and Ricardo Campos (1981), Jorge Duany (2002), Juan Flores (1993, 2003, 2009), Clara Rodriguez (1989), Carmen Whalen (2001), and others argued for an understanding of Puerto Rico as exceptional at the same time that the absence of Puerto Ricans from the growing field of Latino Studies represented a glaring omission in the wider theorization of the Latino experience. The Puerto Rican experience, they argued, because of its unique political and social relationship to the mainland, created distinct frameworks of social and cultural identity (Negrón-Muntaner and Grosfoguel 1997; Godreau 2015). At the same time, despite representing a significant proportion of the Latino population, their experiences as citizens, and as marginalized Afrodescendants, were glossed over when referring to the larger Latino population, and Nuyorican scholars and writers developed creative and scholarly works to rectify that omission.

This articulation was developed against the backdrop of the Puerto Rican formulation of *mestizaje* or racial democracy on the island, in which the dominant narrative of *la gran familia puertorriqueña* presented Puerto Rico as a racial paradise that overcame its racial divisions, even as anti-black stereotypes and stigmatization were, and are, common (Duany 2002; Rivera-Rideau 2015). As Rivera-Rideau argues, Puerto

---

[13] Piri Thomas was of Cuban and Puerto Rican descent. His father, in particular, was Afro-Cuban.

Ricans on the island, like much of Latin America and the Caribbean, embraced discourses of racial democracy and *blanqueamiento* in an attempt to affiliate with European modernity. Devaluing blackness, however, did not eliminate it.

The strategic inclusion of certain constructions of blackness and the rejection of others left open the door of comparison between ideology and experience, and between island and metropole (Duany 2002; Godreau 2015; Rivera-Rideau 2015). In the 1990s, in a dramatic departure from early twentieth-century scholarship on the island that adhered to a *blanquemiento* ideology (Carrion 1993; Godreau 2015), and more contemporary scholarship that painted the practice of those who chose to embrace and identify as black on the island as a product of US imperialism (Rivera-Rideau 2015), some Puerto Rican intellectuals began to challenge notions of an existing racial democracy in Puerto Rico. They did so by asserting that the contributions of Afrodescendants to the island had been systematically ignored and that anti-black racism on the island was pervasive (Rivera-Rideau 2015).

While these new frameworks in Puerto Rican Studies sought in part to recuperate blackness, Godreau (2015) argues that blackness in these new formulations was folklorized, localized, and historicized, emphasizing a specific cultural past. At the same time, as is true throughout the hemisphere, efforts to demonize Afrodescendants in both Puerto Rico and the United States persisted, stereotyping Afro-Puerto Ricans as low-income, hypersexual, and criminal, and therefore outside of the respectable Puerto Rican ideal (Santiago-Valles 1995; Dinzey-Flores 2008; Fusté 2010; Godreau 2015). As Rivera-Rideau notes, "urban blackness thus symbolizes the internal black 'other' against which Puerto Ricanness can be defined as white(ned)" (Rivera- Rideau 2015, 11).

Thus, even as racialized discourse changed over time, efforts to carve out a national identity that relied on notions of white respectability and elite status continued to clash with the experiences of the larger Puerto Rican diaspora, especially in the mainland United States – a population that by the twenty-first century outnumbered that of the island. For those Puerto Ricans, life in the United States was deeply and indelibly racialized toward blackness.

In the decades since the emergence of the assertion of Nuyorican identities in the 1960s and 1970s, Nuyorican scholars have underlined these contradictions, pointing out the distinct racial regimes and rules on the island versus the mainland, engaging in a kind of comparative analysis of racial identities that both acknowledges blackness and underscores the problematics of the kinds of shifting racial encounters that accompany migration and of racial formation itself (Duany 2002).

The question of blackness as part and parcel of the Puerto Rican diasporic experience, and yet apparently irreconcilable with *Latinidad*, emerged as a core contribution of this body of scholarship. As Juan Flores notes in *The Diaspora Strikes Back*, "Many Caribbean Latinos are racialized toward blackness, not only by the wider US society but to some extent by their fellow Latinos as well. This process has been complemented, and complicated, by relations with African Americans and non-Hispanic Caribbeans, relations which have in some cases – most strongly, again, among young people – engendered an Afro- or Atlantic diasporic consciousness and identity" (Flores 2009, 47). Flores argues that Afro-Puerto Ricans specifically, and Afro-Latinos more broadly, have a special relationship to issues of race and racial identity as shaped not by proximity to whiteness, but blackness. However, this sensibility of being both black and Latino is both erased corporeally, in the broad classification of Afro-Latinos as non-Latinos, as well as theoretically, as blackness has been omitted from discussions of *Latinidad* in the United States. It is only in these specific liminal spaces or encounters, such as Nuyorican enclaves, or in the production of new musical forms, that *Afro-Latinidad* becomes intelligible.

In the urban contexts of New York and New Jersey, Puerto Ricans on the mainland constructed alternative racialized identities defined by, and given value through, their proximity to blackness (Ramos-Zayas 2007; Rivera 2007; Arroyo 2010). This kind of urban blackness is associated with mobility and cosmopolitanism. The transnational projection of rap or reggaetón, representing a kind of flourishing of the Puerto Rican experience and cultural production, was deeply racialized and transnational in ways that convey creativity and productivity, and have exploded since the 1970s despite official condemnations from the Puerto Rican elite (Ramos-Zayas 2007; Godreau 2015; Rivera-Rideau 2015). By extension, these processes opened up new avenues for scholarly inquiry, intended to make sense of this cultural mélange, and its role in shaping Puerto Rican identity.

This experience of migration and encounter subjected "African Americans, Puerto Ricans, and other African diasporic populations in New York to similar (though not necessarily equivalent) systems of racial exclusion [and] produced the conditions of possibility for these groups to forge new political, social, and cultural alliances that contested this marginalization" (Rivera-Rideau 2015, 27) and new racialized perspectives. Moreover, work that examines how Puerto Rican articulations of racial identities and meanings differ from hegemonic discourses on race in the United States can lend important insight to the importance of struggle over racial meanings, and how Afrodescendants in particular can trouble mainstream narratives. It is these multiple and varied insights that opened the door to Afro-Latino Studies.

### FROM PUERTO RICAN STUDIES TO AFRO-LATINO STUDIES

Focusing on issues of distinct racialized regimes and experiences, migration and encounter, localized frameworks of intergroup relations and creative expression, and the importance of structural relations including, but certainly not limited to, segregation, politics, colonialism and national ideology, Puerto Rican Studies opened the door to a wide set of inquiries that sought not only to apply these insights to other populations, but to make them visible by putting them in conversation.

### Rendering the Invisible Visible

In the 1980s and 1990s, Afro-Latinos and Afro-Latin Americans globally began to demand both political and scholarly recognition. Increased globalization through increased trade and changing technology expanded both migration and communication across the hemisphere, alongside a shift toward multicultural politics throughout the region that created an opportunity for Afrodescendants to be counted (Wade 1997; Hooker 2005; Paschel 2016). Throughout Latin America, Afrodescendants had long been marginalized as nonexistent or assimilated minorities under nationalist frameworks that excluded them in an effort to whiten or exalt race mixture through *mestizaje*. By the 1990s, Afrodescendants increasingly claimed that this invisibility was part of a broader political and economic erasure in which they were not only made invisible but systematically deprived of the kinds of resources and opportunities afforded to their white and *mestizo* counterparts. They began to publicly advocate for political and social inclusion (see Chapter 7).

This critique of invisibility in Latin America helped reinforce the critique of invisibility in the United States, where *Latinidad*, as noted, was largely understood as distinct from blackness, absorbing the same anti-black racial ideologies as those held in most of Latin America and the Caribbean. With the exception of Puerto Ricans and, later, Afro-Cubans who arrived in the Mariel boatlifts, in the collective imaginary Afro-Latinos in the United States did not exist. Perhaps unsurprisingly then, issues of invisibility and visibility have been central to the emergence of Afro-Latino Studies as an area of inquiry. This has meant not only the project of acknowledging and naming the presence of various Afro-Latino populations in the United States, but how these groups have been excised from other areas of scholarship.

As Afrodescendants achieved recognition throughout the hemisphere in national censuses and in inclusionary policies that extended land rights, called for affirmative action, and acknowledged racial inequalities (Hooker 2005; Paschel 2016), Afro-Latinos in the United States also called for a scholarship that articulated proof of existence as a mechanism of inclusion. As Jiménez Román and Flores have argued, "Afro-Latin@s have faced virtually total invisibility and erasure as a possible component of either the Latin@ or the Black population" (2010, 10).

As a result of this omission, Afro-Latino Studies has emphasized issues of invisibility and the need for visibility to account for the unique forms of stratification experienced by black Latinos in the United States. This effort includes an expansion of work not only on Afro-Dominicans, Afro-Cubans and Puerto Ricans (Aparicio 1999; Itzigsohn and Dore-Cabral 2000; Bailey 2002; Duany 2002; Greenbaum 2002; Mirabal 2003; Rivera 2003), but also Afro-Mexicans in the United States, Garifuna, Panamanians, Colombians, Hondurans, and other Afrodescendant groups that have been invisible in the United States and in Latin America (Hoy 2010; Jackson 2010; Lambert 2010; Mann-Hamilton 2010). Collectively, these studies seek to integrate Afro-Latinos into one broader understanding of blackness and *Latinidad*, highlighting the unique national origin cultures and practices of each group while simultaneously engaging and challenging the US racial paradigm. In this way, not unlike Afro-Latin American Studies, one avenue of building Afro-Latino Studies was for scholars to look toward places that are conventionally thought to be *mestizo* nations and to recognize the presence of Afrodescended people from across the region who have settled in the United States, while also intervening more broadly in Latino scholarship.

The most emblematic work from this wave of research is the *Afro-Latin@ Reader*, edited by Miriam Jiménez Román and Juan Flores (2010). The volume includes a variety of pieces that sought to provide a broad and varied view of Black Latinos in the United States, and focuses, as they note "on the strategically important but still largely understudied United States context of Afro-Latin@ experience (2010, 3)." The volume is interdisciplinary, including history, music, gender, class, and media representations in more than sixty selections, including scholarly essays, memoirs, newspaper and magazine articles, poetry, short stories, and interviews. This book followed Juan Flores' aforementioned 2009 article, "Triple Consciousness? Approaches to Afro-Latino Culture in the United States," Anani Dzidzienyo and Suzanne Oboler's 2005 edited volume, *Neither Enemies Nor Friends: Latinos, Blacks, and Afro-Latinos*, and works by Agustín Laó-Montes (2005, 2007b), which also sought to make visible Afro-Latinos in the United States and theorize the significance of their presence for Latino Studies.

These scholars argued that, despite their relatively small numbers, Afro-Latinos were distinct among Latinos. Moreover, this distinctiveness called into question the broad framing of Latino Studies as definitionally *mestizo*, reminding Latino Studies that Afrodescendant Latinos in the United States were often from places that adhered to a *mestizo* nationalism that erased black bodies by writing them out of the national narrative. In re-centering Afrodescendancy, these scholars argued that the African diaspora empirically is, and therefore theoretically should be, inclusive of Afro-Latinos and Afro-Latin Americans. It is this critical positioning that made Afro-Latinos worthy of theoretical inquiry.

### Transnationalism, Circulations, and Diasporic Dialogues

A third scholarly approach to Afro-Latino Studies is what I call the transnationalism paradigm. Emerging in the 1990s, but really blossoming in the twenty-first century, this body of scholarship examines *Afro-Latinidad* as shaped by flows across borders of people, culture, ideas, and politics. In emphasizing the migration of people and ideas, as well as speaking to African Diaspora and Latin American Studies, scholars who adopt this approach eschew comparison in favor of putting the hemisphere in dialogue. In many ways, this approach builds on the Puerto Rican Studies model, underscoring both the connections and boundaries between island and mainland to understand racialized social, political, cultural, and economic processes. While these works are not necessarily part of a shared disciplinary or theoretical framework, transnational works in Afro-Latino Studies hold together by arguing that any understanding of Latinos in the United States has to be understood, by definition, as deeply transnational and diasporic.

This model also offers new, pointed critiques of both the Black Atlantic model of African Diaspora Studies, which downplays or ignores the role of Latin America in shaping blackness, and the US model, which undertheorizes the circulation of ideology throughout the hemisphere in race-making. It also suggests that while the literatures on Afro-Latin Americans and Afro-Latinos have been largely conceptualized as separate, much is lost in treating the boundaries between the United States and Latin America as fixed.

Afro-Latino transnationalism is defined by circularity, shaped not only by crossing, migration, and exchange, but also by anti-black racism. At its core, Afro-Latino Studies is a project that seeks to claim *Latinidad* and, therefore, articulates its own variant of transnationality. In part, *Afro-Latinidad* in the United States is deeply transnational due to the realities of hypodescent, where it is possible for *Latinidad* to fall away across generations and be replaced by an experience of black Americanness. What this means for Afro-Latinos, then, is that if *Afro-Latinidad* is to be retained, it must be done through transnational ties – visits to the home or ancestral country, ties to relatives abroad, retention of cultural markers and practices, language, and other types of signaling that are, by definition, not US based.

This type of circularity is increasingly common as part of a globalized world. Changes in technology, communication, and transportation make such transnational ties easier to forge and maintain than ever before. And, as Dzideznyo and Oboler note, such ties reflect back on the United States. "In view of the current circular or return migration patterns of people of Latin American descent to and from the United States and the potential impact of this demographic phenomenon in redefining racial and ethnic relations in this society, understanding the historical and contemporary racial representations in Latin America, as well as how these are being transplanted and reformulated in the context of US racial ideologies, could prove to be useful for the ongoing discussion of racialization" (Dziezienyo and Oboler 2005, 9). Moreover, a transnational frame necessarily reinforces the importance of nation states, foregrounding borders, national ideologies, and citizenship in the production of migrant and racialized bodies, underscoring the politics of racial formation.

At the same time, Afro-Latinos are, by definition, embedded in diasporic dialogues. By this I mean that they are a core part of the African Diaspora – not just voluntary migrants but also part of the Afrodescendant population forcibly dispersed across the hemisphere as part of the transatlantic slave trade, and whose identities and experiences are shaped by that shared history. Race is produced through the movement of bodies, settlement, and resettlement. For Latinos, regardless of race, a set of meanings and experiences that are linked to the migration process binds them as a group. Blackness on the other hand, as African diaspora scholars and activists articulate it, is shaped by a shared experience of slavery and global anti-blackness, built and rebuilt across generations. These twin transnational frames – one of migration and the other of diaspora – are the core of the Afro-Latino experience and the transnational wave. This multidimensional transnationality is explored in a works that aim not only to bring to light the presence of Afro-Latinos here and there, but how circulation is a defining aspect of identity. In *Neither Enemies nor Friends: Latinos, Blacks, and Afro-Latinos*, editors Anani Dzidzienyo and Suzanne Oboler underscore this paradigm, bringing together scholarship from the United States and Latin America that emphasizes "the flow and counterflow of racial ideas" (2005, 5).

One area of research that has been particularly generative in this regard is recent work on the Dominican diaspora. Eugenia Georges (1990), Sherri Gramsmuck and Patricia Pessar (1991), Jorge Duany (1994), Luis Guarnizo (1994), Silvio Torres-Saillant (2000, 2010), Peggy Levitt (2001), Benjamin Bailey (2001), Ana Aparicio (2006, 2010), Ginetta Candelario (2007), José Itzigsohn (2009), Wendy Roth (2012), and others have examined the experiences of Dominican migrants who settled largely in New York, New Jersey and the adjacent Northeast following the Trujillo era, emphasizing the unique relationship to blackness experienced by Dominicans on the island and in the United States, and the role of transnational relationships in shaping race both in US enclaves and on the island. In these narratives, race becomes a question of both accommodation and remittance. This is also reflected in an expanding body of Dominican literature by well-known writers Julia Alvarez (1991), Junot Diaz (1996, 2008), Nelly Rosario (2003) and others, who speak directly to the complex relationship Dominican Americans have to both homeland and home (Moreno 2007, 2011; Flores 2009; Torres-Saillant 2010).

As in Puerto Rican Studies, transnational scholars show that local meanings and emplacements are as important as national ones. Dominicans, like Puerto Ricans and other migrant groups, do not circulate everywhere, but rather settle in enclaves, building revised identities, cultures, and politics that are shaped by both circularity and specificity. Urban centers like New York and Miami in particular serve to shape new racialized diasporic identities, as Anglophone Caribbean migrants settle alongside Afro-Latinos, creating overlapping categories of Caribbeanness and blackness that have evolved over time. New York, for example, is home to nearly half the population of US Dominicans and twenty-one percent of US Puerto Ricans (Brown and Patten 2013; López and Patten 2015). It also home to one-fourth of all black immigrants in the United States, ensuring that place shapes race and vice-versa.

Some Afro-Latin American populations, like Dominicans and Puerto Ricans, may now be better understood as diasporas defined by flows between two core metropoles, rather than from a nationalist framework of exodus and return. Jesse Hoffnung-Garskof (2007) argues that such dynamics better explain the reality of Dominican life, with migration and exchange between the twin capitals of Santo Domingo and New York City as core forces that shape the contemporary Dominican self. "Dominicans who migrated to New York, for instance, did not encounter an abstract or timeless U.S. racial system. They encountered the particular terms of neighborhood racial conflict in Upper Manhattan in the late 1960s and early 1970s. When stories of Dominicans' racial encounters in New York appeared in Santo Domingo, they in turn unfolded within the specific context of that city's urban crisis in the 1980s, and not within an abstract or timeless Dominican racial system" (Hoffnung-Garskof 2007, xvvii). These complex diasporas of multiple threads of transnational movement and the dynamics of local meanings and settlement call attention to the relationship between localities and movement.

Puerto Rican Studies has also expanded and deepened to emphasize circulation (see the concept of *el vaivén*, Duany 2002), bringing blackness into broader dialogue with issues of coloniality, culture, class, and gender. Jorge Duany's 2002 book, *The Puerto Rican Nation on the Move*, defines Puerto Ricanness as a kind of "translocal entity," in which cultural continuities between the island and the mainland are constantly produced and reproduced through circular migration. Ramos-Zayas uses the lens of locality to understand national identity and performance, exploring how Puerto Ricans in Chicago perform nationalism, critique social inequality and colonialism, and seek venues for upward mobility (2003). In Juan Flores' 2009 volume *The Diaspora Strikes Back*, Flores seeks to foreground the Caribbean transnational experience as inherently Afro-diasporic and therefore worthy of regional comparison and analysis. Collecting interviews and vignettes from Cuban, Dominican, and Puerto Rican migrants, Americans, and return migrants, Flores seeks to complicate the "lived transnational action and interaction" experiences of those whose lives "straddle diaspora and homelands" (2009, 141). Flores also turns to music and poetry as evidence of a kind of "transnationalism from below" in which cultural production serves both to knit together diasporic Caribbean communities and to challenge them with new language, styles, and acknowledgment of poverty, racism and affirmations of blackness unarticulated elsewhere.

Cultural studies analysts Petra Rivera-Rideau (2015), Raquel Rivera (2007), Arlene Dávila (2001, 2004) and others have examined the role of culture in shaping Puerto Rican conceptions of race, identity and nation, and the importance of relations between mainland and island Puerto Ricans in producing new dialogues. Rivera-Rideau's work examines cultural production and racial formations in Puerto Rico and the United States through the lens of Reggaetón, arguing that blackness gets articulated, reconfigured, and debated within the context of popular music. Because both the study and the acknowledgment of blackness has traditionally been confined to the domain of culture, Reggaetón and its increasing popularity is an especially fruitful space to examine racial meaning and production in diasporic perspective.

Carlos Alamo-Pastrana's *Seams of Empire* unpacks exchanges between African American journalists, white American liberal writers, and Puerto Rican activists from 1940 to 1972, and the ways in which they worked against "simplistic comparative tropes about race and colonialism. Instead these writers harnessed Black radicalism and critical examinations of the material conditions of Black life on the island and in the United States to more accurately interpret their political milieus and possibilities" (Alamo-Pastrana 2016, 10). These analyses fit Mark Anderson's argument that ways of thinking and practicing race arise not merely from national racial ideologies, nor transnational dynamics, but from the intersections between them (2005).

Historians have also noted the importance of these cultural circulations, such as Lara Putnam's work on how labor migration chains from the Caribbean to Panama's Canal Zone and Harlem played a role in shaping the production of musical genres like jazz, which were heavily influenced by cultural exchange among Afrodescendant migrant populations who were often segregated to black social spaces that were nevertheless shaped by transnational interaction (2016).

Cubanists have also embraced transnationalism. Frank Guridy's work on the exchange of ideas and politics between African Americans and Afro-Cubans in the twentieth century emphasizes the importance of cross-national relationships and ideas about race in negotiating "the entangled processes of imperialism and racial discrimination. As a result of these relationships, Afrodescended peoples in Cuba and the United States came to identify themselves as being part of a transcultural African diaspora" (Guridy 2010, 4). He also notes that these linkages must be understood, as in the Dominican Republic, Puerto Rico, and elsewhere, in a broader context of extraordinary US influence, in which racial formation was shaped in Cuba in no small part by its neocolonial relationship with the United States.

Nancy Mirabal (2017) shows how invisibility obscured important historical transnational relationships that in turn shaped ideas about race, gender, sexuality, and the Cuban nation itself. Unearthing the stories of Afro-Cubans in early 20th-century New York, Mirabal underscores their agency in authoring their own experiences. Despite their long political and intellectual history in New York, Afro-Cubans are rarely acknowledged as "some of the most incisive, powerful, and radical voices in the exile nationalist movement, so much so that by the mid- to late nineteenth century, meanings of Cubanidad were inextricably tied to ending slavery, racial equality, and a promise of enfranchisement (Mirabal 2017, 6)." Mirabal notes that, as Afro-Cuban exiles and migrants were constructing a vision for Cuba, they were informed by US racial concepts, laws, and practices, other migrants and the longstanding African American community in developing their ideas and politics.

Building on early works like Steven Gregory's "Afro-Caribbean Religions in New York City, the Case of Santeria" (1989), McPherson (2007) examines African American and Afro-Latin collaboration in religious communities. She emphasizes transnational relationships not only in terms of translocation (communities located in Chicago and Detroit) but also in bypassing Afro-Cuban centers on the island in favor of direct connections to Nigeria, choosing to locate their religious rites on the African continent rather than the Caribbean island. She finds this is the case even as the religious communities themselves remain African American, Latino, and Afro-Latino (largely Cuban and Puerto Rican) in composition, with few African-origin members.

In my own work, I examine how transnational circulation matters for shaping racial identities and outcomes in both the United States and Mexico. Based on field work in Mexico and North Carolina, I argue that increased migration from more heavily Afrodescendant states in Mexico has, in part, shaped Afro identity in Mexico. Until the mid-1990s, few Afro-Mexicans migrated to the United States. The North Atlantic Free Trade Agreement (NAFTA), however, had a serious impact on the livelihoods of rural towns that rely on subsistence agriculture. Because NAFTA has driven down prices, flooded the market with US agricultural surplus, and closed opportunities for small loans, many rural coastal

Mexicans who had never previously migrated have left their home towns in large numbers, primarily for North Carolina (Jones 2013).

Migration then reshaped the landscape of rural Afro-Mexico. Though Afro-Mexicans have historically been poor farmers, many are now upwardly mobile as remittances from the United States have increased. Meanwhile, when they return to Mexico from the United States, migrants are forced to bring their regional identities into discussion with national ones, creating spaces for new forms of racial formation. This process of increased physical mobility has put Afro-Mexicans in the position of having to explain and justify their origins for the first time, emphasizing their sense of invisibility. In addition to being perceived as outsiders due to their official erasure, a pervasive lack of knowledge regarding Afro-Mexican-origins, culture, and history has forced many migrants to examine their understandings of blackness, even when they had previously been disinclined to do so. Similarly, Mexicans leaving their towns encounter for the first time not only American ideas about blackness but also ideas about Mexicanness. Migration, combined with increasing streams of African American visitors from the United States, shifted the structural and ideological fields in which both migrants and non-migrants construct their identities (Jones 2013).

Literary scholars and critics are also deeply engaged in theorizing Afro-Latinos from a transnational perspective. Antonio López looks to Afro-Cuban American literature and performance as an expression of *Afro-Latinidad*, that is, the "Afro-Latino condition in the United States, which Afro-Cuban Americans share with other Latinas/os of African descent, including, but not limited to, those with origins in Puerto Rico, the Dominican Republic, Panama, Colombia, and Venezuela. Central to *Afro-Latinidad* is the social difference that blackness makes in the United States: how an Anglo white supremacy determines the life chances of Afro-Latinas/os hailed as black and how a Latino white supremacy reproduces the colonial and postcolonial Latin American privileging of *blanco* over *negro* and *mulato* (mixed-race) identities" (2012, 5). In López' analysis, Afro-Cuban American writers and performers "represent overlapping Cuban and African diasporas, which is to say that histories of displacement from Cuba and Africa bear upon them simultaneously, with changing, uneven effects on their relations, both material and symbolic, to race and nation, host- and homelands" (2012, 5–6).

Claudia Milian (2013) proposed the concept "Latinities" to attend to the fluidity and contestations around US Latino identities, in part to emphasize their connections to blackness. In interrogating the concept of Latino and the discursive work that *Latinidad* does, Milian argues that *Latinidad* refers to a kind of racialized grammar and meaning that is provisional and undergoing continue change. As an ideology that is shaped by what she calls a narrow 'color palette,' in that *Latinidad* expunges blackness and dark brownness, she argues that we have largely witnessed the production of a *Latinidad* that, as Richard Rodriguez sees it, is reconciled through brownness as the primary habitus for Latino or Latina personhoods (Milian 2013, 8). In turning to blackness and dark brownness in Mesoamerican contexts and through Central American migration, Milian seeks to both highlight and move beyond the white/ brown paradigm of *Latinidad*. Through recognition, she argues that her approach and attention to blackness opens up a new conceptual space of Latinities, a kind of *Latinidad* without national or racial boundaries, transnational, multivalent, and contradictory.

Much of the cutting-edge scholarship on Afro-Latino Studies today is necessarily taking this kind of transnational approach, in which diasporic and dialectical approaches are necessary due to the type of movements we observe as central to the Afro-Latino experience. Edited by Petra Rivera-Rideau, Jennifer Jones, and Tianna Paschel, *Afro-Latinos in Movement* underscores this approach. Through this book, new and established scholars examine the perpetual movement of people, politics, and culture, undermining the separation of the study of Afro-Latin America from that of Afro-Latinos in the United States and foregrounding the inherently transnational character of *Afro-Latinidad*. In doing so, they stress not only the specificity of the experience of *Afro-Latinidad* in the United States, but also how people, cultural productions, intellectual engagements, social movements, politics, and racial frameworks travel between spaces.[14]

The transnational paradigm in Afro-Latino Studies illuminates the way that thinking about Afro-Latinos changes the ways we think about Afro-Latin America. Transnationalism functions to both disrupt and create new emplacements, producing racialized and diasporic spaces like Miami and New York that are deeply local, specific, and contingent; it also points to the importance of ties and flows in shaping

---

[14] As this body of research expands, scholars also look to multiple intersections to deepen its theoretical reach. They stress the importance of locality and place, the intersection of race with gender and feminist epistemologies, neoliberalism, and the issue of method that plagues Afro-Latino Studies, in which the absence of archives and robust numbers and data require scholars to read silences and absences as well.

identities, practices and political dynamics across the hemisphere. For Afro-Latinos, the simultaneous experiences of blackness and *Latinidad* are continuously being shaped and reshaped through these transnational processes of movement and encounter, both diversifying and codifying what it means to be Afro-Latino. Also serving as a critique of normative blackness, it is this transnational emphasis in both scholarship and experience that situates Afro-Latino Studies as a uniquely diasporic enterprise and a necessary extension of Afro-Latin American Studies.

### AFRO-LATINO STUDIES AND AFRO-LATIN AMERICAN STUDIES

The concept of diaspora emerged as an effort to account for the in many ways forcible dispersal of the Jewish population, and was subsequently extended to theorize the African slave trade and the resulting communities outside of Africa that nevertheless remain entangled. This notion traditionally emphasizes, as Guridy notes, "'routes' instead of 'roots' to stress the importance of relationships between diasporic communities outside of the symbolic homeland of Africa in the reconstitution of the wider African diaspora" (2010: 4). In this way, diaspora refers to a kind of displacement and exclusion on the one hand, and attachment to homeland, feeling of connections, and establishment of group consciousness on the other (Rivera-Rideau 2014).

African Diaspora Studies has served as a critical intervention in our understanding of blackness, anti-blackness, and the political, social, cultural, and economic processes associated with diaspora. Yet studies of the African diaspora in African American, Africana and African Diaspora studies departments have most frequently emphasized the ties between English- and, to a lesser extent, French-speaking colonies and metropoles (Gilroy 1993; Edwards 2001; Nassy Brown 2005), to the overwhelming exclusion of Latin America and the Spanish-speaking Caribbean (Laó-Montes 2005, 2007b).[15] This is not to suggest that

---

[15] To be sure, there are exceptions to this trend (e.g., Hanchard 1999; Patterson and Kelley 2000; Butler 2001; Matory 2006; Guridy 2010), which have been cited more frequently in the broader African Diaspora Studies field. However, many dominant paradigms in the field, notably Paul Gilroy's idea of the "Black Atlantic," exclude Latin Americans and Latinos (Gilroy 1993).

Afrodescendant populations across the Americas go unstudied, but rather that these studies are marginalized within the fields of African Diaspora Studies scholarship and instruction. Instead, they appear in other disciplinary spaces – in Latin American Studies and within traditional disciplinary boundaries. As Laó-Montes argues, "Afro-Latinidades tend to be marginalized and even erased from most mappings of the African diaspora, at the same time that African diaspora perspectives need to play a more important role in Latino/American studies" (2007a, 318).

Likewise, the omission of Afro-Latinos and exchanges of ideas and culture across sites results in incomplete understandings of the dynamics of race and nation As Rivera-Rideau notes: "Scholars such as Jorge Duany and Juan Flores argue that definitions of the Puerto Rican nation must incorporate US Puerto Rican communities that have maintained connections to the island and have made substantial contributions to Puerto Rico's culture and politics. However, the insular nature of dominant definitions of Puerto Rican identity often excludes the community in the United States," which outnumbers that on the island (Rivera-Rideau 2015, 25). This omission of Afro-Latino communities in analyzing Afro-Latin America, as is highlighted by numerous new works in Afro-Latino studies, creates a deep gap in our understanding of Afro-Latin America. Transnational, diasporic relations are not only shaping ideas of blackness in the United States, but boomerang back home, both through intentionally cultivated political and social relations and through distinctly neocolonial and globalized processes.

As a result, Afro-Latino Studies has emerged as a corollary, but largely separate, area of research, in which a diaspora of the western hemisphere (rather than the Atlantic) works to theorize not only the legacies of the slave trade but also the influence of regional rebellion, semi- and neocolonial relations with the Spain, and later the United States. It also emphasizes the ongoing dynamics of diaspora that shape the region, such as migration, the circulation of ideas and culture, political movements, agencies, and globalization, underscoring the contemporary, dynamic, and persisting nature of diasporic formation in the region.

Because race was part and parcel of defining oneself as modern, powerful, and independent, blackness and diasporic relations play an outsized role in shaping the Americas. This is true even as much of the official narratives within the hemisphere sought, and often continue, to assert a kind of racial democracy or *mestizaje* nationalism that claims race is irrelevant.[16] These particular dynamics of Afro-Latin America necessarily include the experiences of Afro-Latinos in the United States.

Black Latinos in the United States are important not merely because they reflect long-standing chains of migration and exchange between the United States and the hemisphere, representing categories of people that are frequently invisiblized in popular discourse, national imaginary, and scholarly archives, but also because they trouble our racial categories. *Latinidad* in the United States has emerged in response to the homogeneity of whiteness by reproducing a form of homogeneity of its own through *mestizaje*. Clearly this is a problematic solution. Not only does it reify troublesome nationalist tropes and racialized meanings, but it continues to erase black Latinos and blackness in the construction of Latin America and Western thought.

As a result, there is much lost in the separation of literature on race in Latin America and that of Latinos in the United States. On the one hand, the scholarship on Latinos in the United States takes as a point of departure that *Latinidad* is inherently raced and transnational. Yet the literature on *Latinidad* also comes with much of the conceptual and political baggage of *mestizaje*, which is being vigorously debated and destabilized in Latin America today. On the other hand, by centering blackness and problematizing *mestizaje*, the literature on Afro-Latin America gives us many conceptual tools for understanding how *Afro-Latinidad* is constructed, how it is lived and contested, and how it changes over time. Even so, it often emphasizes a bounded idea of blackness as being articulated exclusively within the nation-state, rather than through cross-national flows.

While these are distinct frameworks, I would argue that they are better theorized as related and complimentary. Bringing Latino studies into greater conversation with Afro-Latin American studies via Afro-Latino studies is a fruitful intellectual endeavor, not only to better understand the role of sending regions, cultures and politics in shaping US identities and racial frames, but also to provide a more nuanced understanding of how those circulations are not merely US racial constructions imposed on Latin America but products of an ongoing exchange of people and ideas. For instance, some scholars have demonstrated how the traffic of ideas about blackness between geographic sites offered important tools and strategies for local communities fighting against racial inequality around

---

[16] It is important to note that these narratives are often contested and not always as hegemonic as official narratives would suggest (Hanchard 1998; Telles 2004).

the globe (Guridy 2010; Mirabal 2017; Pereira 2016). Furthermore, such exchanges become crucial for establishing and elaborating diasporic connections across the African diaspora, including among Afro-Latin Americans and Afro-Latinos (Brown 2005; Edwards 2003; Rahier, Hintzen, and Smith 2010). In other words, Afro-Latinos can change the way we think about Afro-Latin America and the geography of blackness. Anchoring Afro-Latino studies in Afro-Latin American studies is not only a good empirical fit but creates a theoretical position from which important critiques can be leveled at many of their sister fields.

In expanding the reach of the concept of *Afro-Latinidad* to the United States, Afro-Latin American Studies has the potential to create important analytical interventions, challenging the racial projects of Latin America and United States, and the shared anti-black racism between them. Afro-Latino studies at its core emphasizes both the local specificities of race and the patterns of anti-black racism that exist throughout the Americas. Integrating Afro-Latino studies into Afro-Latin American scholarship makes this research and its important insights more visible across the disciplines.

Finally, in broadening the conceptual understanding of *Afro-Latinidad* to include Afro-Latinos in the United States, we can develop a more complete understanding of both the systemic anti-black racism throughout the hemisphere as well as the specific ways these manifest in state projects, cultural productions, and everyday life. This expanded concept of *Afro-Latinidad* aligns with Agustín Laó-Montes's suggestion that, while the term Afro-Latino refers to the ethnoracial backgrounds of "peoples of African descent in Latino/America," "Afro-Latina/o as a subalternized diasporic form of difference should be transformed into a critical category to deconstruct and redefine...narratives of geography, memory, culture, and the self" that otherwise foster the marginalization and/or invisibility of these communities (2005). In other words, by bringing Afro-Latino scholarship to Afro-Latin American studies, we center the diverse connections forged between Afro-Latin Americans, Afro-Latinos, and other diasporic populations, either through in-person collaborations or through the movement of ideas about blackness, as part of a larger strategy to combat anti-black racism.

### BIBLIOGRAPHY

Alamo-Pastrana, Carlos. 2016. *Seams of Empire: Race and Radicalism in Puerto Rico and the United States*. Gainesville, FL: University Press of Florida.
Alamo-Pastrana, Carlos, and Ginetta Candelario. 2016. "*Future Directions in Afro-Latino Studies*." Afro-Latino Studies Symposium, Williams College.

Alba, Richard. 1990. *Ethnic Identity: The Transformation of White America.* New Haven, CT: Yale University Press.

Alba, Richard, and Victor Nee. 2003. *Remaking the American Mainstream: Assimilation and Contemporary Immigration.* Cambridge, MA: Harvard University Press.

Almaguer, Tomas. 2003. "At the Crossroads of Race: Latino/a Studies and Race Making in the United States." In *Critical Latin American and Latino Studies,* edited by Juan Poblete, 206–22. Minneapolis, MN: University of Minnesota Press.

2009. *Racial Fault Lines: The Historical Origins of White Supremacy in California.* 2nd edition. Berkeley, CA: University of California Press.

Alvarez, Julia. 1991. *How the Garcia Girls Lost Their Accents.* Chapel Hill, NC: Algonquin Books.

Anderson, Mark. 2005. "Bad Boys and Peaceful Garifuna: Transnational Encounters Between Racial Stereotypes of Honduras and the United States (and Their Implications for the Study of Race in the Americas)." In *Neither Enemies nor Friends: Latinos, Blacks, and Afro-Latinos,* edited by Anani Dzidzienyo and Suzanne Oboler, 101–15. New York, NY: Palgrave MacMillan.

Anzaldúa, Gloria. 1987. *Borderlands/La Frontera: The New Mestiza.* San Francisco, CA: Spinsters/Aunt Lute.

Anzaldúa, Gloria, and Cherrie Moraga, eds. 1981. *This Bridge Called My Back: Writings by Radical Women of Color.* London: Persephone Press.

Aparicio, Ana. 2006. *Dominican-Americans and the Politics of Empowerment.* Gainesville, FL: University of Florida Press.

2007. "Contesting Race and Power: Second-Generation Dominican Youth in the New Gotham." *City & Society* 19, 2: 179–201.

2010. "Transglocal Barrio Politics: Dominican American Organizing in New York City." In *Beyond the Barrio,* edited by Gina Pérez, Frank Guridy, and Adrian Burgos. New York, NY: New York University Press.

Aparicio, Frances. 1999. "The Blackness of Sugar: Celia Cruz and the Performances of (Trans)nationalism." *Cultural Studies* 13: 223–36.

Arroyo, Jossianna. 2010. "'Roots' or the Virtualities of Racial Imaginaries in Peutro Rico and the Diaspora. *Latino Studies* 8: 195–219.

Bailey, Benjamin. 2000. "The Language of Multiple Identities among Dominican Americans." *Journal of Linguistic Anthropology* 10, 2: 190–223.

2001. "Dominican-American Ethnic/Racial Identities and United States Social Categories." *International Migration Review* 35, 3: 677–708.

2002. *Language, Race and Negotiation of Identity: A Study of Dominican Americans.* New York, NY: LFB Scholarly Publishing.

Bean, Frank, and Marta Tienda. 1987. *The Hispanic Population of the United States.* New York, NY: Russell Sage Foundation.

Beltran, Cristina. 2004. "Patrolling Borders: Hybrids, Hierarchies and the Challenge of Mestizaje." *Political Research Quarterly* 57, 4: 597–607.

Bonilla, Frank, and Ricardo Campos. 1981. "A Wealth of Poor: Puerto Ricans in the New Economic Order." *Daedalus* 110, 2: 133–76.

Bonilla-Silva, Eduardo, and David G. Embrick. 2006. "Black, Honorary White, White: The Future of Race in the United States?" In *Mixed Messages: Doing*

*Race in the Color-Blind Era*, edited by David Brunsma, 33–48. Boulder, CO: Lynne Reinner Publishers.

Burgos, Adrian. 2009. "Left Out: Afro-Latinos, Black Baseball, and the Revision of Baseball's Racial History." *Social Text* 27, 198: 37–58.

Brown, Anna, and Eileen Patten. 2013. "Hispanics of Dominican Origin in the United States, 2011." *Pew Research Center's Hispanic Trends Project*, June 19. www.pewhispanic.org/2013/06/19/hispanics-of-dominican-origin-in-the-united-states-2011/.

Candelario, Ginetta E. B. 2007. *Black Behind the Ears: Dominican Racial Identity from Museums to Beauty Shops*. Durham, NC: Duke University Press.

Chavez, Leo Ralph. 2008. *The Latino Threat: Constructing Immigrants, Citizens, and the Nation*. Stanford, CA: Stanford University Press.

Colon, Jesus. 1961. *A Puerto Rican in New York and Other Sketches*. New York, NY: New World Paperbacks.

Darity, Jr., William A., Jason Dietrich, and Darrick Hamilton. 2005. "Bleach in the Rainbow: Latin Ethnicity and Preference for Whiteness." *Transforming Anthropology* 13, 2: 103–09.

Dávila, Arlene. 2001. "Local/Diasporic Tainos: Towards a Cultural Politics of Memory, Reality and Imagery." In *Taino Revival: Critical Perspectives on Puerto Rican Identity and Cultural Politics*, edited by Gabriel Haslip-Viera, 33–53. Princeton, NJ: Markus Weiner Press.

2004. "Empowered Culture? New York's Empowerment Zone and the Selling of El Barrio." *Annals of the American Academy of Political and Social Science* 594, 1: 49–64.

2008. *Latino Spin: Public Image and the Whitewashing of Race*. New York, NY: New York University Press.

2012. *Latinos Inc.: The Marketing and Making of a People*. Berkeley, CA: University of California Press.

Davis, F. James. 1991. *Who Is Black? One Nation's Definition*. University Park, PA: Pennsylvania State University Press.

DeGenova, Nicholas, and Ana Ramos-Zayas. 2003. "Latino Racial Formations in the United States: An Introduction." *Journal of Latin American Anthropology* 8, 2: 2–16.

Delgado, Linda. C. 2005. "Jesús Colón and the Making of a New York City Community, 1917–1974." In *The Puerto Rican Diaspora: Historical Perspectives*, edited by Carmen Teresa Whalen and Victor Vasquez-Hernandez, 68–87. Philadelphia, PA: Temple University Press.

Díaz, Junot. 1996. *Drown*. New York, NY: Riverhead Books.

2008. *The Brief Wondrous Life of Oscar Wao*. New York, NY: Riverhead Books.

Dinzey-Flores, Zaire Z. 2008. "De la Disco al Caserío: Urban Spatial Aesthetics and Policy to the Beat of Reggaetón." *CENTRO: Journal for the Center of Puerto Rican Studies* 20, 2: 35–69.

Duany, Jorge. 1994. *Quisqueya on the Hudson: The Transnational Identity of Dominicans in Washington Heights*, New York, NY: CUNY Dominican Studies Institute.

2002. *The Puerto Rican Nation on the Move: Identities on the Island and in the United States*. Chapel Hill, NC: University of North Carolina Press.

Dzidzienyo, Anani and Suzanne Oboler, eds. 2005. *Neither Enemies nor Friends: Latinos, Blacks, Afro-Latinos*. New York, NY: Palgrave Macmillian.

Edwards, Brent Hayes. 2001. "The Uses of Diaspora." *Social Text* 19, 1: 45–73.

2003. *The Practice of Diaspora: Literature, Translation, and the Rise of Black Internationalism*. Cambridge, MA: Harvard University Press.

Ennis, Sharon R., Merarys Rios-Vargas, and Nora G. Albert. 2011. "This Hispanic Population: 2010." 2010 Census Briefs. Washington D.C.: US Census Bureau. Accessed April 30, 2017, at www.census.gov/prod/cen2010/briefs/c2010br-04.pdf.

Fernández, Lilia. 2012. *Brown in the Windy City: Mexicans and Puerto Ricans in Postwar Chicago*. Chicago, IL: University of Chicago Press.

FitzGerald, David Scott, and David Cook-Martín. 2014. *Culling the Masses: The Democratic Origins of Racist Immigration Policy in the Americas*. Cambridge, MA: Harvard University Press.

Flores, Juan. 1993. *Divided Borders: Essays on Puerto Rican Identity*. Houston, TX: Arte Público Press.

2003. "Latino Studies: New Contexts, New Concepts." In *Critical Latin American and Latino Studies*, edited by Juan Poblete. Minneapolis, MN: University of Minnesota Press.

2009. *The Diaspora Strikes Back: Caribeño Tales of Learning and Turning*. New York, NY: Routledge.

Flores-González, Nilda. 1999. "The Racialization of Latinos: The Meaning of Latino Identity for the Second Generation." *Latino Studies Journal* 10, 3: 3–31.

Forbes, Jack D. 1966. "Black Pioneers: The Spanish-Speaking Afroamericans of the Southwest." *Phylon* 27, 3: 233–46.

Fusté, José. 2010. "Colonial Laboratories, Irreparable Subjects: The Experiment of '(B)ordering' San Juan's Public Housing Residents." *Social Identities* 16, 1: 41–59.

2016. "Translating Negroes into *Negros*: Rafael Serra's Transamerican Entanglements Between Black Cuban Racial and Imperial Subalternity, 1895–1909." In *Afro-Latin@s in Movement: Critical Approaches to Blackness and Transnationalism in the Americas*, edited by Petra R. Rivera-Rideau, Jennifer A. Jones, and Tianna S. Paschel, 221–46. New York, NY: Palgrave Macmillan.

Georges, Eugenia. 1990. *The Making of a Transnational Community: Migration, Development and Cultural Change in the Dominican Republic*. New York, NY: Columbia University Press.

Gibson, Samantha. 2017. "Puerto Rican Migration to the US: Primary Source Set." Accessed Feb. 2, 2017. https://dp.la/primary-source-sets/sets/puerto-rican-migration-to-the-us/.

Gilroy, Paul. 1993. *The Black Atlantic: Modernity and Double Consciousness*. Cambridge, MA: Harvard University Press.

Godreau, Isar. 2015. *Scripts of Blackness: Race, Cultural Nationalism, and U.S. Colonialism in Puerto Rico*. Urbana, IL: University of Illinois Press.

Gonzales, Juan. 2000. *Harvest of Empire: A History of Latinos in America*. New York, NY: Penguin.

Gonzales, R. G. 2011. "Learning to Be Illegal: Undocumented Youth and Shifting Legal Contexts in the Transition to Adulthood." *American Sociological Review* 76, 4: 602–19.

González, Nancie L. 1989. "Garifuna Settlement in New York, NY: A New Frontier." *Center for Migration Studies Special Issues* 7, 1: 138–46.

Gould, Virginia Meacham. 2010. "Slave and Free Women of Color in the Spanish Ports of New Orleans, Mobile, and Pensacola." In *The Afro-Latin@ Reader: History and Culture in the United States*, edited by Miriam Jiménez Román and Juan Flores, 38–50. Durham, NC: Duke University Press.

Gramsmuck, Sherri and Patricia R. Pessar. 1991. *Between Two Islands: Dominican International Migration*. Berkeley, CA: University of California Press.

Greenbaum, Susan. 2002. *More than Black: Afro-Cubans in Tampa*. Gainesville, FL: University Press of Florida.

Gregory, Steven. 1989. "Afro-Caribbean Religions in New York City: The Case of Santería." *Center for Migration Studies Special Issues* 7, 1: 287–304.

Grillo. Evelio. 2000. *Black Cuban, Black American. A Memoir*. Houston, TX: Arte Publico Press.

Guarnizo, Luis E. 1994. "Los Dominicanyorks:: The Making of a Binational Society." *Annals of the American Academy of Political and Social Science* 533, 1: 70–86.

Guinier, Lani, and Gerald Torres. 2002. *The Miner's Canary: Enlisting Race, Resisting Power, Transforming Democracy*. Cambridge, MA: Harvard University Press.

Guridy, Frank Andre. 2010. *Forging Diaspora: Afro-Cubans and African Americans in a World of Empire and Jim Crow*. Chapel Hill, NC: University of North Carolina Press.

Gutiérrez, David G. 1995. *Walls and Mirrors: Mexican Americans, Mexican Immigrants, and the Politics of Ethnicity*. Berkeley, CA: University of California Press.

Guzmán, Pablo "Yoruba." "Before People Called Me a Spic, They Called Me a Nigger." In *The Afro-Latin@ Reader: History and Culture in the United States*, edited by Miriam Jiménez Román and Juan Flores, 235–43. Durham, NC: Duke University Press.

Hanchard, Michael George. 1998. *Orpheus and Power: The Movimento Negro of Rio de Janeiro and São Paulo, Brazil, 1945–1988*. Reprint. Princeton, NJ: Princeton University Press.

1999. "Afro-Modernity: Temporality, Politics, and the African Diaspora." *Public Culture* 11, 1: 245–68.

"Harlem Race Riot (1935)." 2017. *Uncovering Yonkers*. www.UncoveringYonkers.com/harlem-race-riot-1935.html. Accessed March 8, 2017.

Hattam, Victoria. 2007. *In the Shadow of Race: Jews, Latinos and Immigrant Politics in the United States*. Chicago, IL: University of Chicago Press.

Hernández, Tanya Katerí. 2003. "'Too Black to be Latino/a:' Blackness and Blacks as Foreigners in Latino Studies." *Latino Studies* 1, 1: 152–59.

2004. "Afro-Mexicans and the Chicano Movement: The Unknown Story." *California Law Review* 92, 5: 1537–51.

Higgins, Shana M. 2007. "Afro-Latinos." *Reference & User Services Quarterly* 47, 1: 10–15.

Hoffnung-Garskof, Jesse. 2010. "The World of Arturo Alfonso Schomburg." In *The Afro-Latin@ Reader: History and Culture in the United States*, edited by Miriam Jiménez Román and Juan Flores, 70–91. Durham, NC: Duke University Press.

Hooker, Juliet. 2005. "Indigenous Inclusion/Black Exclusion: Race, Ethnicity and Multicultural Citizenship in Latin America." *Journal of Latin American Studies* 37, 2: 285–310.

Hoy, Vielka. 2010. "Negotiating among Invisibilities: Tales of *Afro-Latinidad*es in the United States." In *The Afro-Latin@ Reader: History and Culture*, edited by Miriam Jiménez Román and Juan Flores, 426–30. Durham, NC: Duke University Press.

Huntington, Samuel. 2004. *Who Are We? The Challenges to America's National Identity*. New York, NY: Simon and Schuster.

Joseph, Tiffany. 2015. *Race on the Move: Brazilian Migrants and the Global Reconstruction of Race*. Stanford, CA: Stanford University Press, 2015.

Itzigsohn, José. 2009. *Encountering American Faultlines: Class, Race, and the Dominican Experience*. New York, NY: Russell Sage Foundation.

Itzigsohn, José, and Carlos Doré-Cabral. 2000. "Competing Identities? Race, Ethnicity and Panethnicity among Dominicans in the United States." *Sociological Forum* 15, 2: 225–47.

Jackson, Maria Rosario. 2010. "Profile of an Afro-Latina: Black, Mexican, Both." In *The Afro-Latin@ Reader: History and Culture*, edited by Miriam Jiménez Román and Juan Flores, 434–38. Durham, NC: Duke University Press.

Jiménez Román, Miriam, and Juan Flores. 2010. "Introduction." In *The Afro-Latin@ Reader: History and Culture*, edited by Miriam Jiménez Román and Juan Flores, 1–18. Durham, NC: Duke University Press.

———. eds. 2010. *The Afro-Latin@ Reader: History and Culture*. Durham, NC: Duke University Press.

Jiménez, Tomás. 2010. *Replenished Ethnicity: Mexican Americans, Immigration, and Identity*. Berkeley, CA: University of California Press.

Jones, Jennifer Anne Meri. 2013. "'Mexicans Will Take the Jobs That Even Blacks Won't Do': An Analysis of Blackness, Regionalism and Invisibility in Contemporary Mexico." *Ethnic and Racial Studies* 36, 10: 1564–81.

Kasinitz, Philip. 1992. *Caribbean New York, NY: Black Immigrants and the Politics of Race*. Ithaca, NY: Cornell University Press, 1992.

Klein, Christine A. 2008. "Treaties of Conquest: Property Rights, Indian Treaties, and the Treaty of Guadalupe Hidalgo." SSRN Scholarly Paper. Rochester, NY: Social Science Research Network, November 19, 2008.

Lambert, Aida. 2010. "We Are Black Too: Experiences of a Honduran Garifuna." In *The Afro-Latin@ Reader: History and Culture*, edited by Miriam Jiménez Román and Juan Flores, 431–34. Durham, NC: Duke University Press.

Laó-Montes, Agustín. 2005. "Afro-Latin@ Difference and the Politics of Decolonization." In *Latin@s in the World System: Decolonization Struggles in the 21st-Century U.S. Empire*, edited by Ramón Grosfoguel, Nelson

Maldonado-Torres, and José David Saldívar, 75–88. Boulder, CO: Paradigm Publishers.

2007a. "Decolonial Moves: Trans-Locating African Diaspora Spaces." *Tabula Rasa* 7: 309–38.

2007b. "*Afro-Latinidades*: Bridging Blackness and *Latinidad*." In *Technofuturos: Critical Interventions in Latino/a Studies*, edited by Nancy Mirabal and Agustín Laó-Montes, 117–40. New York, NY: Lexington Books.

Levitt, Peggy. 2001. *The Transnational Villagers*. Berkeley, CA: University of California Press.

Logan, John R., Wenquan Zhang, and Richard D. Alba. 2002. "Immigrant Enclaves and Ethnic Communities in New York and Los Angeles." *American Sociological Review* 67, 2: 299–322.

López, Antonio. 2012. *Unbecoming Blackness: The Diaspora Cultures of Afro-Cuban America*. New York, NY: New York University Press.

López, Gustavo, and Eileen Patten. 2015. "Hispanics of Puerto Rican Origin in the United States, 2013." *Pew Research Center's Hispanic Trends Project.* Accessed January 30, 2017, at www.pewhispanic.org/2015/09/15/hispanics-of-puerto-rican-origin-in-the-united-states-2013/.

López, Ian Haney. 1996. *White by Law: The Legal Construction of Race*. New York, NY: New York University Press.

2003. *Racism on Trial: The Chicano Fight for Justice*. Cambridge, MA: Harvard University Press.

López, Ian Haney, and Michael Olivas. 2008. "Jim Crow, Mexican Americans, and the Anti-Subordination Constitution: The Story of Hernandez v. Texas," In *Race Law Stories*, edited by Rachel Moran and Devon Carbado. New York, NY: Foundation Press.

López, Nancy. 2013. "Killing Two Birds with One Stone? Why We Need Two Separate Questions on Race and Ethnicity in the 2020 Census and beyond." *Latino Studies* 11, 3: 428–38.

Loveman, Mara. 2014. *National Colors: Racial Classification and the State in Latin America*. Oxford: Oxford University Press.

Loveman, Mara, and Jeronimo O. Muniz. 2007. "How Puerto Rico Became White: Boundary Dynamics and Intercensus Racial Reclassification." *American Sociological Review* 72, 6: 915–39.

Mann-Hamilton, Ryan. 2010. "Retracing Migration: From Samaná to New York and Back Again." In *The Afro-Latin@ Reader: History and Culture*, edited by Miriam Jiménez Román and Juan Flores, 422–25. Durham, NC: Duke University Press.

Matory, J. Lorand. 2006. *Black Atlantic Religion: Tradition, Transnationalism, and Matriarchy in the Afro-Brazilian Candomblé*. Princeton, NJ: Princeton University Press.

McPherson, Jadele. 2007. "Rethinking African Religions: African Americans, Afro-Latinos, Latinos, and Afro-Cuban Religions in Chicago." *Afro-Hispanic Review* 26, 1: 121–40.

Menchaca, Martha. 2001. *Recovering History, Constructing Race: The Indian, Black, and White Roots of Mexican Americans*. Austin, TX: University of Texas Press.

Menjívar, Cecilia. 2013. "Central American Immigrant Workers and Legal Violence in Phoenix, Arizona." *Latino Studies* 11, 2: 228–52.

Migration Policy Institute. 2013. "Mexican-Born Population Over Time, 1850-Present." Accessed May 10, 2016, at www.migrationpolicy.org/pro grams/data-hub/charts/mexican-born-population-over-time.

2015. "Cuban Immigrants in the United States." Accessed May 20, 2016, at www.migrationpolicy.org/article/cuban-immigrants-united-states.

2016. "U.S. Immigration Trends." Accessed May 20, 2016, at www.migration policy.org/programs/data-hub/us-immigration-trends#Diaspora.

Milian, Claudia. 2013. *Latining America: Black-Brown Passages and the Coloring of Latino/a Studies.* Athens, GA: University of Georgia Press.

Mirabal, Nancy Raquel. 2003. "'Ser de aquí': Beyond the Cuban Exile Model." *Latino Studies* 1, 3: 366–82.

2017. *Suspect Freedoms: The Racial and Sexual Politics of Cubanidad in New York, 1823–1957.* Reprint. New York, NY: New York University Press.

Montejano, David. 1987. *Anglos and Mexicans in the Making of Texas, 1836–1986.* Austin, TX: University of Texas Press.

1999. *Chicano Politics and Society in the Late Twentieth Century.* Austin, TX: University of Texas Press.

Mora, G. Cristina. 2014. *Making Hispanics: How Activists, Bureaucrats, and Media Constructed a New American.* Chicago, IL: University of Chicago Press.

Moreno, Marisel. 2007. "Debunking Myths, Destabilizing Identities: A Reading of Junot Díaz's 'How to Date a Browngirl, Blackgirl, Whitegirl, or Halfie.'" *Afro-Hispanic Review* 26, 2: 103–17.

2011. "'Burlando la raza': la poesía de escritoras afrodominicanas en la diaspora." Accessed April 18, 2017, at http://dspace.uah.es/dspace/handle/10017/11127.

Nassy Brown, Jacqueline. 2005. *Dropping Anchor, Setting Sail: Geographies of Race in Black Liverpool.* Princeton, NJ: Princeton University Press.

Negrón-Muntaner, 1997. Frances, and Ramón Grosfoguel, eds. *Puerto Rican Jam: Rethinking Colonialism and Nationalism.* Minneapois, MN: University of Minnesota Press.

Ngai, Mae. 2004. *Impossible Subjects: Illegal Aliens and the Making of Modern America.* Princeton, NJ: Princeton University Press.

Oboler, Suzanne. 1995. *Ethnic Labels, Latino Lives: Identity and the Politics of (Re)presentation in the United States.* Minneapolis, MN: University of Minnesota Press.

Padilla, Felix. 1985. *Latino Ethnic Consciousness: The Case of Mexican Americans and Puerto Ricans in Chicago.* South Bend, IN: University of Notre Dame Press.

Paschel, Tianna. 2016. *Becoming Black Political Subjects: Movements and Ethno-Racial Rights in Colombia and Brazil.* Princeton, NJ: Princeton University Press.

Patterson, Tiffany Ruby, and Robin D. G. Kelley. 2000. "Unfinished Migrations: Reflections on the African Diaspora and the Making of the Modern World." *African Studies Review* 43, 1: 11–45.

Pereira, Amilcar Araujo. 2016. "The Transnational Circulation of Political References: The Black Brazilian Movement and Antiracist Struggles of the Early

Twentieth Century." In *Afro-Latin@s in Movement: Critical Approaches to Blackness and Transnationalism in the Americas*, edited by Petra R. Rivera-Rideau, Jennifer A. Jones, and Tianna S. Paschel. New York, NY: Palgrave Macmillan.

Perez, Gina. 2004. *The Near Northwest Side Story: Migration, Displacement, and Puerto Rican Families*. Berkeley, CA: University of California Press.

Pérez-Sarduy, Pedro, and Jean Stubbs. 2000. *Afro-Cuban Voices: On Race and Identity in Contemporary Cuba*. Gainesville, FL: University Press of Florida.

Pérez-Torres, Rafael. 2006. *Mestizaje: Critical Uses of Race in Chicano Culture*. Minneapolis, MN: University of Minnesota Press.

Pew Hispanic Center. 2016. "Statistical Portrait of Hispanics in the United StatesPew Hispanic Center. Accessed May 1, 2016, at www.pewhispanic .org/2016/04/19/statistical-portrait-of-hispanics-in-the-united-states/.

Portes, Alejandro, and Rubén G. Rumbaut. 2001. *Legacies: The Story of the Immigrant Second Generation*. Berkeley, CA: University of California Press.

Putnam, Lara. 2016. "Jazzing Sheiks at the 25 Cent Bram: Panama and Harlem as Caribbean Crossroads, circa 1910–1940." *Journal of Latin American Cultural Studies* 25, 3: 339–59.

Rahier, Jean Muteba, Percy C. Hintzen, and Felipe Smith, eds. 2010. *Global Circuits of Blackness: Interrogating the African Diaspora*. Urbana, IL: University of Illinois Press.

Ramos-Zayas, Ana. 2003. *National Performances: The Politics of Class, Race, and Space in Puerto Rican Chicago*. Chicago, IL: University of Chicago Press.

———. 2007. "Becoming American, Becoming Black? Urban Competency, Racialized Spaces, and the Politics of Citizenship among Brazilian and Puerto Rican Youth in Newark." *Identities: Global Studies in Culture and Power* 14, 1–2: 85–109.

Rivera, Raquel. 2003. *New York Ricans from the Hip Hop Zone*. New York, NY: Palgrave Macmillan.

———. 2007. "Will the 'Real' Puerto Rican Culture Pleas Stand Up? Thoughts on Cultural Nationalism." In *None of the Above: Puerto Ricans in the Global Era*, edited by Frances Negron–Muntaner, 217–31. New York, NY: Palgrave MacMillan.

Rivera-Rideau, Petra R. 2015. *Remixing Reggaetón: The Cultural Politics of Race in Puerto Rico*. Durham, NC: Duke University Press.

Rivera-Rideau, Petra, Jennifer Jones, and Tianna Paschel, eds. 2016. *Afro-Latino@s in Movement: Critical Approaches to Blackness and Transnationalism in the Americas*. New York, NY: Palgrave Press.

Rodríguez, Clara E. 1989. *Puerto Ricans Born in the USA*. Boston: Unwin Hyman.

———. 2000. *Changing Race: Latinos, the Census, and the History of Ethnicity in the United States*. New York, NY: New York University Press.

Rosario, Nelly. 2003. *Song of the Water Saints*. New York, NY: Penguin Random House.

Roth, Wendy. 2012. *Race Migrations: Latinos and the Cultural Transformation of Race*. Stanford, CA: Stanford University Press.

Rúa, Mérida M. 2012. *A Grounded Identidad: Making New Lives in Chicago's Puerto Rican Neighborhoods*. New York, NY: Oxford University Press.

Rumbaut, Rubén G. 2009. "Pigments of Our Imagination: On the Racialization and Racial Identities of 'Hispanics' and 'Latinos.'" In *How the U.S.*

*Racializes Latinos: White Hegemony and Its Consequences*, edited by Jose A. Cobas, Jorge Duany, and Joe R. Feagin, 15–36. Boulder, CO: Paradigm.

2011. "Pigments of Our Imagination: On the Racialization and Racial Identities of 'Hispanics' and 'Latinos,'" http://papers.ssrn.com/abstract=1878732.

Santiago-Valles, Kelvin A. 1995. "Vigilando, administrando y patrullando a negros y trigueños: Del cuerpo delito de los cuerpos en la crisis del Puerto Rico urbano actual." *Bordes* 2:28–42.

Sarduy, Pedro Pérez, and Jean Stubbs. 2000. *Afro-Cuban Voices: On Race and Identity in Contemporary Cuba*. Gainesville, FL: University Press of Florida.

Sommers, Laurie Kay. 1991. "Inventing Latinismo: The Creation of 'Hispanic' Panethnicity in the United States." *Journal of American Folklore* 104, 411: 32.

Suarez-Orozco, Marcelo, and Mariela Páez, eds. 2002. *Latinos: Remaking America*. Berkeley, CA: University of California Press.

Stern. Alexandra Minna. 2015. *Eugenic Nation: Faults and Frontiers of Better Breeding in Modern America*. 2nd edition. Oakland, CA: University of California Press.

Sutton, Constance R. 1989. *Caribbean Life in New York City: Sociocultural Dimensions*. Edited by Elsa M. Chaney. New York, NY: Center Migration Studies, 1989.

Telles, Edward. 2004. *Race in Another America: The Significance of Skin Color in Brazil*. Princeton, NJ: Princeton University Press.

Thomas, Piri. 1967. *Down These Mean Streets*. New York, NY: Knopf.

Torres-Saillant, Silvio. 2000. "Diasporic Disquisitions: Dominicanists, Transnationalism, and the Community." New York, NY: CUNY Dominican Studies Working Paper Series 1. Accessed April 18, 2017, at http://academicworks.cuny.edu/dsi_pubs/20.

2010. *"Introduction to Dominican Blackness."* New York, NY: CUNY Dominican Studies Institute. Accessed April 18, 2017, at http://academic works.cuny.edu/cgi/viewcontent.cgi?article=1002&context=dsi_pubs&seiredir=1&referer=https%3A%2F%2Fscholar.google.com%2Fscholar%3Fq%3Dsilvio%2Btorres-saillant%2Bintroduction%2Bdominican%2Bblackness%26btnG%3D%26hl%3Den%26as_sdt%3D0%252C39#search=%22silvio%20torres-saillant%20introduction%20dominican%20blackness%22.

Valle, Victor and Rodolfo D. Torres. 1995. "The Idea of Mestizaje and the 'Race' Problematic: Racialized Media Discourse in a Post-Fordist Landscape." In *Culture and Difference: Critical Perspectives on the Bicultural Experience in the United States*, edited by Antonia Darder, 139–50. Westport, CT: Bergin and Garvey.

Wade, Peter. 1997. *Race and Ethnicity in Latin America*. London, Pluto Press.

Waters, Mary C. 2001. *Black Identities*. Cambridge, MA: Harvard University Press.

Whalen, Carmen. 2001. *From Puerto Rico to Philadelphia: Puerto Rican Workers and Postwar Economies*. Philadelphia, PA: Temple University Press.

Wood, Peter H. 2010. "The Earliest Africans in North America." In *The Afro-Latin@ Reader: History and Culture in the United States*, edited by Miriam Jiménez Román and Juan Flores, 19–26. Durham, NC: Duke University Press.

# Index